Women Out of Order

Jeremiah 8:20

About the Artwork

In contrast to the nameless and faceless "women out of order" on the cover of this book, artist Jean Moessner, at age eleven, offered a portrait of another sort of woman. Jean has filled in some of the finer details of what it means to be a strong, proud, and focused woman with a sense of her own rootedness in her culture.

Artist: Jean McCarley Stevenson Moessner III. All rights reserved.

Contributor Photos

On back cover:
Bottom row (left to right): Pamela Cooper-White, Yoke Lye Jerrymia Lim Kwong, Adriana Cavina, Sophia Park, Teresa Snorton. Second row (left to right): Melinda McGarrah Sharp, Insook Lee, Bonnie Miller-McLemore, Joretta L. Marshall. Third row (left to right): Barbara McClure, Jeanne Stevenson-Moessner, Jacqueline Kelley. Top row (left to right): Elizabeth Johnson Walker, Laura W. Dorsey, Angella M.Pak Son, Kathleen Greider.

On p. 363:
Bottom row (left to right): Insook Lee, Esther E. Acolatse, Jacqueline Kelley, Teresa Snorton, Jeanne Stevenson-Moessner. Middle row (left to right): Nancy Ramsay, Angella M. Pak Son, Melinda McGarrah Sharp, Sophia Park, Suk Yeon Lee, Elizabeth Johnson Walker. Top row (left to right): Barbara McClure, Francesca Debora Nuzzolese, Pamela Cooper-White, Kathleen Greider, Joretta Marshall, Laura W. Dorsey. Painting by Reinaldo Vargas; owned by Lucy Alvarez.

Women Out of Order

Risking Change and Creating Care
in a Multicultural World

Jeanne Stevenson-Moessner
and Teresa Snorton, Editors

Fortress Press
Minneapolis

WOMEN OUT OF ORDER
Risking Change and Creating Care in a Multicultural World

Cover image: *Three female figures* by Kazimir Malevich (1878–1935), ca. 1928. Photo: Scala / Art Resource, NY
Cover design: Ivy Palmer Skrade
Additional credits may be found on p. viii, which constitutes a continuation of this copyright page.

Library of Congress Cataloging-in-Publication Data
Women out of order : risking change and creating care in a multicultural world / Jeanne Stevenson-Moessner and Teresa E. Snorton, Editors.
    p. cm.
 Includes bibliographical references and index.
 ISBN 978-0-8006-6444-2 (alk. paper)
 1. Women—Pastoral counseling of. 2. Church work with women. 3. Women—Religious life. 4. Women—Psychology. I. Moessner, Jeanne Stevenson, 1948– II. Snorton, Teresa E., 1955–
 BV4445.W66 2009
 259.082—dc22
                          2009027602

Manufactured in the U.S.A.

Contents

Part One: Women Out of Order

Part Two: Risking Change

Part Four: Challenges Ahead

Credits

In the case studies and examples used in this book, either names and details have been changed to protect the individual's privacy or permission has been granted to share their stories.

Bread (Brot) by Kathe Kollwitz, 1924, lithograph, Rosenwald Collection (Klipstein 1955 194), is courtesy of the Board of Trustees, National Gallery of Art, Washington, D.C., and used by permission.

The poem "The Blanket Around Her" by Joy Harjo, from Rayna Green, ed., *That's What She Said: Contemporary Poetry and Fiction by Native American Women* (Bloomington: Indiana University Press, 1984), p. 127, is copyright © by Joy Harjo and used by permission of the author. All rights reserved.

The poem "Let the Blanket Remind You" by Gina Jones, from Gina Jones, Maryellen Baker, and Mildred "Tinker" Schuman, *The Healing Blanket: Stories, Values, and Poetry from Objiwe Elders and Teachers* (Center City, Minn.: Hazelden, 2000), p. 138, is copyright 1998 © Gina Jones, Maryellen Baker, and Mildred Schuman, and used by permission of the author. All rights reserved.

Figure 11.1, "Five Elements and Cycles," on p. 191 is used by permission of the Northern Shaolin Kung Fu and Tai Chi Academy.

Figure 21.1. "Cycle of Socialization," and figure 21.2, "Cycle of Liberation," are developed by Bobbie Harro, and in Marianne Adams, Lee Anne Bell, and Pat Griffin, eds., *Readings for Diversity and Social Justice: An Anthology on Racism, Antisemitism, Sexism, Heterosexism, Ableism, and Classism*, 2d ed. (New York: Routledge, 2000), pp. 16, 464, are copyright © 2000 Routledge. Reproduced by permission of Taylor and Francis Group, LLC, a division of Informa plc.

Figure 21.3, "Social Identity Development Theory," is from Rita Hardiman and Bailey W. Jackson, "Racial Identity Development: Understanding Racial Dynamics in College Classrooms and on Campus," *New Directions for Teaching and Learning* 52 (Winter 1992): 21–37. Copyright © 1992 Rita Hardiman and Bailey W. Jackson. Reprinted with permission of John Wiley & Sons, Inc.

Preface

It began when a farmer went hunting for a bird to domesticate. He discovered an eaglet. Happily, he placed the newfound eaglet in his chicken coop along with his chickens. Months passed as the eaglet grew. The eaglet ate like a chicken, walked like a chicken, and lived like every other fowl in the coop. Although the eagle was the queen of the air, she pecked around the farm yard each day.

Once, as the story goes, a naturalist spotted the eaglet in the chicken coop.[1] The naturalist confronted the farmer and said the eaglet would one day rise up and fly into the heavens. To prove this to the unbelieving farmer, the naturalist tried three methods of liberation. First, the well-meaning naturalist placed the eaglet on his arm, but she did not fly. Second, the kind naturalist carried the eaglet to a rooftop. Nothing transpired. Finally, as a last effort, leaving the familiar, the naturalist left the town with the eaglet and climbed a mountain. The eaglet saw a new view, a new perspective, and she gazed toward the sun and the wide horizon. At that moment, she spread her magnificent wings, let out a genuine screech, puffed up, and flew toward the heavens.

Women who have seen an unfamiliar but welcoming horizon have collaborated to write this volume. Some of the women have survived lives of restrictions; some have known false expectations. As they have experienced freedoms and found their own authenticities, they have often been labeled "women out of order." In each chapter, they will carry you to a mountain of metamorphosis, a peak of possibilities. They may even introduce you to an understanding of God as Mother Eagle (Deut. 32:11-12).

For certain, the women writing this volume will give credit to those, like the naturalist, who helped them find their way. There are "guides" listed in the dedication pages. We cannot forget the women of earlier centuries who have steered us and led the way. For example, in the field of clinical pastoral education, H. [Helen] Flanders Dunbar was one of the founders along with Anton Boisen and Seward Hiltner. In practical theology, Sojourner Truth became an activist for equal rights as well as an acclaimed preacher. In women's rights and in biblical studies, Elizabeth Cady Stanton and a "revising committee" of able and astute women composed *The Woman's Bible*. These women rose above slavery's and society's restriction.

Current stories of restriction and violence are ever present in the minds of the contributors to this volume. As I wrote this preface, I read about the poison gas being used by militants in Muhmud Raqi, Afghanistan, to keep young girls away from school:

> Only a few dozen of about 570 female students attended class in eastern Afghanistan on Thursday [May 14, 2009] after an apparent attack with poison gas sickened more than 80 girls this week. It was the third apparent poisoning at a girls school in about two weeks. No one has claimed responsibility for the poisonings, but Education Ministry officials say they believe it is a series of poison gas attacks by militants who want to keep girls home from school. Many students who did return to the Aftabachi school in Kapisa province Thursday said they were frightened. Between 22 and 25 girls of all ages huddled in one room as a teacher tried to give a lesson.[2]

These are young girls "out of order" in an atmosphere of repression.

In the expansiveness of the Society for Pastoral Theology, a series of pastoral care books on women's issues in pastoral care have flourished. In 1988, in a seminar led by Rodney Hunter at a Denver SPT meeting, Rod asked one question that led the way: "If you only had one book to write, what would it be?" I answered: "I would write a pastoral care of women, but it is not the time to do that alone." I was an adjunct professor at Columbia Theological Seminary, new to the field. I was tired of xeroxing articles on women's issues for pastoral care classes; this frustration was the impetus for my outburst in Rod's seminar. On the way to the airport, a senior member of the Society stopped me. Maxine Glaz asked, or perhaps "guided," me with these words: "Why don't we write the book together?" That was my introduction to collaborative work. From this collaboration, *Women in Travail and Transition: A New Pastoral Care* grew with eight contributors. Following five reprintings of this first volume, Fortress Press asked for another. Maxine Glaz was busy working on a project with her husband, Stuart Plummer, and was unable to be a coeditor of volume two, *Through the Eyes of Women: Insights for Pastoral Care*. I edited alone as thirteen women came forward to produce a second volume. Fortress then found "a gap in the pastoral care literature" and asked for a book challenging traditional developmental theory. Eighteen women strode forward as guides through traditional theories of maturation, based on male experience. The resulting volume, *In Her Own Time: Women and Developmental Issues in Pastoral Care*, faced longtime theorists such as Erik Erikson, Sigmund Freud, Abraham Maslow, Jean Piaget, and Lawrence Kohlberg, and engaged in explorations of entirely new territory.

In 1988, Maxine Glaz and I knew that Caucasian women dominated our field and our writings. We mentioned in that first volume that future work would need greater racial-ethnic sensitivity and representation. Thus, in this fourth volume, Teresa Snorton and I have been careful that Caucasian women would be in a minority among contributors. In this way, you will be taken to Himalayan heights to see multicultures and complete new vistas.

Such was the work of Turkish doctor, educator, and advocate Turkan Saylan, who died in Istanbul in 2009. She was a champion of women's rights and education for poor children in Turkey as well as a leader in the fight against leprosy in the 1970s. She worked in rural areas with limited resources and focused primarily on the education of young girls who were often forced to marry and have children when as young as twelve. She was on a watch list; her home and office were raided. She continued to denounce sexual inequality. In 1989, she helped found the Association to Support Contemporary Life; at least 58,000 students have received grants and scholarships from the Association since 1989.

Dr. Saylan was working on a book before she died of breast cancer. She was writing a letter to the girls of Turkey, which was read at her funeral in 2009. "You, my dear daughter, stop asking yourself, 'Why am I born a girl?' and aim at becoming the best you can be."[3]

For this we may need a guide, a vision, a vista, and elevation. May this volume be a guide book as you continue to be the best you can be.

Jeanne Stevenson-Moessner, coeditor

Acknowledgments

As we women have risked change and created care, we appreciate and acknowledge the encouragement along the way. A faculty research and travel grant from Perkins School of Theology, Southern Methodist University, supported the meetings and meals that were formative in the cohesiveness of this volume and in the collegial relationships of contributors. Over dinner at the Society for Pastoral Theology in Denver, San Juan, and finally Los Angeles, we women began to see more clearly our differences and similarities. We began to trust our work together.

Perkins associate dean Richard Nelson offered sabbatical wisdom as Dean Bill Lawrence proffered hope in this undertaking. Graduate student Meredith Minister compiled the index in a superb fashion. Martha Robbins and Christie Neuger contributed their faith in this undertaking. All along, we had the companionship of Pamela Johnson and Susan Johnson of Fortress Press, and later David Lott and Margaret Ellsworth. We thank Michael West of Fortress Press for assuring that Pamela joined us at the table in Los Angeles. Michael caught the vision for this volume and never wavered in support. My husband, Dave, and my two children, David and Jean, have cheered this work to completion. We women salute you all for encouraging "women out of order."

Jeanne Stevenson-Moessner

The work on this volume would not have been possible without the support, generosity, and encouragement of the Association for Clinical Pastoral Education, Inc., its Personnel Committee, and the ACPE national office staff. A special thanks is also due to Rev. Brenda Wallace, who gave of her time to proofread manuscripts. I am grateful to my husband, Charles, for his encouragement and to my sons for their curiosity about what I was writing. A final word of appreciation is also extended to the many women in ACPE, the Christian Methodist Episcopal Church, and the Racial, Ethnic, Multicultural Network who have contributed directly and indirectly to this volume.

Teresa Snorton

Dedications

This volume is dedicated to:

My mother, Mercy Acolatse, and the men who broke the rules and propelled me on my journey—*Esther Acolatse*

Lucrezia Cavina, my daughter—*Adriana Cavina*

My mother in ministry, The Reverend Brenda J. Hayes—*Karla J. Cooper*

Macrina Cooper-White, and all our daughters—*Pamela Cooper-White*

Laura Loomis Whitner, my mother, mentor, and a cancer survivor—*Laura Whitner Dorsey*

My dad, Rev. Jesús M. Figueroa, who opened doors for me—*Miriam Figueroa*

My mother, Conyers Donna Kelley, and my CPE mentors, Rev. Drs. Cecelia Williams and Patricia Wilson Cone—*Jacqueline Delores Kelley*

My grandmother, Ah Po, whose voice is remembered—*Yoke-Lye Lim Kwong*

Native American women in ministry and the grandmothers who have helped us on our journey—*Michelle Oberwise Lacock, Carol Anuklik Lakota Eastin*

Elizabeth Conde-Frazier, boundary crosser, truth teller, community builder, beloved teacher, and precious colleague—*Kathleen J. Greider*

My beloved mother, Hun-Il Lim, who has dedicated all of her life to people she loves—*Insook Lee*

All the leaders who have taught me so much—*Barbara J. McClure*

Marsha Foster Boyd, pastoral caregiver and leader in theological education—*Joretta L. Marshall*

Maxine Glaz, wonderful friend, encouraging colleague, leading woman in the field, I still miss you—*Bonnie J. Miller-McLemore*

Lidia Nuzzolese, my sister and friend—*Francesca Debora Nuzzolese*

My mom, Monica Ahsook Do, and Dr. Herbert Anderson, my teacher and mentor in pastoral theology—*Suk Yeon Lee*

Bong-Ja Choi, my mother, and Kyong-Yol Kim, my mother-in-law, two women whose spirituality, strength, and wisdom I strive to embody and pass down to my daughters—*Sophia Park*

Marsha Foster Boyd, Teresa Snorton, and Carolyn Stahl Bohler, pastoral theologians who have provided leadership in bridging the divide that racism poses—*Nancy Ramsay*

Lucy Claire McGarrah Sharp, my daughter—*Melinda McGarrah Sharp*

All the black women in my life who taught me how to be a woman, especially my grandmothers Josephine Watkins and Katherine Snorton, my mother Princella Johnson, and my stepmother Mary Garrett Snorton Frye—*Teresa Snorton*

My mother, Chung Hee Kim—*Angella Son*

Jean McCarley Stevenson Moessner, III, my daughter—*Jeanne Stevenson-Moessner*

Elizabeth Sarai Walker, my daughter, and all the African American women of my heritage—*Elizabeth Johnson Walker*

My mother, Sarah, whom I honor and love dearly, and my daughter, Yolanda, who I hope will break the legacy and reframe the notion of the icon of the Strong Black Women—*Beverly Wallace*

Introduction

While there are many similarities among women's experiences, there are undeniably many differences as well. In her book *White Women's Christ, Black Women's Jesus*, womanist theologian Jacqueline Grant describes the triple impact of sexism, racism, and classism as distinctive markers in the lives of women of color. When thinking multiculturally about the care of women, it is important to keep these variables in mind, for inevitably they set up differences and disparities in the lives and experiences among all women. For instance, although many people generally regard sexism as something that most women experience more or less similarly, one must always be aware of the cultural nuances of sexism. The sociopolitical history of any given culture will dictate the level of sexism that is condoned, supported, tolerated, ignored, or challenged within a particular culture. The ways in which the culture has or has not engaged sexism may differ as well as the way in which change has or has not occurred around the appreciation of women's voice.

When women must also contend with the variable of race, it is easy to see how some women's experience may differ from others. For example, when the society sees one not only as woman but as black woman, that woman's access to education, career options, and other social experiences may be limited because of racial history. The same is true when considering the variable of class. So pervasive is classism in a global economy that any effective pastoral/spiritual caregiver must always give consideration to the impact of economics and social location when considering appropriate interventions for any specific woman as well as in understanding her particular worldview.

A final variable that most certainly has an impact on women's experience is that of generational location. An effective pastoral/spiritual caregiver understands that the worldview of a baby boomer is different from that of a Generation X-er. In the same way, the worldview of a twenty-five-year-old woman in

1

Iraq differs from that of her counterpart in the United States. Women's lives are shaped by the events of the larger world, so caregivers must always be willing to be informed about and aware of the global context in the lives of women.

Teresa E. Snorton, coeditor

While there are many differences among women's experiences, there are undeniably some similarities as well. One similarity is the childish dream of a land called "make-believe." It is a state of utter goodness and fine intentions, of perfectly formed people, and of happy endings. There is abundance and fairness. There is no famine of body or loneliness of soul. It is like a promised land.

As women mature, we note that both the various socioeconomic and racial-ethnic subcultures are like distinct countries touching each other at the boundaries. Women are well aware of the borders or borderlands that form around our cultures of origin or cultures of affiliation. While fluent in our own tongues, we can slip into a common language. I believe that versatility comes from land that we hold in common. This land has been cultivated out of stories of hope; it has been ploughed with stories of harm until seeds of promise have rooted in the furrows. We tend this land in common as we women nurture the narratives of new life and transformation. I call this common land the land of "we-believe."

As the statistics of intimate and impersonal violence, sexual abuse, rape, exploitation, cultural shaming, degradation through stereotyping, and disempowerment are compiled, we have the empirical data to substantiate what we had intuited: "all women grow up within a context that includes the threat of violence, particularly sexualized violence."[1] Therefore, the land we have in common is cultivated with these principles:

a. a recognition of interconnection, particularly that of body-mind-soul-culture;
b. a stance that no one deserves to be exploited, violated, degraded, or suppressed;
c. a resistance to any culture that does so;
d. awareness that the body is a place where God or the holy or the Higher Power can dwell, which results in actions that respect that sacred space;
e. a belief that the worth of a person is not based on contour, color, clothing, creed, or capabilities;
f. a commitment to the importance of community in upholding these principles.

Recently, I was in a workshop to raise cultural sensitivities. The facilitator designated four chairs as representative of four emotions: anger, sadness, happiness, fear. We were asked a series of questions and had to stand by one of the predominant emotions. The group was a mixture of gender, age, ethnicity, sexual orientation, economic background, and nationality. We were moving all around the space, standing beside different "emotions" until the facilitator asked, "What feeling did your family [family of origin] try to convey to the world?" The majority positioned themselves by the "happy" chair for that was the "face" their families tried to convey to the world. However, one lone woman stood by the "fear" chair. It made such a singular impression that the facilitator veered away from her protocol and asked if the one woman might share why the family chose to exude fear. First quietly, then with great emotion, the woman said her father was proud that he ruled the family with intimidation tactics.

What happened next illustrated to me the "land we have in common." Unrehearsed, as gentle as a flow of wind, there was a spontaneous wave of connection and support for other women. The arm of a second participant reached over and rested on the lone woman's shoulder, a third participant stretched to connect with the second, then a fourth participant reached her arm to touch the third participant. Each of the women said in turn: "I can connect with that." While remaining at their respective stations, three women were able to remain distinct yet connect with the narrative of fear. Their connection is a narrative of hope.

Jeanne Stevenson-Moessner, coeditor

PART ONE

Women Out of Order

Women have often been thought of, talked about, and written about in stereotypical ways. The many prevailing stereotypes of women, their behaviors, their thoughts, and their motivations persist in society so much so that when a woman fails to fit the stereotype, she can be viewed as an aberration. Sadly, women who do not fit are often written off, dismissed, discounted, or simply misunderstood. The authors in this section write about the various ways in which women can be perceived as being "out of order," out of sync with the stereotypes, or simply too complex to understand. Their particular multicultural views suggest and affirm that the experiences of "women out of order" are valid, and can be understood with a different set of lenses, perspective, or worldview.

Sara, with her rosetta quilt

Com|plicated Woman

Multiplicity and Relationality across Gender and Culture

Pamela Cooper-White

"At the entrance to our house [when I was growing up] there was a rosetta quilt. Each piece was a rose sewn from 2 folded circles—it took a lot of folds. Each rose was made of scraps of fabric, many colors, polyester, anything and everything, woven together by delicate threads. My grandmother and I would do things like that together. I have one now in my house—4 x 5 feet square. It makes me think of her, doing all these things—cooking, cleaning, helping people, being active in her church. . . . She influenced me to be a fluid person who can move in different spaces and be comfortable."

—Sara[1]

"What always matters is folding, unfolding, refolding."

—Gilles Deleuze[2]

My friend Sara's life looks a lot like the beloved rosetta quilt that hangs on the wall of her house today. Sara's grandmother taught her to quilt—to take brilliant, multicolored scraps of cloth, to cut them in circles, and then to fold them together into bunches and pleats until they took on the shape of a rose, and then with "delicate threads" to weave them all together in an ever-widening pattern that would dazzle and delight.

Sara's life, too, is a weaving and folding together of many parts. Born in Puerto Rico in 1962, she grew up bilingual, and it was her spirit of adventure in her twenties that prompted her and her husband of one year, Nelson, to move to the continental United States to pursue his Master of Divinity degree. Returning together to Puerto Rico for Nelson's first pastorate, Sara began an M.A. in comparative literature, devouring postmodern French philosophy while encouraging Nelson in his ministry. After seven years of being told by doctors that she was infertile ("the seven lean years, like the seven lean cows in the Bible!"), she became pregnant. Her first child, Noelia, was born, and life began to change radically as she fell in love with her baby, and then had a second little girl, Paula. The family moved back to the States where Nelson began his doctorate. Two more children, Celeste and Laura, were born in short order.

Today, she describes her activities in terms of "devotion": in the order in which she herself describes her many commitments, she creates a warm and aesthetically beautiful home fragrant with wonderful meals for her four daughters and her spouse (now a seminary professor); she is very active in her church in both liturgical and programmatic ways; she makes meals and volunteers for the local interfaith homeless network; she is a board member of a shelter for battered women and their children; and she works full-time as the administrator for the graduate degree programs of the seminary (where she also frequently volunteers in a variety of tasks that call upon her artistic, creative, and organizational talents). In addition, she does translating for the national Evangelical Lutheran Church in America, and still somehow finds time to read everything from the Harry Potter books to Jacques Derrida. Her friends marvel at her capacity for multitasking and wonder if, like Hermione in *Harry Potter and the Prisoner of Azkaban*,[3] Sara has mastered the magical art of being in two places at the same time!

When I ask her how she herself understands all her multiple commitments and identifications, she demurs, saying, "One does these things—I don't think about how. It just flows—it just happens." But then, on reflecting, she credits her grandmother with a gift for moving seamlessly from one activity and set of relationships to another:

> I grew up in a family, somewhat traditional in the Latino context, where my mom and I lived with her parents and an uncle and two aunts. We lived in a small town with one of everything except markets—one barber, one seamstress. The Catholic church was at the center of town, on the Plaza, and I went to Catholic school there. . . . Before I started school, even, I would go with my grandmother on her rounds. She was a traditional country woman who went to the market each day to buy the food to cook for that day. And she was a big influence on me concerning relationships. She would negotiate, but also *visit*. Sometimes we would stop in at a merchant's even if she had no business there that day, just to ask about a family member or how someone was doing. She went to the funeral home around three times a week, just to see who had died and to pay her respects! She would walk around town just to see people. This influenced my own desire to move in different spaces. The next generation, my parents and aunts and uncles, settled into jobs. They were settled in one place. But my grandmother *navigated*.

Valuing Multiplicity

The purpose of this essay is to argue that *multiplicity* is a more generous and apt description of women's lives, and indeed a better metaphor for women's hearts and minds, than the logic of "integration" that pervades much of modern psychology.[4] Women, I would argue, are "com|plicated"—literally, we are a folding together (*com-plicatio*) not only of multiple roles and relationships, but also of multiple internal states of emotion and identity. Sara's rosetta quilt offers a rich image for conceptualizing women's psychology and women's pastoral needs in the context of our postmodern, multicultural world today. "Selfhood," particularly ideas of what constitutes a healthy self, has been regarded in terms of "congruence," "cohesiveness," "integrity," or, more popularly, "having it all together." Yet at least as far back as Freud's writings, psychology (especially psychoanalytic psychology) has pointed to a more complex, messier understanding of how human persons—and particularly human *psyches* (minds/souls)—are constituted. Our very selves might be understood as quilts, in which our thoughts, feelings, memories, deeds, and desires are woven throughout our lives into an ever more complicated and colorful pattern of consciousness and identity.

The idea that we are not monolithic—that our minds encompass both conscious and unconscious domains—was at one time revolutionary, particularly to the Enlightenment rationalist for whom the very act of thought was the defining moment of selfhood: *Cogito, ergo sum*—"I am thinking, therefore I exist" (René Descartes). Such complexity, however, has become almost commonplace, and is the prevailing paradigm in most models of human psychology. In Freud's classical division of the mind into the "institutions" of ego, id, and superego,[5] the unconscious was understood to be created by the child's internalization of paternal/parental and societal prohibitions (around the age of five, during the "oedipal crisis"), creating a repression barrier in the mind between the id's instinctual desires and the superego's moral dictates.

We have come to think of this model in terms of vertical "depth," in which our understanding of ourselves is achieved by plumbing downward, digging like an archaeologist or continental explorer for "deeper" truths.[6] While elusive, the contents of the unconscious (at least in part) may be carried up into consciousness on such vehicles as dream symbolism, accidental actions (slips of the tongue and the like), and therapeutic conversation (especially as manifested in the "transference"—the projections onto the therapist of childhood feelings toward original caregivers that are "caught in the act" to be analyzed, yielding new insights[7]).

In contemporary psychoanalytic theory, however, particularly a school of thought called "relational psychoanalysis,"[8] this vertical "depth" model is increasingly being accompanied or replaced by an appreciation of an even greater multiplicity. In this new model, the human mind is understood more horizontally or spatially, across a wider spectrum of states of consciousness and accompanying emotion (often called "affect states" or "self-states"). In contrast to Freud's conflictual model of repression as the mechanism for removing certain mental contents from awareness, relational theorists regard *dissociation* as a significant, if not the primary, means by which a multiplicity of self-states is generated.[9]

Dissociation in this model (as distinct from the *fragmentation* model) is understood as a normal mental process.[10] Unlike Freud's theory of repression, which could be imagined to resemble a hydraulic system of pressures and counterpressures, dissociation is understood as a more organic process, occurring naturally as consciousness moves across a web of mental states and contents. The mind develops through ever-increasing organic associations among bodily experiences, memories, desires, moods, and fantasies—in one author's detailed description, "a multiply organized, associationally linked network of parallel, coexistent, at times conflictual, systems of meaning attribution and understanding."[11] The unconscious itself becomes multiple in this understanding. To quote relational theorist Jodie Messler Davies,

> Not one unconscious, not the unconscious, but multiple levels of consciousness and unconsciousness, in an ongoing state of interactive articulation as past experience infuses the present and present experience evokes state-dependent memories of formative interactive representations. Not an onion, which must be carefully peeled, or an archeological site to be meticulously unearthed and reconstructed in its original form, but a child's kaleidoscope in which each glance through the pinhole of a moment in time provides a unique view; a complex organization in which a fixed set of colored, shaped, and textured components rearrange themselves in unique crystalline structures determined by way of infinite pathways of interconnectedness.[12]

Dissociation is no longer being regarded primarily as pathological, solely as the outcome of trauma. As Philip Bromberg, another relational thinker, has observed,

> The process of dissociation is basic to human mental functioning and is central to the stability and growth of personality. It is intrinsically an adaptational talent that represents the very nature of what we call 'consciousness.' . . . There is now abundant evidence that the psyche does not start as an integrated whole, but is nonunitary in origin—a mental structure that begins and continues as a multiplicity of self-states that maturationally attain a feeling of coherence which overrides the awareness of discontinuity. This leads to the experience of a cohesive sense of personal identity and the *necessary illusion of being 'one self.'*[13]

Healthy subjectivity, then, is far from monolithic. To explain this more concretely, each of us experiences ourselves at a given point in time as being in one particular state of consciousness ("self-state"). Each self-state comes laden with its own thoughts, memories, physical sensations, emotions, and fantasies. In this sense, none of us is a wholly unitive "self" or "being." This nonmonolithic understanding of self/selves as more than a singular individual with an isolated consciousness or will accords well with non-Western conceptions of persons. In fact, as anthropologist Clifford Geertz has pointed out, the Western notion of the person as a "bounded, unique, more or less integrated motivational and cognitive universe" is viewed as quite peculiar in most of the world's cultures,[14] where identity is conceived more in terms of belonging to one's community.[15]

Further, this web of ourselves develops not in isolation, but always *in relation*. Contemporary infant observation studies confirm earlier "object relations" theories that the earliest experiences of self appear to be organized around a variety of shifting self-states formed through the internalization of affect-laden experiences of primary caretakers and others in the early environment.[16] The very capacity to move smoothly and seamlessly from one self-state to another, and to regulate one's own bodily affect-states, is facilitated (or not facilitated) by primary caretakers' responsiveness (or lack thereof). The quality of the boundaries between self and other is gradually established through mutual recognition and regulation, or, in less desirable scenarios, impaired by parental nonrecognition and/or intrusion.

We are better understood, then, as a *folding together* of many selves—personalities formed in identification with numerous inner objects or part-objects (not just id, ego, and superego). Each of us is in ourselves a multiplicity of "selves in relation."[17] At any given moment, we may experience ourselves as one indissoluble Subject, a singular "I," but behind, beyond, or alongside every subject-moment are all the other subject-moments that comprise the whole of this web.[18] We are made up of many parts, with varying degrees of accessibility between and among them as our consciousness shifts more or less seamlessly from one to another, without our paying particular attention to the flux. It is precisely this subjective feeling of seamlessness that creates the illusion of being "oneself," but this very illusion of seamless going-on-being from one self-state to another is in itself a developmental achievement.

Imagine yourself for a moment as more multiple than you had ever considered before—a complex quilt of subjectivities, flexible enough to bend to new circumstances, to form new relationships drawing on an inner world of memories, experiences, and identifications. In a postmodern world, with its ever-burgeoning flow of information—verbal, visual, aural—and instantaneous communication around the globe, is it any wonder that contemporary psychologies are exploring and celebrating this possibility of a more fluid and variegated construction of self and identity? Perhaps it is such "identity complexity"[19] that is the healthiest and most responsive form of "selfhood" most able to cope with the continual flux of the world in which we live.[20]

Com|plicated Woman

The challenge to unitive notions of self is, *theoretically*, gender neutral. In relational theory, consciousness is understood, in both men *and* women, to be multivalent, fluid, their realities continually being constructed and reconstructed in the matrix of individual and social relationships. Why, then, include multiplicity in a pastoral care anthology specifically about women?

The first and more pragmatic answer is that women probably more readily identify with multiplicity as having an intuitive resonance with our own experience. Our lives often *feel* complicated. The book *I Don't Know How She Does It!*[21] points to the challenge of multitasking that confronts middle- and upper-middle-class women, especially those of us who embraced the liberal feminist battle cry of the 1960s and '70s that we could "have it all." "Having it all" has been repudiated by some younger women of both the upper and middle classes because of the stress, and the separation from home and children, that "having it all" seemed to demand. However, women's personal declarations of liberation from sexism never could produce genuine liberation, unaccompanied as they were by a parallel liberation of men. The socioeconomic structures of white male political power and monolithic, stoic constructions of masculine identity continue unabated. So "women's liberation" increasingly came to mean economically privileged women's running faster on the hamster wheel of multitasking, and increasing pressure to master multiple roles as equally true and full-time identities—wife, mother, daughter, professional, volunteer. Of course, such multiple roles, touted as new pressure by the publishing classes, were not at all new to working class and poor women, who for centuries had already been doing it all—and having none of it!

The extent, then, to which we can readily identify with multiplicity of identities as women may have as much to do with externally imposed (and sometimes internally embraced) expectations about juggling multiple roles—involving multiple personas (the faces we show to others in various arenas of our lives)—as it does with the creative, dynamic potential of our true inner complexity and diversity. Sara says, "I don't think there is a woman or girl who can say she does just one thing or is just one thing. . . . Women are more open to 'go with the flow.' Maybe because we're forced to do that, because of expectations on us. I try to fight them, but they are so ingrained. I can't resist." Such socially imposed external demands for increasing flexibility in our lives and relationships, it might be argued, may even be inhibiting the flowering of our internal potential, because we have been so well socialized to inhabit the scripts others have written for us, rather than to explore freely the stories of our own unlimited becoming.

Multiplicity, therefore, has resonance with women's lives at a more complex psychological level—of *inner* creativity and flux. This level of multiplicity is better illuminated by a postmodern feminist analysis that addresses the social construction of gender, and the linguistic mechanisms of reinforcement of patriarchalism embedded in the very language by which we come to know ourselves and others. Although women have made great strides in some arenas, especially as measured by a liberal feminism that demands political and economic equality for women (such as the first viable campaign of a woman presidential candidate in the United States), the social construction of gender difference(s) and the psychosocial category of "Woman" continue to pose problems for individual women's lives, as feminist psychoanalytic and postmodern theorists have shown.

It is by now a commonplace among liberal feminists, from the psychologist Carol Gilligan[22] to presidential primary candidate Hillary Clinton,[23] to speak about the importance of women's "finding their own voices." As part of a larger liberationist movement, feminist pastoral theology has warmly embraced this ideal of helping to give voice to the voiceless, and to "hear" the marginalized, including women, "into speech."[24] As French feminist philosophers have pointed out, however, language itself is part and parcel of the patriarchal infrastructure of Western societies, following Jacques Lacan's linguistically focused version of Freudian theory.[25] Lacan proposed that as babies we all experience a certain shock and alienation upon realizing that the image of ourselves in the mirror is false—a chimera of seeming wholeness, agency, and integrated motion that exceeded our infantile experience of fragmentation and erratic sense of control. We are plunged into an irremedial state of alienation from ourselves as we identify with the illusion of the unified self seen in the mirror. We trade our embodied selves for a false and inverse identity in the glass, in order to defend against the infantile experience of being a "fragmented body" (*corps-morcelé*), "still trapped in his motor impotence and nursling dependence."[26] This unconscious trade-off comes at a price—our first sense of self is inextricably linked with an experience of alienation and lack.

This "mirror phase" of development coincides with the recognition of the mother as a separate subject in her own right, with her own thoughts and feelings. The differentiation from the mother also occurs increasingly alongside the encounter with the father as an "other" whose "Law of the Father" (or "Law of the Phallus") enforces the oedipal rule of further separations, and suppression of spontaneity in favor of survival in compliance with the norms and demands of civilization. Culture itself is the vehicle of the Law of the Father, and as language is intrinsic to culture, patriarchal social structures are imbued with the very acquisition of language itself. There is consequently no coming to speech, or even *thought*, apart from patriarchy, because there is no thought apart from the "Symbolic" (Lacan's term for the world of language and culture by which all operative reality is constituted). Lacan considered this to be absolutely and universally determined, based on biological gender characteristics. In particular, the penis as Phallus—the symbolic role of principle social organizer—engendered what Lacan believed to be a universal phallo-cracy.

It is in this regard that Luce Irigaray, a French postmodern feminist philosopher and psychoanalyst, raised the question: "Can women speak?"[27] Irigaray, however, leaves room for a possible—albeit as yet unknown—construction of femininity, a "feminine god" for "divine women" that would not be so thoroughly conditioned by patriarchal sociolinguistic structures.[28] Irigaray's work entertains "the divine [as] a movement . . . a movement of love."[29] How can we imagine subjects/ subjectivities that are no longer sub-jected (thrown under) by phallocentric language and culture? Such an "imaginary" would require somehow circumventing the patriarchal stamp of language, and of civilization itself. Irigaray's writing style itself is full of circumlocutions, poetic images, and suggestive gaps in logic, as an attempt to inscribe women's resistance to phallocentric language and culture.

As part of this effort at resistance, Irigaray writes frequently of images and themes that appear to derive from female bodily existence—fluidity, flux, folds, lips,[30] even mucous membranes[31] as a counterpoint to the masculinist "logic of the Same"[32] in which truth is equated with linear, rational thought and the straight-ahead movement of progress informed by Enlightenment ideals.

Another postmodern philosopher, Gilles Deleuze, has offered an extensive meditation on the aesthetic theme/image of "the fold."[33] Elsewhere, I have already shown how Deleuze's work provides useful metaphors for the embracing of multiplicity, both in reference to human subjectivity and theology—especially in his revaluing of the image of the *rhizome* as a counterpoint to the frequent psychological and theological "depth" metaphor of "trees" and "roots."[34] This resonates well with conceptions of the unconscious in terms of horizontal or spatial multiplicities of subjectivity and affect, as an alternative to Freud's and Jung's unconscious "depths."[35]

Deleuze links the process of creation to a chaotic, groundless preorigin from which all beings do not so much emerge upward, as they "unfold." Deleuze describes this bottomless origin or "chaosmos" as a "matrix" (literally, womb)[36]— a maternal image for the divine. Deleuze contests the linear logic of Enlightenment conceptions of space and time, posing a trinitarian dynamic of "folding, unfolding, and refolding"[37] as an alternative vision of creative process that, literally by implication, is less phallocentric and patriarchal. Feminist theologian Catherine Keller draws on Deleuze, as well as the ancient church theologian Nicolas of Cusa, to propose an "origami of creation":

> . . . Deleuze cannot resist [the] formula: "the trinity *complicatio-explicatio-implicatio*." This is a trinity of folds, *plis*, indicating a relationality of intertwining rather than cutting edges. *Complicatio*, "folding together," in Cusa folding of the world in God, signifies "the chaos which contains all; . . . *explicatio*: that which "unfolds" what otherwise remains "folded together"; . . . and that relation, the "relation of relations," may be called by *implicatio* the *spirit of God*. . . . So the third capacity thus signifies the relationality itself.[38]

She cites Elizabeth Johnson's affirmation of divine Love as "the moving power of life, that which drives everything that is toward everything else that is."[39]

The fluidity of the fold, like the roses on Sara's quilt, offers a compelling image for the multiplicity of women's lives, both outwardly as we live between and among various spheres of activity and relatedness, and inwardly, as we contemplate the nonpathological—and even life-giving—fluidity of movement within our psyches. We are *com-plicated*—an inner folding together and togetherness of folds. We are inwardly constituted by an ongoing "folding, unfolding, and refolding" as various emotions and ideas unfurl to meet the challenge of each new moment.

Sara comments, "I like reading Derrida. And I think a woman must have come up with it—reading his autobiography, I see his mom's influence!" I ask, "Why do you think his ideas are like a woman's ideas?" "Because he has to undo and redo things. That's what I have done. I had expectations—I thought life was one way. Life takes turns. You have to redo and keep going." Reflecting back, she says, "When Noelia was born I just wanted to be with my baby and enjoy. I didn't feel like I was less of me. I had to make choices—conflicting choices—but I felt it was right. I had to rebuild myself. . . . And I just said, 'Let's keep going! No regrets!' Now the first one is in college and it feels awesome! I am rejoicing in that." Of course regrets, or the specter of regrets put away, and the weathering of hard losses also are threads within the texture of Sara's sense of self. But it is precisely this complexity, this ability to weave strands of experience together, that contribute to her resilience and determination:

> My creativity is always hands on. . . . I find time to cook an extra meal for Northwest Interfaith. I find creative ways to manage my time. I teach Sunday School—it's an outlet—you always have to have one more trick under your sleeve. . . . And being involved in other places, and with my own children—it pushed me to think outside the box: You have to use what you have. I could sit down and complain, I didn't have this opportunity, but this is what I have, how can I use it? This is a thread in everything I do. And lo and behold, you can do a lot of stuff! Could I do more with more resources? Yes, but I can *do lots* with what I *have!*

Furthermore, as liberal feminism has insisted for decades, the personal is also political. Multiplicity becomes a feminist model of resistance to the phallocratic logic of the One or the Same. Deleuze's image of the fold has political implications. As cultural historian Gen Doy has written:

> For Deleuze, [the image of the fold] is not confusing or disorientating, but empowering. . . . The methods of thinking and being of 'possessive individualism' are destroyed. . . . Indeed, the trope of 'the fold' seems to be in the right place at the right time in our postmodern era, where liberal humanist hopes of progress and freedom for all are confronted by wars, famines, indeed barbarism of all kinds. . . . [40]

Jane Flax, drawing on Irigaray, articulates how a concept of multiplicity of selves/subjects is not merely a boon for individual women (and men), but also opens space for an ethic that contests the failed promises of Enlightenment oneness with a new promise of social and political liberation:

> I believe a unitary self is unnecessary, impossible, and a dangerous illusion. Only multiple subjects can invent ways to struggle against domination that will not merely recreate it. In the process of therapy, in relations with others, and in political life we encounter many difficulties when subjectivity becomes subject to one normative standard, solidifies into rigid structures, or lacks the capacity to flow readily between different aspects of itself. . . . No singular form can be sufficient as a regulative ideal or as a prescription for human maturity or the essential human capacity. . . . [I]t is possible to imagine subjectivities whose desires for multiplicity can impel them toward emancipatory action. These subjectivities would be fluid rather than solid, contextual rather than universal, and process oriented rather than topographical. Emancipatory theories and practices require 'mechanics of fluids'. . . .[41]

Michel Foucault translated the need for multiplicity into just such political terms when he wrote, "We must not imagine a world of discourse divided . . . between the dominant discourse and the dominated one; but as a multiplicity of discursive elements that can come into play in various strategies . . ."[42]

This postmodern view resonates well with Homi Bhabha's postcolonial formulation of hybridity in relations between subjects, where hybridity is defined as the capacity of two partners, or two subjects, to join together without losing the distinctiveness of either.[43] Unlike a dialectical relationship, in which each subject must somehow be transformed or even dissolved into a transcendent solution to the problem of difference, hybridity suggests the possibility of a new, more egalitarian intersubjectivity in which particularities, differences, and even conflicts are retained and respected. This image of multiplicity has to do not only with the gendered nature of relationships, both social and political, but the way the "other" has been constructed in global relations of domination, war, racism, and colonization of indigenous peoples.

Gayatri Spivak asks the parallel question to Irigaray's question about women: "Can the subaltern speak?"[44] Where the *subaltern* (the subjugated other) has been constructed through colonial conquest, is there space for resistance? Postcolonial writers have argued that there is no going back or romanticizing earlier, precolonial times, but resistance to the hegemonic influence of the dominant colonizing cultures becomes possible through creative strategies of reassertion of indigenous cultural values and identities. Hybridity becomes a resource for claiming the threads of multiple cultural inheritances, *post*-colonialization, without the need to surrender to dominance via assimilation. While the term *postcolonial* itself represents a hoped-for future that is not yet achieved,[45] postcolonial theorists offer a strategy of multiplicity through which new forms of life may flourish both locally and globally.

Folding, Unfolding, Refolding—Making the Quilts of Our Lives

I have attempted in this chapter to argue that multiplicity is a more generous and apt paradigm for understanding women's lives, both social/relational and internal/psychological. This argument depends in part on the assertion that gender is socially constructed. There will always be an objection to this, that the biologies of male and female bodies (however uniquely constellated in individual human beings) cannot be ignored. Hormones are powerful. Men's psyches may be no less characterized by multiplicity and unfolding/refolding than women's. But we are differently constituted by the sheer biological distinction that while both women and men are birthed from the womb of a woman, only women have a womb like hers (whether we become biological mothers or not). Irigaray draws considerably in her theories from women's more diffuse bodily sources of desire and sexual pleasure.[46] Nevertheless, as "gender" participates in language, it is already embedded in culture. There is no pure biology of gender—all notions of gender are *already interpretations* of biological experience. And these interpretations are laden with implications for power and domination.[47]

As Elaine Graham, Judith Butler, and others have pointed out,[48] however, it is precisely because these categories are finally constructs, and not immutable facts of nature, that gaps and inconsistencies within them may provide spaces from which both women and racialized, subaltern, and queered subjects can speak. Subjugated voices can erode and "jam the machinery" of dominance much the way fluids can erode seemingly solid rock.[49] "If the regulative fictions of sex and gender are themselves multiply contested sites of meaning," Butler writes, "then the very multiplicity of their construction holds out the possibility of a disruption of their univocal posturing."[50] There are spaces within multiplicity from which subversion and critique can still unfold. Deleuze's "fold" and Irigaray's powerfully seductive writings about the fluidity of women's experience lived in the body can be invoked as alternative interpretations to dominant discourses, in which gender, race, and sexuality are constructed and assigned lesser political power and social worth through hierarchical, linear polarities and binary oppositions (male-female, straight-gay, and by extension, white-black, Christian-Muslim, and so on).

A distinction must now be drawn between this new "imaginary" of multiplicity, folding, and flux—which indeed may serve as a helpful corrective to patriarchal insistence on an ideal of the (male) One—and an essentialist rendering of gender difference as innate and biologically determined. Words like "matrix" (womb), "flux," "*jouissance*" (an untranslatable term used by Irigaray to refer to female pleasure, including orgasm, but also a superfluity of internal pleasure, a "reservoir yet-to-come" that may spill over into artistic creativity, writing, or play[51]), and even "fold" (especially when juxtaposed with phallic imagery that is "hard," "straight," and "penetrating") have clear associations with characteristics of the female body. Femininity itself has been associated with the internal in contrast with the masculine as external, although there is a danger here in reinforcing sexist stereotypes.

A too-glib reading of Irigaray could locate her with essentialist feminists who believe that women are inherently or "essentially" different from men, and that the feminist task is not to contest femininity as an immutable "truth," so much as to advocate its being valued equally alongside masculinity. While this may be a temporary strategy for living within patriarchy, Irigaray's appropriation of the postmodern tool of "deconstruction"[52] reveals a more revolutionary agenda, in which the falsity and poverty of patriarchal culture itself is uncovered and repudiated through the play of linguistic analysis.

An additional meta-caution should also be raised—against over-theorizing! The more abstract our discussion of gender becomes, the more it finally flows into an *aporia*—a philosophical dead end. Following Jacques Derrida, there is no construction of gender (or race, or anything, for that matter), dominant or otherwise, that does not already contain the seeds of its own deconstruction.[53] Precisely because gender is socially constructed, as soon as any certainty is claimed about it, the exceptions will sprout up—or unfold!—to undo it. The only way out of this dead end, then, is not finally through further theorizing, but through *practices*. As Graham writes,

> The impasse of postmodernism is resolved not by turning away from the critique of metaphysics and dominant rationality, but by insisting that purposeful, coherent and binding values can be articulated from within the core of human activity and value-directed practice. Such a perspective translated into theology would speak of the contingency and situatedness of human existence and knowledge, and the provisionality of our apprehension of the divine. 'Truth' would be understood as realized within and through human practices and material transformation. . . . Thus, the centrality of practice—as self-reflexively reflecting and constructing gender identity, relations and representations—is confirmed as the focus of critical attention for a theology of gender. It would however add a feminist critique of such claims to truth and value by attending to latent aspects of domination and exclusion in the formulation of such values.[54]

Practical Im|plications—The Quilts of Our Lives

Although my writing is admittedly very theoretical, I am convinced that finally it will not be through new and better theoretical formulations, but it will be through *practices*, of multiplicity that women's creativity and authentic power will come to fruition. What in this postmodern time *practically* keeps us com|plicated women from just flying apart, or falling to pieces? If a psychological model of *integration* comes too close to homogenization and a suppression of creative inner voices, what, if anything, holds our internal diversity together?

It should not be stated that there is no *wholeness,* or sense of cohesion, in this model of multiplicity. Far from being an image of endless iterations of existence without any sense of connectedness (which *would* be fragmentation), the figure of the fold is illustrated by Deleuze via an image of a labyrinth—a whole that is constituted *by* the multiplicity of its folds: "A labyrinth is said, etymologically, to be multiple because it contains many folds. The multiple is not only what has many parts but also what is folded *in many ways.*"[55] Our sense of wholeness, then, as distinct from a monolithic oneness, depends upon our being able to move fluidly and gracefully, *in many ways,* among all the many parts of ourselves, continually drawing from our complexity new strengths for the journey.

In Sara's words, "There is a thread that pulls it all together. And that is very spiritual. I have a sense of gratitude to God that pours out in different ways for different things. In my upbringing, it was important to give to others who are not your family, not just your obligation." Sara's spirituality is a crucial source of strength and has a strongly relational quality:

> I think: This life is our one chance—make it or break it! I believe in a promise of eternity, a reconciliation with God, some unity where wrongs are made right, a reunion of believers, people you will see again. I hold on to that—even if it's not true—because it helps. I expect to see my grandma, my grandpa—even my dog! I have a sense of God's creation [gesture of her arms encircling]—there's got to be something like that. . . . The God I'm praying to—I have to meet some way. There is this force or power I've seen in my life—there has to be a point of looking and recognizing that, in a more tangible (can I say tangible?) way. We expect, we look, we see . . . in prayer . . . good things happen that we didn't expect, and we attribute that to God's good hand and help.

A Threefold Braided Thread

There is still a thread that holds the quilt of our lives together—but I would argue that it is not the thread of "the" executive ego, although that is usually present as an aspect of subjectivity that very usefully carries the mature illusion of being one-self,[56] seaming all our disparate parts and self-states together in a continuous sense of "me" going on being. Rather, I would propose that there is a *threefold braided thread*—the experience of *inhabiting one body in relation to other bodies,* a mature sense of *spirituality,* and a commitment to a coherent set of *embodied ethical practices*—by which the roses of the quilt are bound together.

I would even venture further to suggest that this threefold braid is not a single straight line, but, like the filaments tying each rosetta to the next in Sara's grandmother's quilt, is itself a *network*, a *weaving*. It is not, finally, *one* thread or braid, but a web of threads that, taken together, constitute a "whole"—a whole whose very coherence and binding power is made up of our embodied relationships (including our multiple cultural inheritances and our internalization of others across the lifespan), our spiritualities, and our moral commitments. Each woman (each person, I would argue) is thus a complex community within her- or himself. By recognizing and valuing this communality of self/selves, we are all the more likely to be able to value the pluralism of the many communities with which we intersect, and even those "others" beyond our immediate safe, familiar context.

Weavers of Connection

As women familiar with navigating the web of connections both within and without, we can become weavers of connection and empathy, not only creating personal ties, but building political coalitions through relational acts of *capacitación* (= creating capacity/empowerment). Sara describes her own role in such a moment of weaving, which engaged her at the inner level of emotions and multiple identifications, while externally evoking her best political, cross-cultural, and linguistic skills:

> It had to do with some awareness of "crossing" identifications or something like that. I kept thinking about that and remembered this experience. Last year I attended a MLK day of service at New Creation Church in North Philly. . . . [One of the groups] at New Creation was Rebuilding Together Philadelphia (RTP), an organization that helps qualifying poor homeowners with house repairs, free of charge. People apply and they receive a visit from an evaluating team to verify the information, assess the repairs that need to be done, and approve that person to receive the services. RTP was going to make some thirty visits to people in the immediate New Creation area on that same day. All their members were primarily men (just two women) and all of them were white. Almost all of them lived in the suburbs. They needed a Spanish-speaking person to visit these homes with them. That's how I ended up joining [one of their] teams. Never before did I feel so fortunate and capable. I gained their trust immediately. Furthermore, people they initially ruled out because of misinterpretation of their circumstances and demeanors, were accepted after a brief discussion and some explanations. The contrary also happened. But what I experienced was that I was accepted by both the disenfranchised Hispanic as well as the white, suburban group. I do not know how. I guessed knowing both languages was a real asset. But also my understanding of the two cultures helped, too. I came home so exhausted and sad about what I saw, but very excited about how I might have helped some people who would have been so misunderstood and, therefore, disqualified.

I continue to believe that the more willing we are to explore all the parts of our multiply constituted selves (including our own inner multiculturality—known and unknown to us), and to become curious about encountering the "others" within us—the parts of ourselves we have disavowed or otherwise split off from conscious awareness—the more open we will dare to be toward the "other" in our world. The model of pastoral care and counseling that I am advocating[57] seeks to help individuals (both women *and* men) come to know, accept, and appreciate all the distinctive parts—the many voices—that live within them. This openness to inner "others" may then allow women and men to bridge relational gaps, not simply by liberal Enlightenment values of "unity" and "solidarity" (a form of oneness), but by unfolding to embrace the other.

Might such unfolding lead to new social constructions, new recognitions, across gender, race, sexuality, and religion, to disrupt and replace existing power dynamics of dominance and submission with a new, political intersubjectivity— even among nations? This relational unfolding and refolding together—this com|plication—is the heart of an ethics for a postmodern world. We cannot have empathy for "others" whom we are too afraid to know, either within ourselves, or in the social realm beyond superficial, anxiety-laden politeness or paranoid projections that inflate "others" into enemies, agents of evil, or justifiable targets of war. The more paranoid we become, the more we are likely to behave as the other's fearsome "other," continuing what has already become an endless cycle of provocation and retaliation.

In our relations, from the most intimate circles of lovers, family, and friends, to our immediate communities, to the wider world, and even to God—as Christian theism itself is unfolded and refolded in new, more multiple conceptions of the divine[58]—we will find new sources of justice and creativity to sustain our efforts for justice and peace. At a time when there is so much simplistic rhetoric of "us and them," "good and evil"—especially with regard to race and racialized stereotypes of "other" religions and cultures—I continue to believe that it is precisely a turn toward multiplicity that might best help us to envision a generosity toward the "other" that might save us from ourselves.

While this embracing of multiplicity is both informed by a postmodern feminist pastoral theology/psychology, and resonates strongly within it, it is finally worth pursuing passionately by both women *and* men. Multiplicity can offer new, more creative ways of conceiving both self/selves and other(s) as we take up the challenges of living in today's pluralistic, postmodern world—a "fluidity that is not loss but rather source-resource of new energy."[59] Our com|plication unfolds an alternative "imaginary" to the hyper-rational, masculinist "progress" model of the Enlightenment in whose thrall we have dreamed too long. Multiplicity of self and others unfurls a new fold, to reveal a dream of a truly postcolonial age in which justice, care, and creative flourishing can flow freely among living beings.

Just Care

Pastoral Counseling with Socioeconomically Vulnerable Women

Francesca Debora Nuzzolese

"Before we can hope to change the world, we should try to change ourselves. That always seems like a good place to start. . . ."
                                        —My grandfather, a strong believer in God and Justice

This chapter is about caring for women who live in the subcultures of poverty and powerlessness, and who strive for wholeness and justice in the midst of socioeconomic vulnerability and the unjust distribution of wealth and resources. It is written from the perspective of a woman who, by engaging the psychosocial and spiritual needs of such women through pastoral counseling, was able to experience with them some of the justice and wholeness that are core dimensions of transformative pastoral praxis—or *Just Care.*

This piece hopes to make two contributions: one to pastoral ethics and the other to pastoral methodology. In terms of *pastoral ethics*, it invites practitioners of pastoral counseling to reconsider their commitment to those human groups who have not been considered "educated" or "sophisticated" or "wealthy" enough to engage the psychotherapeutic process, but who need it desperately. The invitation supplies a "try out a new pastoral counseling posture" kit: a few theoretical and practical suggestions to engage the psycho-spiritual needs of socioeconomically vulnerable women, with the promise that a shift in our pastoral attitude may promote therapeutic justice, in their lives as well as in our own. In terms of *pastoral methodology*, it seeks to demonstrate the relevance of pastoral-contextual experience to the construction and pursuit of creative models of care, particularly with those human groups whose voices and experiences have not always been adequately heard. The *Just Care* model proposed here is, in and of itself, a concrete example of how the engagement of a particular context of care (i.e., pastoral counseling with socioeconomically vulnerable women) helped me rethink the universality of certain norms and values and construct a new, contextually and therapeutically viable model of care. Creative attempts such as this are, I believe, one of the distinctive contributions of an *essentially pastoral* theological methodology,[1] a methodology that trusts the wisdom of pastoral experience with all its heart and soul.

Minding the Socioeconomic Context: Some Insiders' Perspectives

What kind of help do poor women seek through pastoral counseling? How does their vulnerability to socioeconomic inequality have an impact on the unhealthy relationships in which they find themselves trapped? Is pastoral counseling their best option for healing? Or is their call for help misplaced? The best way to get a realistic perspective of the struggles, dilemmas, and crises brought to counseling by women in the subcultures of poverty and socioeconomic disparity is to listen to their stories. Here are a sample three.

> Rosa: *A young and charming Mexican girl, Rosa found out about pastoral counseling through a small ad in the local newspaper. She was not familiar with the kind of counseling she would receive, nor did she particularly care. What motivated her call was the line in the ad, which highlighted fees as low as $5.00 per session. She made an appointment by herself and then showed up with her boyfriend of three years, Ricky, an African American young man with a questionable past and an explosive personality. Coming to counseling was more her priority than his. She wanted to know if he would change (for better, I took), after she agreed to marry him. Her marrying him seemed a very scary prospect to me, due to the multiplicity of issues they were presenting, such as the incompatibility of their personalities (or the compatibility of their pathologies); the different cultural, religious, and family values; the unequal access to and availability of resources; the power imbalance; and Ricky's violent behavior and drug abuse. Yet, Rosa's perspective was legitimately different from my own, given where she came from and where she could be headed.*
>
> *On her escape from poverty, Rosa, at twenty-three, risked everything, including her life, and gambled the very little she had to undertake the dangerous crossover into the U.S. territory. It took about a ten-day bus ride through Mexico, $2,000 cash (and a year of work here to pay it back), a seventeen-hour walk through the national border, and a three-day car ride across the country (without restroom stops) in order to reach her destination. The invisibility and statuslessness of undocumented migration, along with abusive working and living conditions and the prospect of marriage with this unlikely candidate, were not as scary to her as the alternatives left behind in her country of origin. Making choices dictated by both despair and hope is a familiar dilemma in the lives of those who feel like they have nothing more to lose. Yet, familiar does not mean painless.*

A few weeks into the therapeutic process, it became obvious that focusing on the intrapsychic dynamics that lock women into abusive relationships and black men into drug and alcohol abuse would not suffice to address the contextual web of interdependencies that entangled both Rosa and Rick in this tragic predicament of hopelessness and resilience, perfect sense and total craziness. Rosa's questions, after Ricky threatened to leave her if she did not stop this therapy nonsense, pushed traditional therapeutic parlance to a new level. One day she asked: "Francesca, do you really think everyone can afford to live a healthy and fulfilling life? Are healthy choices really free for all? Don't you think some people are just stuck—they have to work hard, put up with many struggles, all their lives . . . just to stay alive?" Indeed, a serious engagement of Rosa's situation would urge a pastoral counselor to redefine what good and/or healthy choices look like for those whose choices are extremely limited. An evaluation of the communal dimension of her dilemmas would also force one to recognize that freedom and dependency are complex and intricate dynamics for those who cannot afford to survive on their own means, and yet bear responsibility for those entrusted in their care. The problem with life dilemmas such as these is that they do not tend to lead to clear-cut solutions.

Pam: *It took weeks of counseling before I was able to collect biographical data or to move in any particular direction with Pam, a soft-spoken, fragile-looking, middle-aged woman. Most of our time would be spent in a predictable manner: she would list all the symptoms of discomfort she experienced in her body—from the familiar backache developed during her first pregnancy, through the dizziness that preceded her anxiety attacks, to the latest symptoms of random shaking, weakness in her knees, and muscle cramping. Before leaving, she would bemoan the inadequacy of her faith to help her overcome these physical ailments, then, patting me on the shoulder, she would depart saying something along the lines of: "You are a saint to do this job. I don't know how you can stand to see so much helplessness." Indeed, at times her helplessness felt excruciatingly unbearable. "Pam is a very special lady, with a very strong faith. She just needs lots of listening . . . much more than I can give her." Thus Father John, one of the local Catholic priests, had gently handed to me the care of Pam, a devout member of his congregation, in the grips of a severe form of depression. The depression was, in my opinion, well motivated by the helplessness she had experienced in accessing adequate medical care for the physical distress debilitating her body and afflicting her spirit. A positive outlook on life and a strong faith in God and all the saints had become insufficient resources to cope with the present crisis, namely the fast and steady decline of her physical health.*

Colluding with her husband's misgivings about her complaints was a medical system that was unable to offer a diagnosis comprehensive of her multiple ailments. Lacking the health benefits she used to enjoy when she was young, healthy, and employed, Pam had found herself stuck in a very abusive marital relationship and had become increasingly sicker, frustrated, and demoralized. "What chances do I have of finding a job or another companion at my age and in my health conditions? What do I have to really look forward to? A miracle to heal me completely? A quick and painless death? That I may win the lottery, even if I can't afford to buy the tickets?"

Pam's questions are troubling, yet very legitimate. What opportunities are there for an unemployed, middle-aged woman, who is caught in an abusive relationship and whose emotional and physical health begins to deteriorate, to access the resources necessary to deal with the present and not dread the future? How can she tend to her emotional and interpersonal well-being, while her medical needs are so overwhelming, the services and resources available are scarce, and the only way to afford them is through her abusive husband's health insurance? According to what scale should her needs be prioritized? What therapeutic route would validate and engage all of her needs so that she can live a more hopeful present and prepare for a less bleak future?

Lynn: *The path that led Lynn to pastoral counseling was also a somewhat unusual one. She was referred by a seminary student, who bartended in a local pub. It was in this pub that Lynn would hang out, drink, pick up men, and occasionally curse God. Her Southern Baptist upbringing, in the rural south of Florida, would have the best of her whenever she got seriously inebriated. Thus, she would start convicting the cruelty of a God who had placed her in the womb of an angry mother, in the lineage of poverty, alcoholism, mental illness, and child abuse. What chances were there for someone with her upbringing to really make it in life? What examples had she gotten from her mom and dad, and from her family at large? What opportunities were given to children who could not do their homework because home was "chaos and hell," or who grew up around so much abusive behavior they eventually got convinced they somehow "deserved it"? And most importantly, what kind of God would allow some people to be so rich and others to be as "hopelessly screwed by the system" as it had been for her family through generations? "Where do you see hope for a screw-up like me?" she had challenged in our first interview, after presenting an almost convincing list of reasons that would disqualify her from "the race to life improvement." The reasons included: a childhood lived in close proximity with abuse, a history of addiction to alcohol and marijuana, a series of abusive relationships, current unemployment, a divorce, an abortion, a charge of DUI, the harsh reminders (on her face and arms) of a grave accident incurred while drunk driving, and her present living arrangement as the "cover-up" tenant in a house, the basement of which was used to grow marijuana. Indeed, an unfortunate CV for someone as smart, witty, and young as Lynn. "How far are people like me really allowed to go? For how long do you think I can keep busting my butt to make it on my own, just to be reminded that there is no better life for people like me?"*

Lynn's questions are also poignant and legitimate. It is not hard to empathize with her plight and wonder whether the opportunities to "make it," to build a more dignified and stable life, are really out there for anybody who works hard, or whether the ones who "make it" are so few and rare that it is hardly worth trying hard at all. Will, indeed, the education she is attempting to get actually help her step up the socioeconomic ladder and somehow break the legacy of poverty, addiction, and inaccessibility to resources to which her family has been *"destined" for generations? Will the obstacles on her way keep pushing her back, until she will be too demoralized to keep trying and will give in to the evidence that "the poor need to stay poor so that the rich can keep their fancy mansions?" How much hope for personal and social redemption can a community college degree grant, anyway?*

The Stories of Few, the Predicament of Millions

These pastoral vignettes introduce a particular pastoral-contextual reality. Such reality, and the therapeutic issues it engenders, is characterized by the socioeconomic locus from which Rosa, Pam, and Lynn approach and access the ministry of pastoral counseling. It is primarily defined by the perspectives and experiences of struggling, hard-working, poorly educated and poorly compensated, hardly insured, unglamorous, generally depressed women living in the lower rungs of American society. Far from being isolated or rare expressions of human struggles within the constraints of socioeconomic disparity, these stories bespeak the predicament in which large segments of the human population exist, namely on the verge of economic and emotional collapse, as well as in a state of passivity and quasi-alienation from sociopolitical participation and economic equity in one of the richest and most powerful countries in the world. Within such a predicament, these women's hopes and opportunities to live in more wholesome and just communities and neighborhoods are limited and far-fetched. This is evidenced by socioeconomic studies and statistical reports that engage the reality of class inequality in America and the phenomenon of vulnerability and powerlessness in which large percentages of individuals and communities are locked.[2] Such studies alarmingly remind us that poverty is degrading, greed is demonic, injustice is rampant, upward mobility is mere myth, exploitation of illegal work is a capitalistic commodity, universal health care is still utopia, and that powerlessness has long-term effects on body, mind, and spirit.[3] They also confirm that more than two thirds of the human population lives in such a predicament, and that within such a predicament free and healthy choices for one's life are severely impaired and contingent upon a multitude of factors, over which the poor do not have much control. These realities make a very hard case for pastoral counselors, who, in the presence of clients, especially women such as Rosa, or Pam, or Lynn, cannot help but quietly wonder: Are you sure you came to the right place?

Old Stories, New Challenges: Pastoral Counseling and Socioeconomic Vulnerability

The need to craft more adequate models for practicing pastoral counseling with those who are vulnerable to the variables of socioeconomic injustice emerges primarily from the poignant questions and dilemmas that women like Rosa,

Pam, or Lynn pose to contemporary practices of care and counseling.[4] Once upon a time, women like them would not have even considered pastoral counseling, worried that they might not be able to afford the process, and that they would sink into further powerlessness and shame, given the complexities of their struggles. What could a therapist who expects a rather high fee for service and receives her clients in a cushy office understand about walking one's way into survival, unpaid bills, underpaid work, and pissed-as-hell people, after all? Even if she did understand, how could she possibly help?

For these and other legitimate reasons, people of the lower socioeconomic classes have been in the past, and continue to remain, ambivalent and suspicious about the compatibility of their particular needs and the help offered by pastoral psychotherapists. The overwhelming evidence that pastoral counseling in America has, from its beginnings, met primarily the needs of the middle and upper classes has shaped this reality for several decades. While this reality is slowly changing, the deeper problem to be addressed is that, truthfully, the values, needs, resources, and means of this particular segment of society are unfamiliar and often conflicting with the ones implicit in mainstream pastoral counseling theories, and the therapeutic practices they inform. Such theories often assume a more homogenous, monocultural, white, middle-class, and Protestant context. The stories of oppression and powerlessness shared by women such as Pam, Lynn, and Rosa, and the particular locus in which they unfold, reveal that such assumptions are neither adequate nor helpful to understand and address the psychosocial and spiritual dimensions of suffering affecting those who sit at the very bottom of the socioeconomic ladder. While the quality of human suffering cannot be evaluated according to the variables of race, gender, sexual orientation, and/or social class, it seems naïve to ignore the fact that those who sit at the bottom of the various socioeconomic ladders of Western capitalistic societies are susceptible to some forms of suffering for which they themselves are hardly responsible. It also seems unethical to continue to imply that an effective reactivation of their free will might indeed lead them to healthier choices and improved lives. While encouraging personal effort and responsibility taking in order to transform the intrapsychic and interpersonal realm of human agency continues to be an essential aspect of pastoral psychotherapy, envisioning ways to improve the social, structural, and economic dimensions of suffering needs to become an integral part of the therapeutic agenda as well. This has not yet fully or adequately occurred.

My personal experience of counseling with a number of low-income, working-class, working poor, and undocumented women workers (and indirectly with their families), and the rather meager literature that directly links pastoral counseling with issues of class and economic vulnerability, suggests that one of the issues to consider is the mutual mistrust between pastoral counselors and potential clients from the lower classes. Put quite frankly, poor women are very hard to counsel: they tend not to trust our ability to comprehend fully the tragic dimensions of their plight; and we tend to be overwhelmed by their issues and secretly (unconsciously) mistrust their potential to change or improve, given the multiplicity and severity of obstacles preventing such changes. Behind the surface of practicality, folksy panache, and matter-of-factness, they reek of the paralyzing effects of powerlessness and helplessness, a condition from which, at some level, they hope and long to be freed. It is very likely that both counselor and client might collude in their reluctance to explore the power of such feelings, for in the process they may discover how far-fetched such freedom really is. Needless to say, those theories that capitalize on the activation of one's free will, sense of freedom, agency, and personal responsibility fall short when entering the reality of those who are dehumanized and victimized by unjust and oppressive socioeconomic systems. Even the slightest hint that their predicament is partly "their responsibility" can cause further ethical and therapeutic damage. While taking responsibility is an essential ingredient in the process of change, one needs to be very careful in defining who is responsible for what.

Another reason women of limited socioeconomic resources hesitate to consult "experts" on issues that are unbearable and shameful is precisely because by intuition and experience they know their problems are much larger than themselves. They know it will take much more than personal/individual effort to take care of them. The fear that pastoral counselors will provide neither enough hope, nor adequate answers, to the complexity of their plight is often confirmed by the limited resources we can provide to tackle challenge and change at more communal and global, interpersonal, and intersystemic levels.

It seems clear that both the ministry of pastoral counseling and the population it has failed to effectively reach could benefit from a united effort at redeeming our reciprocal suspiciousness and mutual mistrust. The question is this: What can help establish a healthier connection between pastoral counseling, as a ministry of care capable of destabilizing the power of powerlessness, and the powerless women and communities on which it has thus far failed to have an impact?

To begin with, I suggest an implicit revision of some of the theological, psychological, and sociocultural perspectives we have indiscriminately and normatively employed in our traditional teaching and practice of care and counseling, and the explicit endorsement of some alternative ones. The goal of such revision/proposition is to challenge the traditional notions that "health" and "wholeness" ensue from the successful resolution of intrapsychic conflicts which, in turn, leads to self-fulfillment and self-realization. Not only do such traditional notions isolate individuals from the social, political, economic, and systemic dynamics that support the possibilities and desire for wholeness; at times they seem to aggravate their sense of powerlessness and helplessness in the pursuit of the unattainable. To coordinate such alternative theoretical perspectives, I propose the construction of a model that upholds a pastoral ethic of *justice-seeking and justice-making* at the intrapsychic and interpersonal levels. (The intersystemic is a more complex one, and can be effected only indirectly by this model). The model is grounded in a relational metaphor that more effectively connects pastoral counselor and socioeconomically vulnerable women, namely the metaphor of "friendship." Unlike other metaphors, traditionally employed to characterize the therapeutic relationship (such as the one of "parenting" clients through crucial developmental stages, or "shepherding" them through stages of spiritual and emotional crises), the one of friendship suggests and embodies a relational posture that is essentially embedded in the ethic of mutual regard. Implementing such changes would result in benefits for both those who have been so far missed as well as the practice of pastoral counseling in particular, which, by endorsing a "justice-seeking and justice-making" dimension of care, could become a more prophetic form of ministry.

Developing a Different Therapeutic Posture: Some Helpful Perspectives

The determination to understand and engage the realities of the women who inhabit the subcultures of poverty has brought me into conversation with inspiring partners, such as Italian political activist Antonio Gramsci (my grandfather's hero!), intersubjective psychologist Daniel Stern, and feminist theologian Mary Elizabeth Hunt. The dynamic interplay of these particular theoretical perspectives helps to challenge the monocultural, therapeutic posture assumed by traditional pastoral counseling (i.e., the therapist behaving as a somewhat detached, immutable, analyzing subject) and contributes to the development of a creative alternative one (i.e., therapist and client mutually committed to a process of transformation that will affect all). Such an alternative posture reveals a strategic potential for the counselor to engage the interpersonal and intrapsychic dynamics that interlock to create and sustain the suffering of poor women.

Organic Pastoral Counseling

What is it exactly that creates the conditions of socioeconomic vulnerability to which women like Rosa and Lynn are subjected? What dynamics actually determine their socioeconomic disadvantage? Who and what exactly limits their choices, or creates the conditions for their often entrapping dilemmas? Is it the lack of economic means per se? Or is it also the fact that they are not involved in the political, cultural, and economic decisional life of the communities in which they exist, and therefore feel victimized by a system that they neither understand nor really control? If active participation, through a renewed sense of political and social responsibility to themselves and their community, could indeed rebalance the socioeconomic disparity that afflicts and limits their choices and access to resources, what prevents it? Who discourages it? Who reaps the benefits and who buffers the losses?

The sociopolitical perspective of Italian theorist Antonio Gramsci, particularly his vision of societal transformation through reeducation of the working classes in the service of participation, is built on a very interesting concept, namely that change of the masses comes from change in those who lead them.[5] Gramsci was a man who personally experienced the systemic objectification of the average working-class person within the emerging European capitalist ethos of the early twentieth century. He constructively protested its negative effects by personally pursuing higher education and by using his education to understand and critique the hegemonic style of leadership of the ruling classes. In order to challenge and change such rule, he encouraged the development, among the oppressed classes, of "organic intellectuals," that is, people from among the oppressed who would represent their interests and articulate their needs accurately and effectively. These would be women and men who, regardless of their particular occupation, would assume the role of "educators" of the lower classes, empowering them to take consciousness of their potential as "historical subjects," meaning potential reformers of their current predicaments. Organic intellectuals would be people who understood, by personal experience, the condition of the oppressed classes, and who were committed to use the power and status achieved through their higher education in order to educate and lead the working classes out of objectification and passive acceptance of economic, political, and social oppression. In other words, they were liberators from within.

What does this have to do with pastoral counseling?

The socioeconomic vulnerability experienced by women such as the ones mentioned above seem unfashionably similar to the conditions of the exploited workers Gramsci had in mind while articulating his analysis of power relations and his countercultural philosophical anthropology.[6] The acceptance of work and relational exploitation, their resignation to an undignified life that is often perceived as something they have deserved, the paralysis of their sense of agency, which makes them feel like there is not much that can be done, and the sense of powerlessness with which they tend to assess their predicament seem very common feelings to those human groups that undergo the demoralizing experience of race, class, and gender oppression. Women, ethnic and racial minorities, and uneducated or exploited people in almost every historical and geographical time end up internalizing some of these feelings and the underlying message that their sense of agency is somewhat "defective." The material limitations, the inaccessibility of resources, and the frustration that comes from lacking the basic necessities for a dignified existence (i.e., adequate health care, fair remuneration and benefits for one's hard work, the opportunity for good education) do combine to demoralize people. However, Gramsci's implication is that what contributes even more to their state of vulnerability, alienation, and powerlessness is the ideology of commodity promoted by the capitalist class.

In modern Europe, as well as in postmodern capitalist democracies such as the United States, such ideology still dresses up as common sense, as religious thinking as well as language, and works hard to maintain the illusion of freedom and equal opportunity for all, while in reality life and life conditions (especially for those who do not have much decisional power) are accepted uncritically and fatalistically—simply part of "the way things just are." Gramsci's anthropology holds the belief that all human beings are "intellectually predisposed" toward critical, or philosophical, thinking. They are inherently capable of assessing the world in which they exist, as well as reflecting on their place within it. This belief is grounded in an epistemological precept: experience and knowledge are dialectically interdependent, or, what we experience and what we come to know as "true" about life inform each other in order to create a consistent whole.

Translated into the language of pastoral psychotherapy, this means that potentially all humans are "psychologically wired" to engage the messages sent by the political dimension (i.e., the legal system, the military system, the state policies) and by civil society (i.e., the school system, the Hollywood culture, the food culture, the sport culture, the religious culture) and to evaluate them in light of what, in their experience, makes them thrive over against what makes them suffer—both at individual and collective levels. It also means that humans are gifted with an inherent capacity to question the morality and ethics of any given ideology vis-à-vis a certain vision of communal life as inspired by God's Spirit. This inherent human potential, Gramsci rightly suggests, becomes frustrated and discouraged not by accident or because some human groups are inherently "defective," but, rather, because an operative ideology is at work to maintain people somewhat locked into "nonthinking," mesmerized by the "common sense" of a culture that promotes materialism, consumerism, dispensability, fast earning, fast living, and fast dying. Somewhere in the process of this kind of living (or living somewhat), people are robbed of the possibility to be as fully human as they could possibly be, paralyzed in a state of "economic objectification," which weighs more heavily on the "have-nots" than on the "haves" of society as a whole.

Sadly enough, oftentimes pastoral counselors respond to the needs of the poor within the limits of their own ideological embeddings, and thus end up reinforcing the very dynamics of oppressions their clients need to fight. That is why Gramsci's diagnosis of "historical objectification" becomes relevant to the ministry of pastoral counselors: it reminds us that our role should be also one of education and advocacy, and ultimately of "subjectification" of those who have become all too comfortable with a diagnosis of chronic helplessness. This means that the pastoral counselor who is willing to act "organically" chooses to enter the reality of objectification and victimization to which poor women are intergenerationally subjected. From such a place, and with the psychospiritual tools to her available, she begins the work of critique of objectified behavior and identity, and the work of reconstruction of women's full subjectivity, emphasizing their right and responsibility to participation in their lives and histories. Thus, the work of subjectification becomes a mutually enhancing and transforming one.

The practice of "organic counseling" is particularly viable to pastoral counselors who have been trained in the art of in depth psychotherapy, for such training presupposes both the willingness and the empathic ability to enter the depth of another human being's experience—in order to understand it and to transform it. Gramsci's organic intellectuals could only be those who knew experientially the yoke of inhumane treatment. By the same logic, organic pastoral counselors can only be those who are willing to ascend into the abyss of their own sense of powerlessness and helplessness, for the sake of seeking together with their clients a renewed sense of hope in human solidarity, compassion, and love. Far from being solely a political strategy of empowerment, this is at the very core of incarnational theology, by which we come to know God through the solidarity he showed to humanity in Jesus of Nazareth: both a saving Christ and a fellow sufferer.

Reenergizing the potential for action and resistance of women of the lower classes, illegal migrants, ethnic minorities, and other exploited groups would bring to the fore their experience as historically specific products of a system of inequalities. These inequalities are primarily material, but they are more than that, insofar as they are interwoven in the thick tapestry of political, cultural, and social dimensions of individual and collective life. In the specific case of socioeconomically vulnerable women, the challenge is for pastoral counseling to become one of the places in which these women can be supported and encouraged to access their inner resources for resisting the oppression they experience, and one of the places in which their ability for self-awareness, historical becoming, and political consciousness can be activated enough that they will begin challenging their predicament from within—from the perspective of "historical subjects." Breaking down the invisibility that comes from civil status-lessness, challenging the myth that middle-class values and capitalist commodities equal a healthy and happy life, redirecting the sense of defeat that comes from trusting institutions that will not deliver what they promise, and unmasking the ideology that links self-worth to material productivity become ways to join women in the struggle for counterhegemonic rule—one of the ways to begin a form of "organic" transformation of society from within. This is, in other words, organic pastoral counseling.

Intersubjective Pastoral Counseling

Could it be that some psychological theories are inadvertently more damaging than helpful to women of the lower classes? Is it possible that the anthropological assumptions implicit in some of them end up pathologizing them, rather than empowering them? *Yes* and *Yes.* Pastoral practice and various postmodern critical voices affirm that such is the case, and that the frameworks sustaining our practices of care are often very committed (overtly or covertly) to protecting the needs of the dominant culture and/or of the ruling class. Hence, the urge to choose psychological theories that can best sustain liberatory praxis, or the practice of organic, pastoral counseling, in the service of empowerment and justice of those who long and need both.

Intersubjective theory seems to lend itself naturally to the therapeutic task of strengthening socioeconomically vulnerable women's sense of self and thus to enhance their potential to function as empowered and participating full "historical subjects."[7] A close reading of human development, especially in the detailed observations and accounts of Daniel Stern, reveals interesting, and therapeutically helpful, anthropological assumptions about the essence and purpose of human existence.[8] The first assumption concerns the *inherent human desire for relatedness* (rather than aggression and libidinal drives), which propels the process of human becoming. Stern explains this in terms of an expanding organizational capacity of the human infant to engage in real intersubjective experience, right from birth. The stimulation to thrive, to develop, and to grow is sustained by the desire and the longing to better connect to "others," rather than by the need to become self-sufficient, independent, and autonomous from "others." Without the intersubjective experience of real others, a full sense of one's own self is not even possible. In other words, the task of becoming "fully human" is reached because of the presence of real, available, committed others, who are experienced and engaged, from birth and throughout life, as fully "subjectively others." Another important inference Stern makes about human nature is the baby's potential for *active engagement and participation.* In order to engage the relational context in which experience occurs, something more than the instinct for survival (postulated by Freud) is needed. That "something more" is, according to Stern, the ability and desire to "participate."

Change, growth, and transformation of the human person can only occur within the dialectic of mutual engagement and participation, with others and with one's environment. Yet another crucial assumption of intersubjective theory is the distinctive and crucial roles that distinct *others* play in the healthy thriving of the human being. Just as the pathology, or character malformation, of the child reflects the pathology of the relational matrix in which that human creature was born, so the pathology or dysfunctions of large societies are transmitted to smaller groups and subgroups within that society (such as is the case with poor women's dysfunctional lives, which reveal the malfunction of the system in which their lives occur). Shared pathology means shared responsibility in the route to healing and well-being. It is the job of all to be involved. One more critical assumption in the intersubjective perspective is the notion that *certain human needs last a lifelong time.* Just like the baby needs constant connectedness and relatedness to thrive and mature through life, so does the adult need the presence of loving and supporting communities in order to maintain an emotionally, spiritually, and politically healthy sense of self—and other—and thus prosper in the task of becoming more fully human.

Closely related to this is one last assumption, concerning the value of psychological *separation/individuation* in the service of independence and autonomy. In slight disagreement with other relational models (e.g., Mahler's), separation, independence, and autonomy are neither the ultimate goal of human development nor the primary concern of therapeutic intervention. Paramount to the intersubjective agenda are those maturational aspects of healthy relatedness, or developed capacities for relatedness, which are built on the bases of intersubjective interdependence. The reason why intrapsychic separation is not a core developmental, nor therapeutic, task is because psychological separation of self from other is a given of human nature. In other words, what the human infant needs to muster through development (and the adult through therapeutic treatment) is not separation, but healthy interrelatedness, or a way of engaging and participating in his/her own well-being while staying connected with and caring for that interdependent, intersubjectively connected world of "others."

How does all of this relate to socioeconomically vulnerable women and their therapeutic needs? Let me suggest at least four key implications of such assumptions to therapeutic intervention:

1. Therapeutic empowerment and possible healing begin by viewing women who are strongly marked by a sense of powerlessness, helplessness, suspiciousness, and vulnerability from the perspective of their healthy potential, their full subjectivity, and their longing and capacity for healthy and fulfilling relationships. When therapists believe in their clients' inherent capacity and longing for healthy relatedness, they intersubjectively communicate it to them, thus heightening such capacity and eliciting responsible and mature responses.

2. When the full subjectivity of women who are systematically oppressed is assumed and activated in the service of their healing (though it may not be eloquently expressed or experienced), the "successful" management (if not resolution) of their struggles and dilemmas becomes a concrete possibility. Encouragement to take responsibility for the changes they can make (however small they may seem) indeed results in increased internal strength and the potential to reciprocate with loving care and accountability.

3. When clients' fear to trust an "expert other" (expressed and often diagnosed as "resistance" or "intrapsychic weakness") is interpreted vis-à-vis the larger systems of exploitation and oppression endured over the years, the therapeutic relationship becomes a place where issues of power abuse can be recast both hermeneutically and experientially.

4. When pastoral therapists surrender the myth of their neutrality and detachment, and accept that encountering the "suffering other" will forever change their own subjectivity, they increase their potential to become "organic pastoral therapists"—committed to carry, within themselves and into the realm of advocacy, the plight of those who suffer because of injustice, exploitation, and oppression.

Stern's most helpful contribution to therapeutic practice is in the invitation he issues to view human beings from the perspective of their healthy potential, rather than from the perspective of their malfunctions. From such a place, it is possible to envision, and work toward, increasingly more mature and more responsible relationships—relationships that are self- and other-defining, self- and other-transforming, and self- and other-fulfilling. Although not explicitly stated, this notion of *shared responsibility* among all human beings permeates Stern's whole psychological construct, thus creating the sustaining ground for this new therapeutic norm of mutuality and accountability so crucially needed by the victims and survivors of intergenerational powerlessness and helplessness.

One last comment about the value of working intersubjectively is the promise of transformation of the entire relational matrix, of which therapist and clients are just a small part. Through them, larger cultures and subcultures of networks and communities become engaged, and affected—or, put another way, intersubjectivity reminds us and makes us more aware of how deeply and intrinsically, interpersonally and intrapsychically interrelated we all truly are, by everything that is: God, creation, the other, and self. Through the intersubjective lens, we are pushed toward a much more evolved and mature form of pastoral work—perhaps a more painful and demanding one, but certainly a more authentic and effective one as well.

Friendly Pastoral Counseling

Ultimately, the practice of therapeutic justice, or *Just Care*, calls for a therapeutic posture that is theologically and ethically grounded and that can engender transformation at the multiple levels of need of socioeconomically vulnerable women and the communities to which they have been entrusted. Lest one be misled by the term, "friendly" pastoral counseling refers to a form of therapy grounded in the metaphor of friendship: a relational posture wherein therapist and client are united by shared concern for each other's being and the well-being of all—God included. While the metaphor of friendship has been explored by feminist theologians in order to expand theological and biblical imagination, its potential to inform constructive pastoral theology (in the service of pastoral praxis) has not been fully explored. My pastoral experience suggests that such metaphor indeed can sustain a more inviting, less intimidating, and ethically appropriate pastoral posture toward socioeconomically vulnerable women.

Feminist theologian Mary Elizabeth Hunt provides one of the most compelling descriptions of how women's friendships, in particular, contribute to the construction of more just and compassionate relational communities, sustained by new ethical norms.[9] In that they have the power to cut across the barriers of race, class, gender, and able-bodiness, such friendships, or coalitions of "justice-seeking" friends, link theology and politics in a way that has not been done in male-dominated traditions.

According to Hunt, the four key features characterizing such friendships are the following: love, power, embodiment, and spirituality:

- *Love* she defines as *"an orientation toward the world as if my friend and I were more united than separated, more at one among the many than separate and alone."*[10] It represents both a desire and a commitment to work toward unity, while fully valuing the individuality of each human being. This theological notion of love supports the sense of solidarity that needs to be fostered in the therapeutic relationship, because in the recognition of our interdependence on each other and on God rests the vision for a reconciled world.

- The notion of *power* is recast by Hunt in terms of *"an ability to make choices for ourselves, for our dependent children, and with our community."*[11] Power dynamics ought to be recognized, named, and worked with, as they sit at the intersection of the social/structural and personal/individual relational grid. In the therapeutic relationship, attentiveness to both sets of power dynamics is crucial, lest women's experience of vulnerability and powerlessness be reinforced rather than corrected.

- *Embodiment* is an illustrative term that refers to the reality of humans as incarnate, physical, sexual beings. As *"virtually everything we do and who we are is mediated by our bodies,"* paying attention to health, nutrition, rest, recreation, functionality, and the general quality of people's lives is an integral part of a therapeutic ethic of justice.[12]

- *Spirituality*, in Hunt's model, is divested of its privatized and sanitized connotations in order to encompass *"making choices about the quality of life for oneself and for one's community."*[13] In this sense, spirituality is an intentional process wherein one's well-being is inextricably linked to the well-being of others, and all become communally invested in the improvement of the world's life.

The harmonious interplay of these elements ensures that friendships, and the communities they sustain, work well. When these elements are out of balance, then tension, stress, and interpersonal distortions ensue to create suffering, injustice, oppression, and mutual exploitation.

The effectiveness of the model, Hunt suggests, ought to be measured vis-à-vis three elements of broad ethical significance: attention, generativity, and community. Ultimately, all three converge in a unifying factor, namely the pursuit of justice.

- *Attention* refers to the important task of "attending" to the details of human existence, in all its magnificence and in all its messiness and triviality. Paying attention in the context of therapy means listening over and over to the list of Pam's physical ailments, as well as to the doses of the different medications she takes, at the different times of the day, for the different disabilities she has. What she seems to be saying is this: my body matters, yet no one else seems to care. Paying attention to the tragic in women's lives means grieving the possibility of Rosa marrying at age twenty-three, despite the abuse she constantly undergoes. Attending to women's lives means zooming in on what hurts, what distorts, what unites, what connects, what makes them laugh, what makes them feel ashamed, and to do it all in a spirit of genuine love, care, and solidarity. It means celebrating that which can be transformed and grieving what needs to be let go.

- *Generativity* is for Hunt the hallmark of all justice-seeking relationships. It means generating something new, transforming something old, removing or working through something outdated and stagnant, such as remorse, fears, or regrets. Within the therapeutic context, it means originating new ideas about how to maximize the skills learned in homemaking, child rearing, and care of the elderly in order to make women of the lower classes more "marketable." Their "marketability" is, indeed, in the awareness that what they have learned to do because of life circumstances is useful, is valuable to society, and should be paid appropriately. With women like Rosa, it means highlighting her bilingual potential and her opportunities to reach and connect with her Mexican community—both for her own good and the good that they could get from her, for example, help with translating work documents or mentoring children who have language difficulties.

- *Community* cannot be forced, states Hunt rightly, but it can be fostered. Friendships come in the plural, and they become contagious. Networks can be encouraged and promoted, and their power can be life transforming. There is nothing that unites more than a common struggle, a common goal, and a common vision. Gramsci would agree. When people find their commonalities, in both celebration and struggle, they are prone to join efforts and move toward action. Connecting women who share in similar socioeconomic predicaments in communities of solidarity and support (i.e., through support groups, community education, and advocacy) could lead not only to their own personal emancipation but also to the transformation of their social settings and so forth in an ongoing circle of mutual transformations.

Practicing Just Care: The Model in Action

The socioeconomic realities in which the lives of women like Rosa, Lynn, and Pam are embedded interlock with their particular personality structures, their personal and family histories, and current interpersonal dynamics to generate some of the struggles and dilemmas they bring to counseling. Mindful that the particularities of each individual person should be respected and remembered, some symptoms that can be generalized to all the socioeconomically vulnerable women are issues of victimization, powerlessness, worthlessness, helplessness, and a sense of suspiciousness, or mistrust, toward the systems in which they operate.[14] The theoretical perspectives presented above offer compatible solutions to engage these issues in the most therapeutically valuable way. The interweaving of pastoral experience and sociopolitical, psychological, and theological perspectives become the grounding for a particular therapeutic model, which emerges from reflection on pastoral practice. Briefly summarized, this model capitalizes on the following tasks:

1. activation of women's potential for self-reflection that leads to action;
2. empowerment and strengthening of their internal and interpersonal resources for the sake of more mature relationality; and
3. encouragement to responsible participation in communities of friendships, which leads to spiritual and emotional well-being.

Holding these basic ingredients in dialectical tension, the pastoral counselor can engage the needs of the socioeconomically vulnerable woman, mindful both of her particular predicament as well as of the broader cultural and subcultural contexts of embeddedness and belonging.

Constructing a General Narrative

Women like Rosa, Lynn, or Pam are not prone to ask for help. They are tough, they can put up with a lot, they are resilient, and they are stubborn. Their ability to navigate the incredible odds of life is truly admirable. Having to turn to a "professional" for help carries an implicit stigma that somehow they have failed the task of surviving on their own means, relying on their own strength and the strength that comes from God. The resistance they initially exhibit, their suspiciousness, their reluctance to trust and to share part of their soul is, in fact, part of their assets. They have learned to protect their vulnerable sides as a means of survival. In a world where you "have to work hard just to stay alive" or where "you are doomed right from the start," displaying vulnerability, focusing on feelings, getting in touch with anger, and dwelling in the state of grief can be lethal. Leading them to those spaces without taking responsibility for the consequences in their lives is, on the part of the therapist, simply unethical. Hence, the need to embody a different pastoral therapeutic posture.

When women who are not accustomed to pastoral counseling find an atmosphere of openness, an attitude of humbleness and compassion, and a therapist who behaves more like a caring and just friend than as a neutral and detached other, they are more likely to "give God a chance." Within a therapeutic space of solidarity, empathy, mutuality, and shared responsibility, "friendships" of a particular kind flourish, and they become the ground on which risks can be more easily taken. It is in this space where justice is intentionally lived out in every aspect of the therapeutic process (e.g., agreement on the fee, mutual respect of time, accommodating scheduling difficulties, mindfulness about transportation issues and childcare) that the human potential for fuller subjectivity is activated, and the possibilities for growth, healing, emancipation, and transformation are greatly increased.

Assuming the therapeutic posture of a "just and caring friend," as informed by the perspectives presented above, is one of the ways by which the pastoral counselor can responsibly and ethically offer care to socioeconomically vulnerable women. The gentle and respectful invitation to openness, trust, and exploration of deep and painful feelings constructs the path that leads to more permanent intrapsychic and interpersonal changes. The willingness to share accountability and responsibility in the therapeutic process paves the path that leads to more just and communal relational patterns. The commitment to engage people's suffering both as a concerned friend and as a political agent builds the bridge between private pastoral practice and sociopolitical advocacy.

If some, or most, of these ingredients are in place, women like Lynn and Pam tend to stick around for a very long time. This is not because they become dependent on their therapist, but because they have entered a deeply intimate relationship of trust and solidarity. In times of need, they know they are entitled to fall back on it. If they forget that they are full subjects, in a world which will tend to objectify them and reduce their critical potential, they know where to find reminders, and if their internal capacities fail them, hopefully they have learned to trust that help is indeed available to them.

The therapeutic process, which begins with "feeling" understood, engaged, and cared for, proceeds then with the implementation of some important therapeutic tasks, such as improving their interpersonal skills, strengthening their sense of self, sharpening their critical abilities, nurturing their spiritual resources, challenging those theological beliefs that are not helpful, and encouraging the engagement of their experience to construct a new understanding of themselves in the world. This process is essentially circular, ongoing, and its rippling effects are not only visible in the lives of the women engaging the process itself but also in the lives of their therapists, whose reality and perception of the world is—on their account—forever changed as well.

The following diagram (fig 2.1, p. 40) provides a visual example of what happens in a pastoral therapeutic process that trusts the suggestions of this model.[15]

The diagram illustrates not only what happens and/or should happen when socioeconomically vulnerable women choose to trust the pastoral counseling process, but also, and just as importantly, when pastoral counselors are ready and willing to shift their theoretical and therapeutic postures in order to engage their needs concretely and effectively. The hope is that, indeed, the process proves mutually beneficial and transforming, and that ultimately both pastoral counselor and clients become part of a larger, global effort at bringing some more wholeness and justice in a world that seriously needs them.

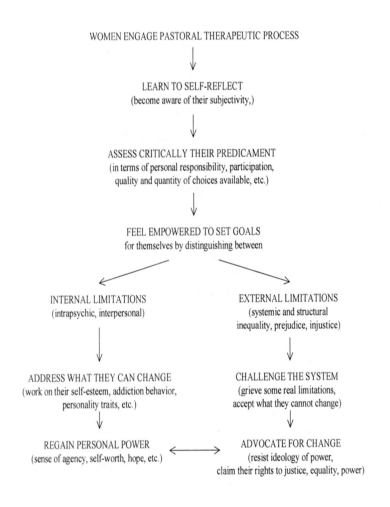

Figure 2.1

Conclusion and Contributions

Is this model of pastoral counseling truly apt to address and engage the vulnerability caused by socioeconomic injustice and inequalities? Does the therapeutic posture of a "just and caring friend" make a difference in engaging the particular struggles of socioeconomically vulnerable women, their families, and communities? Or are there more appropriate, more communal forms of ministry that can better bridge the needs of the oppressed and the mission of the church to bring particularly good news to the poor? While these questions will continue to stimulate the construction of newer and better models of pastoral care and counseling, especially across the cultures and subcultures of human groups not yet fully reached, this constructive effort hopes to have made a modest contribution to the following theoretical and practical dimensions of pastoral counseling.

1. *Socioeconomic context.* The reality of class division, lack of privilege, economic injustice, and inequalities in the United States is still a somewhat uncomfortable and marginalized topic in the field of pastoral care. The invitation has been issued in this chapter to mind the contextual realities of women who are socioeconomically vulnerable, with the purpose of practicing care and justice at the intrapsychic and interpersonal levels and to reconsider what is "normative" in the dominant culture, for the sake of those who live on its many margins.

2. *Political consciousness.* Political consciousness, we learned from Gramsci, is an often underdeveloped function in the lives of those who inhabit the lower socioeconomic classes. The case has been made in this paper that it is also a neglected dimension of psychotherapeutic treatment. As political consciousness is not meant to be an end in itself, but the means to emancipating, liberating, and empowering praxis in the pursuit of a more just society, both clients and therapists are called to work harder at developing a collective and personal political consciousness. The organic engagement of pastoral counseling relationships with the victims of systems of inequalities becomes in itself a way of developing political consciousness, which can in turn inform and transform pastoral praxis.

3. *Intersubjective posture.* Maintaining an intentionally intersubjective posture, as Stern suggests, affirms the full subjective potential of each human being, however damaged their relational abilities and their lives might be. The consistent practice of this posture reveals a powerful therapeutic tool to deal with the deeper, intrapsychic effects of helplessness, powerlessness, and lack of self-esteem, and enhances clients' internal potential for improved relationality. On the interpersonal level, it corrects the power imbalance that women of the lower classes experience in their workplaces as well as in their homes, and grants them concrete

opportunities to practice equality, mutuality, shared responsibility, and participation in the healing process.

4. *A perspectival theological attitude.* One of the core contributions practical theology makes to theological scholarship is the insights it generates from pastoral practice. A theological attitude that values the perspectives of those who are vulnerable to socioeconomic injustice challenges traditional doctrines by reevaluating the role of personal freedom, sense of agency, accountability, and participation. As a result of this brave attitude, our understanding of God is enriched, the possibilities for restoring broken relationships increased, and our visions for a more loving and just world enlarged.

5. *Methodological commitment to praxis–theory–praxis.* The model presented in this chapter began with the pastoral vignettes, or pastoral practice, and returned to pastoral practice. En route, it challenged some theories and adopted some different ones. Beyond mere application of method, the purpose of expanding theological reflection to include the experience of those who have been marginalized, excluded, and exploited in the "theologizing process" was in itself a political act, or a way of practicing *Just Care* while attempting to describe it.

6. *Psychospiritual growth of all parties involved.* My pastoral encounters with women across the cultures and subcultures of poverty for the past ten years have been, and continue to be, life transforming. Indeed, partaking of their joys and tragedies through this intersubjective, organic, and friendly pastoral posture keeps stretching my heart and deepening my soul beyond my expectations. As my awareness of their lives and predicaments propels me to use my own power and privilege in the service of education and empowerment, I am certain that the hope and solidarity generated by our work propels them to stay on the journey toward healing and wholeness. And as I proceed on my own path of healing and growth, and they on theirs, we continue to meet each other in the more loving and caring relationships we are able to weave—all of us guided by a divine spirit, much larger and wiser than us, all of us bound by a shared desire for justice and wholeness, which reaches across and beyond the many cultures and subcultures of divisions and strife.

A Womanist Legacy of Trauma, Grief, and Loss

Reframing the Notion of the Strong Black Woman Icon

Beverly R. Wallace

G rieving people often develop narratives about the death experience involving the person who died, the death itself, and aftermath of the death. For grieving African Americans, the narratives are also often about the larger societal context for the loss and the grief.[1] Understanding grief, using the narrative of African Americans, can therefore prove beneficial. Using the narrative of the lived experience of my mother, in this chapter I will describe what might be considered a legacy of trauma with grief and the losses connected to that trauma, and how the reaction to the trauma manifested itself in the embracing of the icon of "Strong Black Woman." It has been said about the African American woman, "sorrow rolls right off her brow like so much rain."[2] This suggests that African American women cope easily with the many losses in their lives. This coping with losses has been a constant in which African Americans have a long history of knowing—from their separation from their African homeland, to the selling of their children and loved ones during the time of slavery. Yet, the grief experiences of African Americans,[3] and of African American women in particular, have just recently been fully examined as a matter of importance.[4] Models of grief from this vantage point are now being proposed. Margaret Stroebe and Henk Schut's integrative model of grief[5] suggests that African American women's embrace of "controlled triumph empathy,"[6] that is, remaining emotionally strong in the grief process, is reinforced by African American women's adherence to the cultural icon of being "Strong Black Women."[7]

Grief and Loss: An African American Woman's Perspective

It is often easy to assume that grief is a basic human process, analogous to breathing, sleeping, or walking. And while it may be so, even as the processes of breathing, sleeping, and walking are complex if we fully examine them, the grief process is also complex. Much research has been done to help understand this very human yet very complex dynamic of grief.[8] Yet to understand fully how individuals live with grief and to have a comprehensive knowledge of the grief process, especially after a trauma, it is also important to consider the impact that particular cultural, historical, societal, and religious traits can have on a group's experiences.

In many studies about grief, trauma, and loss, cultural nuances are considered. As noted by Robert Neimeyer in "Meaning Reconstruction Model of Grief," one's adaptation to loss is shaped by personal, familial, and cultural factors.[9] Researchers Stroeb and Schut also suggest that in order to understand how individuals experience grief, one has to understand cultural relationships and ways of life that reinforce particular worldviews.[10] As it relates to African American grief and loss, most researchers and practitioners understand theoretically that the African American grief experience is linked to distinct aspects of African American culture as well as past and present racism inclusive of economic and health disparities. As such, these nuances help bring a better understanding of the complexity of the grief and loss experiences of individuals, families, and communities.

"Controlled triumph empathy" is recognized in grief literature as women's willingness to remain strong in the grief process.[11] African American women not only ascribe to "controlled triumph empathy," but they are also influenced by the cultural and societal ideal that says that it is important for African American women to remain strong. The icon of the "Strong Black Woman" describes this attribute typically used to explain African American women's determination and emotional strength that enables them to deal with the many adversities associated with being an African American woman.[12] The idea of being "strong" refers to African American women's emotional and psychological power. Oftentimes this strength is considered as resiliency. African American women have been able to handle and overcome adversities. Yet in remaining strong, African American women often have emotional reactions that are either considered a liability or disguise. African American women's anger, loneliness, and denial of pain, it appears, are shaped by the expectation that African American women are to adhere to the cultural icon of being invincible. While women of all cultures might have experiences of loss, the controlling and cultural mandate that applauds African American women for their strength also makes the way they deal with grief and losses different from other women.

Sarah's Story[13]

My mother is a womanist,[14] yet she does not know that she is. She embraces that which has been defined by Alice Walker as one who "loves the folk."[15] She has always been one to care for the well-being of others, especially members of her family and the community wherever she lives. In New York, she was active in the Parent-Teacher Association (PTA), though she would have to travel more than an hour by subway to participate in the monthly meetings. Oftentimes she was one of only a few African American parents attending these meetings. She felt it was important to have a presence not only for the sake of her two children but to be present for the other African American children who were attending this predominantly European American school during the early days of integration.

In her small hometown in North Carolina, my mother continues to care for her community through the Family Life Center she developed with little or no financial resources, attempting to offer educational programs for children in her community. She recognizes again the need for a place for African American youth in this rural area to receive after-school care and support. When the church she attended refused to support her idea of a youth after-school-care and senior-care project, my mother took her meager disability income and used her resourcefulness to write grants to fund this passion. Although the funds for this center are now drying up, she continues to try to keep the doors open. Rather than have her funeral at the Episcopal church she now attends, my mother says she wants her funeral to be held at the center she developed and funds for the sake of the youth in the community.

This determined mother of mine had a traumatic childhood experience. The ninth child of Callie and James, my mother, Sarah, was born on a farm. When she was six months old, as was the case for many children during the thirties, she contracted polio. Yet, unlike European American children who received health-care treatment sooner, my mother was unable to receive treatment for her polio until she was six years of age.

The health-care system was not kind to the black community. Separate hospitals and clinics for black people and white people were normative in the 1930s. In the local public health clinics, all the doctors were white and the nurses were, too. The clinic where my mother was first taken to be diagnosed suggested that they did not know what was wrong with her. Over several months and perhaps years, my mother's illness was undiagnosed, which left lots of questions and suspicions about what was wrong with her. A consequence of this unknowing was that my mother's older sister, working as a cook in the home of a white family, lost her job because of the fear that my mother's illness was contagious, creating additional financial hardship for the family, as the income was indeed needed. With their own persistence and the assistance of the woman with whom they sharecropped, however, my grandparents were finally able to get help for their youngest daughter and were told that my mother had polio. That very day, my mother was taken directly to the hospital by car by the Department of Social Services. My grandparents did not go with her.

My mother was taken to a hospital more than ninety miles away. In today's terms, the distance would not seem to be much. But for my mother's family in the rural South, with no means of transportation, my mother's family could rarely visit her. For six months, my mother remained in the hospital with no visit from her parents. This hospitalization occurred twice. My mother was thirteen years old when she returned to the hospital for another three-month stay, again with little contact with her family.

My mother says that it is difficult to think of this period of time in her life. She does remember that during her first hospital stay she cried a lot. She cried mostly because other children in the unit had parents to visit them, but her parents could not do so. The economic situation of this time relegated most black folks to poverty—meager funds and limited resources. She remembers receiving tutoring but missed attending school. She was not old enough to write and also received no letters from her parents, as they could not write either. She was in a leg cast as well as a full body cast and could not move. It was a very lonely time for this six-year-old little girl. My mother says she resigned herself to how things were because there was nothing else she could do. She learned at the age of six how to be "strong."

Upon her return home, my mother could not work on the farm as did her other siblings. She still had a cast on her leg, which remained on six additional months. (She recalls that when the doctors finally took the cast off, she fainted.) She also tells how she often felt like a burden. She would attempt either to make herself helpful in any way that she could or would make herself invisible, spending time reading. This, however, often garnered the wrath of her siblings who had no such luxury; they had to work the farm. One of her brothers did assist her by carrying her when needed and then later building her crutches so that she could walk. (Crutches were not provided by the hospital.) My mother became quiet and self-conscious, especially as her illness was visibly evident with the limp that she developed; her left leg had been in a cast for too many months.

Her hospital stay at the age of thirteen was also difficult but a little better, she recalls. Her stay this time was three months, and her parents visited her once. She was old enough to write letters home and although her mother and father could not write, her brothers and sisters could and did. What seemed to bother her most was the fact that even though she received tutoring, upon her release from the hospital it was too late for her to return to school that year.

My mother continued healing from her illness at home. She was proud and determined that she was going to be like everybody else, not depending on others for assistance but managing despite what others might have perceived to be a handicap. Education was very important to her and, despite missing time away from school when hospitalized, she graduated at the head of her class. She wanted to attend college but, because of financial constraints, she was unable to do so. Perhaps this is why education of youth is so important to her to this day.

At the age of eighteen, my mother followed her older siblings' migration to the North. She married my father, who also moved to New York to find a better life. Unfortunately, city life was difficult for all, and my mother found herself in an abusive marriage. My father told her that she was lucky to have him, as who would want to marry someone who was crippled. My mother continued in this physically abusive relationship. She was still very quiet and kept most of her abuse and pain to herself, as she was also very private. She continued to care for her two young children, even as she also attempted to care for her other family members as well. She became the matriarch of the family, although she was the youngest female sibling. She prepared all Sunday meals and hosted all holiday functions. It was expected that when there was to be a family gathering, my mother would be in charge of making certain that it occurred.

As I reflect on the life of my mother, it appeared that she wanted to please her family, perhaps to repay her family, even if it meant sacrificing herself. My mother upholds the icon of the Strong Black Woman and, at the age of seventy-four, she continues to embraces this controlling image.

The Icon of the Strong Black Woman

The concept of the Strong Black Woman describes the specific sociocultural phenomenon of African American women's sense of strength and resilience.[16] It is the culmination of African American women's experiences of relational losses, gains, hopes, celebrations, and defiance in the context of racial and gender oppression manifested in the way that black women psychologically resist oppression.[17] According to Regina Romero, the concept of the Strong Black Woman has two primary themes:

a. African American women are strong, self-reliant and self-contained; and

b. African American women's role is to nurture and preserve family.[18]

Additional adjectives that describe a Strong Black Woman include the following: determined, resilient, responsible, humorous, controlled, private, and proud. These are the characteristics that describe my mother. Hamilton McCubbin would define the black woman's resiliency as the properties that enable her to maintain her established patterns of functioning after being challenged and confronted by a risk factor.[19] These risk factors may include emotional, and even physical, assaults to African American women's well-being. The Strong Black Woman is therefore one who can continue to endure and withstand emotional pain. My mother's risk factors, including that of low self-esteem, made her an easy target of domestic violence. She endured the abuse for more than fifteen years, and though resilient and finally able to escape the abuse, she continues to deny the pain.

Strong Black Women are also described as being self-reliant. They are seen as capable women able to function independently, thus making it difficult to garner support or even sympathy, since it is presumed that the black woman is able to handle situations well alone.[20] According to D. J. Gandy, the Strong Black Woman is one who "constantly gives out love, attention, and affection, but does not ask for it, nor appear to need it or require it in return."[21] This describes the way my mother functions, though at times you can tell she desires love.

Strong Black Women nurture and preserve the family. They are responsible caretakers and have typically internalized the idea that it is their job to take care of others both physically and emotionally. Striking a balance between her own needs and those of others, especially the needs of her children, is very difficult for the Strong Black Woman.[22]

While the experiences of African American women are not monolithic, it can be said that African American women who adhere to the icon of being strong also feel guilty when they or any member of their family falls short of expectations for accomplishments.[23] This guilt creates further obstacles in their capacity and willingness to take care of themselves. In the narrative described above, as a child growing up on a farm yet unable to assist her siblings in the work, my mother probably felt guilt. She continues to care for everyone else more so than herself and still feels guilty.

Historically, African American women have used humor to vent their feelings,[24] since other means of acknowledging painful emotions are difficult and are often unacceptable for Strong Black Women. "Crying is a secret act not to be shared in public but when shared, done only with the closest few."[25] Therefore, the Strong Black Woman's emotions and actions are controlled. She functions as if she is fine, but in actuality, she is numb. Becoming numb is the typical way many African American women survive painful and psychological insults that would normally be responded to more assertively. She isolates herself when she is feeling vulnerable, thus, she is self-contained.[26] Others do not know how to respond to her whenever she finally does reach out and ask for help. Defined by Patricia Collins and later described by bell hooks, the sociopolitical status imposed on African American women leads to their addiction to being tough.[27] Dr. Jacqueline Grant's womanist theology[28] helps to frame an understanding of how racism, classism, and sexism all contribute to the enduring idea that African American women are to be strong.

The Icon as a "Controlling Image"

Patricia Hill Collins writes about controlling images that are used within the American culture describing how African American women and systems within which African American women live support particular attitudes. Controlling images are those symbols, ideas, and qualities that are attached to African American women and then manipulated and used to justify their role, position, and oppression.[29] According to Collins, each of the images is connected to the relative value of the African American woman in a racist (and I might add sexist) society.[30] These controlling images, such as the image of the "mammy," originated during the slave era and were later exploited and used to fulfill society's needs. Even when the political and economic conditions that originally generated controlling images disappear, such controlling images are retained and even endure.[31]

The ideal images of African American women—these controlling images, typically framed in positive terms—are appreciated. Society, for example, values the idea of a good, dutiful woman, caring for children and the family. The African American family, too, loves the self-sacrificing and emotionally strong woman and mother figure. However, pastoral care theologian Teresa Snorton, in "The Legacy of the African-American Matriarch," in unpacking one such controlling image—that of the matriarch—recognizes that while these images are often affirmed, African American women are also criticized for adhering to these images.[32] As it relates to the icon of the Strong Black Woman, culture both praises and criticizes the African American woman for her strength.[33] Snorton suggests that there needs to be reexamination of these controlling images within our practice of pastoral care.[34]

Intergenerational Transmission of the Strong Black Woman

The icon of the "Strong Black Woman" is transmitted intergenerationally. Most African American girls are reared to be independent and confident and are taught to survive and adapt. This intergenerational transmission of socializing African American young girls to be nurturing, self-reliant, and self-sufficient is the process that E. J. Bell and S. M. Nkomo call "armoring."[35] It is a form of socialization whereby an African American girl acquires the cultural attitudes, preferences, and socially legitimate behaviors for two cultural contexts, that of being an African American and of being a female in the majority cultural context.[36] This socialization is considered a "political strategy for self-protection," whereby a girl "develops a psychological resistance" to defy racism and sexism.[37]

According to Leslie C. Jackson, many African American young women, in the process of armoring, are often taught to mask their anger and to internalize the experiences of the numerous micro-insults and micro-aggressions they experience.[38] Armoring therefore forces many African American young women to adhere to the message that it is important for them to be strong.[39] Many learn from their mothers how to be strong, thus the legacy is continued.

In armoring or socializing young African American girls to be strong, there are risks, however. The question has been raised as to whether or not being strong heightens some young African American girls' need to become superwomen with the consequences of losing the ability to seek help or to allow themselves to be out of control.[40] This critique suggests that some young African American girls may not be able to admit when they are in pain—not even to themselves. This phenomenon further suggests the need to find ways to assist African American young girls and women who do have difficulties and to help them acknowledge grief and losses so that healing may occur.

Understanding Grief and Trauma in the Context of the African American Woman

African American grief is like European American grief in all its cultural, social, and religious diversity. Yet there are differences between African American and European American grief because there is much that is different about the cultures. African American grief might be like European American grief in the core processes of dealing with loss. But African American grief is dissimilar because the history and experiences of African Americans provide different and unique insights into the meaning of the loss.[41] More often than not, racism is implicated in African American experiences of loss and, by extension, in how African Americans grieve and cope with the loss.

African American grief sometimes stems from trauma. In the case of my mother's life story, the trauma occurred when at the age of six years old she was hospitalized. Imagine how frightening it must have been for her to be separated from her parents and siblings and not to have her parents visit for six months. It would seem that she was retraumatized when she returned to the hospital seven years later to be left alone once again.

Trauma is described as a "bodily or mental injury usually caused by an external agent."[42] What makes an event traumatic is, first, the nature of the event itself. The event may involve actual or feared death or serious physical or emotional injury. Second, the event may be traumatic because of the meaning attributed to the event. According to Dena Rosenbloom and Mary Beth Williams, when trauma is imposed from outside, it can undermine a basic sense of trust in others; it can make intimacy with others difficult; and it can disrupt one's sense of self-worth and self-esteem.[43] To understand African American grief as presented in this chapter, we must also consider the emotional injury imposed by systems outside oneself, often unacknowledged by the victims who are affected by the event.

Grief is the emotional, psychological, and physical response to loss.[44] In the African American experience, this grief is compounded by the multiple factors that may accompany the grief experience.[45] African American grief occurs in the context of a substantially shorter life expectancy. African Americans experience early loss of parents, children, siblings, and spouses. Health disparities are a leading cause of death.

While my mother's life was spared, it did not spare her from the grief associated with the trauma of her childhood experience. Institutional racism imposed by the medical-care system relegated my mother to a delay in receiving timely health care and admission to an already hard-to-access health-care system. Societal oppression that relegated my mother's family to fewer life options allowed a little girl to be left alone at a crucial time in her life. The effects of racism and oppression on the African American experience must therefore be considered in understanding grief and loss experiences.

African American Grief and Racism: Family Dynamics and Gender Expectations

Grief includes the collective losses from the ongoing oppression as one tries to deal with and confront many other losses.[46] Growing up in a racist society with issues of injustice would therefore have an impact on family dynamics. As was the case for my family, especially my mother, the emotional losses manifested themselves in strained relationships and life-destructive behaviors including the choice of the wrong life partner, culminating in physical abuse. The African American community and family often helps to reinforce the idea that it is the role of African American women to be strong, denying the expressions of African American women's emotions, even in abusive situations.

African American women, the community, and the African American family's embrace of the controlling image of the Strong Black Woman also has an impact on gender expectations. There appears to be an expectation that in life, and especially during times of grief and sorrow, African American women should be responsible. African American women are often the caretakers within their families. They are expected to hold their emotions in check so that other family members will do the same. If the matriarch in the family "breaks down," then others may also; there is a need for someone to be strong. The willing matriarch will thus suppress her own emotion, present herself as strong, in order to live into this mandate. As noted by Sharon Smith, African American women prioritize the thoughts and actions relative to loss in terms of maintaining first the well-being of the family.[47]

Critique of the Controlling Image

The controlling image—that of the strength of African American women—may prove beneficial for some but may also have negative consequences for other African American women and, by extension, the African American family. Martha Robbins critiques the idea of African American women adhering to the idea of being strong.[48] In examining the dynamics of mother-loss, she recognized that "by internalizing cultural norms (that of being responsible for the care of parents while at the same time maintaining emotional distances), many adult women were confused by their responses to their loss and often buried their grief behind a wall of silence only to feel weak or deficient if grief seeps through."[49] She suggested there is a need to give public expression to African American women's grief over their losses.

Bridgett M. Davis also critiques the idea of being strong. In examining her own response, also to the loss of her mother, Davis suggests that while being strong may have been helpful at the time, in the long run it may not have been beneficial. Davis recognizes that she did not know how to grieve, nor did she have the luxury to grieve because she was taught to be strong: "Everything in my genes, in my family tradition, has coerced me into being strong. Both of my parents came from a line of strong, willful people. That ability to be strong has saved me day to day, but I wonder if it has slowed my overall healing process."[50]

These critiques suggest that while it may be helpful for survival, being strong might also hinder the process of healing from losses. A more inclusive model of care must acknowledge feelings and cognition, empathy and control, and cultural and structural influences, especially in grief-coping responses to death and losses.[51] I concur with Smith that "understanding the ways in which gender socialization and racial-ethnic culture influence experiences may lead to better assessments of coping strengths and weaknesses, as well as the development of viable interventions."[52]

Addressing African American Grief and Trauma: Implications

As noted earlier, there are some similarities in the grief, trauma, and loss processes that are experienced by all persons. And as mentioned, to understand grief and loss more fully, one must take into account the social location of people and the effects of that location in understanding grief and loss. A person not familiar with African American cultures could have a difficult time understanding important aspects of the African American grief experience.

In their article "Narratives in African American Grief," Paul Rosenblatt and Beverly Wallace suggest that a view of African American grief and loss that is not sensitive to issues of racism in the American experience may lead to less than optimal support and counseling.[53] While Stroebe and Schutt suggest that there is a lack of applicability of some grief-work concepts in some cultures where there is adaptation without confrontation, as it relates to their chapter on the Strong Black Woman, they also suggest that regulation or even the disassociation of negative emotions may be appropriate adjustment to loss because they help maintain high levels of functioning.[54] While this may be true, this adaptive coping method of maintaining the image and regulating emotions may only further help support the adherence of the role of the "Strong Black Woman."

A pastoral care provider who is not well grounded in dealing with issues of racism and discrimination could also be harmful to African American women. Pastoral care providers who are not culturally competent or grounded may not recognize how the nature of racism has historically had an impact on the ways in which African American women respond to the many insults of institutional racial and gender discrimination. These people might allow African American strengths to get in the way of their providing pastoral care, as Teresa Snorton warns,[55] thus failing to provide the help and support that African American women may need. They also may not recognize significant coping responses, such as remaining strong and resolved, as some African American women deal with their pain, rather than crying and announcing their hurts and grief. The consequence of this unawareness is that the legacy of remaining strong is upheld, the method of coping remains the same, and healing may not take place.

To what particular things should pastoral care providers and counselors therefore be sensitive in designing grief interventions, support, and programs? First, pastoral counselors and professionals should keep in mind that there is diversity in the life experiences of African American women. These differences include not only gender differences but also socioeconomic differences as well. And as mentioned above, the sociopolitical nuances that complicate their life experiences are issues professionals must consider.

Second, the continuation of the effect of the historical and systemic trauma ought to be unpacked. The experiences of trauma imposed by systems and institutions give important information to help understand the lived experiences of those affected by the trauma. For many African Americans, it is at unexpected times that this grief deferred shows up. For example, one way that African American grief is expressed is in delaying the expression of the grief.[56] African Americans are living with traumatic grief. Assisting African American women to become aware of their grief (when appropriate) will in fact give African American women more strength and control of their lives. Unpacking the trauma, though painful, will help African American women begin to heal themselves.

Third, racial injustice, distrust of clinical and research institutions, fear of stigmatization, and lack of comfort with clinicians could be potential barriers to African American individuals seeking support.[57] African Americans may be reluctant to participate in grief support groups out of fear of racism and discrimination by white participants and organizers. Support groups provided by African American churches could prove to be helpful. Provision of a safe place where African American women can express their full range of emotions and responses to their suffering with appropriate therapeutic approaches is essential.

Fourth, the religiosity and spirituality of African American women should be examined. Diversity in the life experiences of African American women also includes their religious and spiritual experiences. While African Americans who are active religious participants often adhere to religious belief systems, not all African Americans attend church. Assumptions about the religiosity and spirituality of individuals and support of the church should not be made. And while religious ideas keep many African Americans strong, those same religious beliefs and theological ideas may sometimes also reinforce, for example, the impossible ideal of African American strong women. The task for African American women is not to become weak but to discern how and when to use strength.[58] This can assist with the healing process.

Fifth, the ecological systems that collectively keep Strong Black Women in their place must be examined more closely. This system includes not only the macro-system, such as societal institutions, but also familial systems, including that of the African American community and family. This type of critical investigation and analysis would examine and reflect upon ideological beliefs to see how contemporary social practices and cultural concepts and traditions can or cannot be rationally justified. Such an examination would uncover those traditions cloaked in silence that, as feminist writer Audre Lorde said, may not be helpful:

> I think of how important it is for us to share with each other the powers buried within the breaking of silence, about our bodies and our health, even when we have been schooled to be secret and stoical about pain and disease. But that stoicism and silence do not serve us nor our communities, only the forces of things as they are.[59]

There are high expectations of African American women supported by the ideology that African American women are to be strong: "The shoulds [of being a black woman] are so demoralizing and dehumanizing. It takes away my whole humanity."[60]

The icon of the Strong Black Woman and the toll that grief and trauma may have on the emotional well-being of some African American women is therefore an important concept to understand. The cost of adhering to this icon is enormous as the legacy of having to be strong continues. As Julia Boyd says, being black and being a woman can be viewed as a blessing and a curse: "We're expected not to deviate from the mold of how we are supposed to be as Black women. It is expected that our loyalty to our race must and should override our loyalty to our individuality as women."[61]

There is a need for professionals, including pastoral care practitioners, to become aware and make use of appropriate therapeutic measures to assist African American women in unpacking their grief and historical trauma experiences. These measures include, as Snorton suggests, a safe place where African American women can express their anger, sadness, grief, anger, fears, and all of their emotions and responses to their losses—known and unknown—with appropriate therapeutic approaches.[62] Disclosure intervention[63] and womanist models of care[64] are such appropriate examples.

For the purpose of healing, there is a need for African American women to talk about these expectations of being strong. African American women's grief groups with discussions on the icon of the Strong Black Woman, led by knowledgeable facilitators, would be helpful in assisting African American women to move toward healing. Gender and cultural awareness for all counselors and therapists is essential.

There is also a need for African American women to redefine the ideology of the Strong Black Woman, employing what is called using "power from the periphery," the redefinition of one's involvement in an oppressive system by establishing alternative ground rules and accepting the consequences of not doing politics according to the system's rules.[65] This would entail African American women using their strength to look at the trauma and to examine its impact on their well-being. This might include the African American woman exploring her coping behaviors, including the cost of caring for others at the expense of herself. This might involve defining rules of engagement within the workings of societal and familial systems for purposes of health, noting that systems and the way systems function might have to change. The challenge in doing so might be that the African American woman may be perceived as being "out of order," meaning not adhering to behaviors as others had scripted them to be.

When working with African American women, it is the understanding of this concept of the icon of the Strong Black Woman and the toll that it may take on the emotional well-being of some African American woman that may prove to be crucial. The cost of adhering to this icon is enormous, though the legacy of having to be strong continues.

Summary

This chapter has shown how systemic trauma and experiences of grief and loss and African American women's response to grief and loss may manifest itself in upholding the icon of the "Strong Black Woman." This dynamic was illustrated using the life-story of my mother's childhood experience of polio as a case in point. I hope that informative themes gleaned from "Sarah's Story" could be useful in understanding and addressing the adaptive coping method used by African American women. This chapter presents "a" perspective about African American women's grief and trauma experiences. It does not propose to suggest "the only" perspective about African American grief, trauma, and loss; as each individual is unique, each life experience is also unique. Respectful, knowledgeable support of African American women will always require attention to the uniqueness of each individual, situation, and community. It is my hope that this perspective will highlight matters in understanding the complexity of grief, trauma, and loss as it relates to African American women.

Breaking the silence of African American women's pain is important and, at the same time, the strength and legacy of African American mothers must be honored. Historically, African American mothers, for example, provided roots of strength that their daughters needed in order to work through the traumatic history and legacy of being African American and female in this country. However, African American women's roots are also entwined with violence, pain, and silence imposed by systems and institutions whose sole purpose is to maintain itself. Recognizing social institutions, including health-care systems, from a historical perspective can assist in developing a deeper understanding of the lived experiences of African American women. African American women can begin to acknowledge their pain as well as their strength and the source of their grief and trauma. African American women can redefine their strength by reexamining their involvement in systems that benefit from African American women's continued adherence to the "controlling image" to be strong. African American women can then also envision healing—a healing strengthened by a new definition of what it means to be a "Strong Black Woman."

Pastoral Care of Korean American Women

The Degeneration of Mothering into the Management of an Inadequate Sense of Self[1]

Angella M. Pak Son

Motherhood is usually perceived as one of the most noble human identities and activities. It would not be an exaggeration to say that motherhood is often surrounded in mythological meaning. Motherhood is understood as an ability and power that transcends the very human ability and power. Mothers are seen as the most loving, giving, understanding, patient, wise, and even strong persons that can extend themselves beyond the normal level of human effort. While women are perceived to be weak and fragile, mothers are seen as women who suddenly acquire superhuman ability and powers that are beyond all measures of human possibility. Mothers are available to us with endless time and emotional capacity. They are both cheerleaders for our successes and accomplishments in life and comforters in our times of failures and pains. Motherhood is thus regularly revered and held in utmost respect and love. This highly elevated status and celebration of motherhood is abundantly demonstrated by the respectful extravagance expressed for mothers on Mother's Day in our society.

It is, however, alarming to note the discrepancy between this romanticized picture and ritualized celebration of motherhood and the reality of the daily experience of people. Undeniably, while there are those who truly love and respect their mothers, there are also, at best, those who are ambivalent about their mothers and, at worst, those who hate their mothers with the very fiber of their being. Because of the societal discourse that highly elevates motherhood, there are also many who struggle with the dissonance between their own individual discourses that vary greatly from the societal ideal characterized as a loving relationship. The undesirable side of motherhood, which is more or less an underground discourse in the society, contains the opposing characterization of mother as domineering, invasive, controlling, indulgent, selfish, unreliable, and perhaps even stupid. While a certain extent of discrepancy between our understanding of ideal motherhood and our real experiences of mothers should be granted to exist, the wide gulf between the two should not be ignored but be

examined closely. I propose that, when motherhood is closely examined, sacrificial motherhood, however paradoxical it may sound, is one of the responsible
factors for the wide dissonance between the highly elevated motherhood held by
the society and the deeply resented motherhood experienced by some people in the
society. Sacrificial as well as neglectful mothering is used to manage mothers' own
low self-esteem and self-development.

In this chapter, while myths of motherhood are universal and especially
troubling in the United States, I offer greater understanding of the particular
cultural myths of Korean American mothering. The cultural myths of Korean
American mothering are shaped by Confucianism, challenged by immigration
and gender role changes thereof, and complicated by the interlocking dynamics of racism and sexism. I propose that many of the arguments in this chapter
apply to women with other ethnic or societal backgrounds: motherhood, when
both neglectful and sacrificial, is used to manage an inadequate sense of self. It
is, nonetheless, beneficial to focus on one ethnic group of women and on the
particularities of the group in order to respond with more tailored and appropriate pastoral strategies for the group. Closely examining the discrepancy between
the ideal notion and real experiences of motherhood by observations of Korean
American women affords a heightened clarity of the influence of the patriarchal
system in the society, Confucianism. While it is important to address pastoral
care of women in various situations including single women, older women, bar-
ren women, widows, and so forth, I have chosen to examine the experiences
of the first-generation Korean American mothers, including both biological
and nonbiological such as adoptive, step, foster, surrogate, and the like. I chose
these particular women because they make up the current majority of Korean
American mothers. In addition, their plight is most challenging among Korean
American mothers, including their inevitable uprooting and rerooting experiences and their particular need to negotiate between two different cultures,
Korean and American. In addition, the simplicity afforded by focusing only on
first-generation Korean American mothers can deepen the discussion, and the
study's implications for pastoral strategies can be made more relevant and specific. While the discussion is focused on the first-generation Korean American
woman, it can be easily applied to 1.5- and second-generation Korean American
mothers with some modifications as well as to women from other ethnic and
social backgrounds.

Unlike the conventional precedent of blaming mothers themselves for not
measuring up to the ideal notion of motherhood, I will argue how the societal
norm of a subordinate role for women (sexism) and an inferior status due to their
ethnicity (racism) are major contributing causes for the inadequate sense of self
found in Korean American women. These societal expectations, in turn, reduce
mothering into a means of managing women's inadequate sense of self. This
degeneration of mothering into the management of an inadequate sense of self is

responsible for the labels attached to the negative side of motherhood. I will further point out the danger of a mother's inadequate sense of self being transmitted to the next generation. I will then discuss some theological dimensions and propose several pastoral strategies for the care of Korean American women that have implications for the care of Korean American men and children as well. In particular, I posit that Korean American women use their understanding of sacrificial motherhood to manage low self-esteem and lack of self-development. Pastoral strategies thus must focus on building strong selves rather than just on warning against excessive self-sacrifice.

The societal attribution in both Korea and America of inferior status to Korean American women has an unavoidable implication for the development of their psychological self. Heinz Kohut,[2] who is the originator of the psychology of the self, is helpful in guiding us to a more appropriate answer for the discrepancy between the ideal notion of and our actual experiences of motherhood; this understanding is an alternative to simply pointing our finger at some mothers for their inadequate mothering. By consulting Kohut's psychology of the self, I argue that the subordinate role imposed on women by society is the cause for the lack of the development of the self or an inadequate sense of self that is characterized by insecure, indulgent, inadequate, selfish, controlling, intrusive, and domineering behaviors. In particular, in the case of Korean American women, Confucianism—as the key factor in attributing the subordinate role to Korean American women—causes the lack of the development of the self. I additionally claim that Korean American women are at risk of further stagnation of self development because of the following: (1) the damage to their self-identity as mothers, which is mainly associated with the education of their children in Confucianism, due to their lack of knowledge about and their inability to deal with the education of their children in the United States; and (2) their dehumanizing experience of racism due to the inferior status of their Korean ethnicity attributed by American society.

Women's Inadequate Sense of Self Based on Self Psychology

While many developmental psychologists have described the psychological process of development as one that moves from being dependent on mothers to becoming an independent self, their descriptions of the developmental process of children lacks the delineation of the specifics of the quality of mothering. They have mainly developed various theories on what the children's maturity from dependence to independence from their mothers entail, while assuming the universal understanding of the trusting and caring mother's love. For instance, John Bowlby[3] has described the dynamic of a child's psychological development in the dialectic of attachment and loss—a child's growth by a successful attachment to the mother that eventually leads to independent individuation of the child as opposed to a child's pathological state of anxiety and anger due to a repeatedly experienced loss of the mother. Margaret Mahler[4] has described the process of psychological development as the separation-individuation process and offered three different stages: (1) *hatching*: the beginning of separation from the symbiotic relationship with the child's mother and the shift from inward-directed to outward-directed attention by the child; (2) *the practicing period*: the repetition of the child's assertive and autonomous actions demonstrating the physical separateness from the mother approximately between ten months and sixteen months of age; and (3) *the rapprochement phase*: the reestablishment of the child's attachment to the mother while maintaining the separateness from the child's mother. D. W. Winnicott[5] has made a claim about an infant's progress in the relationship with the mother developing from object relating by a symbiotic child to object use by a child who experiences the mother as an independent object. Erik Erikson[6] also described how a person goes through eight different psychosocial stages in life; identity formation emerges as the core task in the fifth stage, occurring during one's adolescence. While the insights from the developmental psychologists have been invaluable, most of them have defined psychological development generally as one's development of autonomy from others. In particular, none of them has distinguished the necessity of mothering or parenting needed for the child to make developmental progress. Most of them assume that people already understand what necessary care is for an infant or a child, that is, the provision of a trusting and responsive environment.

Heinz Kohut, the creator of the psychology of the self, takes an exception. Kohut delineates the specific shape of a mother's responses necessary for a child's psychological development as well as the nature of the developmental process of a child. Kohut has specifically defined psychological development as the development of a cohesive self that is self-assured and able to claim its independence from other selves. This self also flexibly negotiates independence and interdependence from other selves as needed by different situations. Moreover, he elucidates the specific quality of the care that a child needs to develop a cohesive self. According to Kohut, in order for one to develop a cohesive self, empathic responses to meet three major functions are needed from the primary caregiver: (1) one's healthy self-assertiveness needs to be affirmed in order to develop sound ambition and purposes in life; (2) one's healthy admiration for another needs to be affirmed in order to foster ideals and values in life; and (3) one's talents and skills need to develop to match one's ambition and ideals.[7] Kohut thus defines both the types of people who can serve as our primary caregivers and the types of responses from them that are necessary for us to mature and be self-assured in facing life's various and complex challenges in human relationships. We need someone who is able to see the good in us as we grow up, no matter how nonsensical or even immoral we may seem or sound; we then eventually form adequate ambitions and purposes in life. We also need someone to admire, who allows us to share in and own the very greatness we admire in that person. What is more, we need someone who encourages and facilitates our development of appropriate talents and skills to pursue both our ambitions and ideals in life.

While women's movements have made certain things more readily accessible to girls today in both Korean and American societies, though in different degrees, it is nonetheless plain to see how the still imposed subordinate role on women hinders in all three functions mentioned above the development of a cohesive self among women. Girls are often not affirmed of their own greatness. Instead, they are regularly affirmed only when they mold themselves to the restricted roles defined by society. Girls are consistently affirmed only when they manifest those traits prescribed by the society as the "feminine traits," such as being fragile, passive, submissive, dependent, and so forth. They are frequently scorned as being not feminine enough or being mannish if they exhibit some of the traditionally understood male traits such as being strong, active, or independent, or taking the role of providers, protectors, or leaders. They are thus likely not to develop appropriate ambitions or purposes in life. Society also imposes whom their ideal figures should be—that is, the ideal woman defined by society. If girls find in some men their "ideal traits," it is often unlikely that those men would allow the girls to join in their achievements. Women's talent and skill training is likewise geared more toward becoming women with the highest "feminine" virtues. For instance, women's talents and skills would not ordinarily be formed in building leadership. On the contrary, their abilities would be directed toward such things as reading other people's emotional state or toward satisfying needs such as hunger for food, need for comfort, need for an extra hand, and the like.[8]

The Damaging Influence of Confucianism on the Development of the Self among Korean American Mothers

Undisputedly, this subordinate role for Korean American women in today's society can be traced back to the influence of Confucianism, which was chosen as the national orthodox teaching at the founding of the Choson Dynasty in 1392.[9] The influence of Confucianism on the Korean people has been far-reaching, comprehensive, and pervasive since it is a whole way of living that incorporates both ideology and the practice of daily life. It has moral, philosophical, and spiritual teachings as well as specific notations of rituals, customs, and even educational curriculum.[10] While Confucianism emphasizes the Way of harmony and the cultivation of the self, its pursuit benefited mainly *yangban* (aristocrat men) and not women or *sangnom* (servant-class men). The subordinate role of women is evident in its emphasis on *nam jon yu bi*, which means that men should be respected and women should be lowered. It is the virtues that represent the inherent superiority of men and inferiority of women. Moreover, a woman's identity under the influence of Confucianism is characterized mainly by obedience as reflected in *samjong chido*, the rule of threefold obedience— women are to obey their fathers in their childhood, their husbands during marriage, and then their sons in old age when they become widows.

A woman's subjectivity is thus rarely mentioned and girls are almost invisible in the teachings of Confucianism. While girls are mentioned indirectly in *samjong chido*, which teaches women to obey their fathers in their childhood, they are not referred to in the five major relationships in the society by Confucianism: the right relationship between father and son, between ruler and subject, between husband and wife, between elder and younger both within and without family, and between friends.[11] It is easy to note how daughters or girls are not mentioned in these relationships, although one can argue that girls are included in the fourth and the fifth relationships. This invisibility of girls and the low status of women are clearly evident in the following characteristics of the traditional Confucian family system: (1) only the paternal line of relatives were regarded as relatives; (2) social class and rights were transmitted only from fathers to sons; (3) the sole authority in the family rested with the father who held control over the children; (4) marriages were allowed only with those outside the blood clan; and (5) firstborn males held the right to lineal succession.[12] What is more alarming about the influence of Confucianism on the status of women is that, while the lack of women's positive self-regard in Confucianism is inherent because of Confucianism's classification of women as being inferior to men, it is further reinforced by its narrow restriction of women's roles to that of wives and mothers.

Confucianism emphasizes women's virtue as *hyun mo yang cho*, which literally means the wise or sacrificial mother and submissive wife. This is time and again reflected in further descriptions of women's virtues. The goal of life for a woman is to develop the virtues of filial piety, loyalty, chastity, and fidelity. Women's filial piety was explained further as "her filial piety towards parents and parents-in-law, assistance to her husband and education of her children."[13] In Confucianism, the identity of the woman depends greatly on how good a daughter or daughter-in-law she is, how submissive a wife she is, and how wise a mother she is. A Korean woman's identity depends mainly on her ability to practice what Charisse Jones and Kumea Shorter-Gooden call "shifting," the African American practice of subterfuge for survival. They argue this practice is most pronounced in black women's lives, stating: "Black women are relentlessly pushed to serve and satisfy others and made to hide their true selves to placate White colleagues, Black men, and other segments of the community. They *shift* to accommodate differences in class as well as gender and ethnicity."[14] A Korean woman learns to shift her self-identity in various relationships in order to placate herself to others such as her parents-in-law, husband, children, and so on. This shifting is extended to include Korean American women living in the United States. This subordinate status of Korean American women persists because the influence of Confucianism in the Choson Dynasty has lived on in the Korean national consciousness[15] and continues to be the main paradigm in the relationship between Korean American men and women.[16]

Renegotiation of Korean American Women's Sense of Self in the United States

Due to the change in their community context, their uprooting and rerooting experiences, this restricted designation for women as sacrificial mother and submissive wife creates a complex dynamic for Korean American men and women. Specifically, it creates both the enhancement of a cohesive self and a further stagnation and deepening of the inadequate sense of self in Korean American women with respect to their relationships to their parents, parents-in-law, and husbands. With respect to their relationship to their children, however, I will argue that Confucianism's narrow definition of motherhood, which focused solely on the education of children, causes grave damage to women's identity as wise mothers and thus brings further stalemate to the cohesiveness of their selves.

One of the most drastic changes in the lives of Korean American women is their direct economic participation in their families. While many Korean women are stay-at-home mothers, most Korean American women work outside the home because of necessity. The majority of Korean American women enter the labor force in small businesses, and many work together with their husbands in their own family-owned small business such as a dry cleaning store, grocery store, deli, restaurant, and the like. There is a smaller fraction of Korean American women who hold professional positions such as a bank officer, pharmacist, accountant, real estate agent, lawyer, doctor, and so on. Because their occupational role is added to those assigned to them in Korea— that is, domestic, marital, and parental roles—their "role proliferation" or "a coterminous, continuous, and additive combination of two (or more) disparate, high-commitment activities"[17] becomes more intense in the United States and they inevitably face the helpless condition of the "scarcity of resources for role fulfillment."[18] In other words, their economic participation creates the biggest hurdle in their ability to keep up with the expected responsibilities toward their parents, parents-in-law, husbands, and children. They simply do not have enough physical hours to tend to the needs of their various family members. They are not able to spend as much time in cleaning and tidying up the house, cooking the nice meals and doing the laundry for the family, or observing all the traditional holidays, family birthdays, or other significant events.

This situation becomes even more complicated when their parents or parents-in-law remain in South Korea. Physical separation heightens the sense of abandonment for both the women and their parents or parents-in-law. Their parents and parents-in-law feel abandoned by their daughters or daughters-in-law as they receive less physical contact and/or phone or mail/e-mail contact from their children. The adult children also feel inadequate from a sense that they have abandoned their parents even though that is far from their intention. Korean American women thus have a sense of not quite measuring up to the role of "good daughter" or daughter-in-law since they are so heavily tasked with simple daily survival. While they are under extreme stress internally about not being "good-enough" daughters or daughters-in-law, they often experience a certain amount of relief from the high expectation. Because of the inevitable fact that they simply do not have much time left to attend to their parents, parents-in-law, and family and traditional matters, they are justified in excusing themselves from traditional expectations on them, although hidden expectations still linger and weigh heavily on them. Additionally, living outside of South Korea and apart from many of the relatives, friends, and other significant social acquaintances automatically reduces their heavy responsibility for maintaining traditional observances and respectable relationships with this social circle. This also means less physical and emotional support from others. They are as a result less driven by relational and traditional obligations externally placed on them and more able to live lives based on their own decisions and initiatives while they still carry an internal sense of expectations and responsibility.

A simultaneous increase and decrease in the adequate sense of self in Korean American women is also observed in their relationship with their husbands. As Korean American women bring significant financial resources into the home, more and more household decisions are shared between them and their husbands. Shared decisions result in an increase in the power of Korean American women within the family. Several studies confirm this development of a more egalitarian attitude in the relationship between Korean American men and women on some decision matters.[19] While this redistribution of power in the Korean American family brings empowerment to Korean American women, it nevertheless simultaneously puts a greater burden on them as well. An overwhelming amount of both physical and psychological strain is placed on them. Some studies have noted that the actions, roles, and lifestyles still reflect a strong gap in the status between Korean American men and women, and the increase in the economic participation of Korean American women is not matched by a corresponding increase in the household participation of Korean American men.[20] Korean American women are thus forced into a double bind of being responsible for both economic and household duties, like a superheroine who brings in the bread, keeps the house clean, ensures the children's education is up to par, feeds the family, and so on. They are physically overworked and psychologically stressed out with this overwhelming amount of responsibility. More importantly, they live with a sense that they are not doing a good job in any of these areas.

Yet, a Korean American woman's expanded role as co-breadwinner for the family also creates opportunities for her to increase self-esteem and enhance her adequate sense of self. While women participate in the labor market, the nature of work they engage in usually does not correspond to the level of their education. Some find a boost in their self-esteem by the affirmation received from their supervisors for being a good worker in nondomestic jobs. Sometimes they receive even better praise than their husbands since these women have learned to follow directions whereas their husbands only give directions. Others demonstrate a superior ability to that of their husbands in running a small business. This may result from the fact that their main role as a housewife taught them many basic principles and skills useful in operating small businesses.

The increase in a Korean American woman's power within family, however, generally causes acute tension to arise within the traditionally defined dominant husband/submissive wife relationship. Several studies have noted how the growing independence of Korean American women creates more conflict between Korean American women and their husbands than between their counterpart Korean women and their husbands.[21] Some Korean American men experience frustration since they are not the only authoritative voice in the family. In some cases, they experience inadequacy and rage as they are less able than their wives to work in a job or run a small business. As a result, the shift in Korean American women's role from housewife to co-breadwinner brings a substantial decrease in Korean American men's adequate sense of self. Some Korean American husbands thus try harder and harder to claim a traditional status as the sole figure of authority in the family by harshly demanding submission from their wives. A few even resort to violence as Pyong Gap Min and Young I. Song suggest from their study.[22] As noted by E. Chun, according to the records of the Los Angeles County Attorney's office, the number of Korean American men accused of domestic violence was the highest among all Asian American men.[23] The grueling stress brought on by redistribution of power within the relationship between Korean American women and their husbands produces significant damage to the level of intimacy and a number of these relationships end in divorce. While Korean American women experience an increase in self-assuredness by having more of a voice in family matters and by receiving recognition of their ability as a qualified worker or successful business entrepreneur, they also experience a precariousness in their identity as submissive wives. This is due to the increase in marital tension and conflict resulting from a corresponding decrease in their husbands' sense of self-assurance.

Further Stagnation of Korean American Women's Self in the United States

While Korean American women's relationships to their parents, parents-in-law, and husbands in the United States brought both enhancement and damage to their sense of adequate self, Korean American women's identity as wise mothers is most at risk. Since their concept of motherhood is defined singularly by their role in the education of their children, they are supposed to be the expert on children's education and carry out what needs to be done to ensure the best quality of education for their children. In South Korea, a Korean woman's concern is to find out what is the best way to prepare her children to enter a prestigious college or university and then implement those things, including participating in PTA, garnering help from school teachers, sending their children to the best possible *hakwon* (an outside-school academy), to strengthen both academics and special talents such as music, art, dance, and so forth. Some mothers would even work as nannies or housemaids to afford these for her children's education. Those who cannot afford them experience the inadequate sense of self as mothers. In the United States they are, however, no longer experts on their children's education. In fact, they suffer extremely heightened anxiety because of a lack of knowledge about the intricacies of the U.S. education system, which is completely different from the South Korean education system. For many, owing to a lack of language proficiency and cultural familiarity, they encounter extreme frustration and anxiety by not being able to accomplish things well even when they understand what they need to do. Even for those whose level of English proficiency is adequate, they may still experience a sense of incompetence because some of the things requested by the schools can be very taxing for them.

They thus need to depend on others, whether for good or bad, to handle their children's education in the United States. For instance, if their husbands have a better mastery of English and are willing, they may take the expert role in educating children. If that is not the case, Korean American women must often depend on others, although the level of dependence may vary. As a consequence, they have inevitably relegated their most important role as the one responsible for the children's education to their husbands or another and predictably experience some amount of resignation and helplessness. In addition, they frequently have to depend on their own children to learn about the school system and to prepare for college entrance exams and applications, and so forth. In many cases, they must also depend on their children to write the correspondence to teachers, school administrators, or others. This role reversal between mothers and children has the effect of compromising their authority for nurturing their children and "the children experience the ebbing of parental authority, including parental moral value systems."[24] While the rise in the number of Korean American businesses providing various services that assist with high school education and college applications alleviates some of this problem, the constant and pervasive uncertainty about mothers' ability to provide for their children's education brings further impasse to an adequate sense of self.

Confucianism's limited designation of the role of mother as the educator of her children, combined with the loss of a sense of her expertise as an educator, is not the only major reason causing further fragility in her cohesive self. The interlocking reality of sexism and racism experienced by women of color in the United States is an additional experience of dehumanization of Korean American women's dignity as human beings.[25] While they are working or handling household matters, they often experience racial prejudice in the external community that treats them as ignorant, inferior, or imperfect human beings. Their efforts to deal with coworkers in the labor force, or with retail customers and business-related persons as small-business owners, almost always require an extra amount of emotional energy. Even delivery persons repeatedly give them disrespectful treatment, implying that Korean American small-business owners do not deserve to be business owners. When they deal with banks and other business establishments, they usually try to be prompt and proper, with everything in order, so as not to cause any irregularity. This is because dealing with any irregularity, however insignificant it might be, may become an unwelcome occasion for them to incur a dehumanizing experience.

For instance, Young Hee, who with her husband Chan Ho runs a grocery store in the Bronx, feels that her employee, Diane, is disrespectful to her. This manifests itself by the fact that she always has to repeat instructions to Diane three to five times before Diane will actually do what Young Hee wants her to do. Young Hee feels that Diane treats her as a subordinate instead of as her boss who pays her wages each week. She often takes care of things herself instead of requesting that Diane do them in order to avoid the dehumanizing experience of losing her dignity at the hands of this employee. Similarly, Sook Ja and her husband own a sizable dry cleaning store in Manhattan. While their work is appreciated by many of their customers, Sook Ja lives in constant fear of her customers because a few bring their dry-cleaned clothes back and complain about the damage done to their clothes, treating her and her husband like unworthy slaves. These customers belligerently imply with their tone of voice and attitude that Sook Ja and her husband are imbeciles to have made such simple mistakes. They call for immediate action to meet their demands. Just to avoid any more problems and further dehumanizing experiences, Sook Ja will submit to the demands of these customers despite knowing that she does very careful work and that these customers are raising complaints unreasonably. These are only a few examples of numerous and uncountable instances of dehumanizing experiences of racism that Korean American men and women encounter. Kelly Oliver's definition of racism points out the profound and exacerbating nature of alienation in their experience of racism. Kelly Oliver calls racism the "alienation of colonization and oppression"[26] or the "debilitating alienation" and depicts clearly the harmful effects of racism on subjectivity.[27] Similarly, this new additional experience of racism adds to further alienation of the Korean American women's cohesive self and robs them of their subjectivity.

The Degeneration of Mothering into the Management of an Inadequate Sense of Self among Korean American Women

The Korean American woman's insecure sense of self has a devastating impact on her children. According to Kohut, people with an insecure sense of self or lack of the development of a cohesive self create children with the very same problem. When the mother as the primary caregiver does not have a self-structure developed, she has to turn to others to fill the functions of her self and, in turn, is unable to provide empathic mirroring or idealizing responses needed for her children. There are three different cases of the misapplication of empathic responses, "faulty empathy, overempathy, and lack of empathy,"[28] and Kohut elaborates on them:

> (a) [T]he mother's self-absorption may lead to a projection of her own moods and tensions onto the child and thus to faulty empathy; (b) she may overrespond selectively (hypochondriacally) to certain moods and tension in the child which correspond to her own narcissistic tension states and preoccupations [and thus to overempathy]; (c) she may be unresponsive to the moods and tension expressed by the child when her own preoccupations are not in tune with the child's needs [and thus to lack of empathy].[29]

Mothers whose selves are not cohesive are primarily preoccupied with their own self needs and cannot feel other people's self needs.[30] Such a mother would use other people's concern as an occasion to bring up her own self concern. For instance, a good example of faulty empathy is a mother's inability to celebrate her son's pride in his accomplishment of getting an 85 on his math test. The mother's rather empty self structure is unable to celebrate her son's pride in his achievement and, instead, the mother responds to the child with her sense of inadequacy and points out to the child how the test score *85* is not good enough. She then goes on talking about how she used to get As on her tests; unconsciously, she does this in order to ward off her own sense of inadequacy. The pride of the child is crushed and the subjectivity of the child as the focus is quickly replaced by the subjectivity of the mother as the focus.

In other words, these mothers engage in the noble role and task of mothering not to nurture their children but to manage their own insecure sense of self. Mothering thus degenerates into a means to maintain the mother's own intact sense of self. This mothering is no longer focused on facilitating the maturity of children by allowing them to be the center of the universe. The mothering is instead used to keep the mother as the center of the universe in a way that she never had the chance to be previously. This sounds like mothering gone bad demonstrated in the neglect of children and the selfishness and self-absorption on the part of the mother. A crucial point is that this degeneration of mothering also manifests itself in dedicated and sacrificial mothering. For instance, here is an example of overempathy: a mother, who is in need of high achievement, overly affirms her child's high achievement in school while she allows the child to ignore other of life's important lessons, such as being respectful to others or being responsible for his or her own share in the family or community. This mother sacrificially dedicates herself to helping the child excel in school to the point of doing things herself that are the child's responsibility, not just in school but also in other non-school duties. This is precisely the reason why the great gulf between the highest love portrayed in the romanticized picture of mother-hood and the negative love in degenerate mothering is misleading and ambiva-lent. The paradox about mothering noted in the beginning of the chapter thus is not a paradox after all. Unlike the conventional understanding of the quality of mothering, where mothering is characterized by good or bad mothering, sac-rificial or neglectful mothering, I argue that quality mothering contributes to the development of a cohesive self in children and both neglectful and sacrificial mothering might indicate a lack of quality mothering. What is crucial is whether the mothering is done to support and expand the subjectivity of children and not whether it is sacrificial or neglectful. To put it differently, mothering should be examined on the basis of whether the children are treated as an extension of their mothers (subjectivity of mothers) or as independent agents motivated by their own initiative and making their own decisions (subjectivity of children).

Korean American mothers are under more intense pressure because of the influence of Confucianism. As a result, Korean American mothers seek with single-minded effort to become dedicated and sacrificial mothers for their chil-dren. This, in fact, should serve as a wake-up call to the Korean American com-munity. Korean American mothers put all their time, effort, and resources to help their children attend the most prestigious universities, ultimately striving to see their children in the Ivy League. Because of this devotion and sacrifice for children, motherhood is without a doubt elevated to the highest regard among Korean Americans. To their credit, some Korean American teenagers, 1.5 or second generation, do enter these upper-echelon universities. It is, however, dis-turbing to note another trend among Korean American college students and college graduates. Among Korean American teenagers whose high school rank-ing was someplace between good and outstanding, many of them maintain good grades in college, but others fail to maintain the corresponding ranking and fall precipitously into a ranking between poor and extremely poor. A number of these experience a serious depression so that they barely graduate or sometimes fail to graduate from college.[31]

Even among those who manage to keep up with their college work, a quantity of them later manifest similar adjustment problems as they enter the workforce following graduation from college. They too fall into depression and find themselves unable to hold jobs or find themselves changing jobs frequently without making much progress in their careers. As a result, instead of pursuing a career based on their college education, they choose to help out in their parents' small businesses with the plan to take over the business after their parents' retirement. This pattern is a good indication of how some of the most highly functioning Korean American high school teenagers are not really living their own lives but that of their mothers and fathers. They more or less have followed their mothers' decisions, and their accomplishments during high school were the accomplishments for their mothers and were not really their own. The myriads of decisions required in college are experienced as overwhelming because all prior decisions were more often than not made for them. When they start making their own decisions, they often, as to be expected, wind up making bad choices. Their repeated bad choices, combined with the overwhelming sense that they are faced with too many decisions that have too many options, reinforce their heightened insecurity and helplessness. Many Korean American teenagers are like highly functioning computers—as long as mother is at the keyboard inputting information—but they become like obsolete computers when no one is at the keyboard but themselves. Numerous Korean American teenagers consequently lose the much-needed opportunity to grow up to be their own persons. These teenagers subsequently become confused about their ambivalent feelings or possibly even hatred directed toward their devoted and sacrificial mothers. Those who choose not to trust their own experience as real experience walk further down the road of deepening depression as they continue to forfeit the opportunities to benefit from their own experiences.

Theological Dimensions and Pastoral Strategies

Before specific pastoral strategies are offered, it must be noted that the issue at hand is not just a social or psychological problem but requires careful consideration of theological dimensions. Church and theology offer specific contributions to the issue that social science cannot. I suggest that at least two theological contributions can be set forth: (1) the church and its implicit and explicit theology have a big influence on ideals and ways of life in families; and (2) the theological metaphor and narrative of pilgrimage and wilderness provide hope and guidance. First, with respect to the theological influence on ideals and ways of life in families, we only need to turn to a very fundamental difference in theological positions in the church between that of treating Eve as the origin of evil and thus women as the cause of evil in the daily lives of families and that of treating everyone, both men and women, equal as God's children based on the

apostle Paul's exhortation (Gal. 3:26-29). It is apparent that the former theological position will reinforce the arrest of self development among women and
result in the degeneration of mothering into the management of an inadequate
sense of self while the latter theological position will encourage the development of self among women and avoid the use of mothering for the management
of self inadequacy.

In addition, two particular theological issues are noteworthy to be mentioned
in this discussion: (1) the church must use its language of sacrifice with greater
care and consideration; and (2) the church must expand its narrow notions
of interior spirituality to include acts of social justice. While I address both
of these theological issues below in my discussion of the pastoral strategies,
the theological issue of sacrifice warrants a few words here. As it is explicated
below in the discussion of pastoral strategies, the intentional examination of
the church's current theological position with an open mind on the issues of
sacrifice will point to both the necessity of sacrifice in human life and the crucial importance of the issues of justice in defining the who, what, when, where,
and how of sacrifice. More importantly, the theological issue of sacrifice has
a far-reaching relevance to other theological issues. Bonnie Miller-McLemore
astutely indicates this very point in her book written with Herbert Anderson,
Faith's Wisdom for Daily Living. She posits that discussions on sacrifice extend
immediately into a bigger theological debate about Jesus, atonement, the Lord's
Supper, and the place of self-sacrificial love in Christianity.[32] Consequently, it
is both urgent and essential for the church to engage in critical conversations
about and to reexamine its theological position on sacrifice and other theological issues in order for theology to be relevant and constructive in directing and
steering ideals and ways of life in families.

Second, I suggest that the theological metaphor and narrative of pilgrimage
and wilderness provide hope and guidance. I further suggest that the pervasive
experience of uprooting and rerooting is for Korean Americans a God-given
opportunity to redefine and enhance the various relationships in which they
engage, such as those of women-men, wife-husband, and parent-children. Sang
Hyun Lee's Asian American theology of "called to be pilgrims" is helpful in
making a biblical image and narrative of pilgrimage and wilderness relevant
to the lives of Korean Americans. Lee developed an Asian theology based on
the experience of alienation among Korean Americans who do not experience
belonging fully to either Korean or American culture. By drawing a parallel
with Sarah and Abraham's journey away from home into a foreign land and
the journey of the Israelites in the wilderness before entering the promised land,
he suggests a theological meaning to the marginalized experience of Korean
Americans and posits marginalization as a sacred calling from God. He thus
concludes that Korean Americans have a special vocation to be pilgrims and
work toward realizing God's work in this world. He states:

Having left behind us the securities of belonging to just one world, we are now free enough to dream bigger dreams and to see larger visions than we might have been otherwise. In other words, our alien predicament is something we can turn into a sacred vocation—that is, into a vocation of the pioneers who introduce creative advances and imaginative changes into human society in order to do God's will here on this earth. Such servants of God lead the often uncomfortable life of sojourners, pilgrims.[33]

Lee may not have been so presumptuous after all; we can envision the Korean American community redefining and reshaping relationships that God desires and wills for human beings.

Redefining roles and relationships is the key rather than focusing on what problems are created by the processes of uprooting and rerooting as experienced by Korean Americans in the United States. The unique situation of heightened suffering and pain among Korean Americans can be seen as an inevitable component of life in the wilderness before entering into the promised land. I propose that their wilderness experience affords a God-given opportunity to reconfigure the system of various relationships. By being faithful and taking advantage of this opportunity in spite of inevitable pain and suffering, Korean Americans can contribute toward aiding all women and men to truly appreciate and love one another by means of their example of living in ways that deepen intimacy. It rarely happens that traditional things are shaken enough for new things to appear, yet Korean Americans have been given such opportunity. I suggest that one of the vocational responsibilities of Korean Americans is in redefining traditional relationships and practicing the new relationships that God desires and wills for human beings. To this end, proper pastoral strategies are urgently needed for Korean American churches. This is particularly the case since the role of churches for Korean Americans is very crucial as "church participation has indeed become a way of life among the Korean immigrants in the United States."[34] While many strategies can be devised, I will limit my discussion to four major pastoral strategies.

First, a clear understanding of the dynamic tension between self-sacrifice, mutual love, and adequate sense of self is needed. Many feminist scholars such as Barbara Hilkert Andolsen and Brita Gill-Austern[35] have directed our attention to the harmful effect of self-sacrifice by women in the family. Feminist ethicist Barbara Hilkert Andolsen revisits the notion of *agape*, Christian love, in Christian ethics. Andolsen brings feminist critique to the dominant understanding of *agape* as reflecting the centrality of other-regard and emphasis on self-sacrifice, and proposes mutuality as the apt paradigm for *agape*. She further suggests the ethical implication of *agape* as mutuality and calls for a widespread change in societal structure including both public and private spheres.[36] Similarly, Gill-Austern astutely calls for the replacement of self-sacrifice with mutual self-giving as the paradigm for love in the relationship between men and women. While she acknowledges the possible necessity for the inclusion of self-sacrifice in achieving mutual love, she denies any possibility of self-sacrifice as the love's desirable aim. She nevertheless sees the value of self-sacrifice in parenting and families and posits the importance of distinguishing between life-giving and life-denying self-sacrifice.[37]

Miller-McLemore extends Gill-Austern's concept of life-giving and life-denying self-sacrifice and proposes a new notion, "salvageable sacrifice," which she distinguishes from exploitative sacrifice, the former being life giving and the latter being life denying.[38] Recognizing the inevitable component of intense self-sacrifice required in mothering, she points out the one-sided position on self-sacrifice by both traditional and contemporary theology. She states: "Mutual love is the ideal. But particularly with children, mutual love does not begin mutually, and their care involves a certain measure of parental self-loss and self-renunciation."[39] She calls the parent-child relationship "lopsided mutuality and authority."[40] In light of this necessity of self-sacrifice in the nature of mothering, she makes a crucial move beyond treating sacrifice as altogether an altruistic category, as held in the traditional viewpoint, or as a despairing category, as held by many contemporary feminists. To her, Christians should neither idealize nor dismiss self-sacrifice. Thus is her notion of "salvageable sacrifice," and she cautions us both to be aware of all the damage that the idealization of self-sacrifice has caused for women and to grasp its necessity in family, society, and world politics. She further suggests a "more radical justice in the distribution of domestic labor both within and beyond the private family"[41] as a way to handle salvageable sacrifices in caring for children. Her concept of "salvageable sacrifice" enhances the notion of mutual love and the reflection of a structural change in society called for by Andolsen.

While Miller-McLemore's appeal for the practice of a just distribution of domestic labor without making it into a tit-for-tat kind of struggle is a needed step in redefining the relationship between self-sacrifice and mutual love, her suggestion is still one-sided in that it treats self-sacrifice as a cause of a sense of inadequacy among women. It ignores the aspect of self-sacrifice that results from the inadequate sense of self as implied in Kohut's discussion on the formation of the cohesive self. Women resort to self-sacrifice because it brings stability to their sense of self or it fills them with assurance by satisfying their craving to feel that they do indeed exist or are worthy to exist. Telling them simply not to be self-sacrificing or merely raising their awareness about the exploitative nature of some forms of self-sacrifice will not help them depart from being self-sacrificial. In other words, we need to focus pastoral strategies that enhance the formation of a cohesive self in women in addition to warning them about the harmful effects of self-sacrifice on the part of women. Pastoral strategies for enhancing the cohesive self in Korean American women and pastoral strategies for raising awareness about the danger of self-sacrifice thus need to go hand in hand, but perhaps with far more weight on the former.

Second, in order to address a few of the problems associated with the rigid role distinctions for men and women found in the traditional Confucian system, pastors will need to change their own leadership style and pastoral image. Following the insight found in Bowen's family-systems theory, which observes that the most effective change in a system is brought on by the changes made by the healthiest member or the most differentiated member of the system,[42] changes should be sought first in pastors. In Korean American churches, the healthiest members of the system may likely be the pastors. Korean American pastors as a rule are given an enormous idealized identity that paradoxically combines the authority of the Confucian father with the sacrificial love of the Confucian mother. Instead of simply taking double identity for granted, and developing their style of leadership from that background, Korean American pastors need to take a bold step and assert a different leadership style and pastoral image. In this regard, Jeanne Stevenson-Moessner's suggestion of employing the parable of the good Samaritan is helpful for envisioning a different kind of leadership style and pastoral identity.[43]

Stevenson-Moessner points out a neglected, but crucial, aspect of the parable: the Samaritan finished his journey by employing communal support in the form of the inn and the innkeeper. She argues for two very important aspects of interconnectedness in pastoral leadership. They are the interconnected love of God, others, and self and the interconnectedness among various disciplines. She argues for the importance of love of self as well as love for others and God, particularly in light of current women's inclination to excessive self-sacrifice to the point of self-abnegation. Moreover, she emphasizes the importance of teamwork as a primary paradigm in which the pastor avoids trying to do everything herself but entreats others, both laity and other professionals, to share in the responsibilities. Pastoral leadership should therefore be based on the compassion anchored in the balanced love of God, others, and self and in teamwork reflected by letting go of over-control and sharing the responsibility and authority. When Korean American pastors embrace the pastoral image of the good Samaritan as their leadership style, then Korean American women and their husbands would naturally follow their leadership and embrace that new way of life.

Third, churches need to focus on a variety of programs that can cultivate additional development of a cohesive self in Korean American women and men. Korean American churches already function by helping Korean American families deal with the otherness of U.S. culture, education, business, and so forth. These churches can be more intentional about that role and expand it toward helping people reroot in U.S. society. Similar to children's programs that enhance student skills, Korean American churches need to create programs specifically for adults. These classes could include those that teach English, provide orientation to the American educational system, enhance job skills, and provide employment information. To help Korean American women deal with difficulties arising from dealing with their children's education, something like an education hotline could be provided, perhaps as a concerted effort by multiple churches.

It is vital that Korean American churches realize that many Korean Americans struggle all the more because of their socioeconomic location. In the United States, Asian Americans are considered a "model minority" and their upward mobility in society is often taken for granted. This label pays honor to Asian Americans' hard-working lifestyle and high emphasis on educational achievement in addition to strong family relationships. This stereotype, however, presents a skewed picture of the entirety of Asian Americans. As Jamie Lew profoundly points out, some Korean American high school kids drop out or do very poorly in school because of their difficult socioeconomic conditions. They are plainly ignored by society when it paints a broad picture of "problem-free" Asian Americans.[44] In order to help these people with few resources, churches could mobilize older men and women who are familiar with and able to handle the educational system as volunteers. They could help mothers, both within and outside church, who would benefit from their expertise. In addition, churches can offer more programs or classes to enhance couple and family relationships by addressing a new vision for structuring female-male relationships, taking into account the cultural differences between the relational mode of Korean culture and aggregate mode of U.S. culture. Korean American churches also need to be more explicit about the issues of racism and its influence on Korean Americans so that their sense of adequate self can be better sustained.

Finally, Korean American churches need to eliminate the inconsistency caused by the dualistic division of spirituality and social actions. Korean American churches tend to focus more on the inner state of spirituality and habitually ignore or shy away from a call to social justice. Korean American churches need to embrace both a contemplative spirituality in solitude and a practicing spirituality in connectedness. Although she was formulating a notion of spirituality in the chaos created by highly demanding parenting, Bonnie Miller-McLemore's suggestion of contemplation in chaos is a helpful paradigm that can move us beyond the dualism in aspects other than mothering.[45] She calls us to find spirituality in our ordinary daily activities in addition to traditionally defined arenas for contemporary spirituality.

The foremost step in this process would be to raise awareness on topics such as mental health issues including depression and addiction, domestic violence, racism due to societal structural oppression, and so on. For instance, the awareness related to mental health issues for Korean Americans should be addressed. Korean American churches often treat psychology as a proponent of human desire and they silently ignore it, at best, or publicly denounce it as evil, at worst. In the wake of the April 2007 massacre at Virginia Tech University in which a young Korean American student, Seung Hui Cho, shot and killed thirty-two people and wounded twenty-five others before killing himself,[46] churches need to help Korean Americans address mental health issues and feel safe in dealing with their own or their family members' mental health issues. Korean American churches need to pay attention to both mental health issues in general and particular mental health issues brought on by Korean culture. They thus need to pay heed to the discovery by the World Health Organization that the symptoms of depression manifest differently in various cultures in spite of the presence of the core characteristics of depression defined by DSM IV-TR (*Diagnostic and Statistical Manual of Mental Disorders*, fourth edition, Text Revision).[47] For example, Korean Americans tend to show depression more in somatic symptoms such as headache, backache, stomach problems, and the like than in a psychological symptom of sadness.[48] The reverse is also true. A well-known illness known as *hwa-byung* in Korea can be treated effectively once it is recognized that there are significant similarities between its symptoms and those of major depression as categorized by Western mental health professionals.[49]

Conclusion

Korean American churches are at a critical juncture. They have an opportunity to help not only themselves but also lead others toward creating a better loving relationship characterized by mutual demand and sacrifice with joy and appreciation. It is crucial for the pastors, the leaders of the Korean American churches, to realize that the change has to start with them. One of the implications of this means that there exists a certain amount of responsibility for seminaries to establish closer relationships with Korean American pastors and create relevant continuing-education courses for their further reflection on these issues. It is essential to keep in mind that self-sacrifice of women imposed by society is not only a cause of the arrest in the development of self among women but is perhaps more the result of the lack of the development of the cohesive self. It is thus far more important to focus pastoral strategies to enhance the development of a cohesive self. By doing this, the cause as opposed to the result is addressed and it avoids futile attempts to try to eliminate a result, something that cannot be fully accomplished until the cause is addressed. It is also important to take into account that women's health is not just an issue in relation to women but concerns men and their children as well. Care for women thus should be seen from a multirelational rather than from a single vortex.

More importantly, all of us—both Korean American and non-Korean American communities—face a major shift in our understanding of what good mothering is: good mothering depends on the quality of mothering that actually benefits the children for whom they care. Sacrificial and devoted mothering does not automatically indicate good mothering but the aim of such sacrificial mothering needs to be closely examined to discern if such sacrificial mothering indeed benefits children. Since both sacrificial and neglectful mothering are ways for mothers to manage their inadequate sense of self, simply distinguishing sacrificial mothering as good mothering and neglectful mothering as bad mothering is gravely misleading. We need to be more sophisticated and able to penetrate into the silent cries for help both by mothers with lack of development of the self and by children who are surrendering their chances to develop their own selves. In order to respond adequately to those silent cries, churches need to face squarely the stark reality of the harms brought on by sexism and racism reflected in our cultural practices as well as in our theological understandings. It is time for churches to own up to their own call to God's ministry to all—both women and men, colored and noncolored, have-nots and haves, recent immigrants and early immigrants—so that the grace of Jesus Christ may not be experienced to be lacking but be sufficient for all.

Gyn|Ecology

Woman as a Symbol of Carrier, Protector, and Nourisher of Life

Laura W. Dorsey

Although strangers to one another standing in the hospital elevator, they begin to talk as they move into the damp parking garage. "I have stage 2 breast cancer." "I'm stage 4 ovarian."[1] Their bald heads signal that these women are fighting a terminal illness. They are literally under siege. A 2007 study published in *CANCER: Interdisciplinary International Journal of the American Cancer Society* says that "comprehensive surgical care for women with ovarian cancer is independently associated with multiple factors, including age, race, payer (provider), cancer stage, surgeon volume, and surgeon specialty."[2] Perhaps this is a commonality among women. How are women cared for under siege and what does theology bring to it? Literature and art are full of stories and images of women's struggles within the tension of life and death in all cultures. Around childbirth and the rearing of children, women's willingness to engage in the struggle for life moves them forward. As a carrier of the egg or seed from which life springs, women with cancer come for care out of their own history and relationships. They manifest a need to be seen and accepted where their souls are honored. As distinguished from men, women are often reluctant to experience others caring for them. Women have traditionally been the caregivers. With cancer, women are the receivers. This reversal upsets the "normal order" of organism and environment! Care is shaped in dialogue as unique patterns of meaning emerge.

This chapter unfolds in four parts. The first, "Care of Women Under Siege," brings together feelings that women experience around the diagnosis of cancer using a reflection on the book of Jeremiah;[3] this is followed by statistics of the cancers that are most often experienced by woman and by the significance for diverse cultures. The second part, "Significance of Symbolic Memory," connects us as women to the larger world, its history, and its varied cultures through two examples: a quote from Pearl Buck's *The Good Earth* and a reproduction of Kathe Kollwitz's lithograph *Bread!* The third part, "Potential to Respond

Authentically," highlights the efforts to respond to cancer patients across the disciplines and the world with creativity and intention. The final part, "Service in Dialogue," is a reminder of what we have learned, what it can be like at the bedside, what being authentic can create theologically, and how all of this brings the divine image of God as *mother* and *covenant maker* into clearer focus. Both presence and ritual serve a meaningful role in the health and recovery of women, a recovery that is interlocked with decisions we make about the larger environment, mother earth.

Care of Women Under Siege

Ecology is defined as the relationship between an organism and the environment. The women mentioned above have active, full lives, whether in the private or public arenas or in some combination of both. How do they respond to the diagnosis, treatments, and prognosis? They feel as though they are on an elevator to the unknown. The elevator seems to be out of control as it goes up and down. Sometimes they push the buttons and nothing happens, or the elevator stops, but the doors won't open. They are never quite sure which floor to stop on next. The buttons light up for surgery, chemotherapy, radiation and its side effects. Individual sensitivity varies. Sometimes the experience is similar to a free fall, as though the cable has just snapped. Other times it is like the design of the finely tuned specialists with advanced technology and medicines at his or her command. The jolts come between floors in spite of insurance coverage or lack thereof. These women reach out for some control and coherence in what feels like chaos. The reality of a cancer diagnosis heightens the threatening aspect of being a woman. Intrusion anxiety increases with the concern of actually being taken over by the disease and treatment. In this instance "the female's defense in the face of threat of harm and of her own impulse seems to be more usually withdrawal and avoidance of threat."[4] It is a response shared among women of all cultures.

Like the prophet Jeremiah, many want to cry out to God in anger and despair, "Is there no balm in Gilead?" (Jer. 8:22), but most cannot or will not. They search for safety and health. Their passion is for recovery and solace. Their hope is to somehow make sense of this tragedy, to recover their identities and live. Those of us who visit or sit with a woman through an ordeal of this nature are humbled daily.

Anatomical realities distinguish women with cancer from men.

> For good or ill, much of women's existential life is oriented toward the body and the physical, psychological, emotional, and spiritual aspects of reproduction. Corresponding to bodily issues, women deal with the theological realities of identity, embodiment, generativity, rhythmicity, guilt and shame, limitation, and loss and grieving. The pastoral care needs around the gynecologic issues of contemporary women are great, but the

task of breaking through our learned defenses and creating a viable language and a credible theological presence is difficult, given a patriarchal history and cultural assumptions.[5]

We bear witness to tears, upheaval, and patients' buried feelings of outrage and despair. Their bodies, minds, and spirits are under siege, intruded upon, by the disease and the treatments. The rhythmic balance of their lives is disrupted or destroyed with this disease.

Chaplains and students in clinical pastoral education (CPE)[6] voice several stories during a didactic, a peer learning environment in which chaplains in residency retell their encounters with patients. For instance, a young seminary student shares that her mother died from cancer when she, the student, was only nine years old. Now as an adult she learns that her aunt in a rural area of the South doesn't have enough support to get her to a hospital an hour away for cancer treatment. We can feel the intensity of feelings as she speaks. Her encounters with patients awaken both memories and emotions.

A chaplain who serves in a large metropolitan hospital tells of receiving a referral to visit a patient on the oncology unit. She knows the patient and her husband from earlier hospitalizations. As the chaplain sits at the bedside and listens, she learns the severity of the prognosis. The patient is almost paralyzed at the thought of sharing with her mother, sisters, and daughters. She weeps and keeps saying, "I'm not sure I can trust God."

A chaplain from Africa explains that women come to her at the church for support. One woman who was refusing cancer treatment took refuge in the church. She died there while hoping for a miracle. Another came for prayer and guidance. This parishioner was willing to receive treatment, and she survived. The chaplain shakes her head in anguish.

For some guidance in understanding and reflecting on these experiences I find Kathleen O'Connor's chapter in *The Women's Bible Commentary* helpful.

> Jeremianic themes of weeping and lamentation call upon common human experience, but it is women who are particularly familiar with weeping and grief—grief for their children, for their loved ones, for themselves, for the world. Jeremiah's weeping may help women recognize and express their own unnamed grief, and perhaps it may help them place their sufferings before God, not a God who threatens and punishes but a weeping God who takes up women's pain and weeps with them.[7]

This reflection on the Jeremianic themes of weeping and lamentation brings the possibility of an understanding God alongside women. God sees and accompanies their pain and the tears that are often too overwhelming for words.

I wonder how the experience of ovarian cancer for women is a symbolic crucible, "an alchemical symbol for transformation through dissolution, purification, and union?"[8] A woman is a symbol of carrier, protector, and nourisher of life. Under the siege of cancer she is an earthen vessel tested as if by fire. Her preoccupation with the body and need for curing or alleviating ill is then a physical crucible. It is a crucible that bears an elemental power that transcends boundaries. Cancer in many ways holds significance for our varied cultures to see and respond to the tears of women, to come alongside them also as God does. It is conceivable that issues of living together and caring for our world are being revealed through this disease in particular women. Some diagnoses may be the result of early environmental exposure. It is as though the suffering of the whole environment manifests in the individual. As far back as 1209, St. Francis of Assisi modeled reverence and tender concern for all of life. In 1962 scientist Rachel Carson wrote *Silent Spring* to sound an alarm by highlighting the consequence of indiscriminate and careless use of this earth. Are these Gyn|Ecology[9] questions indicators of larger environmental questions?

The cancers that most frequently affect women include breast, lung, colorectal, endometrial, ovarian, cervical, and skin cancers. According to the American Cancer Society, approximately 23,400 cases of ovarian cancer occur annually; it causes about 14,000 deaths a year, more than any other cancer of the female reproductive system. This is largely because signs and symptoms of early ovarian cancer are often subtle and nonspecific. "When detected in an early stage, ovarian cancer can be cured more than 90 percent of the time, simply by removing the afflicted ovary. Unfortunately the majority of women with the disease aren't diagnosed until stage three or four, after the cancer has spread," writes Hilda Brucker in an article about the Atlanta-based Ovarian Cancer Institute.[10] Issues that are now being raised publicly, such as the frequency of mammograms, mutations in the tumor suppressor gene BRCA1, and pivotal choices a woman can face, are highlighted by the following:

> The study, led by a University of California, San Francisco radiologist, looked at more than 1 million women over age 40 who received mammograms between 1996 and 2000. The data shows African-Americans, Hispanics, Asians and Native Americans are less likely than white women to get mammograms every one to two years, as recommended.[11]
>
> Pathogenic mutations in the tumor suppressor gene BRCA1 confer high risks of breast and ovarian cancer. Although mutations in BRCA1 are rare, they are more frequently present in individuals with multiple relatives having breast or ovarian cancer, early-onset breast cancer, or of Ashkenazi Jewish ancestry. Among African American, Asian American, and Hispanic patients in the Northern California Breast Cancer Family Registry, the prevalence of BRCA1 mutation carriers was highest in Hispanic and lowest in Asian Americans.[12]

After her mother's death, at the suggestion of an acquaintance, Jessica Queller opted to discover whether she carries the breast-cancer gene; indeed, she tested positive for the BRCA1 gene mutation, which gave her an 87 percent chance of breast cancer before age fifty and a 44 percent chance of ovarian cancer in her lifetime. With this knowledge in hand, Queller began the journey toward her pivotal choice: a prophylactic double mastectomy at age thirty-five.[13]

There is a fear and apparent gap in education for African Americans, Hispanic Americans, Asian Americans, and Native Americans about the value and/ or availability of mammograms in their community. If the results of genetic testing increase fears among specific population groups, are they helpful or detrimental to overall health care? And what would you or I do with the information Queller received? Under these circumstances, what does it mean to take responsibility for your health care?

Significance of Symbolic Memory

When I think about women's suffering as a group, I can see the way it symbolizes the pain of nations, peoples, and the earth. As a young woman I awoke to a painful awareness of the difficult history of women. Several experiences, growing out of impressions in literature and art history, were formative for me then, prompting me to reread certain paragraphs in a book or to return to a particular visual impression. I realize now that many women today have the freedom to make their own choices. They hope to assure that opportunity for the generations to come as they expand their contributions and participation in health care and society as a whole.

The first formative experience I remember was reading *The Good Earth* by Pearl Buck, first published in 1931. In almost pastoral style it describes the cycle of birth, marriage, and death in a Chinese peasant family. The book is written realistically, without any overt attempts to awaken sympathy for any of the characters. It is the absorbing story of Wang Lung's life on the farm, his trip to the city when starvation threatens, and his last years until it is time for him to be claimed by the good earth. His wife, Olan, worked in the field beside her husband even on the day she bore their first son.[14] Toward the end of their life together, Pearl Buck sketches a visual impression:

> Because he could not be rid of this unease toward her, then, he kept looking at her as she brought in his food or as she moved about, and when she stooped to sweep the brick floor one day after they had eaten, he saw her face turn grey with some inner pain, and she opened her lips and panted softly, and she put her hand to her belly, although still stooping as though to sweep. He asked her sharply, "What is it?"
>
> But she averted her face and answered meekly, "It is only the pain in my vitals."
>
> Then he stared at her and said to the younger girl, "Take the broom and sweep, for your mother is ill." And to Olan he said more kindly than he had spoken to her in many years, "Go in and lie on your bed, and I will bid the girl bring you hot water. Do not get up."[15]

It is as though Olan has no voice to express her own needs, her own pain. She received permission from outside of herself to rest and be cared for by another. Wang Lung and Olan spent a lifetime together with children and extended family, yet this was simply the way it was. There was no request, no tears, or expression of relief. There was obedience. I was stunned and speechless. It is this way for some cancer patients.

The second experience that awakened my awareness was seeing and studying the work by Kathe Kollwitz, an artist of German Expressionism and a Northern European who witnessed two world wars. Kollwitz was attuned to women's experiences and documented women's existence and their roles in society. Kollwitz grieved deeply for humanity. The word *war* triggered various pictorial responses at the time. For Kollwitz it meant the armed conflict of nations and the senseless destruction of family. In her lithographic print *Bread!*, the female experience with its pain and melancholic intensity is revealed for all to see. A particular woman is portrayed within the larger social context of senseless destruction, a facet of the earth's scars.[16]

Bread (Brot) by Kathe Kollwitz, 1924, lithograph, Rosenwald Collection (Klipstein 1955 194), is courtesy of the Board of Trustees, National Gallery of Art, Washington, D.C., and used by permission.

The image is a lithograph in tones of black and gray. A woman's frame is bent as though hiding. Two young children cling to her. The youngest child looks up to her with a saddened and sorrowful expression. The other child, who is taller, grabs hold of her skirt and pleads, begs for food. The woman bends over in anguish. One of her hands rests across the mouth of the crying child who pleads with her. The other arm appears to cover her face as she weeps. The hunger, dislocation, and loneliness of a woman who is trying to live through a war shows in stark reality. How will she feed and nurture her young? How will a woman with breast cancer nurture her young? How will a woman with ovarian cancer have (give birth to) young? I grieve for all the women for whom this image is daily reality.

Over many centuries women found their identity primarily in motherhood. Their group identity was first as mothers, long before they began to conceive of the possibility of "sisterhood."[17] Alice Walker writes in her 1988 collection of essays, *Living by the Word*, "there is no story more moving to me personally than one in which one woman saves the life of another, and saves herself, and slays whatever dragon has appeared."[18] Walker's emphasis on the sacrificial nature of women is even more true for women's concept of motherhood.

We continue each in our own way to search for our identity and discover who we are as women, mothers, and soul sisters. Joan Borysenko expresses the need for role models, wise elders, and sisters in *A Woman's Book of Life*.

> Aging white women have precious few role models to look to because the aging mystique has disempowered so many of our elders. Black, Hispanic, and Native American cultures, in contrast, venerate older women. These cultures view women elders as becoming more wise and beautiful than they were before, rather than fading into something physically, emotionally, and spiritually less than they were in their youth. Wise elders are a tremendous source of knowledge, having lived long enough to understand the delicate, and sometimes invisible, web of interconnections that link our every action to a network of tangible and intangible results.[19]

Volunteer programs and support groups for breast cancer survivors attempt now to connect women with role models, both to empower and heal. These efforts tend to bridge across racial and cultural barriers to create symbolic memory and affirm its role in the healing process.

Potential to Respond Authentically

In the medical effort to respond to this siege of cancer, there is a creative partnership among all disciplines. A primary example is the dedication, innovation, and collaboration that mark the efforts of the Ovarian Cancer Institute, a nonprofit organization founded in Atlanta. The sheer size of the tissue bank gives researchers the statistical power to identify subtle molecular patterns among ovarian cells that might otherwise go undetected. In addition, the concept of a virtual lab allows scientists from different disciplines to collaborate and share data electronically. With sophisticated technologies, researchers have already been able to demonstrate that malignant cells express different genes than normal cells, differences clearly distinguished in the lab.[20]

In the fall of 2007 Benedict Benigno, M.D., one of the world's leading gynecologic oncologists and founder of the Ovarian Cancer Institute, remarked: "It's like removing ants from fine porcelain. We can do better in the treatment of women with cancer through earlier diagnosis and less toxic methods." Porcelain was originally named after the Venus Shell and is the finest of earthenware, differing from ordinary pottery, being more or less translucent. Porcelain is a feminine symbol linked with a woman's conception and regeneration in many traditions. Ants, on the other hand, are like cancer. They are excessive in number and are usually involved in ceaseless activity that is blind to the transience of human life.

The training of new nurses on the Gyn|Oncology unit also represents a variety of disciplines working together. The intern nurses are knowledgeable with strong academic credentials. Their internships cover a lot, everything from cancer treatment modalities, oncologic emergencies, and cancer symptom management to care of the post-op Gyn|Cancer patient. Other topics such as physical therapy, wound and elimination care, infection control, pharmacy, pain management, nutrition, and psychosocial support are covered in this training. The final lecture is spiritual support. Nurses receive a page outline that is designed to increase their comfort level. At the top of the sheet in bold print it reads: "Spiritual care is an integral part of caring for the whole person." Cancer is not an abstract subject, one that we can keep at a safe distance to maintain our professionalism. When asked about their own connection to the disease, the nurses within a minute or two have touched on their own stories; their eyes may fill momentarily with tears. Whether through a family member, friend, colleague, or ourselves, each of us has been touched by the terror and loss this illness brings. As a clinical team, we don't dwell here but agree to proceed with understanding the significance of spiritual care in the treatment process. We represent the dedicated human beings who serve at the forefront of cancer care.

Cancer care is all around us through education, prevention, screenings, diagnosis, treatment, research, and support as well as rehabilitation services, not to mention the laparoscopic robotic surgical procedures. The National Women's Health Information Center and the Women's Environments Network[21] are options online to raise our awareness. Another item of particular interest is a study undertaken to assess the life views, practices, values, and aspirations of women with various stages of gynecologic cancer. A self-administered questionnaire was completed by 108 women with various stages of cancer and thirty-nine women with benign gynecologic disease. The questionnaire included items on cancer demographics in addition to sixteen multiple-choice questions, and four true-false items related to criteria of good care, degree of involvement in decisions, psychosocial well-being, religious experience and aspirations, which form the basis of this study. The list of variables included age, ethnic group, marital status, education, other life-threatening conditions, religious preference, children living at home, and disease status.

> Roberts et al. (1997) surveyed 108 women with gynecologic cancer to determine factors influencing views about end-of-life decisions. Subjects were recruited from the Oncology Service Department of Obstetrics and Gynecology at University of Michigan Medical Center in Ann Arbor.
>
> Approximately three-quarters of patients indicated that religion had a "serious place" in their lives. Another 49% indicated that they had become more religious since having cancer, whereas no one indicated they had become less religious. Almost all patients (93%) believed their religious lives helped sustain their hopes, 41% felt their religious lives supported their self-worth, and 17% indicated that religion gave their suffering meaning.[22]

Spiritual care is very much a part of caring for the whole person. At Northside Hospital in Atlanta, each day after morning report, chaplains to the oncology units review the hospital census. Who's a new patient, who has had surgery scheduled, who will get a pathology report back today? Which patients have family coming from out of town, or a family consultation scheduled with the doctor? Who is receptive to support, angry or unavailable, despondent? Is pain a primary issue? These are some of the queries raised.

So often faith traditions and spiritual symbols provide an important cultural setting through which an individual patient can endure and even articulate the mystery of pain in a meaningful way. When a patient wants to express feelings associated with pain and/or to share ways the current illness has brought change in their religious or spiritual health, chaplains are available to listen and offer prayer, meditation, and guided imagery. Life and death issues emerge in story form. Some patients feel strongly supported by their pastors and church communities. Their gratitude is deeply felt and expressed. Others feel dismissed by church authorities and/or abandoned by God. Our visits can be informative but also a time of prayerful intercession. As representatives we come alongside the patients and/or family as they try to voice needs. We bear witness to suffering and celebration. What do we do? We seek God's love and presence to empower patients and to hold them as they approach the unknown.

In *Deep Is the Hunger* Howard Thurman wrote, "Human understanding requires great artistry; the touch of the artist may be light, but it is sure. This is one of the reasons why conversation and good talk are of such immense value. They provide moments of direct quickening in contact that instructs the emotions and feeds the understanding with revelations of interests, slants, and overtones of the other person, without which there can be no deep sure respect for personality."[23] Pastoral care is in many ways an art form. Authenticity is as genuine as a painting. The subtle or slight variations in communication around the experience of cancer are as significant as shades of color.

Service in Dialogue

Our introduction to the world of the Gyn|Oncology patient underscores the fact that spiritual care is an essential part of the whole, not merely an incidental extra. In dialogue we hear the uttering cries of the young and old who fear. We are witness to an endless succession of clinical, individual, and communal efforts to save lives. A sense of community enables us to support one another and reflect on our experiences as we seek to be a part of the expression of God's love through a thoughtful, personal connection. One of the greatest lessons of the Cancer Help Program is shared in the words, ". . . if you spend a week with a small group of people with cancer, you come to see and appreciate the beauty of each individual way of encountering cancer."[24] The commonality and the individuality of cancer are striking!

Conversations with Gyn|Oncology patients hold particular human situations in the light as if in a transformation. Fruitful dialogue tends to emerge. Women who are under siege are provided the opportunity to till the soil of their own experience sensitively and truthfully. Although short at times, the "reciprocal dynamic"[25] is both healing and spiritually supportive, with powerful implications for understanding. Those of us who offer pastoral care risk being in this dialogue. The conversation is reciprocal in that something is given or felt by each of us toward the other. It is dynamic in that under the pressure of the diagnosis and/or prognosis, the patient is responding and seeking some form of equilibrium.

There are times when, like Jeremiah, we want to cry out to God in anger and despair, anger at the disease and form of attack. A woman is a symbol of receptor, carrier, animator, protector, and nourisher of life. At the bedside we meet a person who is both a particular woman as well as a symbol of the depiction of women in art, mythology, and religion in early traditions. This depiction may include the qualities associated with women in traditional symbolism such as soul, intuition, and emotion. Whatever their story, spiritual care is offered to provide the individuals living with cancer resources to draw upon their faith and traditions. Our hope is for each one to experience a meaningful quality of life during what is a trying time and unknown culture. Continuously we support and reevaluate their needs, hopes, and resources, and respect the uniqueness and history of each. Often when our eyes meet, and we create a quiet space, a shift takes place, subtle but major, and the wholeness of the world is revealed beyond our diversity.

During critical illness, particularly with end-of-life or life-altering situations, certain existential questions of ultimate meaning arise: Why me? Why my child? What purpose does this serve? What does it all mean? Since the questions may have intangible, unanswerable qualities, formulating responses may require a shift to the spiritual domain that can be defined as a concern for what exists beyond oneself and the physical world.[26]

It is important to me to meet each patient, really meet each patient. I introduce myself and look her directly in the eyes if possible. I let the patient know that I am aware she is here in the hospital and that I know it must be difficult. Although some cultures are more hesitant to make eye contact than others, I find eye contact is fundamental to the development of trust.[27] If she agrees, I sit with her, and I am quiet. Some of the reciprocal dynamics are conscious, and some I suspect are unconscious. I give my attention to her and my willingness to accept what she wants to share. I ask if I might have her in my prayers. Often I will ask if there is anything particular she would like for me to have in my prayers for her or her family. Again I am quiet. Together we begin to resource her faith tradition, fears, ways of expression, anger, and hopes. Below are three different experiences.

The patient is a young woman in her twenties. I first met her in ICU, with her fiancé and parents. She hadn't come back for chemo after her surgery about three months earlier for ovarian cancer. She now has small bowel obstructions. I know from a physician the gravity of her condition. Her doctor has spoken with her and her family. I introduce myself and sit with her again. She says, "Thanks so much. I can use some spiritual care right now, really can. I've gotten some kind of virus. They don't know what it is. Need prayers. Want to get over this and to get out of here. I have lots of people praying for me."

"May I have you in my prayers?" I ask.

"Oh, yes. Prayers are what keep me going!" she says.

"Anything specific you want me to include?"

"Ask God to help them figure out what this is, what antibiotic I need?" she replied. At this point the staff comes into the room. I agree to follow up with her.

Another patient is a single mom. Her twenty-five-year-old son is seated on the window seat next to her bed. They are both very quiet. I know her from earlier hospitalizations. We met at the time of her diagnosis. She had waited before she came to the doctor. Later I sat with her when the treatments proved very difficult, and she requested support. Now there is nothing else that can be done for her, and her depression is heavy. "This isn't what I wanted. I appreciate your coming," she said. "I'm grateful to everyone."

We sat quietly. "This is painful and not what you expected," I replied. "As I sit with you I am wondering if you've had a chance to say what you really want your son to know and remember?" Again it is quiet.

She speaks to her son. "I want you to have the house. I have put it in our names together so you won't have any problem. I want you to know that," she says tearfully.

Her son says, "Mom, you've done a good job. I'm going to be all right. We'll take care of the house." Then he wipes the tears from his face.

The door opens suddenly, and the patient's mother enters the room briskly.

The third encounter involves a patient and her husband. He guarded the patient's room consistently. He checked everything. He sat by her bed or stood at the door. He did not want his wife to know the prognosis, although she was competent to make her own decisions. He was her husband, and he didn't want her upset. The staff was concerned. The patient was still a "full code,"[28] and he was not ready to consider hospice. The nurse asked me to stop by the room. The patient was sleeping soundly. Her husband and I spoke briefly just outside the door to her room. I introduced myself and waited. He carefully weighed whether to trust me.

"I realized she's here." I said. "I've been with her before." He began to relax.[29]

"Is there anything I can do for her now? I know this is difficult. She's fought this for a long time."

"She is resting now; best to let her rest." As he talks, we walk into the room. As he looks toward the bed, he speaks of getting her to rehab. "She sat on the edge of the bed earlier today. If we can get her strength up then I think she will be ready."

"And how are you?" I ask.

"I want more time; not ready to let her go." He responds tearfully.

"I hear you. She means a great deal to you and your children. Prayers continue." After a brief hug, he moves back across the room to his chair.

"You can leave the door open now," he says as I leave. Perhaps the door to his denial opened as well.

These are three distinct adult women. They are women who are or have been in mature relationships. They and their families are learning a whole new language. Each patient is coping in the best way she knows how with a life-threatening illness and is most probably overwhelmed by grief and uncertainty. How they respond to this responsibility is as unique as they are. The specifics of their illnesses may differ. The stage when each received the diagnosis of cancer differs from noninvasive, to no evidence of spread to lymph nodes or other parts of the body, to tumor size with no evidence of metastases, to large tumor with lymph nodes involved with no distant spread, or to evidence cancer has metastasized and is growing in other parts of the body.[30] The treatment issues vary. Some of these cancers are fast growing while others are slow. I have learned time and time again to respect each woman and where she is in her journey with this illness. When we show respect and provide witness, these women and their families become empowered. They are empowered to share a sense of themselves and claim the time they have to live, which is sacred time.

While in seminary in 1987, I studied in Berlin. I stood in the place where Dietrich Bonhoeffer was imprisoned and where he later died. He wrote in December of 1943 to a close friend, Eberhard Bethge, "I must know for certain that I am in God's hands and not men's."[31] In another book, *Spiritual Care,* Bonhoeffer wrote,

> Truth belongs at the sickbed. The pastor should never come with cheap and false comfort that life will soon be all right once more. How is [he] to know that? On the other hand [he] shouldn't say that it will soon be all over. [He] has no certainty of that either. What the sick need to know in any event is that they are special and uniquely lodged in God's hand, and that God is the giver of life whether in this world or the next. Vision and heart must always be made opened up to that other world. "Be at peace and let life rest quietly in God."[32]

It's that "let life rest quietly in God" that is hard, so hard, to grasp in the midst of the suffering and unknown aspects of cancer. I return to the book of Jeremiah.

In the book of Jeremiah God weeps. In no other prophet in the Hebrew Scriptures do we have a comparable reflection of the spiritual struggle with God. In her commentary O'Connor highlights two poems in which the weeping figures of God and Jeremiah become almost indistinguishable. In chapter 8 Jeremiah speaks and acts for God, and God identifies with the people. In chapter 31, God is depicted as a mother attached to her child through the unending bonds of love, and God is a covenant maker who pursues relationships of mutuality and fairness. O'Connor writes, "These divine images of God as *mother* and *covenant maker* provide women with the theological bases to claim a place for themselves within the Jewish and Christian faiths."[33] Similar to God, women love their young unconditionally and seek new relationships of trust as they bear and nourish new life. Love and relationships come as gifts from God that connect and extend life even in the darkest hours.

Each day is a learning process. A weary and restless patient feels abandoned by God as the treatments intensify. God's love seems very distant or nonexistent. Another patient accepts God's presence as a given even in the struggle. Non-patients feel inadequate in themselves to stop the progression of the disease and the side effects of the treatment regime. They face their own limitations and mortality as well. There is a growing awareness of the human desire for some kind of refuge and a ritual of exchange. Women claim this support as they make the decision to seek treatment, to find an experienced surgeon, to talk with family, and to create life within difficult and uncertain circumstances. Although they do not always know it, these women are worthy of care and hopeful of dialogue with God and possibly the church if the interaction is not intrusive and overbearing.[34]

Around the significance of ritual and repetition in religion Ann Belford Ulanov, professor of psychiatry and religion at Union Seminary as well as a faculty member of the C. G. Jung Institute in New York City, writes:

> In its positive role ritual marks off the necessary space and time to acknowledge our relationship to an essential otherness, to coordinate our response to the address of the transcendent. Such ritualized awareness of the power and meaning of being happy occurs at the expense of denial, linking the here and now to the eternal NOW. A surprising sense of mutual enhancement grows between our finitude and the infinite. Awareness of this otherness, this transcendent mutuality distinguishes ritual from mere repetition.[35]

This can come in the form of a familiar prayer, scripture verse, solitude, or the verses of a significant hymn. Somehow through the grace of God we discover together the resources of faith and community at hand. Stories of suffering link with God's stories and initiate insights to strengthen and bless. "Souls are watered like gardens" (Jer. 31:12).

The struggle of each woman with Gyn|Cancer is our struggle, our pain. Their lives are ongoing improvisations. Unfortunately, these are quite ordinary sequences of day-to-day events that continue to unfold. The time of change in our world today is filled with interlocking messages of our commitments and decisions. The health and survival of individual women is connected with the health of the earth. Love of the earth and our relationships around its use are paramount.

> The well being of the ecosystem of the planet is a prior condition for the well being of humans. We can not have well being on a sick planet, not even with our medical science. So long as we continue to generate more toxins than the planet can absorb and transform, the members of the Earth community will become ill. Human health is derivative. Planetary health is primary.[36]

In the world today we can see and feel the connection between the earth and its inhabitants. We are confronted with the challenge of caring for our mothers and Mother Earth. We are together whatever our nationality. Margaret Kornfield suggests that "just as God holds the wholeness of creation, our connections hold and sustain us."[37] The care of women and Mother Earth require attention to the wholeness of both. Our commitment to the health of the earth and of human beings is a multicultural message pregnant with possibility. The organism and the environment are interrelated. Life and death are in the balance. To respond to a woman's personhood with gratitude and acknowledge her particular health situation through dialogue, whether we are male or female, does not diminish us. Reuel Howe wrote in *The Miracle of Dialogue* that "dialogue requires a disciplined attention to and acceptance of the content of the exchange and its meaning. Many people draw back from it because its meaning is painful and disturbing. They would like to have the benefits of relationship without its cost."[38] But if we accept that woman is a symbol of carrier, protector, and nourisher of life, then she warrants our attention and love. With a diagnosis of cancer and its treatment, the normal order of her life is disrupted.

To see with respect, really see, the uniqueness of a woman with cancer and to affirm through faith her existence in dialogue is to offer her the potential for connection and commonality. It means breaking though our avoidance or denial and stepping beyond our fears. It means recognizing the realities of the illness that distinguish it from a man's. It means claiming an alternative way to think and live that is often at odds with the normative cultures. It provides for a woman with cancer the opportunity to respond instead of withdrawing in fear. In the exchange there exists the hope that love and relationships intercede into fellowship with God and that the possibility of healing and wholeness is nurtured.

The pace of our lives has increased to unheard-of speeds. E-mail, and text messages keep us connected at a frantic rate. But in hallways, living rooms, parking lots, and even elevators there are moments of dialogue, celebration, and transformation. God meets us there in ways beyond our imagination. We are called to see and respond with pastoral care and/or counseling at the bedside, in our offices, in the church, and in the community. We are called to support a woman who is seeking care and to walk with those who love her. We are called to all of the above, whether we are comfortable or not. New ways are being born to approach and to relate to female cancer patients, ways that are more sensitive and knowledgeable. For this we can give thanks and participate.

We Hold Our Stories in Blankets

Pastoral Care with American Indian Women

Michelle Oberwise Lacock and Carol Lakota Eastin

Maybe it is her birth
which she holds close to herself
or her death
which is as inseparable
and the white wind
that encircles her is a part
just as the blue sky
dangling in turquoise from her neck
Oh woman
remember who you are
woman
it is the whole earth.

—Joy Harjo, "The Blanket Around Her"[1]

In preparation for a baby's birth, Native American women gather and create a blanket as a gift for the newborn as a celebration for her or his life. This blanket is a gift made from the women's hands, either woven from wool or from pieces of saved material artfully collected and placed together to form a quilt. Each strand of pure wool, each thread, and each piece of cloth are tenderly stitched together to make the blanket just right for the newborn. The blanket will provide the infant with warmth and comfort for the journey ahead.

When a Native American couple is married, the wrapping of the couple in a new Pendleton blanket[2] represents the unity of their relationship. It symbolizes that they will live under one roof, under one blanket holding them together, which gives security and well-being. At the time of death, a blanket is wrapped around a person as a way to honor the individual, which will ease their journey as they cross over to be with the Creator. Another way a blanket is used is as a shawl, worn by a woman as a reminder of the womb that birthed her and her role as nurturer in the community. The blanket nurtures, protects, and provides comforting strength during each aspect of a person's journey. It reminds us of the women who made the blanket for us, of their support during these various seasons of life, and helps us walk through the next of life's passages.

In the process of counseling Native American women, the authors have experienced the telling of stories as the gentle unfolding of blankets. We have been blessed by the gifts of their lives, and have been honored to share the pain and the grief that the blankets have concealed. In this chapter we will explore the stories that have been rarely shared. We will look at the process that happens when the silence is broken and the stories are told. We will explore the historic traumas affecting Native women and the impact on their health and relationships today. Through the use of specific examples gathered by interviewing a number of Native American women across the United States, we will share key patterns observed.

One model of healing that has been found useful is narrative medicine. Like the many threads that make up a blanket, narrative medicine is the weaving together of the history of a woman's family, her tribe, and her nation; her belief system and worldview; her spirituality; her connectedness to the land; her view of healing and health; and her understanding of her future story. The counselor enters into the woman's story to hear it and to participate in it. By doing so, there is the possibility of weaving new strands of hope for her life and generations to follow.

Naming the Pain

Native women have many roles, including the following: being a part of the political and economic structures of society; teaching; working productively; giving birth to a new generation; being in relationship; creating exquisite quilts, bead work, baskets, and crafts; singing; and telling stories. Native women are "dynamic members of their communities and families; their lives and actions will assume importance in their own right."[3] Yet how much of their wisdom has been lost and smothered by the great changes that they have and are facing? A review of the literature reveals a long list of significant statistics about Native women. Since Native American persons make up only 1.5 percent of the U.S. population, the outstanding statistics are often hidden by this invisible place in society.[4]

Some of the facts that are covered by the suffocating blanket are partially identified in the 2000 U.S. Census report.[5] The population for American

Indians and Alaska Natives (AIAN) is 4.3 million people.[6] The census reports that 34 percent of the AIAN people live on the various Indian reservations while 64.1 percent live outside of the reservation. Currently the United States federal government recognizes 567 tribes, with many more being recognized at the state level. There are over two hundred languages spoken, although many of these languages are only known by a few of the elders.[7] *The Status of Women in the States*, written by the Institute for Women's Policy Research, reports that "the median annual earnings of Native American women who work full-time, for a full-year in the U.S. are $25,500, and they make only 58 cents for every dollar white men in the country make."[8] The report says 25 percent—one in four—of American Indian women in the United States live in poverty. The number is even greater for Native American single mothers; more than a third (38 percent) of families headed by a Native American single mother live in poverty.[9] The poverty rate for Native American people is three times higher than any other ethnic/racial group in the United States.[10]

When the poverty rate is high, other risk factors include poor health, poor diet, early death, and related diseases. This makes Native women more susceptible to HIV and other STDs, diabetes, and tuberculosis. Tuberculosis is twenty-two times more common among Native Americans than other races in the United States.[11] The life span of Native American women is five years less than U.S. women of all racial ethnic groups. The leading causes of death for Native American women include heart disease, homicide, accidents, alcoholism, meth/drug addiction, suicide, and cancer.

Poverty is an important dynamic in considering a woman's accessibility to quality health care. This lack of access contributes to shorter life span, poor preventive care (including an annual cancer screening), lack of prenatal care, and higher infant mortality. According to a 2004 report, "Only 69% of Native American mothers begin prenatal care in the first trimester of pregnancy, compared with the rate of 83% for all women. The death rate for American Indian infants is also higher: nearly 10 American Indian babies in 100,000 die before their first birthday, compared with nearly 6 white babies in 100,000."[12] Poverty also contributes to a sense of powerlessness, keeping women at home and at times in violent and abusive relationships.[13] Native American women are seven times more likely to be the victims of domestic violence and rape than any other racial ethnic women in the United States.[14]

Behavioral-health illnesses have an impact on 21 percent of the American Indian population, costing approximately 1.07 billion dollars.[15] These illnesses include: alcoholism, depression, anxiety disorders, mental illness, post-traumatic stress disorder (PTSD), emotional trauma, child abuse, sexual abuse, attention-deficit hyperactivity disorder (ADHD), antisocial behavior, conduct disorder, juvenile delinquency, and "postcolonial stress disorder," a communitywide PTSD related to the collective historic trauma due to loss of place and culture.[16]

Drug and alcohol addictions are often tied with the other disorders causing dual diagnoses, such as alcoholism and depression, in many patients. Death from alcoholism is 550 percent higher and suicide rate is 60 percent higher than the general U.S. population.[17]

Environmental health factors from living on or near reservations have an impact on the health of women. In 1979 the largest U.S. nuclear accident occurred on the Navajo reservation, located in Arizona, releasing 1,100 tons of uranium waste into the water supply. This health hazard causes cancer, which leads to early death. Exposure to environmental hazards such as mercury, uranium, radiation, and toxic waste can also lead to sterility and birth defects. One thousand atomic explosions have occurred on Western Shoshone land.[18] In total there are 317 reservations that are threatened by environmental hazards, such as reservations being used as nuclear waste dumps.[19]

With all of these problems, Native American women need a place to name their pain, yet there are a variety of complicating factors that prevent them from seeking health care and counseling. One factor can be the physical location of the reservation and the distance to agencies or health-care institutions. The reservation may be surrounded by mountains or frozen plains (as in Alaska), with only one way in or out of the reservation. There may be no safe haven or medical facility near enough to assist in a time of crisis. Another factor can be the tribal government, politics, history, and/or the role the woman has in the tribe,[20] which may say that seeking help or being treated medically outside of the tribe is inappropriate or not sanctioned. Family and friends are often not supportive when women report abuse or if the woman seeks to leave the situation. Child abuse is high, which can lead to children being traumatized by the violence, later being removed from the home, and never learning about their heritage, traditions, or culture. These children who are placed in foster care or into adoptive families will often search for years when they become adults to reconnect back with their families. This loss of connection can cause depression, which can lead to drinking or drug use.

Suanne Ware-Diaz stresses that Native Americans struggle with invisibility, especially in urban settings. Young women may be cut off from their extended families and are forced to assume the role of "elder." They find themselves raising their children in a culture that identifies Native Americans as sports mascots, which may cause them to find it easier to "just not be Native American."[21] Women in this situation often grow tired of having to "explain themselves" to others. When families move to urban areas, there is often a loss of community and identity, which leads to a sense of isolation. In efforts to "fit in," families may give up their culture, language, and customs, which can then lead to feeling a deeper sense of isolation. Women who feel isolated in this way may find themselves in abusive relationships with their partners and may interpret violence as affection.

Learning how to access social services and health care is complicated for the American Indian woman. When someone is in pain, it can be very difficult to navigate through the process. Even if she gains access to health services, the unilateral nature of health-care diagnosis and treatment may be at odds with her more multidimensional worldview of illness and health that affirms the interconnectedness of life. Again, the perspective of the tribe comes into play, and if the Native community from which she comes is not supportive of seeking assistance, the woman may ignore her symptoms and not seek the help that she needs. One pastor told us that in her area, people are afraid to seek counseling. To do so is to admit that they may be crazy. Counseling is associated with insanity or "you are crazy," rather than life guidance. Yet many need that guidance, and the pastor has found they may be responsive to practical interventions such as vocational counseling and interview skills. Many do not graduate from high school, and if they do, they find themselves spending their money on food for their family rather than college.

When the Native American woman lives in an urban area, she may be underemployed and may find herself without community support and without the intergenerational role models available on her reservation. Quality educational opportunities may have been or are limited and this can lead to low self-esteem, anxiety, and low-paying jobs. This can produce a continuous spiral downward to despair and hopelessness unless an intervention takes place. She may find herself in continuous crisis, including homelessness.

Mary,[22] living in an urban area for many years and struggling to overcome her alcoholism, finally was having success in her life. She completed treatment and has been sober since January 2006. She felt grounded in her being and even though her work was paying minimum wage, she could now see hope. She said, "Through the help of feeling connected to my spirituality, [through] finding a deep faith in a loving Father, and through the help of my faith community, I have found hope." She stated she was being granted visitation rights to her daughter, and in time, she might be living with her once again. Mary's face glowed, and she looked years younger than before. Peace and hope were present, giving her a radiating joy that touched everyone around her. Her life had been transformed, and this change affected other women around her; they witnessed the potential of something better for themselves and their children.[23]

Remembering the Past

Important to understanding Native American women and their concerns, pastoral counselors and faith leaders need to have a basic knowledge of Native American history, the importance of land, and the impact of colonization on Native people. Understanding this history became very important in a clinical pastoral education group we led that consisted of seven Native American clergy—five women and two men. During the group each student shared their genogram; in those presentations the connection to their family's history was rooted to their tribal history and to the impact of the relocation from their ancestors' land.[24] During that class we discussed the importance in understanding systemic grief and the impact this sadness had on the students, their ministry, and their tribe today. We honor that importance by including a brief remembering of the past and the impact it has had on Native women and men.

Prior to the European ships landing in 1492, America was called Turtle Island by the indigenous people. Turtle Island was populated by at least twelve to fifteen million inhabitants who had lived on this land for over forty thousand years.[25] In the early 1500s there were over "six hundred autonomous societies in what is now the United States and Canada, each following its own way of life."[26] Each culture was diverse, "the way of life finely adapted to its own local environment and producing" many complex cities, organized governance, spiritual traditions, ceremonies and rituals, social life, medicinal healing practices, tools, living quarters, weapons, artworks, crafts, and music.[27] Each society had developed many ways to provide for food by fishing, hunting, and farming, with the societies having similar understandings that the land was a "common resource rather than a commodity that could be owned."[28]

Food was abundant; in fact, many of the foods grown, produced, and preserved—such as potatoes, corn, chocolate, tomatoes, peppers, spices, and squash—provided food for the hungry Europeans upon their arrival. Later, the export of these foods to a starving Europe transformed that continent in ways "that centuries of prayer, work and medicine had been unable to do: they cured Europe of the episodic famines that had been one of the major restraints on the population for millennia."[29] The food that was discovered in America caused a dramatic change in food and cuisine that continues today to lead "the world's largest array of nutritious foods and the primary contributors to the world's varied cuisines."[30]

New societies shattered Native American culture, and by the mid-1500s, life changed dramatically due to smallpox, typhus, scarlet fever, measles, and influenza. These diseases that came with the Europeans were unintentionally and intentionally used to destroy the indigenous population. "It is also estimated that between the sixteenth century to the beginning of the twentieth century there have been as many as 93 serious epidemics among Native people, epidemics which have caused significant death and invaded Native people at intervals approximately every four years."[31] Of these diseases, smallpox was the greatest killer; ironically, one method of creating an intentional smallpox epidemic was the distribution of infected blankets to the freezing cold Indians in the East and in the forced relocation of the Cherokee and others, which was called the Trail of Tears.[32] During the sixteenth and seventeenth centuries these diseases brought massive destruction and eliminated whole tribes.[33] Gradually, resistance and some immunity began to be developed and by the 1800s diseases did not eliminate entire tribes. Instead, the mortality rate ran between 55 and 90 percent. The massive demographic destruction and deaths caused an irreplaceable loss of leadership, knowledge, cultural traditions, stories, and language.[34]

Diseases alone were not to blame for all of the deaths. Diseases' lethal effect was also due to the inadequate and nonexistent access to medical care. In 1928, the Meriam Report noted that every aspect of activity assumed by the U.S. government for the promotion of Indian health, education, and overall care was below a reasonable standard of living.[35] In response to the report, conditions on the reservations began to improve with the development of better health conditions, hospitals, nursing care, and salaries for health-service personnel. Although conditions improved, the mortality rate of Native Indians at that time was still 50 percent higher than that of whites.[36] The disease that was the number-one killer was tuberculosis.

Important to understand is the complicated relationship that the federally recognized American Indian tribes and Alaska Natives have with the United States. It is a government-to-government relationship that was established through a variety of treaties, Supreme Court decisions, legislation, and executive orders. Indian Health Services (IHS) has been the principal federal health provider and advocate for Indian people since the Synder Act of 1921. Later Congress passed the Indian Self-Determination and Education Assistance Act (Public Law 93-638, as amended) and then the Improvement Act (P.L. 94-437), which both gave the option for tribes either to assume the Indian Health Service administration and operation for themselves or to remain under the federal IHS administration. Health care again improved when the responsibility of IHS health services moved in 1955 from the Bureau of Indian Affairs to the U.S. Department of Health, Education, and Welfare. When this restructuring occurred, Native peoples had better access and availability to health care; however, there were still problems in the system. Those health-care problems still plague both the reservation and urban communities of today.[37]

Another aspect of the massive grief was the loss of land. For hundreds of years the indigenous people of North America called and still do call this land home. The land provided them with crops, hunting, water, fishing, sacred sites, burial sites, homes, and their way of life. Native women often held high status in many tribes because of the tribal matrilineage where matrons managed the "long houses" and women cared for the land, which was passed down through the mother's family. This also included the postmarital residence, where a woman could divorce her husband and send him back to his family.[38] In the tribes that were patrilineal the women also had clearly defined roles of honor and power within the families and communities. When the Native peoples were forcibly removed from the land of their ancestors, from their tribal homelands, immense grief occurred; grief still occurs. By the late 1800s and early 1900s the Native people had lost over 95 percent of their homeland. As more and more people came to North America, the need for land intensified; the official policy of the U.S. government was the dispossession of Indians from their rich resource of land. Land was a means to wealth, power, and greater freedom for anyone who could acquire it. The loss of the land also meant loss of a way of life, loss of role and place for women, and a loss of sacred sites, food, and resources; removal meant loss of life due to famine, poverty, and poor health care and living conditions.

The current delivery of pastoral care is further complicated by the historic relationship the Christian churches had with the American Indians and Alaska Indians. Initially, the Spanish royalty decreed that the "Indians of the New World were vassals of the Crown."[39] By 1512 Pope Julius II issued a decree on the humanity of the Indians and stated they were descendents from Adam and Eve. The Fifth Lateran Council in Rome later issued the "dogma of the 'Immortality of the Soul' and declared Indians did have souls."[40] Thus, there was value in saving them. Initially, once the missionaries and soldiers landed, their point of view was that the Indians were to convert or were to be killed. Later the Europeans learned there was value in keeping the Native peoples alive; they could be used as slaves. Native women were forced to cook, maintain homes, make their bed with their slave owners, and serve as experts on valuable resources.

Gradually there were missionaries and soldiers who had a gentler approach and sought to reach out through love and care to understand the culture, spirituality, and language of the various tribes. The underlying intent, however, was to convert the Native people to the Christian religion. By the 1870s, "President Grant gave control of the Indian agencies and Indian schools to Christian missionary denominations after Congress passed a law prohibiting army officers from holding the post as Indian agent."[41] Later, the U.S. government allotted to the mainline Christian churches certain reservations with the intent of converting the Native people. This also led to the development of boarding schools where children were forcibly removed from their mothers' arms so they could be acculturated into the "European/American society." While there, their hair was cut and their clothing was removed, replaced with "European/American clothing." They were given English names, and they were told not to speak their Native language or they would be punished. They were forced to speak English and to become Christian. Tragically, once the children were removed, oftentimes the mothers never saw their children again. Thus, the women lost the ability to teach their children their history, culture, music, preparation of food, clothing or dress,[42] their language, spirituality, and the meaning of what it meant to be the daughter or son of their family and their tribe.

With Christian churches now on reservations, suggestions were made to make it illegal for Native people to practice their spiritual traditions. It was believed that if those were not practiced, they would be able to acculturate and assimilate more quickly into the Christian American life.[43] The U.S. government created and broke over eight hundred treaties. Despite these broken promises over decades, the Native American community continued to survive.

The indigenous people were the majority of the population in the North American continent up until the mid-nineteenth century. "By the end of the nineteenth century, the combination of war, disease, famine, conversion at sword point, the appearance of railroads, and Indian removal programs had conspired to destroy tribes and to decimate the rest."[44] The numbers of independent indigenous people were reduced to less than 300,000; they now lived for the most part on reservations that were away from their homelands. However, these "demographic facts should remind us that Native people did not disappear nor vanish, although they certainly experienced severe and dramatic" challenges.[45]

Unfortunately, in the 1900s it was outlawed for tribes to practice religious observances such as the Sun Dance and Ghost Dance and to play the drum, sing certain songs, or use the pipe in ceremonies.[46] From 1953 to 1964 "termination" became the official American Indian policy, which meant that the U.S. government could terminate a tribe's trust status. This meant their land could be sold, they could be required to start paying taxes, and they would have to provide for their own education and health care. The policy of termination was outlawed in 1962 by the Kennedy administration; however, this was not enforced until 1970 by President Nixon. The American Indian Religious Freedom Act became law in 1979. This law stated, "It shall be the policy of the United States to protect and preserve for American Indians their inherent right of freedom to believe, express, and exercise the traditional religions of the American Indian, Eskimo, Aleut and native Hawaiians, including . . . access to sites, use and possession of sacred objects, and the freedom to worship through ceremonials and traditional rites."[47] However, many states did not abide by the law. Later in 1990 the Supreme Court ruled that states could outlaw religious Native American practices. In 1993, Native American Free Exercise of Religion Act was introduced into law to overrule the Supreme Court's decision. The United Nations inaugurated the Decade of Indigenous People to run from 1996 to 2005 in order to acknowledge the damage done by the world society and to celebrate the contributions of indigenous peoples.[48]

This is an extremely brief rendition of history. We would encourage those who are working with Native American women to learn more about the story that is not told in mainstream history books. This small portion gives a sense of the relevance of the immense losses and systemic grief over hundreds of years. The losses of land, culture, language, sacred sites, people, knowledge, leadership, stories, and familiar roles can and do have an impact on Native Americans today. A few years ago we attended a conference in California on Native American spirituality and heard the story of one California tribes' search to learn their language. The last elder had died, and no one knew how to pray or speak the name of the Creator in their language. The pain of this loss was enormous. A discovery was made at the Smithsonian museum of some early sound recordings of their elders and chiefs. From these sound recordings from over a hundred years ago, they heard their language and how to speak the name of God. One of the elders of the tribe shared her tribe's story, with tears streaming down her face; in looking around the room, we noticed everyone was moved. Finally, the tribe had a way to speak from their heart to the Creator's heart and to recapture that which they thought had been lost forever.

Important in working with Native American women is to understand the legacy of these losses, by acknowledging the complications from the grief and developing a trusting relationship with each woman. It is also true that Native Americans have been able to forge strategies for physical, cultural, and spiritual survival, and it is essential to remember and tell these stories.[49] By remembering the successful stories women have lived, heard, or known, it will help them restore harmony and balance in their lives and move to believe in their future stories.

Stories of Survival

Despite this traumatic past, Native Americans have demonstrated a tremendous resiliency. Being connected to community is a way they find restorative healing. Extending one's family beyond the biological one enables persons to create those connections that will be supportive. Pride of heritage, flexibility and adaptability, a good sense of humor, and a deep spirituality are among the things that have helped Native American women and men survive.

A number of United Methodist clergy and laywomen were interviewed about the experiences of women in their context, including their issues and their sources of resiliency. When reviewing the issues discussed by these women, an image of a whirlwind came to mind. The Native American woman can be caught up in a whirlwind of destruction; unless she finds the courage and resources to get loose of its hold, the results can be devastating. In the whirlwind image we wanted to capture how the many issues whirl around and around Native women, attempting to pull the life out from under them.

Tweedy Sombrero is a Denai (Navajo) pastor who has lived on and off a reservation. She has worked as the director of a domestic-violence shelter in addition to her pastoral work. Tweedy identifies violence and abusive relationships as the biggest area of concern for women on the reservations in the Southwest. Yet there are no domestic-violence shelters on these reservations; often a man's story is believed over a woman's. Sadly, if women in many of these tribes would claim their traditional role as women, they could force their husbands to leave. In this traditional culture, a woman owns the house and land; she has relatives who

Addictions
Diseases
Oppression
Lack of education
Low Self-Esteem
Mental illness

Invisibility
Loneliness
Divorce
Violence
Oppression
Prison
Suicide
Early Death

Poverty
Unemployment
Lack of resources
Homelessness
Spiritual disconnection
Isolation

Figure 6.1

could support her. However, the internal shame of failing in marriage causes many women to stay in destructive relationships.[50]

Another clergywoman[51] stated that in some tribal communities, a divorced woman might as well have a red "A" tattooed on her forehead. If the marriage fails, people will say "she just didn't have what it takes to make a marriage work," or "she can't keep a man." If there is physical violence, they will say that "she drove him to it." Unfortunately, the woman who stays with a violent husband may be making the children vulnerable to abuse.[52]

In the city, Tweedy identifies poverty and unemployment as the top concern, mentioning that education makes the difference. She notes women suffer high rates of STDs, HIV/AIDS, and diabetes. The tribes in this area include Apache, Zuni, Navajo, and Hopi. These women come from rich cultures with powerful stories about women. Tweedy believes the Native women need to reconnect to their tribal stories, the core stories of their culture, and to remember who they are. They need to remember stories of Changing Woman and Spider Woman.[53] Changing Woman embodies the changes of the earth, its seasons, and is associated with the various rites of passage of women. Spider Woman helps sustain the world. By teaching the Denai people how to weave blankets from wool, she teaches them how to sustain themselves. These stories and the ceremonies associated with them can empower and instill pride in these women as keepers of their tribe.

Connecting to a community is a key means of survival for a young urban woman. A Native American center[54] or local church can become an extended family for her in providing the elder women she so desperately needs, and elder men who honor her with the respect she is due as a mother. Sometimes the best therapy will not be that which we provide in the clinical setting. It will be found in community where she hears others' stories, laughs hard, and learns traditional arts and ways.

When women hear each others' stories, women then see how their story connects to the story of others. When women make the connection, they feel less alone and understand their place in the larger story of context, place, and culture. Sharing stories is how a group's identity and rituals are constructed and sense is made of life. "The larger stories in which we often unconsciously dwell have been called 'master narratives' and provide the meanings and values within which people position their identities."[55] Through identification with the larger story, we come to understand that our personal story is important. What we learn shapes us and calls us to make choices about our place and our part in that narrative. What we choose to do as a result of our past creates a beginning of a new story, an "a long time ago when the world was new" or a "once upon a time" story. In Mary's case, the story she believed for a long time was that she was a drunk and a bad parent. She kept acting out that role. Now with her new community and people who believed something different about her, she has a new role, a new story. Now she is a recovering alcoholic who has the potential to raise her daughter and to be the parent she now believes she can be.

Building Trust, Making Sacred Space

Building trust begins at the very first phone call and continues to the first visit. It is critical that this contact set the tone for the therapeutic process, which will be based upon developing a caring relationship. It is important that the initial contact be with a person who is genuinely concerned and interested in the caller. A "too formal" process that seems similar to filling out a loan application or another government procedure will often lead to the rapid exodus of the individual. Patience and time may be needed in order to complete all the needed paperwork (perhaps some can be saved for future visits and not all done on the first visit). Assistance should be offered for the completion of any documents or diagnostic materials. Consideration of literacy and the person's primary language is necessary whenever written materials are required. It is essential that the first visit, which may take longer than the usual fifty-minute time frame, includes a preliminary assessment of the person's risk level, given the overall population's high incidence of chemical dependency, violence, and suicide.

Developing rapport with a Native American woman may require techniques not typically used by the counselor or pastor. When one of the authors worked as a pastoral counselor in an urban medical setting, she found that Native American clients were often not comfortable in that setting. This clinical context, which requires arriving at a specific time and staying for exactly fifty minutes, was a strange arrangement for some women. This led the counselor to schedule two-hour sessions for one woman who was an abuse survivor. This allowed enough time to include going out of doors to take a walk, burn some sage or cedar together, sit on the ground, draw, and sing songs.

When doing assessment and diagnosis, the counselor needs to be sensitive to cultural and religious belief factors that may affect results of standardized assessment instruments. In a study of Native American women in Albuquerque, it was determined that the use of traditional assessment tools such as the CIDI (the World Health Association's Composite International Diagnostic Interview) were less effective than an interview by a competent, culturally sensitive mental health counselor.[56] A sensitive, caring counselor will be able to assess the client's status by taking time to listen to her story, and by living the qualities that are so necessary in a healer: honesty, genuineness, vulnerability, and warmth. Given the unique worldview of Native Americans, their responses to tests such as the MMPI (Minnesota Multiphasic Personality Inventory) may lead to a clinical diagnosis and a label that is not appropriate. It is important to compare responses to a Native population group, and to look closely at the specific questions that have led to any significant response groupings. For example, a report of seeing visions or hearing voices could be related to traditional spiritual ceremonies and not psychopathology.

The counseling process includes the following: making sacred space, telling the story, listening to the story, and mutual interpreting of the story. Among Native people, stories are often shared while sitting in a circle around a fire at night. The fire represents protection and safety from wild animals, and there is a trust that develops among those who share a fire. How can the counselor create a safe place for the sharing of stories that are powerful and painful? The lighting of a candle at the beginning of the session and the presence of flame can signal that the counselor and client have now entered a safe place. The holding of a "talking stick" or feather while one is speaking, and then passing it to the other(s) reminds us of proper listening and of the sacred nature of conversation. By listening with empathy and acceptance, the counselor helps the client to weave new threads into her life story.

Breaking the Silence

Stories are powerful when they are kept silent. They are powerful when they are told. The very telling of a story changes it. Every time it is told, there will be changes, subtle or significant, in its interpretation by the teller. The counseling process is the telling and hearing of stories. The pace at which stories are remembered and shared is a delicate thing. "Once a story is told it cannot be called back. Once told, it is loose in the world. . . . You have to be careful with the stories you tell . . . stories are wondrous things and they are dangerous."[57] Silence is a defense mechanism. When silence is broken, new defenses must be set into place. A healthy defense can be a fresh interpretation of a person's core narrative.

The pastoral counselor, in listening to these stories, will discover embedded theologies.[58] At the same time that history is being taken, a theological assessment is being done. The process includes discovering the client's worldview, and how that perspective affects her interpretation of her life experiences.[59] The counselor has now entered the story with the client, and together the two, like warp and weft, can weave the new telling and meaning of it.

An example of this occurred in a clinical pastoral education (CPE) Native American group. Students shared a particular story from their life; they had to identify God's presence in that story. One woman's story was of a time growing up when she had endured physical and sexual abuse. She had never thought about God's presence at that time in her life. Her embedded theology was that God was absent and had abandoned her in her time of need. As each student listened to her deep pain, heard and acknowledged her feelings, she was open to hearing where they saw God's presence in her story. As each student shared, she experienced her story in a new way and felt God's presence in her pain. A new perspective on her life, a shift in her theology, occurred as new meaning was made through the telling of her story.

Just like the student, we all have a story we believe about ourselves—a core narrative. It is a tale we spin. It starts like a woven blanket with one simple thread—a memory of an incident or a word spoken to us. And we weave other threads into this blanket that we wrap around ourselves, and we say to ourselves, "This is my story; this is who I am." With a change in perspective a new core narrative emerges with a new meaning.

Our past is always with us. We carry our individual and communal past as bundles. Native Americans place a high value on family, community, and tribe. Individualistic thinking is not the norm. A person's history includes not only individual incidents but also the stories of family and ancestors. Given the historical trauma experienced by Native Americans, many current problems are exacerbated by that trauma, and the individual carries a bundle (an identity) that reflects all that.

Many Native persons possess a medicine bundle. Traditionally, this bundle is a *parfleche* bag, or a blanket containing sacred items from a person's history. It is a very personal bundle, rarely opened in the presence of another. To be invited to see the contents of another person's medicine bundle is a great honor and sign of deep trust. The bundle will contain such things as a stone or some soil from a special place, a vial of water, a memento of an event, and an object that belonged to one's mother, father, grandmother, or grandfather. Buttons, pins, small objects, tobacco, sage, and other sacred herbs each have a story. These objects wrapped and bound together are a person's medicine bundle.

To Native people the word *medicine* refers to any and all things that contribute to one's healing, one's balance, and one's wholeness (*shalom*). Upon hearing a beautiful piece of music or seeing children happily playing, one might say, "That is good medicine!" Medicine bundles contain items that bring good health and balance. The medicine bundle is not excess historic baggage—but the very resource from which one draws courage for the journey and the strength to survive.

The therapeutic process includes taking an inventory of what we carry with us, deciding what we will keep, choosing what we wish to abandon and what we might need to add to our bundle that might give us renewed strength and hope. Letting go is not forgetting. It is reframing. . . reinterpreting the events. We cannot change what happened to us in the past, but we can change what it means to us.

Christie Neuger has described a narrative approach to pastoral counseling with women. It includes a repositioning, or reframing, of the story by the client. The goal of the counselor is to help the client position herself as the reteller of the story. The counselor listens actively and deeply to the story, believes the client's story, and then looks for where the problems are in the narrative. Helping the client tell the story as "I struggle with depression" rather than "I am a depressed person" is the kind of shift in story that can make a significant difference in the client's sense of power to change the story's outcome.[60]

Throughout her life Sally's brothers had told her that she was a failure as a wife because she was divorced. They told her it was her failure as a wife that led her husband to be a drug abuser and a controller. Even though now she had a successful vocation and was considered an excellent pastor, she still carried with her this core story of not being good enough. By opening the bundle, breaking the silence, and retelling her story, Sally was able to say that her husband's behavior was not her fault, and her divorce was not her failure. It was, rather, a brave choice not just for survival, but for becoming the person her Creator would want her to be.[61] She claimed her voice and her power and saw that her brothers' version of her story was not the one she had to live by any more. She had the power to create the outcome of her life and had been doing that for many years. She had reframed her story and saw herself as good.

Community and Healing Ritual

"We live stories that either give our lives meaning or negate it with meaninglessness. If we change the stories we live by, quite possibly we change our lives."

—Ben Okri, Nigerian storyteller[62]

Counseling is an art. It requires the intelligent processing of information and the creation of a treatment plan that is tailored specifically for a particular person.[63] This is especially true with Native American women. The use of standard treatment protocols should not be neglected, but should be used as a beginning place in designing the individual's unique plan. The multidimensional, global, and community-oriented worldview of the Native woman will help inform a plan that is not linear, but many faceted. Treatment may include family sessions, community involvement, spiritual and ritual tasks, expressive arts, and sharing of dreams in order to understand their meaning.

We have emphasized the telling of story, the use of narrative, the oral tradition. Sometimes, however, there are story lines that are only known in the unconscious mind. There are parts of the story that are not understood by a counselor whose frame of reference is a different worldview. There are parts of the story that may elude both the woman and the helper. The writing and sharing of dreams in a journal that contains not only words but also pictures, painting with watercolor, or molding an image in clay may reveal a story line otherwise unnamed. In the old days, people would tell a story by drawing a series of pictures in a ledger book or on a deer hide, or even on a wall. The pictures use a universal language that transcends words. One technique is to have the woman storyteller create such a storyboard—a series of images that tell the story. By doing this in a concrete way, it may be easier to insert new story pictures, or to create an alternate ending from the one already imagined. One medicine tradition involves the making of a painting with sand, which is then destroyed after the healing is done. The picture has served its purpose and is not kept. Sometimes a ritual letting go of pictures or journal pages is recommended; at other times the story pictures are kept as a reminder of the healing that has taken place.

It was mentioned earlier that Carol found the clinical setting a difficult place for some Native American women. Many never seek out counseling because of that setting. Carol worked to establish Seven Circles Heritage Center in a rural setting at the edge of Peoria, Illinois—a place where persons can come to hike, paint, garden, or participate in a talking circle (an open forum for sharing concerns and ideas).[64] Individual counseling is available, but many persons participate in groups or support settings, which include expressive arts and ritual. Ongoing groups have included a remembrance circle (a grief sharing group) and a healing circle (for persons with chronic health conditions).

In this setting a holistic approach includes cooperation between a woman's medical doctor, traditional medicine healer, counselor, pastor, and community. It is not unusual for the counselor to support and encourage the traditional healing practices of a Native person. A medicine man or woman will often provide the very rituals needed for the individual to be empowered and transformed. In his book *A Seat at the Table*, Huston Smith states that many elders often call the recovery process the "Good Red Road":

This is the spiritual path that emphasizes the community and the great web of life. The return to this ancient way of life, the way of native ceremony and orator, of ethics and morality, has helped build a sense of hope about a future that weaves together the best of the two worlds in which native people find themselves. But even this effort to walk in both worlds, Indian and Anglo, is difficult if the inhabitants of these worlds don't share a language. "The fundamental factor that keeps Indians and non-Indians from communicating," wrote Vine Deloria Jr. in 1979, "is that they are speaking about two entirely different perceptions of the world."[65]

This may seem to be too great a challenge to bridge; however, in our experience, we have found that there are counselors who have been able to do this because they are grounded in their own identity and story. Since they have walked their own road, this then becomes the bridge that breaks through the different perceptions of the world and allows the discovery of the common thread between the woman and the counselor. When taking this "journey with a client, wherever and however it happens is the path of transformation not only for the client but for the counselor, health practitioner or pastor as well."[66] The empathy from the counselor, along with the bonding and sharing that takes place, is the substance for growth and change.

Giving Our Daughters Voice

"You as a woman have the strength to change the world."

—Ni o gishi goo ikwe (Ojibwe)[67]

When we interviewed Rose she introduced herself by telling us not only her own name, but the name of her clan and her tribe; then she told us where her umbilical cord is buried. As an adoptee, finding the connection to her biological Denai (Navajo) family has meant finding her connection not only to her people but to the earth and its sacred places.[68]

Belonging is not only about belonging to the community, but also about belonging to the earth. Belonging to the earth means learning what it truly is to be a human being. Sometimes in describing a person who has achieved this state of being (in Rogerian terms, someone who has "become a person"), an Indian will say, "She is a true human being." To be a true human being is to live in an existential now; it is to fully feel and express, to think and know, to live and love what it is to be a human being. In her beautiful song "Held," Christian songwriter Christa Wells describes the terrific pain that comes after the loss of a child: "This is what it is to be loved, to be held."[69] When Carol lost her son to cancer, this thought ran through her mind: "So, this is what it is . . . to be a human being. . . . I get it now. I get all of it. The Viet Nam war vets when they talk about holding young men dying in their arms or mothers holding their hungry children or Mary holding the body of Jesus. I get it now. This is what it is to be a part of the circle of life, to be a part of the earth."[70]

At Seven Circles Heritage Center, young girls are taught by women to design and sew their own dance outfits.[71] A girl learns that everything about her outfit has a meaning, and she can tell a story about it. The choice of fabric, color, and design is purposeful. Young women are encouraged to stand and tell the story of their outfit, and when they do they are telling about themselves. Telling a story about oneself is an important step in claiming one's identity and worth.

In a national Native American Youth Peer Leadership training program sponsored by the United Methodist Church, lead faculty member and storyteller Ragghi Calentine helps youth reframe situations through games, role playing, and an intimate sharing time called "talking circle." "No problem is hopeless," Ragghi instills in them. "You've got a problem? Let's make a plan." Making a plan is made possible through education, learning new ways of responding, and seeking out supportive peers and community.[72]

It is critical for young women not to become isolated from their people. Young women need to be with grandmothers and mothers who tell them who they are and help them know their place in the world. If a woman's family does not provide this connection, alternative family communities can be found in a local Indian center, spiritual circle, or church.

In places where connection to elders has been broken, pairing youth with elder mentors may need to be an intentional part of a therapeutic plan. In Rapid City, South Dakota, where Native young people are losing their traditional ways and turning to gangs for a sense of belonging, the Lakota Project[73] was born to help the youth recover their language and culture. One of the unique features of this program is that it takes the youth into the rural areas to spend time with elders. These elders can help by weaving healing threads of "grandparenting" into these young people's lives, helping them know that they belong to something bigger and more ancient than any gang.

The Seventh Generation

A concept that is of deep significance to Native people is the Seventh Generation. We are taught that it takes Seven Generations to heal brokenness. In our decision making we are reminded to consider the impact of our decisions for the next seven generations. It is believed that the ripple effects of our lives will travel across a great distance. The seventh generation is sometimes called the healing generation. We look to our little children as the hope of our people—that their generation may be the one finally to let go of some of the historic trauma with which we live.

In the Native American Fellowship Dayspring United Methodist Church, when babies are baptized, they are brought barefooted.[74] After the baptism of water and the laying on of hands, new moccasins are placed on the child's feet for their new walk with Jesus. Often they are given an Indian name by a grand-parent or other relative. Each child is held up to face the four directions as they are introduced to the world. As the child is carried about, everyone in the circle greets her with her new name saying, "You are Laughing Cub," or "You are Horses Carry Her." They are telling her who she is and who she will become for the people.

When she reaches womanhood, at the time of her first menstrual cycle, the women gather with her to have a ceremony to welcome her to womanhood. Each tribe has its own ceremony, but these ceremonies always celebrate the beauty and power of womanhood, and they instill in the young woman a sense of pride. In one ceremony, a braided rope is held between the mother and the daughter, representing the umbilical cord that has tied the girl to the mother throughout childhood. Ceremonially, the leader cuts the cord and says, "You are no longer tied to one another in the same way, but you each still hold a part of the other, and will always be connected." The cutting of the cord symbolizes the girl's independence and her power to break any patterns that it is not desir-able to repeat in the next generation. As women sit in the circle, the girl is taken into the confidence of the women gathered. Each takes a turn giving her advice about life, men, and self-care. Often, these women will mention mistakes that they have made and admonish the girl not to repeat them.

In one such ceremony, a woman wrapped a blanket around the girl saying, "My daughter, I am giving you a blanket—not to hide or conceal your pain but to warm and comfort you. This blanket belonged to your grandmothers and your aunties and to me. This blanket holds all of our strength, our love, and our hope for you. It is the loving embrace of your sisters who stand with you in a circle. We wrap this blanket around you, to wear, and then to share with your daughters yet unborn."[75]

There is a dance that the younger girls dance at powwows. It is called fancy shawl; it is supposed to represent the butterfly. A Ho-Chunk elder was at a powwow, watching the girls dance this athletic dance. "You know how you can tell the good ones, don't you?" he said. "They are the ones who start in a cocoon, with their arms still close to themselves, then as they dance their arms are opened gradually, and then eventually they are in full flight. So many of them start dancing with their arms open right away, but that is not how it is supposed to be."[76]

He was speaking not only of the dance, but of the real unfolding of these young women and their stories. It takes time to leave one's protective cocoon. The cocoon is like a blanket that holds the young women until the time comes for emergence. This is similar to the counseling setting: in the safety of a coun-seling relationship, these shawls may be opened, stories shared, and wings emerge. The lesson of this teaching is that the cocoon is a necessary part of the transformation of each woman's lives. The unpeeling of the layers of protection is a process that is gradual, unhurried, and beautiful to see. The challenge for the counselor is to invest time, patience, and expectancy that something beautiful will eventually unfold. This is a sacred task, a call to journey, a call to build bridges of healing that will transform not only the story of the Native women you meet but also your personal story. It is our hope that each of you will take this journey and discover the blessings we have found.

> Let the blanket remind you of the tears.
> Let it remind you of the struggles,
> Of the needs,
> Of the rights.
> Let it remind you of your ability to heal.
> Let the blanket remind you of the tears.
>
> Let it remind you of your power,
> Of your dignity,
> Of your love.
> Let it remind you of your honor.
> Let the blanket remind you of the tears.
>
> Let it remind you that we are all related,
> To shelter and to comfort,
> To acknowledge,
> To do.
> Let the blanket remind you of the tears.
>
> Let it remind you of your beginning.
> Let it remind you of your end.
> Let it remind you of our beginning.
> Let it remind you of our end.
> Let the blanket remind you of the tears.
>
> Wear the blanket.
> Offer the blanket.
> Put the blanket down
> And heal.

—Gina Jones, "Let the Blanket Remind You"[77]

PART TWO

Risking Change

In the realm of pastoral care, certain methodologies have inherently emerged as the "mainstream" methodologies to offer care to hurting persons. Theoretical understandings of the psyche, the human condition, and processes like grief have birthed a body of knowledge on how to facilitate effectively a process of healing and restoration. While this is generally helpful in pastoral practice, it can be limiting if the practitioner fails to adapt the methodology to fit the particularity of the person in need. This is especially critical in instances of cultural difference. Because the distinctiveness of women's experience was not usually the basis of historic pastoral theory and theology, it is also crucial for pastoral practitioners to be willing, able, and equipped to employ other methodologies with women from a variety of cultures. The authors in this section highlight the ways in which today's practitioner must be able to "risk change" by utilizing other theoretical constructs and methods of intervention and praxis in order to offer relevant care to women of other cultures.

Where Race, Gender, and Orientation Meet

Karla J. Cooper and Joretta L. Marshall

Authentic pastoral care requires the integration of one's prophetic voice into concrete acts of care and counseling. Without such integration, pastoral care turns one-dimensional by focusing so much on individual experience and feeling that it misses the call of God "to do justice, and to love kindness, and to walk humbly with your God" (Mic. 6:8b). Perhaps there is no greater test of the integration of the prophetic voice and the priestly office than that of tending to issues at the intersection of race, ethnicity, gender identity, and sexual orientation. Consider these situations:

- A young African American woman asks her pastor what the Bible says about homosexuality because one of her friends has just told her she is lesbian;
- A Euro-American woman and her Asian American partner have asked their pastor if she would perform a "marriage" for them;
- A Latino explores with the college chaplain feelings and thoughts that he has about being "born in the wrong body" and wonders what it would mean to live as a Latina;
- Two female pastors, one African American and the other Euro-American, join as allies in their work for racial/ethnic justice but disagree deeply about the role and involvement of lesbians in the "movements of liberation."

These, and a multitude of issues like them, confront pastoral leaders in the United States and beyond.

This chapter will address some of the intersections of racial/ethnic identity, gender expression, and sexual orientation. In so doing, we especially want to note the way in which power and the social construction of multiple identities have an influence on our pastoral care and to suggest strategies for responding to parishioners and other care seekers while working toward justice. Since the broader topics that surround this chapter cannot be fully explored, we will confine our examination to reflecting on the intersection of race/ethnicity, gender, and sexual orientation in the context of pastoral care through the exploration of two case studies.

We write as colleagues in ministry in the United States who experience our culture in very different ways, largely because of the social construction of race/ethnicity. Karla is African American and from an area rich in southern charm and laced with hospitality. Joretta is Euro-American and born in a small midwestern farm community. Karla's vocation sets her at the intersection of parish ministry and college chaplaincy, while Joretta's setting is largely theological education and pastoral counseling. Both of us are ordained in Methodist traditions (African Methodist Episcopal and United Methodist), although Karla is also recognized in the United Church of Christ. We are both committed to addressing racial/ethnic justice as well as liberation for persons who experience the oppression related to gender identity and expression and sexual orientation. Ultimately, we believe that women in pastoral care must build cross-racial/ethnic alliances in order to battle systemic sins such as racism, sexism, and heterosexism, among others.

Two pastoral care cases provide the context for examining these intersections. The stories are both built around real situations in which we have been involved, yet they are fictional in their presentation. After describing each case, we explore aspects of race/ethnicity, gender, and orientation embedded in the stories. We conclude the chapter by returning to the importance of proactive, prophetic pastoral care in hopes of contributing to justice in light of racial/ethnic, gender, and sexual oppression. We are eager to build healthy alliances that can strategically resist multiple -isms, including racism, sexism, and heterosexism.[1]

The Concerned Grandmother

Mrs. Hill stands up one morning to ask for prayers, as is the custom in this particular African American church. Often this is the time that people confess their sins in a public way or voice prayers of thanksgiving and petition. Mrs. Hill pleads for prayers for her family and for the sin that surrounds her nineteen–year-old granddaughter, Evangeline, who has self-identified as lesbian. Evangeline, her parents, and her grandmother are all members of this church, although only Grandmother Hill is present on this Sunday. Mrs. Hill notes that she and Evangeline's parents are deeply concerned for Evangeline's soul and her prayer is that, "if Evangeline could just remember who she is—she's a good, black Christian girl—she would return to God." The pastor struggles to respond, unsure about how to stand with Evangeline while acknowledging that many in the congregation—including Evangeline's parents and grandmother—will be adamant that homosexuality is a sin.

Claiming one's identity and being named by others as a lesbian is a complex reality in the culture and in the church. In this case, Evangeline carries her self-identity as an African American lesbian alongside an identity given to her by her family as a sinner who is betraying her African American heritage by her choice to love other women. Her parents, grandmother, and congregation members live out of self-understandings and perceptions that provide meaning for them about being African American Christians in our culture.

The pastor believes that Evangeline has not sinned by self-identifying as lesbian and would like to support her. She is also aware that a public stance on this issue in the congregation could cost her dearly, as many people would challenge her perspective and pastoral authority. As a single woman who is the pastor of this church, she also knows that people are curious about her own beliefs and her life. Her internalized self-images and understandings about what it means to be female, a pastoral leader, and an African American are part of what she brings to the situation. Because Evangeline and her family are her parishioners, she feels caught in the uncomfortable situation of discerning how to bring her prophetic vision of liberation from heterosexism into the lives of a family and community that will not be particularly open to it. For some members of this congregation, Evangeline's racial/ethnic identity is more salient and important to her identity than is her sexual orientation, and they wish the pastor would be clear about where she stands.

At one level, some might suggest that this situation is not unique to the African American context. Indeed, many pastors face similar situations of potential conflict in various denominations situated in diverse racial/ethnic communities, including within Euro-American Christianity. Racism, heterosexism, and sexism are embodied in every context in multiple ways as individuals and communities live with constructed meanings of gender, orientation, and racial/ethnic identities. Our argument here, however, is that there is something distinct about self-identifying as a lesbian of color within the African American church community. Any pastoral response must be conscious of the historical and contextual realities for African Americans and for this particular congregation, as well as attentive to the various meanings that race, ethnicity, gender, and orientation have for Evangeline and those who surround her.

Although the multiple dynamics in this case cannot be explored fully, we would like to note four concerns essential for the pastor to consider in providing authentic pastoral care to Evangeline, Mrs. Hill, and the rest of the family, as well as to the members of the congregation. First, the pastor needs a complex and multilayered approach to understanding race/ethnicity, gender, and orientation. In particular, the pastoral leader will be helped by understanding that we all live with multiple identities whose meanings are created in the context of the world around us. In the last several years, critical race theory, gender identity, and sexual orientation studies have moved from essentialist notions of race/

ethnicity, gender identity and expression, and sexual orientation toward more postmodern understandings that recognize the power of social construction. Our self-understandings and our interpretations of the identities of others are shaped by our systems of belief, our experiences in the world, and the messages we receive from the dominant culture, which is largely white and heterosexual. Pastoral caregivers are increasingly aware that one's identity is shaped not simply by one's inherited genetics, biology, skin color, or sexual orientation. Instead, meanings attached to race, ethnicity, gender, and orientation become part of broader social constructs that influence our understandings and our experiences. It is no longer assumed that people have "an" identity; rather, people's lives are constructed around multiple identities that intersect and interact in dynamic ways.[2]

In this case, the pastoral caregiver has been shaped to understand herself, her racial identity, her gender, and her pastoral identity through a milieu of multiple influences. Everything from her own family of origin and cultural context to her experiences in theological education to her self-understanding and practice as an African American pastoral leader have an influence on how she begins to respond to the situation presented in this morning prayer by Mrs. Hill. As she begins to reflect on Evangeline, her family, and the congregation, the pastor must remain conscious that everyone involved brings an interpretation about self and others that will have an impact on how they perceive her response or judge what she "ought" to do.

Second, this more complex understanding of the social construction of our identities enables the pastoral leader to recognize the interlocking systems of oppression that exist for Evangeline and her family, for the members of her church, for herself as a pastoral leader, and for the community that surrounds her. In this case the systems that keep structures of oppression in place are multiple and quite powerful in overt and covert ways. For example, members of the church, including the pastor, experience on a daily basis what it means to be African Americans in the culture of the United States. At the same time, Evangeline not only experiences the margins constructed by racism but also experiences heterosexism and the oppression of gender as her family and members of the congregation whom she has known most of her life are clear about the expectations they have of her as an African American Christian female. These expectations do not include being a self-identified lesbian.

Heterosexism and the negative constraints of gender in the context of this particular faith community are distinct because of the African American context. In his book *A Whosoever Church*, theologian Gary David Comstock notes the struggle of many African American churches as they wrestle with homosexuality. While he notes that it would be unfair to say that the African American church is more homophobic and/or heterosexist than other churches, the story of Evangeline's family represents ways in which internalized racism, sexism, and heterosexism converge in a particularity that is unique. Pastoral leader Yvette Flunder notes as well the power of potentially destructive dynamics as an invisible marginalization emerges within a visibly marginalized group. While feeling the effects of racism in our culture, congregations that feel marginalized face increased diversity and are not always sure about how to proceed in ways that keep the community safe and open.[3] The interlocking dynamics of oppression press upon this congregation and its members in ways that are complex and not life-giving.

Outside of this quasi-homogenous group, racial/ethnic identity and sexual orientation place Evangeline on the margins of the culture. Given the intersecting experiences of oppression, it is likely that there will be pressure on her to feel as if she needs to justify her blackness to one group and her sexual orientation to another. As an African American in a predominantly white culture, Evangeline lives with the meanings that have been constructed from the history of slavery in the United States. She cannot walk in the world—in her own church or in the broader community—without being aware of her "blackness" and the multiple meanings that are placed upon her because of the color of her skin. The racism she experiences on a daily basis is real and constant. Equally true is that the communities of lesbian, gay, bisexual, and transgendered people who will accept her orientation may not have dealt adequately with racism. As psychologist Beverly Green noted over a decade ago, lesbian women of color live in "triple jeopardy" as women, as lesbians, and as members of a group that experiences racialized oppression.[4] Sadly, lesbian, gay, bisexual, and transgendered (LGBT) communities are often colorblind and have not done enough work around racism to be able to understand the differences Evangeline faces compared to Euro-Americans.

The pastoral caregiver in this situation must recognize not only how oppressive structures have an impact on her life or on the members of her congregation, but she needs also to be aware of the way in which multiple oppressions collude in keeping all kinds of people in structures that are not life-giving or liberative. The potential for ongoing fragmentation and hurt increase with the multiple realities of oppression that exist in the various contexts in which Evangeline, her family, the church, and the pastor all participate. Racism, sexism, and heterosexism are interlocking structures that cannot be separated one from another. A good pastoral caregiver will work with care seekers in ways that engage wholeness and that promote the deconstruction of paradigms of oppression. In turn, this will model to the family and the congregation new ways of imagining identities and their complexities.

A third issue important for the caregiver to recognize is the conflicting messages people give and receive about human agency in connection with the divine. The ability to act and to make decisions can be construed by religious communities as either something positive or something sinful, depending upon their theological commitments about God and the human creature. For example, the ability for women and men to make choices about traditional marriages and weddings is often celebrated in the church as something that is embraced by God. Because sexual orientation is seen as a "sin" by many within Evangeline's family and within the broader mainline church, however, her behavior may be interpreted as a sin that has been willfully chosen rather than a part of her wholeness that has been given to her by God.

This negative implication that homosexuality is a choice has two consequences. First, focusing on the act of choosing sometimes colludes with other dynamics to reinforce the false argument that homosexuality is a sin that arises from the deliberate use of one's agency. This communicates that sexuality is something that is powerfully dangerous, particularly when it is not expressed in heterosexual ways. Second, the negative connotation given to matters of choice can result in a strong suspicion of agency and power. From postmodern perspectives, it is important to retain a positive sense that individuals, families, and communities have agency. Anything the pastor can do to both demythologize the belief that homosexuality is a sin and support notions of agency are positive pastoral care interventions for Evangeline, for her family, and for the church community.[5] This might be particularly true in light of the intersecting oppressions of racism where agency is already experienced as diminished.

Agency is especially important to recognize in Evangeline, her family, congregation members, and the pastor of this African American church for personal and social reasons. Patricia Hill Collins suggests that black feminist thought demonstrates African American women's emerging power as agents of knowledge. A significant dimension of Collins's work is its potential to reveal how the social relations of domination are organized with other axes of power such as religion, ethnicity, sexual orientation, and age in order to diminish the flourishing of life. While it would be easy to assume that such external dominant discourses create passivity in women of African American heritage, Collins suggests that it is essential to recognize the power and agency of women to resist oppression, not out of some heroic stance, but out of a genuine sense of authentic agency.[6] Helping Evangeline, members of her family, and members of the church articulate and act out of their own sense of agency will counter the impact of domination and contribute to movements toward wholeness.

A fourth dynamic that the pastor recognizes in this case is, undoubtedly, that Evangeline's family and perhaps the majority of parishioners in her church still understand homosexuality to be something for which they ought to feel shame or regret. It is not unusual or uncommon for gay and lesbian individuals to experience shame about orientation and relationships, largely because the culture around them reinforces the images of shame.[7] Shame, however, is not confined to those who are lesbian; rather, it extends beyond to the family and others who have a relationship with the individual. In this particular case, this may be evidenced in the matriarch of the family, Mrs. Hill, whose age and standing in the church community has always been "respectable" and cherished. Once again, the interlocking systems of oppression—including ageism—increase negative feelings among individuals and within the community of the church.

Pastoral theologian and caregiver Horace Griffin notes that the family in African American churches often suffers from a sense of shame in response to the self-identification of their sisters, aunts, mothers, or grandmothers.[8] Shame constricts agency and encourages people to think they are of little or negative value. The church family in Evangeline's case may experience such shame as well. Explicit and perhaps covert conversations among church members deny not only nurturing Evangeline in her lesbian identity but also sends a message to other lesbians and gays who may be hiding in the congregation or in their families that there is something wrong with who they are. The deep contradiction with the historical characterization of black women as those who have been nurturing, embracing, loving, and forgiving is lost in the process. Drawing upon the agency for offering life-giving support, the pastor might engage the mothers and grandmothers of the faith by helping them note how oppression and domination have had an impact on their own lives, thus countering the power of shame.

The pastor in Evangeline's case stands in a different place from many within her congregation. She is called to be the pastoral caregiver for persons who will be angry at her for taking a stand against heterosexism in the community while, at the same time, she receives quiet support from others who might want to send a different message. Lest Evangeline be ostracized or asked to leave, the pastor's ability to stand in the middle and to remain pastoral with the family and congregational members as well as with Evangeline is a heavy responsibility. For this work, the pastor will need the support and guidance of persons outside of her particular church. Indeed, this may also be difficult work. The shame and anxiety about issues of orientation, sexuality, race, gender, and other aspects of our identities are difficult for many pastoral leaders to confront and often cause them to move away from conflict rather than engage differences of understandings and perceptions. Finding colleagues in ministry who can be conversation partners with the pastor about these aspects of her work will be essential, even while it might be challenging.

By tending to the four concerns articulated above, the pastor can offer care that assists Evangeline and her community in moving toward wholeness, naming places where heterosexism, racism, and sexism merge, and identifying their own agency. Encouraging the pastor to find ways to stay engaged with the community of faith and to dismantle the heterosexism, racism, and sexism that persist in every part of this particular church will require a collaborative group of allies who can support the pastor in her work. A second case illustrates, however, the systemic forces that sometimes work against building alliances that resist multiple oppressions.

Allies In Racial and Sexual Justice?

> With an eagerness that seemed contagious, a vibrant female Euro-
> American parishioner asked her Euro-American pastor, Pastor Sue, to
> bless her same-sex union. Her same-sex union was with an African Amer-
> ican woman whose pastor had shunned her. While Pastor Sue welcomed
> the invitation of the parishioner, internally she was hesitant because of her
> denomination's stance on holy unions. Not only did she pray for wisdom,
> but she also began to seek guidance from an African American pastoral
> colleague, Rev. Jean, who worked with her on a Dismantling Racism Task
> Force in the community. Both pastors are heterosexually married and have
> come to appreciate one another's commitment to racial justice. To Sue's
> surprise, her intelligent, academically well-prepared, and theologically
> trained colleague said that "under no uncertain terms should you perform
> any such ceremonies." Reverend Jean noted that, "This was a trap by the
> devil and it didn't line up biblically, plus the denomination will take your
> ordination papers." Greater tension between the two began to emerge
> when Rev. Jean noted her concern that if others on the Dismantling Rac-
> ism Task Force discovered that Pastor Sue had participated in such a ser-
> vice, she would no longer be seen as an ally in the fight against racism.

Building alliances across racial lines in order to dismantle racism and promote racial justice is essential in our culture and context. If we are to be pastoral leaders who can assist people like Evangeline and her church family and who can help churches envision a more just way of being together, we must be will-ing and able to work toward justice on multiple fronts. But what happens when dismantling heterosexism appears to distract or threaten the work of actively resisting racism? The challenge of dismantling oppressions and reckoning with the structures of power in which oppression persists, as well as the perceived value that it is best to work on one oppressive structure at a time, creates unique challenges in this moment in history. Three distinct practices will assist Sue and Jean in staying in dialogue and working together to resist multiple oppressions.

First, it is important for Sue and Jean to recognize that privilege and power are operative in their relationship with one another in ways that could destroy their ability to work together. While they share the similarity of a common gender and probably both have experienced sexism, their distinct places within the broader social structures of the culture because of the color of their skin should not be overlooked. They are two women engaged in a committment to racial justice in a historical context where white women and African American women have often been turned against one another. Against the historical reality of slavery in the United States, Jean and Sue come to this moment in their lives together.[9]

While slavery as an institution predates the presence of race as part of slav-ery, the United States cannot separate the impact of race upon contemporary dynamics. The United States embodied the first system of slavery where all slaves shared a common appearance and ancestry. Prior to this, the enslave-ment of others had to do with conquest or debt relief, and not with physicality. African American and Euro-American women carry different residual effects of slavery. The developing chasm between the African women and Euro-American women was exacerbated by a value system that viewed the African slave women as breeders in an economy that needed more slaves for more labor. An African slave woman could be raped by the slave owner, yet her sexuality was never valued. Euro-American women were encouraged to hide the fact that their husbands were philandering into the forsaken slave women's sacred space. Women from Euro-American descent were placed upon a pedestal as dolls. It is no wonder, then, given all the infidelity, that sexuality was closeted, qui-eted, silenced. The African slave and the Euro-American woman shared in the dynamics created in a constructed moment of history, yet there was no way for them to become allies. The privilege of some was not shared in just ways.

Historically this dynamic of difference between women of African Ameri-can and Euro-American contexts has always been present and has threatened the ability of women to join together to dismantle the structures that oppress. Sojourner Truth spoke about it in her rhetorical reminder, "Ain't I a Woman?" reminding the audience of her place as both a slave and a woman. The dynamic of difference and privilege was present in the abolitionist movement as women attempted to move toward a more holistic understanding of the world yet faced the divisions created by slavery.[10]

African American women have always had to prove their "womanness." The social construction of race and gender in our culture creates a matrix for the symbolic and real violence that has been passed down through generational intolerance and through the construction of oppression. The mistrust of women across racial lines can be linked to the effects of slavery and the way in which the white male patriarchy benefited from keeping women—both slave and free—in their respective places. In similar ways, critical race theorists and others make the connection between racism and other interlocking oppressions such as clas-sism in the United States.[11]

Power as embodied in privilege and represented through the differences of race and the ability to be legally married is present in the matrix between Pas-tors Sue and Jean and the issues they confront. Signifiers of difference—race, class, gender, sexual orientation, bodily ability—have come to carry different kinds of power. Euro-American women, for example, continue to experience less oppression and more privilege than black women in our culture. Sexuality becomes yet another signifier of difference that carries weight and power. In his book *A History of Human Sexuality*, French philosopher Michel Foucault states that as time progressed sexuality became equated with other layers of oppression, and was classified by the "church" as the most heinous of sins if per-formed outside of the institution of marriage. Foucault states that body and soul cannot be disconnected, yet the power and control of sexuality often reduced its importance to productivity and reproduction.[12] In the case of Pastors Sue and Jean, they are both women and both heterosexually married. On one level it would appear that they are "similar" in the balance of privilege. On the other hand, their differences in racial and ethnic heritage create a distinct imbalance of privilege that must be attended to in the context of their relationship.

Against this backdrop of privilege and power, Jean and Sue work to dismantle racism as women from different racial/ethnic backgrounds. Some would suggest that precisely because of the power differential between Sue as Euro-American and Jean as African American, Jean's wisdom around dismantling racism ought to be privileged. We would suggest, however, that to begin with the argument that heterosexism can deter the work of dismantling racism is another way of colluding with the status quo and dividing women one against another.

This leads to the second strategy the two women pastors must attend to in their work to dismantle racism and struggle with heterosexism. It is clear that each woman has work to do in understanding the impact of multiple oppressive structures on their own lives and the lives of others. While Pastor Sue must continue to be aware of her place of privilege as a Euro-American, Pastor Jean is invited to struggle with the realities of oppression as experienced by sexual minorities. For Pastor Jean, including heterosexism in their common agenda is experienced as a distraction to the dismantling of what she experiences as a more powerful oppressive structure, namely that of racism. What is most clear is that if Pastor Sue and Jean are to be allies in dismantling racism, they must also become more aware and conversant with the way in which all structures of oppression feed into one another and are intricately linked. Both Sue and Jean have their own work to do around issues of privilege and the corresponding dynamics of oppression. The call of the gospel is to work to dismantle oppressions for all, not just for one group at the expense of another.

Building upon the recognition that the powerful dynamics set in place by the institution of slavery in the United States continue to have an impact on the experiences of all persons, it is possible to begin to understand how race might be seen as more significant. Some who seek to dismantle racism in the United States suggest that it is better to isolate race from sexual orientation because of the perception that sexual orientation negates race. Again, Horace Griffin notes that, for some, race must be placed as more important in the formation of one's identity as an African American. Griffin writes,

> lesbians, gays, and bisexuals must challenge black church homophobia, biphobia, and sexism and resist the notion that we are 'sellouts,' not committed to black causes and the black community, when we refuse to go along with black church and social exclusion against us simply because we are gay. The needed work against homophobia and sexism should never be preempted by the needed work against racism.[13]

Pastor Jean, as a traditionally married African American clergyperson, lives with the privilege of heterosexism in the culture while also experiencing marginalization because of race and gender. The social construction of these various oppressive structures are dynamic and never simple.

To complicate the issue further, LGBT communities have often reproduced the dominance of the culture around them by ignoring or participating in the perpetuation of racism in covert and overt ways. This is true around the systemic oppression known as racism as well as around sexism. Scholars E. Patrick Johnson and Mae Henderson point to a parallel construction within the academy. For many decades white men controlled the academic disciplines, including theology. Since the 1960s Euro-American women who were once marginalized began to realize gains in academic institutions and in denominations and judicatories, yet they did not tend substantively to issues of race. African American women began to challenge Euro-American feminists because of their lack of attention to the politics of race/ethnicity. In a parallel situation, African American male academics in race theory marginalized the work of African American women.[14] If we are to embody justice as pastoral caregivers, we must pay attention to the multiple ways in which oppression and privilege are used to keep people in their places, including our own unwitting participation in these structures. Sue and Jean are living out the dynamics of oppression in ways that are not new, but that could potentially divide them.

In order for Jean and Sue to move beyond their current impasse, they will each need to recognize that a lack of awareness about privilege can collude in ways that prevent them from addressing structures of oppression. In spite of their most well-intentioned efforts, collateral damage to one another is the consequence of the structures themselves. Homosexuality has often been seen as a "wedge" issue, threatening to divide movements of liberation around the issues of orientation. This false claim results in persons fighting one another about which oppression is worse rather than joining forces to combat the structures that negatively affect all kinds of persons in multiple ways. Ultimately, this divisive approach is not simply unhealthy for the liberation of lesbian, gay, bisexual, or transgendered persons; it also works to support systemically the hegemony of white, male power in ways that do not serve the work of dismantling racism or any other oppression.

What is clear from the case is that building coalitions and alliances requires each woman to do work on whatever issue most challenges them (race, gender, class, orientation, etc.). Dismantling power structures ought not be seen as competing goods that require only one issue to be addressed at a time. Instead, intersecting oppressions are powerful structures that create imbalances of power, privilege, and agency and that insert themselves into our everyday lives in ways that are insidious and destructive to all, including the community of faith.

This latter reminder moves us toward the third strategy for Jean and Sue. Building resistance and creating alliances is difficult and painful work, even when it points to the embodiment of God's *shalom*. The pain and injury that occur because of unintended hurt is set against a backdrop of living in the midst of multiple oppressions. If we walk away from one another because of disagreement or hurt or difference, the structures of oppression are reinforced and upheld. In order for Sue and Jean to do the work they are called to do as prophetic pastoral caregivers, they must remain in conversation and dialogue with one another, working to develop deeper levels of trust.

In a powerful article noting the power and struggle of being allies working to dismantle racism, pastoral theologians Marsha Foster Boyd and Carolyn Stahl Bohler speak of the importance and potential pain when telling truths about issues of oppression.[15] They suggest that in order for women to be allies against racism and other structures of oppression they must have a strong ability to establish the characteristics of trustworthiness that come with taking risks, making mistakes, and seeking understanding. Because tensions in the context of our differences are likely to arise, clarity and conviction need to be met with honesty and grace. The kind of self-awareness and mutual work required if we are to be allies in dismantling racism and heterosexism is that which remains humbly open to the narrowness of one's own perspective even as one takes risky stands for justice.

What is clear is that taking stands against sexism, racism, genderism, classism, and heterosexism can marginalize and even victimize pastoral caregivers. It is not easy work. Our human condition makes it easier to question the motives of others who are different from us, creating the potential for unintentional pain and injury. At the same time, it is only in building alliances that we will gain the kind of wisdom needed to take risks and stands that contribute to the wholeness of individuals, families, and communities.

Pastors Sue and Jean can access the strategies on analyzing how privilege and power work in their individual and corporate relationships, as well as identifying the personal work that each must do on issues important to one another. Building trustworthy relationships where truth-telling can occur without causing permanent damage to one another will move these pastoral colleagues toward embodying authentic pastoral care with one another, even as they work together to dismantle structures of oppression.

Conclusion

Pastoral caregivers have, historically, done best in responding to the needs and concerns of individuals in their churches. We have done less well in understanding how our pastoral care for individuals and families sometimes misses the more prophetic nature of our call. The two case studies in this chapter illustrate how impossible it is to do effective pastoral care without attending to the dynamics of multiple structures of oppression. If pastoral leaders care only about the individualistic needs of parishioners, they miss the call to be part of the building of communities of faith in new and visionary ways.

Racism, sexism, and heterosexism are but three of the multiple structures of oppression that pastoral caregivers face in the context of our work. Providing authentic pastoral care requires that we constantly ask questions about how these structures have an impact on our own lives, the lives of our parishioners, and the broader communities of which we are a part. Such awareness leads to a stronger prophetic approach to pastoral care that includes attention to multiple issues at a time. In April of 1977 the Combahee River Collective, a group of African American women in Boston, wrote a statement that articulated their vision of political activism. It included this reflection:

> The most general statement of our politics at the present time would be that we are actively committed to struggling against racial, sexual, heterosexual, and class oppression, and see as our particular task the development of integrated analysis and practice based upon the fact that the major systems of oppression are interlocking.[16]

More than thirty years later we continue to invite the church to address oppressions created by racial/ethnic, gender, sexual, and class oppression. As pastoral caregivers we also continue to see how these structures of oppression keep people from living whole and full lives.

Pastoral caregivers must continue to find ways to integrate our ability to respond to the frailties and struggles of individuals and families while working to change the structures that support domination and oppression. The latter structures work against the very things that we are attempting to promote in our church communities as we seek to build safe spaces that tend to justice and liberation and loving care. Authentic pastoral care holds together the prophetic call to justice as we create alliances and relationships that cross boundaries of division and the need to care for those who live in our churches and communities.

Womanist Pastoral Care Using Narrative Therapy in Addressing Multicultural Issues

Jacqueline Kelley

"The entire world is in my street, in my city, and every big city. Keep eyes and ears open: African boubous, North African djellabas, Asian faces, and musical accents. In the space of a few seconds people pass by whose gait, physical features, skin color, language, gestures, and behavior display a wide variety. As in a kaleidoscope, forms and colors are constantly transformed. Thanks to the present mingling and merging, humanity has never been in a better position to recognize its extreme diversity. We instinctively search for indicators. We primarily use geographical reference points when we try to situate people somewhere on the face of the earth."

—Jacques Audinet[1]

As I began to approach the subject of multicultural issues in pastoral care, it became apparent to me that I needed to define what I meant as "multicultural" or "cultural." The word *culture* is a relatively recent addition to everyday vocabulary, at least with the meaning we give it. At the end of the nineteenth century, the Grand Larousse dictionary used it in the sense of agriculture and conceded a derived meaning: a cultivated person. The word began gradually to have a different meaning. Ethnologists began to use *culture* instead of the word *race*.[2] Subsequently, culture gained a precise meaning. It no longer referred to the universal person of classic humanism, that ideal personality who could be considered a "cultured person" due to a good upbringing and well-rounded knowledge. Now ethnologists focused on human experience, diversity, the multitude of experiences, outlooks, lifestyles, and the uniqueness of people due to their specific modes of existence, representations of the world, and values.

Anthropologists put an end to the illusion that all human groups are similar, with "white" being the normative role. This enabled other traditions, other human groups, and other cultures to exist in their own right. Now they were no longer minorities who deserved to be scorned. Sharing in the human adventure could be done in multiple ways, all equally deserving of respect. Humanity began to include a rainbow of situations and traditions, as varied as a cornucopia of colors. The word *culture* became a heuristic tool, helping people to recognize and to give value to diversity.[3]

Defining Culture/Multiculturalism

"Cultural identity has a profound impact on our sense of well-being within our society and on our mental and physical health. Our cultural background refers to our ethnicity, but it is also profoundly influenced by social class, religion, migration, geography, gender oppression, racism, and sexual orientation, as well as by family dynamics. All of these factors influence people's social location in our society—their access to resources, their inclusion in dominant definitions of 'belonging,' and the extent to which they will be privileged or oppressed within the larger society."
—Monica McGoldrich, Joe Giordano, Nydia Garcia-Preto[4]

I find this quote helpful as I look into providing pastoral care to people of different cultures. As an African American female, and Clinical Pastoral Education (CPE) supervisor, my practice is within a hospital setting and involves working with patients, staff, families, and CPE students from diverse cultures. My understanding of teaching pastoral care has been enhanced as I have looked at womanist theology and narrative therapy as structures to define my methodology. I think it is important to understand words like cultural identity, cultural diversity, multiculturalism, culturally sensitive practice, and cultural competence because they have ambiguous meanings depending on who is using them.

In the twenty-first century, "cultural diversity," "multiculturalism," "culturally sensitive," and "cultural competence" are phrases that are heard daily. "Culture" is used in a multifaceted way, which allows reinterpretation and misunderstanding. It is used synonymously with the terms *gender, race, ethnicity, social class*, and *sexual orientation*, which creates confusion. It does not matter if a person is looking at news journals, the evening news, psychiatric journals, magazines, cable news, census reports, listening to the radio, or surfing the Internet—he or she is bombarded with the idea of multiculturalism and diversity.

People in caring professions (pastoral care providers, mental health-care practitioners, educators, pastors, ministers, rabbis, imams, etc.) are being exhorted to become culturally competent in order to provide ethnic-sensitive practices. This means that we need to educate ourselves about the characteristics of others and to develop an understanding of people with origins different from our own. Learning about others is learning about ourselves.

Defining culture begins with understanding that it operates from the inside out and includes behaviors that may have been learned through socialization. These values "have been passed down to us through generations."[5] For example, ethnic groups vary in their response to problematic behaviors and to problems as well as their attitudes toward seeking help. Not all cultural practices are ethical, according to a womanist perspective. Womanist views help us look at sexism, racism, classism, and ageism and how these have an impact on the treatment of women, children, gays, lesbians, old and young, those who have been disrespected, as well as those who have been abused emotionally, physically, sexually, and spiritually. Subsequently, culture is a vast interdisciplinary topic that has generated many books, new literature, research in the social sciences, and discussions in academia, organizations, and professional conferences within the last decade.

The purpose in this chapter is to focus on narrative therapy and womanist theology as they allow marginalized women to develop their voices and to realize their value, worth, and the importance of their stories. Naming and externalizing are concepts of narrative therapy, which empower women to speak the unspeakable. In most cultures, women have adopted the views of what society says about them based on a patriarchal model. Women are viewed as "less important" in most cultures. Even though experiences of oppression vary, there are some commonalities that cross cultural and racial barriers. The process of change occurs as we engage one another's stories and experience, then reflect, document, deconstruct, and create alternative narratives. We do this by employing music, books, short stories, movies, poetry, and dance. Listening to others' stories deepens cultural sensitivity and expands the awareness of helping professionals. As a result, this listening informs strategies and interventions that are more precisely refined. Let us begin with the historical perspective.

Historical Context of "Culture"

At the Bandung (Indonesia) Conference in April 1955, "culture" acquired a new meaning. This large-scale conference consisted of Asian and African states, most of which were newly independent. The organizers were from Egypt, Indonesia, Burma, Ceylon (Sri Lanka), India, Iraq, and Japan. Twenty-nine countries were represented. The purpose of the conference was to promote Afro-Asian economic and cultural cooperation and to oppose colonialism by the United States, Soviet Union, and any other imperialistic nation. Although the conference met for these reasons, an additional effect was the raised level of awareness concerning multiculturalism. This allowed the "two-thirds world" (developing countries) to have a voice in deciding how they should be developed and to be less dependent on the industrialized nations. These countries affirmed a role for themselves not aligned with either of the two blocks: the capitalist West or the Marxist Soviet Union. The key words of this affirmation were *cultural freedom*.

Ten years after the Bandung Conference, China underwent its *Cultural Revolution*, with its cortege of destruction and death, which profoundly shook and troubled the country. It heralded the worldwide appearance of new and malevolent forces. The rich and powerful countries were no longer the only ones deciding the rules of the game. The word *culture* became a weapon in the conflict between groups. This combat did not take long to reach the developed countries. In the United States, the word *culture* became a subject of debate. During 1968, from Santiago to Mexico City to Paris, students demonstrated in the name of *cultural revolution*. Sometimes they paid a heavy price of physical attacks and death for challenging the established order. These student movements—sometimes lightheartedly, sometimes tragically—made governments everywhere tremble, eventually causing the departure of Charles de Gaulle in France and a bloody repression in Mexico. The tidal wave challenged the very underpinnings of developed societies.[6] By contrast, the Cultural Revolution in China was an oppressive force to promote communism, rather than free thinking—in many ways, it supported the establishment. This is quite different from how "cultural revolution" happened in the rest of the world.

The word *culture* is multivalent. It can express values for a group referring to social and political standing, then include economics, etiquette, and personal freedom. It can also morph to become an oppressive structure that takes away personhood and liberties.

The Blind Leading the Blind: The Crisis of Our Limited Awareness of Multiculturalism

"If a blind man leads a blind man both will fall into a pit."

—Matt. 15:14

In an article entitled, "Becoming Multicultural Dancers: The Pastoral Practitioner in a Multicultural Society," K. Samuel Lee raises the questions, "What makes a pastor?" or "What makes a chaplain?" or "What makes a pastoral practitioner in our multicultural society?"[7] It is imperative that we open our eyes. All around us, our communities are changing. Lee uses the metaphor of dance in ministry and pastoral care and counseling as we deal with the "shift in music." The dance partners have shifted, and they have their own preference for music, which may be different from ours.[8]

The waltz, two-step, polka, square dance, boogie-woogie, American slide, twist, and Big Apple are being intersected with the samba, tango, Afro-beat, belly dance, and reggae, just to name a few. There has been a "multicultural revolution"[9] taking place on every dance floor, so to speak, in the United States.

Nearly one-third of our dance partners in the United States today come from non-European American cultural traditions. According to the U.S. Census Bureau information released in April 2000, ethnic minorities in the United States made up 28.4 percent of the U.S. population as of March 1, 2000.[10] About 45 percent of the students in the public school system today are ethnic minority communities.[11] The U.S. Census Bureau conservatively estimates that by the year 2050, ethnic minorities will make up 50 percent of the U.S. population.[12] We also live in a globalized community. "Globalization" has become a household word in theological schools since mid-1980. Multiculturalism and globalization are here to stay. They describe the reality of the society to which we belong. We cannot simply close our eyes to the reality of our society, which has changed and is still changing.

Listening to the Music/Learning How to Dance

> "What we do need is one another! We need one another's stories, pain, honesty, laughter if we are to discern the power and the pain of our mothers' gardens in a way that bears fruit for the work of new creation."
>
> —Letty M. Russell[13]

> "Having a sense of belonging, of historical continuity, our identity with one's own people is a basic psychological need. Ethnicity, the concept of a group's 'peoplehood,' refers to a group's commonality of ancestry and history, through which people have evolved shared values and customs over the centuries."
>
> —Monica McGoldrich, Joe Giordano, and Nydia Garcia-Preto[14]

Our ethnicity is retained whether we are aware of it or not. Religion, race, and cultural history join our values to create our identity and patterns of thinking, feeling, and behavior. Thus, culture determines how we live, eat, work, celebrate, make love, and die. It is not easy talking about ethnicity in our American culture. It often becomes a volatile discussion, which evokes deep feelings, and the discussion can become polarized or judgmental. We tend "to focus on the nondominant groups' 'otherness,' emphasizing their deficits, rather than their adaptive strengths or their place in the larger society, and how so-called 'minorities' differ from the 'dominant' societal definition of 'normality'."[15]

What becomes the norm for society is generally based on "white" people as the dominant group. In general, Americans are viewed as having European ancestry. This creates a problem for those of us who have other ethnicities. Until this myth is acknowledged we will not see the need to become culturally competent. Within the narrative model, there is a sense of "curiosity," which allows one to ask questions and to dialogue in order to gain clarity. In a social constructionist model, there is the realization that "truth" is learned by hearing the experience of all parties. Human development begins within an ethno-cultural base. Many Western cultures see the individual as a psychological being and define development as growth in the capacity for autonomous functioning, whereas this is not the case in Eastern cultures. They are defined as social beings categorized by growth in the human capacity for empathy and connection. In order to understand human behavior we need to look at intra-psychic, interpersonal, familial, socioeconomic, and cultural factors. As Derald Wing Sue notes,

> Race, culture, ethnicity, and gender affect communication styles. There is considerable evidence that theoretical orientations in counseling will influence helping styles . . . [and that] different cultural groups may be more receptive to certain counseling/ communication styles because of cultural and sociopolitical factors. Indeed the literature on multicultural counseling/therapy strongly suggests that American Indians, Asian Americans, Black Americans, and Hispanic Americans tend to prefer more active-directive forms of helping than nondirective ones.[16]

In studies done on Asian Americans and African Americans, results showed that they value restraint of strong feelings and believe that intimate revelations are to be shared only with close friends. As a result, this causes problems for the counselor who is oriented toward insight or feelings. These clients seem to be more inclined to a directive approach. "Asian Americans seem to prefer a logical, rational, structured counseling approach to an affective, reflective, and ambiguous one."[17] Such techniques as reflection of feelings, asking questions of a deeply personal nature, and making in-depth interpretations may be perceived as lacking respect for the client's integrity. These clients may not value the process of insight into underlying processes. The blind application of techniques that clash with cultural values seriously places many Asian Americans in an uncomfortable and oppressed position.

Voices of Women

> "Training in pastoral care, if it is to be of any effect, has to enable people to acquire the attitudes and 'ways of being with others' which will be most beneficial to the people they are with. Attitude formation involves the developing of cognitive (thinking), affective (feeling), and conative (behavior patterns) abilities. Pastoral formation necessarily is attitude formation. It is who the pastoral caregiver is, and who they are becoming, that is the crucial thing. This is especially so in the way they relate with others."
>
> —Emmanuel Lartey[18]

As pastoral care providers "who work with culturally diverse populations, we need to move decisively in educating ourselves about the differential meanings of nonverbal behavior and the broader implications for communication styles. We need to realize that the proxemics (the study of personal space), kinesics (study of communication and body language), paralanguage (nonverbal vocal communication), and high-low context factors (the text and conditions surrounding the meaning of the word used) are important elements in communication."[19] Use of self in pastoral care is a key factor.

In order to dance, we need to "hear all of the music." The music comes from listening to different voices speak. An acronym for active listening is the following (LISTEN):

> **L**ook and be interested,
> **I**nquire with open questions,
> **S**tay alive to the speaker,
> **T**est your understanding by checking,
> **E**mpathize,
> **N**eutralize your feelings.[20]

The dance begins when the pastoral care providers and the client are able to send verbal and nonverbal messages, which are read clearly. Pastoral care providers need to be able to shift their therapeutic styles to meet the developmental needs of those served. It is clear from research that white counselors (by virtue of their cultural conditioning and training) tend to use the more passive attending and listening skills in counseling and therapy, while racial/ethnic minority populations appear to be more oriented toward an active listening/influencing approach.

Whereas pastoral care providers have learned to do the two-step of empathy and listening, developing a multicultural model of pastoral care involves developing sensitivity and awareness of culture, racism, classism, ageism, sexism, gender, power, and oppression. Understanding multicultural women requires more than an understanding based on gender issues from the perspective of white females (feminism). Within the feminist model, the primary issues are the oppression of woman as a denial of equal rights and of access to opportunities, whereas a womanist model involves these and other issues. I have chosen the following excerpts, which allow us to hear various voices in this chapter and to understand the reason for distinguishing womanist theory from feminist theory.

Letty Russell Speaks

Letty M. Russell was a professor of theology at Yale Divinity School.

> ... I find myself having to confess that as a white middle-class North American woman I have inherited benefits that accrue to me disproportionately

because of the social structures of racism, classism, and imperialism. I also have to confess that a great deal of this results from my fathers' gardens and binds me to the patriarchal family structures out of which they have come. Perhaps confession is good for more than the soul.[21]

Ada María Isasi-Díaz Speaks

Ada María Isasi-Díaz is a Hispanic American who is an associate professor of theology at Drew University Theological School. She was born in Cuba and feels like a foreigner in a strange land.

> . . . by belonging to a minority culture within another culture, the changing dynamic of my culture becomes a nonorganic force. The changes taking place in the Hispanic culture in the United States do not start from within but are imposed from without. These inorganic changes do not enhance the culture but rather negate it. . . . A culture forced to change by outside forces suffers violence; its values begin to deteriorate. A culture that is not valued, whether by being ignored or by being commercially exploited, is in danger of losing little by little its will to live.
>
> This is what happens to Hispanic culture in the United States. It is sacked and raped every time we are told that our children cannot learn Spanish in school, when our customs are ridiculed, when our cultural artifacts—typical dress, music, etc.—are commercialized. No wonder I have never been able to plant my garden successfully in this society.[22]

Mitsuye Yamada Speaks

Mitsuye Yamada is a second-generation Japanese teacher and poet.

> . . . Asian Americans as a whole are finally coming to claim their own, demanding that they be included in the multicultural history of our country. . . . When the Asian American woman is lulled into believing that people perceive her as being different from other Asian women (submissive, subservient, ready-to-please, easy to get along with Asian women), she is kept comfortably content with the state of things. She becomes ineffectual in the milieu in which she moves. The seemingly apolitical middle class woman and the apolitical Asian woman constituted a double invisibility.
>
> I, personally, did not "emerge" until I was almost fifty years old. Apparently, through a long conditioning process, I have learned *not* to be seen for what I am. A long history of ineffectual activities had been, I realize now, initiation rights toward my eventual invisibility. The training begins in childhood; and for women and minorities, whatever is started in childhood is continued throughout their adult lives. . . .
>
> We must remember that one of the most insidious ways of keeping minorities powerless is to let them only talk about harmless and

inconsequential subjects, or let them speak freely and not listen to them with serious intent. We need to raise our voices a little more, even as they say to us: "this is so uncharacteristic of you." To finally recognize our own invisibility is to be on the path to visibility. Invisibility is not a natural state for anyone.[23]

Judit Moschkovich Speaks

Judit Moschkovich is a Latina—Jewish, immigrant born, and raised in Argentina. She speaks about her experiences of the blatant ignorance most Anglo-American women have about Latin cultures. Her greatest challenge was to choose whether to pass for American rather than being Latina or Jewish.

> I believe that the lack of knowledge about other cultures is one of the bases for cultural oppression. I do not hold any individual American woman responsible for the roots of this ignorance about the other cultures; it is encouraged and supported by the American educational and political system, and by the American media. I do hold every woman responsible for the transformation of this ignorance.
>
>   . . . Anyone that was raised and educated in this country has a very good chance of being ignorant about other cultures, whether they be minority cultures in this country or those of other countries. It's a sort of cultural isolationism, a way of life enforced on the people in this country so as to let them have a free consequence with respect with how they deal with the rest of the world or with subcultures in America. . . . We've all heard it before; it is not the duty of the oppressed to educate the oppressor. Yet, I often do feel pressured to become an instructor, not merely a "resource person."[24]

Barbara Cameron Speaks

Barbara Cameron is a Lakota Indian who experienced racism. This affected her childhood as she saw Indians who were treated unjustly on the reservation in South Dakota. She spent a great deal of time attending funerals of relatives and friends. One year she went to funerals of four murder victims.

> I spent a part of my childhood feeling great sadness and helplessness about how it seemed that Indians were open game for the white people, to kill, maim, beat up, insult, rape, cheat, or whatever atrocity the white people wanted to play with. There was also a rage and frustration that has not died when I look back on reservation life. . . . Native Americans are the foremost group of people who continuously fight against pre-meditated cultural genocide. I've grown up with misconceptions about Blacks, Chicanos, and Asians. I'm still in the process of trying to eliminate my racist pictures of other people of color. . . . My personal attempts at eliminating my racism have to start at the base level of those mind-sets that inhibit

my relationships with people. Racism among the third world people is an area that needs to be discussed and dealt with honestly. We form alliances loosely based on the fact that we have a common oppressor, yet we do not have a commitment to talk about our own fears and misconceptions about each other.[25]

Atoosa Nowrouzi Speaks

Atoosa Nowrouzi is an Iranian seminary graduate and a first-year CPE resident at Princeton Baptist Medical Center. The racism she describes is fueled by prejudices toward and misconceptions about Iran.

The major perception of most Iranian immigrants, especially women, is that American culture and society provide more rights and opportunities for women. My understanding of American culture and society was based on the fact that the early immigrants came to this country due to many injustices, oppressions and inequalities in their society. Thus, it seems so unrealistic for any woman to come here from Iran or from any other country and not want to take advantage of her increased rights, her opportunities in education, profession and other forms of personal and social achievements. However, that initial excitement did not last long after coming here since as an Iranian female Christian, I faced special complications because of gender and nationality.

As an Iranian woman, I have faced occasional sexism and racism in the past few years of my new life in America. While sexism may seem more blatant in the present Iranian society, I would contend that life in the US with its white male dominant culture and negative view toward Iranian society presents challenges to Iranian women like other minorities such as African Americans, Latinas, Asians, Native Americans, etc. Sadly, my experience was not limited to the secular society; it also extended to the faith communities.

As a female Iranian seminary student, I had sad experiences in the Christian setting of my seminary. I was not received with great warmth and love as any Christian individual would like to be embraced by his/her brothers and sisters in Christ. For some people I was not welcomed because of being a female who pursues God's calling in ministry since some denominations do not believe women should be part of active clergy life. For some others, the cause of rejection was my nationality: Iranian, a Middle Easterner. I remember some male students would sit in front of me in class for several consecutive semesters and would never speak a word to me. I find those experiences so hurtful. The sadness, rejection, and loneliness from one side, and the pain of missing loved ones, homeland, and living in a foreign country from the other side, had become an inseparable part of my life during those years. I came to realize that I am accepted by God. I am part of God's family. Why should I seek acceptance from people? My only anchor and stronghold was Jesus Christ. He experienced similar feelings of rejection, loneliness, sadness and pain. Therefore, I was not alone in my journey but He was walking with me in every step of my path. Jesus says in 2 Corinthians 12:9: "My grace is sufficient for you." This was my daily source of strength at that time.

It was shocking for me to experience such lack of knowledge, misconceptions and wrong presumptions about my culture, background, history, reality of Iranian society, and quality of life and education in my home country. I was often asked very primitive questions either regarding women and their status in my country or concerning obvious life situations. My response has always been simple. I would explain that even though the cultures, traditions, and ethnic rituals were different, at the end we were all human beings with similar needs, desires, ways of living and life values. Women in today's society of Iran are actively involved in every aspect of life, education, business, health care, art, and literature. We have Iranian women among scholars, university professors, physicians, attorneys, teachers, musicians, authors, artists and any other aspect with national and international accomplishments in the present society of Iran. The information about Iranian culture is so widespread with today's latest technologies that I think not only it is educational for people to learn from it but it would eliminate so many cultural misinterpretations about Iranians.

In my opinion, even though there are some general restrictions for Iranian women due to the present Islamic government, immigrant Iranian women experience sexism and racism differently but on a daily basis in the American society within work environments, faith communities, and social classes.[26]

Williadean Crear Speaks

Williadean Crear is an African American seminarian and a first-year CPE resident at Princeton Baptist Medical Center. She describes how she came to her own narrative.

I Have Found My Voice and I Will Not Shut Up!
There was a time when I was told when to talk and what to say
There was a time when I was told not to talk
So when I met the Lord, I didn't tell anybody
I just wrapped myself in His grace
There was a time when I thought my voice was not mine
That it belonged to someone else
And they had to tell my story the way they wanted to
I dare not tell it the way it was
So when Jesus healed me and strengthened me
Taught me how to sift through the rubble that covered my voice

Let me know it was mine to tell my story
The way He wrote it
That my voice was shaped by my pain and my silence
Colored by my disappointment
And it was the size of my determination to praise His name
Then I knew it was big and it was bright and shaped to fit my mouth
The way Jesus described my voice, it sounded like His
Shaped by pain and silence
Colored by disappointment
And determined to glorify God, I couldn't miss it
With Him encouraging me to find it
I could toss all the rubble aside
Didn't matter if it cut me, hurt me, or brought physical pain
I was on a mission and would not be stopped
PRAISE THE LORD, I found it![27]

Communication Styles and Pastoral Care

"Pastoral care consists of helping activities, participated in by people who recognise a transcendent dimension to human life, which, by the use of verbal or non-verbal, direct or indirect, literal or symbolic modes of communication, aim at preventing, relieving or facilitating persons coping with anxieties. Pastoral care seeks to foster people's growth as full human beings together with the development of ecologically and socio-politically holistic communities in which all persons may live humane lives."

—Emmanuel Lartey[28]

Pastoral care has been likened to a dance. How can two persons dance together when they hear different musical tunes? How do you learn to appreciate the rhythm of the music that is of a different beat? It is apparent that women from different ethnic groups perceive themselves to have problems that are similar. However, the challenge is to take the time to listen to one another tell our stories in order to pick up the cultural nuances. Whether we are talking about racism, classism, ageism, sexism, abuse, oppression, and so forth, the pastoral caregiver needs to be able to dance with any music.

If counselors share their perception, they may take a more active role in the sessions, giving advice and suggestions, as well as teaching strategies (becoming partners with the client). It is important for counselors to become knowledgeable about how race, culture, and gender affect communication styles and seek to obtain additional training on a variety of theoretical orientations and approaches beyond those that are primarily taught (namely, programs that are psychoanalytically oriented, cognitively or existentially oriented, person centered, or behaviorally oriented).

I recognize there is not one helping style of counseling and therapy that is appropriate for all populations and situations. I remember in seminary being coached by my advisor, Howard Stone, to be eclectic in my techniques as I studied "schools and techniques of psychotherapy." Multiculturally competent caregivers will focus on oppression, racism, classism, ageism, sexism, and other "-isms" as they make their assessments of the clients' needs. Consequently, I find that narrative therapy and womanist theology are approaches to pastoral care that help me to bridge a variety of helping styles and roles in order to work with diverse populations.

Womanist Perspectives, Narrative Ideas, and Practice Principles: Assuming a Narrative Stance

"Womanist pastoral care provides a way of remembering and attending to what is meaningful in life."[29] It gives the pastoral caregiver a format to follow, which allows her or him to enter into a person's experience by listening to the person's story. Helping people to explore their story as social construction enables them to recognize how their behavior and context contribute to suffering. In addition, womanist pastoral care identifies the destructive effects of oppression and lifts up alternative stories of endurance, courage, hope, and wholeness. Developing a culturally sensitive practice is crucial. It gives the care seeker a place to be heard as an individual without feeling the need to be responsible for packaging their story in the language (music) of the caregiver. In addition, it allows the expression of a variety of ideas and feelings; it avoids blame and searches for strengths in individuals, which helps them to identify areas of responsibility. In the process of healing, people are able to tell their cultural stories of oppression and marginalization without being ashamed. In this way, suffering may become redemptive, even in a situation of multidimensional oppression, so that healing and liberation are possible.

Womanist pastoral care enables an individual to author an alternative story. As it begins to emerge, the new story empowers and helps the care seeker to move from victim toward freedom. Freedom comes as the person continues to recreate her or his story. Our role as pastoral caregivers is to care for the souls of the persons who come to us for help. We are to remember and consider the meaningful aspects of our personal stories and those of others, as well as remember to attend to what is meaningful to God. From an African American perspective, our presence represents the life-giving breadth of God.

Womanist consciousness is thinking and acting simultaneously in two contexts: (1) the context of the oppressed black community's concerns and struggles, and (2) the context of women's struggle for liberation and well-being.[30]

Alice Walker popularized the term *womanish*. The womanish idea was birthed from the experiences of women of color; however, a *womanist* is anyone who loves, commits to the survival and wholeness of all people, and has integrity and vision. "A Womanist is one who has developed survival strategies in spite of the oppression of her race and sex in order to save her family and her people."[31] A womanist theological perspective is fivefold: (1) eschatological, (2) liberating, (3) historical, (4) based in reality, and (5) transformational.[32] This fivefold perspective is like a thread that creates a pattern for living in the African American community, becoming a credo for survival and transcending suffering. God is seen as being personal, powerful, compassionate, and liberating. God is mother to the motherless, father to the fatherless, sister to the sisterless, brother to the brotherless, and friend to the friendless.

Womanist theology is a multidimensional theology, which includes racism, classism, ageism, and sexism. As previously stated, its roots are grounded in the experiences of the African American community. However, its beliefs about sin, salvation, grace, and God's relationship to us are developing over time. Womanist theology is primarily concerned with the faith, survival, and freedom struggle of African American women. It opposes all oppression based on race, sex, class, sexual preference, and physical disability. It recognizes the responsible freedom for all humans, and it is dialogical with a variety of theological voices: liberation, white feminist, *mujeri sta*, Jewish, Asian, Native American, African, classical and contemporary, as well as nonfeminist, nonwomanist female voices.

Even though there are commonalities in the various ways of recognizing oppression, there are schisms as various groups become too introspective and begin to exclude others. For example, two-thirds-world feminists see themselves as being excluded by white American feminist groups. Black feminists see themselves as being excluded by both white feminists and black males. Because of this tendency toward exclusion, womanist theology proposes to look at oppression from an inclusive perspective.

Womanist theological praxis encourages all people to look at the trilogy of their life stories (1) with a sense of history, (2) with a sense of self, and (3) in relation to God. This is important because one needs to understand and know how his or her personal story has an impact on the way one encounters others. Initially, we must understand that history is universal. From a womanist theological perspective, women must learn to value their personal story enough to use it as a tool to measure and evaluate their personal experience. It is important to understand how we are connected and how we relate. The Ashanti say, "I am because we are: and since we are, therefore I am."[33] The community of which that person is a part defines the basis of the worth of the individual; this includes the shared beliefs, values, expectations, and behaviors of the society.

In black philosophical tradition, the identity of the individual is never separable from the sociocultural environment. It is based on shared beliefs, patterns of behavior, and expectations. In contrast to the Cartesian way of thinking ("I think; therefore, I am"), there is a different message: individual identity and sense of self is grounded in social interaction and the life of the community.

Gaining self-knowledge has long been the quest of many enlightened persons. It is important to stop and ask ourselves, "To whom and to what do I belong?" Seeking God's presence in the ordinary is a valuable means of examining one's relationship to God. As ministers, meeting people at the point of their need allows us to connect and to feel God's presence as we touch the sacred places of those around us. By recognizing the value of each encounter that we share in our practice as ministers, we learn that our theology is not stagnant. It is forever transforming, consequently requiring a womanist pastoral caregiver to act as a sage or griot, a moral teacher. The womanist gains insight and ethical inspiration, which is channeled toward the betterment of the community, while "preserving the cultural memory of his or her people in the re-telling of his or her tradition."[34]

Ultimately, one can deduce that helping persons find wholeness and healing evolves as they come to "voice" by divine inspiration. This interpretation of one's particular history, sense of self, and relation to God enables womanist theology to make unique contributions to pastoral care and counseling.

Narrative Therapy

Narrative therapy may be used to develop a person's understanding of individual and community stories in a specific sociocultural environment, interpreting suffering and liberation with renewed knowledge of self and relation to God. Narrative therapy encourages the expression of multiple ideas and possibilities; avoids blame or pathologizing; searches for strengths rather than defects; is grounded in a value; and fosters transparency on the part of the therapist (i.e., a situating of the therapist's ideas in her or his own experience). Narrative therapy is based on these constructs: (1) externalization, (2) relative influence questioning, (3) discourse, (4) deconstruction, (5) reconstruction, and (6) alternative stories. It is a stance uniquely suited to culturally sensitive practice.

Culturally sensitive practice allows the caregivers to operate out of a model of freedom, which allows them to be curious about other cultures. No one is an expert on another person's life. This allows the caregiver to learn from the narratives that other people give. People can learn to voice their cultural stories of oppression, marginalization, and find help as they are empowered to tell their stories in a new and larger context. In narrative therapy, there is an argument that stresses "that every therapeutic act is a political one, and that clients need to be helped to deconstruct not only their self-narratives but also the dominant cultural narratives and discursive practices that constitute their lives."[35] "Deconstruction" means to explore how these dominating discourses are shaped, to examine whose interests they serve and whom they subjugate, while exposing the marginalizing possibilities. "Deconstructing the cultural self-narrative means listening, questioning and exploring how the client's cultural meanings and cultural premises (whether linked to race, ethnicity, social class, gender, sexuality, work, religion or mourning, etc.) are being performed and how they are influencing both the self-story and the problem." [36]

However, the postmodern, narrative social constructionist viewpoint blends in well to develop the skills that a culturally sensitive practitioner needs. You look at power, knowledge, and truth as they affect the person's story. As Jill Greenberg and Gene Combs note,

> The only worlds that people can know are the worlds we share in language, and language is an interactive process, not a passive receiving of preexisting truths. . . . Using the narrative metaphor leads us to think about people's lives as stories and to work with them to experience their life stories in ways that are meaningful and fulfilling. Using the metaphor of social construction leads us to consider the ways in which every person's social, interpersonal reality has been constructed through interactions with other human beings and human institutions and to focus on the influence of social realities on the meaning of people's lives.[37]

Key factors in deconstructive listening are to be curious about the client's story and not to take a stance on being an "expert." It requires being a good listener, who is willing to dialogue with people, along with asking questions about things that seem to have gaps. It also includes being able to look not only at individual life narratives, but at cultural and contextual stories. Ultimately, clients tell their story, and they become the interpreter of their own experiences.

Externalization helps the clients realize that they are not the problem; the problem is outside of them. This enables them to vocalize the internal discourses. This leads to deconstructive questioning, which allows people to examine their stories from different perspectives, in order to unpack the narrative and to become aware of other possibilities for their story.

Embracing the Complexity of Multicultural Lived Realities: Utilizing Narrative Questions/Deconstructive Questions

> The questions, struggle, pain, and insight of those at the bottom were the basis of our learning together. . . . The task of [emancipatory historiography] was to learn about the social, political, economic, ecclesial structures that oppress women in all parts of the world and to work . . . on how oppression has come about and how to take steps together with others to work for change.
>
> —Letty Russell[38]

In the dialogical model of pastoral care, the utilization of questions is the key to helping people express themselves clearly. In narrative therapy the idea of "curiosity," "not knowing," are key elements to forming questions, which give the therapist insight to the person's story. As Don Locke notes,

> To meet the needs of culturally diverse populations, helping professionals that work with them must have an understanding of culturally consistent assessment, evaluation, and treatment skills as well as theoretical content. . . . Effective education and counseling of the culturally diverse can only occur when teachers and counselors have knowledge of both education/counseling theory and the particulars relevant to the individual and groups they are trying to help.[39]

The following deconstructive questions are examples, within an externalizing conversation. The idea is to remember at least these five categories: the "history" of a person's relationships, contextual influences, the effects or results, its interrelationships, and the tactics and strategies of narrative and social construction.

Cultural Assumptions about Some Mysteries of Human Existence[40]

1. What does it mean to be a person (a "whole person")?
   - *A male or female, young or old, rich or poor, healthy or sick, physically able or physically handicapped, normal or deviant*
2. How should persons relate to each other?
   - *As male/female, young/old, husbands/wives, parents/children, partner/ partner*
   - *As leaders/followers, teachers/students, employers/employees*
   - *As peers, colleagues, fellow workers, fellow citizens, etc.*
3. What does it mean to belong to a biological or social group?
   - *A family, kinship, group, clan*
   - *A peer group, secret society, gang, club*
   - *Various forms of community (including religious groups)*
4. What is a "good" person? (virtuous, mature, responsible, etc.)
5. What is the "good life"?
6. What is the meaning and purpose of life?
7. What is the meaning of death? What happens when we die?
8. What is "good" and "evil"?
9. What is "health" and "illness"?
10. Why do we have pain? Why do we suffer?
11. What is anxiety and why do we experience anxiety?
12. What is time? Space? Causality?
13. How do we understand and relate to our natural environment?

14. How can we understand and relate to that which transcends human knowledge, time, and space (the supernatural, the Spirit or spirits, God or gods, eternity, infinity, immortality, eternal life, etc.)?
15. How can we know anything for sure?
16. What is "good" and "bad" mothering?
17. What is your role as a woman?
18. What stories have prevailed in the shaping of your cultural narrative? Are they nurturing, strengthening, or potentializing stories or are they self-defeating?
19. Do your self-stories trivialize or render invisible some of your life experiences?
20. Do your self-stories demean you and your ideas while privileging the ideas and interpretation of others?
22. How do you respond to stories that contain contradictions or double binds that are invalidating?
23. Do we interrogate subjugating narratives? (For example, "bride burning in India," "supercision of young males in New Guinea—puberty rites," "clitoridectomy of young females in some African tribes.")
24. Are there any stories to affirm the identity narrative of gays, lesbians, bisexuals, or transsexuals?

The process of standing on the boundary involves using this list of questions to understand and compare perspectives on the mysteries of human existence that are found in different cultures.[41] As Freedman and Combs write,

> Through story development questions, people plot the actions and content of their preferred stories. Through meaning questions, we invite people into a reflecting position from which they can regard different aspects of their stories, themselves, and their various relationships. These questions encourage people to consider and experience the implications of unique outcomes, preferred directions, and newly storied experiences. In naming the meaning of these experiences, they are constructing them.[42]

Womanist Perspectives for Pastoral Care Aided by Narrative Therapy

Womanist concepts look at racism, classism, and sexism. Womanist praxis encourages all people to look at the trilogy of their life stories (1) as a sense of history, (2) with a sense of self, and (3) in relation to God. This is important because one needs to understand and know how his or her personal story impacts the way one encounters others.

"Pastoral care is essentially a literary narrative enterprise of relinquishing stories, submitting to stories, and being transformed by stories," writes Old Testament scholar Walter Brueggemann.[43] Stories function in the caring setting to bring healing and wholeness to the lives of persons and families within the pastoral care context. As Edward Wimberly notes, "These narratives suggest ways to motivate people to action, help them to see themselves in a new light, help them to recognize new resources, enable them to channel behavior in constructive ways, sustain them in crisis, bring healing and reconciliation in relationships, heal the scars of memories, and provide guidance when direction is needed."[44]

While narrative therapy is not synonymous with pastoral care, there is sufficient affinity so that an eclectic approach to pastoral care will find it a helpful aid. The insights of both narrative therapy and womanist theology can be integrated into a ministry of care. Of particular importance is their mutual recognition that suffering, troubled, or oppressed people can be brought to health, healing, wholeness, and hope by telling and hearing their life stories with a sensitive pastor or therapist who draws upon the resources of narrative therapy.

The listening and discourse dimensions of narrative therapy necessitate sharing life stories. Through listening and discourse, the pastor or therapist attempts to liberate persons from the effects of the negative or oppressive discourses that have narrowed their worldview and self-perceptions. This enables them to assuage their fears of failure and rejection that have ensued from the dominant discourses experienced in their social settings. The healing process moves toward the reshaping of life stories, new chapters, and new growth. In all of this, there must be active collaboration between the participants in the process of reconstructing a narrative of substance and value for the person seeking care. Both teller and listener may be enriched in this process.

From a Womanist Pastoral Care Perspective

Narrative therapy is a strong foundation to build upon as one approaches listening to patients, students, parishioners, family members, and others. This theory suggests that everyone has a story to tell and that it is important enough to be heard. Naming is an important part of the womanist concept of coming into "being" by giving "voice." From a womanist pastoral care view, we must consider how racism, sexism, ageism, and classism influence the care that we give, and be aware of how multiple oppressions (shame, guilt, anger, low self-esteem, mental/physical/emotional abuse, self-hate, invisibility, voicelessness, etc.) have affected the lives of the people whom we encounter.

Questions, which motivate the development of womanist pastoral care in a Christian context, continue to be posed: How can I use the experience of women of color as an element of caring for persons who need to find liberation and healing? How have these women used Scripture as a means of empowerment? How has the revelation of God's goodness and God's power in the resurrection of Jesus Christ been a factor in their willingness to remain steadfast and hopeful in the face of many struggles? We can respond to these questions with the answer that African American women have placed emphasis on the humanity of Jesus Christ who challenges us to ask new questions demanded by the context in which we find ourselves.

We know that we are not alone in the face of the struggle. Jesus is the source of our strength. God's action, through Jesus Christ, has destroyed the power of death as the end of struggle and suffering. For non-Christians it is just as important for them to express their belief. From a Christian perspective, there is a transformation from suffering into wholeness. We can no longer accept all suffering as potentially good. Suffering due to injustice is seen as a tool of oppression, which often leaves people without the means to examine the conditions of their oppression. However, pain caused by oppression may move the victim to confront the situation that is causing the suffering. As the oppressed become aware of their pain, a narrative approach encourages them to reflect on their past and to recover subjugated "truths" as they deconstruct and reconstruct their life stories.

Conclusion

Survival, resistance, and liberation are the three keys to following a womanist pastoral care model. Just as Hagar was able to survive in the wilderness with the resources revealed to her by God, oppressed persons can be led to see the resources within their stories and God's story through the listening presence of the womanist pastoral caregiver. The womanist pastoral caregiver must always be prepared to consider all of the information brought to light as the oppressed tell their stories, remembering that there are "no essential truths." Womanist pastoral care helps suffering people to name the things that have caused them to be in bondage, to resist the elements of oppression, and to understand individual and community stories of suffering and liberation in new and redemptive ways.

The dance of health, healing, and wholeness will begin when we incorporate cultural knowledge into our theories and into our therapies, so that clients of the less dominant culture will not have to feel lost, displaced, or mystified. Working toward multicultural frameworks in our theories, research, and clinical practice requires that we challenge our society's dominant, universalist assumptions. Rather than placing blame on "others," we need to look at ourselves and begin to correct the problem by coming to an understanding of our history (where we have been) and the present (the cultural assumptions and blinders that we wear). Then we can begin to understand those who are culturally different from us.

Learning about culture is not done by gathering facts about another's culture. It is by changing our attitude. One has to be open to those who are culturally different in order to expand cultural understanding. It is necessary to add cultural lenses to our psychological assessments in order to get past our assumptions and to get to the "truth" of understanding the experience of others.

Learning how to dance requires that one follows rather than leads in the beginning. In establishing relationships, we must work to see the limitations of our own view so we can open our minds to hear the music (experience) of others. Womanist pastoral care calls us into community with others and God. We have our Healer, our Sustainer, our Liberator, and our Empowerer. The Holy Spirit (Paraclete) invites us to the dance.

La Veglia—Keeping Vigil

The Power of Storytelling and Story Sharing in Women's Lives— A Study in Mediterranean Culture

Adriana P. Cavina

The evening shadows were longer now. The women knew that soon the winds of winter would sweep away their time together. Families would gather around the fireplace at night but there would be no more time for chattering with neighbors sitting outside the steps of each house along the narrow village street. Life was going along in cycles, as grandmothers used to tell the children. As soon as spring would warm up into summer, *la veglia*[1] would resume. In the evening, from the open kitchen window, one woman would call another. Families would bring chairs into the street and keep vigil together, enjoying the cool of the evening and chatting away the facts of the day. Men would gather in circles of men, and women would form circles of women. Children would play together not far away; puberty was the accepted time to enter one of the two circles, the sign of adulthood. Then, as the nights would again grow too cool for a warm sweater to brush off the shiver, *la veglia* would stop, and the evening chat would continue only among the generations of the same family around the supper table.

This was the life of the Italian country town on the slopes of Monte Amiata in Tuscany when I was growing up. *La veglia,* "the vigil," was a time of gathering, a time for discussion, a time for sharing. Newspapers or television were still a rare commodity. In any case, what would ever have been more important for my grandmothers than gossiping along with other women, or just sharing hopes and dreams and fears and joys with other female friends? My grandmothers and their friends were too busy cultivating live relationships among them to be attracted by the prospective of sitting in front of a television screen where strangers would talk of things and events too far away to be really interesting. Clearly, *la veglia* was the best time of the day, as grandmothers used to say. Often women would sing at those gatherings. Arias and traditional songs would fill the evening sky, and laughter too. At times, the song would be softer and more sober, as a memory of a departed loved one or an individual crisis would come to the center of conversation. One woman would sing in the background, as the choir of classical Greek tragedy. Other women would chime in and out of the tune, or call for a different song. One rule, however, was sure, not even to be discussed among the group: What song could be sung if not a woman's song, a female story? Men were busy chatting in their circle about the events of the day, smoking pipes and marking the talk with big gestures and loud laughter. Only women would lift their voice to sing a story.

La veglia was a local cultural tradition. I witnessed its slow disappearance from the Italian life-scene as individual and communal life took on a new pace with the appearance of shopping malls and media screens. With the passing of *la veglia,* something else died, the demise of which, I realize today, still has universal significance. With *la veglia* a habit of talking, a linguistic exchange, disappeared too.

Language and the Shaping of Worldviews: How Do I Compose My Own Song?

Language is the main means we have to describe our inner and outer world of experience and to communicate it, exchanging with others the different ways we face events and learn from them, as we attempt to make sense of our individual and communal lives. It is the tool that helps us to weave the threads of a shared narrative, providing us with common symbols. The way we see the world is shaped by language and, in turn, our perspective shapes language. It is our connection with self and story, individuals and community. We make sense of events and our accompanying emotions as we engage in the effort of translating an experience into a symbolic expression and then communicate it to others. Paradoxically, the uniqueness of my story is highlighted and affirmed when I find the similarity of that story with other people's stories. My story is my own, unique and unrepeatable. Yet, I find its value affirmed when I see it reflected in similar stories and similar themes, like the thread of blue color that appears brighter when woven together with other shades of blue. Meaning is individual but it needs to be validated through the act of sharing it through words, symbols, music, art, and emotions.

In a Romance language—such as French, Spanish, and my native Italian tongue—grammatical gender gives life and form to our world of perception.[2] In the absence of a neuter gender, in the Italian language everything assumes an identity that projects our cultural views on sex and sex roles onto the world of things. All nouns are either masculine or feminine. The mental associations with a gendered view of the world are inescapable. So, in Italian a chair that welcomes your sitting in a comfortable embrace is female, while a hammer that pushes nail into a hard wood is male. Trees are masculine, and water is female. Every aspect of creation has a gender; we view, describe, understand, and build the world around us through the two genders. This process deeply reflects our cultural way to live in the world. Language is "gendered" from its deeper roots into our collective unconscious. There is a female way of discourse and a male way in our communal conversations. As the author of my linguistic expression, the "I" that is spoken by me is a female one, as my describing, reflecting, exploring, and explaining is also. My grammatical discourse is in the feminine. The female gender marks all aspects of my spoken sentence whenever I speak of myself and my experience: female endings will give the structure of my spoken sentence its specific feminine connotation. My male counterpart is expressed in his masculine linguistic view of experience. Speaking of himself, he will structure the sentence in the masculine. In describing my view of reality I will use a feminine grammatical structure, and he will use a masculine one.[3] Community is made of a female "me" and a male "you," and vice versa; both subjects are reflected in our linguistic interactions. The issue, however, is complicated by the fact that the two gendered linguistic expressions do not share equal power. The masculine form always prevails and is assumed to be normative or standard, the universal voice for all. This has profound implications for the way men and women describe personal experience that may have common significance. To give power to my discourse and generate interest for it, I, as a woman, will have to speak or write using a male grammatical gender and giving my sentence a male grammatical structure.

In Italy, most small towns and villages still today remain perched on hilltops, living remnants of a medieval way of defense against the invaders from the plain. The focal point of the *polis*, the communal life, is the main square with its three places of social power and interchange: the cathedral with its spiritual authority; the town hall with its political power; and the marketplace, the locus of commerce and social interaction, the place of storytelling and story sharing, the meeting place of young and old, families with families, men and women, locals and visitors. On the main square, the language is mixed, both genders equally present, but with no equal power. If a common view is to be expressed, it will be expressed in the masculine grammatical gender, the only voice of authority. Female gender is left for gatherings of only women. If one man is present, the common conversation will have to turn into the masculine grammatical gender, no matter how many women may be present. Families speak in the masculine, so do all members at social gatherings.

La veglia was different. With its circles of gender separation, it actually provided a space of freedom for all. The female circle and its cultural practice of female linguistic exchange would ensure that my grandmothers' voices would find full space of expression. No wonder it was such a precious time for women! At *la veglia* women would talk of birth and death and instruct the younger ones into the mystery of sexuality and of expected female roles. It was the place of socialization into the larger world, but it was also a place of freedom because individual experience, communicated and shared through a female voice in a female language, would receive full acceptance and be given common significance. For me and for my young female friends, who used to leave the city and spend summer vacation time with our elders, *la veglia* had a mysterious attraction. It was a different society, a gathering of shared learning about the relationship with the other sex, its excitement and its dangers; fertility and motherhood were discussed freely, and we were also well instructed about cultural role expectations, well-proven customs, and solid norms of behavior. The women at *la veglia* had no awareness of being feminist pioneers; they shared in the common culture, but they knew well about women's power and its societal repression. *La veglia* provided a place and a time to claim that power among sisters of equal power and not be bashful about it.

La veglia was more than the place where conversation could remain in the feminine with no need for further accommodation; it was also a precious opportunity for country women whose voice or place in society was rarely noticed. Women shared views that did not need to be translated into a so-called neutral masculine linguistic counterpart. Conversations could relax into one grammar, one voice, that had all the freedom and the authority to affirm and to judge, to discern and discriminate, to support and challenge. The language of the mother (*la lingua materna*) was given unrestricted power. The language of the father (*la lingua paterna*), with its patriarchal order, was set aside during those cool breezy evenings of summer.

Language and Power: How Can I Sing a Song That Will Be Heard?

The power of language is mirrored in our social relationships. *La lingua materna,* "the female-gendered voice," is not given power in a society that makes use of only one grammatical gender in any form of public speech. Italian women have long denounced the unequal distribution of power when society assumes the neutrality of language and at the same time privileges one linguistic expression over another. For decades French philosopher Luce Irigaray has repeatedly raised a lonely voice to denounce the falsity of "neutral language." She has clearly unveiled the hidden power of language to impose worldviews and the danger of a society that ignores the "gendered" or "sexed" view of verbal expression.[4] She affirms:

> How could discourse not be sexed when language is? It is sexed in some of its most fundamental rules, in the division of words into gender in a way not unrelated to sexual connotations or qualities, just as the lexicon is sexed too. Differences between men's and women's discourses are thus the effects of language and society, society and language. You can't change one without changing the other. Yet while it's impossible to radically separate one from the other, we can shift the emphasis of cultural transformation from one to the other, above all we must not wait, passively, for language can be deliberately used to attain greater cultural maturity, more social justice.[5]

Our individual and communal views are expressed through people, and people are men and women, expressing themselves in many world languages and societies through male or female grammatical genders. Men and women speak out of their respective experience. Biology does not limit us, but it certainly provides two ways of being in the world. We are embodied beings. Language is a tool that comes out of shared embodied experiences that reflect our two sexes and their different ways of being human beings on planet earth. It then connects us to the here and now of our political and social interactions with one another, thereby reflecting the power imbalance of our culture.

> Sexual difference is not just biological, as it was commonly said, and it is not just the product of social stereotypes, as it is now affirmed. It is actually a *difference of relational identity*. . . . Man and woman represent two *different worlds* that cannot communicate with each other if first they do not recognize their diversity and then elaborate some strategies to address the other while respecting their mutual differences. In fact, we believe we can communicate if we stop at the level of primary needs, such as eating, finding shelter, sleeping, and so on; or if we belong to the same culture. But this is our illusion, because culture has been elaborated by men with the help of language and its syntactical structures and conceptual contents, and so on. Even if a woman can understand, as one can understand a foreign language, she cannot express herself in this culture which she supported only through silent presence and silent work. The medium that should represent our ability for mutual communication is not the result of mediation; it does not equally represent man and woman.[6]

During the 1970s and '80s, as Italian women were moving into larger places of visibility in professions and in society at large, the feminist movement called *Il Pensiero della Differenza* ("the language of difference") was formed, and many women's groups initiated habits of gathering and reflecting on thought and language. One of these groups gave birth to *Diotima*, an association of Italian women in philosophical and theological research. The choice of the Greek name of the first woman philosopher ever recorded in history was not casual. It affirmed women's right to philosophical and theological investigation and proclaimed its perennial and universal worth. The women who took part in *Diotima* began to engage in dialogue among themselves, with the wider feminist movement, and with the prevailing culture about language, gender, and female identity, denouncing the "sexed expression" of every communal conversation with their different power of significance for female and male views. Many *Diotima* women, including Luisa Muraro and Adriana Cavarero, studied the birth of female identity in relation to language and the negligible value given by society to the mother's voice compared with the power of the father's voice to establish rules and lines of command.[7] What is the disguised message that girls receive in schools and in society when the female grammatical form can never be used to signify anything of common value or to describe the experience of both men and women, and therefore the female discourse is deprived its contribution to a universal expression?

Diotima's answer to the question woke many people up to a form of exclusion and suffering that had never been named before and to the necessity to reform education and language.[8] In a famous article, Adriana Cavarero narrates the process through which women learn to describe their experience using the masculine grammatical gender in order for their discourse to be given any universal value. First, she writes that: "Every discourse carries in itself the sign of the speaker, the narrating subject that describes oneself and one's vision of the world through it."[9] Then, Cavarero denounces the "monstrous" process that assumes the masculine gender as the universal gender: "The male-neuter subject, a monster that cannot be represented and yet is so familiar to everyone who affirms: 'man is a rational subject' or 'man is the child of God,' etc."[10] Cavarero notes that while the process of recognizing oneself in similar universal affirmations is easy for men, women need to "add something" to the same process of recognition: "Woman is the 'universal man' with an addition, the female gender. We know well that this addition does not increase power, actually it decreases it, because this 'plus' is in reality a 'minus.'"[11] Then, she goes on describing how girls learn to articulate their thought-processes and experiences in family and community:

> The mother tongue in which we began to speak and to think is in reality, the language of the father. There is no language of the mother because there is not a [universally recognized] language of women. The language we women speak is a foreign language. . . . Pulling down the veil that hides the false neutrality of the language and its externality from women's experience is the first step towards articulating a thought that includes woman as the speaking subject, and a self-reflecting subject.[12]

The challenge sparked by the sophisticated articulation of the women of *Diotima* called for a fast response in the Italian intellectual landscape. Many women raised their voices to claim space for the "female order of language," *la lingua materna*, in conversation with Luce Irigaray, who became personally involved in Italian political and academic circles and an active participant in the movement. They asked that another voice be added to the formation of the *polis* in its three components: the cathedral, the town hall, and the marketplace. Another voice, a female voice, to contribute to the building of political theories and structures, to the many ways of describing our relationship with the sacred and of living it in worship, and to the establishment of just, peaceful, and creative societal relations, was heard.

In parallel, a group of Protestant and Catholic women pastors and theologians gave life to *Sophia,* an association of women who had set their hearts and minds to bring the female voice of difference into the larger community of churches and the theological academia. *Sophia* joined other women in the Italian society and took part in a female collective political effort to create a new Italian vocabulary for women in traditionally male professions. The word *pastora* ("a pastor who is female") was coined, and the women pastors asked the churches to call them using that name and to abandon the traditional masculine word *pastore* ("a pastor who is male") to address women in ministry. This linguistic act brought a revolution in the way church members and people at large began to perceive the role of pastors who are women. Women in the congregations felt empowered. Men encountered the depth of their resistance. It forced everyone, however, to think of women in ministry from the point of view of women, using a grammatical feminine form, and therefore accepting a female way of being a pastor instead of covering the female specificity under the false universality of a masculine name and a linguistic male expression.

As the word *pastora* began to be used for a woman in ministry, *le pastore* ("the women in ministry") began to feel a freedom of theological and pastoral expression that they had never before experienced. They could now preach and teach more spontaneously, occasionally referring to themselves or to female colleagues in the feminine. Parishioners could now address them in the feminine, using the usual conversational grammar employed with other women. Awkward conversations were replaced by easier ones. Women who were pastors felt recognized and given worth as women in authority.

Joining my female colleagues and claiming an appropriate grammatical gender for myself was one of the most revolutionary acts of my life as *pastora* in active ministry. As a member of the women of *Sophia*, together with my colleagues and the women of *Diotima*, we realized that the problem of the insignificance of women's voices and intellectual contribution in our society was centered in the language and was deeply rooted in the culture. It was necessary to bring this fact to the attention of Italians, and reclaim the right to use feminine nouns and feminine sentence agreement when speaking of a woman in any traditionally male role.[13]

Diotima and *Sophia* knew, and affirmed against all odds, that there is a power that has the potential of transforming society: *il potere della differenza sessuale* ("the power of sexual difference"). This power goes unnoticed and when it is voiced, it gets easily dismissed. If a society deprives itself of the contribution of the female gender, not only women encounter discrimination, but the whole society suffers. Gender denotes more than identity; it unveils the attribution of power in the patriarchal construction of the world.

Language and Identity: How Many Voices to Sing a Solo?

Italian feminist thought with its *pensiero della differenza* acknowledges the different voice critically explored by Carol Gilligan[14] but goes beyond it. The voice of women is a voice of difference, not a different voice. It is an integral part of the human voice, which is by nature a "dual voice of equality." There is not a male or female subject in the world. There is only *un soggetto duale* ("a dual subject"), one voice with a dual expression, one subject with two ways of being, sensing, relating, and speaking. Since one of the two voices is consistently suppressed in the social arena, at times it is necessary to meet separately, and to affirm women's place and voice, as in the practice of *la veglia*, but the separation is not one of exclusion or of hierarchy.

The distinction is subtle but important. If we affirm two subjects, no matter how much equality we may try to give to both, still one will eventually prevail in the common discourse, whether it be the masculine or the feminine. Bringing the "dual subject" to the forefront is much more revolutionary and requires a stretch of imagination and will that has the potential to transform the world we live in. Irigaray writes,

> Being attentive to sexual difference implies respect for the other in light of being faithful to oneself. . . . Being two implies building history together, cultivating humankind in its incompleteness, without dominion or subjugation, but also through the happiness of shared energy, and the joy of treading a common path.[15]

The "dual subject" forces us not to change the language but to become aware of the language. It does not ask us to invent awkward new expressions of supposed neutrality, but simply to accept that there are two ways of being and speaking, a female and a male one. The whole picture, the real picture, can only appear when we see male and female as one subject, and when we bring both voices to speak together with *equal power of expression, interpretation, and representation*. We can get a glimpse of the revolutionary power of this process if we move our attention to our multilingual, multicultural, multispiritual society. By moving *il potere del soggetto* ("the power of the speaking subject") into our present context, we are called to accept "a plural power of naming." The consequences for our communal discourse are noticeable.

The power of language, since its inception in the history of humankind, is the power of "voicing" and "naming," and therefore of giving norms of interpretation for the structuring of the collective perception of reality. What happens when this power is given to multiple individual expressions of being human? Our reaction may be one of excitement or fear at the prospect. It certainly does not leave us indifferent. Are we going to lose our power by giving others, so different from us, the same power of naming and interpreting, voicing and sharing, categorizing and norming that we have?

Our emotional response does not change much if we think of the "dual subject" of male and female expression. How would the world change when our views of it would be commonly expressed through a female grammatical gender instead of through the unquestioned "universal" masculine grammatical gender of our languages and cultures? For example, could we indeed speak of the Italian people using the expression *le italiane* (female plural noun) interchangeably with *gli italiani* (male plural noun)? As a native Italian speaker I know that my mind immediately shifts the focus as I hear male or female nouns used to describe a collection of people. When I hear *gli italiani*, my mind goes to include all the Italians due to habit and socialization. When I hear *le italiane*, my mind is only able to include the females that are part of the Italian population. Generation after generation, the use of the language has engraved in our psyche the male noun as the only one able to signify the whole.

Even languages that have a third neutral gender use the masculine gender to denote universality. The process goes beyond grammar and includes power and its ownership, as reflected in culture and societal norms. Languages other than those of Latin roots may not have different grammatical voices, but the power of the *linguaggio della differenza* transcends grammar because gender difference is a symbolic order in the shaping of the communal web of meaning and inter-pretation. The *veglia* taking place in villages around the Mediterranean shores reminds us that storytelling and story sharing is at the core of the *polis*, the communal society based on democracy and equality. It also provides substance to our symbolic interpretations of our life in the cosmos. We need to speak our truth, sing our individual songs, in order for a multiple multitone, multivoice choir to lift up a genuine hymn of praise in one voice to the one Creator. Only by singing together can we be one voice.

Multicultural societal practices that are based on the acceptance of a "lan-guage of difference" from an ethnic-cultural point of view begin the process of raising awareness of the coexistence of "equal differences" within the home and then take it into education and social structures. When difference in its linguis-tic and cultural forms finds space and celebration, it reverberates its potential for profound transformation in the lives of individuals and societies around the whole world.

Conclusion: How Can I Keep from Singing?

The tradition of *veglia* brings new insights to multicultural pastoral care. Deprived of the power of naming their pain or of sharing their ideas in the context of the "village," or relegated to a female vocabulary that cannot be expressed in the pres-ence of males, women from different cultures feel oppressed. Conversely, opening up to "new listening" and "new hearing" when the "voice of difference" begins to speak, individual men and women in the collective marketplace of communal life undergo a shift in perception. Inclusive language liberates new views and fresh thinking. "The sky is now painted with two strokes," as an old Latin proverb says. It requires two painting hands to look like one whole picture.

The memory of the Italian *veglia* with its creative exchange of women's voices and experiences calls for our celebration today. Around the world, other cultures speak of similar gatherings, limited spaces for a vocal sharing of views that the whole society needs to hear, to absorb, and to bring into the larger commerce of ideologies and languages that forms our world.

The practice of storytelling is the way the people of the world have always used to contribute to the common culture, its traditions, structures of norms and values, and institutions. If there is no more time or space in our busy cities for sitting outside on porches and streets for an evening gathering, we can still be creative and find unexpected places of connection and collective story sharing where different views, dual subjects, and multicultural subjects can receive equal power of describing and naming the collective experience. Town-hall meetings, as well as advocacy and support groups, are all different ways to shape new communities gathered around common topics of interest. Our societies are changing rapidly in their composition and the present need is to find creative ways to add multicultural voices and a whole new range of verbal expressions.

The power of linguistic difference helps us see that if we want to shape a balanced view of human experience, we always need the convergence of multiple expressions, from the two genders of grammar to the coexistence of multiple cultures. Places of faith and worship are in the forefront of this movement toward the inclusion of different voices and cultural expressions into one community. This is not an easy process, but it is more and more demanded of us as societies become variegated expressions of different beliefs, values, and cultural practices. I have personally witnessed the challenge evoking emotions of excitement and fear, opportunity and danger.[16]

Making space for *il linguaggio della differenza* is much more than just linguistic integration. It is a political act, because it calls us to new forms of taking care, paying attention, and communicating in ways that are inclusive of all in our community. It is a theological act, because it requires a more nuanced and varied vocabulary to enrich our metaphorical language about God. Enlarging our way to speak about God and including female images and symbols help us to connect theological discourse and liturgy with the experience of all those who join us in reflection and in worship. In some languages, such as those belonging to the Romance domain, if we use a female metaphor for God, we need to structure the whole sentence in a female grammatical form. The effect for women, as I have often witnessed in my life of *pastora*, is to find a God that "finally speaks and thinks like me," as one of my parishioners said one day with amazement.

As women speak their different embodied experience, new relational contracts are formed. By their storytelling, women sitting at the *veglia* used to weave a web of meaning that built their view of human existence into the larger whole. In our memories, they are still sitting there calling us to be visionary. Without their and our gendered voice, the commonly shared view of the world will always bear a flaw, our choirs will miss a voice, and our vision will always have one blind eye to the future.

Aggression in Korean American Women

Cultural Adaptation and Conceptual Reformulation

Insook Lee

The overnight flight from Korea to the United States places Korean immigrants in a strenuous situation of surviving, as well as thriving, in a foreign land. This struggle begins the very moment they land in any one of the airports in the United States. I remember my first day in the United States in 1983. In a crowd of mostly American people at a New York airport (I had never seen such a huge crowd of Western people until that moment), I was simply overwhelmed with trying to figure out where to go, what to say, and how to interact with people who spoke a different language and appeared to behave in puzzling ways. In order to deal with such a new and urgent situation unfolding before me, I literally had to grab and utilize any and all of my available resources, both inner and outer. Survival greatly matters and thriving is crucial for Korean immigrants, as for all racial/ethnic immigrants.

Sudden cultural change has a major impact in all spheres in the lives of Korean American immigrants, including the personal, familial, social, and economic areas. Having already formed self-identities and basic personality structures within the Korean Confucian culture, Korean immigrants are suddenly, and naïvely, exposed to American culture without proper education and information about the ins and outs of mainstream culture, which soon dominates every detail of their ordinary immigrant lives. In the process of slowly adapting to a new culture, they, whether intentionally or unintentionally, experience some degree of a reintegration of their self-identities, personalities, value systems, and worldview in response to this new cultural need. This need to survive a radical cultural change can never be underestimated when we consider its substantial impact on their psychological, emotional, and physical well-beings.

The differences between Korean culture and American culture can be described from various perspectives. For example, there are differences in the modes of interpersonal relationships: how people greet each other; how they relate with each other; how they show hospitality, love, and respect to each other; what they value most in their personal and social lives; what kinds of people are considered mature and capable; what personality characteristics are considered strong; how they make a decision in a crisis and what their priorities are; how they deal with conflict and disagreement; who has the power in a group and why; and so forth. These differences in everyday life often create serious misunderstandings, prejudices, hostility, and pejorative indifference amongst people from different cultures.

Considering all these numerous differences, Korean American immigrants, in general, experience a sudden transition from the Confucian communal culture of Korea to "a post-communal" culture,[1] that is America, which is described mostly as democratic and individualistic. A communal culture emphasizes corporate well-being and maintains its corporate system mostly by requesting that individuals limit and suppress their individual need on behalf of the corporate good. On the other hand, a post-communal culture focuses on individuals' self-actualization and encourages an "active" expression of individual needs and desires. These contrasting values of the two cultures often clash with each other in the lives of Korean American immigrants and create turbulence, confusion, conflict, and maladaptation, which can significantly threaten their emotional and psychological well-being.

This radical cultural change, of course, influences both Korean American men and women. I believe that it has a stronger impact on Korean American women, however, because of the unique social system of their native Confucian culture. The traditional Korean Confucian culture prescribes the roles of men and women strictly on the basis of a patriarchal social system and expects women to stay in a passive and subservient position as clearly formulated in the Confucian social ethics. These ethics are summarized as "Three Bonds" and "Five Relationships" and will be discussed in detail later in this paper.

Deeply embedded in this Confucian culture, Korean American women are now challenged to survive and function in a heavily individualistic culture that greatly values an assertive expression of individual thoughts, desires, and needs. Their old survival mode of being "humbly" quiet, "elegantly" passive, and "maturely" altruistic often leads to a failure to survive and thrive in the assertive, self-expressive, and even aggressive American culture. Faced with this challenge, Korean American women may feel that they are inadequate, incapable, and "less than normal." Self-doubt pressures them, whether willingly or unwillingly, to start a long journey into the wilderness of self-exploration in a new culture. The question "Who am I?" is the main force that pulls them into that uncertain wilderness. Unfortunately, like the Hebrew people in the exodus story, some may wither and die in the dry wilderness, some may wish to stick to their familiar Egypt, while others may successfully transform their identities to thrive in the new soil of American culture.

Korean American women, out of lack of immediately available survival strategies in a new land, are psychologically pressured to cross over the conscious dimension of survival modes in order to probe new inner resources and strengths. This process often happens on an unconscious level, just as in crisis situations.[2] This search for new resources continues in a lifelong process of their cultural adaptation and self-transformation. I contend that one of the newly discovered inner resources could be women's aggression, which the Korean Confucian culture has systematically suppressed in order to maintain the status quo of its patriarchal system.

To argue this point, I must first explain the major difference between Korean Confucian culture and American individualistic culture. For the purpose of illustrating the contrast between the two cultures, I am using Philip Rieff's psychosocial theory of cultural changes. I have chosen Rieff's theory because his theory historically and systematically demonstrates well the major differences between a corporate culture and an individualistic culture, findings that can then be applied to the immigrant context of Korean American women. Then, using various psychological theories,[3] I shall show how human aggression is one of the "innate instinctual drives," which persistently demands its healthy expression for authentic humanness; therefore, the repression of aggression can cause various problems and "less-than-humanness."

Finally, I shall discuss feminist pastoral theology in order to reformulate the concept of aggression for Korean American women. I believe that such a reformulation can help Korean American women clarify the confusing experience of their aggression discovered in a novel cultural background, and be able to value it, rather than condemn and feel "shameful" of it. Aggression is a powerful and creative source for change and transformation in an immigrant context.

Post-Communal American Culture

According to Philip Rieff's psychohistorical theory of cultural changes, every culture has the tension between "controls and releases."[4] In other words, every culture has a system that serves both communal purposes and individual purposes. For the communal purposes, each culture develops a moral system that demands individuals' commitment to communal well-being. The communal moral system often demands individuals to limit, control, and suppress their individual desires and needs for corporate harmony. Renunciation of the individual's need is considered a virtue in a culture where a controlling force for corporate well-being is stronger than a remissive one for individual good. In this cultural system, human instinctual desires—such as sexual, emotional, psychological, and physical desires and expressions—are perceived morally "bad" because these instinctual desires are thought to primarily serve only the individuals.

On the other hand, Rieff also asserts that each culture has a "remissive" system that attempts to ease the communal pressures for individuals.[5] Every culture, he continues to argue, has this tension between control and remission and these two forces of control and remission have been the constant source of cultural changes in history. In other words, a cultural change takes place when the remissive pressure grows more compelling than the controlling one. Different from a controlling culture, a remissive culture becomes skeptical of communal moral demands as well as their authorities and instead tends to "trust instinct."[6] The release of individuals' instinctual impulses is thus the ultimate aim of an extremely remissive culture, which counteracts a communal controlling force and its demands.

Based on this explanation, Rieff argued that America in the 1960s was experiencing a radical cultural revolution. The antecedent American culture was a unitary communal system. The communal culture established a moral system, and people submitted to its authority and limited their instinctual impulses on behalf of communal purposes. An individual self was realized and satisfied through the limitation and renunciation of instinctual needs and desires. This kind of American culture belonged to Rieff's "mandatory" system of "commitment."[7]

As Rieff rightly argued, the American culture is becoming a "post-communal culture."[8] It is experiencing the radical release from the mandatory systems and the shift toward impulse release. People free themselves from the sense of community and preoccupy themselves with their individual selves and with their utmost concern about their sense of individual well-being. Well-being is a personal achievement for the individual, and thus modern individualism is born. As the self becomes the ultimate concern of contemporary American culture, people resist any moral demands that oppose the expression of the instinctual part of the self.

The extreme ethos of individual well-being of humanistic psychology has deepened this cultural tendency. Humanistic psychology celebrates the values of "freedom, spontaneity, introspection, and self-actualization."[9] Carl Rogers, a prominent humanistic psychologist, describes the humanistic ethos: "Fully functioning individuals are individuals who rely totally on their own actualization tendency rather than on the expectations of others. For them, doing 'what feels right' proves to be a competent and trustworthy guide to behavior which is truly satisfying."[10] American culture has been steadily moving toward a freer release of individual impulses as a means of self-actualization.[11]

Korean Confucian Culture

In 1392, Yi Song-gye and his supporters overthrew the Koryo Dynasty and founded a new dynasty called Chosun. As soon as the Chosun Dynasty was established, Confucianism replaced Buddhism of the Koryo Dynasty and became the "official state orthodoxy."[12] After that, the conflict between Buddhism and

Confucianism became a major issue for the Chosun Dynasty. One of the reasons why Confucianism was chosen as the state orthodoxy for Chosun was the underlying structure of Confucianism that suggests a strong concern for social ethics. Such a strong ethics helped the new dynasty create social stability and order at a critical period of historical transition and change.

Different from Buddhism, Confucians have a this-worldly orientation and try to deal with concrete mundane affairs by providing specific guidelines and standards. They insist that a human being should be embedded in a given set of human relationships and that the relationships should be the point of departure in any ethical reflection. Three Bonds and Five Relationships are the "ethical cores of human relationships for Confucians."[13] Three Bonds refers to authority (1) of the ruler over lesser governmental figures, (2) of the father over the son, and (3) of the husband over the wife. The Three Bonds is obviously based on the system of dominance/subservience that underscores the hierarchical relationship as an inviolable principle for maintaining social order. The primary concern is not the well-being of individuals but the particular pattern of social stability that results from the prescribed rules of conduct.

Five Relationships specifies a pattern of interaction between two groups of people. The relational pattern emphasizes (1) righteousness or mutual faithfulness between ruler and minister, (2) intimacy between father and son, (3) distinction or division of labor between husband and wife, (4) order between old and young, and (5) faith or mutual trust between friends. The Five Relationships focuses more on mutuality than the Three Bonds does. However, Five Relationships also expresses its basic agenda to establish social stability and harmony on the basis of "rank, gender, and age."[14] The Chosun Dynasty strengthened these Confucian ethics and politically implemented them to control its new regime at a most turbulent historical moment in Korea.

Since then, this "politicized Confucian implementation of the ethics"[15] has continuously operated as being exploitive of Korean women. The strict authoritarianism based on power and domination has become increasingly an oppressive system that undermines the value of women both at home and in society. In Confucian culture, authority is respected as an important virtue. Women, however, are systematically alienated from possessing authority and power. A woman's dependence on her father, husband, and son for the sake of the communal harmony and well-being is regarded as one of the highest feminine virtues. Women's individual well-being is constantly overshadowed by the communal well-being whenever these two purposes conflict with each other.

Thus, the politicized Confucian culture systematically teaches Korean women to actualize themselves by limiting and repressing their desires and impulses, thereby denying their potential powers of individual creativity, autonomy, and sense of freedom. The Confucian culture has a controlling function of renunciation and puts men in a position of exercising control and power. Korean women internalize its moral system and, without thinking critically, accept the culturally prescribed belief that women's self-fulfillment and happiness can be acquired through the limitation of personal and instinctual need and desires.

Suddenly being exposed to the American "remissive" post-communal culture, however, Korean American women may get in touch with new parts of themselves that had not been reached in the Confucian culture. One of these new parts is human aggressiveness, a form of the instinctual impulses, which has long been hibernating under the Confucian ethics of renunciation for women. I have often found in my pastoral relationships with many Korean American women that this unexpected and abrupt encounter with a new part of themselves often puzzles them, as well as those around them, enough to disturb their emotional equilibrium and to produce anxiety and fear.

One of my Korean American clients shared her story of how she had to change herself to become a "tough" businesswoman who shouted at and physically struggled with her male business partner who tried to cheat her. Her daughter saw this scene and was shocked. She confronted her mother by saying, "You were a decent, graceful lady in a beautiful dress in Korea and you've changed. Now look at you, and I feel shameful of you. You don't care for others any more, and you don't care for me either." This client came to the United States alone right after the divorce from her violent ex-husband and left her two daughters, thirteen and fifteen years old, with her ex-husband's mother in Korea. As soon as she had secured her financial status, however, she brought her daughters to the United States to provide them with a good education and a happy life together. The two daughters were initially happy to come to the United States but soon became extremely rebellious; my client felt helpless and frustrated, without knowing what to do. My client said, "They miss their 'old' mom back in Korea. They are right. I was a very decent and respected woman in our community. Yes, I've changed [she sighed]. They just don't understand that I have to be tough and strong here to survive and to support them." Understanding this aggressiveness that was new for both my client and her daughters was crucial in reestablishing their relationships with each other after several years of separation.

In the next section, I explore the psychological meanings of human aggression. The exploration includes definitions, origins, functions, potentials, and the powers of human aggression. The purpose of this discussion is to show how human aggression can be an essential part of being human; the systematic suppression of aggression might cause Korean American women to experience themselves as "less than themselves" and therefore "less than human."

Psychological Understanding of Human Aggression

When my daughter, Ellen, was about two months old, I bought a set of cloth human figures on a string and hung it on the headboard of her crib. For the next couple of weeks, I observed her playing with the toy and was amazed by the intensity of her exploration of the toy. I took lots of pictures of her movements and placed them in her scrapbook. Fifteen years later, I came across a book written by psychoanalyst Henri Parens, *The Development of Aggression in Early Childhood.*[16] Parens did a longitudinal study from 1970 to 1979, based on research into human aggression, and he used direct observations of children's behavior. I was struck by the similarity between my observation of Ellen as an infant and his research report.

Parens observed an infant of nine weeks who was playing with a set of plastic rings on a string. The female infant began to explore the rings busily by pulling them apart, sucking them, and waving her arms to reach them when the rings were pushed inadvertently away. Her entire body was involved in her effort, and her serious facial expression and entire body posture indicated the tension of that protracted activity. After eighteen minutes of continuous effort, she paused as if she was tiring. An observer noted signs of displeasure on her face. She put her thumb in her mouth and lay quietly, giving the impression that she was recovering from her tiredness and frustration. Soon, however, her body curled up again, her legs kicked up, and she alternated between exploring the rings and thumbsucking as if she were experiencing some frustration again. This activity lasted for about twenty-five minutes until her mother picked her up to comfort her.

Parens, as I, was impressed by this intense "work-like affect" of the infant and the constancy of the effort the infant invested in exploring the rings. This observation led him to believe that this type of pressured, driven, exploratory activity was compelling the infant and was not elective. This "inner-drivenness"[17] of the activity was observed in all of the healthy infants of his research objects from the ages of eight to sixteen weeks. An infant seemed driven to explore and "gratify the push from within to assimilate, control, and master her visual experience."[18] After having presented this observational data, Parens asks a theoretical question: What is the source of the energy for this activity? Parens relates this inner-driven activity to human aggression. That was exactly what I observed in Ellen's struggle in her assertive and determined movements toward her new toy.

Historically, there have been many controversies over human aggression, and the controversies have revolved around two major questions. One of them is as follows: Is human aggression an innate instinctual drive or the secondary impulsive trend? In other words, are people born with aggression as an instinct, or do they develop aggression after they are born? The other question is equally provocative: Is human aggression innately destructive or neutral?[19]

Sigmund Freud was one of the theorists interested in human aggression. He developed his theories of instinctual drives, which changed over the years in his life. As a consequence, he formulated two slightly different theories of instinctual drives, and each presents a different understanding of human aggression.

His first theory consists of sexual instinct and self-preservative instinct. While Freud initially implied that aggression might arise from the sexual instinct, early on he concluded that aggression arose from a mastery instinct that struggled to preserve and maintain itself,[20] thus coming from the self-preservative instinct. In other words, aggression became subsumed under the self-preservation instinct, and this means that the aggressive drive has an inherent adaptive trend. Freud's first theory implies the existence of the innate, not secondary, positive function of human aggression.

In his later years, however, Freud revised the first theory and postulated the dichotomy of life and death instincts. He put the sexual drive and the self-preservation drive under the life instinct, and the aggressive drive under the death instinct. He often used aggression and destruction interchangeably and wrote that "this instinct of aggression is the derivative and main representative of the death instinct."[21] The primary adaptive aspect of aggression of the first Freudian drive theory is lost in the second, as Parens correctly argues in his critique of Freudian theory.[22]

Heinz Hartmann is another well-known psychoanalyst who was interested in human aggression. He rejected Freud's definition of the death instinct as "the destructive and aggressive force that only seeks to sever connection and thus destroy."[23] According to Hartmann, aggression powered the thrust into the separation-individuation process and propelled the individual forward developmentally. Hartmann proposed the concept of differentiation as nondestructive and thus implied that human aggression is innate and self-preservative. His theory is closer to the first theory of Freud, which affirmed the innate, positive trend of human aggression.

Hartmann, however, argued that self-preservation was not an id but an ego function. This is a major difference between Hartmann and Freud's first theory of aggression. For Hartmann, this self-preservation was an ego function and did not come from the conflictual relationship with the id. Hartmann thus rejected the assumption of "id-ego conflict of the earliest model of psychoanalysis"[24] begun by Freud. Instead, he postulated "a conflict-free sphere"[25] and "innate noninstinctual neutral ego energies."[26] This conflict-free sphere refers to the processes that have an intrinsic potential for development, such as language, productivity, thinking, walking, crawling, and other maturational and learning processes. These spheres belong to ego functions and do not require conflictual experiences between id and ego. Hartmann's theory of aggression is another step toward an affirmation of the innate, positive, and self-preservative forces of human aggression.

Anthony Storr, a psychoanalyst who did significant work on human aggression, also proposed that aggression was inherently adaptive and self-preservative. He further elaborated this idea and distinguished two types of aggressive behaviors. One type is "active strivings,"[27] and the other is aggression as "destructive hostility."[28] The first type is the drive toward mastering the environment and is both desirable and necessary for survival in striving toward obtaining food, space, and the acquisition of a mate. The second type of aggression is "hostile destructiveness" which "militate[s] against survival,"[29] as shown in sadism in the most extreme sense.

In sum, Storr's theory rejected Freud's death instinct basis of aggression (second theory) and affirmed the view that human aggression is not destructive only. Storr's theory is thus based principally on Freud's first instinctual drive theory but, different from Freud's first theory, it considers aggression as primary. The contributions aggression makes to adaptation and self-preservation are primary, not secondary, in nature.

Each of those theories discussed above has made its own significant contribution to the topic of human aggression, particularly in moving toward a positive affirmation of human aggression. However, I argue that Parens's theory of aggression, which builds on these earlier theories, is the most helpful for understanding the experiences of Korean American women and their struggle to survive in the American culture. In the next section, therefore, I discuss Parens's theory and show why the theory is an effective tool for explaining Korean American women's experiences.

Parens prefers Storr's theory to Freud's and Hartmann's. First, Parens takes issue with Freud's second theory, which suggests that human aggression is inherently destructive and does not have a self-preservative function. He thus agrees more with Freud's first theory. Parens, however, keeps a point from Freud's second theory, that aggression is one of the two primary human drives. Thus, Parens keeps the nondestructive, self-preservative quality of Freud's first theory of aggression and then locates it in the place of primary human drives as Freud did in his second theory.

Regarding Hartmann, Parens is troubled by the "possibility of an originally neutral, noninstinctual energy in the ego."[30] Rather, Parens believes in the existence of the id energy of human aggression, which is neutral with respect to the ego. On the basis of this belief, Parens argues that there is "*a trend of the aggressive drive that is inherently nondestructive, that while it is represented in the id, it inherently serves the ego without requiring neutralization.*"[31] While Hartmann postulates the "conflict-free neutral ego" energy for self-preservation, Parens postulates the "conflict-free neutral id" energy.[32] The contribution that Parens has made is that he has promoted human aggression as a *neutralized, nondestructive instinctual drive* that exists prior to the development of the ego's capability of neutralizing instinctual-drive energy.

Parens's contention is similar to Storr's theory, which distinguished aggression from hatred and which regarded aggression as inherently adaptive and self-preservative. Parens, however, thinks that Storr's theory needs further development to achieve "metapsychological status."[33] Parens thus elaborates his argument and develops the theory of "a spectrum of aggressive tendencies."[34] This spectrum forms a continuum that includes "four trends of aggression"[35]: "nondestructive aggression discharges," "nonaffective destructive discharges," "unpleasure-related discharges of destructiveness," and "pleasure-related discharge of destructiveness." The discussion of each trend is beyond the scope of this paper; therefore, I focus on the idea of *nondestructive aggression discharges* as a useful tool for helping Korean American women.

So, what does Parens's thought mean for Korean American women who have immigrated from their native Confucian culture to the American culture? As we already discussed, the Confucian culture fits Rieff's description of a communal culture that demands its members, particularly women, to control, suppress, and even renounce their individual instinctual need and desire if necessary for communal purposes. Rieff described such a communal culture as anti-instinctual.

Parens's findings of human aggression as the *conflict-free neutral id energy* provides a significant perspective for Korean American women and their struggle in the American culture. Human aggression has a compelling, not elective, force for discharge from within to outward. Such a compelling force is one of the characteristics of instinctual drives, and Parens elevated human aggression to such a compelling position.

Therefore, we can safely assume that, as a form of id energy, aggressive instincts have been embedded in the personality and humanness of Korean American women all the way from the beginning, even though those instincts were systematically denied and suppressed in their expressions and utilizations in the Confucian culture. Then, we might ask what would happen if such an impulse of aggression was constantly blocked in its expression? In the next section, I briefly discuss this in relation to the context of Korean American women.

Korean American Women's Aggression: Hwa-Byung Syndrome

There is a psychological and emotional disorder labeled *hwa-byung* in the Korean medical diagnostic system. *Hwa* means "anger" or "fire" and *byung* means "illness." *Hwa-byung* thus can be correctly translated as "anger illness" or "anger syndrome." The origin of this medical term is Korean, but it was formally registered as a psychological diagnosis by the international medical organization in 1996.[36] *Hwa-byung* is also listed in the Diagnostic and Statistical Manual, Fourth Edition (DSM-IV), as a culture-bound syndrome,[37] though there is not a consensus as to whether the syndrome should actually be classified as culture bound.[38]

According to the theories of traditional Oriental medicine, fire is one of five universal elements.[39] If found to be excessive in the body, this element of fire is believed to disturb the balance of bodily elements, thereby resulting in disease.

Koreans commonly describe anger as fire. If anger is suppressed for a long time, patients experience excessive fire in their bodies and a group of symptoms develops that is identified as a somatization disorder. *Hwa-byung* patients have experiences that "cause hurt, damaging, boiling, exploding [sensations] inside the chest or body."[40] Sometimes, the term *wool-hwa-byung* is used, in which *wool* means "dense, thick, or pent-up."[41]

Sung Kil Min, M.D., Ph.D., of the department of psychiatry at Yonsei University,[42] College of Medicine in Seoul, Korea, explains that Korean patients' cultural inclinations to keep the family in harmony and peace and to preserve social relationships dictate that anger must be suppressed, pent up, and accumulated. Then, he continues, the anger becomes like a dense mass "pushing up" in the chest, resulting in a distinct syndrome of *hwa-byung*, which is accompanied by characteristics of major depression or dysthymic disorder, a mild or low-lying chronic depression, combined with somatization disorder.

Hwa-byung is more frequently found in females in their forties and fifties, in less-educated people, those of lower socioeconomic status, and those from rural areas where a conservative lifestyle prevails. Many of these stratifications represent oppressed classes within Korean society and, therefore, it is not surprising that many *hwa-byung* patients relate their condition to the psychology of *haan*, a traditional, culturally determined emotional state, not a disorder or disease. *Haan* refers to a deep feeling of suffering, despair, "everlasting woe," and "being trapped" and "victimized"[43] in the face of enduring injustice and oppression that are far beyond their resistance and control. Many Korean people agree that *hwa-byung* can be called "women's disease"[44] and the psychology of *haan* describes particularly well the emotional state of many Korean women.

As Parens theorized, human aggression is a *conflict-free neutral id energy* that serves self-preservation and constantly looks for an opportunity to express itself to affirm what it means to be human and alive. Culturally and systematically stripped of this opportunity, Korean women have developed the anger syndrome, *hwa-byung*, which threatens their full humanity and well-being.

Unfortunately, the Korean Christian church, which lives within the larger cultural context heavily influenced by Confucianism, has not been "good news" to Korean American women who desire to express their positive aggression. Rather than liberating Korean women from the disorder of *hwa-byung*, the Korean church has historically allied with Confucian culture in suppressing and oppressing women's aggression and assertiveness. The Confucian ethical codes of Three Bonds and Five Relationships have been bolstered and strengthened by culturally biased, patriarchal exegesis and interpretations of Paul's household codes (Eph. 5:22—6:9, Col. 3:18-25) regarding women's status in family and community.

For example, Confucius taught: "Women are no doubt human beings. But they are inferior to men. They will never reach the equal status to men's. Therefore, the purpose to educate women is not to enlighten or cultivate their minds but to teach the total obedience to men."[45] This teaching has been affirmed and confirmed by Paul's selective teaching toward women, "Wives, submit to your husbands as to the Lord. For the husband is the head of the wife as Christ is the head of the church, his body, of which he is the Savior. Now as the church submits to Christ, so also wives should submit to their husbands in everything" (Eph. 5:22-24, NIV).[46] The culturally prescribed Confucian ethics has now become the preordained "God's will" for Korean women and thus an unbelievably effective means of controlling women's aggressive instinctual energies. Korean women are trapped by this deleterious alliance between culture and religion.

In the next section, I shall discuss how an understanding of this primordial and natural instinctual energy can be theologically reformulated to help Korean American women who are suddenly exposed in the American culture to the previously prohibited and suppressed instinctual energy.

Theological and Sociopolitical Understanding of Human Aggression

As I showed above, Parens has elevated human aggression to a compelling position of a *neutralized, nondestructive instinctual id energy*. Theologically interpreted, it represents a life-force that is an essential part of being a creature, which requires a constant expression of id energy to make life alive and full. Kathleen Greider, a feminist pastoral theologian, effectively argues this point in her book *Reckoning with Aggression: Theology, Violence, and Vitality*. She argues that human beings do not have a choice about whether or not they will be aggressive because aggression is a sacred and "basic dimension of our creatureliness."[47] We are made in the image of God and born with aggressive life-force that comes from God. The biblical narrative of creation affirms the aggressive life-force as "part and parcel of the drive to survive and thrive":[48] "Be fertile and multiply; fill the earth and subdue it. Have dominion over . . . all the living things that move on the earth" (Gen. 1:28, NIV).[49] Based on this analysis, Greider elevates human aggression to the level of "significant energy, vigor, agency, enterprise, boldness, and resilience."[50]

Greider, however, is not naïve in discussing human aggression because she sees it as an essential life-force in "a form of power."[51] She therefore has developed a feminist "hermeneutic of suspicion"[52] for studying aggression. She contends that "aggression is not simply a psychological category or personal issue"[53] but that it is a "politics of aggression."[54] Her major point is that, in a society that mostly depends on the hierarchical system of dominants and subordinates, human aggression is often used as a means of controlling and suppressing the power of the subordinates. The other corollary of her major point is that persons and groups being subordinated need constructive and positive uses of aggression for the purpose of freedom.

The traditional Korean Confucian culture depends on a highly hierarchical system; men hold all of the legitimate leadership, power, and authority while women are usually dependent on men economically, socially, and politically. For the maintenance of social equilibrium, Korean women are systematically taught to yield their aggressive instinctual tendency and are allowed to express this assertive life-force only to serve others.[55] Korean women internalize this manipulative teaching and learn to feel "shameful"[56] when they develop and nourish this life-force to present themselves as strong, powerful, and assertive. They feel "shameful" because they have deviated from a culturally designated place, in other words, the norm of being "feminine" in the patriarchal system.

Walter Wink, a theologian and biblical scholar, has developed the concept of "the Domination System"[57] and systemic evil. His provocative theology defines the Domination System as an "overarching network of Powers"[58] that overtakes people like a blind fate. According to his theology, all organizations, groups, or institutions elicit some kind of power, and every power has the following progression; "The Powers are good; The Powers are fallen; The Powers must be redeemed."[59] Any power would turn into the "demonic"[60] if the institution violates its own divine "vocation" of "humanizing purposes."[61] I argue that the distorted form of Korean Confucian culture that has systemically attempted to suppress women's innate, creative life-force is demonic because its ultimate purpose is not to serve women's God-given humanizing purposes but instead serves to exploit women's aggression to maintain its Domination System.

Implications for Pastoral Care of Korean American Women

A "heavily remissive" American culture that requires and encourages people to express freely their individual desires and needs, doubled with an immigrant context of urgent survival that calls for assertiveness, boldness, and resilience, would often drive many Korean American women to get in touch with their aggression, from which they have long been alienated in their native Confucian "communal" culture. They, as well as others around them, would be puzzled and confused by this new source of energy when they need to mobilize this energy to survive and thrive in a new immigrant context.

This powerful and previously untapped energy that Korean American women encounter in an immigrant situation can cause a crisis that threatens their personal, familial, and social lives and relationships. For example, a Korean American husband may welcome his wife's use of aggression for a successful management of their home business,[62] but he cannot tolerate his wife's assertiveness in their marriage or private life. When his wife becomes assertive in their relationship using her newly discovered life-force, he regards the new attitude as an unacceptable threat to his authority and power and thus to their family structure. Confronted by this resistance and rejection, Korean American women suffer significant emotional and psychological turbulence and confusion regarding self-identity and self-image.

It is important for a pastoral caregiver and counselor to provide Korean American women who are in such situations with a space where they can safely talk about, explore, identify, and successfully integrate the new resource into their personality structure. It is crucial for a pastoral caregiver and counselor to understand Korean American women's Confucian cultural demands on them, without any value judgment of that culture. Korean American women need an empathetic listening ear that will help them be aware of, express, and freely explore their emotional reactions to those cultural demands. There might be a wide range of differences in these reactions. In the long run, Korean American women have to negotiate to what extent they can and want to incorporate the new resource of positive aggression in their lives. Based on their decisions (these decisions might change in the course of their journey), they need to be aided in acquiring concrete strategies and skills to implement those decisions in their daily lives, as well as in developing religious and theological foundations that support and embrace their decisions.

In the Bible, there are many different models of how women with wisdom and courage have used their aggression and assertiveness to survive and thrive in oppressive cultures. Some women struggled and fought within the system itself and some outside of the system: Sarah (Genesis 12–21), Rachel (Genesis 24–33), Abigail (1 Samuel 25), Deborah (Judges 4–5), Jael (Judges 4), and Ruth and Naomi (the book of Ruth) are among the models in the Old Testament; Mary Magdalene who delivers the first message of Jesus' resurrection (John 20:1-18), a Canaanite woman who challenges Jesus regarding his mission boundary (Matt. 15:21-28), and a woman who pours perfume on Jesus' feet (Luke 7:36-50) are among the models in the New Testament. These are just a few of the many examples that are in the Bible. Pastoral caregivers and counselors can discuss these stories with Korean American women, focusing on how women's aggression and assertiveness can be used for the purpose of accomplishing God's will and plan. However, a premature discussion of these biblical materials can produce an emotional resistance to them. The timing is crucial, and the discussion must be carefully tuned in to the extent they would want to incorporate this new resource of positive aggression in their life.

This decision making should be owned and processed by the Korean American women and not be imposed by therapists for any reason. The decision making itself is an empowering process and a journey, not a one-time event, and requires careful support and guidance. To make this happen, a pastoral caregiver or a counselor has to understand the complex dynamics of cultural, sociopolitical, psychological, and theological dimensions of human aggression and its impacts on Korean American women's personal, familial, and social well-being, particularly during the active process of successful adaptation as immigrants into American mainstream culture.

Pastoral Care with Korean Goose Moms

Suk Yeon Lee

The Ironic Symbol: Wild Goose (*Gireogi*)

In a traditional Korean wedding held at the bride's house, the bridegroom's first act upon arriving is to offer to the bride's family a wooden goose as a token of lifelong fidelity. After the groom bows twice to his future mother-in-law, he then hands the wooden goose to her. Once the mother-in-law accepts the wooden goose (*Gireogi*) into the house, the wedding ceremony continues. According to Korean tradition, there are three reasons to use a wild goose (*Gireogi*) as a wedding symbol. First, wild geese keep their promise of love. They ordinarily live for about 150 to 200 years, and if their partners are lost, they never take another partner. Second, wild geese keep a public order in their vertical formation. When they fly, the leader makes a noise and the others follow and imitate. Third, wild geese leave tracks, meaning that people follow them, leaving great achievements.[1] The symbolic image of a wild goose is strongly connected with Korean family values and structure. The groom's act of handing over a wild goose to his future mother-in-law is a symbolic gesture of how he will lead his future family. It represents the promise that he will be faithful to his wife until death separates the couple.

However, the wild goose (*Gireogi*) is an ironic symbol for the twenty-first-century Korean mind. The irony arises from the fact that the wild goose spends a lot of time away from home, but maintains unyielding devotion to its family. Similarly, Korean "goose families" maintain their loyalty and devotion within the family, despite being separated by great distance. The term *goose family* came from this ironic use of the wild goose as a family metaphor.[2] A Korean goose family is a family in which fathers live in Korea to earn money, while mothers and children move to an English-speaking country for the children's education. It is very ironic that most people in a goose family have to sacrifice their personal needs for the sake of family. Nonetheless, the number of goose families increases every year. This article will share the story of the goose family in women's perspective and examine pastoral theological exploration of the experiences of women living in America as goose moms, apart from their husbands and extended family.

Stories of Three Goose Moms

Love for Children

Eunji[3] is a very respected woman in her congregation. She has many talents that she contributes to the church, where her musical talents and gifts of cooking are particularly famous. People have a lot of respect for her continuous service in many areas of ministry, yet she is always humble. She grew up in the southeast part of Korea in a large family, as the first of four children. Although her family was economically comfortable, her mother was busy with taking care of her siblings and other extended family members. As she grew up, her mother often relied on her to help with household chores like cooking or shopping. Her strong sense of responsibility and loyalty to the family seemed to develop from a very young age.

Eunji's plan for marriage was her first rebellion against her parents' authority. Her parents could not accept the fact that their daughter had fallen in love with someone they did not know. They wanted her to marry someone whose family they knew, and with whom they could make the customary arrangements. Eventually, she persuaded her parents to agree, got married, and had two children. For her husband's graduate program, they stayed in America for about five years and then returned to Korea. Her husband is a highly respected professor in Korea and busy with various projects. Although her husband heavily relied on her to take care of most of the family affairs, their marriage was strong and happy. She joined her family-in-law's publishing business and successfully ran the business. The trouble started when her son did not adjust well to the Korean school system:

> My relationship with my husband was troubled before I became a goose mom as we fought over how to raise our son. My husband's parenting approach is different than mine. My relationship with our children in Korea was not good. I used to be a disciplinarian, and my husband was more permissive in everything. In Korea, there was strong academic pressure, so I criticized my children harshly, and pushed them to study harder. My husband was the one who patronized our children and talked to them nicely.

Since her son is an American citizen, the idea of sending her son to America for school seemed like a good plan at the time. Many of her friends had already sent their children to America. The promise of an American guardian family sounded convincing, so she sent her son to the United States. When her son was not happy with the guardian family, her family had to make a difficult decision.

> I was not planning to become a goose mom. My son had difficulty in the Korean school system so we sent him to America for an exchange-student program, but he had some problems with the host family. My husband and I talked about it. I did not want to live apart from my husband. However, my husband insisted that I should go to America to be with my children. He said that it would be a good opportunity for our daughter to learn English, and that he could take care of himself. Also, we had lived apart for six months before. We thought it would be fine.

Even though Eunji did not want to be a goose mom at the beginning, her transition to America with the two children seemed to be working well. Her only obstacle was getting a visa to stay legally in America. Fortunately, she was able to get a student visa, which enabled her noncitizen daughter also to study in an American public school. However, giving up her career in Korea and separating from her husband were not easy for her:

> I heard that becoming a goose mom could be very hard. But I thought that I could sacrifice myself for my children whatever it took. I did not know this when I was in Korea. Since I had a job, I was busy. But now I know that I love my children so much I would do anything for them. Although I miss my family, I miss my husband, and I am struggling with English, I do not regret that I became a goose mom. I knew that the Korean education system was not working for my son and I am happy now that my son likes his school and his friends. I made the best decision in my situation. Even though I had to give up my business. . . . I can start my business later when I go back to Korea. I don't want to spend my time in here for myself. I want to do my best to support my children. Children come first. My son needs a lot of my attention and I have to take care of him in every detail.

Eunji realized that she would sacrifice anything for her children's sake. Her children's well-being is more important than anything else. Actually, she is very excited to have an opportunity to study again, but she does not want her studies to disrupt taking care of her children. Her biggest concern right now is her husband, who has not been adjusting well to living by himself. Being a single parent is another concern for her.

> I thought that my husband would live well in Korea. But he often tells me that he is having a hard time living alone. I am worried about him. However, I do not feel guilty about it because this living arrangement is not for myself but for our children. I actually like living in America. I do not have to take care of the extended family or other complicated relationships in Korea. Here, I only have to take care of my children. I enjoy a simpler life. But parenting by myself is hard. I am worried if my children do not get good grades. I feel a strong responsibility. When I lived in Korea, we

shared responsibilities of parenting. I am worried about my in-laws' criticism, when the result is not good. My daughter is having a problem adjusting to an American school and friends. She wants to go back to Korea.

Living in America is considered a luxury for most Korean women because
they are excused from the responsibility of taking care of their husbands and
extended families. But they feel strong pressure to devote themselves toward
their children's academic success and to ensure that their children will enter a
prestigious college in America. After all, the main reason for becoming a goose
family is for the children's welfare and success. Eunji has been a goose mom for
fourteen months. This has brought about some good changes and bad, but she
believes that this is the best choice for her children. She is planning to stay two
more years before going back to Korea. While she stays here, she is planning to
finish a degree in music.

Listening to Eunji's story, I kept thinking about the self-sacrifice these goose
moms endure for their children. She had a successful business and loving husband in Korea, but she needed to become a goose mom in order to stay with her
son and take care of him. For those goose moms who are willing to do anything
for their children's education, the reflections on the concept of "beneficial sacrifice" will be helpful to discern their decisions to maintain healthy families.

Beneficial Sacrifice

Many mothers today still wonder about how much sacrifice is enough. Bonnie Miller-McLemore addresses women's issues of sacrifice in her book *In The
Midst of Chaos*. She asks, "While we have assurance that God is holding us, we
still must work out the nitty-gritty details of care. Who along with God or on
God's behalf or in the midst of God's care, cares for the caregiver?"[4] Despite the
cultural differences, the questions are the same for a Western white professional
woman and a Korean goose mom.

Most goose moms are willing to give up their responsibility to take care of
their husbands and extended family for the sake of their children. But they still
feel guilty when they cannot totally devote themselves to their children. To some
extent, it is worse than the previous situation because of their responsibility of
functioning as single parents. Therefore, I think it is important to reevaluate
the virtue of traditional Western Christianity as well as the Asian Confucian
concept of "self-sacrifice" of women.

In Western culture, according to Miller-McLemore, many conservative ministers, such as Horace Bushnell and Henry Ward Beecher, "virtually created" a
sentimentalized approach to family life in which women "endlessly sacrificed
themselves" because they saw this as their primary role. Bushnell, for example,
compares God's love to a mother's exhaustive love for her child. Beecher says
that "the love most like God is an 'unselfish' love that 'makes suffering itself

most sweet, and sorrow pleasure,'" a love best exemplified by mothers, who are by nature "unselfish and long-suffering."[5]

Romanticizing women's sacrifice is not just Western Christian tradition. Korean folktales are full of stories that praise and encourage this virtue in women, especially young women who sacrifice themselves for the family. The most prominent of these female virtue stories directed at young girls is the story of Shimchong, the blind man's daughter who sells herself to a merchant and becomes a human sacrifice for a safe sea sailing. She does this to raise money to cure her father's blindness. The story concludes with a happy ending. Shimchong is rescued by a sea turtle, becomes a queen, and is reunited with her father. However, the story obviously praises her self-sacrifice for her family and how it is rewarded later. In addition to folktales, there were many gates in the entrance of small villages established from the Choson Dynasty, called *Yealyeamon*, that were dedicated to women who sacrificed themselves[6] for their husbands or their in-laws. The virtue of self-sacrifice in women is widespread in many cultures and religious traditions.

In recent years, however, many Western feminist Christian theologians have challenged the concept of self-sacrifice as a virtue for women. This concern widely surfaced throughout the 1980s, largely as a result of a classic publications by Beverly Wildung Harrison, Rita Nakashima Brock, Joanne Brown, Rebecca Parker, and Christina Gudorf. Each of these authors connected the problem of sacrificial women with bad Christology. They argued that sacrificial love is not the right religious ideal to hang over the heads of women who are already overprogrammed to give and give. This leaves them feeling ashamed of the self-interest that accompanies their love. Nor is a Father God bent on sacrificing his Son, Jesus, the appropriate image to promote from pulpit and communion table, condoning passivity before violence and perpetuating abuse.

According to Christina Gudorf, the portrait of maternal love as heroic self-sacrifice results not just from a "radical misunderstanding of parenting" and "personal relationships in general," but also from a misunderstanding of Jesus. In Gudorf's words, "Jesus did not come to earth to give himself disinterestedly to save us. Jesus was motivated by a mutual love with 'Abba'" and "felt impelled not only to love others, but to bring others into the relationship he shared with 'Abba.'"[7] Although Jesus did urge sacrificial action, he did not pursue sacrifice as a good in itself. He connected the demand for sacrifice—losing one's life, being last—with the promise of reward in the kingdom to come, of which the present rewards of mutual love are already a partial taste.

In an essay titled "The Power of Anger in the Work of Love," Beverly Harrison rules out sacrifice completely, ultimately declaring, "Mark the point well: *We are not called to practice the virtue of sacrifice*."[8] She reaches this conclusion in the context of a larger argument about the undervalued but powerful reality of women's history of bearing and nurturing life and the need for a fresh ethic of radical mutuality that encompasses this. Reappraisal of women's relational capacity to nurture others does not, however, imply a return to sacrificial womanhood. Harrison connects this directly to misconceptions about Christ. Christians have taken the crucifixion "out of its lived-world context in [Jesus'] total life and historical project and turn[ed] sacrifice into an abstract norm."[9] Jesus did not seek death by crucifixion as an end in itself. He faced it because he refused "to abandon the radical activity of love," now redefined as "solidarity and reciprocity with the excluded ones in his community."[10]

While others consider self-sacrifice from the perspective of adult life in relationship to partners, spouses, and children, Brock as well as Brown and Parker regard it through the eyes of children with abusive parents. They accuse the traditional doctrine of sacrificial atonement of promoting what they christen as "cosmic child abuse," in which the "father allows, or even inflicts, the death of his only perfect son." In Brock's own reading, salvation comes not through sacrifice but through intimacy, the highest form of Christian love. Genuine love requires "self-awareness, self-affirmation, and concrete presence," not "egoless self-sacrifice."[11] The feminist reexamination of self-sacrifice in connection with theological exploration of the meaning of the cross has empowered many women and contributed to recognizing the destructive influence of self-sacrifice in the Christian tradition. Some Korean feminist theologians also have supported these perspectives. In spite of the contribution to pastoral care of women, however, those notions of giving up self-sacrifice altogether are based on Western individualism that excludes the experiences of women of non-Western/communal cultures.

For the effective pastoral care of Korean goose moms who have been living in a bicultural context, it is important to find a more balanced notion of self-sacrifice, one that will create and sustain healthy family dynamics. Striving to sustain this balance is at the heart of faith when it is active in family living. Bonnie Miller-McLemore presents the idea of "salvaging sacrifice" as an alternative way of looking at the theory of self-sacrifice. *Webster's Dictionary* defines "salvage" as the "act of saving or rescuing property in danger" of destruction by a calamity, such as a wreck or fire.[12] Miller-McLemore says, "Salvage implies a moderate path because the property has some value, despite all the damage, but the entire piece itself is not worth saving."[13]

Drawing on the work of Barbara Andolsen, Miller-McLemore specifies three occasions in which sacrifice is justifiable: (1) when practiced by the privileged on behalf of the oppressed; (2) when a party in greater need has a *prima facie* claim on others; and (3) when occasions of sacrifice can be balanced out over the long run.[14] Miller-McLemore suggests that more explicit standards must be developed to assess the legitimacy of sacrifice to identify different kinds of sacrifice. In order to discern the difference between exploitative and salvageable sacrifice, Miller-McLemore presents a series of complex questions raised by feminist and womanist theory pertaining to the motivation and aim of sacrifice and the nature of the person's selfhood. Is the sacrifice and surrender chosen and invited rather than forced or demanded? Is it motivated by fear or genuine love and faithfulness? Does the person remain a subject or is she turned into an object and a means to someone else's end? Does sacrificial "loss" actually gain in some deeper way and enrich rather than destroy life? Does sacrifice, in essence, lead to more just and loving relationship?[15]

The issue for this chapter is how Western society and Korean society perceive the different issues of self-sacrifice; the latter society is wondering how to find a place for self-sacrifice within families for the benefits of children, while the former is looking for liberation from forced self-sacrifice. Both, however, want to find a healthy balance between sacrificial love and self-fulfillment. Especially for a goose mom, those questions are extremely important for discerning her choices: whether she wants to be a goose mom or not, whether she wants to pursue a career in America or not, and, more importantly, whether or when she returns to Korea. Interestingly, instead of polarization between sacrifice and self-fulfillment, the sacrificial love of many goose moms for their children gives an opportunity to find a way to self-fulfillment.

Most goose moms I interviewed agreed that their experience is a beneficial sacrifice. The sacrifice of intimacy between couples somehow allows couples to see each other with compassion. According to Herbert Anderson, the central paradox of marriage is found in holding in vital tension the human needs for intimacy and for autonomy. He says,

> Living side by side does not always make a clear seeing of the other. Couples may rather see what they would like the other to become or a mirror image of themselves or the other as an object to be used. Couples who are able to love the distance that exists between them are more likely, however, to see clearly the uniqueness of each partner.[16]

Besides the benefit of deeper relationships with their husbands, many goose moms experience increased self-confidence because they have been learning independent living skills in a foreign country. The life of the goose mom is motivated by sacrificial love for her children, but it also provides a perfect opportunity to discover a new self-identity. Self-sacrifice has weight and bearing in a goose mom's life. However, the word *sacrifice* originally means "to make sacred." Self-sacrificial love in families does have the potential to bless and sanctify, transforming family life. At the same time, it has a danger of casting oneself as a victim and eventually destroying the family itself. It is an important task for many goose moms to discern their choices in the light of beneficial sacrifice for themselves as well as their children.

A Maid No More

Sunni seemed to be a very self-confident woman when I first met her. Her calm and soft voice showed that she was a very intellectual and thoughtful woman. Sunni became a goose mom three years ago. For the first two years, she stayed in Canada with her three children before she moved to California a year ago. Her elder daughter is already in college. Sunni married a firstborn son who grew up in a closed family system. Her family-in-law placed a lot of demands on her; as a first daughter-in-law, she had a lot of responsibilities to look after her extended family. Her story illustrates why many women in Korea choose to be goose moms.

> One of the reasons that I wanted to become a goose mom is very personal. I found out that in Canada, most of the goose moms are the oldest daughters-in-law or only daughter-in-law. I heard that many women who used to live in other countries came back to Korea in tears. Social pressure of a daughter-in-law can be a critical motivation. I myself took care of almost twenty extended family members for fifteen years. My family had so many events, and I worked so hard. My younger sisters-in-law might not want to be a goose mom. Their lives in Korea are comfortable enough. I could not have come here if my mother-in-law was still alive. She died five years ago. I had breast cancer surgery right before I came here. My family was concerned about my stress level. Maybe that is why my family allowed me to go. I think many goose moms have the same reason. In Korea, I spent more than 80 percent of my time taking care of extended family. I even missed my children's pick-up time from school to serve my parents-in-law. I knew that I could take care of myself. I was a very smart girl in college. I was an editor of the school newspaper. But after I married, I just became a cook and maid. That was very difficult to accept, especially when I heard about a friend who succeeded in her career. Now, I have more time to think about myself.

In the traditional Korean family, taking care of the husband's family is the responsibility of the first daughter-in-law. Sunni's role as first daughter-in-law took too much time and energy from her. She needed to take a break from it. However, the decision to be a goose mom was made for different reasons. It is not common in Korean culture for a woman to leave her husband and extended family to take a break from family responsibilities in pursuit of her own dreams. However, many Korean families have a strong desire to educate their children in an English-speaking country. This creates new opportunities for many middle-class moms to explore a new horizon for themselves. Sunni explained how they decided to become a goose family.

> We decided to become a goose family because of my daughter. All her friends went to study in an English-speaking country. She kept pushing us to send her to America. But my husband is a very conservative man and he could not imagine that a "girl" could leave her parents to study abroad

at such a young age. But when she was [a] sophomore in high school, she went to America as an exchange student. Once she was in America, she did not want to come back. My husband and I also wanted to teach English to our two sons. It was the best choice for me to move to Canada with my children. The decision was made by my willpower. I strongly insisted to go. After my daughter got into an American college, I decided to move to America. I finally got a student visa for myself and moved here. My plan was to go back to Korea after my elder son enters college, but my husband thinks that we have to give equal opportunities to all three children. However, it will take seven years until my youngest son enters college. I wanted to become a goose mom at first, but now my husband wants to continue for seven years. He witnessed one family who has been separated for eight years and returned. They seemed okay, without any marriage conflict. He thinks he can do it, too. However, he will be lonely.

The Korean media criticizes the goose family as a concept that promotes infidelity between couples and dismantles the family unit. Experiences show that there is some validity to that criticism, and that many goose moms have that concern. However, if their marriages have been built upon solid foundations, the couples can sustain their relationship through the separation process and develop even greater compassion toward each other. Sunni noted:

> My relationship with my husband became deeper. We have become more considerate of each other. I failed the driving test three times. It was very painful to admit the fact after long years of driving in Korea, I could not pass the test. It was the most difficult thing for me to rely on other people's favors whenever I needed a ride. I called my husband every day, and he comforted me in many ways.

It was Sunni's decision to become a goose mom, but her life as a goose mom has not been easy. She shares many of the same issues as other goose moms. Parenting is a big issue. Her strong extended family support is not there anymore. Although she can experience a certain amount of freedom from her extended family, their absence also presents concerns about her two sons' developmental process for the lack of available male role models:

> If anyone knew beforehand what is involved in the life of a goose mom, nobody would ever do it. It is very hard. There is a big responsibility to take care of children. My husband never imposed that kind of responsibility on me. I worry about my role as a parent. My two sons need a good male role model. Our family used to gather every weekend. We are very close as a family. But living in the U.S., we do not have any support from the extended family.

Sunni also struggles with language. Since this is the first time living in America, learning English became a big stress in her daily life. Learning to speak English at a later age is very difficult for all the goose moms I interviewed.

This is often the biggest barrier to pursuing available opportunities for their own development in America. It also prevents many goose moms from participating in their children's school activities. Moreover, many goose moms are often discouraged from studying in America, starting a new business, or looking for new jobs. However, the language barrier has not stopped Sunni from pursuing her own dreams. She has been studying English very hard. She knows that being a goose mom is giving her a wonderful opportunity for herself as well as her children. She is planning to enter a master's program in early childhood education.

Sunni's story helps us to understand that the Korean woman's role in taking care of her extended family can be burdensome. As noted, this is especially difficult for the first daughter-in-law in a family. She has to be in charge of all family gatherings and do most of the cooking and cleaning. Most first daughters-in-law do not like big Korean holidays like *Chusukk* (Korean Thanksgiving day), *Seol* (New Year's day), and other special family gatherings because they have to serve the entire family all day long. There is no sense of fairness or justice in the family system. If a daughter-in-law refuses to do the cooking or serving, she is often criticized as undutiful. It is understandable why many goose moms do not want to go back to Korea after all those years of freedom. Sunni refused to be treated as a maid by her family-in-law family any more and started to pursue self-fulfillment. The discussion of justice in the family in the following section is essential, as Sunni's case illustrated. It has important implications for many Korean goose families.

Justice as a Family Value

Although most goose moms miss their families and want to reunite with their husbands, they are afraid to go back to Korea. If they were looking for personal freedom to escape from the rigid family system in the first place, it is not surprising that after several years of experiencing personal freedom and being exposed to emphasis on self-fulfillment in Western culture, they wouldn't want to go back to Korea unless they saw some changes in the Korean family system. In some cases, the husband eventually joins his family in America. If the wife insists on staying in America after the children's education, the couple could end up divorcing. This trend is prevalent especially when a goose mom has found means of financially independent living in America.

Korean family structure has been changing very rapidly. Many parents-in-law do not have the same expectations of their daughters-in-law as in previous generations. Many young husbands are willing to share domestic duties with their wives, due to the increased number of working women in recent years. But still Korean society fails to provide an alternative way of family life to traditional Confucian values. In this section, I shall explore issues of mutuality and equal regard among American family theorists, and examine how one can implement justice as a family value in Korean society.

One might argue about whether or how Western family theories can be beneficial to the Korean family. However, I believe that the fundamental issue of justice for women is cross-cultural. According to Carolyn Osiek, most cultural systems that attribute wisdom and consequent authority to elders also incorporate a gender bias in favor of male authority, sometimes with explicit statements and beliefs in the superiority of males over females.[17] She observes that there is hardly a culture in existence even today that does not disadvantage women either politically or socially, even though the stated goal of a culture is to eliminate these disadvantages. In most cultures, women are seen as the guarantors of legitimate offspring. To the extent that men feel it necessary to control that process and assure legitimization, women will be closely guarded. That fundamental importance of women is then domesticated and sacralized into the embodiment of family virtue and integrity. Thus, women in today's families often bear the entire responsibility for maintaining relationships through the extended family and across generations while they are sacrificing the opportunity of self-fulfillment.

As a means of defining and promoting a healthy Korean family value system, I found Paul Kleingeld and Joel Anderson's article "Justice as a Family Value" to be a very intriguing and accessible resource for Korean families. This article raises concerns regarding the widespread view that justice stands opposed to (or at least in tension with) the nature of characteristics that we associate with loving families. Kleingeld and Anderson see that this view is reflected in a deep and highly politicized opposition between "pro-justice" and "pro-family" approaches in the debate about the family as a social institution.[18] They argue against the assumption that love and justice are opposing commitments. There are ways of being committed to justice as an essential and internal component of familial love.

Kleingeld and Anderson illustrate four standard notions that love and justice are opposed to each other in family. According to the standard model of love, the nature of genuine love within families stands in sharp contrast to the motivational, emotional, and normative character of interpersonal relationships in public domains, where claims of justice are appreciated. This notion of a love-justice opposition is based on conceptual assumptions regarding the nature of genuine love. It also includes psychosocial assertions about the practical implications of introducing claims of justice into love relationships. The first assumption is that love is thought to be a matter of spontaneity and affective immediacy: to act out of love is to act without having to think about principles or to calculate effects. Second, love is thought to be a matter of particularity, that is, of a special dedication to the particular other. Third, love is thought to be a matter of self-sacrifice and the dissolution of the barrier between one's own interests and those of the other.[19] However, Kleingeld and Anderson argue that these three points about what constitutes a genuinely loving relationship or action seem to exclude any serious concern with intrafamily justice.

The tension between love and justice in the family comes from the false perceptions about justice as a threat to love or as a fallback system. Some conservative critics have assumed that current cultural trends—the decline of tradition and the increasing pressures to choose one's own form of life autonomously—lead straightforwardly to a "breakdown of the family," and that we had better brace ourselves for a time dominated by cold egoism of negotiated arrangements rather than loving families. They see the gender-justice critique of the family as a symptom of this general trend.[20] Others see that justice does have a place within the family, but there is always uneasy tension between the two. Finally, there are those who see bonds of love as a threat to justice, because they think that the talk of providing a family zone of love seems to block any criticism of domestic violence, exploitation, and other forms of injustice. Despite the differences, they all hold the concept of the logic of the family in opposition to the logic of justice. Kleingeld and Anderson write,

> None of these views is able to integrate the concern with justice into the conception of the family. Even those who find it important to "apply" principles of justice to the family system betray, in such locations, an understanding of the family as organized around something other than justice, such that justice needs to be brought to bear on the family, from the outside as it were.[21]

Thus, making room for the possibility of justice as a family value requires more radical thinking. The most distinctive aspect of the justice-oriented family is that members of a family see the realization of justice within their family as a shared, cooperative, and intentional enterprise. In order for the demands to be experienced as a shared pursuit, justice needs to be not merely the outcome of family structures, but also an explicit, shared goal. To accomplish that goal, family members should reflect on basic family arrangements and the way family members are treating each other.

Another aspect of a justice-oriented family derives from the recognition of human limits—limits of mood, attention, time, energy, and memory.[22] Kleingeld and Anderson think that the justice orientation is already more present in the interaction between parents and children, but the idea is not that the distribution should be equal in all respects; rather, it should be fair, and this intuition should be extended to the interaction of spouses.

In reality, justice requires one to work well with one's own spontaneous and loving inclinations. Doing the right thing does not need to be a burden, and being just toward a loved one would seem to be a natural inclination. Even at times when a person is not spontaneously moved by affection to do what is expected of a loved one, it would be better to perform the action out of a sense of justice than not to do it at all.

The idea of justice-oriented family clearly can accommodate the perception that love necessarily involves promoting and protecting the welfare of one's family and loved ones. However, there is an important difference between the self-sacrifices motivated purely by love and those motivated also by a commitment to justice. Kleingeld and Anderson ask a very important question regarding this:

> As a result of deep-rooted patterns of socialization, women and girls tend to be more self-sacrificing and feel more uncomfortable than men and boys in sticking up for their own interests within family, difficult questions arise as to whether these sincerely felt desires to make sacrifices for the family are authentic and free or the result of ideology and gender-biased socialization. It does complicate matters to acknowledge the possibility that one's willingness to make sacrifices for loved ones may be the unfair result of gender-biased socialization.[23]

In other words, if and when these choices are really made freely and voluntarily, acting out of love in an extravagantly generous way fits easily into the justice-oriented family. But it does need to be possible to ask the difficult questions, and it is hard to see how that can be done within drawing on the vocabulary of justice. One of the key advantages of the model of the justice-oriented family is that it does situate these questions of justice within the core concerns of a loving family.

Kleingeld and Anderson caution that women's sacrifice for loved ones may be the result of gender-biased socialization instead of authentic decision. It is important to ask difficult questions, as Miller-McLemore has suggested. If the decision was made out of true love for the family, it will conform to the standards of a justice-oriented family system. As we see in Eunji's story, many goose moms are ready to sacrifice for their children's sake at any cost. Before we praise their motherly love, we must address questions related to the application of justice within the family, and whether any double standards exist.

There is no denying the difficulties involved in keeping a family together today, and many of these challenges result from social transformations demanded by justice. But Kleingeld and Anderson believe that withholding the application of justice within the family system will not make these challenges and problems go away. What is needed is more attention to ways of enabling families to meet the challenges within justice-oriented families. Moreover, they add, the justice-oriented family develops the capacity to handle these complex new decisions. The capacity to listen and the willingness to take the wishes of the other seriously are needed to maintain justice within the family and maintain genuinely loving family relationships. In this sense, a commitment to justice actually serves to make loving relationships more flexible, adaptive, and enduring.

In order to promote justice in the family, the social perception of the essence of marriage and family must be changed. The members of family and the society at large should accept the idea that a commitment to justice fits well with a commitment to loving relationships. Instead of seeing family as only a source of love, a family can be a source of justice. Justice within families is reconcilable with love and affection. In this sense, one can be always both pro-family and pro-justice.

For the Korean goose moms trapped in conflict with two different cultures, the idea of being both pro-family and pro-justice is a liberating concept. In reality, most Korean families are far from accepting any sense of equal justice for each family member. It is hard to say that the decision to be a goose family is derived from the idea of justice-oriented family values. However, unlike the traditional Korean family dynamics, which are based on gender inequality, members of a goose family are experiencing a fair share of discomfort or suffering in their own way. If goose families can learn how to be more sensitive to each other's voices within the family, this sensitivity will promote a deeper appreciation for each other, a desire to maintain the harmony that comes with this, and a desire to safeguard their sense of being a justice-oriented family.

I Can Do It

I have known Minji for several years. Her family did not belong to a church but she used to send her children to Vacation Bible School. She seemed a little shy about bringing her children to church, but she was always eager to help out whenever she came. Minji's husband was a manager in the American branch of a Korean company. Her husband's employment enabled the family to receive a green card, and the family have been living comfortably in California. Her husband had to go back to Korea after his six-year term was completed. Although Minji did not want to be left behind in California with her children, her family eventually made a decision to be a goose family for three years. She reflected on this experience in this way:

> I wanted to go back to Korea, but my husband heard from others who went back to Korea after they stayed in America more than several years. They have been experiencing difficulty adjusting to the Korean school. I don't want my children to get into that kind of situation. It would be my fault if they became a wrong person. My husband said to me that it would be better if I would stay here. Both of my sons have been here for five years and they like to study here. My kids grew up in Hong Kong when they were younger. So they did not know about the Korean school system. My friends in Korea told me not to come. They said my kids would be called "stupid."

There are several reasons Minji wanted to go back to Korea. Unlike other goose families, Minji's children mostly grew up outside of Korea. In her opinion, helping their children to develop a strong self-identity as a Korean is very important. However, her main concern is living without her husband. Minji's husband had been very involved with their children's education as well as taking care of household business. She depended upon her husband for many things ever since they got married. This is her first experience of "standing alone."

> I cried when we decided to live as a goose family. My husband always took care of everything for me. Now I have to take care of everything. My husband used to play basketball with the children, but I cannot do it. There is no male role model for my boys.

However, her fear of living as a goose mom changed to a new discovery of self-confidence. In comparison with many other goose moms who do not have legal status to work in America, Minji was lucky to find a job in a good environment. While working in America, Minji has been discovering hidden power within herself.

> Right now, I am enjoying working as a cashier at the college cafeteria. It is a perfect job for me. I like America because people do not seem to judge others by their jobs. I would never have a cashier job if I lived in Korea. Korean people are always concerned about how they are perceived by others. Here, I felt a freedom to explore what I like instead of worrying what others think about me. I used to live in Korea very comfortably. However, my life in Korea was more like living in a trap. I did not have a lot of friends or my own family around. My family-in-law was the only relationship I had. I was an extremely introverted person. Now I am very active, and interested to help others without any expectations. I learn to appreciate small things. I realize that I have depended on my husband in everything. Now, I keep telling myself that I can do this. I am doing great. I have more confidence about myself now. I never wrote a check before. Now I can do it.

Minji smiled warmly as she told me how she can do so many things now that were previously not in her repertoire. It turned out that her experience as a goose mom was an important step in her life for self-discovery. Because of the protective nature of her husband and in-laws, this personal evolution could not have otherwise occurred. Her new self-discovery in herself extended to helping others and developing a greater appreciation about life. For other goose moms like Minji, who are able to create a new identity in America, H. Richard Niebuhr's ethical reflection about the "responsible self" will provide a good foundation. He developed the concept of the human as responder. In Niebuhr's terms, humans are most themselves as responder, in I-Thou relationship. And the dialogue begins when the human answers the greeting or the cry of need of the neighbor.[24] It is an important task to expand his idea to goose moms' new identity making.

Responsible Self: New Identity Making for a Goose Mom

It is impossible to understand the choices of a goose mom without evaluating the social, historical background of Korean family life. It is also important to explore the personal memories and experiences, as well as hopes and fears, of each woman. Korean women's responsibilities to themselves have not been fulfilled throughout their history. This repressed self-fulfillment may influence their choice to become a goose mom, as Sunni's story illustrates. The choice of becoming a goose mom carries a significant risk of upsetting family stability. However, it may also be viewed as an opportunity to shape a new identity for Korean women.

H. Richard Niebuhr viewed self as a reflexive being. He insisted that the human is a responder to a situation, reflecting the world in the process of interpretation. Here the human being is in dialogue with and responds to the actions taken upon him or her. As responsive beings, humans act in accordance with their interpretation of what has happened to them, what they have seen, or what has been done to them. The decision to become a goose mom is one response to the challenges faced by Korean middle-class women who do not have a chance to explore their self-identity. It is also a decision in response to the challenges their children have to endure in the Korean educational system. Instead of being abused by the system, goose moms make a radically different choice for their children and themselves. That choice is not, by any means, the traditional image of relational self in the Korean society. However, it shows that a responsible person can rise against the system and make new changes in one's life journey.

Niebuhr understood that one's identity is not static, nor simply abstract, but involves living interpretations and reinterpretations of one's "self" in time. And it is this "self" that is experienced and defined in relationship to and by others. Identity is crafted not in a solipsistic vacuum but in a web of relations with other people individually and within community, with one's memories of other people, and one's memories of his and her relationship to God. Many goose moms are experiencing some confusion in breaching the gap between the newly developed "self" and the responsibilities to others. However, without a sense of self, it is difficult to develop a sense of self available to offer others. For Korean goose moms, it is not enough to emphasize the importance of self-development in fulfilling their public responsibility to use their God-given gifts on behalf of the greater community and the common good.[25]

Niebuhr also points out that how one characterizes one's relationship with God affects how one will view one's life, as well as how one views others. Niebuhr believes that since God is in every action, if we can steer a course in conjunction with God's will for us, our response to that central relationship will move us into trust and faith with God. Most goose moms I interviewed put their faith in God in this dangerous journey. One of the goose moms said:

I do know that I trust God more than before. If I did not have faith, this would be very hard. I am praying God to lead me where he wants to be. I open my options to God. I don't know how long I will stay here. I think whether I live here or in Korea, if God has a plan for my life, then God will open the door for me.

The choice of viewpoint depends upon whom we perceive God to be. Faith is not a simple maxim to be shared; it is an orientation to God who is trustworthy and compassionate. One who has faith in a trustworthy God will find strength to reinterpret past memories as well as one's present pain and suffering.

Niebuhr's reinterpretation of memories in the light of trusting God will bring new hope and empowerment for many Korean women who were forced to sacrifice selfhood for the sake of family in the Confucian culture. Concurrent with Niebuhr's emphasis on being responsible to one's self, he also reminded us that one can't live by abandoning one's own natural responsiveness to others. Often many goose moms feel like fragmented or unbalanced people because of identity conflict. However, in relationship with God, they can fashion new responses and habituate reactions and trajectories of balance, strength, and wholeness. Niebuhr provides a new vision of being a relational self, which includes freedom to develop one's own gifts. With this understanding, the goose mom may have courage to live in a way that transcends her previously fragmented life and to find an authentic self.

While I was listening to the stories of goose moms, it became clear that many goose moms are developing strong autonomy through their experiences. At the same time, they also try hard to meet the expectations of the traditional woman's role as a mother and wife. However, it is not an easy task to reconcile two different values in the traditional Korean family system. It is an important task as a pastoral caregiver to explore the possibility of finding harmony in the Korean family, while promoting self-fulfillment for each family member. In the following section, I will suggest a new framework for family values, which apply to Korean families living in the twenty-first century.

Multicultural Approach to Mutual Family

Some multicultural pastoral theologians have raised questions regarding the application of principles of mutuality and justice as a family value in a multicultural context. In the book *Mutuality Matters*, Samuel Lee raises this issue of balancing the cultural identities for Korean American families today who are facing difficult and distinctive questions about the nature of love.[26] As we see in the goose mom stories, the Korean American family presents issues about opposing and contradictory cultural forces that are difficult to reconcile. The Korean Confucian traditional familial practice often places more emphasis on the obligations of sacrificial love for family members, while North American familial practice calls for the mutual love of individual family relationships. Lee argues that this apparent contradiction between hierarchy and mutuality results from the theoretical construction that allows only the forced choice of either-or between the two cultures in which Korean American families live.[27]

While recognizing the importance of mutual love and the problems of sacrificial love, Lee argues that extreme emphasis on mutuality or equality alone ignores the multivalent complexity of human relationships. The concept of mutuality alone cannot cover the many complexities of human identity and relationship. To resolve effectively the tension between the Confucian hierarchical influence and the more individualistic and egalitarian influences in North American culture on Korean American families, Lee introduces the concept of "complementary dualism" over the "conflicting dualism" that exists within Western culture.[28]

According to Lee's terminology, the concept of complementary dualism derives from the Asian *yin-yang* philosophy, which is described as a "hermeneutical key" to understanding the Korean "cosmo-anthropology." The *yin-yang* philosophy views the world as complemented by seemingly conflicting forces of *yin* (negative) and *yang* (positive). Lee says the linear model of cultural identification positions *agape* (sacrificial love) against *caritas* (mutuality), on complete opposite ends. On the other hand, the orthogonal cultural identification model poses two separate questions in search of one's cultural identification. Since one's identification with *agape* is not necessarily correlated with *caritas*, both virtues complement each other in a theologically and psychologically healthy family.[29]

In a collection of essays entitled *Is Multiculturalism Bad for Women?* feminist political scientist Susan Okin raises a difficult issue. She points out how certain unjust cultural practices can be perpetuated in the desire to respect cultural diversity.[30] I strongly agree with her observation that many patriarchal cultures are unjust because they suppress the necessary and faithful navigation between complementary values that must be foundational for healthy and just family relationships.

I appreciate Lee's effort to embrace both cultures through the complementary model of bicultural identification. But Lee's concern to find a healthy balance within a bicultural Korean American family is based upon a false assumption; he views Korean culture as *agape* and American culture as *caritas* and expects a conflict between these two values that have an impact on family life. Although the conflict might be possible in the beginning, true *agape* will embrace *caritas* in any culture.

Kleingeld and Anderson point out the danger of the cultural assumption that an orientation to justice and equality in the family tends to overwhelm families by individualistic modes of interaction that require complex and difficult negotiations. As a result, people seek to act out their own impulses of individualism in the conflict between love and justice. People who have had no experience with justice-oriented families assume that the interdiction of claims of justice will make families cold or heartless.[31]

In practice, Korean society might not be a good role model for a justice-oriented loving family. However, there is a key philosophical principle that can conceptualize the justice-oriented family in an Asian context. As with the concept of *yin-yang*, *Sangsheng* is also an important hermeneutical principle that provides a path for understanding cosmic principles of the creator. According to Chinese philosophy, there are five elements in the universe and these elements are used for describing interactions and relationships between natural phenomena. These five phases describe both a creation (*Sheng*) cycle and a destruction (*Ke*) cycle of interaction between phases (fig 11.1).

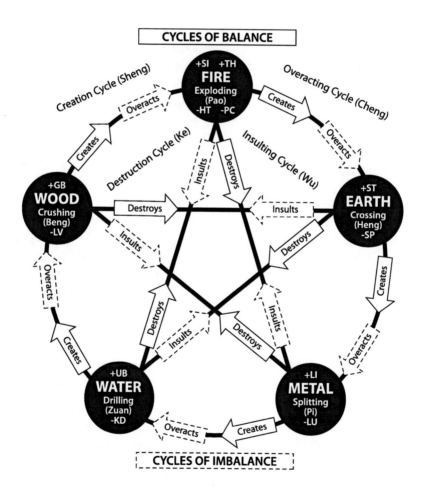

Fig. 11.1 Five elements and cycles

The creation cycle is sometimes called "mutual giving" and "mutual conquest." They are cycles of balance. If any of the elements are overabundant, they can disrupt the balance. For example, water can create wood, but too much water will kill the wood. The overacting (*Cheng*) cycle and insult (*Wu*) cycle are an imbalanced cycle.[32] As we can see in figure 11.1, water can control fire, but too much fire will evaporate water.

Sangsheng refers to the creation cycle, which is a mutual life-giving spiritual force between five elements. In daily life, *Sangsheng* (mutual life-giving) means to work for the well-being of others. Contrary to people who prospered at the expense of others, people who practice the principle of *Sangsheng* only prosper by helping others. The concept of *Sangsheng* can be interpreted as promoting both just and loving relationships and life-giving affirmation for each member within the family at no one's expense. As we can see in the five elements chart, when the force of creation moves in the right direction, it gives new life to each element. If the force is overactive, however, it will break the balance of the cycle.

If I apply this concept to family life, when a husband forces his wife to take care of his parents, the wife feels abused and will lose the joy of taking care of the weak, old parents. Likewise, if the wife insists on pursuing her own interests and does not pay attention to her husband and children, it will create a conflict in the family. The concept of *Sangsheng* teaches us how important it is to find a right balance between love and justice in the family. If family members learn to maintain the balance between love and justice in their relationship, the whole family will be happy and find harmony. However, it will take some effort and skill to negotiate each family member's need.

As we recognize the need to respect the traditional cultural concept in family life, we do so by rediscovering the concept of *Sangsheng* and redefining it in postmodern Korean family life. When that is clear, we can challenge the injustice in family life and promote a more justice-oriented and loving family life in Korean society. Furthermore, through the process of examining choices using this concept, goose families will find the fine balance between justice and love in family life and move forward to truly life-affirming and life-giving mutuality.

Conclusion

To support their children's academic success, many Korean mothers become focused on their children's education. Lack of social support for working moms, along with increased responsibility for children's education and in domestic chores, limit many highly educated middle-class women in pursuing self-fulfillments. The goose family phenomenon is the result of Korean families' commitment to children's education and of women's alternative way of escaping from the traditional family system.

Despite the many obstacles, risks and challenges that come with the endeavor, the number of goose families has been increasing. Also, the number of children coming with their fathers has also increased. Children either stay with their father or mother; long-distance relationships can be problematic for the entire family. Traditional Confucian principles of hierarchy, inequality, and duty often define the relationships between husband, wife, and children. It is an urgent task to present more fluid bonds of equality, intimacy, communication, and mutual trust. Instead of viewing the family system as a network of rigid hierarchical relationships, each member should make room for each other so they can develop respect for one another's particularity. As Augustus Napier and Carl Whitaker write,

> We feel that the family capacity to be intimate and caring and its capacity to be separate and divergent increase in careful synchrony. People can't risk being close unless they have the ability to be separate—it's too frightening to be deeply involved if you aren't sure you can be separate and stand on your own. They also can't risk being truly divergent and separate if they are unable to count on residual warmth and caring to keep them together.[33]

Being separate selves who are capable of being together with other selves is necessary for a vital society that both celebrates diversity and honors community. In that sense, the goose family has already introduced a new family system in Korean society. However, praising women's self-sacrifice is still a huge barrier for embracing their choice of the goose mom and for developing an autonomous self-identity.

The task of maintaining a goose family is challenging because goose moms and their children have already tasted the cultural freedom that the West has to offer. This is a huge departure from the traditional family system, which husbands and extended family members still want to maintain. Unless the whole family can respect each member's individual identity and rights, and actively practice justice-oriented loving relationships, conflict cannot be avoided. This should not imply that I am just emphasizing individual freedom at the expense of family life. Herbert Anderson has used the phrase "being separate together" to convey the equal importance of both community and the individual. It is not possible to be an individual except in relation to community. In sum, commitment to community need not exclude freedom to be one's self.[34] Creating a harmonious balance between the individual self-interest and the interest of the community requires mutual trust and good communication among family members. I strongly believe the concept of *Sangsheng* should be applied to the family system to create the right balance between justice and love.

Community and the individual cannot exist without each other; neither can justice and love be separated. Without support and encouragement from their husbands and other family members, the journey of discovering self-autonomy for many goose moms can be a dangerous process. It is also true that family members who love each other deeply will eventually figure out how to have just relationships. For the goose family, it can be a tricky task, because both wife and husband often feel that they are making a greater share of sacrifices for their children. However, they both might be victims of the competitive education system in Korea. They never are victims of one another. Although they choose the path for their children, they always can use the opportunity to maximize one another's best interests. The goal for the goose family should be developing compassion for each other, supporting and encouraging each other to make the best of their time together as well as their time of separation.

I believe that the journey of these goose moms, who are courageous enough to live independent lives in a foreign country with their children, will lead to creating a new identity for other Korean women. These women must be wise enough to maintain a sense of justice within their loving family relationships. They must have qualities of compassion and adaptability, and they must freely share their experiences with many other women. Women need encouragement to develop their sense of self-autonomy while they are responsible to their own family and extended community. The future of healthy families in Korea will be greatly benefited by new insights of goose moms.

Pentecostal and Female in Puerto Rico

Risking All to Pursue a Call

Miriam Figueroa

The present Pentecostal movement in Puerto Rico can be traced to 1916 with the return of Reverend Juan L. Lugo, the pioneer Pentecostal missionary, a Puerto Rican who had been living in Hawaii.[1] Lugo was converted in 1913, and three years later he felt the call to evangelize his homeland. His wife, Isabel, "has been credited with having contributed much to the couple's ministerial success."[2] They began an effort in Santurce and then moved to Ponce, Lugo's hometown. Several congregations emerged from these efforts and affiliated with the Assemblies of God in 1921, with Lugo serving as its executive director. This movement grew rapidly and was the cradle of the biggest and most powerful Pentecostal churches of the island: Pentecostal Church of God International Movement, Assemblies of God, and Church of God Mission Board, among others.

Another important event was Francisco Olazábal's revival rally in the 1930s, when people gathered by the thousands every night in Ponce. The revival was well covered by Puerto Rican reporters, who wrote about the healings, miracles, and thousands of conversions during this spiritual awakening.[3] Then a second revival was held in Ponce by Tommy L. Osborn, an American evangelist who came to the island during 1950–51. The "Pentecostalization of Protestantism" or a "Puertorican Pentecostalism" began with this revival.[4] Since then, Pentecostal churches in Puerto Rico have grown as a powerful influence in our society. Although Puerto Rico is still considered a Catholic island, it is also known as a missionary stronghold; the Protestant churches, including Pentecostal churches, are well respected by the local government and ecclesial leaders.

Responding to God's Call

Since its beginnings, the Pentecostal movement has attributed much of its growth to the role of women. Women have influenced our churches as teachers, missionaries, pastors, leaders in all areas, and planters of new churches. However, response to both God and the church's call has been a struggle for Pentecostal women. There is always a tension between responding to the call and realizing the lack of the recognition by church leaders in administrative positions. Women do not have the same privileges in governing the church.

As *mujerísta* theologian Ada María Isasi-Díaz notes,[5] women are in a struggle for survival and a struggle to be fully human. To survive one has to have the power to decide about one's history and one's vocation or historical mission. There has to be an analysis of the reality of the oppression.

What is our struggle as Pentecostals in Puerto Rico? As ministers and pastors dealing with the "cure of souls," we are convinced that God has called upon us and has called our names. We women have responded to that wonderful call. As Pentecostals, we believe that the Holy Spirit empowers Christians to testify about God's power, and also this same Spirit has given us gifts in order to serve in whatever mission the Lord appoints us. I can claim what Paul said in Galatians 3:27-28: "For as many of you as have been baptized into Christ have put on Christ. There is neither Jew nor Greek, there is neither bond nor free, there is neither male nor female; for you are all one in Christ Jesus."

Nevertheless, women in my church struggle because denominational policy only allows women to exert pastoral ministry in secondary positions or in a second rank (level or category) of credentials,[6] according to the Church of God's administrative system. I understand that, although in Puerto Rico the Church of God has surpassed many limitations, such credential policies are influenced by prejudiced theological constructs against women in the ministry. This is not simply an administrative dilemma but a theological issue, for it marginalizes women in the ministry. Somehow we must examine such theological constructs in order to be consonant with the liberating struggle of women; in practical and concrete terms, this implies the recognition of women's capacities to hold leadership and authoritative positions within our church.

Mujerísta theology highlights the process of conscientization. What Isasi-Díaz[7] is saying is that women must be aware of the oppressive structures that affect their lives. This is an ongoing process of critical reflection on action, which leads to critical awareness; this in turn becomes an essential building block in deciding the next action that Latinas—and, in our case, Pentecostal women in Puerto Rico—must take. As we look into this theology, we also discover that it is important for women to understand how much they have acquiesced to the present structures. We must ask ourselves if we are doing something unintentionally to sustain the oppressive structures. If so, we can make changes after conscientization of our oppressive situation. Once that conscientization has taken place, a woman can overcome the androcentric system, not just by herself but in community or communality. Conscientization is personal but not individualistic; it also involves the totality of the person[8] and a critical mass of support.

What have we done regarding conscientization? We have made others conscious of the oppression and discrimination as well as the sexism among many of our leaders. We want to be treated as completely human; we want to use our full capabilities in order to expand the kingdom of God. As I explained, we are sure God called us to be ministers and pastors. We were called by the Holy Spirit, who has confirmed that call. So, how is it then that our brother ministers and colleagues from the Church of God cannot accept the will of God for women?

Sexism is a sin; it is a structural sin. Eldin Villafañe, a Pentecostal social ethicist, wrote in his book *The Liberating Spirit* that oppressive structures must be confronted in order that justice shall be done.[9] Justice for women should become a reality inside the church as a model to the rest of society and not the other way around. It seems that we women in the church have been left behind. Although Pentecostal women are very much engaged in laboring at their local churches, many times they are not considered when decisions are made or when strategies are devised. Sometimes the rest of society seems more understanding and advanced in accepting women at decision-making levels. The androcentric model must not be tolerated in church where we preach and teach that men and women are both equal before God.

In conclusion, struggle and conscientization are important elements in our Pentecostal experience. Women have struggled against sexism while convinced that the Holy Spirit has called upon them to serve in the *basileia* of Christ. Our call is the fuel that drives this realization. We know we are complete in Jesus Christ. Nevertheless, Christ's justice is claiming to be heard in order for the church to be more of a testimony to communities around us. Conscientization is also taking place. Some Pentecostal groups like the Pentecostal Church International Movement and the Missionary Church of Christ are ordaining women as ministers. In these groups, women are allowed to share the structures of power with men. In our denomination, the Church of God Mission Board, conscientization of the situation of women has begun. With the support of male ministers, women are gaining access to the decisional and service bodies of our church.

Dealing with Anger and the Sense of Not Being Completely Human

Delores Williams's *Sisters in the Wilderness* is an exquisite book[10] that elucidates the suffering of so many African American women, their struggle, and their survival. Womanist theology has provided a way for understanding the sense of anger that comes with feeling despised and devalued. Womanist theology reflects on the incarnation of suffering among African American women. One way of embracing suffering is by embracing the Bible. As Pentecostals we consider the Bible to be the word of God. That word inspires and nurtures our entire life. The Bible is our comfort in times of tribulation, our guidance when seeking wisdom, and the answer to our questions and doubts. We Pentecostals promote the reading of the Bible in order to have intimacy with the author of it. It is interesting to find out how this same Bible plays an important role in womanist theology. For instance, womanists have taken the story of Hagar and given it a new dimension in order to understand their struggle and suffering in life. Just as theologians of liberation validated their experience of oppression and preferred option for the poor using the story of the exodus, so have womanists used the story of Abraham, Sarah, and Hagar.

Cecil Cone explains how certain parts of the Bible became important to African religious history.

> The slaves' appropriation of the Bible was made easier by the fact that certain parts of scripture, especially in the Old Testament, were in keeping with the slave's African religious tradition. Slaves already possessed the concept of a Supreme Being who created, sustained, and ruled the world. This meant, of course, that the Old Testament's Almighty Sovereign God did not seem unfamiliar to him [the slave]. What this God did for the children of Israel was in harmony with the slave's own understanding of the divine. Gradually through this conversion of Christianity, slaves accepted and utilized the Bible as one of the sources of black religion.[11]

Now, Delores Williams challenges black theology in its use of the Bible. She does not oppose it but has called for a broadened hermeneutical interpretation of the words in the text. Still, she recognizes the importance of Scripture:

> Womanists have a slave cultural heritage of which to be mindful. This cultural heritage, patterned by biblical motifs, is the context of the early Christian origins of African Americans. It was this cultural heritage and its biblical patterning that transmitted to slaves the hope for liberation and the belief that God's power sustained their survival's struggle. This slave way of using the Bible must be affirmed. Thus the Womanists also engage in a hermeneutical posture of affirmation as they attempt to discern both the Bible's message to black women and the meaning for black women of the biblically derived black cultural patterns.[12]

African American slaves, female and male, created an oral text from the written text (the King James Version of the Bible). They composed this oral text[13] by extracting from the Bible or adding to biblical content those phrases, stories, biblical personalities, and moral prescriptions relevant to the character of their life's situation and pertinent to the aspirations of the slave community. They took from the Bible those things that assured them that they were under God's care and God's justice because "God has the whole world in God's hands."[14]

As Pentecostals we have done the same thing. From its beginnings in Puerto Rico, Pentecostalism has been deeply rooted among the poorest people of the island. They have internalized that the Lord is their provision, sustainer, and, of course, their healer, because there is no other way to be healed. The word of God from the Bible is to Pentecostals the way of living, their air in order to breathe; it is a way of survival. As Pentecostal women, we see ourselves in the eyes, acts, and thoughts of Deborah, Ruth, Anna, Esther, women disciples of Jesus, Martha and Mary, Lydia, Phoebe, and many others like them. From our point of view, these women in the Bible, by gaining access to God and Jesus, trace a path to be followed, where women are able to participate, taken into leadership, and are partners.

Luke 13:10-17 (CEV) narrates the following:

> [10]One Sabbath, Jesus was teaching in a Jewish meeting place, [11]and a woman was there who had been crippled by an evil spirit for eighteen years. She was completely bent over and could not straighten up. [12]When Jesus saw the woman, he called her over and said, "You are now well." [13]He placed his hands on her, and right away she stood up straight and praised God. [14]The man in charge of the meeting was angry because Jesus had healed someone on the Sabbath. So he said to the people, "Each week has six days when we can work. Come and be healed on one of those days but not on the Sabbath." [15]The Lord replied, "Are you trying to fool someone? Won't any one of you untie your ox or donkey and lead it out to drink on a Sabbath? [16]This woman is a daughter of Abraham, but Satan has kept her bound for eighteen years. Isn't it right to set her free on a Sabbath?" [17]Jesus' words made his enemies ashamed. But everyone else in the crowd was happy about the wonderful things he was doing.

This woman was ill for many years. Being in that synagogue that Sabbath day changed her completely. She can represent so many women who are oppressed for so many reasons and circumstances. The prophet made her aware of her and called her a "daughter of Abraham." This is unusual because there was no daughter of Abraham; men were the sons of Abraham. All of a sudden this woman was not on the periphery but was the center of attention. She received the benefits of those who can be called sons of Abraham. Jesus changes the paradigms. Nowadays leaders (supervisors, superintendents, male ministers) can also change paradigms. They must recognize female ministers as equals. Much dialogue is needed among fellow pastors, ministers, and educators. Rethinking of ideas, both theological and cultural, must be articulated in order to promote understanding. Understanding is a key element for respect, which in turn will impel action toward justice. It is imperative to position women (as well as men) in the center as Jesus did and not the periphery. This act of repositioning can transform the Pentecostal generations to come.

Also in Mark 16:1-11 (CEV) we have this narration:

> [1]After the Sabbath, Mary Magdalene, Salome, and Mary the mother of James, and Salome, bought some spices to put on Jesus' body. [2]Very early on Sunday morning, just as the sun was coming up, they went to the tomb.

³On their way, they were asking one another, "Who will roll the stone away from the entrance for us?" ⁴But when they looked, they saw that the stone had already been rolled away. And it was a huge stone! ⁵The women went into the tomb and on the right side they saw a young man in a white robe there. They were alarmed. ⁶The man said, "Don't be alarmed! You are looking for Jesus of Nazareth, who was nailed to the cross. God has raised him to life, and he isn't here. You can see the place where they put his body. ⁷Now go and tell his disciples, and especially Peter, that he will go ahead of you. You will see him there, just as he told you." ⁸When the women ran from the tomb, they were confused and shaking all over. They were too afraid to tell anyone what had happened. ⁹Very early on the first day of the week, after Jesus had risen to life, he appeared to Mary Magdalene. Earlier he forced seven demons out of her. ¹⁰She left and told her friends, who were crying and mourning. ¹¹Even though they heard that Jesus was alive and that Mary had seen him, they would not believe it.

But in 1 Corinthians 15:3-9 (CEV), women are completely ignored in this narration of the apostle:

³I told you the most important part of the message exactly as it was told to me. This part is: "Christ died for our sins, as the Scriptures say. ⁴He was buried, and three days later He was raised to life, as the Scriptures say. ⁵Christ appeared to Peter, then to the twelve. ⁶After these, he appeared to more than five hundred other followers. Most of them are still alive, but some have died. ⁷He also appeared to James, and then to all of the apostles." ⁸Finally, he appeared to me, even though I am like someone who was born at the wrong time. ⁹I am the least important of all the apostles. In fact, I caused so much trouble for God's church that I don't even deserve to be called an apostle.

There is no mention whatsoever of the role of Jesus' followers who were women. According to the Gospels, women were witnesses of the resurrection even before Cephas, but that fact is ignored in this account. They were also disciples and were at the cross. Women played an important role in Jesus' ministry. It is important then to reread the Scripture and rediscover, reteach, and recover those narratives that will do justice to women.

Justice means that women shall be considered as equals, that their efforts and works are recognized and appreciated, and also that they are allowed to be part of the decisions made for the church. Women are called by the same Holy Spirit and are invited by the same word of God to become partners in the building of God's kingdom. When women are treated like "second-class members," no justice is delivered; when they are sent to be laborers but not permitted to vote or to be elected in a General Assembly, no justice is delivered. When the Bible is used to marginalize women but not used to condemn men's behavior, no justice is delivered. This is an example of misusing the word of God. God's word must be used to liberate and not to enslave people. This liberation is much needed for both men and women. Instead of understanding women at church as a threat, they must be considered as collaborators.

The Cure of Souls through Pastoral Care

How will we accomplish the liberation of Pentecostal women in Puerto Rico who struggle as they receive the call to become ministers and pastors within the structure of the church? Since we love and appreciate our church, we don't want to abandon it. We need to transform it according to the Holy Spirit's desire. How? Conscientization of oppression must come first. Second, we need to reread the Bible with suspicion[15] and rediscover the stories that will liberate us. Finally, we need to propose a reconstruction of our theology that will have an impact on our ecclesiology in order to acquire the third level of credentials[16] that will allow us to fully participate as equals within the structures of this great Church of God. Pentecostal women need to achieve our own historical project in the Church of God in general and Puerto Rico in particular.

Pastoral care is vital during this process of realization. Pastoral theology is a science of action or praxis. Casiano Floristan[17] understands it as a theology that moves from reflection to action. Christians understand the universe of events through reflection and dialogue. They formulate objectives and express those objectives among people. Pentecostal women could rely upon pastoral theology to promote the changes needed without experiencing feelings of guilt. Answering our dilemmas through reflection on our practices will certainly free us and will point to new roads to walk. We propose conversion as a result of repentance in the higher levels of authority of the church. Spaces are needed for women to be represented in a more unbiased manner, in order to benefit the body of Christ. This church cannot continue ignoring women who comprise more than half of this precious body among our Pentecostal community.

As part of that Pentecostal community, females in Puerto Rico received a legacy from North American missionaries. As they came to the island, they also brought their administrative structures. As we began our journey responding to God's call, we followed their model. Nevertheless, Pentecostal women began doing things differently because they were needed and their ministry was accepted as given by the Holy Spirit. They were preaching, planting churches, and doing missionary work, among other tasks. But the idea of the administrative model, where men made decisions for everybody, was too entrenched and women were unable to confront those structures at that moment. Men at the church understood that moment as a time to "surrender" those ideas. Colonization has always been an important issue in Puerto Rican lives; surrendering was part of our mind-set. Thus, Pentecostal women, although allowed to engage in some ministries, were excluded from the administrative organization where decisions were made.

There have been some gains to date. Our church in Puerto Rico has a woman supervisor in one of its fourteen regions. In addition, women in Puerto Rico are part of the Church and Pastor's Council of a local church.[18] Moreover, in our last local assembly four women were elected as members of the Executive Council of the Church in the Island. This was the outcome of a motion passed and approved in January 2006. In that assembly, women with the second rank (level) of credentials, ordained ministers, were accepted as eligible members of such an important and honorable body of our national church. Also, women are now being invited to preach at our National Convention. These achievements in Puerto Rico are not found in the U.S. Church Of God. At our General Assembly in San Antonio, Texas, in August 2008, a motion was presented to allow women to be part of the Church and Pastors Council, a local body that works with the pastors and looks after the church. The motion was defeated, preventing loyal members of our churches who happen to be women to be part of that body. So then, in the United States, Church of God female members cannot be part of that important body while in Puerto Rico the vast majority of our churches have women in that position.

Although we have accomplished this among our people, we call upon our male brothers who are not watching over their sisters to join in solidarity. Sisters and brothers must take care of each other in every family. In the narration of Cain and Abel in Genesis we find God asking Cain for his brother. Cain's question to God, "Am I my brother's keeper?" does not excuse him from his obligation and responsibility. He as the older brother was expected to protect his younger brother. God could be asking the same question again today to our brothers, "Where is your sister?" Would God be surprised by their answer? Am I my sister's keeper? Solidarity is needed in order to secure the wellness of our people and all of those around us.[19] Writing about pastoral care as a spiritual discipline, Roberto Rivera says the following: "This concept of a Christian community as an ecological system of care and vocation implies remembrance and care of the other as intrinsic qualities of what it means to be part of God's family. It is a contradiction to be a believer independent or isolated from the community of faith without thinking how to help others in that community."[20]

Our vision is an optimistic one, although we recognize that a collective transformation of character is most needed. What do we hope? *Mujerísta* theology believes in the historic project of inclusion of women. We hope for that project in which both women and men could be collaborators in forming a society and community that is more just, that shares power, and that makes decisions as a reality in the near future.

Final words from Justo L. González's *Mañana* are appropriate words with which to conclude. González recognizes three macro-events in theology, the third one being:

. . . those who were silent are now demanding to be being heard and are accomplishing so. Women from various cultures and countries are rising and are bringing about a movement from its base. Although the author recognizes disagreement among some issues of feminist theologians, what they all have realized is that they need to claim their space and place in the scheme of things that are happening.[21]

We shall do so: claim our space and place in the scheme of things happening in the church in Puerto Rico that were given to us by the Holy Spirit. "We have arrived at the end of our arduous journey. . . . The meeting and conversation . . . have provided the imaginative space for our critical feminist conversations. . . . Jesus goes ahead of us on the open-road to Galilee signifying the beginnings of the still-to-be-realized *basileia* discipleship of equals."[22]

PART THREE

Creating Care in a Multicultural World

The phenomenon of the concept of "global village" has changed the world in which we live and provide ministry. Assumptions about homogeneity, value systems, and spirituality previously widely accepted in the academic, religious, and clinical world are being constantly challenged by changing communities. These communities are confronted with adjusting to the presence of many cultures and languages within their borders. The luxury of monocultural thinking is now a liability for those striving to be competent theoreticians, educators, and practitioners. The authors in this section write from a variety of cultural backgrounds, emphasizing what care looks like in a multicultural world.

What About All Those Angry Black Women?

Teresa E. Snorton

The "angry black woman" is a force to be reckoned with or, better yet, avoided. In the African American community, she is known as "b–t–h". On television she is the "know-it-all, nagging, castrating" wife. In real life, she is filled with pain, and anger is her only apparent means of coping with that pain.

When I was asked about my anger in my first CPE (clinical pastoral education) internship, I was puzzled. What suggested that I was angry? Not me—the gentle, soft-spoken, always cordial, accommodating member of the team. I had no idea what I was being asked. Unlike the outspoken, verbally aggressive women portrayed as angry in the media and in our communities, I did not see myself as angry. My anger was suppressed. It had taken another form, repressed into a quasi-politeness, but my CPE supervisor could see it, feel it. To him, it was quite palpable, just below the surface of my emotions. To me, my anger was hidden.

This chapter will explore the nature of anger in the lives of African American women. I suggest that many African American women struggle with anger and what to do with it. Some become "raging women," abhorrent and frightening to others. Other black women become "proper women," yet full of rage and no way to express it. Society in general does not tolerate the former, and the latter is affirmed for her appropriateness, but never given space for her angry feelings to be expressed and explored. The judgmentalism experienced when anger is expressed and the misplaced affirmation of those who "suck it all in" force black women into either over-expressing their anger or into minimizing and discounting it. Very little is said about the healthy and healing ways in which black women can express their anger in a society that tends to silence them on two fronts—racism and sexism. The dual marginalization of black women has resulted in a miscalculation of the depth of their anger. Even more, there is often the apparent hint that her anger is unwarranted, and that she should be appreciative—appreciative that she has a job, grateful that she has a man, thankful for whatever opportunity has come her way.

In order to be taken seriously, particularly when she experiences racism and sexism (and classism), the black woman often feels she must over-express her anger, lest it be ignored. And if and when she chooses the other polarity, to "dress up" her anger into socially appropriate garb, the cost is to her own internal sense of self and worth. What then are the alternatives? How can black women express their anger in ways that are empowering for them, without resorting to either extreme of over- or under-expression? How can the expression of anger be encouraged, even in the midst of a culture that would rather have that anger disappear?

Why Are Black Women Angry?

The Collective Pain of History

It may be important to first establish why black women are angry. I am not attempting to suggest that black women are any more or less angry than white women or women of other cultures. However, the peculiar circumstances of being a black woman in America has created a kind of anger that is unique and quite often misunderstood. I contend that the ordinary black woman bears the collective pain of the history of African Americans. Embedded in the DNA of African American women is the memory of the enslavement of their ancestors, the horror of the Middle Passage, and the atrocities of slavery and Jim Crow. Black women in Africa, on ships, and on plantations in the United States and the Caribbean had their children snatched from them and their bodies repeatedly raped and violated. Hard work, harsh living conditions, and lack of basic necessities were commonplace variables in the slave woman's life. The trauma inflicted on black women (again, not to suggest it was more or less than that inflicted on others in history) surpasses what any human ought to be asked to endure. The notion of the collective unconscious, a term coined by Carl Jung[1] and later described as the "reservoir of the experiences of our species,"[2] suggests that the legacy of the survivors of slavery includes an inheritance of the strength and power that helped them survive the tribulations. At the same time, the post-traumatic stress of those experiences is a part of that inheritance.

The numbers of Africans transported to America and the Caribbean through the transatlantic slave trade are staggering.

> Half of the more than 20 million Africans captured and sold into slavery never even made it to the ship. Most died on the march to the sea. It is impossible to determine how many more lost their lives through the crossing. Current estimates range from 1 million to 2.2 million.[3]

The above estimates suggest that at least eight million native Africans ended up in the Americas as slaves. This number does not include those slaves who were later born in America. The perpetuation of slavery transferred from the hands of the slave traders to those of the slaveholders, with legal sanction. Slavery was legally recognized in 1641 in Massachusetts.[4] Georgia was the last of the colonies to legalize slavery in 1750.[5] Between 1680 and 1690, the Royal African Company in England shipped an average of 18,000 slaves a year, exceeding 45,000 slaves during one of those years.[6]

While the slave trade was banned in the northern colonies in the years following the Revolutionary War,[7] it continued to be legal to engage in slave trading in the southern colonies. After the prohibition on slave trading, slavery continued to thrive because of the phenomenon of perpetual slavery—those born into slavery remained in slavery until death.

The number of slaves in America supported an economic system that thrived, but one from which the slaves did not benefit. "By 1861, there were over 4 million slaves in America,"[8] representing the largest percentage of the total workforce in the country. There is no reliable number on how many of those were women, but we know that there were no special provisions to exclude the black female from slavery. The slave traders captured men and women alike. The slave owners bought and sold women the same way as men. Gender made no difference in the world of slavery, except that black women probably experienced more sexual abuse and exploitation than black males. Slave women were overworked, beaten, tortured, separated from their mates and children, and brutalized as were slave men.

In the slave woman's experience there was no way for her to express objection to her treatment. There was no way for her to refuse to give up her children or demand their return. The choice to say no was not a choice available to her. Even those who attempted to fight back or rebel were only able to do so in ways that continued their victimization:

> After seven years of being one of the "disappeared," Harriet Jacobs dared join the world again. She had eluded her abusive master by folding herself into a crawl space in a building, a space which never allowed her to stand upright. Burdened with a mother's pain, she observed the growth of her children through a peephole and watched almost daily the master who hunted for her and who had sexually threatened her for almost half of her life.[9]

The anger at being violated, and abused, victimized remained unarticulated except in the recesses of the black woman's soul and psyche. From this internal pain and unexpressed anger, a tension in black mother-daughter relationships was born.

> The need to be exceedingly harsh or enterprising where their children were concerned often created emotional distance between mother and child. . . . The tension was greater . . . when the child was a daughter, whose "almost certain doom is to minister to the unbridled lust of the slaveholder" . . . it is not difficult to imagine the anxiety of a mother whose daughter had reached the age of puberty. . . . In the world of the slave

mother, there was little room for compassion, because there was no room for weakness. This was especially true when the mother herself had been compromised. A Northerner who settled in Mississippi spoke of mothers who were concubines there: "They had too much pride and self-respect to rear their daughters for such a purpose," he said. "If driven to desperation, she destroyed herself to prevent it, or killed them."[10]

A willingness to destroy self as an option to expressing anger at the one who was inflicting pain became one of the only ways black women could fight back. This kind of selflessness persists in the African American female community today. It is often admired and glorified, to the exclusion of recognizing that this ultimate sacrifice of self is due to the inability to express one's anger at oppression without fear of retaliation.

The Controlling Images

The collective pain of the past and subsequent anger is embodied in the lives of black women as these kinds of dynamics persist in the African American female world. At the same time, contemporary culture has also adopted "controlling images" of black women in its attempt to define and describe the experience of the postslavery African American female. The impact of these externally imposed images is a reworking of the control previously imposed on black women by slaveholders. In her book *Black Feminist Thought: Knowledge, Consciousness, and the Politics of Empowerment*, Patricia Hill Collins describes four "controlling images": mammy, matriarch, welfare mother, and whore.[11] While there is no specific controlling image that exclusively typifies the angry black woman, the implication of these controlling images is that anger is not encouraged for African American women. The mammy image is the nurturing, caring presence—desired because she is not angry. The matriarch is the antithesis of the mammy, and is considered undesirable because of the way in which she dominates males. The welfare mother is another failed mammy, according to Collins, and thus not to be emulated (in the eyes of the dominant culture). She is to be grateful for the help offered to her by the mainstream. Finally, the whore image reworks and rejustifies the sexual exploitation of black women, portraying them as oversexed and promiscuous, excusing their exploitation as being their own fault. In any case, these controlling images more than infer that black women should not be angry.

A twenty-first-century reimaging of these post-Reconstruction archetypes can be observed in today's visual media as well. The television show *Everybody Hates Chris* is loosely based on the childhood experiences of popular African American male comedian Chris Rock. The mother on the show, Rochelle, is played by actress Tichina Arnold. Rochelle is the postmodern angry black woman. She yells at her kids. She yells at her husband, Julius, even when he is trying hard to support the family by working two jobs. She is frequently portrayed as a demanding, critical mother. It seems that nothing can make her happy. She is the angry black woman that you want to like, but you just can't.

Another television show, *Ugly Betty*, likewise presents an image of the angry black woman. Wilhelmina Slater, played by actress Vanessa Williams, is co-editor-in-chief of a successful fashion magazine, *Mode*, following her career as a supermodel. She has also become a surrogate co-owner of the magazine as the result of her scheming to produce a child from the harvested sperm of the publisher, Bradford Meade, after their wedding was tragically aborted when he died at the altar from a heart attack. As a result she came out on top, sharing responsibility for the magazine with Meade's ex-wife and children. In spite of this good fortune, Wilhelmina is still an angry black woman. She is beautiful, but so very angry and bitter. At every turn she is on the lookout for who is out to get her next, so that she can get them first. Despite some efforts to show a softer, more vulnerable side to her character, the message is clear: she is an angry black woman, and no one likes her!

The subtle (or not-so-subtle) message in these two present-day images is simple. Black women, do not be angry or no one will like you! This mandate transcends social location and applies to black women regardless of their station in life. The well-beloved mammy is no longer on the television screen. But her antithesis, is and she is not lovable! The choice given to black women to express even legitimate anger is suppressed and eliminated.

The power of these kinds of images can best be understood through the lens of W. E. B. Du Bois's concept of double consciousness. For Du Bois, double consciousness is the "sense of always looking at one's self through the eyes of others, of measuring one's soul by the tape of a world that looks on in amused contempt and pity."[12] It is not difficult to imagine that the mainstream audiences of these two shows despise and pity Rochelle and Wilhelmina.

While Du Bois was writing of the duality of being black and American, his thoughts can apply to those women struggling to simultaneously be black and female.

> The concept of Du Boisian "double consciousness" has three manifestations. First, the power of white stereotypes on black life and thought (being forced into a context of misrepresentation of one's own people while also having the knowledge of reflexive truth). Second, the racism that excluded black Americans from the mainstream of society, being American or not American. Finally, and most significantly, the internal conflict between being African and American simultaneously. Double consciousness is a convergence of two identities from two different cultural realities. When one of those cultures represses a traditional oppressor, the danger of double consciousness resides in conforming and/or changing one's identity to that of how the oppressing culture perceives the person.[13]

Black women live with the reality of being stereotyped and misrepresented. When it comes to anger, the strong message of how to "be" or "not to be" are clear. To be accepted by her American culture, the African American woman must deny her anger or risk alienation. Yet, she has reason to be angry. Moreover, for black women, the "double consciousness" dynamic has often meant that the black woman be an advocate first for the rights of black people, subjecting her unique experience as a female and any related exploitation further down on the ladder.

Disparities in the Life of the African American Woman

Aside from the collective unconscious of historic pain and the impact of controlling images, African American women have valid reason to be angry in the twenty-first century. One might argue that awareness and some deep therapeutic work should help overcome the generations of pain and suppressed anger. One might argue that with insight, the African American woman should be able to see the controlling images for what they are—distortions intended to limit and proscribe. But a close examination of the data that reflects the lives of African American woman reveals that there is still much about which to be angry. The disparities that exist in the lives of black women are real and undeniable. These disparities point to the enduring nature of racism, sexism, and classism. Black women have yet to experience the coveted liberation dreamt about and yearned for by their foremothers. Certainly, the lives of black women are greatly improved over that of the slaves in the eighteenth and nineteenth century. Strides made through civil rights and the feminist movement during the twentieth century have made a difference for black women. But, in reality, black women remain at the bottom of the barrel. Consider these realities:

- The 2005 United States Census revealed that when comparing incomes, males of all races (white, Asian, black, and Hispanic) and white and Asian women made more money than black females. Only Hispanic women were paid less than black women.[14]
- African American women experience intimate partner violence at a rate 35 percent higher than white women and two-and-a-half times the rate of women of other races.[15]
- In 2005, black women (who are 8 percent of the U.S. population) accounted for almost one third (29 percent) of all female victims of intimate partner homicide.[16]
- African Americans are about twice as likely to have diabetes as whites of the same age and they are more likely to have other serious health problems caused by diabetes. Among women, about two out of three new HIV cases are African American women. African American women are less likely to receive health care; when they do receive care, they are

more likely to receive it late. For example, African American mothers were twice as likely to have late or no prenatal care compared to white mothers in 2004.[17]

Black women today live with the pain of the past, the impact of controlling images, and the reality that their social location is fraught with contradiction and compromise. Black women continue to live in poverty, even those with jobs. They continue to be victimized and assaulted. Their needs continue to be ignored.

When the United States was developing its gender definitions of what it means to be male and female, the fate of black women was sealed. Dr. Love Henry Whelchel speaks of the "identity theft" that has been endured by African Americans. In a 2009 lecture he identified the four ways in which this has occurred: dehumanization, depersonalization, desexualization, and desocialization.[18] In the dehumanizing process, Whelchel asserts that for African Americans, the male/female roles are reversed. Where mainstream society encourages males to be independent and females to be dependent, the dehumanization inflicted on African Americans creates the opposite. African American males are dependent and females are independent. According to Whelchel, this leaves the African American woman without a provider and without the protection normally afforded to women. He further posits that in the desexualization process, black men have learned to avoid attachments to black women. Historically, white men, not black men, determined the course of the lives of African American women and families. The centuries-long process of dehumanizing and desexualizing black men has created difficulties in black male/female relationships and families. Black women feel cheated and robbed. In addition, it is common in the black community for African American women to say they cannot find a good relationship because out of four black men, one is married, one is in jail, one is gay, and the other one is undesirable as a mate (unemployed, addicted, emotionally wounded, and so forth). Myths like this persist in part because of the historic disruption of black male/female life and in part because of statistical realities in the African American community. It should be no surprise that black women are angry! The question then is, What do they do with that anger?

Anger and Religion

Religion plays a central role in the lives of many African Americans. Black women represent the largest group of regular churchgoers, outnumbering men two to one.[19] Because of the core religious beliefs[20] held by many African Americans, black women tend to look to religion for guidance on all kinds of matters—fiscal, relational, emotional. In the context of faith, maintaining favor with God, seeking and accepting God's will, and not questioning God are primary values. For the African American woman, one's religion is a crucial determinant in how she understands the feelings and dynamics of anger.

Anger Discouraged

In the Christian tradition, anger is regarded as one of the seven deadly sins. Andrew Lester writes, "The anger-is-sin tradition declares that anger was not present in humans at creation, but has its roots in the original sin of pride and disobedience."[21] In his subsequent summary of the sin of anger, Lester traces how humanity has been taught to avoid anger, to view it as negative. He also points out how this narrative about anger has victimized women.

The black church has bought into the notion of anger-is-sin, most likely a remnant of native African religious beliefs that emphasized harmonious living.[22] Part of the success of the nonviolence movement of the civil rights era in the 1960s was due to the way in which the principle of nonviolence fit with the typical belief system of the African American Christian.

When I was a child, an argument with a cousin or sibling was met with the following admonishment from a grandmother: "Don't let the sun go down on your anger," a paraphrase of a Scripture passage from the New Testament book of Ephesians (Eph. 4:26: "Be angry, and yet do not sin; do not let the sun go down on your anger" [NASB]). The intent was to encourage rapid apologies and speedy resolution of the conflict. When women were arguing, it was common to hear "It is better to live in the desert, than with a contentious and angry woman" (Prov. 21:19 [NASB]), an attempt to remind women that it was unladylike to argue, and that men did not like it anyway! Finally, at virtually every annual Women's Day celebration in a black church across America, Proverbs 31 is read, including verse 24: "She opens her mouth with wisdom, And on her tongue *is* the law of kindness" (NASB). These and other Scripture texts are why many African American women have difficulty expressing their anger and, when they do express it, are often filled with guilt and remorse for their misbehavior.

Anger Encouraged

Lester points out the key role feminist theologians have had in rescripting the narrative on anger as sin: "the feminist theologians have long recognized that anger did not originate in sin and evil, but in the Creator's blessed creation— a gift with significant positive potential for assisting with our well-being."[23] Womanist writers have also contributed to the rescripting of the anger narrative. Author bell hooks writes of her own transformative experience with anger:

> Like all profound repression, my rage unleashed made me afraid. It forced me to turn my back on forgetfulness, called me out of my denial. It changed my relationship with home—with the South—made it so I could not return there. Inwardly, I felt as though I were a marked woman. A black person unashamed of her rage, using it as a catalyst to develop

critical consciousness, to come to full decolonized self-actualization, had no real place in the existing social structure.[24]

bell hooks insists that black people, black women in particular, must see their anger as constructive, rather than as destructive. She encourages African Americans to embrace anger as a force for growth.

Anger and Healing

In 1990, I came to the Emory Center for Pastoral Services as the second female CPE supervisor, the first black female. I was recruited, in part, because of the difficulties encountered by the white male CPE supervisors with black women students. These women were seminary students, many breaking down barriers erected by their faith groups to keep women out of ministry. They had stories of adversity overcome and of challenges of every kind. In CPE, they were invited to share their feelings, but when they did, the CPE faculty was overwhelmed with the depth and force of the anger of the black women.

During subsequent years as a CPE supervisor, I consulted with many others in the field about working with black female students. The story was almost always the same: the black female student was invited to share her feelings and the white (male or female) supervisor did not know what to do when the anger came. In response to these queries for consultation, I developed the following tool [fig. 13.1] to help non-blacks understand black women.

Figure 13.1

Supervising African American Women

Gender development
- Females tend to have a higher capacity for emotion than males
- Western women are taught to value this emotional capacity in the relational realm and to devalue it in the professional/business realm

Cultural development
- African American women experience tri-level oppression (gender, race, class)
- African American women are taught to hide their emotional capacity for the sake of survival
- African American women are taught to maintain strong relational ties even when they are not mutual

---

- The African American matriarch is both revered and resented, creating a "double bind" for most African American women

Black church life for African American women

- African American women are often regarded as the "backbone" of the church
- African American women are encouraged to play nurturing roles more than leadership roles in the church
- African American women experience both overt and covert sexism in the black church
- Black church continues to use patriarchal language, God-images, hymns, etc.

Learning styles

- African American women value concrete experience over abstract conceptualization
- African American women expect relationship even in the context of a teacher-student or mentor-mentee relationship
- African American women regard external validation as an aspect of community assent to her work/performance
- African American women engage in learning to "transcend" and/ or "to return" to their communities, therefore tangible results of learning are important
- African Americans, in general, enter into environments outside their own community with suspicion and mistrust

Dynamics to remember

- African American women experience considerable violence within their own community, in addition to the social violence of racism and sexism
- African American male/female relationships are affected by the social-political factors of the larger community/society
- African American women must mediate the tension between dependency and independency in view of social-political-economic realities
- African American women's aggressiveness and anger can often be misinterpreted as inappropriate or extreme, while it is actually being expressed out of a sense of empowerment

The last point in this figure—that black women's aggression comes out of a sense of empowerment—is intended to demythologize the anger of black women. When a black woman feels safe enough to express her anger, it is to be celebrated, not feared. The realities of racism and sexism in the daily lives of black women remain largely unaddressed in the academy and the clinical setting, resulting in a lack of familiarity with the plight of the black woman. The controlling images of the dominant culture tell us that an angry black woman is dangerous and undesirable. Religion tries to convince us that anger is sin. But I am convinced that black women and their liberation are dependent upon the freedom to give voice to the pain of their individual and collective lives. Theologian Evelyn Parker uses these adjectives to describe black women who have found liberation: "courageous, tenacious, audacious, bodacious."[25]

As diversity and difference become more widely accepted, perhaps the impression of the angry black woman will also change. Perhaps there is hope that she can be seen and understood in her fullness—filled with pain, yet with room for hope.

Black women poets and writers like Maya Angelou, bell hooks, and Delores Williams, to name a few, have been writing for the past two decades about the contemporary manifestation of pain in the lives of black women and the search for hope in the midst of sexism, racism, and classism. Their words serve as an excellent resource for practitioners engaged in a helping relationship with an angry black woman.[26]

The challenge to pastoral care providers is similar to the challenge that Parker gives to the black church:

> In light of the realities of racism, sexism and classism, if the church—in which women and girls have long been the majority—is to be a relevant institution, then the church must discern ways to let girls tell their stories and receive God's miraculous healing in the process.[27]

When working with African American women, we must be willing to hear their stories, to see their anger, to assist them in naming the anger, and to walk with them through the anger as a means of empowerment and a vehicle for growth.

Unraveling the Relational Myth in the Turn Toward Autonomy

Pastoral Care and Counseling with African Women

Esther E. Acolatse

The current trend in concepts of the person as "self-in-relation" is not new to the African. "I am because we are, and because we are, I am" is the primary myth, the story-forming principle that people are called to live. It is the principle that undergirds familial and group relationships and, in an ideal situation, ensures the well-being of the whole group. In reality, however, women are the ones who make the sacrifices that ensure the expected welfare of the family and community, usually to the detriment of the formation of a healthy self. Overt messages from the faith perspective combine with the covert traditional messages based in proverbs and stories to point to disastrous consequences for women who step beyond their expected roles. Self-autonomy is not encouraged in the general population in Africa, especially not in women.

The notion of the development of the self as moving from dependence in infancy to independence in adulthood, in the West, has been challenged by feminist psychological theorists like Carol Gilligan, Mary Field Belenkey, Blythe McVicker Clinchy, Nancy Rule Golder, and Jill Mattuck Tarule. Their research and findings indicate that women experience the growth of self from dependence to mutual *interdependence*, rather than to *independence*, as a sign of maturation. In fact, what is commonly acknowledged now is that all human development follows the trajectory that was ascribed to female self-development, and the understanding of growth toward autonomy perceived in male development (which was once assumed to be normative for all) has been critiqued as unattainable. In each of these notions and critiques leveled at the effects of autonomy on persons, autonomy has been only apparent rather than real in what can be termed "the abstraction of autonomous man." Catrina Mackenzie and Natalie Stoljar propose that what is perceived as autonomous living in men, and that which has been critiqued by feminist psychologists like Gilligan, are merely abstractions of autonomy, since a completely autonomous life is unattainable by anyone. At the same time, they acknowledge that especially in Western men, socialization has tended to be geared toward greater autonomous living and away from appearance of dependence. If the above observation is true, then it is reasonable for feminist critiques that seek to correct for autonomous living (even abstractions of it) to be based on the need for relationality and mutual interdependence, and the benefits of communal living that emanate from such a relational ethos. While in most African cultures and many societies the relational ethos is expected and esteemed, however, women do not receive equal benefits from the group-centric identity. In such circumstances, the call to relationality and interdependent living, without equal attention to issues of lack of autonomy, does not bode well for women.

This chapter aims at debunking current notions of relationality within African cultures, including African feminist appropriations of it, and insists that what is termed "relational ethos" benefits only some of the people. In fact, the African conception of "relational ethos" works against the very purpose of its existence—the welfare of the entire group. The chapter then proposes ways for nurturing individuated "selves-in-relation" to promote healthy relationships in women and thus for all, while keeping in mind traditional and faith values that sustain such selves. The implications are offered for pastoral care and counseling.

Current Perspectives on Notions of the Self

The turn to the relational ethos in self-development has gained ascendancy in both psychological and theological writing with the rise of the feminist movement and with the challenge feminists pose to existing understandings of the development of the individual from dependence to independence as indicative of maturity. Noting gender differences in growth and development of the self and social bonds, earlier studies in the psychology of gender by second-wave feminists indicate that women are motivated more toward community, while men are oriented toward agency. Agency is characterized by traits such as assertiveness, self-confidence, and a sense of autonomy, while women oriented toward community are seen as warmer and more expressive, with demonstrable empathy for others.[1] The tendency toward agency or community is noted as being internalized into the self-concept of males and females, but agency, the motivating factor in men, serves as the criterion for evaluating both genders. This dynamic creates the problem of assessing women as lacking in qualities assumed to be universal human characteristics. For this reason, men especially are reluctant to adjust to new roles in a changing society for fear of taking on what are assumed to be female characteristics.

Further, studies by second-wave psychoanalytic feminists like Nancy Chodorow and Jessica Benjamin[2] suggest that not only is the standard for evaluative assessment of maturity flawed, but that characterizing men as active and independent and women as dependent and passive is not universally valid. More recent studies and writings influenced by postmodern thought and spearheaded by women, Chodorow and Benjamin among them, recognize both the universality and intractability of gender, but argue also for its particularity and multiplicity.[3] Moreover, attention has now been drawn to the fluidity rather than rigidity of formation of the gendered self. Rather than assuming fluidity only at the preoedipal stage of infancy (before an individual has differentiated him- or herself from the opposite-sex parent and then later identified with the same-sexed parent at the oedipal stage), it has been suggested that a post-oedipal stage of adult maturity returns to the fluidity of the preoedipal constitution of gender, but without the narcissism that attends it.

Studies in gender differences in sociality that seek to understand attachment and relationality reveal that connectedness is different for men than for women. While both need and seek connectedness, women are seen to favor relational or dyadic relationships while men move toward collective bonds. Thus, while women primarily are self-described by their one-on-one relationships, men are self-described by their affiliation to groups.[4] The difference is thus in types of relationality rather than presence or absence of the need for relationality. Such findings, therefore, emphasize the gender-neutral nature of such characteristics and tendencies, and allow us to think in ways that overcome the apparent intractability of gendered existence that works against all humanity.

Problematizing Self-in-Relation Theories

The fact that all selves come into being in relation to others, however, is no longer in dispute. In reality, there is evidence that growth and development of the self is toward more and more connectedness even though the *type* of preferred connectedness differs with the gender.[5] It is in relation to others that authentic identity emerges. Authentic identity is a prerequisite for mutual intimate relationships in which each is enabled to live into her or his full humanity and is changed and enlarged by the encounter. Erikson, in his analysis of psychosocial stages of development, has this to say about identity formation:

> Accepting the fact that the human environment is social, the outer world of the ego is made up of the egos of others significant to it. They are significant because on many levels of crude or subtle communication my whole being perceives in them a hospitality for the way in which my inner world is ordered and includes them, which makes me, in turn, hospitable to the way they order their world and include me—*a mutual affirmation*, then, which can be depended upon to activate my being as I can be depended on to activate theirs.[6]

If the above statement is a correct description of how one forms identity, and I believe such to be the case, then there ought to be mutual responsibility among all peoples for the formation of authentic egos, because from those "ordered inner worlds," which are cocreated by the individual and the relational environment, all relationships find their life-spring.

Theologian Martin Buber gives this same thought a psychological foregrounding when he proposes that the measure of an individual's narrative integrity is a measure of the integrity of the individual's relationship with other people.[7] He asserts that while "persons appear by entering into relation with other persons,"[8] "egos appear by setting themselves apart from other egos."[9] The former is lauded while the later seems to be deplored. While Buber is right in asserting that becoming a person transcends becoming an ego—for the ego is not self-sustaining—his observation overlooks the fact that the setting apart of one's ego from those of others is a necessary prerequisite for true I/Thou relationships and thus for becoming a person. Object relations psychology points to the essential need for the emerging ego to recognize and negotiate the clear boundaries between self and other in order for a full relationship of self and other to emerge. Without this clear boundary between the growing child's self-concept and the acknowledgment of the other, fusing occurs and results in unhealthy enmeshment later.[10] The ability to move between egocentricity and exocentricity is perhaps the task of the emerging self-in-relation if both the self and the other are to be attended to with integrity. To focus on one without the other is to lose both or at least to short change both.

Women for the most part have been socialized to negate the self, the sense of I-ness, and to attend to other selves as a way of proving their worth. Self-sacrifice for the good of others is held up as a virtue for women much more than it is for men.[11] But nowhere more than in collectivistic cultures like those found in Africa are the worst manifestations of the effects of the indoctrination of being-in-relation to be seen, as well as gender disparity regarding who carries the weight of sustaining the relationships.

Understanding Relationality in African Traditional Systems: Corporate Personality

The African conception of the world is one in which all of creation is intertwined for common good. In its worldview, the cosmos is divided into four entities that exist in a three-tiered, hierarchical world in close relationship. At the apex of this worldview is the Supreme Being, believed to be the creator and general overseer of the whole universe, though not conceived as involved in the day-to-day life of creatures. Closely tied to the Supreme Being are the lesser gods, who are believed to be the messengers acting on behalf of the Supreme Being. Next are the Ancestors, those known as the living dead and who are custodians of the clans, rules of engagement, humans, and all creation, but especially other spirit beings who are believed to inhabit the Underworld and who infiltrate the human world and wreak havoc. A three-tiered world, not unlike that held in all ancient belief systems, is assumed here. But what sets the African worldview apart is the close affinity among all these entities and the importance of striving to maintain a harmonious and balanced environment at all times. Harmonious living, especially among people to please the custodians of the spirit world, ensures blessings that translate into fecundity for humanity. The human family is further broken into tribal units and then into clans by bloodline. Bloodlines are either patrilineal or matrilineal, where individuals belong to their mother's clan and receive inheritance through their maternal uncle. Matrilineal clans hold the belief that at conception the mother gives *mogya*, or blood, and the father gives *ntro*, or his essence, to the child. Each individual belongs to one of these bloodlines and is not known without reference to the immediate family or the clan, which is usually the smallest social unit.

African culture assumes the connectedness of all beings and believes that an imbalance found or wrong done in one part of the system affects or harms all. Yet in many ways, this ideal is not lived out in the daily lives of the people. The mutual interdependence that is to be forged by the knowledge of interrelatedness and interdependence of all beings is a noble ideal, but in reality, any existing imbalance is muted by the silence of the women who carry the bigger burden of responsibility for maintaining relationships, even if to their own detriment. Usually the conflictual situations created by the recognition of one's potential and the need to make autonomous decisions, and the insistence of the culture toward conformity of gender roles, have been linked to the rising levels of depression in women.[12] Depression that is not related to chemical imbalance in women is claimed to be a direct result of their experience of loss of power and thus of self, often in their primary relationships, and especially with their partners.[13]

Women and the Relational Ethos: Focusing the Problem

Women's sense of self, which develops from infancy, especially through gendered nurturing, is always one focused on the interaction between the self and the other.[14] An attunement of the developing self with that of the primary caretaker, usually the mother, fosters "a more *encompassing* sense of self, in contrast with a more boundaried, or limited, self that is encouraged in boys from a very young age."[15] The encompassing self, which can be assumed as embracing the other into one's life rather than insulating oneself from others, exhibits the need for connectedness. This becomes the motivation, as well as the goal, of the self. In this way, the need of the female for connectedness is seen as essential for the survival of the self, and yet this need in certain cases also becomes the source of the death to the self. A culture that promotes a relational ethos and denigrates individual autonomy ought to be the fertile ground for growing female selves, and evidence of this should be seen in the flourishing of its women (both at home and in the diaspora) and, by extension, in the whole population. The cultural ethos, "I am because we are, and because we are, I am," and the natural growth of their core essence should work with, rather than against, each other.[16] But the reality belies this ideal, and instead, the obverse is true. While women care for all from cradle to grave, any relief they might get is from other women, usually distant relatives who function as servants with their more affluent family members in the cities.[17]

Perhaps what is missing is that too much attention is focused on the corporate self, without equal attention to the autonomous self. The negation of the self from without, as well as self-negation from within, persists where collectivistic and corporate personality is overemphasized. Surprisingly, the result of such overemphasis of the corporate self not only leaves the autonomous self inadequately formed, but the corporate self is shortchanged. What is most alarming is the expectation that women carry the heavier end of the load of what it means to live into a corporate identity, but with little reward or respect. When women speak up against the inequity, they are seen as destroyers of the communal ethos; thus, they find it difficult to attend to themselves without undue guilt. While the communal existence is extolled, individuals, especially women, are bogged down by the weight of that which ought to make their existence lighter. To ensure that the status quo is in place, women are nurtured early into keeping to their place.

In her book *Daughters of Anowa*,[18] Mercy Oduyoye, herself a woman from a matriarchal Akan clan who has experienced the patriarchal extension via marriage in a Nigerian culture, probes the way in which language in the form of proverbs, folk tales, and myths—what she terms "folktalk"—has been employed to subjugate African women over the years. Selecting proverbs that describe and define women and other female creatures, Oduyoye compares them with other parallel proverbs that apply exclusively to men. For instance, the Akan say: "Like hens, women wait for cocks to crow, announcing the arrival of daylight"; "[I]f a tall woman carries palmnuts, birds eat them off her head"; or "[W]hen a woman makes a giant drum, it is kept in a man's room."[19] The only proverbs that speak well of women exclusively are ones that allude to their mothering roles. So one hears: "[W]hen the hen is caught, her chicks are easily collected"—a mother's misfortune is expected to lower the aspirations of a child or, in short, it is far better to be fatherless than motherless. The underlying assumption is that mothers are important. Womanhood by itself is still second-rate at best; it is the striving to be good mothers and daughters that provides recognition and affirmation, which, as I have indicated earlier, is necessary for the growth of the self. It means that being single (and this is often the blight on attaining higher education) and childless leaves many women feeling insignificant and incomplete. Similarly, in a culture in which age is exalted because it is equated with wisdom, many older and wiser childless women find, however, that they are not proffered the same deference shown to their married counterparts or even younger colleagues.

Aside from these proverbs, myths abound in which mishaps befall strong women who have tried to wield power or assert their autonomy. The import of this "folktalk" is clear: in male-female relationships, males have preeminence, and any woman stepping out of line is a shame and a disgrace to womanhood and only misfortune (especially the lack of a husband, who is termed a woman's glory) will follow her. Women who step out of their roles often find themselves shuttling between their need for competence and guilt for their competence.[20] All wise mothers are tacitly enjoined to take heed to bring up their daughters to know their culturally acceptable position vis-à-vis men. They must be seen and not heard, at whatever cost to them; they must not be seen as being better than men. Thus, studies of proverbs, folk tales, and myths have not only uncovered neglected or glossed-over dimensions of gendered socialization in Africa, but have also challenged traditional assumptions and conclusions drawn from these premises. The hope is of diffusing the telling of *Anansesem* (tall tales according to human beings based on the trickery of Ananse, the spider) and of encouraging the retelling of *Nyankosem* (stories according to Nyame—their Creator).[21]

When we tell the human story according to the Creator, and offer a theological anthropology, we are invited first to understand (stand under) the Creator's own inner life—a life of autonomous relationality, the prototypical self-in-relation. We are enjoined to imitate the *imago Dei*. From a Christian perspective, the language in which we usually address God often fractures the trinitarian concept of God and leaves us with a weak monism at best. Regardless of whether doctrinally we affirm a triune God or not, the everyday God image of the average believer is inherently of a single being (sometimes referred to as God or Jesus and, albeit rarely, the Holy Spirit), rather than three persons in one God. This same inability to properly name God as three distinct persons in one without lapsing into monism is demonstrated in our tendency to collapse the individual into the group and thus lose the individual, or focus on the individual and lose the community. We thus move toward individualism or communitarianism. Later on, we will see how attention to the inner life of the triune God provides both language and a conceptual frame for navigating self-in-relation.

What I am advocating here is a turn toward attending to the ego and its development. I am suggesting that though the self is the overarching archetype and the core of the person, we nevertheless set it within bounds that free other archetypes to cooperate with the self in the interest of the person. Furthermore, the self, like the other archetypes, is still developing and, as previously observed, progression is not linear but rather moves in a spiral and regresses as it moves to the next stage, as Robert Kegan points out.[22] A strong ego might come to the aid of the self in the moments of its downward spiral and as it journeys back up toward the next stage in development. Additionally, Mary Lynn Dell, Carolyn Wilbur Treadway, and Bonnie Miller-McLemore have dealt with the need to understand that women's growth in development is also marked by distinct rites of passage such as menarche and childbirth.[23] Thus, their growth would follow a different trajectory to that of men.

While the self develops in relation to other selves, it requires autonomy to develop as an authentic self-in-relation. Autonomy entails the ability to chose and live in the best sense after one's own values and beliefs and to make meaning in self-reflexive ways about one's decisions. It is a personal process that encompasses both the affective and the rational. Sometimes, however, it is difficult to tease out what is socialization and what is coercion, especially in more traditional cultures focused on maintaining the status quo. In the African setting, for instance, when a woman has her daughter circumcised[24] because it is a requirement of her religious and cultural heritage, how does she distinguish what is socialization from what is coercion when she is cognizant of the ramifications for the daughter in future marital and familial life? Or when a mother cautions a daughter about being outspoken in mixed company? Or when female teachers publicly deride the boys in her class for allowing a "slip of a girl" to ace each subject and place first each school term? If this girl lives in dread of excellence, sabotages herself academically, and exists in the tension between remorse for mediocrity and fear of excelling, where does socialization in conformity with culture end and coercion begin? Cultural stereotypes of appropriate striving for the different genders account for this phenomenon.[25] Studies show that women who not only deviate from traditional occupations but succeed in nontraditional occupations can suffer negative consequences. On the whole, results indicate that such women are less likely to be found desirable as romantic partners and are also likely to lack female friendships. Thus, such studies indicate that men wield considerable power, even if tacitly, in limiting the occupational choices of women. For the African woman especially, since marriage and motherhood is what affirms her as a *person*, to succeed in assumed male occupations means that her striving toward attaining her optimal potential (which is needed for self-fulfillment) is directly proportional to paving her path for social negation. In addition, the culture perceives a woman who has few female friends but several male friends as "loose." If her fears overcome her desires, then the woman is likely to sabotage herself and avoid succeeding, or relegate herself to the stereotypical occupation.

The drawback to the lack of autonomy in these instances is what it takes away from the individual, as well as the society.[26] In short, being different in a relationally bounded social world with a strong familial ethos, especially where women are told in both overt and covert ways that they should be seen and not heard, means that a significant portion of the population is kept from living into its full potential. The impact of this state of affairs, which is often ignored, is that society as a whole is deprived of the full participation and contribution of half of its members.

The Double Bind of Mothering: Agency and Subjectivity

Women continue to grow girls into women like themselves. Mothering allows the cycle of "femaleness" to go on, because without a paradigm shift, there is always a tacit understanding of "femaleness" as tied to the roles of wife and mother. Marital life and motherhood are what elevate woman to status in African society. Bearing male children is further advantageous. It is not uncommon for an Akan man to be asked if his expectant wife gave birth to a human being or a girl. Women who know the injustice of the situation are often disempowered and unable to protest; they are in a double-bind situation.

Women's identity as mothers is constructed through forms of subjection and their subordination as women. At the same time, they gain their power or agency through their identities as mothers. Yet the fact is that while this power that both constructs and subordinates mothers, and severely limits their freedom, the tendency is, nevertheless, to compensate by investing *more* in motherhood. Thus, mothering takes on gigantic importance, especially in the sphere of limited freedom. As Chodorow points out, the mutuality of interpersonal relationality and the attendant affirmation of women's identities (which are denied them in their primary spousal relationships) are found in their dyadic relationships with their children.[27] This is especially true with daughters who grow up with an experience of sameness and continuity with their mothers. Boys, on the other hand, grow up with an early experience of continuity with mothers and later differentiate when gender difference is recognized.

In a culture in which what is named has its own existence as such, and is believed to be called into being once spoken, it is reprehensible that the source from which the pinnacle of creation emanates is not allowed full autonomous existence and is regaled with *anansesem* (male folktales) in the name of relationality to continue less-than-optimum existence. In a society in which many female children are currently named without reference to paternal identity (as typified in the giving of Western-style surnames), one would expect that females would be accorded the same rights as men, and that their autonomy would be affirmed rather than denigrated. This naming of a child thus from birth, sometimes even during gestation, suggests that though the individual belongs to a family and even a larger clan within a given tribe, that individual nevertheless came with its own destiny and path on this earth. Yet while naming gives autonomy and reality to substances, a woman does not have such autonomy in a substantive way. The traditional understanding of family somehow subsumes the individual that preceded the family and gave rise to it. Idealizing and sentimentalizing the family above the individual, without the necessary balance between common shared ends and the hopes and needs of the individual, almost always denies justice to some, usually the women. They are often encouraged to make sacrifices for the sake of the common shared ends, but ironically, they receive little if any of these goods, such as money, time, leisure, sometimes even necessary nurturance, and so forth. Often women are the ones who do without when the proverbial "not enough" shows up.

Reframing Autonomy: Toward a New Relationality in the African Context

All selves, male and female, possess a need for recognition and a need to understand the other, and these needs are compatible. This two-pronged need is created in the context of mother-child interactions and is satisfied in a mutually empathetic relationship. Right from birth, and especially in the first few years, both infants and mothers give and take in a way that not only contributes to the satisfaction of their needs as individuals but also affirms, as Virginia Held states, the "larger relational unit" they compose. Held further suggests that the maintenance of this "larger relational unit" then becomes a goal of the individual, and maturity is conceived not in terms of individual autonomy but in terms of competence in creating and sustaining relations of empathy and mutual intersubjectivity.[28]

As argued above, the creation and maintenance of this positively nurturing "larger relational unit" seems often to be a matter of appearance as the reality is that women are both the creators and sustainers of these units to their own intrapsychic and sometimes somatic detriment. Mothering fosters and perpetuates this phenomenon and its social repercussions, which produce conflictual responses in women who need to move away from the status quo. Attempts in counseling women who find themselves burned out by the demands on their time and resources in the name of the ethos of a collectivistic culture and the role of a "proper woman" do not show promise if the counselor begins to unravel the relational myth and introduces notions of autonomy. What is heard in such concepts of autonomy, especially when they come from Western trained counselors, is seen, at best, as foreign and inapplicable to their context. At worst, women fear that their significant others would judge such autonomy a corruption of all that they deem "good" and a disruption of their homes. I have already indicated above the double-bind situation that is produced for African women in navigating what seems to be a difficult terrain. Oduyoye uses a popular cultural game to illustrate this situation. In this traditional game played by girls, each steps to the mat in fetters. As the game unfolds, a "voice" asks participants how they are feeling and though they indicate that they are miserable, they chose to remain in the game. To the follow-up question addressed to each player, "Fatima, doesn't that hurt?" they respond "Sure! I am miserable." "Then pull it out," the "voice" comes back. But the girls playing the game say, "No, I may not do that. It is the practice of my father's town/It is the practice of my mother's town."[29] Therefore, how can African women be encouraged to hold on to life-giving aspects of the relational ethos that formed them, while jettisoning aspects that stymie them?

We do not change until we address our myths. These myths should be of our own telling and not what has been told *to* us or *about* us by others. It cannot be in this sense *anansesem* (folktales), though it can be *yankosem* (stories according to Nyame—our Creator). Nevertheless, the creator's story about us ought to coincide in a life-giving rather than death-dealing way with our self-stories, our personal myths. How do we encourage life-giving stories without being led back into a dualism of self and other that is antithetical to what it means to be a person in African perspective? For the African woman especially, the need for, movement toward, and maintenance of "homonomy" (harmonious coexistence of all created reality) is of primal importance. Since both intrapsychic and inter-personal harmony extends to encompass the spirit world, which can adversely impact earthly life if disrupted by conflict that may ensue with change, care must be taken in encouraging African women toward autonomy.

Evelyn Fox Keller's concept of "dynamic autonomy," which she contrasts with "static autonomy," is helpful in this context. For Keller, the notion of autonomy, which should probably be termed "static autonomy," is a concept that carries the notion of fierce competence and independence. On the other hand, the concept of dynamic autonomy is one that does not deny connectedness but understands itself as both related and differentiated from others at the same time. One is oneself in the world of others and related to them without loss of agency; one is also at home with oneself in equal measure; thus, one is in a world filled with "interacting and interpersonal agents" and cognizant of others "as subjects with whom one shares enough to allow for a recognition of their independent inter-ests and feelings—in short for a recognition of them as subjects."[30]

Yet one owns that the sense of dynamic autonomy requires a level of matu-rity and a willingness to "surrender" the self when needed.[31] In making the suggestion for a reframed autonomy, from a static concept of autonomy to a more dynamic autonomy, one might hopefully overcome resistance in women to claiming themselves and their voice and to "remyth." I am aware that there still remain risks of even a reframed autonomy in the African context for men and women alike, because it means that attention has first to be directed toward new concepts of masculinity and femininity in postcolonial Africa. Strict gender-role expectations in the past were the defining characteristics of people, and people saw themselves in relation to their roles. With the social changes taking place because of opportunities for equal education and voca-tion for women, many men especially are finding that they are unsure of their identity and role as husbands and fathers. Role confusion is leading to identity crises, which are affecting family life for many, but still there is the reluctance to embrace the necessary change that would forge new ways of being. For the religious, especially in Christian pastoral counseling, Scripture and theo-logical insights will offer the added impetus for overcoming the inertia about change.

Perichoresis: A Theological Map for Dynamic Autonomy in Relation

The foregoing discussion has framed a psychosocial basis for a return to the autonomous self, what I have called a dynamic autonomy so as not to lose the self, especially female selves in relationships. Here I adduce theological reasons to emphasize points earlier raised. Trinitarian life of the Godhead is the lynchpin to understanding how human relationality ought to function in light of creation in the image of God. It is on this foundation that we insist on the need for autonomy in spite of the understanding of the self as always being in relation. Keller's notion of dynamic autonomy has theological echoes, which in fact precede it because they stem from the inner life of God. Further, I propose that the autonomous self be given formal priority over the relational self based on the nature of the perichoretic life of the triune God, who exists as autonomous beings in relation without conflation and yet one.

A dynamic autonomy, which in practice is demonstrated by the perichoretic life of the Trinity in which each member of the Godhead is allowed full personhood and yet cooperates together in creating, redeeming, and sustaining with none dominating in their cooperative life, is the prototype of the life human creatures are enjoined to imitate. Thus, a self-story within the larger corporate story lives on. The story of Attanaa Nyonmo Greatfather/Greatmother, for instance, cannot be told without the story of the Son who confers parenthood, or the Spirit in whose power the Great Parent sends the Son. While the story of the whole can be mapped out, it is impossible not to delineate each person's story in the whole. Each allows the other the freedom of surrender and embrace in this perichoretic dance for the fulfillment of their life.

Conclusion

This chapter set out to unravel the relational myth that has been wrapped like a blanket around African people, but most specifically its female populace. In calling for an unraveling of the relational myth, I have suggested that it is for the betterment rather than the detriment of the corporate self that the myth is unraveled. In its place, a new myth can be rewoven from the cloth of "dynamic autonomy" in which the individual strands may stand out, rather than be muted, to display a richer tapestry of relationality that uplifts the essence of the corporate self. Since the call to spearhead this new relationality starts with women, the traditional custodians of relationships, I am aware of the moral quandary of the extra burden it places on already burdened women. The hope is that the sense of self and purpose derived from agency will allow women to establish the necessary boundaries within their relationships, and that this will gradually spill over into the larger family units and the society at large.

Pastoral Care for the 1.5 Generation

In-Between Space as the "New" Cultural Space

Sophia Park

The Virginia Tech shooting in April 2007 put the spotlight on Korean Americans. The perpetrator, Seung Hui Cho, a senior student, intentionally and indiscriminately shot students and professors, killing and wounding dozens, and then killed himself. Through this tragedy, realities and problems of families living in multiple cultures (culture of origin and Western culture) in the United States have come to light. These families, living on the margins, the outside of the dominant culture, have been brought into the center of attention, the inside of the dominant culture. Although they have been brought into the inside, they are still classified or labeled as outsiders. Who are they and what is their reality of life in America?

Many social descriptions of Seung Hui Cho have been made. At the time of this event the American media had classified Cho variously as a Korean, a Korean immigrant, and a Korean with a green card. On the other hand, the Korean media in Korea portrayed him as a 1.5 generation[1] of Korean American who is caught in between Korean and American cultures. There has been no consensus on understanding who the 1.5 generations are or where this group belongs in the social map of America. Who, then, are the 1.5 generation of Korean Americans? Where are they located in terms of cultural space?[2] And how do we provide pastoral care for them and their families?

My aim in this article is threefold. First, I want to explore the multicultural context of Korean American families, consisting of first, 1.5, and second generations. Second, how can pastoral care be effective and relevant for families simultaneously living in multiple cultural spaces? Third, how can I, as a 1.5-generation Korean American woman counselor, offer pastoral care? In this article, I explore the identity of the 1.5 generation not only in terms of characteristics but also from the perspective of their cultural location and space. I propose to rethink the space of the 1.5 generation as a "dynamic"[3] cultural space where both cultures, Korean and American, can come and interact. I extend the 1.5-generation space to pastoral care to demonstrate that this dynamic cultural space of pastoral care brings people who are on the *outside* and disconnected, remaining in their own personal space, into connection. We are not only bringing those from the outside into the inside but creating together a new dynamic space where there is no inside or outside, but only interactions and interrelations.

Multicultural Reality of Korean American Families

Before going further, we must first understand the multicultural context of Korean American families. In a typical Korean American family, members live in multicultural spaces. Even though family members live in the same physical place under one roof, they live in different cultural space. Language and cultural differences as well as inadequate awareness of each other's cultures prevent the necessary intercultural dialogue between parents and children as well as between Korean Americans and the larger American society. The result has been that while living in the midst of people, many are isolated because they are not in relationship with family nor with the outer society. They remain locked in their own space. How then do we provide care for families who are disconnected from each other? What is the relevant care for both the first-generation parents and their 1.5-generation children? How do we bring them into connection with each other and also with the larger society?

Most Korean American family members are divided into first generation, second generation, and/or the 1.5 generation. The division is not only based on generation gap within the same culture but also cultural gap between cultures. Even though these three categories have been widely used to identify the different groups within the Korean American people and families, corresponding definitions have varied slightly, especially on who exactly the 1.5 generation is.

The term *first generation* generally refers to the immigrants themselves, who have immigrated to America as adults. Often with an inadequate command of the spoken English language, they have a limited desire to assimilate into the Western culture. They want to preserve the way of Korean life and maintain their Korean values, beliefs, and traditions, including Korean language. They gravitate toward having relationships with other first-generation people and remain connected in the Korean immigrant society.

Second generation refers to the children of the first generation who have been born in the new country. They are not only born in America but are culturally Americanized. In contrast to their parents, their cultural propensity is to reject the way of Korean life and to accept the American way. Though their physical appearance is of Korean ethnicity, they are Americans who think with Western values and speak in the English language.

In between the first and second generation is the *1.5 generation*. The term *1.5 generation* was coined by Ruben Rumbaut, a sociology professor at the University of California at Irvine, to refer to the people who are *in between* cultures, a group whom Rumbaut has been studying since the 1960s. They are not children and not yet adults but old enough to speak and know the culture of their origin. However, because they have not yet been intellectually and socially formed, they have less difficulty adjusting to change than their first-generation parents.

Both Western and non-Western social theorists have made many attempts to define this large middle spectrum of the immigrant continuum. The widely accepted criterion for the definition has been "when or at what age one came to America," suggested by some to be anywhere between ages four to eighteen. However, one's age of arrival has not been proven to determine one's ability to integrate and assimilate well into both cultures. Some people have chosen to remain in the Korean immigrant community, limiting one's exposure to the dominant Western culture, thus remaining in the cultural space of the first generation. Therefore, rather than having one's age of arrival as a deciding factor, the term *1.5 generation* needs to be understood in terms of one's degree of knowledge and the command to navigate in both cultural systems. In this sense, because "Korean American" is a culture-oriented term, "1.5 generation" should also be understood from a cultural angle. In this article I propose to rethink the 1.5 generation from a cultural-spatial perspective (cultural space).

Often the 1.5 generation has been portrayed "negatively" as those who are caught in between Korean Eastern and American Western cultures with nowhere to stand. Unfortunately, this is a dilemma most Korean Americans experience, particularly the 1.5 generation; they are not quite American but not really Korean either. The reality is that they are considered and classified as *outsiders*, who are out of order from both the dominant Western and the Korean immigrant society. However, on the positive note, these persons are bilingual and bicultural. Being in between and in both the Korean and Western culture, they can function as a bridge, becoming a connecting point in the multicultural context of America.

Effects of Living in Multicultural Settings (Spaces)

First-generation parents and 1.5- or second-generation children live in different cultural spaces. In order to consider relevant ways to bring care to families living in multicultural spaces, it is necessary to know how the distinctive reality of having multicultural space affects relationships in Korean American families.

First, within the Korean American family, two cultural mores, values, and languages exist: one that the parents live by and enforce on the children; the other that children pick up in Western society. Korean family values of obedience, interdependence, and harmony are in direct competition with Western-based value systems, stressing individuality and autonomy taught in schools.[4] Conflicts are inevitable when such cultures, which are antagonistic in values, are present within the same living space, within the familial relationships.

For the first-generation parents, their assumptive values and the way of family life have been formed and firmly set in their Korean cultural upbringing, rooted in and shaped by Confucian teachings through thousands of years.[5] Family, in Confucian teachings, is considered to be the basic unit of human community.[6] As such, harmonious family relationships are believed to be crucial for a peaceful society. From this belief, Confucius put family harmony and loyalty, especially between parents and children, as the most important responsibility, even over social duties. Hierarchical social order with specific roles are believed to be the stabilizing force to maintain peace and harmony. Both the parents and the children have specific roles and responsibilities: parents owe their child care, moral formation, and an education necessary for success; children owe parents absolute loyalty, obedience, and respect. In addition, the primary responsibility for family harmony is laid on the children. The cause of any conflict between parents and children is believed to be in the latter's lack of respect. Whenever a conflict arises, it is the children's responsibility to seek reconciliation by unconditional apology. For a long period of time, this solution contributed to stable family structure at the children's expense.[7]

Education is important in Confucian values. The sole purpose of learning for Confucius was to promote virtuous actions and cultivate moral characters that would in turn produce peace and harmony in families and thus in societies.[8] Education is important to "put into practice the core values fostering a spirit of self-discipline, family solidarity, public morality and social responsibility."[9] Even though the rationale for education is different nowadays, the importance of education has nonetheless been passed down as one of the important Korean cultural values.

In the Korean American family, first-generation parents believe it to be their duty to provide well financially so the children are able to concentrate solely on learning. While parents try to fulfill their duty as a good parent, some working long hours, they expect their children to do the same: respect parents, obey their commands, and study hard. However, parents' expectation of their children's absolute obedience goes against what the children are taught in school and by the larger community: the Western-based value system stresses individuality and autonomy that are often in conflict with the Korean ways of family- and community-centeredness, interdependence, and harmony taught at home.[10] The combinations of different values and unfulfilled role expectations the parents and children have of each other lead to divides in relationships. First-generation parents entrenching themselves further into traditional beliefs create an insurmountable impasse. In addition, cultural expectations of the children to bear the responsibility of conflicts in silence disallow further engagement. However, when children protest and question their parents' "unfair" demands, their acts are seen as those of defiance and of "disloyalty." Both parents and children are left with feelings of betrayal, resentment, and anger. As a result, many children withdraw into their own personal space after repeatedly experiencing the futility of trying to reach into the cultural space of the parents.

Second, language is another barrier disconnecting Korean American families. First-generation parents come to America lacking a command of the English language, both understanding and speaking. Even though many do have a good grasp of the written word learned in school back home, learning to speak fluently as an adult is very difficult, if not impossible. Often cared for by mothers or grandparents, many children's first language is Korean. However, the children slowly lose their Korean language and cultural influence as they start school and make friends. Increasingly, as the children grow, English is spoken more often and becomes the dominant language. In communicating with parents, both are able to get by with each others' limited command of English and Korean. However, this disparity in language abilities does not permit parents and children to communicate emotional matters in a manner that requires more in-depth language skills. Thus, for many families, relationships remain hollow without a deep connection with each other.[11] Lacking language as a means for intimate connection, parents and children are unable to make a way into each other's spaces.

Third, relatively few Korean immigrants are salaried employees in large corporations.[12] Rather, they are drawn toward small businesses such as dry cleaners, grocery stores, and liquor stores. Because the nature of their businesses requires long hours of work, often more than twelve-hour days, including weekends and holidays, many Korean parents and children do not have much time to spend together. Not being in the same physical space, gradual loss of common language, and increasingly diverging cultural values make connecting at a deeper level progressively more difficult. Family members are limited in their ability to enter freely into the space of the other; as a result, each individual remains in his or her own personal space.

This is a phenomenon that can be seen in many Korean American families, including the family of Seung Hui Cho. Cho's parents worked long hours at their dry cleaning business. They worked hard to support their two children financially, fulfilling their duty as parents. Both of their children were good students academically, fulfilling their duty as children. Because of this, the parents did not foresee serious problems with their son, Seung Hui, nor with his sister, a Princeton graduate. Rather, they were proud of their achievements. Unfortunately, Seung Hui's parents were not in touch with their son's troubled inner world. His sister, who was an employee at the U.S. state department, said after the tragic incident that she did not know "who this person" was. This person was not the brother she knew. She was not aware of Cho's disturbed inner world either. She was a "valued" member of society, contributing to the welfare of the nation, being in the dominant societal space yet outside of her brother's space.

The parents remained in their own space, working very hard, secluded from society, remaining outside of the dominant society and apparently outside of the Korean immigrant society as well.

Cho, too, remained outside of the systems, both the dominant society and the Korean immigrant society. Cho suffered from being taunted, rejected, and labeled as a "loner" since age eight when he came to America. Neither did Cho belong in his parents' Korean immigrant culture with the rift of cultural differences becoming wider in their relationship. He was not welcomed into the spaces of either. He may have felt that there was no space to stand in society. Cho probably felt he was an "outsider" in every sense of the word. Rather than finding ways to connect and other possibilities of relating, Cho seems to have chosen to withdraw into his own personal space. Whether he wanted to be in isolation, or was in it as a result of being rejected, he was disconnected from society. He also was disconnected from his family. Cho chose to remain in his own personal space, creating his own inner world, that is, the only space over which he had control. In his space, Cho was able to control who came in and out, who was an "insider" and an "outsider." Unfortunately, he chose to close his space to others, not allowing entrance. Inside his own space, he seems to have become a powerful figure, having internal control. Cho was repeating the behavior of exclusion inside his own space, becoming the exact figure of what he "hated" in the dominant cultures. As he was reducing the space for others, Cho was opening up his own space, enlarging it through engaging his own ideas and fantasies. He had a relationship with his ideologies, actively engaging his own fantasies, and creating enemies within his space. Unfortunately, Cho decided to enter into the actual space of others, where he was not welcomed, to take revenge on his own internal enemies. Cho's enlarged space, created from being unwelcome and unable to enter relational spaces of others, became the source for his violent actions that destroyed him and others.

It is important to point out that Cho's story is an extreme case and should not be generalized. And yet it makes one think about what can happen when people are disconnected from society and from families, remaining in motionless space.[13] Living in detached spaces is a reality for many Korean American families and individuals, split by cultural and language barriers. The space Cho created was an isolated, closed, violent, motionless, and "folded" space[14] in the in-between space of societies. How can we reach into the "in-between" space of the 1.5 generation and their families who are disjointed and out of the system because of different cultural understandings and lack of common language? How do we bring isolated individuals who are outside of the system into connection with each other, back into relationships? Is there hope for the 1.5 generation and their families?

Not all members of the 1.5 generation living in multicultures stay caught "in between" cultural spaces, but function as a *connecting point* in the multicultural context of America and a junction where all sorts of people can meet. Unlike Cho, his sister, Sun Kyung,[15] was connected with other people.[16] She had relationships with Korean Americans through an on-campus Bible study group. She also had relationships with others in the dominant Western culture. Sun Kyung received an Ivy League education and was employed by a government agency. She did not remain within her parents' cultural space nor only in the dominant cultural space but was actively engaged in both. Rather than remaining in her personal space or her comfort zone, she was able to move beyond the "in-between" space of the 1.5 generation and engage in the space of other cultures.

Through the Cho sibling narrative, we have seen the divergent path to which the space of the 1.5 generation, or the "in-between space," can lead: one that is life destroying, the other that is life enhancing. Obviously many factors, such as personality and gender differences, may have influenced the outcome of the lives of the Cho siblings. However, Sun Kyung's story can attest to the hope and potentiality imbedded in her identity, and thus the "in-between" space of the 1.5 generation.

According to the Gospel of Luke, during Jesus' crucifixion, two men accused of theft were also nailed on the cross. For the two men, the space on the cross was the "in-between" space; a juncture between life and death, between salvation and destruction. One of the criminals who hung with Jesus hurled abuse at him, saying, "Are you not the Christ? Save yourself and us!" (Luke 23:39). But the other answered, rebuking him, "Do you not even fear God, since you are under the same sentence of condemnation? And we indeed justly, for we are receiving what we deserve for our deeds; but this man has done nothing wrong" (23:41). And this other criminal said, "Jesus, remember me when you come in your kingdom!" (23:42). And Jesus said to him, "Truly I say to you, today you shall be with me in Paradise" (23:43). The space on the cross, between life and death, became an "in-between" space where one criminal—who refused to repent by engaging his own space as a sinner, and who closed off others—brought eternal destruction to himself. The other criminal engaged his own location by acknowledging his sin and reaching out to another—namely, Jesus—and in so doing ended up bringing life to himself. Two criminals located at a juncture, in the in-between space, ended up going two different directions: one that destroyed life and the other that gave life. A couple of observations need to be noted. First, Jesus is placed outside of the system and is located at the shadow of death where Jesus meets two criminals. Second, Jesus is portrayed as in-between space and as a juncture where two criminals can cross over and attain, through connection, salvation. Yet one criminal is willing to connect with Jesus and the other refuses to be connected with Jesus. As a result the two had opposite outcomes: one, new life, and the other, destruction.

Pastoral Care as Understanding of Cultural Reality and Location

Even within one Korean American family, members live in different cultural spaces. Societal structures and inadequate awareness as well as language and cultural differences prevent the necessary intercultural dialogue between parents and children as well as between Korean Americans and the larger American society. The result is that while living in the midst of people, many are isolated, not being in relationship within the family or with the outer society, remaining locked in their own space.

In order to address what is relevant care for families living in multicultural spaces, it is essential that the counselor understand the cultural reality of the 1.5 generation. It is important to understand not only *who* they are but also *where* they are, that is, their social location. In addition, we will also consider *why* they end up in the "in-between" space and the resulting effects of remaining in it.

The 1.5 generation is squeezed in between the American and the Korean culture. The space where the 1.5 generation ends up is the *in-between* space of the two cultures: Korean immigrant and dominant Western. "In-between" space is the interstitial space that is between cultures. However, it is also marginal space in the sense that people in this space are not included in the dominant cultural systems. The late Jung Young Lee, in his autobiographical book *Marginality*, also has termed this space as "marginal," adapting the terms of "marginality" and "marginal person" as defined by prominent Western sociologists[17] who focused on racial and cultural determinants to refer to minority groups, including the 1.5 generation.

By being born into a life of two or more cultures, the unique social environment of the 1.5 generation forms different characteristics and behaviors in its people. Heinz Kohut, the founder of self psychology, indicates how living in two cultures diminishes the formation of self in ways fundamentally different from how the self is formed for those living in one culture. His theory of self focuses on the formation, growth, and interruptions of the self. The self or self-concept is continually formed and reformed through continual interactions between self and what Kohut terms *self-objects,* which are those persons or objects that are experienced as part of the self or that are used in the service of the self to provide a function for the self.[18] For the healthy self to form, according to Kohut, empathic understanding as well as healthy mirroring is crucial.

Kohut's assumption, however, is constructed upon a hypothesis when only one cultural setting is present. Adding a bicultural factor challenges this assumption. Adding another culture to the mix "de-forms" the possibility of a strong and healthy self, which is characterized by the ability to tolerate loss, failure, and disappointments without breaking down under pressure. According to Kohut, a healthy individual has the capacity to be attuned with the other, maintain relationships, and also enjoy them. Living in a bicultural setting provides different cultural self-objects that mirror back different values, priorities, and ways of life. Inconsistent mirroring and differently valued reinforcements disturb the formation and growth of self. Since the consequence of living in between cultures is that bicultural settings cannot provide a needed consistency to form and nurture a strong sense of self, the most critical symptom of living in between cultures is the development of an inconsistent identity. This is similar to Kohut's idea of the weakened self, which is the opposite of his idea of a healthy self.

For those of the 1.5 generation who live in more than one culture and have formed a particular way of being in the world, rather than having their distinctive characteristics and ways of being acknowledged and affirmed, their differences are continually pointed out by their Korean parents and Western friends. These criticisms and nonacceptance become the basis for further exclusion, pushing this generation into an outer social space.

People in power within dominant societies dictate who can be an "insider" and who is an "outsider" based on the characteristics that are acceptable to them. Moreover, they also dictate the social locations where groups of people, especially minorities, are to be placed.[19] Korean Americans, even the second generations, cannot embody the American identity because "fundamental, structural discrimination and racial prejudice are too great to transcend."[20] Thus, 1.5 generations (and other minorities) remain in the marginal space because they feel "psychologically restricted and emotionally imprisoned."[21]

Then why does the 1.5 generation remain in this marginal space? One major reason is that as a group, they lack the common collective stories that can provide interpretations for identity. Having been left out of the dominant culture's discourse and without their own contextual analysis and adequate language, the 1.5 generation has not had the foundations to start to describe their plight. Furthermore, because there have not been adequate theories of what "normalcy" and "health" would be for people living in between two cultures, their idiosyncratic ways of life have been deemed "unhealthy," even "pathological." It is important for this population, as well as the dominant society, to know that their experiences are adaptive, not pathological, and that these are part of the larger experience of the 1.5 generation.

This leads to the question, "What are the effects of remaining in the marginal space of society?" To say that one's identity is negatively affected seems to be stating the obvious. To be "in between worlds," on the margins of society, according to Lee, means to be fully in neither. Experiencing alienation from both cultures impairs one's sense of self. One feels "invisible." One feels as if one is living within neither perspective of two (or more) dominant worlds that impinge upon him or her. This can bring a sense of dehumanization.[22] Consequently, the ill-formed self and its effects of low self-esteem foster further self-alienation and self-marginalization. Being in the midst of this alienation and loneliness is debilitating, preventing one from seeing or imagining the possibilities of another form of life. Thus, a limited horizon is created by remaining inside one's own boundaries.

When there is no awareness of words to define the self, you can only accept what has been defined for you, internalizing the term *marginal* and applying it to your own character. Being told what you are, where you belong, and why you belong in that space restricts the boundaries of your thoughts and, more importantly, imagined possibilities of the self. It puts you in a motionless space. The message communicated is that you are insignificant. Being confined to a bound static space leads one to lose the potentiality of having his or her future unfold in the journey of life. Thus, one's life remains folded, pressed, compacted, unable to open out into numerous potential directions and in multiple ways. The multiplicity and potentiality of the self cannot be realized.

The parable of the mustard seed as found in the Gospel of Matthew can be a powerful analogy to show potential transformation within the 1.5 generation. The seed is seen as small and irrelevant. It is not useful in and of itself. However, the seemingly insignificant seed possesses the possibilities and potentialities to grow, to branch out, to produce fruit, and to bring forth new life that will carry on to the next generation. Within the small and insignificant seed, there is potential space that can unfold to multiple spaces to produce life for self and for others. The 1.5 generation, like the seed, is constantly seen by both the dominant Western and the Korean immigrant culture as insignificant. The 1.5 generation has not been given the opportunity to unfold, but is placed on the margins of dominant cultures and "controlled" to remain as seeds.

In-Between Space as Potential Space

As many have tried and failed, the 1.5 generation cannot conform to become like those in the dominant culture or to enter the dominant cultural space and be unconditionally accepted. The place where the 1.5 generations will find healing and nurturing is where they are standing now, in the in-between space, in the margins of the dominant cultures. I am contending that the 1.5 generation also has its own cultural space, in between cultures, that needs to be claimed. This is the space where this generation's creative potential can work to bridge and transform cultures. The in-between space has the potential to become *in-both* and, furthermore, *in-beyond*[23] space where cultures merge and connect often-antagonistic societies, serving as the catalyst in creating a "beautiful mosaic of colorful people in this nation."[24]

The potential of the 1.5 generation as the new cultural space starts in the in-between, outside the space of the dominant cultures. Awareness of pain, suffering, discrimination, and alienation of others can escape those who live in monocultures where the particularities of their stories have been taken for granted. Their cultural and social systems are fixed, and when a person fits, those systems become "normal" for the person. However, for the 1.5 generation that has been located on the outside of the dominant systems—unable to fit into the fixed, prescribed, dominant ways of being—they are able to objectively look into the central system. Moreover, they are able to look into the experiences of people living in other cultural spaces. Empathy that is needed to connect, to relate, and to reconnect with different others is possible for the 1.5 generation. Their self-understandings, which have been formed through experiences of being on the outside, have made it possible for them to appreciate and relate to others who are different, transcending fixed social and cultural systems. Where people living in monocultures know of one story, the dominant one, the 1.5 generation has multiple stories that give its members reference for understanding, connecting, and relating with different others. With their multiple stories and their ability to understand many different narratives, those who belong to the 1.5 generation can provide the space that can transcend languages, cultures, and values to connect people and bridge societies.

As opposed to the dominant cultural space as being fixed and static, where there are clear values, ways of being, and boundaries of who is "in" and who is "out," the new cultural space of the 1.5 generation is dynamic, full of movement and change. It is not a fixed and closed space but an open space where anyone can come in, connect, and be transformed. There is no longer "insider" or "outsider." There is no membership requirement and everyone can come and belong. In this space, there is not only movement of many people but also movement of growth within each individual. No one is considered insignificant by others. This space allows individuals to open up the spaces within themselves that were folded, pressed, and compacted. They can extend their shoots and branches out of their own life as seeds and live lives of potential—emotional, intellectual, and spiritual. The new cultural space of the 1.5 generation is a potential fertile ground where transformations can happen.

In-Between Space as Connecting Space, Creating New Dynamic Space

The space of the 1.5 generation is a dynamic one where both cultures, Korean and American, can come and interact. As a 1.5-generation Korean American pastoral counselor, and a woman out of order in all the dominant cultures of which I am a part, I can function as a juncture or a connecting point, providing space where first-generation mothers and second-generation children can cross over into each other's space. As my feet are both in the Korean and American society, I was and am still seen as both an outsider and an insider who can connect others, creating together a new dynamic space where there is no inside or outside. In this sense, a pastoral office can be described or should function as a new, dynamic cultural safe space.

The dynamic cultural space of pastoral care brings people who are on the outside, disconnected and isolated, into connection; they are changed by the encounter of reciprocal relations. Pastoral counselors not only bring those from the outside in, but also create together a new dynamic space where there is no inside or outside, but rather interactions and interrelations.

People come to counseling because their relationships have been disconnected. Counseling entails reconnecting them back with people and places who give meaning to their lives. In a sense, the pastoral counselor is like the 1.5 generation, positioned in between the counselee and her world, to bring creative energy into the counseling room to empower and bring connection and healing into the counselee's life. The counselor has to be in both worlds, able to see from the perspective of the counselee but also from the outside. Furthermore, the counselor moves together with the counselee to the beyond, a new dynamic space, to find transformation. In this sense, pastoral counselors are like the 1.5 generation who can see from both inside out and outside in.

Pastoral Care as Going Outside of the System Boundary: Taking Risks, Creating Change

Jesus was a member of the 1.5 generation. Jesus came to the world, became a human, dwelled among people (John 1:14), and moved "in between" God and humankind. Yet he was both divine and human (Phil. 2:6-7; Rom. 1:3-4). Jesus was both insider and outsider. Jesus came to the outside to humans, to forgive sins and offer salvation. Salvation began from the outside and in between. A new dynamic space was created from the outside and in between.

The central power system during Jesus' time was the Jerusalem Temple.[25] The religious leaders exercised power by categorizing people as a means to maintain order. According to the purity rules,[26] the religious leaders decided who was clean and who was unclean, who could enter the Temple grounds and who had to leave. Women, the poor, the Samaritans, and the sick were forced to stay outside of the Temple and holy community. The hierarchical system of the Jerusalem Temple had a clear boundary, and the Temple authorities controlled and monitored the daily activity. The social system of Jerusalem was fixed and static.

Jesus was not of the system; he was an outsider. However, Jesus often overturned the system of purity through his ministry. He ate with tax collectors,[27] healed the sick on the Sabbath (Luke 6:9-10), and associated with a Samaritan, a woman no less. He came to save the lost (Luke 19:10) and those who sat in darkness and in the shadow of death (Luke 1:79). In other words, he went where the outsiders were and transformed their lives. Jesus forgave sins and brought salvation from the outside. The lives of many who struggled in the margins of society, were changed. Jesus brought people who were out of the system back into relationships by connecting with them. Jesus challenged fixed dominant systems, creating a new dynamic ministry. Jesus, who was not of the Temple system, challenged and changed that system from the outside by proclaiming salvation in Galilee, outside of the Temple and the city of Jerusalem. Jesus brought in a creative power, a new dynamic space, from the outside and was able to confront fixed structures.

Just as God and Jesus are depicted as connectors who go outside of the system to bring back into relationship those who are disconnected, pastoral counselors should also bring into connection those who feel caught in between,[28] isolated in their own motionless space. Pastoral care should become a new, dynamic cultural space where there are no longer insiders and outsiders but interactive relationships.

Counseling Grace

A Pastoral Theology

Elizabeth Johnson Walker

Pastoral theology is regarded as the science of the care of souls. A clearer understanding of grace as a source for the care of souls emerged from my experience working with African American women who present in therapy for individual counseling and who conceptualize the experience of a crisis of disconnection. These African American women are suffering from a sense of falling apart in relationships with self, God, and others; for them, Christian grace is a norm of healing. Hope is often conceptualized and imagined as experiencing reconnection with self, God, and others through spiritual healing sought in therapy.

The women represent persons who are single heads of household, have at least a secondary educational degree, hold professional and service roles of employment, are divorced, and, in most cases, are caregivers of previous generations. Their feelings manifest in the counseling relationship as a crisis of being dynamically divided and estranged from self, God, and others. It is important to understand and conceptualize the psychological adaptation tasks of African American women for appropriate assessment and treatment in Western culture.

Cultural racism deprives some developing African American women the opportunity to experience adequate empathic relationships. One reason for inadequate empathic relationships in Western culture is the historical, cultural, and social location of African American women, which limits their access to such empathy. I propose to correlate the phenomena of normative narcissistic development (conceptualized by Heinz Kohut[1] and which I explicate in my dissertation for the purposes of a pastoral counseling theory of grace) and the existential experience of disconnection with the concepts of empathy and grace.

Conceptualization

The nature, purpose, and meaning of a pastoral counseling theory of grace has been conceptualized in my dissertation, "A Model of Counseling with Some African American Women Clients,"[2] where I use practical correlation to illustrate African American women's dilemma of falling apart and feeling disconnected in relationships in various contexts. The method of practical correlation is an interdisciplinary and ecumenical dialogue that enables intervention strategies for pastoral counseling. In addition, this method, supported by a womanist theological response, provides a locus for engaging a conversation with theological and theoretical disciplines to construct a pastoral counseling theology.

The Pastoral Counselor

It is important that the pastoral counselor's professional preparation includes developing the capacity to respond to the nature of the client's suffering with empathy. The pastoral counselor must be mature, having undergone extensive experiences of self to be aware of the use of self and empathy in the counseling relationship. The role of empathy is to form a psychological perspective regarding how the self experiences meaning and value in pastoral counseling. Empathy is the basis of care and informs the therapeutic responses to the client's condition and the counseling engagement. The pastoral counselor's engagement is broad in scope, especially where the counselor has the capacity for sustained empathic attendance to the particular harm rendered in relationships to African American women in this culture. There must be the capacity to take seriously—that is, to understand, interpret, and communicate—that awareness to African American women as they bring their experiences and capacities to the therapeutic relationship.

Stages of Grace

There are three stages of pastoral counseling grace in which the self structures meaning and healing. The stages are (1) discernment; (2) interpretation; and (3) reconnection. The stages are interrelated, interdependent, and inseparable. The condition of the person initiating the pastoral counseling relationship is assessed to be disconnected in relationships.

The *discernment* stage has two movements: estrangement analysis and the assessment of the social nature of the self's estrangement. Estrangement analysis in the pastoral counseling relationship is concerned with how the client understands and conceptualizes her condition and what she understands about her inner world. The social nature of the self's estrangement is concerned with the client's capacity for self-curiosity about her inner world and her ability to interpret meaning for herself.

The *interpretation* stage involves the pastoral counselor's assessment of three ongoing interpretive dimensions: the pastoral counselor's interpretation of the client's experiences of her inner world; the client's experience of optimal frustration and self-acceptance; and the client's internalization of the self-worth functions of the counselor's attitude. The pastoral counselor, as much as is possible, immerses herself in the experiences of the client in order to help the client to understand her personal and historical experiences and how those experiences have been shaped in regard to her gender, class, race, and social location in this society.

The third stage is the dimension of *reconnection* when the client feels the goal of therapy has been reached. At the reconnection stage the client exhibits faith in her capacity to participate in her community with a sense of connection with her own goals and future aspirations, with others, and with her sense of self as spiritual. The hoped-for good outcome of therapy is to experience healing or reconnection through a process of grace. Grace is accessed using the mediums of reason, imagination, and revelation in an empathic pastoral counseling relationship. Grace, for the clients in this article, represents a sense of spiritual connection that assists the clients in locating themselves in relationships. The pastoral counselor's primary role is empathy, understanding, and interpretation of the client's experience. While the pastoral counselor is essential to the healing process, the agency of healing is understood as the manifestation of the activity of the mystery of God and identified as an activity evoked by Christian grace that grounds the client in relationships of worth and value.

The Variables

The case studies I offer here involve three representative African American women. The participants in the project were middle-class, Christian, divorced, heads of households, ranging in age from twenty-seven to seventy-two. They hold advanced academic degrees, have professional employment status, and, in most cases, are primary caregivers of three generations. They place high value on family of origin and church affiliation. The African American women share both the ancient African heritage and the American legacy of slavery with the destructive implications for acculturation in Western culture. Their collective faith stories give evidence to a firm belief that spirituality is an important source for discerning meaning and healing in relationships.

The case studies also represent persons who have sought counseling on at least two occasions with psychotherapists, pastoral counselors, pastors, and/or close friends. At a time of crisis, these women initiated pastoral counseling with an African American woman pastoral counselor whom they felt confident could help them precisely because of the counselor's gender, race, social, and cultural location in this society. Their sense was that the counselor could understand their suffering as spiritual and assist them in their personal inquiries. The women exhibited self-empathy in their desire to care for themselves in a particular way by choosing a particular counseling relationship. They self-analyzed their condition as a spiritual crisis, evidenced by a sense of disconnect from self, God, and others.

The Analysis

Brenda

Brenda is a forty-five-year-old woman. She is a teacher in the public-school system. Brenda is the second of five children, divorced, has one child in college, and cares for her aging parents. Brenda came to therapy because she was depressed and had difficulty with relationships. She stated, "I have it all to do, and there is no one to care about me." Brenda explained that she felt she had spent a lifetime supporting others at the expense of nurturing or even getting to know her own self. She added that she even felt distant from God and wondered if she ever really connected with her spirituality in a way that was not colored by her investments in others. Her goal for therapy was to find herself and to become connected in meaningful ways. It was her stated goal that she felt she wanted to develop the capacity to use the empathic pastoral counseling relationship facilitated by the therapist as a model for developing spiritual relationships beyond the counseling session. Her experience in counseling was described as very similar to the kind of relationship that would help her feel connected in relationships with herself and others.

Early in the counseling relationship a sense of fragile self surfaced. Brenda expressed that she felt her sense of self was related to a negative self-image and low self-esteem. Brenda attributed her experiences of her self, in part, to family-of-origin roles, messages, and expectations that she often experienced as non-empathic. In her own awareness she felt that her historical, cultural, and social location in this society tended to reinforce destructive familial images of herself in relationships. This self-exploration was a lengthy process for Brenda, but a time in which she began to see the counseling relationship as a model of a connected relationship. This insight was crucial to her potential to move forward into the subsequent stages.

Juanita

Juanita is a forty-four-year-old woman. Juanita is the oldest of five children, a widow, and the mother of one adult child who lives outside the home. Juanita's only sister died at a young age. Her brother died from complications of cancer. Her parents are well advanced in age and are needy. Juanita lives alone and describes herself as the primary caregiver for family and extended family, and as having no friends. Relationships with family members are close. Church life is important, but like other relationships, does not sustain her in ways she expected.

Juanita describes her life as fulfilling, having accomplished more than she hoped for, but sad because she somehow missed getting to know her own self, "like someone asleep, or in another person's dream." Juanita reports that she had somehow missed the messages from her family that she should be curious about her own self and develop a sense of self-awareness and self-appreciation. When considering counseling, she surmised that she wanted to sit with an African American woman pastoral counselor who might have a sense of the importance of having been invited to navigate a personal spiritual crisis, with another African American woman, in an environment where, among personal difficulties, the pain of cultural oppression must be reckoned with as well. Angry and disappointed with the "superwoman" role she adopted, she concluded that the false images of being able to sacrifice herself were just that—false. Early in the pastoral counseling relationship she discovered that the woman who does it all carries a burden of never quite doing enough and being objectified. Exploring these concerns helped Juanita to know that she needed to develop the capacity to care for herself. She surmised that her problem was spiritual.

Her experiences in therapy were described as an experience of being awake and spiritually alive. The purpose for therapy was her desire to reconnect in relationships by reconnecting with her spirituality. Her goal for therapy became to experience and engage the sense of awakened reality in her various contexts beyond the therapy room. She likened her forty-five minutes of therapy to the hymn "Amazing Grace"[3]—particularly the stanza "I was lost, but now I am found/I was blind, but now I see"—in relationship to her increasing self-awareness of her experiences of her inner world. The empathic therapeutic relationship helped Juanita feel a sense of spiritual connection to the pastoral counseling relationship and provided her with the expectation that she could develop the sense of connection with others.

Susie

Susie is a sixty-year-old African American woman. She is the second eldest of seven. Her father, oldest brother, and younger sister have died from complications of cancer in recent years. Relationships with siblings are both close and conflictual. She reports special closeness with the deceased siblings, as well as close relationships with her mother and deceased father. Susie's parents divorced when she was ten years old. There was a lapse in the relationship with her father when her parents divorced. The relationship with her father resumed when Susie was in her late forties, and she describes that as very meaningful.

Susie entered an arranged marriage at the age of twenty. She married a soldier and traveled with him and their children until he retired. She divorced her husband after his retirement. Susie describes herself as a dutiful child and woman. Prior to therapy, Susie experienced a heart attack and the break-up of a significant relationship. These events caused Susie to come to know herself in a crisis where she experienced herself to be out of touch and far away from the source and strength of her life, God. She reports that she knew she was out of touch because she did not feel her spirituality, which had functioned to ground her in her value systems that guided her relationships in the past. Without that sense of God's presence, and suspecting that she may have psychological malfunction, Susie sought pastoral counseling. She eventually determined she wanted to sit with a woman pastoral counselor who may know something about a spiritual crisis and might be able to help Susie rediscover sources that would help her make sense of her faith and her spirituality and thereby facilitate her in relationships.

Susie's experiences in the discernment stage, where the counselor's relationship patterns of attentive listening and attending to her experiences and meaning of her inner world of reality, evoked Susie's own self-curiosity about the social nature of her condition, and enabled her to interpret meaning for herself. The persona of the dutiful self camouflaged a fragile sense of self that emerged during counseling. The fragile sense of self was a result of instances during development where Susie received messages of her flawed self from her environment.

These three vignettes describe a condition that the three representative clients experience in common, that is, the experience of feeling disconnected in relationships, resulting from pervasive familial and environmental lack of empathy. Pervasive lack of empathy in the multiple systems of relationships for these women failed to strengthen their sense of self. Family-of-origin roles and rules influenced by powerful and destructive cultural messages reinforced their defenses to resist anxiety and move the self toward adaptive behaviors to survive in this society. Adaptive behaviors often manifest in unrealistic and flawed expectations for the client about the self in relation, a perpetuation of a lack of self-empathy, and consequently the crisis of a sense of disconnection to self and others in relationship.

The Process of Discernment: Stage One

As noted above, the discernment stage of pastoral counseling is comprised of two movements: estrangement analysis and the assessment of the social nature of the self's estrangement. The pastoral counselor assesses the client's understanding and experience of the sense of a crisis of disconnection in relationships. The pastoral counselor assesses the client's cognition and understanding of her inner world, how her relationships are related to her inner world, and the client's own curiosity to discern the relationship between her inner world and her relationships.

In the discernment stage of pastoral counseling the client needs to experience acceptance, affirmation, understanding, attention, and empathy to herself. This includes her historical, social, cultural, and spiritual dimensions. The condition of the client that emerges is that of feeling disconnected from self and others in a dynamic way as a consequence of internal distorted images of the self and the self's relationships.

In the first case study Brenda felt alone and disconnected in her sense of community and from a sense of herself in important relationships. She felt at a loss to identify internal and external resources in her life that would allow her to engage meaningfully with the painful self-images that were given to her. She suspected that there was a way to shed light on resources—internal and external—that would enable her to participate in interpreting her reality. In this stage of pastoral counseling Brenda gradually began consciously and unconsciously to gain self-value and self-empathy in the pastoral counseling relationship. Memories emerged of self-value experiences during childhood that she had forgotten. She began to realize that her inner world of meaning and her responses to others seemed to reenact continuously some of her childhood experiences in relationships, and that those reenacted feelings tended to form her understanding of current relationships. Brenda attributed her response to the empathic pastoral counseling relationship as the doorway to her memories and to her self. The function of the pastoral counseling relationship facilitated Brenda's ability to utilize therapy as she became curious about herself. Curiosity indicates the possibility to describe and engage definitions of self-affirmation and self-acceptance. Pastoral counselors conceptualize it as the courage to manifest faith in the self's capacity to exist and discern meaning in community. Brenda eventually described her pastoral counseling session as an encounter with God. She reported that she likened her time in therapy to the Christian hymn "Amazing Grace," which was written by a one-time slave owner.

The activation and mobilization of transferences for Brenda, Juanita, and Susie represent the precursors for the experience of grace in the pastoral counseling relationship. The first stage of pastoral counseling, estrangement analysis, the process of grace is experienced in two phases in the counseling relationship. The exploration of the inner world of the client in light of her social, cultural, and spiritual concerns helps to assess the social nature of the self's disconnection in relationships and the capacity of the client to experience self-curiosity and self-value. The exploration of the inner world of the client also allows the client to gain access to the empathic therapeutic pastoral counseling relationship that assesses and discerns the nature of the client's feeling of disconnection in relationship.

Discernment of Faith

The pastoral counseling relationship becomes a healthy experience of transference and one in which hope and trust can emerge. These facilitate the client's capacity to access her own resources, which will later be apprehended by grace. The attitude and empathic responses of the pastoral counselor supports the process. The pastoral counselor listens deeply, witnesses, attends to the client's experience, discerns, and assesses the hope and trust of the client in therapy. Brenda connected her experience of the therapeutic relationship with God's good will for her in the therapy session and in other relationships. She experienced this understanding of her therapy relationship with her capacity to use her faith as a door to get connected to her spirituality. Her spirituality helped her to interpret meaning and value in relationships.

Brenda's and the pastoral counselor's inquiry into faith patterns for interpreting meaning and value is what makes the pastoral counseling process pastoral. The inquiry enables the client and the counselor to notice and discern the truth for the client. The truth for the client points to the client's center of value and meaning. The inquiry facilitates the potential for Brenda to experience what is most important for her, her faith.

Regardless of the client's faith, the first stage of pastoral counseling is characterized by the discernment of faith. The discernment of faith is manifest in counseling in part by an openness of the client and the counselor to having curiosity about the client's truth; the attitude and the expectation of the client and pastoral counselor; and the client's capacity to access her own resources for healing. An open attitude of faith helps the client and the counselor to assess the social nature of the self's disconnection in relationships.

The Social Nature of the Self's Disconnection

The persons in this chapter described their sense of disconnection to be related to the personal, social, and spiritual dimensions. Disconnection was pervasive and plunged them into a crisis in all of their relationships. They indicated that they believed that their faith was a resource that could help them through their suffering and to more helpful relationships. They also indicated they believed that exploring their concerns with a pastoral counselor would help them understand how to be in relationship with themselves and others. Discernment (coming to know self in relationship to others) and faith (trusting in another) in the counseling relationship helps the client conceptualize her own self-understanding in significant relationships. This observation is based upon the approach that the client has the capacity to participate in the counseling relationship to discern and interpret meaning or truth for her self in an empathic relationship. The length of time spent in the first stage of pastoral counseling is related to the capacities of the client.

In the first stage these women explored images that helped shape their self-understanding and self-experiencing. Juanita came to know that the limitations and disconnections she felt were related to gender and role assignments she was given by her family and her culture. Juanita's faith helped her to recover the capacity to validate herself, thereby gaining permission from her self to challenge some self-images that were painful and to privilege more helpful images from her familial and cultural resources. Brenda accessed images from her faith tradition that helped her feel connected spiritually, particularly biblical stories where women seemed to find ways to sustain relationships, get their needs met, and be in a leadership role of ministry. The New Testament story of the character of Lydia and her aunt helped her recover experiences of empathy in her youth. Susie interpreted her tendency to be dutiful as a childhood response to relationships that implied little power and granted no responsibility to participate in developing and sustaining relationship. She understood the childhood tendency to be dutiful until her dad came back home. Assessing and interpreting her own capacity to find ways to transform her relationships, Susie moved toward increasing her own sense of agency in relationship with herself and others.

In the discernment stage the client has the potential to restructure meaning by coming to recognize the sources of disconnection and coming to know the sources of connection and reconnection. For the purposes of this theory, discernment of faith moves the counseling relationship toward grace for those clients who experience empathy as analogous to grace. In order to approach the dimensions of personal and social experience in a crisis of disconnection that some African American women bring into the therapeutic relationship, the attitude and approach of the therapy must be characterized with empathic engagement.

The Process of Interpretation: Stage Two

The second stage of a pastoral counseling theory of grace involves generative interpretation. Generative interpretation is the pastoral counselor's introduction of the client to herself which helps the client to foster new meaning and value. The client begins to understand ways to preserve and express her inner world. She notices her capacity to be able to make a decision about the meanings given to her about her self and others. She recognizes resources to help her come to terms with meaning for her self, an awareness of alternative self-images. Three things occur: (1) the inner world is illuminated as being composed of disconnected and connected relationship images that contribute to understanding of meaning and value; (2) the hopelessness and powerlessness in the social and personal dimensions of self-experiences are recognized as being consequences of distorted perceptions and interpretations from internalized conscious and unconscious familial and cultural messages; (3) the empathic pastoral counseling relationship is received and facilitates restructuring.

The interpretation stage of pastoral counseling helps the client interpret the interpersonal and spiritual concerns in which she is embedded. The counseling relationship mediates grace, invites the client into an alternative movement from disconnection in self-destructive behavior to connection and self-empathy, wherein the client moves from self-judgment to self-acceptance in relationship. Defensive behavior is understood, explained, and given new meaning. There is a movement from powerlessness to transform relationships to a good outcome for the client.

This stage is characterized by therapeutic explaining and working through interpretations of dynamic understandings of the client's inner world. In order to facilitate this stage the pastoral counselor must have an adequate theory and understanding of the nature of the relationship between the self and its self-objects, and needs to provide accurate empathic interpretations of the client's interrelatedness to her self-objects. Empathic interpretations facilitate the client's capacity to move from fixation on flawed images to a gradual decrease in fixation intensity, and from intensity of the use of the pastoral counselor as an object to a more mature self-object therapeutic relationship. The client gains some self-awareness, self–understanding, and self-acceptance as the self begins to emerge from disconnection.

Ongoing interpretive movements occur in stage two. The pastoral counselor interprets the client's experiences. The client experiences optimal frustration and self-acceptance as she begins to shift her empowerment for self-interpretation from the pastoral counselor. The client internalizes the functions of the pastoral counselor in the counseling process and interprets self-object relationships for her self. In stage two the client is involved in self-agency as she becomes a resource for her self.

For Brenda, interpretations focused on her unrealistic expectations in professional and personal relationships. Working through them, she became aware of the nature of her social isolation during her childhood development, and the development of her defenses as adaptive mechanisms to resist the condition of isolation that she was feeling.

Juanita began to interpret her experience of disconnect in failed relationships as her response to what she characterized as never getting the emotional support, love, and affirmation she needed in significant relationships growing up at home and then in adult relationships, i.e., what the pastoral counselor characterized as her experience of chronic lack of empathy. Juanita's search for grace in her life was interpreted in the counseling relationship as a need for self-empathy. In the cases of Brenda and Juanita, transformation took on similarities, such as: (1) gradual self-awareness; (2) gradual awareness of the pastoral counselor as a separate person; (3) reduction in the levels of anxiety induced by ambiguity as interpretations were appropriated; (4) enhancement of the activity of self-interpretation; (5) risking responsibility for relationship; (6) gaining self-acceptance.

The anxiety and frustration of the second stage indicates vulnerability and highlights the tension that occurs when the clients come to terms with their dependency in relationships. Dependency in relationships with others is threatening because of the possibility of rejection and/or deception. Dependency is experienced as the limitations previously masked by unrealistic expectations. Ongoing internalization of generative therapeutic interpretations helps the pastoral counseling process of working through issues.

Reconnection: Stage Three

The third stage of the pastoral counseling theory of grace refers to the client's movement of reconnecting with her history and spiritual relatedness through interpretation and by the internalization of more appropriate self-images. In the light of generative therapeutic interpretations, the client has the capacity for self-love that discerns and moves from interpretations based on flawed and distorted faith patterns and interactions of meaning and value to more helpful faith patterns and interactions. Some responses in this stage are the following: (1) increased self-awareness; (2) increased preservation of freedom and accountability; (3) increased self-relatedness; (4) increased transcendence in an attitude of faith. The termination process of counseling is actively envisioned in the third stage of counseling.

In the cases presented in this chapter the clients reconnected in relationships as they searched to discern the nature of God's proximity to their suffering and hoped for God's movement of grace in their suffering. For them, therapy represented the potential to become reconnected in relationships by this grace that is the initiative of God. The reconnection manifests itself and is experienced in ongoing dimensions of processes in the client's history—past, present, and future. Reconnection promises to transform personality and social relatedness both inside and outside the traditional church, especially beyond the trappings of religion where God is free from the idolatry of distortion and is encountered in the counseling process employing reason, imagination, and revelation . . . where God encounters relationships in the human condition.

The Method of Reflection

The method of reflection in this theory refers to the individual's capacity to gain self-awareness and insight about her use of faith to get at important concerns of meaning and value. The focus of this method is to understand and interpret one's faith by attending to the inner world of the self and its self-objects. I derive the implications for a pastoral counseling method of reflection by applying the method of practical correlation to explore the suffering and the hope of individuals represented in three cases in this chapter. The method of reflection engages the individual in ongoing conversations about subjective experiences of meaning and value that lead to ever-increasing critical self-awareness. The pastoral counseling theory of grace is a contextual theory and model of pastoral counseling, and a method of reflection developed to explore the nature and dynamics of assessment and treatment of persons suffering a crisis of disconnection.

Postscript

Since developing the pastoral counseling theory of grace, I have used the theory with various individuals and groups suffering with crises of disconnection. These persons represent varying faith traditions and commitments. In my practice I have found that the greater promise of the theory is its insistence that systemic cultural analysis of the clients' reality and truth and the inclusion of the clients' own experiences as source is important for assessment and treatment. Pastoral counseling must seek to engage all dimensions of the clients' experiences. This is important working with African American women with whom this theory was developed. Moreover, a contextual approach to all persons is paramount when providing a pastoral counseling ministry. There must be in the person of the pastoral counselor a profound respect for the ways in which culture, history, and the "-isms" of life bear upon and help interpret the profound vulnerability of suffering persons who find themselves in the presence of others and the Other.

Silent Cry

In Search of Harmony on Gold Mountain—The Yin-Yang Way of Pastoral Care

Yoke-Lye Lim Kwong

Silent Cry—A Story Remembered

A woman from China journeys to Gold Mountain,[1] the Chinese name for the United States. This is the story of her silent cry in America.

> The old woman remembered a swan she had bought many years ago in Shanghai for a foolish sum. This bird, boasted the market vendor, was once a duck that stretched its neck in hopes of becoming a goose, and now look!—it is too beautiful to eat.
>
> Then the woman and the swan sailed across an ocean many thousands of *li* [miles] wide, stretching their necks toward America. On her journey she cooed to the swan: "In America I will have a daughter just like me. But over there nobody will say her worth is measured by the loudness of her husband's belch. Over there nobody will look down on her, because I will make her speak only perfect American English. And over there she will always be too full to swallow any sorrow! She will know my meaning, because I will give her this swan—a creature that became more than what was hoped for."
>
> But when she arrived in the new country, the immigration officials pulled her swan away from her, leaving the woman fluttering her arms and with only one swan feather for a memory. And then she had to fill out so many forms she forgot why she had come and what she had left behind.
>
> Now the woman was old. And she had a daughter who grew up speaking only English and swallowing more Coca-Cola than sorrow. For a long time now the woman had wanted to give her daughter the single swan feather and tell her, "This feather may look worthless, but it comes from afar and carries with it all my good intention." And she waited, year after year, for the day she could tell her daughter this in perfect American English.[2]

Chinese women have come to America in search of harmony, community, a safe haven, and gold. While there has been an increasing number of publications and workshops on pastoral care pertaining to women in the United States, few specifically address pastoral care to immigrant women from China and the Asia-Pacific in general.[3] Kwok Pui-lan, one of the foremost Chinese American feminist theologians, writes and speaks with a passion on various issues faced by Asian women in the United States today. Her appearance in the 2007 Racial Ethnic Multicultural Network (REM), sponsored by the Association for Clinical Pastoral Education (ACPE), introduced to the chaplaincy community a powerful awareness of the urgency to recognize issues of oppression and displacement in Asian communities in America and particularly the advocacy of Asian immigrant women.

The urgency I feel is born out of the reality that pastoral care in general has traditionally been written and practiced in a North American, Western-dominant culture and from a Judeo-Christian European perspective. In the discussion of pastoral care of Chinese women immigrants, a number of sociocultural aspects must be taken into consideration. These aspects include philosophy, spirituality, language, culture, third-world theologies, racism, sexism, classicism, Chinese tradition, Confucianism, and their relationships with one another in the light of current theoretical and practical models of pastoral care in the West. When we begin to learn from listening to the stories of Asian women immigrants, are we responding to their voices calling us to rethink and reimagine pastoral care *differently*?

While the shared fundamentals of pastoral care grounded in an understanding of human dignity and respect hold, there is the critical need to recast a model of pastoral care for Asian women immigrants. We must resist the temptation to move into a "common difference" approach that denies the unique experiences of Chinese female immigrants. The "common difference" approach on issues of feminism, for example, makes the assumption that all womens struggles are similar and universal. This "common difference" approach unites women of all cultures to speak with one voice to common themes and issues. However, there are critical issues that Asian women immigrants face that are different from Euro-American women in relation to immigration rights, religion, language, family systems, colonization, and imperialism. These dimensions produce a unique struggle that is particular to Asian women immigrants.

My writing of this chapter presents the experience of immigration and its impact on *Chinese women* out of many sacred encounters and ministry with my "neighbor." My passion is fueled by many journeys between the East and West as a female, a theologian, a clinician, an educator, a pastor, a mother, a wife, and a spirituality birthed out of engaging fearlessly with perils from both worlds. It is important to state that I do not claim to represent all Chinese women immigrants nor do I imply there is only one experience for all. When I worked in a Chinese restaurant for a year as a waitress in 1997, I learned much and saw plenty in the way Chinese women immigrants were treated. They faced issues of immigration, health, and poverty. They worked very long hours and were paid below the minimum wage. The true stories of these Chinese women immigrants did not reflect the image of the "model minority" in America. This chapter is part of my larger effort to bridge the East and the West on behalf of the voiceless, particularly those whose first spoken and written language is Chinese.

The beginning step in engaging the *Yin-Yang*[4] way of pastoral care is for us to acknowledge the reality of the twenty-first-century demographics in North America influenced by the influx of Asian immigrants. For the majority of these immigrants, their first language is not English and Christianity is not their religion. For those who are Christians, they understand the Bible from the Asian experience. The immigration journey is intertwined with socioeconomic/political, cultural-linguistic, and spiritual layers. Like other immigrants, they leave their homeland in search of a better life. For the Chinese women immigrants there is more: a quest for "harmony" in the new world. For a period in history, the Chinese were ostracized by exclusion laws and were considered a "yellow peril," a threat to white wages that supported higher standards of living.

The "model minority" myth supports a social definition that Asians in general are, as a minority group in the United States, a distinguished example of success. It is a stereotype that denies the suffering that Asians in America have silently endured. This chapter is written with the hope that, in breaking the silence of suffering, Chinese women immigrants in particular will experience social redemption where they are recognized, respected, and treated as equals in the changing American social landscape. My hope for the pastoral care community is that we nurture our ability and sensibility to embrace cultural humility,[5] and then ask how we might revamp current models of pastoral care or create new models of pastoral care for Chinese women immigrants so that we do not perpetuate our neighbor's "silent cry," but yield the floor for their voices to teach us the *Yin-Yang* way of caring.

In Search of Harmony on Gold Mountain

Harmony, the unity of opposites, the fundamental philosophy of *Yin* and *Yang*, defines Chinese spirituality. For Chinese families that are traditionally rooted in Confucianism, a harmonious life is not only reflected in prosperity of material gains, but includes meaningful *relational connection* within the communities where they live and work.

Gold Mountain was the name the Chinese gave to America when gold was first discovered in California in 1848. Those who emigrated from China experienced the forces of "push" and "pull." Negative conditions resulting from the

Opium Wars in China, which brought about poverty, political oppression, and hardship in the beginning of the nineteenth century, pushed many to leave their native land. Positive conditions in America, including the California gold rush of the mid-1800s, pulled many Chinese to embark on a long voyage to America. Working head on with this "push-pull" circumstance, Chinese "coolies" (laborers) came to Gold Mountain with dreams of prosperity for their families in China. Seeking harmony and prosperity began the three waves of Chinese migration to America.

The first Chinese people movement took place in the early 1800s, the second in the 1940s, and the third in the 1980s and 1990s. Looking at the context of the first wave, it is important to note that American interests in China antedated Chinese immigration by more than a half-century, going back to the 1700s. Much like Great Britain, America was interested in Chinese goods, such as tea, porcelain, paintings, silk, and art from the Far East, to feed a culture and style of Western art known as *chinoiserie* that swept the West among wealthy businessmen. However, there was very little merchandise from America that benefited the Chinese.

When opium was introduced into China in the 1770s by the British East India Company, the drug swiftly helped to destroy Chinese society. The government of China ordered an end to the flow of opium into the country, for which the British retaliated with an armed navy. The conflict known as the Opium Wars, which China lost, lasted from 1839 to 1842. With the loss of property and land, cycles of suffering and civil disputes ensued among Chinese peasants. It was around this time that the tales of Gold Mountain in America sparked hopes among peasants.

Chinese men dreamed of going to Gold Mountain to strike a quick fortune and to return home with enough wealth to provide for their families. In poor living conditions on board ships and the long voyage, many died on the way to America. Those who arrived in San Francisco, of which 90 percent were men, wasted no time in joining many others to work the gold mines of California. Initially, Chinese miners were welcomed by white miners and employers. As the Chinese became more successful in the gold mines, growing envy among white miners led to anger and violence toward the Chinese immigrants.

In 1852, the government of California imposed the Foreign Miners' Tax on the Chinese as a measure to calm the conflicts. This law stated that no Chinese person could work in a mine without paying a fee in gold dust to tax collectors. It was a law that supported racism. More violence was directed at the Chinese, with the tax collectors as the perpetrators. The linguistic limitations of the Chinese in speaking English deepened their pain and suffering when they could not explain themselves about the unfair treatment to the authorities. To protect themselves, the Chinese lived in ghettos where they shared their common language and customs. The springing up of "Little Chinas" or "Little

Cantons" gradually turned into a large "Chinatown" in the city as more and more Chinese started restaurants and became grocers. Chinese women worked in the laundries, since washing and ironing were traditionally "women's work" in the old country.

By the early 1860s, gold mining slowed down as the mines were emptied. In 1862 the building of the transcontinental railroad to connect the east and west coasts of America was approved by Congress with the support of President Abraham Lincoln. The story of the Chinese having undertaken the largest construction in the world, the Great Wall of China, lent credibility to the Chinese to be hired to build the transcontinental. The work was dangerous and difficult. Many Chinese lives were lost to granite rock explosion accidents. In addition to working long hours, many were mistreated, often beaten or whipped by the foremen. In praise of the hardworking immigrant Chinese railroad laborers, the governor of California and the president of the Central Pacific Railroad extolled the Chinese as industrious, patient, and economical to the public. Once again, praises of Chinese work ethic caused jealousy, anger, and violence from white laborers. As in the days of mining, the Chinese faced similar threats and violence on the railroad. Upon the completion of the railroad on May 10, 1869, celebrations were held with photographs of the momentous historical event. Sadly, no Chinese were invited to the celebrations, nor were they allowed to appear in the photographing of the event.

During the Long Depression of the 1870s in America, there were more people than jobs. Many Chinese were hired because of their willingness to work long hours for very low wages. Whites accused the Chinese for "taking away" jobs that belonged to "real Americans." Once again, the emergence of anti-Chinese sentiments caused the government to step in to address the issue through the enactment of the Sidewalk Ordinance. The law prohibited the Chinese from walking on sidewalks while carrying baskets on both ends of a pole. The Queue Ordinance in particular caused a great deal of humiliation to Chinese men who were forced to rid their queue of long, braided hair. The laws caused more hardships on the Chinese people. Furthermore, the Chinese were barred from becoming American citizens.

On May 6, 1882, President Chester Arthur signed the Chinese Exclusion Act into law. For the first time in American history, a group of people was singled out to limit severely their immigration rights. Except for certain classes of Chinese, such as merchants, teachers, or American-born Chinese, all other Chinese were not allowed into America. In 1910, a new immigration processing center was established on Angel Island, a small island in San Francisco Bay. The Chinese who were held as prisoners at Angel Island poured out their pain, despair, and anger into Chinese poems.[6]

In 1924, another immigration act was passed prohibiting Chinese women in general from entering the United States with the exception of wives of certain classes of Chinese. During the Second World War, the law was challenged when America and China became allies against their common enemy, Japan. Chinese Americans supported the war by joining the army or by working in weapons factories. The war helped close the gap between the Chinese and the whites.

In 1943, the Chinese first lady, May Ling, wife of Chiang Kai-Shek, leader of the Republic of China, visited America to promote friendship between the two countries. At her request to repeal the Chinese Exclusion Act, President Franklin Roosevelt asked Congress to acknowledge their mistakes of the past by lifting the immigration ban to correct a historic mistake. On December 12, 1943, the Chinese Exclusion Act was repealed. This was the beginning of the second wave of Chinese immigrants to America, which brought a greater number of Chinese women. Indeed, Madame Chiang demonstrated unusual courage in those days of setting a liberation movement in a land that was not hers and gained recognition by the key male American politicians.

The arrival of more Chinese women was especially important as they restored family life and brought harmony in Chinese immigrant families. In 1965, President Lyndon Johnson signed the Immigration and Nationality Act that increased immigration to America from all nations. For the first time, more than half of new Chinese immigrants were women, among whom were doctors and college professors from China. However, because of their limited English language facility, many Chinese women immigrant professionals worked as waitresses, cooks, and domestic maids in America. Again, work was taxing, with few to no benefits. Their perseverance for liberation ensured their children equal rights to education. In 1974, a U.S. Supreme Court ruling began bilingual education in America. First-generation Chinese immigrants, however, did not return to school to be proficient in the English language. They would, rather, continue to work in low-paying jobs to feed their families and raise their children for a more harmonious future. Their posterity, American-Born Chinese (or ABCs), stepped through the doors of universities not only with rights as American citizens but also with awareness of the sacrifices of their parents.

As the relationship between China and America was steadily improving, a third wave of Chinese immigration took place during the 1980s and 1990s. Two groups of people marked this wave of immigrants. First, entrepreneurs, intellectuals, and those with skills in technology and computer science. Second, the unskilled, similar to the immigrants from the first and second waves. Like their ancestors, this third group also worked long hours in low-paying jobs and under poor conditions in such places as garment factories, laundry shops, and restaurants. Among the entrepreneurs, skilled and unskilled, one observed a widening gap between the wealthy and poor within the immigrant Chinese community, a kind of internal classism that began to divide the community. In addition to "classism," there was "nativism," a prejudice in favor of people born in the country and against immigrants who settled in America. Even though ABCs are no less American than Caucasian Americans, typically, they have been perceived and treated as "immigrants." For the Chinese female immigrant this nativism added another factor to her already many-layered socioeconomic/political, cultural-linguistic, racial-ethnic, and interrelational/gender power dynamics of dislocation and festering disharmony within and without one's soul. Harmony seemed like an unattainable ideal.

At the close of this twentieth century, it appears that the Chinese are thriving in America. They hold political office, are university professors, heads of corporations, winners of the Nobel Prize, Olympic game competitors, and outstanding artists in music and theater. Identified as the "model minority," it has been assumed in the American consciousness that the Chinese in America can and should succeed. However, a closer study of the status of Chinese Americans does not support their success story. Apart from being a tourist attraction, Chinatowns in America are also ghetto areas stricken with unemployment, poverty, health problems, and legal issues. Keeping in mind the story of Chinese immigration and its historical contexts, Chinese women immigrants in particular face a much greater challenge in fitting the mold of the "model minority." The spiritual, emotional, and mental health fallout among them is enormous. Here lies their untold and unheard soulful "silent cry" on Gold Mountain, the United States.

As described earlier, immigration laws have huge and often decades of unfavorable impact on Chinese immigrant families. After 1965, Chinese women immigrants, a majority of whom were wives of high-tech workers on H1-B visas, were prohibited by the federal immigration law from employment. Hence, they were rendered completely dependent on their husbands for income as well as for their legal immigration status to remain in America. For those who were employed they were discriminated overtly and covertly in areas such as (1) speaking English-only rules, (2) accent, (3) job promotion, and (4) harassments.[7] For Chinese women immigrants who speak English, but whose first language is not English, the inclination is to remain *silent* because of their minority status in their respective places of employment. Their experience is one of downward mobility, earning less than their white counterparts. Although equally qualified, they have less access to administrative promotions than their white colleagues. For those who gain such opportunities, subtle oppression continues to cause silence and suffering. Thus, unbeknownst to them, many Chinese women immigrants today are reliving the cycle of the first and second wave of Chinese immigrants who could not voice themselves to their appropriate authorities. It is a twenty-first-century "silent cry."

In Search of Self in Community: Within and Without

To appreciate a Chinese woman's place and belonging in her family, one must understand Confucianism. Confucianism is the life force of the Chinese people.

It has been the cultural DNA of the Chinese people within and beyond China for more than twenty-five hundred years. This life force nurtures the core values of virtue and ethics that define essential human relationships for family, neighbor, and community. Rooted in Confucianism, the traditional Chinese family relational dynamics speak of respect and obedience in a hierarchical relational structure. It is shaped by a five-dimensional filial piety of parent, sibling, heaven, spouse, and friend. Filial piety and fraternal submission provide the foundation for the five classic virtues: (1) benevolence and love of all persons; (2) propriety and attendance to ritual, ceremony, and courtesy; (3) obedience to communal values; (4) knowledge and intellect; and (5) harmony of life with heaven, earth, and people. The Chinese writing for filial piety, namely, *Hsiao*, is composed of two Chinese writings that mean "an old man" and "a boy," an image depicting patriarchal respect of a responsible son who bears up his father and the family name in his father's old age.

As revered as Confucianism may be by the Chinese, some aspects of it pose cultural-emotional ambivalence for Chinese women in particular. A Chinese woman is expected to obey her father before marriage, her husband after marriage, and her son after her husband's death. In the crucible of the immigration experience and such cultural conditioning within the Confucian family system, Chinese women immigrants wrestle between filial piety and Western individuality in the new world of Gold Mountain. In essence, she becomes a marginal person twice! Within immigrant Chinese families, the parent-generation Chinese depend on their English-literate American-Born Chinese (ABC) children to make sense of, say, a letter from the U.S. government or a parent-teacher meeting. An immigrant mother often worries that her children may not use their native names,[8] culture, value, and language; hence, she fears raising a "rootless" generation in a new land.

Confucianism permeates Chinese Christian communities and their theology in America. This is especially true on the view of women in general and women in church leadership in particular. The ordination of women into the Christian ministry remains a controversial and sensitive issue in many Chinese churches today. Governed by the cultural mores of Confucian hierarchical and patriarchal structures, women are welcomed to teach the children's Sunday school, cook meals, and decorate the church, but not to pastoral leadership. The *lack of,* if not, *void of* a female voice from the pulpit contributes to the *theological famine* in empowering women in their need for liberation. Ken Uyeda Fong, a second-generation, American-born, male Chinese pastor from Los Angeles writes:

> In contrast to many of their denominations' white churches, which have already seen fit to confer equal status on women, more than a few theologically moderate and conservative Asian churches in America continue to preach and teach variations on the principle of authoritative-male/submissive-female model. These unresponsive Asian congregations cite that they are only acting in accordance with the teachings of Scripture.[9]

As to the administration of the sacraments and preaching, Chinese women are rarely welcomed and involved. Many immigrant Chinese women educated and trained in theological institutes have a difficult time finding their place in the church and being respected in their leadership. The Chinese church becomes a double-edged sword: on one hand, a much-needed support and resource for Chinese women immigrants in America; on the other, a perpetuation of the cultural interrelational/gender dynamics of Confucianism in a religious form. This causes cultural, emotional, and spiritual ambivalence within themselves as Chinese women and relational conflicts with their faith communities. The story of Li Ling is one such story.[10]

> Li Ling is a fifty-five-year-old woman immigrant from China. She came to the United States upon her graduation from a seminary in Hong Kong in 2000 to marry Pastor Ting, the senior minister of a large Chinese church in New York. Li Ling was excited about this marriage because she considered herself "old" and past the appropriate child-bearing age. It would have been impossible for her to marry a man in China. She saw this marriage as God's divine favor upon her. Not only was she to be married, she was marrying a Chinese American citizen.
>
> As soon as they were married Li Ling was involved in the church as expected by the congregation as the pastor's wife according to the "help-mate" biblical teaching. She worked many hours serving the congregation by making home visits, teaching children's Sunday school, and praying with the women. As a theologically trained church worker, Li Ling could qualify as an associate pastor and be compensated in any way as a staff-person. After several years of active involvement in the church, she was emotionally depleted. When conflicts arose in her ministry, she did not have the resources and support that she needed from the church leadership or her husband. In his sermons, Pastor Ting often used illustrations with humor that consistently carried undertones that portrayed women as inferior, needy, and incompetent. Younger church women complained to Li Ling that they felt put down by her husband. But Li Ling did not have the courage to speak to her husband about it, even though she was asked by the women to do so. Feeling stuck, Li Ling became depressed. She had no one inside or outside of the church to talk to for fear that she might cause her husband to "lose face."
>
> In her desperation for help, she located a Caucasian female counselor after failed efforts in finding a Chinese counselor. When Li Ling came for the session, she was highly anxious, feeling unworthy and sensitive to the interethnic/racial counseling relationship and the focus on her problems. She stated that she would like to have gainful employment outside of her church for additional income and personal freedom. While she eagerly talked about her difficulty in leaving the church, she was also afraid that the counselor might report her to her husband. There was also the unspoken expectation that the counselor would find her a job. The counselor worked

hard to understand Li Ling, offering her a listening presence and support. The counselor assured Li Ling that she would not "cross" Ling's boundaries by giving her advice and by fixing her problems. The counselor clarified her role and practice as one who guides her clients to discover their paths.

With difficulty, Li Ling tried to understand her counselor's approach and was "respectful" as not to disagree with her counselor. In addition, Li Ling felt a great deal of shame about spending her husband's money to talk about her disappointments with her husband. She felt that she had disgraced her husband. In her failed attempts to get part-time work, her counselor remarked that she needed to be more "assertive." The counselor underestimated the challenges faced by Li Ling in culture, language, mannerisms, and accent in particular. Li Ling felt embarrassment from the counselor's comment but kept it to herself.

Li Ling continued to come to the sessions out of her politeness toward the counselor. She continued her attempts to explain her conflicts in the sessions. She disclosed her fear of disobeying the God who gave her a husband, brought her to America, and made her a pastor's wife if she were to stop supporting her husband's church ministry. As a Chinese wife nearing fifty-five years of age, she could not give her husband a son in return for God's favor toward her husband. Feeling caught between her cultural obligations and her resentment for the lack of support by the counselor, Li Ling said, "I just want to become a rabbit running into the woods and hide beneath green trees, never to return to the field and expose myself lest I get hunted down by uncaring people."

Furthermore, Li Ling mourned losing her immediate family and friends in Hong Kong and China to come to the United States. A part of her wanted to return "home"; another part of her questioned "Why?" especially after everything that God had done for her, to bring her to America to serve in a large church and to be married to a godly man.

Li Ling became increasingly depressed and guilty. The counselor used the empty-chair technique and suggested that Li Ling imagine her husband was sitting on the chair next to her. She asked Li Ling to express her *feelings* about being a pastor's wife and her stay in America. Li Ling "obeyed" her counselor, expressed her negative feelings over two sessions, and subsequently quit counseling altogether.

The counselor who worked with Li Ling failed to take into account the complex cultural-linguistic, socioeconomic, racial-ethnic-cultural, and interrelational power dynamics intertwined with immigrant issues. As an immigrant Chinese woman in America experiencing all of the above, Li Ling's "silent cry" was profound.

Xei Xong Xon Tan—"Gifting Burning Charcoal in the Midst of a Cold Winter"[11]

This Chinese proverb simply says: when a person is experiencing a cold winter, the giving of burning charcoal for warmth is what is needed. Li Ling's counselor could be more *culturally relevant* to her if only the counselor recognized that her comments to Li Ling regarding her "lack of assertiveness" undermined Li Ling's resiliency and self-esteem in her Chinese worldview. While listening to Li Ling's story, recommendation of employment resources would have been appropriate and empowering to Li Ling. In short, these are examples of "the giving of hot coals in a cold winter." Instead, the counselor was bound within the confines of her theory of exploring with the client her feelings and practical involvement in the client's need for employment was seen as a violation of boundaries. Furthermore, in implementing the empty-chair technique, the counselor overlooked cultural relational power dynamics between Li Ling and her husband on one level and, on another level, the counselor's exertion of dominance over Li Ling.

As responsible pastoral caregivers and counselors, ethical caring requires us to connect with our clients' worldviews and spiritualities, which are often *veiled* in their stories; this includes what is *not* storied. Sometimes their unspoken stories are their truth and authority, *not secrets* as defined by Western family-system analysis. Therefore, in constructing a model of pastoral care for immigrant Chinese women, attention to their stories spoken *and* unspoken, along with the practice of "giving of coal," is a dynamic intervention that nurtures hope and healing for both givers and receivers. This is a vision of cultural relevance and an ethically just relationship, which was actualized in the story of Ah Ping.

> Ah Ping was from China. On the same day she was born, her father became very ill. Ah Ping was told by her parents that she was born with bad luck, that is, *disharmony* between her and her father. When Ah Ping turned sixteen, her parents gave her in marriage to a man that she had never met before. After several years of marriage, Ah Ping did not conceive and bear any children. She was described by her father-in-law as having bad fate. Soon her husband married another woman and this woman bore him a son. Ah Ping's role was to serve his second wife and his son. Feeling shame, Ah Ping gathered enough courage and ran away from home.
>
> She joined others who escaped to America in a boat for a better life. She was promised a good job. When she arrived in Los Angeles, she was taken to a restaurant to work where she worked long hours every day, seven days a week. She lived in the basement of an apartment with many others who were in similar situations. She was required to turn in most of her income to the owner of the restaurant to pay for the boat trip from China to America. Not having a legal status or the ability to speak English, Ah Ping was careful to obey the requirements to avoid being sent back to China.
>
> After three years of hard work, Ah Ping became ill. She missed work for many days. Eventually, she was admitted to a hospital for treatment and was diagnosed with end-stage kidney cancer. The social worker and chaplain secured resources for her to receive medical care. Ah Ping was very afraid because other than her restaurant coworker friends, she had no family.

The chaplain offered her steady and silent companionship in the midst of her despair and homelessness. Such companionship provided Ah Ping unspeakable comfort as she experienced the chaplain joining her in her solitary despair. Eventually, Ah Ping made her wish known to the chaplain and social worker that she did not want to die in America where she saw herself a "drifting" seed in an ocean with no place to settle. She said she wanted to die in China, the place of her roots. She then thanked the chaplain and social worker by using a Chinese proverb, that is, for being "gift-carriers of burning coals" to keep her warm in the winter season of her life.

Ah Ping's story was translated from Chinese Mandarin into English. What is written above is only a brief summary of her life. Both the chaplain and the social worker contacted a Buddhist temple that was willing to sponsor Ah Ping's return home to China to be with her parents.

To understand Ah Ping's story, one must appreciate the Chinese sense of self in terms of its family and its complex web of relationships. Belonging to a family unit was what gave Ah Ping identity and meaning. Such belonging parallels the story of Ruth in the Bible who wanted to stay with her mother-in-law, Naomi, after Ruth lost her husband. In Ah Ping's circumstances, her parents with good intentions dealt with Ah Ping's bad luck by having her marry a man with hopes that good fortunes would be restored. Ah Ping's search for *harmony* in self and her circumstances embodied her strength and resiliency of soul and spirit when her fate was out of order. Essentially, what brought order to Ah Ping's life was the chaplain's offering loyalty of companionship, and the social worker's bringing resources that would unite her with her family in the homeland. Harmony, the peace of God, is at the center of these actions.

From Being Out of Order (Disharmony) to Being in Order (Harmony)

Returning to the story of Li Ling, the pastor's wife, her attempts to exercise her right and power to acquire gainful employment was futile. Turning back to her community, she only had her husband and the church. Until her husband could step out of his own culture of gender domination and change the way he related with Li Ling, the dominant-subordinate relationship would continue Li Ling's silent cry. Unfortunately, within the cultural community of his church, it is unlikely, although not impossible, for Pastor Ting to use his position of power as a man, a pastor, and a husband to empower Li Ling.

Korean feminist theologian Chung Hyun Kyung says, "What Asian women want from Asian men is not their generous understanding on 'women's problems' but their repentance, a genuine commitment to end their oppression over Asian women."[12] Two indigenous Asian feminist theologians who understand Western theological frameworks yet who are firmly grounded in Asian theologies speak a theology that engages Asian women's stories. Kwok Pui-lan (Hong Kong) and Chung Hyun Kyung (Korean) introduced Asian women's theologies in addressing their respective sociocultural and sociopolitical contexts.

In light of the virtue of "sacrifice" among immigrant Chinese women, images of the "humble Christ" or the "suffering Christ" that appeal to them may be employed in the counseling relationship. Thoughtful use of these images can empower, while careless use may lead to further deterioration of the client. Kyung offers the following to raise our awareness around the issue of "sufferings" in helping Asian women in general:

> Making meaning out of suffering is a dangerous business. It can be both a seed for liberation and opium for the oppression of Asian women. These two conflicting possibilities shape Asian women's experiences of encounter with Jesus. Asian women have believed in Jesus *in spite* of many contradictory experiences they receive from their families, churches, and societies. Believing *in spite* of great contradictions is the only option for many Asian women who are seeking to be Christian. Jesus is only good for these Asian women when he affirms, respects, and is actively present with them in their long and hard journey for liberation and wholeness. Asian women are discovering with much passion and compassion that Jesus sides with the silenced Asian women in his solidarity with all oppressed people. This Jesus is Asian women's new lover, comrade, and suffering servant.[13]

In the Asian women's context, the "suffering Christ" is one who empathizes with their suffering versus one who calls them to suffer by sacrificing themselves. The "humble Christ" is one who *companions* them in their experiences of being humiliated versus one who calls them to endure humility quietly and passively in the face of injustice. In addition, the use of scriptural images of Christ portrayed as the *compassionate human Jesus* to women may be employed. Interspersed in the Gospels are such examples as: Jesus weeping when he learns from Mary and Martha that their brother Lazarus has died (John 11:35); Jesus telling his disciples that the woman has performed a good service for him when she anoints his head with costly perfume (Matt. 26:7); the resurrected Christ first appearing to a woman, Mary Magdalene (Matt. 28:1). Even upon his death, Jesus shows love and care to his mother by asking the disciple, John, to look after her upon his death (John 19:26-27).

Kyung uses an insight from Virginia Fabella of the Philippines:

> For Filipino women Jesus is neither a masochist who enjoys suffering, nor a father's boy who blindly does what he is told to do. On the contrary, Jesus is a compassionate man of integrity who identified himself with the oppressed. He "stood for all he taught and did" and took responsibility for the consequences of his choices even at the price of his life. This image of Jesus' suffering gives Asian women the wisdom to differentiate between

the suffering imposed by an oppressor and the suffering that is the consequence of one's stand for justice and human dignity.[14]

Where West Meets East in Harmony

In recent years, the number of female Asian theological students engaging in counseling and other related forms of training, including clinical pastoral education (CPE), in America has increased. Most, if not all, have been trained in Western theological frameworks, theories of education, and personality theories. Granted, CPE supervisors trained in Western models will likely train their students in the same. While opportunities abound with more international students engaging in CPE, there is still much to be desired in the level of exposure and learning by certified CPE supervisors in third-world theologies and non-Western models of education and psychologies in their training of and learning from their students. Culturally relevant models of care are urgently needed as globalization of America increases. Third-world theologies are out there and available if one is curious enough to seek them out.

Intercultural counseling and education call for a process of change through imagination, self-reflection, education, critique, and cultural immersion experiences. Peter Phan and Jung Young Lee[15] suggest that those who hope to be helpful must begin to think and see things from the margin, that is, "from the other side" versus the center or "dominant side." Marginality and centrality are so mutually exclusive that unavoidable disharmony emerges, as it has been proven by history, when centrality is stressed and marginality is ignored. Only in illuminating marginality, not shadowed or covered by centrality, can harmony of justice and rightness be experienced beyond the intellectual level. Caregivers can then begin to adopt an attitude that will help them to see their clients clearer in what it means to live on the edges of existence. Such a movement to "see things from the margin" requires the counselor to do the following: (1) shift from an individualistic to a communal-relational model (in the latter, individual personal boundaries are defined by the community to which the client belongs); (2) equalize power by "declassing" oneself—that is, one's white privilege, position, or title—to one of mutuality as an equal; (3) join in their emotional "homelessness" with its challenges; (4) focus, recognize, and acknowledge resiliency and strengths of the counselee; and (5) use a cultural consultant. In some instances, with the client's consent, it is appropriate to invite the cultural consultant to accompany the client in the counseling session.

There is still a long journey in actualizing the *Yin-Yang* way of ministering to immigrant Chinese women. Often, after we have made some attempts to do so, we come away with more questions. However, the journey of a thousand miles begins with the step just beneath us. Any one of the following points can be the first step:

1. Go beyond intellectual study to acquire an emotional appreciation and connection for people movements as a growing global phenomenon.
2. Divest of the attitude that Western thought is superior to Eastern thought. Whether it is philosophy, psychology, sociology, or theology, recognize differences in worldviews rather than the assigning of values.
3. Be open to learning the great philosophical, religious thoughts and traditions of the East. These include, but are not limited to: Buddhism, Taoism, Feng-Shui, Chinese myths, legends and superstitions, face and palm readings, ancestral veneration, and the worship of gods and goddesses. Acquiring these understandings will enhance the Judeo-Christian perspective in caring for the spiritual and pastoral needs of immigrant Chinese women.
4. Think and practice the "harmony" of *Yin-Yang* in these basic and simple ways in a helpful relationship: (a) take the relational-communal approach by becoming a "family" member of the client; (b) be a social equal by sojourning with the client in her social and cultural sphere. This is the balance of interrelational power that promotes harmony in the counseling relationship.
5. Seek to listen to their "silent cries" so these cries are released and translated into sacred stories.
6. Engage in a cultural immersion experience in a foreign country and culture for a season.

As a community of caregivers, if we envision ourselves to be a growing, compassionate, and effective healing community that attunes our hearts to the "silent cry," then we must move out of our comfort zone and narrow minds and step into the East-West sphere with humility in order to be taught so that we might be wise.

Women, Professional Work, and Diversity

Pastoral Theology in the Midst of Globalization

Barbara J. McClure

Though my primary identity is as a pastoral theologian and clinician, I have extensive experience working in corporate settings as a leader and organizational development consultant. An academic colleague once asked me, "What business does a pastoral theologian have working in corporate America?" He elaborated, saying, "Your work puts you right in the middle of the corporate machine, doesn't it? Aren't you just gilding the iron cage of capitalism by working in the business world?" He was not the only person to express this concern during my tenure as a full-time consultant in a leadership development firm; others had posed similar questions and, indeed, I had wondered about the work myself.

In this chapter I use the above critique of my work in the corporate sector as a way to examine the vocation of pastoral theology more broadly. I propose the possibility of an expanded role and place for pastoral theology in the work lives of those for whom we seek to care. I build my argument in four movements: first, I explore the effects of immigration and work in the corporate sector on the well-being of professional immigrant women through a case study of one woman; second, I use the reflection on this woman's experience to invite pastoral theological engagement in corporate settings; third, I describe what such work might look like; and fourth, I argue why I think pastoral theologians are especially equipped to engage in the institutions that organize our work lives. My purpose here is not to defend my decision to enter the corporate sector, nor to be an apologist for corporate capitalism. Instead, the goal is to explore my experience in that context and examine what we pastoral theologians may be missing when we fail to take on the challenges of the work-a-day world and the institutional realities that structure the lives of our parishioners and clients. I want to remain open to the lessons of my experience and explore how caregivers like me (and probably you, the reader) can better care for those of our parishioners and neighbors who seek their own flourishing, in part, within the context of the corporate world where, for good or ill, they spend a good part of their waking hours.

Pastoral Theology: A Changing Vocation

The field of pastoral theology is in a state of flux (perhaps even confusion) about its purpose and context, particularly as it begins to grapple with multicultural variables. In response to this uncertainty I would argue that at its core pastoral theology seeks to define and promote flourishing, and develops theories, theologies, and practices toward that end. Such a broad purpose can fund a wide variety of engagements, and in fact the general theme in recent literature has been the recommendation that we expand our horizons, both theoretically and practically. This expanding pastoral theological imagination has led some to suggest novel contexts for the application of pastoral theological expertise and practice in a changing world. I want to enter this discussion and suggest that we think about corporate settings as one important place for pastoral theologians to work.

Change is at the heart of our work in other ways as well: pastoral theology is a vocation in which practitioners support positive change. Historically, the change we have sought to support has been at the personal or interpersonal level. In the last twenty-five years especially, however, pastoral theologians have been encouraged to support change in new ways and new contexts, expanding our attention from personal to systemic and even public-policy levels. This trend is a result of the growing awareness that personal distress and dysfunction recommends not only psychological diagnosis and treatment but institutional critique as well. Indeed, I argue that persons' feelings of distress carry at least as much information about our social/institutional/cultural worlds as they do about our individual limitations and psychologies.

I begin by framing this discussion with a case that highlights the situation of a minority woman in the service sector and foregrounds issues of oppression, isolation, relational difficulties, role changes, and other challenges that pastoral theologians could address more effectively than we do currently. What I learned in working with this individual, an immigrant woman in a white-collar job, is that some of the challenges many of our clients face daily have both personal and organizational etiologies. In this way my client's story offers us new possibilities for doing the deep individual work we have always done well and invites us into new work, helping us imagine possibilities for pastoral theologians' engagement within organizational life.

Case Study: "Shape up or ship out"[1]

I was invited to work with a mortgage-lending team experiencing internal conflict, low morale, and high turnover. One of the employees I was asked to work with was a middle manager who, because she was an Asian immigrant, had been assigned to serve the financial needs of the local Asian community. The company's leadership felt she was a valuable asset they wanted to keep but she was struggling to meet the expectations of her job. I was told that this manager had been coming to work after 9:00 in the morning, too late to attend the 8:00 a.m. production meeting. She seemed to have difficulty holding her direct reports accountable, and her communication skills were described to me as "quite poor." The company's expectation was that I would help her understand what was expected from her in terms of her management role and that I would facilitate the development of her leadership skills so that she could lead a more productive team that would be better equipped to meet the challenges of a highly competitive market. Though the company had hired me, my coachee was grateful: she wanted to experience less stress on the job, to get along better with her team, and to have more job security by meeting company expectations of her. She was motivated to keep her job and to resolve some of her inner and interpersonal conflicts, so we got to work addressing the most pressing issues: how to learn to lead "American style," how to increase her and her team's performance and cooperation, and how to manage her work/life balance.

I quickly learned, however, that my client's internal and interpersonal struggles were not simply indicative of her own psychodynamics or her inability to "assimilate" effectively. They were also indicative of challenges, even debilitating organizational dynamics, in which she was caught.

Immigrant Women, Work, and Personal and Familial Well-Being

Overview of Data

In what follows I explore immigrant women's experience as they move in greater numbers into white-collar jobs, using the experience of one such woman. This chapter cannot address all the issues facing all immigrant women such as full-blown harassment or violence, wage discrimination, exclusionary hiring and promotion practices, or challenges faced in non-wage-earning work such as that in the domestic sphere, though these are all of critical importance. It does seek to explore more mundane (though perhaps not less important) issues as they bear on women's ability to keep their wage-earning jobs and help support their families. The challenges the woman in the case experienced threatened her family's financial stability and diminished her abilities to parent well, partner well, and maintain her own mental and physical well-being. While the dynamics highlighted by the case are experienced by nonimmigrant women as well, being foreign born has the potential to exacerbate one's challenges in navigating the work-a-day world in the United States.

My client's story is, of course, unique. But it must also be viewed within a larger national context and conversation about immigration that is being played out at our borders, in our politics, and in the media. Her experience is set against a backdrop of immigration, globalization, race relations, sexism, insensitivity toward immigrants, and the challenges of diversity in the workplace. The Immigration Act of 1965, which was a turning point in the history of U.S. immigration policy, widened the door to immigrants, especially from Asia and Latin America. Immigrants and their children account for over half the net annual population growth of the United States, in which over one million immigrants (legal and not) are added to the U.S. population annually. Though the trend itself has both supporters and critics—as does the response of the United States to it—its impact is undeniable: foreign-born workers accounted for more than half the total workforce growth from 1996 to 2002 (data from the most recent census still being compiled), and in the Midwest, New England, and Mid-Atlantic states, foreign-born workers accounted for more than 90 percent of the employment growth from 1996 to 2002, and they are gravitating to the highest-skilled and lowest-skilled jobs in almost equal measure. This data would create an hourglass shape if it were graphed, with the thin middle demonstrating immigrants' more limited presence in mid-skill jobs.[2]

The move of immigrant women into professional (or "white collar") jobs poses particular challenges for the employees that fill them, raising interesting issues for professionals such as pastoral theologians interested in supporting human well-being. The increasing number of service-sector jobs require less in terms of manual labor and more of what have been called emotional intelligence ("EQ") capacities such as relationship-building, socially and culturally appropriate assertiveness, and managing and motivating others.[3] In other words, the industrial skill set is giving way to postindustrial requirements that focus more on EQ and the "soft skills" of human relations. Thus, in the professional sector, the new economy demands new skills from its workforce, including the ability to communicate clearly, to know the subtleties of national and corporate culture, to handle conflict, and other typical leadership and management tasks. At the same time, U.S. companies are hiring more foreign-born workers who often do not have—or value—these abilities, often for cultural reasons.

Psychological Effects of Immigration on Women and Families

The effects of immigration go beyond the numerical, of course. Immigration profoundly affects many spheres in the lives of its participants, including family dynamics, interpersonal relationships, and personal well-being. Indeed, studies on the effects of globalization and immigration show that while immigration is often positive in financial and other terms, it can have negative psychological effects, especially for women and children.[4] These links are worth studying since by 2020 women and minorities will comprise more than two-thirds of the net workforce entrants.[5]

While all immigrants face difficulties as they acculturate, acclimate, and integrate into their new countries, foreign-born women are entering the work force in larger numbers than ever before and are facing unique challenges and significant psychological effects that have an impact on their families—factors that concerned me in relation to my work with the woman in the opening case. For example, one study demonstrated that although women are more realistic than men about the requirements of their new lives, are more active in trying to improve their life conditions, and are more resilient and able to cope (exhibiting higher ingenuity and adaptability than their male counterparts), they also experience more depression, stress, and lower self-esteem than their male counterparts.[6] Sociologists Cynthia Coll and Katherine Magnuson demonstrate that immigrant women and their families fare far worse psychologically after they immigrate than they had before: marriages fail at higher rates than in their sending countries, and children's stress levels rise, they become more violent, exhibit antisocial behavior, and are more likely to drop out of school.[7] The stress immigrant women and mothers are under can lead them to be less nurturing to their children, more likely to use physical means of control, and to abandon their families with higher frequency than they might if they were more supported and empowered.[8] Migration to the United States erodes family ties and other strengths immigrants bring with them. The challenges immigrants face in their new home countries diminish hope and aspirations for success, reduce their ability and willingness to work hard and be productive at work, and increase the likelihood of the somaticization of psychological distress.[9]

Immigration also can create challenges for women in their intimate relationships; they encounter culture clash and the disorientation wrought by gender roles and expectations shifting at home and at work. In their studies of immigrant families, Caroline Bretell and Patricia DeBergeois have shown that while men's stress levels are high immediately following immigration and decrease over time, women's optimism is high and stress is low, and over time optimism wanes and stress rises, leading to depression, insomnia, loss of appetite, complaints of frigidity, and increased use of both prescription and illicit tranquilizers.[10] It is important to note that these negative effects are not the whole story: working outside the home and earning wages that help support the family also bring benefit to immigrant women. They are increasingly empowered to make important decisions about the home and family—and have the money to support those decisions. As we might expect, however, even these gains are ambiguous: men can be glad their wives or girlfriends work, but the increased informal power their female partners gain also can increase relational strife, physical means of control, and attempts to undo the newfound power by asserting traditional gender roles.[11]

Professional Immigrant Women and Organizational Dynamics: Identifying Challenges

The effects of immigration on women can be overwhelming; they tend to have primary responsibility for taking care of families, the burden of maintaining intimate relationships and families in an environment of change, and for navigating the sociocultural and institutional challenges of work in their new home countries. Entering the U.S. labor market poses challenges on other fronts, too, as I will discuss below.

Despite the complex challenges they face, however, more immigrant women than ever are entering the U.S. labor market and are bearing the brunt of the change in their families' lives, taking the lead in supporting and establishing their families in the United States.[12] Women are more willing than men to undergo occupational reversals in order to bring in a steady income, requiring them to learn new skills or new professions as they seek employment;[13] as a consequence, immigrant women are increasingly taking service-sector or white-collar jobs upon their arrival in the United States, even if that means a steep learning curve and significant challenges on the employment front in addition to those already mentioned.[14]

From an organizational perspective the influx of foreign-born employees helps meet the goals of diversifying the workplace. However, while immigrant women's employment by U.S. corporations helps meet the needs of both the individual and her family as well as the company for which she works, it also presents ethical and moral issues in organizational life: immigrant women at work in U.S. corporations represent one of the most concrete opportunities for exploring and redressing complex issues such as racism, sexism, xenophobia, labor exploitation, and the hegemony of companies' singular commitment to financial gain.[15] In fact, immigrant women report experiencing marginalization, discrimination, isolation, and feelings of powerlessness over their situations at work, which are significant contributors to their psychological conditions and their abilities to parent and care for themselves and their families.[16]

Much of this stress is a factor of a steadily increasing diversity in the U.S. workforce amidst confusion about how to integrate foreign-born workers into the culture of American business; though many companies seek to diversify their workforce, attention to genuinely integrating immigrant hires is scant.[17] Most organizations operate out of a model of diversification that is limited. For example, among the reasons for making diversity hires, these three tend to be the most common:[18]

1. In an attempt to comply with Equal Employment Opportunity Commission (EEOC) requirements, organizations are pressed to hire a certain number of minorities and women. Under the guise of equality and

fairness in hiring, organizations operating under this model are primarily motivated by compliance and concerned about ratios and can otherwise be color- and gender-blind. Because they are concerned primarily with numbers as signs of inclusion rather than changes in corporate culture as means to inclusiveness, they expect minorities and women to blend into the existing organizational environment and structure, no matter the cost to those individuals.

2. In order to better serve their minority customers (and gain market share in an increasingly racially and ethnically diverse society), organizations hire employees who can serve the new clientele. The diversity directive is market driven. Organizations operating in this model value the business possibilities of diversification but fail to appreciate the implications for the organizational culture or work environment such inclusion will necessarily mean, and minorities and women often feel exploited and devalued—hired only to increase the financial stability of the company.

3. Organizations diversify in hopes that female and minority employees will offer varied perspectives and approaches to the enterprise. This perspective values the contributions of diverse employees and appreciates the ways diversity "may affect work group abilities to process information, perceive and interpret stimuli and make decisions."[19] It does not, however, recognize the mutual give and take that real diversity in organizations requires, more about which will be said below.

Theological Considerations of Engaging Business Organizations

Theological critiques of corporate America and capitalism are many, well documented, and familiar: we find admonition in the Bible against trying to serve God and mammon, and the World Council of Churches has issued reminders that there are important values that for-profit businesses and the free market do not nurture, including compassion and genuine cooperation. Capitalism has been criticized as an imperial ideology precisely for its potential to exploit labor and natural resources for the benefit of a few and for its capacity to dissolve all difference by translating all goods and values into the unitary currency of the dollar.[20] The argument is that differences do not go away; they are merely obscured by the narrow moral logic of capitalism. Though these are some of the reasons religious folk have eschewed explicit participation in the lives of business corporations, they are the very reasons I argue that the corporate world is one place in which pastoral theologians ought to be engaged.

My overview of the toll of immigrating to and working in the United States makes concrete the ways issues of gender, class, and race come together in oppressive and unjust ways—and how organizations are mediators of discrimination and injustice and significant contributors to dis-ease.[21] The data highlight the ways personal and interpersonal distress can be exacerbated by organizations that are not sensitive to the particularities of their employees—particularly in this case of racial/ethnic minorities and women. While nonimmigrant women experience similar dynamics, these issues are exacerbated when English is one's second (or third or fourth) language, when one is confused about what is culturally appropriate, when personal issues are compounded by a work environment that is demanding, sexist, ethnocentric, inflexible, and strange.

Pastoral theologians such as Archie Smith, Pam Couture, and Larry Graham are among the most astute observers of the challenges and suffering our contemporary social and economic systems create. Because for-profit organizations (and, we might note, many not-for-profits as well, including the church) are driven by fierce competition to maximize profit, to enhance growth, and to increase productivity, they can require the heart and soul of their members, killing the life spirit and limiting the definition of "flourishing" to numerical terms. They too often seem to transmute human souls into human resources—it is the alchemy of the modern world. And it is precisely for these reasons that the corporate sector, for all its dangers and pitfalls, is an appropriate context for the work of pastoral theologians and practitioners. To make this argument I challenge four assumptions implied by my detractor who suggested that corporate America is not an appropriate context for pastoral theologians' engagement.

First, his critique rests on the assumption that the self can and should be autonomous—that institutions are necessarily and always a threat to its well-being. I argue below that this is a perspective that is not nuanced enough, though one that persists in much of our current pastoral theory and practice. It reveals a socially inadequate theological anthropology, and is limited theoretically, theologically, and practically. A more socially adequate theological anthropology recognizes, in part, that institutions mediate selves and are essential to well-being. I presume that pastoral theologians are called to promote flourishing, which I am convinced requires critical and productive engagement *with* the social order.

Second, and perhaps more significantly, the charge implies that the world of work is not within the purview of pastoral theology. However, by avoiding the arenas of work and focusing primarily on the realms of familial relationships and self-actualization, pastoral theologians are avoiding key social contexts that are important sources of psychic and spiritual distress and thereby are losing opportunities to address some of the common roots of contemporary dis-ease. Indeed, possibly for all, but especially for professional and white-collar workers, work is an essential dimension of a meaningful life. My experience working in the corporate sector has convinced me that our theories and practices of care can and should be directed toward a broader range of human experience than the personal. People experience some of their greatest distress (and yes, joy) on the job. Thus, the world of work is an important horizon of response-ability for pastoral theologians.[22] A robust theology of work is needed both to critique current labor practices and to provide both client and caregiver with a realistic and practical vision of the purposes and meaning of "good work." It is too easy to treat work and the contexts in which we undertake it as profane, and thus dismiss them as not worthy of pastoral theologians' attention. However, good work—an opportunity that rewards commitment to excellent performance, in which one can express one's values and ethics, and that offers a meaningful sense of engagement—surely is something we all would value.[23] I can only begin such a project here, but because work is elemental to human flourishing, it is an important area of human experience to be addressed by pastoral theologians.

Third, the critique implies that economically driven institutions are irredeemable; that is, because they are economically driven they are, *by nature*, alienating and exploitative. While this is often true, pastoral theologians need more than a critique of the alienating and exploitative dimensions of our economic institutions; we also need to think of ways to participate in changing them for the good, to make them more conducive to human flourishing. We need to imagine (and help others imagine) economic institutions that are life giving rather than life denying, and to find ways to make them so. The option of living without economic relationships, without markets, without business, without the institutions of work is not merely utopian, it is untenable in the modern, developed world. Businesses are a *necessary* part of the contexts within which we live; they are fallen and can/need to be redeemed—organized in such a way that they breed life and not death.[24]

Fourth, my challenger's comment fails to recognize the ways "-isms" (ethnocentrism, sexism, and classism, to name those most salient in this case) are mediated through organizational policies and structure, and that institutional life is thus an appropriate context for pastoral (and prophetic) engagement. I further flesh out each of these points below.

1. Pastoral theologians are called to promote flourishing, and institutions affect persons' ability to do so.

At a basic level, the goal of our field is to promote flourishing.[25] Our theological and theoretical perspectives as well as our practices all have that goal in mind. How we define the Good and strive to achieve it is an important part of the pastoral theological conversation. The operative assumption here is that the Good for human beings includes meeting the basic requirements for life, including food, shelter, rich and positive interpersonal interaction, and spiritual depth. It also requires opportunities for good work, a conscious relationship to the transcendent, meaningful interpretation of life's experiences, and emotional nourishment. But the task of pastoral theology has never been merely definitional:

we also develop practices that will *contribute* to such wellness, an issue to which I return below.

Many pastoral theologians' definitions of "wellness" are rightly expansive. The pastoral vocation, in the words of Larry Graham, is twofold: "the care of persons and the care of worlds."[26] Yet critics have noted that for much of the twentieth century, despite attempts otherwise, pastoral theology has been practiced primarily in a personalistic mode and has not recognized the centrality of institutions in the ordering of human lives.[27] As pastoral theologians our vocation surely is not to stand outside institutions (as if this were even possible) and merely critique them, but to operate *within* these institutions and the organizations that instantiate them and to *humanize* them—to join with those whose lives are, like ours, structured *by* them.

Thus, wellness, wholeness, and health in this expansive mode will mean engagement with the social order, working in and among organizational life to help humanize it, holding organizations accountable. To imagine a different and more humane way for institutional life to be constituted is important work for pastoral theologians.

2. Pastoral theologians are invited to reclaim the importance of work and attend to its contexts.

Although Sigmund Freud directed therapeutic attention to the dynamics of love *and* work, pastoral theologians have attended primarily to intimate relationships.[28] It is time to return to considerations of work and its contexts. Work is part of the created order and God's gift to us. God has ordained us to work, and to find meaning and fulfillment therein. The author of Genesis tells us that *before* the fall, there was work (Gen. 2:15), and the reformers insisted that all have a vocation in the world, connecting our *doing* in the world with God's *being* in it.

Theologian David Jensen writes that work has value because "Meaningful human work responds to the divine work that pulses at the heart of the universe. Though God's work is not dependent on ours, when our labors respond to the divine work, we also contribute to the life of the world."[29] In other words, work is not secondary but elemental to human flourishing.

Too often, however, churches have been curiously silent on issues of work. Indeed, as theological ethicist David Miller argues, though the church "could be one of the best resources to help people live balanced and meaningful lives at work . . . [by offering] theological and ethical [and, I would add, practical] resources to help transform corporate life and its impact on society, it remains largely silent."[30] Similarly, theological ethicist Max Stackhouse argues that critically engaging institutions and the organizations that incarnate them is indeed the work of theologically trained persons, noting that "the patterns of [organizations] in a civilization constitute the basic fabric of social authority. . . . One of the tasks of social ethics is to analyze and critically evaluate the perceptions of needs, requirements, or desires on the one hand, and the definitions of what is right or good on the other, to see whether that which is institutionalized is morally valid."[31] Pastoral theologians need to be in this conversation and we bring not just the ability to critically evaluate and analyze organizational life against a vision of flourishing, but have already and can develop further the skills and practices to help change organizations in light of that vision as well. As Larry Graham argues, pastoral theology should contribute to the common good by analyzing critically the norms and practices that structure our common lives and by developing strategic practices to intervene with an eye toward the well-being of individuals, cultures, and the order—which includes the natural environment and the "basic" structures of our lives together.[32]

Besides, the context of the modern workplace is worthy of pastoral attention since the basic structural issues of labor have far-reaching implications. The way we organize different kinds of labor, employer and labor-market expectations (such as the "shape and length of the working day and the form and status of sex segregation and gender stereotyping in more public paid occupations"), and the dynamics of an increasingly globalized labor market all bear on the issue of human flourishing.[33] Indeed, the values and prejudices carried by institutional policies and practices often operate to enforce and reinforce injustices and create contexts in which individual employees suffer. They affect significantly a person's abilities to flourish and as such are worthy of our pastoral attention. Alternatively, labor practices that are fair and life affirming, that seek justice and consider the human costs of decisions can increase human flourishing. While no corporation is perfect, some are better than others, and all would benefit from the prophetic critiques of pastoral theology done well.

3. Organizations are the necessary contexts within which we live and work; we are utterly dependent on them in modern life.

Pastoral theologians have been mining social theories and theologies with increasing interest for several decades now, and leaders in the field have been pressing for a more socially adequate understanding of what it means to be human—our theological anthropology. Crucial to such a theological anthropology is the understanding that the self is formed by and within social contexts. The self and society cannot be seen as discrete entities; rather, the self is a node within a web of personal and institutional dynamics.[34] To understand the particularities of selfhood requires understanding social and institutional conditions. As pastoral theologian Archie Smith puts it, the self is not given at birth, but rather "originates in activity and in a social process, and unfolds through interaction, and communication and reflection" with others and the social world.[35]

If the self is fundamentally social, so too are the origins of some of its deepest struggles. Pastoral theologians such as Pam Couture, Christie Neuger, Archie Smith, Edward Wimberly, and James Poling have delineated the direct connection between social structures and individual suffering.[36] This observation does not prescribe removing the self from society in the attempt to heal but instead recommends tending to the social context as a way to help heal the self. Being socially inattentive is not an option if we want our care to be adequate. We all live in and through institutions and organizations that frame our lives and determine our possibilities. As one student of organizational life puts it, "Almost every aspect of life is affected by organizations. . . . Organizations are indispensable to human civilizations' progress in meeting societal needs, but they can also be a force of destruction. . . . Today modern organizations shape values, set structural roles and norms, change human destinies and perform a wide range of functions from integration and human fulfillment to disintegration and individual alienation."[37] Organizations are central to our lives and can support or impede our well-being.

My detractor's comments suggest the degree to which pastoral theology is still captured by the hegemony of individualistic understandings of the self. However, this perspective fails to understand that all selves are organizationally situated and that organizational transformation is required to sustain individual well-being. Withdrawal from the social field is not an option: being "doctors of the soul" means we must be doctors of the social order as well. Being clear about the social nature of selfhood opens up a focus of care that we have not yet fully developed: the critique and reformation of the organizations that shape our lives. These insights offer arenas for the contributions of pastoral theology beyond those typically thought of (the individual and the family), expanding our spheres of influence to organizational structures as well.

The response of pastoral practitioners historically has been to deal with issues such as those identified above one-on-one with a client in therapy, emboldening her to be differentiated and to stand strong in the face of structural challenges. Indeed, sociologist Ann Swidler suggests that the weakening of our public institutions/organizations that has occurred over the past generation puts increased demands on individual selves to be strong, and certainly empowering individual selves has been an important aspect of our work. But this cannot be our only answer to persons' distress. As Swidler puts it,

> We do not create our own lives. What we are and what we can be depends upon an endowment—moral, intellectual, social and institutional. . . . We depend on a culture and a set of social institutions that we did not make, and could not have made, for ourselves. . . . [I]t is only by recognizing the irreducibly collective nature of a cultural and institutional endowment that we can begin to take responsibility, not for ourselves, but for beginning a process of social rebuilding.[38]

If we are truly committed to human flourishing, then, we need to contribute to the building of a strong, living human *and institutional/organizational* web.[39] This requires that pastoral theologians become students not only of the self and its intrapersonal and interpersonal dynamics, but also students of the institutions that shape the self, attending to the interdependence of social and individual dynamics.[40] We must recognize the connection between institutional integrity and personal wholeness. We cannot have one without the other, and a pastoral theology that only addresses the private tribulations of the soul or the dynamics of interpersonal relationships while neglecting the wider context misses opportunities to address significant roots of distress and participate in deep healing. This is being done at the ecclesial level, especially in the genre of congregational leadership, but I argue that attention should also be paid to other organizations as well.[41] In fact, we might even be able to extend our knowledge derived from attending to church organizations to the ways other organizations work, and offer prophetic witness to the ways organizations are or are not aligned with social and moral goods, something that is surely of pastoral interest.

4. Organizations are prime mediators of injustice and need pastoral attention.

Pastoral theologians have begun to expand the foci of care to include "public, structural, and political dimensions of individual and relational experience."[42] The field's attention to personal self-actualization is being "enlarged to include responsible agency."[43] We have become concerned not just with helping individuals understand better their social contexts, but are asking ourselves how we can contribute to—or at least support—the transformation of these contexts as well. This has been our challenge—to expand our focus and practices to dynamics beyond the intrapsychic or interpersonal.

I have argued that organizational life is one place where sexism, racism, and class prejudice come together in complex and oppressive ways. For-profit companies who have racially/ethnically diverse and female persons in their employ are prime examples where this is often most significant. Blindness to or ignorance of the issues that come into play in the process of making diversity hires creates systems that disadvantage and discriminate against those hires. As Iris Marion Young puts it, "People who are perceived as racially or ethnically different by dominant groups . . . often find themselves regarded as deviant in relation to conventions of politeness, articulateness, or the appearance of honesty and trustworthiness, which matter a great deal for the attainment of positions of authority or significant responsibility."[44] The gap between what is and what could be in these contexts presents rich opportunities for pastoral theologians.

As an important basis of prophetic critique, we might use our understanding of the dynamics and nature of sin. In the theological tradition, sin is not just an individual alienation or act but an aspect of social life;[45] the discourse of sin gives us insights into the workings of power. Indeed, theologians have drawn on the biblical language of "powers and principalities" to describe the institutions and structures that "weave society into an intricate fabric of power and relationships."[46] This system of power is both embodied in the actual structures of organizations and their leaders, and it takes on a life and spirit of its own.[47] This organizational structure determines what we can imagine as possible, and orders all our lives. These dynamics of power surround us on every side, and we are dependent on them. They are not bad in and of themselves (indeed, who among us would want to live without organizations that provide meaningful work and decent livelihoods?).[48] In fact, organizations are in place, at least ideally, to serve the common good and to support the flourishing of all. Consequently, the institutions and systems that order our lives are not inherently evil. Rather, they are good, have fallen, and can be redeemed. The system of power does not simply destroy; it also makes the good possible. The reality, of course, is that it often does good and evil at the same time.[49] This understanding of the ambiguous role of systems of power and the organizations that mediate them funds my invitation that business corporations come within the purview of pastoral theologians' attention: we can be instruments of change in these contexts, helping harness positive forms of power while critiquing and helping resist the abusive forms. This contention has at its heart a faithful hope: I see the modern world—both the persons and social systems within it—as part of the reign of God, created for good but fallen and redeemable. Social institutions can serve as iron cages, but they can also serve as vehicles for God's grace. They can be the context within which the good life is lived—important mediators of flourishing—though they often fail to live up to such an ideal.

Imagining Organizational Engagement: Returning to the Case

Coming back to the case above will ground this discussion again in concrete experience. As I began to know my coachee, I learned that she had come from a small country in Asia as a young girl, escaping a country of war and trauma. She had been raped and her brother had been murdered. She seemed to be suffering from post-traumatic stress disorder (PTSD) and debilitating depression. Furthermore, she was essentially a single mother since her husband was in town only on weekends, "visiting" from his job eight hours away. She struggled to get her children to school on time and herself to work in time for the first sales meeting of the day. She was supporting an extended family, many of whom do not speak English and some of whom were unable to work for various reasons. Because of the trauma she had experienced in her life, she was afraid to live outside what felt like the safety of a close and closed Vietnamese community. She desperately missed her home country and resisted acculturating to life in the United States by speaking Vietnamese as often as possible and by resisting Western business culture. At the same time she was both good at the technical aspects of her job and desperately afraid of losing it because her leadership and management skills were lacking. I began to understand her lateness, her lack of assertiveness, and her "quite poor" communication skills as expressions of more complex personal, social, and cultural dynamics.

Through my engagement with this employee we both came to understand better the challenges she was facing, the complexities of her situation, and the fact that many of her difficulties at work stemmed from her personal struggles as well as the organization's culture and expectations. Her employers hired persons who could meet the unique needs of a changing market without considering the unique needs and situations of a racial/ethnic employee or attending to the development of the skills required for her to succeed in her job as a midlevel manager. This woman's work life had begun to feel unsafe and unstable, and she felt confused and afraid. I now understood this sense to be the result of both her PTSD, her challenges to adapt both at home and at work, and a corporate culture that expected diversity but did not support genuine multiculturalism.[50]

My client was facing difficulties at multiple levels: as an *immigrant* she struggled with the language; she felt marginalized and isolated and misunderstood. She had been raised in a culture that did not value assertiveness, directness, outspokenness, or open conflict, especially from women. As a *woman* she was facing the responsibilities of supporting her family financially by working outside the home while also shouldering the majority of the domestic labor. She struggled to manage her grief about the many losses she had experienced (including that of her "real" cultural home, her brother, her personal and cultural identity), and eventually shared with me the difficulties she was facing in her marriage and in parenting her two children. As an *employee*, she struggled to perform the duties expected of her such as dealing assertively with poor performance or dysfunctional behavior among her team members, being present at all meetings no matter the time of day, and being a full participant of the company even as it did little to help her develop the skills she needed to succeed and even less to support her integration into the corporate culture. She was trying to lead her team even as her authority was sabotaged, and she was (subtly and not so subtly) made fun of for her accent, some of her behaviors, and her views of work and business protocol.

While I realize that our efforts are only a modest beginning, they provide insight into possibilities for pastoral theologians' work in organizational life. Because of the particular location I held in the lives of this woman and the organization, I was permitted to do a different kind of pastoral work: we integrated personal change and organizational change in ways unusual for a pastoral practitioner or a corporate consultant. In effect, my work bridged these two professions. By tending to personal symptoms we also gained insight into organizational dynamics and the challenges they posed for her. In our work together we were able to address both individual and organizational change, at least in small ways, and she began to strategize how to get professional support for her personal psychological healing. Because of my role as a consultant for leaders at multiple levels in the organization (not just the woman in the case), I could intervene in the system in a variety of ways, opening lines of communication, deepening understanding among various employees about the situation(s) they were all facing, helping set more realistic expectations for the employee and her management, increasing support (both material and emotional) and coaching individuals toward developing particular skills. I was able to offer the client in this case some realistic hope that the company's leadership was open to something other than the status quo and that they were open to (at least some) organizational changes that would promote better the well-being of their team members. She and I addressed the culture clashes she was facing—in and outside the company—in both our one-on-one work and in discussions with her managers. In addition, I began to articulate with her managers a vision of an antiracist, multicultural organization that went beyond EEOC compliance—a normative vision informed by my own commitments to liberation theologies, feminist and multicultural perspectives, and the values that I seek to embody as a Christian practitioner.

Hiring and employment practices often are geared toward diversity without significant consideration of the basic structure, mission, or culture of the system; however, organizations benefit most, as do their employees, when, in addition to the reasons articulated above, employers are also open to being challenged and changed by their diversity hires, recognizing them for the unique perspectives and contributions they can provide and responding in creative ways to the unique needs and challenges that diversity presents.[51] Part of my work in this case was to help create an organizational environment and relationships between this woman and her managers in which it was safe to address the conflicts and speak one's needs.[52] She was able to get some of the management coaching she needed to succeed and her managers supported her leadership and addressed challenges to her authority in her group. One manager in particular came to see her with new eyes, appreciating her as a human being (not just a human resource), and becoming an ardent advocate for her at work.

After many conversations with my coachee and her managers, I helped frame the challenges as both personal and organizational; managers began identifying and implementing small changes that benefited both the individual and the organization.[53] After beginning to trust that the leaders of her organization cared about her as a person as well as an employee and beginning to believe that they wanted to find ways to address her challenges at work, my coachee enrolled in English classes, which her manager committed to paying for with company funds. She began to negotiate with her supervisor a shared work schedule with a colleague during the week as well as a day during the weekend when she could work from home when she had help with childcare. Together we complexified our understanding of and responses to what originally were taken to be primarily personal leadership challenges. My client began to feel freer, more empowered, more courageous, and more hopeful.

This change was possible because of my theologically informed perspective on human wholeness coupled with a unique form of pastoral practice: I was meeting my client in one-on-one sessions, but I was also meeting with the people to whom this woman reported, which meant I could address the systemic and organizational contributors to distress and poor performance. In fact, because the company *and* the individual employee were my clients, and because I was coaching her managers in the two levels above her, I was able to share, within reasonable expectations of confidentiality, her managers' personal commitments and values, and could inquire into the ways personal and corporate values and their management expectations and policies were not aligned. I found that her managers were interested in supporting their employees' professional development, though their policies and practices did not always indicate this.[54] Because of my role as a coach and organizational consultant, I was not simply offering solace and encouraging adjustment to her employing company's culture; I could also be an institutional guide, trying to humanize the larger structure within which this woman found herself. By forming professional relationships with leaders at several levels in the organization, I could do the work this particular employee's situation invited: I was able to analyze critically the needs and expectations of both the employees, the management, and the company itself to see whether what was being practiced was in line with the identity and mission each wanted to live.

My role as organizational and leadership consultant gave me an opportunity to do deeper institutional work and connect it to the realities of the individuals trying to find safe passage within the larger organization. In this way I was doing both pastoral and prophetic work. This expanded role, I think, accounts for the satisfaction that often attended my sense of a good day's work.

Pastoral Theologians Have a Unique Contribution to Make Toward Organizational Change

Using Professional Skills in New Ways

Pastoral theologians could expand their contexts of engagement and bring to this work a commitment to help create organizations that are more flexible, responsible, and just. We might, for example, put our shoulders to the work of developing truly multicultural organizations in which employees are seen as full participants and change agents as the system works to overcome racism, xenophobia, and sexism, and play a significant role in the shape and direction of mission and policies and practices of the organization that are inclusive of diverse cultures, lifestyles, interests, and abilities. Since the flourishing of persons is heavily dependent upon the organizations that hold them, it makes sense that this would become a subject of our attention and context of our work.

Of course, participating in organizational change will mean we pastoral theologians will have to make room for ourselves in an arena already crowded with leadership consultants, industrial psychologists, management specialists, organizational development professionals, leadership coaches, and corporate chaplains. While these groups may be doing important work, they are not often tasked with changing the organization as much as they are called to adjust individuals within it. While this can be true, too, of consultants such as myself, pastoral theologians offer a needed and increasingly valued perspective and prophetic voice that is unique. When my clients inside these organizations learned that I had a graduate degree in theology, they opened up in deeper ways than they might have if my title were "organizational psychologist." I was permitted to inquire about deepest aspirations, moral dilemmas, questions of meaning and purpose, highest values of both the employees and the company leadership. Members of nontheologically oriented professional organizations are doing their best and do provide useful interventions, but such work would be greatly enhanced by a theological and socially critical perspective as well as practices that are theoretically, theologically, and practically sound. For example, in the case above I was able to support my coachee and her managers in the development of their analysis and understanding of the situation that led us to a more inclusive understanding of self- and corporate-interest, one that went beyond individual income, status, and stability in the economic hierarchy to embrace the well-being of employment base more broadly.[55]

Pastoral theologians and practitioners are uniquely qualified to do such work for at least five reasons.

1. Pastoral theologians are guided by theological principles, psychological insights, and practical training, and we bring these together in powerful ways. We can articulate a normative vision of what could/should be in any given situation and can devise practices to close the gap between what is and what ought to be.

2. Pastoral theologians are increasingly versed in the intersections of personal experience and sociocultural/systemic context, a perspective that is required for the work I am inviting us to consider. We can offer appropriately complex diagnoses that account for the ways past personal experiences shape and intersect with organizational contexts to inhibit growth and well-being.

3. Religiously/theologically trained persons may be able to harness the values and meaning-making potential as well as make explicit fulsome visions of flourishing that other professionals may not be interested in

or equipped to address. This ability is important since religion increasingly is finding a place in the work world, and studies on immigrant persons have shown the importance for them especially of incorporating religious perspectives into one's attempts to meet the challenges of life in the new world.[56] Pastoral theologians are uniquely able to engage and use for positive change this level of human experience while also attending to intrapsychic, interpersonal, and systemic dynamics that impede well-being.

4. At the individual level, pastoral theologians can participate in the personal development of individuals (as we have always done well), guiding and supporting them as they gain increasingly complex understandings of themselves and their world. We can harness the opportunities for growth women in these situations can face, helping persons devise strategic and effective interventions toward individual and organizational/systemic change. Pastoral theologians can also help women who, like my client, must navigate the increased antagonism and relational strife that can result from new forms of power, guiding the development of new confidence, empowerment, and courage; such work surely is within the realm of the compassionate, resisting, accompanying roles recommended for us by fellow pastoral theologians.[57]

5. Women (especially racial and ethnic minority women who are often isolated and marginalized in predominantly white organizations) benefit from efforts to provide safe spaces to acknowledge and deal with the deeply negative effects of sexism, xenophobia, and racism. We might help support their efforts to build networks of relationships that help them strategize their resistance to the policies and dynamics that undermine employees' flourishing.[58]

Changing Places: A Challenge to Professional Identity?

Pastoral theologians might struggle with their professional identity if they expand their role to working in organizational settings, but it may not be as far a stretch as some imagine. We understand the importance of whole persons within healthy systems, and recognize that well-being includes a spiritual or religious dimension of life. These dimensions of wholeness (individual/psychological, systemic/organizational, and spiritual/religious) are coming together in intriguing ways: as I indicate above, data suggest that an attention to religion increasingly is being integrated into corporate culture, and employees are being more explicit about bringing their religious and spiritual lives into the workplace. Companies are hiring chaplains and professionals are hiring "spiritual coaches" with greater frequency (though, granted, this is usually for their own personal benefit and not for the purposes of helping transform organizations). Pastoral theologians may be able to take advantage of these trends and gain access to contexts unusual for our work. By so doing we may be able to serve the needs of populations that are currently not commonly seen in our offices and undertake work that is more prophetic than that of other consultants or even, perhaps, of clinicians working strictly at the personal level.

Working at the individual *and* organizational levels will require an intentional engagement with leaders of organizations, including capitalistic, for-profit ones. Rather than demonizing and avoiding such organizations and ignoring people's experiences at work, pastoral practitioners can seek to understand better how deeply dependent we all are on such enterprises, and might develop perspectives and practices that can increase organizations' abilities to support a good society that supports human thriving. We are technically adept at developing practices that support and effect change, and we are experienced at addressing the complex resistances to it. Pastoral theologians bring to this work the tools to help individuals develop into differentiated but connected, mature, compassionate, and conscientious participants who can better redress the corporate injustice and discrimination that impede flourishing. Ideally, our engagement in the institutions that organize work lives could help create contexts that are less stressful, that expect and support mature relationships, and provide opportunities for more creative and meaningful labor. Because of the deeply transformative potential in this work, we might even begin to go home with more energy and enthusiasm for our own vocations and the organizations within which we undertake them. Good work, indeed.

Part Four

Challenges Ahead

In spite of all that can be learned in the previous sections, it is clear that many challenges still lie ahead in the field of pastoral theology/pastoral care. These challenges compel us not to get comfortable with a bit of new knowledge, but to embrace cultural competence with humility and to understand it as a lifelong process. The authors in this section conclude the volume with words of caution and prophetic vision of the emerging frontier of multicultural care.

Soul Care Amid Religious Plurality

Excavating an Emerging Dimension of Multicultural Challenge and Competence

Kathleen J. Greider

In the United States generally, and in the field of pastoral care and counseling specifically, work on multicultural issues has only barely begun to address the specific challenges of religious particularity and plurality. This is the case despite the fact that the United States is now argued to be the most religiously diverse country in the world.[1] Across the nation, more and more frequently, we are encountering persons of religious identity different from our own in our public institutions, workplaces, neighborhoods—and even in our families, religious communities, and religious schools. If we came to these encounters well educated and nonviolent in our attitudes, speech, and action with regard to religious particularity and plurality, the religious dimension of multiculturalism might not need specific attention. However—as with race/ethnicity, gender, sexuality, ability, and other dimensions of diversity—segregation, attitudes of superiority, and patterns of domination have tended to characterize human interactions in regard to religious differences. Consequently, interreligious encounters tend to be hampered at least by ignorance and insensitivity, and too often by subjugation and hostility. Where religion is concerned, there is very little multicultural competence, and that insufficiency is undermining our progress toward genuine intercultural dialogue and cooperation.

In pastoral care and counseling, considerable progress has been made toward attending in theory and practice to many dimensions of multiculturalism, especially race/ethnicity, gender, and sexuality. Still, the majority of us have been practicing monoculturalism in regard to religion. This is less true of those who teach and practice chaplaincy—these colleagues have been on the leading edge of an approaching tidal wave of interreligious encounter in soul care. Especially in chaplaincy, where religious professionals typically are expected both to restrict their care to the dimensions of religion or spirituality and to provide soul care to persons of religious traditions different from their own, teachers and practitioners have had to grapple more intentionally and explicitly with interreligious encounters. Their learnings are beginning to be reflected in the English-language literature and pedagogy in chaplaincy.[2] To a lesser degree, religious diversity has also been acknowledged in the counseling literature that informs pastoral psychotherapy.[3] But for the most part, religious diversity has not been addressed in the field of pastoral care and counseling, and the demands of soul care amid religious plurality far exceed the field's resources.

This has been understandable, since the majority of scholars, teachers, and practitioners of "pastoral" care have been Christian and focused on congregational settings and practices. A few texts explore pastoral care in the context of Judaism.[4] But, understandably, given the origins of the field of pastoral theology and care in Christian contexts, its literature and teaching have tended to assume Christian caregivers and Christian care seekers and, thus, the adequacy of Christian categories and values for soul care. Of course, Christian theory and practices in pastoral care and counseling have important contributions to make amid religious plurality. Indeed, some professionals in religious traditions other than Christianity are looking to Christians in theological schools and clinical pastoral education (CPE) programs for education about how they might better provide care within their own religious communities.

As religious plurality more widely influences everyday life, however, Christian traditions of "pastoral" theology and care are no longer sufficient by themselves to carry out adequate care of souls. For all religious leaders, not only Christians, the increasing frequency of interreligious encounters presents special challenges and calls for new competencies, especially in our practices of care and counsel. The integrity of soul care and of its practitioners will increasingly require attention to the reality of religious plurality within and beyond our specific communities, questions that plurality raises relative to the Christian origins of theory and practice in soul care, and the new resources for interreligious soul care that can be developed only through sustained and collaborative scholarship by religiously diverse teams of religious caregivers.

In this chapter I reflect on just a few of the challenges and opportunities presented by soul care amid religious plurality.[5] I identify and speak to these issues as a Christian, which will make my ideas more likely to reflect and speak to the experiences of Christian readers, though I also have in mind and am trying to address a religiously diverse readership. Similarly, I have in mind diverse practitioners: not only chaplains but also leaders of religious communities (pastors, rabbis, imams, others) and teachers of soul care. In recognition of an immediate question posed to Christian traditions in soul care—What terminology will respect religious diversity?—I will use the designation *pastoral* only when referring to Christian tradition or practices in the field and otherwise will use the less limiting terms of "soul care" or "religious caregiving." (I do not use the terminology of "spiritual" care/giver because the focus of this chapter is on encounter between adherents of religious traditions, not on care of the nonreligious or of those who designate themselves "spiritual but not religious.") Though the relationship between caregivers and care seekers is in the forefront of my attention, the issues and practices we will explore are also likely to be active when there is religious difference between teachers and students or supervisors and supervisees.

Interreligious encounter may seem a rather distant reality for readers who are not chaplains, and so in the next section, I offer a few vignettes through which to bring to life some of the everyday ways that religious pluralism is complicating human identity and challenging Christian traditions in soul care. Then I note two issues of theory that become significant when religious diversity is considered from the perspective of soul care. To close the chapter, I explore some practices that have special importance when we seek to offer soul care in interreligious encounters. It is important to emphasize that—like an archeologist excavating a very limited area of an ancient site with a small brush—my efforts here are limited and tentative. We are just beginning to recognize the parameters and depth of the challenges posed by religious plurality to the traditionally Christian field of pastoral care and counseling. Therefore, I can name only a few dimensions of the challenge and offer only provisional suggestions for praxis.

Before moving to these matters, two final introductory comments are needed. First, religion will be the aspect of culture and multiculturalism in the center of our attention in this chapter, but it is important to remember throughout our reflections that a focus on any one aspect of culture falsely simplifies the complex, dynamic, and often divisive interplay of all elements of culture. For example, if we really take religious particularity and plurality seriously, we cannot ignore how racial-ethnic particularities and conflicts loom over our discussion. Consider, for example, how the history of Christian evangelism is to a large extent a record of white missionaries dismantling the indigenous religions of other peoples—Native Americans, indigenous Hawaiians, tribes throughout Africa, Buddhist and shamanistic Koreans, and many more. Similarly, the challenges of religious plurality have specific cultural shapes when viewed from the perspectives of girls and women. We need only think of the ongoing debates within and between religions over Christian women's rights to ordination and Muslim women's rights to determine their use of head scarves and other coverings to see how religious plurality and gender differences are intertwined. The dynamics of race/ethnicity, gender, and other dimensions of cultural difference are mostly in the background in this essay, but their importance relative to soul care amid religious plurality is an important area for further investigation.

Religious Pluralism Comes Home

Consider these three vignettes that portray dimensions of religious pluralism in the context with which I am most familiar—Christianity. Each are fictional composites of experiences familiar to me and my students, but they show realistically how religious pluralism and interreligious encounter are not distant realities but rather come home to us in everyday ways.[6]

> *The monthly newsletter of a New England congregation in an old-line Protestant denomination contains an announcement inviting everyone to a meditation group. The group was started quietly a few months earlier by a few members who have long been struggling in private with some sort of disability or chronic illness. When the men's fellowship meets over breakfast the week after the announcement, the meditation group becomes a topic of conversation. A number of the men nod in agreement when one says, "Why should a Christian church advocate meditation—isn't that some sort of New Age thing?" The next month, the newsletter announces that a Buddhist monk will come to give instruction to the meditation group. With this news, and the news that the pastor is participating in the meditation, the controversy grows. At the next meeting of the church council, the majority of which represents the demographics of the congregation—white, sixty-five to seventy years of age, little traveled—all eyes focus on Rev. Grace Kim when one council member forcefully asks the young 1.5-generation Korean American pastor to defend her actions.*

How can this pastor caringly approach the education that is needed to address this tangle of issues related to religious particularity and pluralism? Growing religious illiteracy leaves new and old members of religious communities ill-informed about other traditions—in this case, the role of meditation in religious traditions other than Christianity. But religious literacy is also declining *within* traditions—the council members appear unaware of their own religious particularity, about the history of contemplative prayer in Christianity. Thus, they see meditation only as religiously foreign and theologically suspect, the kind of fear-engendering misinformation that can lead to dismissive labeling—"some sort of New Age thing"—or worse. Most of the members at the breakfast and the council meeting also seem unaware of and insensitive to the religious particularity and diversity in their own congregation—by asking the pastor to defend her actions, implying criticism, they are also implying criticism of their fellow members with disabilities or chronic illnesses, who may already be feeling marginalized. In all fairness, those raising complaint may have been taught (explicitly or implicitly) that Christianity *requires* an attitude of superiority or evangelization toward other religions. So, what looks from the outside like theologically fueled religious superiority or intolerance may be for them an insistence on religious purity they think is required if they wish to be considered faithful Christians. For Christians formed in this way, hosting the Buddhist monk for education and conversation is irrelevant at best, and perhaps blasphemous.

But the notion that religious purity is possible also makes it difficult for us to recognize how persons are themselves often religiously plural. In this case, it may be difficult for both the pastor and her congregation (and this would be no less difficult if her congregants were Korean) to recognize the reality—much less reconcile themselves to it—of Buddhism's inevitable effect on Koreans.

Due to its historical and ongoing significance in Korean culture, Buddhism is likely to be culturally or religiously significant even for the most devoted Korean American Christian pastor—a part of her family's religious history or otherwise a part of her religio-cultural DNA, impossible to simply discard, even if she desired to do so. Her youth and gender will likely make it more difficult for her to address the needs of those raising complaint, the needs of the disabled and ill seeking holistic spiritual sustenance from meditation, and the needs of her own religiously pluralistic soul.

> *The Reverend Theodore Jones, an African American Christian pastor, receives a phone call from Marcella, a young woman who has been a leader among the youth in Rev. Jones' congregation. Marcella and her family became active in the congregation in her teenage years, just after they immigrated to the United States from Ghana. The family was drawn to this particular congregation because its worship services combine elements of African traditional religion with the rich history of African American Christianity. With excitement, Marcella tells her pastor the news of her engagement to a man who shares her passion about religion—Martin is an observant Jew and a grandson of German Jews who died in concentration camps during the Shoah.[7] Reverend Jones is surprised to find himself concerned and suddenly realizes that, despite his good experience of interreligious encounter in the context of his clinical pastoral education and service as a chaplain, it never occurred to him that religious diversity might come home to his congregation. He is momentarily reassured when Marcella asks him to participate in the wedding ceremony, alongside Martin's rabbi. However, Rev. Jones is again surprised by the depth of his dismay when in their first conversation about the service Marcella quickly assures Rabbi Smith that she and Martin will raise their children in the Jewish tradition and then goes on to say that lately she has found herself considering conversion to Judaism.*

Here we see aspects of religious pluralism similar to some in the previous vignette. Reverend Jones and his congregation are religiously plural, though more intentionally and positively so than Rev. Kim's congregation—pastor and members alike appear comfortable with being Christian and at the same time expressive in their worship life of spiritual values and religious practices inherited from African traditional religion. As in the previous vignette, we see here the interface of two religious communities—this time Jewish and African-Christian. Here, though, the encounter is not fleeting, as would be the case in the educational exchange at Rev. Kim's church, but a more substantial partnership required for creating an interreligious wedding—and marriage. Like Rev. Kim, Rev. Jones has been developing a theological stance in which he values religious plurality, though here pluralism asks him not simply to embrace religious difference but to release Marcella and her family to a different religion, should she choose conversion.

But in this vignette, our attention is drawn to an additional important dimension of religious pluralism, and one where neglect by pastoral caregivers has been addressed in the literature: religiously plural families. One aspect of this challenge manifests in what were once called "interchurch" marriages— marriages between Catholic Christians and Protestant Christians or between Protestants of different denominations. Even when the pluralism has been of this relatively limited degree, these Christian—but still religiously plural— families have long suffered judgment and consequent neglect at the hands of their pastors. In a 1988 essay, one Catholic priest went so far as to call the degree of neglect malpractice.[8] George Kilcourse noted that couples who challenge the theological and social proscriptions against intermarriage are often invisible to their respective clergy because both spouses tend not to be assimilated into each other's religious communities. "The 'other' partner, and hence eventually both members of the couple, constitute a seemingly unassimilable [sic] foreign body; parishes cannot make accommodations for them."[9] This situation is exemplified by the story Kilcourse tells of a Protestant woman who, after a year of attending church, was invited by her pastor to join a widow's group: "My husband's not dead," she had to inform her pastor, "he's just a Roman Catholic!"[10] Also neglected have been couples with children;[11] for example, the religious communities of each parent both expect to be chosen as the environment for the children's religious education; if not chosen, the community tends to overlook other opportunities for caring for the family.

Feeling welcomed and at home in each other's religious communities is rarely reported by religiously plural families. Rather, the literature notes that the failure of religious communities to assimilate both members of a couple or the whole family into both communities seems to contribute to religious disaffiliation of the whole family.[12] Given that attention to religious plurality has barely increased in pastoral care education, it would not be surprising to hear from Rev. Jones that his theological education did not give attention to interreligious marriage, or to how he might best support Marcella, whether she continues to be related to his congregation through family ties but herself chooses conversion, or whether she does not convert and thus faces even more substantial challenges as she and her husband try to create a religiously plural family.

Professor Monica Smith walks back to her office mulling over the group of students she has just met in the first session of her introductory course in pastoral care and counseling. A Christian clergywoman educated in Christian schools, she now teaches in a progressive Christian theological school where the students in her classes increasingly represent the diversity of religion. This year there are a half dozen Unitarian Universalist (UU) students and, because they have grown accustomed to being assumed by their professors and classmates to be Christian, a few of them introduced themselves by noting that most UUs are not Christian, and they need to learn how to provide pastoral care in congregations that are not only religiously diverse but are also havens for humanists, agnostics, and atheists. There are two Muslims and a Buddhist studying to become chaplains, and all of them enrolled at a Christian school because the kind of education expected by professional guilds for the certification of chaplains is rare or nonexistent in their own religious traditions. There is a Jewish rabbi from the Conservative tradition enrolled in the D.Min. program and a woman from the Reformed branch of Judaism who has been to rabbinical school and is now considering whether to pursue a degree in counseling, maybe pastoral counseling. And then there are the Christians, in all their remarkable diversity: preachers' kids steeped in Christianity and ministry; new converts, many of them learning the Christian tradition for the first time; Christians from Korea and Africa and Armenia; progressive Christians, liberal Christians, conservative Christians, evangelical Christians, fundamentalist Christians, orthodox Christians, Buddhist Christians. . . .

The need to provide care in religiously plural contexts happens frequently, but, at least in the Christian tradition, education for caregiving amid religious plurality appears to be uncommon. Even where future religious leaders get instruction in religious diversity and interreligious engagement, *caregiving* receives little attention. Interreligious *dialogue* is not the same as—and too often stops short of—interreligious *care*. Rare indeed are curricula that address how religious caregivers should undertake the care of someone from a tradition different from their own. It is especially puzzling that the Christian pastoral care and counseling literature on interreligious caregiving is so sparse, given the extensive literature on interreligious dialogue and the prominence of education in care of souls as a part of preparation for Christian ministry. Though Christian academics and practitioners in pastoral care and counseling characterize ourselves as more engaged than many scholars in theology and religion with the real circumstances of diverse human communities—more attentive to "the living human document" and "living human web"—thus far we have tended not to extend our attention beyond Christians.

Professor Smith's classroom helps us see nuances in how and why religious particularity and increasing interreligious encounter call for changes in the education of religious professionals. First note the extreme diversity of the Christian students brought together by Professor Smith's course. Encounters between persons of the same religious tradition are not typically considered to be interreligious. However, the interpretations of Christianity held by the Christian students are likely so divergent and polarizing that it may seem they do not belong to the same tradition, that there are Christiani*ties*. Professor Smith is likely to find that, for example, it is more difficult for the so-called liberal and conservative Christian students in her class to interact caringly with each other than to treat their colleagues from other religions with respect. Debates *within* a tradition—such as those about sexuality and gender—are often more personally hurtful and therefore difficult for adherents to navigate than differences *between* religions. Given the extent of sectarian conflict within many religious traditions, it may be time to admit that *intra*religious encounters challenge us to change our attitudes and behavior at least as much as *inter*religious ones.

If Professor Smith intentionally uses the intrareligious differences and divergences among her conservative and liberal Christian students as an opportunity for teaching care, her students will be better equipped to react constructively amid the bitter theological disputes that too often divide congregations and split denominations.

Of course, it is enormously significant and challenging that there are persons of other religious traditions trying to learn soul care from the Christian tradition. Professor Smith's school has enrolled this religiously diverse group of applicants and the students have paid tuition, all in mutual good faith that this traditionally Christian school has education to offer that will benefit all these students. Just as genuine response to the racial/ethnic and gender particularity of students leads to changes in curriculum and pedagogy, so also will genuine response to students from traditions other than Christianity cause professors of pastoral care to begin the long process of reworking our theory and practice with religious diversity in mind. Professor Smith's education has not prepared her for this—could not have, given the mostly Christian identity of the field of pastoral care and counseling thus far. But she cannot and need not take on this revision by herself. Respecting the expertise of her students in their own traditions, she can engage her students as collaborators. As K. Samuel Lee has noted relative to our efforts to revise pastoral care and counseling theory and practice in light of racial/ethnic diversity, making theory and practice in pastoral care and counseling more responsive to religious particularity and diversity can begin with professors and students engaging in "collaborative inquiry."[13] Currently, most students who are not Christian are engaged in a constant and difficult process of translation—trying on their own to figure out how to make theological education steeped in the Christian tradition a resource for their tradition. But if Professor Smith is able intentionally to collaborate with her UU, Muslim, Buddhist, and Jewish students in considering the relevance or revision of Christian pastoral care theory and practice for their contexts, together they will begin the process of invention and revision that is called for as a response to religious particularity and pluralism.

However, such collaboration will benefit not only Professor Smith and the students who are not Christian, because interreligious encounter is increasingly required of religious professionals in all traditions. As we have seen, her Christian students will benefit from learning how to care for multireligious families and for persons and communities who find spiritual nurture in more than one religious tradition. Professor Smith's open collaboration with students from diverse traditions will empower all her students to recognize and provide education when religious illiteracy impairs interreligious and intrareligious encounters. All her students will be faced with the challenges of responding to religious diversity and pluralism in their professional roles, and so our wrestling with the Christian basis and bias of the pastoral care and counseling literature will benefit Christian students as much as students from any other tradition.

Soul Care and Religious Pluralism: Two Theoretical Issues

Of the many theoretical issues where exploration is required if soul care is to be more responsive to religious pluralism and interreligious caregiving, I will briefly describe two.

Religiously Plural Persons and Communities

I have grown accustomed to hearing people describe themselves as biracial, bilingual, bisexual, bicultural. Recently, however, it was quite striking to hear a colleague refer to herself as "bi-religious."[14] Postmodern scholarship in soul care has identified the insufficiency in the modern notion of a unified self and drawn our attention to the often functional reality that human identity is composed of a multiplicity of self-experience and self-presentation, as appropriate in different contexts.[15] Thinking of this multiplicity in terms of religious identity, however, remains less common. Theory and practice in soul care has tended to assume "pure" religious identity—persons are assumed to belong to *a* tradition; religious communities are assumed to embody *a* tradition. But as our vignettes have suggested, this internal religious pluralism occurs relatively frequently *within* persons and communities.

Religious pluralism within persons and communities tends to be judged negatively. Why? Being religiously plural seems in many traditions to be considered unfaithful. Or, to put it positively, those persons and communities who are considered most mature in a tradition are normally persons who identify with only one religion—they are, if you will, religiously monogamous. In some traditions, desire for religious purity is fueled by concern that syncretism (like intermarriage) threatens the survival of a tradition and dilutes the meaning of doctrine. Quite disdainful judgments are leveled at persons who are said to take a "supermarket approach" to their religion and/or spirituality—persons "pick and choose" beliefs and practices indiscriminately, or according to personal taste, without substantial knowledge of the traditions from which they are "borrowing," and so use those traditions without integrity. "True" converts (communities as well as persons) embrace their new religion completely and, if they previously practiced another religion, divorce themselves from it. There is also well-founded concern about whether religions can be combined meaningfully in this way, without violating the integrity of both or being overwhelmed with the discipline and time required adequately to learn and practice more than one tradition. For all these reasons, singular religious identity has been assumed and argued to be preferable.

However, religiously plural persons and communities also are formed in other, less dubious, sometimes unavoidable, circumstances. Though it seems the majority of persons do indeed know only one religion, and happily so, others find that such religious purity and loyalty is not an option. Some persons seek to know more than one tradition because of an inherent limitation in their native tradition[16] or, even more commonly, because their native tradition has done them harm. Some persons are born into religiously plural cultures.[17] Others are born or marry into religiously plural families—children who learn the different religious traditions of their parents; spouses who do not convert to the different religion of a spouse but do desire sincerely to learn and practice with their loved one, as much as possible. Where conversion takes place, whether of a person or of a people, it cannot obliterate all vestiges of prior religious beliefs and practices: converts, however devoutly drawn to a new tradition, cannot simply abandon prior religious culture and history, any more than a person can abandon their mother tongue by becoming bilingual. Some people cannot fail to be affected by their religiously plural cultures—the literature in pastoral care and counseling is beginning to explore this reality, considering for example, how Confucianism, Shamanism, and Buddhism are threaded through the beliefs and practices of Korean Christians,[18] and African traditional religious practices are embedded in African American Christians and congregations.[19] And even where a person converts with genuineness and integrity, it takes many years, even decades, to learn a new tradition thoroughly. If we allow that the degree of diversity within Christianity can also be argued to be religious pluralism, the widely referenced description and distinction between embedded and deliberative theologies in Christian faith development can help us see how Christians themselves are religiously plural.[20]

Care for persons of mixed religious identities is mostly uncharted territory. Given this, we can find help from Peter Yuichi Clark's discussion of similarly uncharted territory—the experience of mixed-race persons.[21] Clark suggests several emphases for care with mixed-race persons that can be adapted for care with persons of mixed religious identities. First, caregivers can be mindful that a religiously plural identity, especially because of the historic judgments against syncretism, can carry with it feelings of confusion, aloneness, and even alienation. Offering deep listening to these feelings may help the care seeker to become more aware of these challenges, the social imposition of many of them, and perhaps more at peace with the complexity of their religious identity. Second, the caregiver who welcomes and affirms the richness and wholeness of the religiously plural care seeker may assist care seekers to consider that their complexity might be one dimension of "the pluralistic, multi-faced, multi-voiced goodness of God's creation."[22] Third, religious caregivers can honor the experience of marginality experienced by many religiously plural persons, first by not minimizing it but also by exploring with the care seeker the gifts that their marginality might yield—for example, compassion for other marginalized persons, their unique perspective, and the capacity to bridge the gaps that normally exist between the religious cultures they embrace.[23] Fourth, religious caregivers can affirm and make space for identity development as it is experienced by religiously plural people—not necessarily linear and consistent but rather characterized by "context and contingency, with multiple affiliations and particularities."[24]

Philosophies of Religious Plurality for Caregiving

For the sake of effective interreligious soul care, religious caregivers need to have a nuanced philosophy through which to understand the variety of religions and their often competing truth claims. The field of Christian pastoral theology and care has tended to address this question pragmatically, through its widely accepted argument that authentic and ethical soul care requires that caregivers not impose on the care seeker the caregiver's religious identity, beliefs, and practices but rather honor those of the care seeker. While this standard for care is well founded, the field of pastoral theology and care has tended to sidestep the question of how the caregiver is to accomplish this, given different philosophies in Christianity regarding the value of religious pluralism. However, scholars whose primary interest is in religious pluralism and interreligious dialogue have created a nuanced discussion and substantial literature that can help religious caregivers sketch the parameters of this difficulty and some of the ways it complicates meaningful interreligious soul care. Addressing this issue from a Christian perspective, Paul Knitter offers a nuanced and even-handed description of four common ways that Christians approach the oftentimes conflicting truth claims of different religious systems.[25]

In what Knitter names the *replacement* approach, Christians' deep commitment to Christ and to the Bible leads to the position that only through Christianity can G-d[26] and salvation be known—for this reason, interreligious dialogue has value but, ultimately, "Christianity is meant to replace all other religions."[27] The *fulfillment* approach is shaped by an equal commitment to the universality of G-d and the particularity of G-d's revelation in Jesus Christ—these Christians pursue interreligious dialogue because G-d's universality assures there is value in other religions, value that is ultimately fulfilled through G-d's particular revelation in Jesus Christ. *Mutuality* is the aim of a third approach, Knitter says, in which Christians' commitment to the universality of G-d's love makes interreligious dialogue an imperative, so much so that they relativize their claims about Jesus' particularity in hopes of creating a "level playing field" for dialogue in which persons of all religions are mutually enlightened. Finally, the *acceptance* approach is in part a corrective to the mutuality approach, which has been criticized for emphasizing dialogue and religions' similarities at the cost of overriding religions' particularities. Christians using this last approach instead emphasize that there are radical, essential differences between religions that cannot be adjudicated but must simply be accepted—this approach emphasizes the limits of interreligious communication (even more so with dialogue) given the degree of differences among religions. One of the most remarkable and valuable aspects of Knitter's work is that he refuses to idealize or demonize any of these approaches. Those espousing the more "conservative" replacement and fulfillment approaches and those espousing the more "liberal" mutuality and acceptance approaches often caricature each other's positions and fall into competitive and disdainful disputes over which approach is most faithful. But Knitter does a masterful job of discussing the insights of each approach and identifying the questions each one leaves unanswered.

As among Christians in general, all four of these approaches are found among Christians who provide soul care. But we must raise a delicate question—Do all four promote interreligious soul care equally well? If we take into consideration the starting point and basic standards for interreligious soul care noted above— respect for others' religions and carefulness not to impose the caregiver's religion on care seekers—it seems that a combination of the mutuality and acceptance approaches best assures these two standards. Indeed, though not stated as such, the stances of the mutuality and acceptance approaches have dominated the theory and practice of soul care. Several values account for this. First, both approaches provide a philosophical rationale for a widely agreed-upon priority in soul care: care of persons and communities is given priority over preservation of a religious tradition or faithfulness to a doctrine. This priority emerges from a second confluence: both the mutuality and acceptance approaches affirm the possibility that divine revelation is possible in all religious traditions, an extension of pastoral theology's foundational theological assertion that the holy can be revealed in human experience of all kinds. Third, the literature and standards for practice in soul care suggest that all human encounters occasioned by suffering require not merely tolerance but the further respect of nonjudgment and affirmation inherent in mutuality and acceptance approaches. Fourth, both these approaches seek to privilege the subjectivity of religious others, which is congruent with the caregiving standard that the caregiver take steps to avoid projection and refrain from acting out countertransference.[28]

The mutuality and acceptance approaches are so widely and highly valued among professionals teaching and providing soul care that they are sometimes embraced uncritically. However, both present problems. For example, the mutuality approach affirms the ministry of presence so prized in soul care—compassionate presence can create a relational bridge over religious gaps. But both the mutuality model and the ministry of presence risk emphasizing similarity at the expense of fully engaging religious difference. Joseph Viti admits a truth with which few of us have adequately wrestled: "there are times when the relational quality of pastoral care relationships is not sufficient to bridge the [religious] gap."[29] Another problem is the relativism that characterizes both the mutuality and acceptance approaches: If we say that all religious traditions provide pathways to the divine and to sanctification, what criteria do we have to identify and seek to abolish wrongdoing, which is so often the cause of the suffering that soul care seeks to alleviate? Third, emphasis on difference—the radical otherness of others—is highly valued in the acceptance approach, and in soul care. Ultimately, however, caregivers' responsibility is to try to make human connections amid difference, a responsibility that suggests the mutuality approach is most often used by religious caregivers but which leaves us always vulnerable to its overemphasis on similarity. Professional standards call for practitioners to maintain their own religious integrity while providing care for people in other traditions. However, this is very difficult to achieve, and it is common that practitioners resort to genericism—assuming or trying to identify religious understandings and practices common to all traditions. Some say this genericism poses problems in soul care—it becomes shallow, disingenuous about the extent of our differences, unable to adjudicate between life-giving religiosity and that which thwarts life.[30] Perhaps more important for meaningful relationship is a lesson learned through decades of interreligious dialogue—meaningful encounter cannot occur by hiding differences but rather requires that all participants are able to maintain a clarity of identity and find ways to articulate their particularity as part of the encounter. Interestingly, Knitter observes that one of the insights of the replacement and fulfillment approaches is that they enable their adherents to maintain a valuable clarity of religious identity, a clarity Christian pastoral care has been accused of underemphasizing.

Finally, both the mutuality and acceptance approaches are widely embraced because they espouse humility about one's own religion and respect for difference in other traditions. But persons espousing these positions are not immune from the audaciousness and intolerance of which the replacement and fulfillment approaches are often accused. Even if we can at an intellectual level accept radical difference, we may have little heart for authentic engagement with those radically different others and even fall into judgmentalism. We see this dynamic when "liberal" practitioners of soul care find it remarkably difficult—especially where personally charged issues like sexuality or gender are at stake—to offer the mutuality and acceptance they espouse to "conservative" care seekers, students, or supervisees. This gap between principle and practice is not surprising though, as it takes uncommon depth of spiritual maturity to offer soul care to someone whose beliefs judge us or violate our most precious beliefs. Many of us will retreat, even involuntarily or unconsciously, again revealing the limits of the mutuality and acceptance approaches.

Building on our earlier discussion of multiple senses of self, perhaps it is both possible and preferable for religious caregivers to have the capacity to embody elements of more than one of these approaches, depending on context and the needs of others and self. It seems this happens in practice—for example, persons who hold replacement and fulfillment theologies as their personal theologies are able as professionals to convey care to persons from other traditions. Knitter discusses these approaches as four distinct approaches, but perhaps they are not necessarily mutually exclusive. And perhaps in this way religious caregivers are required to be religiously plural—for example, to be able to state clearly, without apology, their own particularity and its necessity for themselves, but also offer unconditional positive regard to persons of other religions, and be willing to engage with others to adjudicate between life-giving and death-dealing religious interpretation.

Practice of Soul Care amid Religious Plurality

The effect of religious pluralism and diversity on the theory and practice of soul care is of sobering magnitude and barely studied. Therefore, religious professionals are obligated to be extremely cautious not to settle early and facilely on standards for such care. Anything we can articulate about the practice of soul care amid religious diversity must be asserted and enacted tentatively. However, providers of soul care are also morally obligated to respond in situations where interreligious soul care is desired or necessary (short of doing harm because of our lack of preparation). We cannot wait for surety nor be tentative in expressing our desire to do all we can to care for the particularity of all persons, including persons of diverse religious traditions. As in the practice of medicine, where urgent and previously unrecognized forms of human suffering sometimes require physicians to try untested procedures and medications, those offering soul care must—in restrained, cautious, and humble ways—venture into relatively uncharted waters. Therefore, in this section, we take a pragmatic stance and, building on all the usual practices required for excellence in soul care, reflect on several additional practices that have special significance for effective interreligious soul care. Our discussion will be structured via three interrelated perspectives on practice—encounter, evaluation, and preparation—that, taken together, comprise a practical theological approach to soul care amid religious plurality.[31] It may seem counterintuitive not to start with preparation. But at this point in the development of our expertise in interreligious encounter, it is interreligious encounter that typically motivates evaluation and preparation for future encounters, so the order of our discussion reflects the logic of our current practice. Five practices will be addressed: encounter calls us to (1) prioritize difference and (2) develop religious multilingualism; evaluation calls us to (3) consult; and preparation calls us to (4) articulate our own religious location and (5) learn with some depth at least one religious tradition different from our own.

Encounter: Prioritize Difference and Develop Religious Multilingualism

In the encounter of interreligious soul care, it is crucial to give adequate attention to religious and spiritual differences between caregivers and care seekers.

We do this not to exaggerate distance between caregiver and care seeker, but, rather, to see distance that needs to be bridged for care to be possible. The formulation provided by Clyde Kluckhohn and Henry Murray has become a useful heuristic for the theory and practice of soul care: "every human person is in certain respects like all others, like some others, like no others."[32] Care attentive to all three dimensions of human experience is holistic care. As previously noted, however, religious caregivers, in their laudable efforts to serve all people, have been at some risk to underestimate the differences between persons and groups. For this reason, it is arguably the case that we should enter into interreligious soul care attuned at first primarily to religious differences, showing honor to care seekers through our willingness to recognize their religious particularity. The literature of pastoral care has tended to encourage caregivers to begin to build a relationship with care seekers through the practice of empathy. But entering too quickly into empathy, without sufficient sense of the irreducible otherness of the care seeker, risks running roughshod over difference. Judith Berling calls us "beyond empathy" in our effort to bridge religious differences and draws our attention instead to an alternative more fitting in the context of religious difference.

> However well-intentioned, the ideal of empathy is problematic, for it severely underestimates the challenge of understanding across lines of difference. Empathy, looking with the eyes of another, is impossible. The point is articulated well by anthropologist Clifford Geertz. The ethnographer (or scholar of religions) "does not, and in my opinion, largely cannot, perceive what his informants perceive. What he perceives, and that uncertainly enough, is what they perceive 'with'—or 'by means of,' or 'through' . . . or whatever the word should be." He reports on his own experience. "In each case, I have tried to get at [cross-cultural understanding] not by imagining myself someone else . . . but by searching out and analyzing the symbolic forms—words, images, institutions, behaviors—in terms of which, in each place, people actually represented themselves to themselves and to one another."[33]

Some of us will dispute the adequacy of Berling's conceptualization of empathy. But the most sophisticated argument for empathy will not give us grounds to dispute her main point—that empathic perception is a significantly limited, partial, and often untestable perception. We will return later to the alternative Geertz proposes. For now it is important to stay with the point that making it a priority to observe carefully and act in light of differences between ourselves and care seekers is an essential counterbalance to overly confident empathy.

As part of prioritizing attention to difference, it may be helpful during experiences of interreligious soul care for caregivers and care seekers to speak explicitly about their religious differences, especially for caregivers to admit our lack of knowledge regarding a care seeker's religious tradition. It is never the care seeker's responsibility to be our teacher, and we will discuss later our responsibilities to educate ourselves about the religious traditions of the persons for whom we are caregivers. However, when we do not name obvious differences in religious tradition (and our silence may serve primarily to protect our ego), we may simply create the proverbially awkward situation in which there is an "elephant" in the room of which, oddly, no one speaks. If the care seeker is willing and able, it can be empowering for the care seeker to help the caregiver in this way. As noted earlier, decades of interreligious dialogue have shown that encounters between persons of diverse religious identities are most meaningful not when differences are obscured but when each person speaks of their religious identity and commitments clearly, nondefensively, and with respect for the religiosity of others in the dialogue. Power analysis is another crucial approach in prioritizing difference.[34] A caregiver effective in interreligious interactions is attentive to how social structures and historical conflicts may have created power differentials that are now affecting an encounter with a care seeker—for example, Christian caregivers and Jewish care seekers meet in the shadow of the Shoah—and the caregiver will try to respond in a way that equalizes power to the degree possible.

A second practice crucial for interreligious soul care is the development of religious multilingualism. Deriving directly from our willingness to see the many differences and power asymmetries amid religious plurality is our realization that it would be a misuse of our power to impose on the interreligious encounter our preferences in language. Robert Anderson names just a few of the most concrete possibilities, and though he seems to be addressing situations where the caregiver and care seeker do not speak the same language literally, his questions apply as well if different *religious* languages are being spoken.

> Not knowing the language of the other person has both literal and symbolic consequence. . . . Is there someone to translate? Is communication even possible? Who is not speaking in their primary language? Effective communication is primarily my responsibility. Does my worldview allow for pluralistic reality?[35]

Anderson's statement that the responsibility for effective communication falls primarily to him and not to the care seeker is exactly the "communication ethic"[36] called for by Daniel Schipani and Leah Dawn Bueckert: it is the responsibility of the caregiver to realize any communication gaps and to try to narrow them. Especially where there are differences in preferred religious language, it is the caregiver's responsibility to become "spiritually and theologically multilingual" so as to be able to provide the language care of translation.

> "Becoming spiritually and theologically multilingual" refers to the caregiver's ability to identify and communicate love, care, grace, and hope in a variety of ways (including through nonreligious spiritual languages). Just as the fluency in several languages (Spanish, English and Japanese, for

example) enhances one's communication abilities, so does familiarity with the variety of spiritual and religious languages.[37]

Though we will address in the next section the importance of becoming a student of religions other than one's own, Schipani and Bueckert are not equating religious multilingualism with scholarly academic knowledge. It is impossible for a religious caregiver to be fluent in the languages of every religious tradition. Rather, by careful listening to and conversation with each care seeker the caregiver discerns what religio-spiritual language (if any) she or he prefers. This is exactly what Geertz, in our prior discussion of empathy, described.

> It is important to attend to the particular words, images, and behaviors through which the other represents himself [or herself]. How is meaning expressed, lived out, understood, and articulated in the context I am trying to understand? Attending to the particular words, images, and behaviors important in the other context helps me to acknowledge the particularity, the difference, of the religion I am trying to understand.[38]

Schipani and Bueckert call this "language care": "caring deeply *for* language itself and communicating care *through* diverse forms of language."[39]

Evaluation: Consult, Consult, Consult

Given that so much is yet to be learned about interreligious soul care, it is especially important to learn from each encounter.[40] But given the sheer volume of the diversity of religious traditions, the process of evaluating interreligious encounters is naturally one in which we are not learning alone but with others. It is crucial to have regular consultatory space, with religiously diverse colleagues, in which to reflect on experiences in interreligious soul care, hopefully to share our learnings and enhance everyone's next encounters. Rarely is it given adequate emphasis that there are circumstances outside our control that circumscribe our capacity to provide effective soul care, and the sheer volume of religious diversity is surely one such circumstance. *No one* can have adequate knowledge of religious diversity sufficient for all situations of interreligious soul care. From this perspective we can welcome Anderson's claim that one marker of a person competent in interreligious care is the capacity to identify one's limitations and other barriers to interreligious communication.[41] As Anderson suggests, the purpose of this consultative evaluation is to provide a transitional space where new competencies can be built:

> A transitional zone is possible as a learning context between my comfort and discomfort zone. A small study group of colleagues might combine articles from literature with personal and professional vignettes and prospective cases to portray webs of meaning and the transitional territory between comfort and discomfort zones, identifying experiences and

providing feedback towards the goal of demonstrating multi-spiritual and cultural interaction and competency.[42]

In this transitional space we might begin simply with description: What did we experience in the encounter—differences, uncertainties, connections? In full awareness that our assessment of this may be different from the care seekers', take note of ways in which our care seemed to be well received and effective. What have we learned in this encounter about the particularity of a tradition different from our own—the preferred language, images, values, and behaviors? What did we learn about ourselves in relation to this other religion? Reflection after the encounter is also opportunity for the language care Schipani and Bueckert say is so helpful for interreligious soul care. We can use this evaluative consultation to refine our capacity for religious multilingualism, to become more adept at speaking with authenticity the linguistic expressions organic to religious locations other than our own, even as we hone our capacity to communicate our own, when appropriate. This looking back at an encounter completed enhances us and makes us ready to use this enhancement in preparation for the next encounter.

Preparation: Articulate Our Religious Location and Learn Another Religious Tradition

Education in pastoral care has tended to focus on cultivating the caregiver's capacity for silence and for restraint in the expression of one's own religious beliefs during caregiving encounters. Thus, it is notable that in the few texts that discuss the overall competencies required for interreligious soul care, caregivers' clarity and capacity to speak about their religious identity and location are emphasized.[43] Why might this be? A. J. van den Blink's no-nonsense words about the difficulties of diversity suggest a reason for this shift in emphasis.

> Diversity can be very enriching. . . . But diversity can also be unpleasant and threatening. Encountering diversity can upset our emotional equilibrium and unbalance and undermine our definition of reality. It can be a humbling and painful reminder of our limitations, our biases, and of our efforts to deny those. . . . [Diversity] may be something we endorse theoretically, but dealing with it in actuality is another matter altogether. This is especially true when it means being pushed to question one's own assumptions, reality definitions, and identity.[44]

Religious plurality, perhaps more than other aspects of diversity, may challenge us in this foundation-shaking way, because it can raise all at once questions about our worldview, our view of ourselves, and our view of the holy—What *is* essential, right, wrong, ultimate, sacred? Religious pluralism can separate us quite suddenly from what we thought was a passionately held commitment to care for others—instead we are reduced to silence or self-preoccupation, go on the offense or fall into defensiveness.[45] Religious diversity can quickly cause us to lose the strength of self that, as van den Blink goes on to address, a constructive response to diversity requires of us.

> It requires . . . a secure enough sense of self and of one's own vulnerabilities, and an attentive awareness to be able to reach out and explore the other, or any situation which is new, different or alien, without prejudgment and without the need to control, reassure, lecture or make immediate sense out of. That is why genuine empathy is so rare. Much of what passes for empathy is not empathy at all, but kindness, a willingness to listen, feeling sorry for the other, overidentifying with the other, or worse, losing oneself in the other through an inability to maintain appropriate personal boundaries.[46]

Uncertainty and insecurity about our own religiosity make it difficult to welcome and move toward persons who are certain and secure in theirs. Or, as Schipani and Bueckert put it more positively: "Ministry based on an ethic of care and respect . . . calls for a balance between maintaining personal and spiritual integrity and responsively attending to the care-receiver's experience, needs, and preferred ways of expressing their spirituality and religious conviction."[47] Preparation for interreligious soul care emphasizes clarity about and capacity to articulate our (ever-evolving) religious, theological, and spiritual history and present location. But it also involves exploring how we articulate ourselves religiously relative to diversity. As Anderson puts it:

> I need to monitor my readiness to emphasize universality, the common traits of human existence (i.e., "we are all the same or we all suffer"), that often overlooks the uniqueness that another wishes to claim. If I express common bonds too readily, I may be exercising presumption and power, interpreting as common what is distinctive or unique for someone else. To recognize the integrity of the other, postured outside my reference, serves as an essential base for preparation.[48]

Power analysis also requires of caregivers an awareness and capacity to speak articulately of how the history of religious conflicts, or current religious conflicts locally and internationally, might inject power dynamics and impede relationality in encounters with care seekers from religions different from our own. For Christians in the United States, this means being aware of and prepared to respond to the ways that, as the dominant religious culture, Christianity and Christians enjoy privileges not accorded other religious traditions and adherents represented among our citizenry.

This preparation is not a call to rigidity or self-righteousness. Rather, our self-awareness and self-articulation in the context of religious plurality involves maturing our religious identity and expression in the direction of humility, ongoing attentiveness to areas of our stagnation and growth, and other aspects of self-care.[49] Here again we encounter a dimension of the "language care"

Schipani and Bueckert ask of us: in the context of religious plurality, language care is the self-aware and self-caring attention that caregivers give to being able to articulate honestly and with integrity their own religious identity while at the same time remaining open to the religiosity of others.

Whether or not we ever speak about our personal beliefs to care seekers, being able to do so for ourselves, and with our consultants and other colleagues, helps us keep our bearings—an internal compass—when encountering difference, and that keeps us able to focus on care of others. Recognizing the contours of our own religiosity makes us more able to discern and respond to the "distinctive grounding of another person,"[50] but also more sensitive to how historical conflicts and philosophical divergences between religions may be clouding a particular encounter. And, on those relatively rare occasions when care seekers need to know our positions, we will have well-considered perspectives to offer, rather than platitudes or imperatives. We will be able to speak from and about our own context in a manner that does not seek to impose our belief but seeks to share it, trusting that if there is something of the holy in what we say, it will influence by virtue of its own power.

Finally, preparation for interreligious soul care also includes progressing in the lifelong effort to work our way out of our religious cultural encapsulation[51] and learn more about religions other than our own. Calls to learn more than one religion often gloss over the fact that the number and variety of religious traditions make it impossible for a caregiver to have a substantial knowledge of many and that it takes years to learn well even one other religion. As we noted previously, some of this learning rightly and more efficiently takes place in encounters with adherents of other religions (consultants or, sometimes, care seekers) who, much better than academic study, can help us comprehend the complexity of a religion—the multiplicity of views and particularity of experiences within it.[52] At the same time it is our professional and moral responsibility to take initiative; especially because of the power attributed to the role of the caregiver, it will attribute more authenticity to our professed interest in the religious tradition of the other if we do not make the care receiver responsible for our education. Realistically, even as we gain a modest competency in the variety of religions, to avoid superficiality, it is advisable to choose one in which we immerse ourselves.

Concluding Thoughts

Unlike archeological excavation, where the subject of study usually is underground, religious plurality and its effects on soul care are happening right before our eyes. But our awareness of the many forms of religious plurality and knowledge of how it can best be addressed by religious caregivers are more difficult to access and will take years of delicate, patient discovery. As noted earlier, our understanding and response to religious plurality is hampered until we engage the more complicated dynamics that emerge when religious plurality is inter-acting with other aspects of cultural particularity and diversity, such as race/ethnicity, gender, and sexuality. Similarly, our understanding and response to religious plurality is hampered until religious caregivers from different tradi-tions regularly come together in teams of scholars and practitioners that can guide our excavations below the surfaces of interreligious encounter. But as we work toward comprehending these more complicated dimensions of religious caregiving amid religious plurality, all of us can also be working—gingerly, with our little brushes, together drawing tentative impressions—on excavating this dimension of soul care, which is emerging more and more amid the diversity in all our lives.

Are There Limits
to Multicultural Inclusion?
Difficult Questions for Feminist Pastoral Theology[1]

Bonnie J. Miller-McLemore and Melinda McGarrah Sharp

The feminist agenda has shifted markedly in the past few decades. Feminists no longer seek a single-minded equality in workplace and family. Although the "problem with no name" captured well the hidden struggles of white, middle-class U.S. housewives in the 1960s, it failed to consider women whose problems had other names shaped by the multiple jeopardy of sexism, racism, heterosexism, classism, ageism, and colonialism. In the years since, women across academic disciplines and social settings have tried to correct this misnaming and rewrite a political program that "includes everyone."[2] This catchphrase marks not only the most recent stage in women's consciousness raising, but a growing global endorsement of multiculturalism, defined as the need to respect distinct groups and voices often omitted. Feminism now involves the effort to challenge wider systemic structures of oppression.

Pastoral theologians and counselors have readily supported this expanding agenda in their definitions and practices of care. Paradigms of care have shifted from a more individualistic focus to heightened attention to wider social and political contexts. Reflection on personal and relational dynamics now includes acute consciousness of the multiple intersecting cultural factors that shape feeling, thought, and action.

Including everyone has not been easy, however. People in different cultures do not always agree about the status of women and children. Some of the more difficult questions about equal rights and liberal views of bodies, reproduction, sexuality, discipline, authority, families, and religion have an impact on women and children most directly. Cultural differences over issues such as the morality of female genital circumcision or mutilation, polygamy, and forced marriage have attracted wide public attention. Intense conflict has also surfaced around homosexuality and recognition of the rights of lesbians and gays. Beyond particular concerns with each issue, general questions arise about the relationship between feminism and multiculturalism.[3] Broadly stated, what happens when claims about women's and children's rights over their bodies and lives come into conflict with particular cultural and religious claims about women, children, and society? Are there limitations to multicultural inclusion? If so, what are they and how are they determined?

These are disturbing questions. Feminists at large have begun to grapple with them in the past decade. Few in pastoral theology have done so. The original proposal for this book as addressed in the introduction states clearly the view that "no one deserves to be exploited, violated, degraded, or suppressed."[4] This is a baseline commitment with which it is hard to disagree. But what do we do when we differ over what we see as violation, degradation, exploitation, and suppression, particularly in relation to children and women? How does one care well across cultural difference?

This chapter only initiates this discussion. As women fundamentally influenced by our own personal histories in white, middle-class U.S. contexts, we recognize our limitations. We do not seek easy solutions or definitive answers. Nor do we assume such questions can be answered without contributions from women in other contexts. We are acutely aware that our very interest in how multiculturalism affects women and children comes directly out of the modern Western ethos of a progressive Protestant worldview and its liberal feminist offshoots. This has inherent dangers. Others have pointed out the problems of the Western feminist script that tempts white feminists to act as "white women saving brown women from brown men."[5] We have tried to check this kind of colonialist feminism by sustaining a self-critical posture and including diverse views.

Our primary argument is therefore fairly simple and straightforward: we claim that pastoral theology has not yet given sufficient attention to difficult questions that arise when feminism engages multiculturalism. After drawing on case examples, scholarship in feminist theory, and resources in pastoral theology, we suggest practical strategies for the road ahead. In general, we contend that the first step in more serious engagement with the tensions between feminist pastoral theology and multiculturalism is to raise questions, acknowledge the problems, and try to articulate some of the complexities before moving toward more formal responses or solutions. We believe pastoral theology has much to learn from the wider feminist discussion. But we also hope that feminist pastoral theology has its own wisdom to offer now and in the years to come.

Disciplining Children and Other Examples

As a common way into pastoral theological exploration, we begin with concrete examples, starting with our own experience and inviting readers into quandaries raised for us when caught between cultures. We then draw on additional examples of children's and women's experiences debated and recorded in international and U.S. law. Although this literature does not often appear in pastoral theological scholarship, it is important to feminist political theory, a central partner in constructing a response to such cases.

Suppose you have been living for a couple of years in a non-Western context with a complicated history of cultural exchange and conflict, as one of us did. You recognize cultural differences and celebrate the variety of people with whom you and your children are friends. You host a gathering that includes representatives of several cultures and subcultures. While playing together, one of your friends becomes upset, for whatever reason, at the way in which her daughter is acting. She reaches for the nearest implement—an umbrella in the corner—with which to reprimand her. Just as she moves toward the child and raises the umbrella to hit her, you intervene. Spontaneously, you reach out to grab the umbrella from the mother's hand.

Silence instantly pierces the room. From the look on your friend's face, you realize that your action in front of her children and community has likely heightened an already tense interaction. You have unintentionally violated accepted norms of adult interactions in relation to children. Yet you believe that hitting other people is always wrong and should be prevented. This is what you learned and what you try to teach your children. But you find it difficult to articulate your reasoning in a way that respects your friend or makes sense across the obvious and not-so-obvious cultural differences. Many questions come to mind. How do you discern what is happening in this moment? Does it matter that you are in your own home? On what do you base judgments about which actions are right or wrong? Was the mother wrong for starting to strike her child? Were you right to intervene in the mother's parenting?

Conflict over practices of disciplining children is not unique to other countries. Recently one of us was talking with several parents in a largely white community in the southern United States when conversation drifted to corporal punishment. A father who had strong opinions about it led the way. He argued that nothing could replace the value of physical reprimand. It is the "only way," he said, to make kids learn what parents expect. His own father had used a belt. After just one such experience, he learned quickly to obey his parents. Other parents chimed in in agreement, describing similar experiences. The inviolability of such discipline dominated the discussion, perhaps in part because of the religious conservatism of the participants and general adherence to the proverbial idea that "sparing the rod spoils the child." Evangelical Christianity is, after all, one subculture in the United States where corporal punishment receives its primary endorsement.[6]

What would you say in such a situation? "Should I object," one of us thought, "and argue that such parental action harms more than helps, diminishing self-esteem and confidence and fostering resentment, hatred, and more violence?" Or does the corporal-punishment approach, expressed by those who comprehend its inner logic, have a cohesiveness and consistency that has its own benefits when thoughtfully employed? In the end, the weight of the discussion in favor of physical discipline seemed formidable enough that all we said was, "Did your father *really* use a belt?"

At first, these examples seem mundane. On further reflection, however, they reveal complexities and ambiguities. The parental right to chastise children, though often hidden from public view, is one of the most challenging cultural matters, as difficult as issues that have received wide attention, such as the parental right to withhold medical treatment from children. Discipline is, of course, not usually a life-and-death issue. It is often considered a personal matter in the United States, sequestered in the private sphere of home and family. Disagreement over parental authority and discipline is actually the main reason why the United States stands alone among developed nations in refusing to ratify the United Nations Convention on the Rights of the Child (CRC), adopted by nearly two hundred member nations as an international treaty in 1989.[7] In the United States, some groups advocate for the CRC, while others fight against it. For example, according to their 1999 and 2007 alerts, the Home School Legal Defense Association warns that the CRC removes rights from parents, including the right to corporal punishment. Their report argues that the CRC gives children rights that radically detract from parental authority.[8] More liberal organizations, such as the Campaign for U.S. Ratification of the CRC and Amnesty International, base their support for the CRC on the unique status of children and their needs to thrive.[9]

The intellectual community is also divided. Two sociologists who describe "elite evangelical parenting" as a discourse that puts a "premium on obedience to parental authority and control of youngsters' behavior through the use of physical discipline" acknowledge criticism of such parental behavior. But then they go on to argue that when corporal punishment is coupled with more affectionate child rearing, higher levels of paternal involvement, and a reduction in the amount of parental yelling, there are positive developmental outcomes.[10] This certainly stands in contrast with other research in which historians, pediatricians, social scientists, and pastoral theologians have linked corporal punishment to a variety of negative outcomes and traced how religious justification for punishment has bordered on and evolved into abuse that destroys rather than shapes a child's will.[11]

The international community first formally took up the issue of parental authority and the rights of children with the Geneva Declaration of the Rights of the Child of 1924. Building on this and the 1959 Declaration of the Rights of the Child, the 1989 CRC recognizes the special status and often difficult conditions for children worldwide.[12] The CRC outlines rights of children, such as the right to survive, the right to expression, the right to participate in family, and the right to protection from violence. Feminist political theorists point to the interrelatedness of rights. Children's right to education, for example, is connected to and just as important as their right to protection from violence.[13] The diminishment of one right diminishes all rights for all people.

Listing rights does not, however, solve problems faced in actual experience. The CRC intends to set common standards. But its vague terminology regarding specific kinds of violation or exploitation makes it difficult to point to universal rules that hold in particular situations. Is striking a child with an umbrella or belt an act of violence, for instance? What about one or two spanks on the buttocks that does not cause physical injury? There are also concerns about who has the power to create such rules. According to developmental economist and activist Devaki Jain, we must consider the difficult question: "Who [is] entitled to define or to name a practice as a rights violation?"[14] How do we determine "whether the risk of harm to children warrants intrusion into parental rights"?[15] Much work across the international community has gone into translating the theoretical standards into practices that actually increase children's well-being.[16]

This is not the first time in U.S. history that communities have argued more generally over parental authority and children's rights. In the well-known 1972 case *Yoder v. Wisconsin*, the Supreme Court ruled unanimously for the right of Amish parents to withdraw their children from school beyond the eighth grade based on freedom of religious expression. In a partial dissenting opinion, Justice William O. Douglas articulated concern for children who might resist an Amish way of life and pursue lifestyles that require further formal education.[17] Findings that demonstrate how gender affects opportunity and creates unequal access for girls further complicate questions about education.[18] Is the belief that girls need less education for their role in life a violation or just a cultural difference? Even among those who believe in equal access, on what basis does one argue for an equal right to education in the face of actual obstacles that diminish educational opportunities for girls compared to boys worldwide?

Even though feminists have focused largely on women, we begin with examples of children rather than women for several reasons. Contradictory views of children's rights and parental authority illustrate well the tension between cultural beliefs and human rights. Such tensions arise not just outside the United States but also in diverse communities interior to our society. Discipline is a tough intercultural issue even in seemingly more homogeneous contexts in the United States. Starting here also allows us to focus on children and women rather than just on conflicts between women and women, men and women, or the church and women. Across cultures, children are still primarily a shared concern of women. Other cultures sometimes offer better approaches to raising children than those of the United States. Finally, children are often overlooked in these discussions. Pastoral theologians have taken a special interest in them, well before childhood studies became a popular topic in religion. Several have focused on child abuse in particular.[19] But few have considered cultural variations in the treatment of children or attempted to define the fine line between discipline and abuse.

We could have begun with the more familiar and heated debate over female circumcision or, as critics call it, genital mutilation, which has served as a lightning rod for concern over women's rights and over Western stereotyping of other cultures. In parts of Africa and southern Arabia, girls undergo procedures intended to initiate them into adult community involving ritual surgery and removal of parts of their external genitalia. Public concern became more visible in the 1990s as those who practice female genital cutting migrated to other countries that often officially declared the practice abusive and unlawful. Although groups such as the World Health Organization and the American Medical Association have denounced the practice, partly because of health hazards such as hemorrhage, infection, and maternal-fetal complications, sometimes women in these cultures do not see the practice as dangerous or destructive of their status, sexual rights, or pleasure. Instead, they believe it contributes to important aims, such as marital stability or their devotion as mothers.[20] Do such women suffer the sexual and social oppression that come with loss of informed choice and control over their own bodies? Or are activists who challenge these rites negligent and destructive of deeply embedded traditions that have their own internal reason and value?

Consider one final illustration. A key event in the U.S. decision to deem female genital cutting unlawful was the 1996 landmark case of Fauziya Kassindja.[21] In 1994, seventeen-year-old Kassindja fled Kpalimé, Togo, to the United States upon the death of her father, who alone had protected her from an arranged polygamous marriage and the accompanying practice of female circumcision.[22] After being detained in prison in the United States by Immigration and Naturalization Service from 1994 to 1996, Kassindja was granted asylum in 1996 by the U.S. Board of Immigration Appeals. Her case set a precedent that opened the door to gender-based practices, specifically "fear of genital operations," as grounds for asylum.[23] According to anthropologist Corinne Kratz, while some of Kassindja's family in Togo considered abandoning the practice, others in the village responded by performing the ritual on preteen girls as young as four as a way around the opposition.[24]

In each case—corporal punishment, girls' education, genital circumcision or mutilation—it is tempting to rush to judgment. But how can pastoral theologians and Christians discern the basis for our judgments? Do they hold in every case? How do we claim particular rights, discover universal aims, and attend to cultural and religious differences? How do we take diversity seriously while also protecting and respecting the full humanity of children and women?

Is Multiculturalism Bad for Women?

In 1997, prominent political scientist Susan Moller Okin published an essay in *Boston Review* whose title put the matter bluntly: "Is Multiculturalism Bad for Women?" Although multiculturalism has many meanings, Okin highlights as her primary focus its aim to protect the special group rights of minority cultures. Many such cultures remain deeply patriarchal, she argues, often shaped by the "founding myths" of antiquity and "more orthodox or fundamentalist" versions of Judaism, Christianity, and Islam that are "rife with attempts to justify the control and subordination of women."[25] Such norms and practices often go unnoticed by multiculturalists or group-rights activists because they do not formally violate civil or political liberties but operate out of sight in the privacy of the domestic sphere. Hence, Okin concludes, protecting groups, whose designated leaders are often men, sometimes harms women. What should be done then when the "fundamentals of liberalism"—the "norm of gender equality that is at least formally endorsed by liberal states" (even if often violated in practice)—clash with the "claims of minority cultures or religions"? Those who seek justice between cultures, she says, "must take special care to look at inequalities" within cultures, especially between the sexes. Securing group rights must not occur at the cost of the "best interests of girls and women."[26]

Okin's answer drew varied responses, some of which appear in a later issue of the *Review* and then in an anthology that includes fifteen leading scholars and concludes with Okin's reply. In the introduction to this anthology, Joshua Cohen, Matthew Howard, and Martha Nussbaum identify four emerging positions, which might be roughly called *women's rights* (Okin's position), *human rights, group rights,* and *cultural difference.* Scholars of the human-rights position agree with Okin that protecting group rights, even of liberal minority groups, is often at cross-purposes with securing women's rights, but think such claims should be extended or nuanced to consider other dynamics of discrimination. Sociologist Saskia Sassen argues, for example, that culture should not be analyzed exclusively around gender, especially when men, women, and children are "oppressed by a dominant/host culture" and may use the minority culture to resist, an argument that has affinity with that of many womanist and feminist theologians.[27] The sharpest contrast lies between both of these views—women's rights and human rights—and the third position of group rights that believes "it intolerant to require that cultures and religious outlooks endorse, in theory or practice, the egalitarian principle and to condition special [group] rights on such endorsement."[28] Finally, some argue that Okin is simply "blind to cultural differences" and that the discussion as a whole falters on a liberal misunderstanding of other cultures that cannot get beyond its own ethnocentric assumptions about the generic human.

Philosopher and legal scholar Martha Nussbaum's response to Okin is noteworthy here because of her scholarly contributions to this subject and her focus on religion. She praises Okin's effort to point out the dangers of cultural inclusivity for women's equality. But she is disturbed by Okin's portrait of religion as "little more than a bag of superstitions." Other respondents, such as law professor Azizah Al-Hibri, agree that Okin oversimplifies religion. Okin is casual in her dismissal. She uses popular sources as evidence, makes sweeping claims, omits reference to religion's role in social movements for human freedom, and bypasses religious debates over gender in traditions that have sometimes made greater progress toward women's equal participation than secular institutions. But even more important, Nussbaum thinks Okin presumes an all-consuming or "comprehensive liberalism" that makes autonomy the singular good and refutes the "existence of a reasonable plurality of comprehensive doctrines of the good, prominent among which are the religious conceptions."[29] In what Nussbaum sees as her own less-consuming "political liberalism," religious capabilities have intrinsic social value and are the "most deserving" of protection and respect.

Nussbaum, along with others such as Seyla Benhabib, have attempted to articulate the complicated position of defending universal claims of human rights for women while also strongly endorsing diversity, pluralism, and multiculturalism.[30] Nussbaum suggests a difficult middle ground that contests religious practices that place an undue burden on women, denying them the liberty and opportunity promised by law, while also allowing practices internal to the tradition that do not impede the state's interest even if they discriminate against women. She thereby hopes "to protect women's vulnerability, while also protecting" the religious choices of women and men. Philosopher David Crocker argues that Nussbaum's capabilities approach "can retain the notion of a culturally invariant (absolute) core to both well-being and deprivation while at the same time construing any *specific* means of provisioning as relative to historical and cultural contexts."[31] Other scholars are not so sure.

In an ambitious overview of feminist scholarship, political scientist Mary Dietz identifies a significant problem in the approaches of Okin, Nussbaum, and Benhabib: Okin's "modified Rawlsian liberalism," Nussbaum's "modified Aristotelian humanism," and Benhabib's "modified Habermasian discourse ethic of interaction" all contain a universalist tendency that does not adequately represent women of all cultures.[32] Dietz observes a partial corrective in more recent feminist scholarship. Older feminist tensions between equality and difference have yielded to current recognition of intersecting factors that bear on identity, a central concern even among divergent scholars. The question then becomes "how to theorize a conception of justice (or equality of rights) that applies to all persons while still maintaining the integrity of and respect for particular, diverse groups and cultural collectives."[33] In other words, in this controversy between universalism (which critics fear silences the most marginalized voices) and particularity (which critics fear lapses into cultural relativism), the challenge before us, according to Dietz, is how to "employ both universal and cultural discursive strategies with a view toward social justice and freedom."[34] Here the focus shifts to specific communal and individual practices, the idea of women's positions within and between cultural groups, and philosophical debates about whether universal claims can be made in a way that does not reinscribe male hegemonic norms or otherwise harm women. Under such circumstances, conflict between people and cultures is an inevitable, maybe even a positive, attribute of healthy feminism. In Dietz's words, "contestations . . . are the reality, and the vitality, of contemporary theories of feminism."[35]

Others before Dietz have pointed to similar problems. Okin jump-started the conversation about the tensions between multiculturalism and feminism in 1994 by insisting that scholars face a "critical juncture for feminist issues in a global context" with the well-being of women, children, and theories of justice themselves at stake. Shortly after, a debate about this between Okin and Jane Flax, a political theorist and practicing psychotherapist, appeared in the journal *Political Theory*.[36] Similar to Dietz, Flax raises concerns about what counts for evidence, issues of adequate representation of particular women's voices, and the problem of so-called first-world theorists speaking for the so-called third-world women and children who actually comprise two-thirds of the world's population. She questions the wisdom of considering an Archimedean theoretical viewpoint from which to craft universal theories of justice. While Okin warns that postmodernism, by problematizing subjectivity, can be a trap for women who have yet to achieve subject status, Flax responds with caution against the normative status and privilege associated with white women's subjectivity and the subsequent, if inadvertent, tendency to objectify all other women as *non-white*.[37] They dispute a question at the core of this chapter and book more generally: How does one balance differences between individual women and their complex identities and affiliations? Whereas Okin stresses similarities between oppressions of all women while at the same time recognizing differences, Flax calls for greater attention to actual stories of difference and to scholarship of women of many races in the United States and abroad.

Okin and Flax raise rather than settle some of the dilemmas that arise when feminist scholars grapple with multiculturalism. These debates among a few leading spokespersons who have addressed the tensions between multiculturalism and feminism give a flavor of the discussion. This allows us to identify some of the contested issues so that we can assess more fully what pastoral theologians have contributed thus far and outline rough guidelines for the road ahead.

Multiculturalism and Pastoral Theology

Seldom have pastoral theologians addressed in depth or detail the tensions involved in including multiple perspectives. This is not due to failure to appreciate multiculturalism. Almost from the start, feminist pastoral theologians have striven toward greater inclusivity. The first edited book on pastoral care with women acknowledges a major problem in the publication's white, middle-class perspective. "We are aware," the coeditors write, "that women behave differently in other cultures and that culture itself bears analysis. As editors, we hope that companion volumes will be written by nonwhite, ethnic, non-middle-class women within Western culture and by other women elsewhere throughout the world."[38] With this fourth volume in the series on women and pastoral care, the original hope for broader participation comes to fuller fruition.

Although conflict between women's and children's rights and group rights has received more attention among scholars at large than among pastoral theologians, a few have acknowledged the challenges of multiculturalism. In moving away from a white, Eurocentric model to greater inclusion of diverse voices, the present book adopts an *intercultural* approach to pastoral care first described by Ghanaian-born, British-trained pastoral theologian Emmanuel Lartey. He uses the term *intercultural* in contrast to the words *monocultural, cross-cultural,* and *multicultural* to underscore the complex reality that most people live at the juncture of several cultures and are "often enigmatic composites of various strands of ethnicity, race, geography, culture and socio-economic setting."[39] "Intercultural" best captures the longstanding recognition in anthropology that people live at the intersection of the particular (like no others), the cultural (like some others), and the universal (like all others). Similar to Dietz, Lartey's definition of intercultural recognizes personal and interpersonal conflict as inherent in the inclusion of multiple perspectives. He actually defines intercultural pastoral care around conflict. Good pastoral care involves "three principles": attention to context, inclusion of different people's voices, and authentic participation by all parties. Conflict is unavoidable because differences in values will arise naturally out of diverse histories and traditions. "I must face the reality," Lartey remarks, "that others from other contexts might disagree very strongly." "What is realistic" is, precisely, conflicting perspectives.[40] In his case studies, conflicts between traditional and newly acquired beliefs surface within individuals themselves as much as between groups.[41]

Lartey prefers "intercultural," seldom uses "multicultural," and questions the ability of "cross-cultural" to move beyond an us-versus-them mentality. His use of intercultural parallels our own definition of multicultural as aimed at "giving many different voices from different backgrounds a chance to express their views," particularly in light of "dominant or powerful groups" that "deliberately or unwittingly seek to impose their culture and perspectives upon all others."[42] "Multicultural" is still more widely recognized in public conversation at large than the term *intercultural* and has rich meaning beyond the narrower definition Okin and others assume of preserving the group rights of minority cultures. As we have come to understand in this chapter, multiculturalism is a word about power. It contests the power of a singular dominant culture to establish universal norms and insists that no single culture and its leaders can set standards for all cultures. It is a word that attempts to claim space for repressed or oppressed voices and communities.

As in the study of religion at large, white feminist pastoral theologians have much to learn here from womanist, Asian, *mujerista*, Native American, and post-colonial scholars. Feminist theologian Kwok Pui-lan draws the distinction between multicultural and intercultural around the role of conflict even more starkly: "By intercultural, I mean the interaction and juxtaposition, *as well as tension and resistance* when two or more cultures are brought together sometimes organically and sometimes through violent means in the modern period." Given the particular history of the West in which cultures are "intertwined with one another as a result of colonialism, slavery, and cultural hegemony," conflict should be expected.[43]

In theology, womanist scholars were among the first to insist, as Sassen did with Okin, that women of color face multiple intersecting social pressures and oppressions, among which sexism is only one. Womanism itself is a term borrowed from Alice Walker to name a theological movement that, in Delores Williams's words, "opposes all oppression based on race, sex, class, sexual preference, physical ability, and caste."[44] Without adequate consideration of these multiple factors, a good deal of pastoral care literature, as pastoral theologian Carroll Watkins Ali points out, is irrelevant and disenfranchising. She finds in Williams and Jacquelyn Grant fresh resources for constructing what she calls a "multidimensional approach" to care that is more inclusive of the needs of poor black women.[45] A leading black feminist at large, Patricia Hill Collins coins the term *intersectionality* to describe the complicated interconnections of race, gender, and social class in black women's lives.[46] She claims that the pursuit of social justice for all (in the face of serious inequalities) is a collective problem requiring multiple, collaborative projects.[47] She also urges scholars to consider whether their position in the academy fosters social justice or reinscribes existing social hierarchies.[48]

Tensions between feminism, liberal values, and multiculturalism receive explicit attention in a few other places in pastoral theology. In an article in *International Perspectives on Pastoral Counseling*, Fred C. Gingrich includes a short section on child abuse and parental authority in his reflections on pastoral counseling in the Philippines.[49] Although he only briefly outlines some of the conflicts we explore in this article, he highlights the tensions surrounding child discipline, abuse, and rights when considering care across cultural differences. Gingrich urges consideration of the "variety of ways in which children are at risk for exploitation," even though he does not develop this suggestion further.[50] In introducing the volume in which Gingrich's article appears, Howard Clinebell urges pastoral theologians and practitioners to consider complications of political, economic, and class oppression. He emphasizes the danger of inadvertently contributing to further suffering by what might otherwise be thought to be healing or liberating.[51]

We can also find a few resources for considering questions about children's rights and multiculturalism among those pastoral theologians who have studied and worked on behalf of children. Pamela Couture confirms a conclusion with which we began: some of the biggest international challenges surface around the questions of what constitutes harm and how different cultures perceive children and adult responsibility.[52] She believes nonetheless that people can agree on core values across cultures, finding support for this position in the human-capabilities approaches of Nussbaum and Amartya Sen. Pastoral theologians could draw even more from these rich philosophical positions that outline various capabilities that allow persons the "substantive freedoms to choose a life one has reason to value" (Sen) and that define "what people are actually able to do and to be" (Nussbaum).[53] A focus on human capabilities could help address some of the difficult issues surrounding children's rights by helping to consider specific conditions required for their fulfillment.

Both pastoral theologians and political theoreticians also reflect on the important theme of moral agency. Within the political-theory literature, Crocker claims that "adults right now, and children, in the future, are assumed to be moral agents, and genuine social development aims to provide the conditions in which they *themselves* acquire expanded and valuable capabilities, including that of substantial choice."[54] For feminist pastoral theologians, such as Bonnie J. Miller-McLemore, advocacy for children has led to fresh definitions of their moral agency in balance with parental authority. She considers children to be knowing agents who are both responsible and vulnerable. Moral agents are not always like-minded adults or static, independent, and mature people presumed in many discussions of human rights but children and adults in various stages of development and dependence. Children have needs and cannot fully reciprocate, while adults in their care for children need the support of others and appropriate means to meet their own needs. Contrary to cultural constructions of children as corrupt or, inversely, as innocent, naïve, and passive, children deserve greater recognition for the particular knowledge and agency they possess.

At the same time, recognition of differences between children and adults leads to acknowledgment of the place of "transitional hierarchies," a temporary inequity between persons—whether of power, authority, expertise, responsibility, or maturity—that is moving toward but has not yet arrived at genuine mutuality.[55] This provocative vision of the caretaker-child relationship as a moving, dynamic partnership that changes over time could respond to feminist theory's call for ways to envision theories as flexible enough to allow for people in various stages of development to participate and contest practices. Seeing cultures as changing rather than static is of importance to children and women in particular because it leaves room for reformers within cultures to challenge traditional norms to improve their social status.[56] Such ideas do not, of course, directly answer questions about discipline, parental authority, and children's rights. But they do provide greater understanding of the dynamics of agency and transitional hierarchies that characterize the tensions between children's rights and parental authority.

Rough Guidelines for Pastoral Theology

How might the field of pastoral theology draw on both its own insights and resources in the wider discussion to address tensions between different forms of feminism and multiculturalism that shape the giving and receiving of care? How do we reconsider children's and women's rights in light of cultural differences? Are there limitations to multicultural inclusion? Some scholars, such as Okin, believe that there are. Protection of women, she insists, imposes limits on multicultural representation and group rights.

Our analysis, however, suggests that such a straightforward claim requires further nuance. Political theorists recognize the tensions between feminism and multiculturalism. Admitting this is a first step in good pastoral care. Caregivers should expect to be torn and to find those whom they counsel torn between cultural demands. "Multiculturalism resists easy reconciliation with egalitarian convictions," as the editors of *Is Multiculturalism Bad for Women?* point out. "After all, some cultures do not accept, even as a theory, the principle that people are owed equal respect and concern."[57] In extending this principle to all women around the world, feminism has questioned the sexual social order that some traditional cultures want to preserve. We should not be surprised, as columnist Katha Pollitt says, to find a political movement that opposes "virtually every culture on earth" in its demand for women's equality at odds with multiculturalism, which demands respect for all cultures.[58] A basic assumption behind multiculturalism itself—the condemnation of intolerance—evolved out of Enlightenment understandings of human nature and is not a value shared across cultures.

At the same time, as Pui-lan asserts, the Eurocentric origins of much feminist discourse has "perpetuated colonialist structures," distorting and stereotyping other cultures. Feminists must be wary of the temptation to use political constructions of gender to justify further colonization of women in other cultures.[59] Even the assertion of women's and children's universal dignity can have hidden problems. Nussbaum insists that there are "universal obligations to protect human dignity" and that women's dignity is "equal to that of men."[60] But postcolonial theorists, such as Meyda Yegenoglu, insist that such claims to universalism have often functioned similarly to masculinist and colonialist claims to superiority, power over others, and denial of difference.[61] An investigator who studied the impact of the Convention on the Rights of the Child on children in Vietnam, the first country in Asia to ratify it, concluded that Western assumptions about universal rights and the superiority of Western approaches led aid agencies to ignore local views about how children should be treated.[62] Nonetheless, "to avoid the whole issue" of conflicting interpretations of women's and children's treatment because the tensions are just too difficult is what Nussbaum describes as "perhaps the worst option of all," worse than either imposing values on others or allowing oppressive practices of local traditions to go unquestioned.[63]

Beyond recognition of the inherent tensions, proponents of feminism and multiculturalism should also see the common cause that unites their efforts. They both question common assumptions of the dominant social order. In his response to Okin, Will Kymlicka is bothered by Okin's view of multiculturalism as threat rather than ally and attempts to show how they might work together. As movements, they share a common enemy, a liberal politic that assumes the primary citizen is a man from the dominant culture. They both criticize liberalism's failure to attend to the social institutions that shape the lives of women and children in diverse ethnic and cultural communities. Finally, Kymlicka continues, they challenge the "traditional liberal assumption that equality requires identical treatment."[64] Women and those in minority groups sometimes need particular privileges and protections to achieve full equality with white men.

Part of Okin's problem is her narrow definition of multiculturalism. Professor of political theory Bhikhu Parekh accuses her of reducing it to group rights, "which is a small and minor part of it." He offers a rich four-part definition that reveals connections with feminism's own aims. Multiculturalism suggests

> that culture provides the necessary and inescapable context of human life, that all moral and political doctrines tend to reflect and universalize their cultural origins, that all cultures are partial and benefit from the insights of others, and that truly universal values can be arrived at only by means of an uncoerced and equal intercultural dialogue.[65]

This final claim is perhaps the most important from our perspective. It affirms that in contesting the attempts of others to impose their beliefs about human nature as universal, those who support feminism and multiculturalism can work together for a common cause.

This suggests a third step beyond navigating the fine line between conflict and solidarity: recognition of culture's complexity. Cultures are dynamic, not rigid and static. They are unbounded, complicated, lived realities rather than the "stable, timeless, ancient, lacking in internal conflict, premodern" communities that liberals often imagine.[66] Other cultures are "less univocally patriarchal" than Okin suggests, and liberal culture is not unambiguously supportive of women, as any close look at current U.S. teen fashion or market advertising will confirm.[67] Nor are minority cultures and those most directly influenced by postcolonialism as pristine and untouched by liberal values as the Western gaze imagines.[68] Cultural identity is forged through a complex intracultural *and* intercultural interaction, as political theorist Sarah Song points out: "Cultures and cultural identities emerge, change, and are maintained through social interactions and political struggle."[69] People, including vulnerable persons with minimal agency such as children, contest practices at many levels.[70] Certainly people are constrained by culture but, as Nussbaum remarks, they "are not stamped out like coins by the power machine of social convention . . . norms are plural and people are devious."[71] Considering human rights without attention to culture's dynamism and the complexity of human agency and subversion is incomplete at best and potentially harmful at worst, especially for children and women.[72]

As a fourth guideline, it is important to recognize that religion also plays a complex and central role. Okin tends to reduce it to its poorest misogynist historical apparitions. But religious traditions and communities are more ambiguous than this. Like culture more generally, religion is also a "living, breathing system" that lends itself to complicated strategies and enactments of "agency, power, and privilege among its members."[73] As both Nussbaum and Bonnie Honig argue, religion is not the sole cause or even the primary perpetrator of sexist brutality. In some places and times over history, including the women's movement, people have used it as a source of liberation from authoritarian oppression and exploitation. In addition, religious practices that people sometimes automatically dismiss as repressive, such as the Islamic practice of requiring women to wear a veil or head scarf, actually serve a multiplicity of purposes, including ones that support women.[74] Finally, Okin ignores the reality that some feminist scholars are also faithful Jews, Muslims, or Christians. To ignore such colleagues is to forfeit potentially forceful allies.

Understanding religion, and distinguishing it from the many local customs that accrue around it, is a "complicated and time-consuming project," as al-Hibri makes clear. Rather than working over against religious traditions, this project involves working through and with particular beliefs.[75] Of course, it also requires recognizing religion's liabilities and dangers. Okin is right in this regard. There are still "hundreds of millions of women rendered voiceless or virtually so by the male-dominated religions with which they live."[76] Although even here she drifts toward hyperbole, some of her respondents agree that "some of the more pernicious forms of sex discrimination are a result of the practices of religious institutions."[77] There is also an important difference, Okin says, between the mature woman who makes an informed choice to submit to authoritarian beliefs and the young girl who is given no choice but to be indoctrinated into sexually discriminatory roles and an exclusive worldview without any exposure to alternatives.[78] Plenty of scholars in religion would agree.

If religion is important as an active ingredient in the definition of culture and tradition, then scholars in religion and theology should have a heightened investment in joining this discussion. Almost every essay in *Is Multiculturalism Bad for Women?* mentions religion. However, even though the authors represent a variety of fields such as law, philosophy, and sociology, theologians are not among them. Perhaps this is because few scholars in religion or theology have explored the conflicts. Pastoral theologians in particular may avoid these delicate issues because we want to model care and avoid divisiveness. But our close study of human nature and interpersonal dynamics and our long therapeutic history of intervening in situations of suffering and healing also give us particular insight into how to approach these problems.

This leads to a final guideline: making judgments about cultural and religious values requires attentive listening that pastoral theologians and counselors know well. How does a certain behavior function psychologically, sociologically, theologically, and so forth? What might it mean? What are some hidden implications and suppressed feelings and convictions? How is religion operative in the lives of women and girls? Westerners in particular need to "defamiliarize" ourselves with our own assumptive worlds and "reflect more critically upon them." As Honig observes, this requires feminists to "hold their own practices up to the same critical scrutiny they apply to Others [sic]" and to refuse "to prejudge the merits of practices that are unfamiliar or threatening to those of us raised in bourgeois liberal societies."[79] In pursuit of gender equity, we need to remain alert to racism and cultural imperialism. In pursuit of multiculturalism, we need to remain alert to gender discrimination and acts of inhumanity of all kinds, seeking to make the tough distinction between "enabling and oppressive cultural norms."[80] The hope is to prevent a universalizable feminist perspective from harming those it intends to protect and to maintain a flexible feminist perspective that respects cultural differences and moral diversity while also including an option for contesting practices from within cultures.

This stance of critical self-reflection on practice is one that pastoral theologians have spent years cultivating. Pastoral theologians and counselors have also practiced the skill of mediation, which is requisite if we hope to move forward in moderating tensions between individual and group rights. Any move forward through these difficult questions must facilitate rather than squelch participation from diverse voices, both within and between cultures. Ultimately, as Corinne Kratz argues in the case of seventeen-year-old Kassindja, it helps to focus on concrete lives and particular cases rather than abstract questions and distant presumptions, a practice familiar to pastoral theologians.[81] In fact, political theorist Brooke Ackerly highlights cultural struggle and contestation over specific practices, such as outlined in the first part of this paper, as the place to begin asking and responding to difficult questions.[82] To make progress, we need to draw the particular and the more abstract into richer dialogue.

Are there limitations to multiculturalism? Exploration of this question has led us to several more focused questions that might inform future investigations into conflicts between feminism and multiculturalism. These questions suggest practical strategies for working collaboratively toward fuller inclusion and better care:

- What are some of the conflicts between different forms of feminism and multiculturalism?
- How might we discover and build on opportunities for solidarity even within difficult tensions?
- Can we work toward full inclusion and opportunity for women and girls while respecting different cultural and religious understandings of gender?

- How can we acknowledge cultural values that feminism may overlook and appreciate the fluid nature of culture, its complexities and ambiguities, and its complicated intersections with other changing cultures?
- How can we acknowledge feminist values and contest practices that harm women and children? Can we avoid hegemonic, colonialist assertion of norms from the outside while also challenging the exploitation of women and children by dominant voices inside cultures? How can we work from within rather than from outside cultures?
- What is the role of religion in relationship to culture and gender and how can we assess its potential to help and harm?
- How can we challenge the public/private divide and its gendered history that sometimes hides the exploitation of women and girls behind closed doors?
- How can we attend to the consequences of multiculturalism and feminism for poor women and girls in particular?
- What will help us sustain a focus on individual women and girls and not just abstract theory?
- Can we hone pastoral skills (such as empathy, attentive listening, and mediation), allow one's own authority to be decentered when within another culture, and learn to study the context closely before speaking or acting?
- Does diverse scholarship in the United States and other global contexts challenge our work? Have we considered the question of representation and who is speaking for whom in what we read, write, and reference?
- Does our position in our various institutions foster social justice or reinscribe existing social hierarchies?

These questions and guidelines are not entirely new to pastoral theology. Over the last few decades, pastoral theologians have tried to balance the care of individuals with careful attention to social and political context.

Nevertheless, the concerns raised by this chapter challenge this delicate balance. More scholarly engagement with the tensions between feminisms and multiculturalisms is needed. Conflict over cultural values is likely to continue to grow. Some Christian denominations have already experienced the divisive nature of differences over sexuality, gender, and ordained ministry within intersecting cultures around the world. Although the technologies and market capitalism that drive globalization can sometimes erase social differences, they can also surface tensions previously submerged by geographical and social distance and boundaries. Globalization brings diverse cultures and people into greater proximity as worldwide neighbors. Meanwhile, the center of world Christianity and religion has shifted from the northern to the southern hemisphere. Tensions between Islam, Judaism, and Christianity have deepened as conflict, violence, war, and terrorism intensify. In a word, including everyone when not all communities have the same standards of inclusion will remain a difficult journey to navigate for quite some time.

Where Race and Gender Collide

Deconstructing Racial Privilege

Nancy Ramsay

Whether teaching a class on pastoral care, writing a sermon, or visiting a patient in ICU who identifies with a different culture, white, feminist pastoral theologians, pastors, and chaplains know well the unease of the precarious hope that we can meet the challenges of intersecting forms of oppression and privilege as we learn to recognize and resist realities such as sexism, racism, classism, and heterosexism that often coexist and collide in our own lives and the lives of those we serve and with whom we work. Two women sit side by side in a seminary classroom. One is a white, middle-class seminarian who self-identifies as a lesbian and yet is closeted due to her denominational affiliation. She knows her African American, middle-class classmate rightly expects her to be an ally in racial justice even as she opposes policies of full inclusion in their denomination. Both women worry about their local judicatory's history of not supporting women students fairly. The relationship of these two women illustrates the ascribed and embodied differences that intersect and sometimes collide as privilege and oppression in women's lives. Even in this brief illustration we can picture the peculiar complexity of women's social identity with its multiple and often competing dimensions that require our vigilance in self-awareness and accountability to one another.

While the above illustration does not exhaust the complexity of oppressive differences that may exist among women, it is sufficient to alert us to the need for theoretical and theological conceptual resources and strategies to inform our conversations and efforts to build relational bridges in confronting oppression as it arises in our lives and the lives of those we serve in ministry. While each of these oppressions is distinct, together they also share common aspects. Iris Marion Young rightly warns against definitions that reduce or oversimplify the differences among oppressions, and she provides us with five criteria for identifying and comparing these oppressions that help us distinguish the effects of each and their often overlapping consequences within and across social groups.[1]

The five criteria she notes include the following: exploitation, marginalization, powerlessness, cultural imperialism, and violence. Briefly,

- *Exploitation* refers to inequalities created and sustained by structural, systematic, and relational imbalances.
- *Marginalization* may be the most dangerous form of oppression because it diminishes the humanity and agency of groups of persons such as women and older adults.
- *Powerlessness* refers to structural, systematic, and relational practices that set in motion enduring limitations on persons' opportunities to exercise agency and creativity and receive acknowledgement for these capacities as well as material consequences for this limited access to agency.
- *Cultural imperialism* describes the way in which those who enjoy the privileges of a dominant status in culture often unreflectively project their own experience and identity as normative, thus paradoxically rendering others such as women, people of color, and those in the lesbian/gay/bisexual/transsexual (LGBT) community as either invisible or as stereotypes.
- By *violence* Young is referring to the way in which systematic violence is apparently at least tolerated as an acceptable social practice when expressed toward persons in certain social groups such as women, people of color, and those who self-identify in the LGBT community; all of these live with the knowledge that they may experience such violence simply because of who they are.

Young rightly claims that persons who experience even one of these criteria are oppressed, and that many people are in social groups that variously experience multiple criteria. Her analysis is helpful because it discloses both the heterogeneity of individual identity with dimensions of privilege and oppression and the similar heterogeneity that occurs across social groups such as we see in the two women whose experience was described at the outset of this essay. Phenomenologically, her observations are helpful because these criteria offer ways to reflect on shared and particular experience and honor the complexity of such experience. Theologically, Young's analysis deepens our appreciation for the complexity of human beings and particularly our efforts to live in community, understand the character of social sin, and appreciate the difficulty and power of love.

With this brief acknowledgment of the complexity of experiences of oppression and privilege, I will narrow the scope of this essay to focus on the sometimes colliding oppressions of race and gender. As a contextual theology that is funded by critical and constructive engagement with theories, normative value structures, and practices that contribute to healing and transformation at relational and corporate levels of communal life, pastoral theology is a useful theological resource for our reflection. I will draw on Young's criteria, relational theory, critical race theory, and pastoral theological reflections to propose resources and strategies particularly for European American women who think of ourselves as feminists and who want to deepen our work in confronting and deconstructing the distorting power of racism in our own lives, in institutions and churches, and in culture. The goal of this exploration of theology and theory is to assist European American women in becoming trustworthy allies in the work of building communities and institutions in which all God's people may flourish. This goal will require deepening awareness of our own racial identities and complicity in racial privilege and identifying strategies for addressing inequities of power that include constructing patterns of accountability as allies.

For nearly two decades women of color and white women who are scholars in the field of pastoral theology have struggled to articulate and embody the challenge of being in relationships of mutual care and regard while we are actively naming and oh-so-slowly deconstructing the barriers that racial privilege erects among us. Whether deepening levels of honesty and understanding through shared teaching or in the contexts of plenaries and workshops at national meetings, we know the importance and challenge of sustaining the conversations and the work of becoming allies. We have identified the common bond of resisting sexism that also yields its grip far too slowly in the institutions where we work and in the churches where we and our students serve. We know the terrain of sexism well enough to navigate with some familiarity, though not ease, because racial difference matters there as well.

Of course, difference in itself is not the problem we need to solve. Politically and theologically this is an important affirmation. Difference is the context in which we live and work. Differences such as race, gender, and orientation disclose aspects of God's rich imagination. Each offers avenues for wonder as we embody variously these intersecting, core aspects of identity. As Young's analysis demonstrates, the complexity of difference arises because of the imbalances of power that accrue and dynamically intersect across individual, group, systemic, and symbolic dimensions as privilege or advantage and as stigma. Women of every racial identity know the reality of asymmetries of power that accrue across these several interlocking dimensions.

The dynamics behind this enduring power of sexism have strong parallels in the reality of racial oppression. The mystification that many men profess about the origin and reproduction of sexism is equally troubling to women of color who urge women of European heritage to recognize the relationship between the economic and political privileges of our racial heritage and their oppression.

This term *privilege* is at the heart of our discussion and reflects what Young describes as cultural imperialism. It arises and endures as interlocking, systemic advantage that usually functions outside the awareness of those who enjoy such privilege. It renders normative the experience and values of one group and subordinates and marginalizes the experience of others. In the context of race, for example, European Americans often seem oblivious about the fact that our security and comfort may well exist at the expense of those whose racial identity differs from ours. Privilege has material benefits for those whose identity is rendered normative as well as invidious consequences for those it renders invisible or marginal. In practice this would mean, for example, that many white persons can live wherever they can afford; will find that those in authority in the legal and justice systems likely look like them and won't suspect them of wrongdoing without cause; and that the curricula of educational institutions reflect their history and values. But those in minoritized groups will likely find financial institutions and landlords whose practices preclude access to housing even when income could assure it; law enforcement personnel who all too often demonstrate a readiness to profile or react on the basis of stereotypes; and curricula that overlook the accomplishments of those who were not central to the preferred narratives of the dominant culture.

A 2002 joint study by MIT and the University of Chicago to measure racism in employment is a remarkable illustration of racial privilege and its material consequences that are alive and well in the United States.[2] The researchers developed comparable resumés using typically European American names and typically African American names. The resumés were created for a wide range of positions from upper-management to service-sector positions in Boston and Chicago. Interestingly, the researchers met with personnel officers prior to the project who assured them that they were so committed to affirmative action in their various companies that there would be a marked, positive response to the resumés of African Americans. Instead, what the researchers found was that resumes with European names were 50 percent more likely to get a positive response. The researchers then tried increasing the skills described in each resumé. There was no change in response to those with African American names but those resumés with fictitious European American names got even more responses. This study is a disturbing illustration of how privilege functions even in the context of intentionality to correct discrimination. What these personnel officers underestimated were the subtle ways their own experience predisposed them to privilege the applications of those they imagined to be like themselves, and the ways, outside of their awareness, that they marginalized the identically qualified applications of persons whose experience they presumed to be different than their own.

This research study illustrates well the underlying, central dynamic of *meritocracy* that gives rise both to such racial privilege and to oppression. Meritocracy presumes that in this country everyone starts on a "level playing field" so that a person's advantages are deserved, that is, they are understood as the result of their effort to succeed. Meritocracy is reflected in the national myth that anyone who really tries in this country can succeed because opportunity is equally available to all. This myth, deeply subscribed to in the United States, provides a veneer of protection to those who would never want to accept advantages they did not "earn." If this is a country where all who are willing to work hard can succeed, then vast differences in rewards can be justified by one's own efforts and the perceived lack of another's. But the truthfulness of this myth is deeply challenged by this employment study when clearly racial discrimination is real and invidious but not justified by the qualifications of the applicants. However, those reading the files were oblivious to their bias and its consequences. They reproduced the effects of racism without any awareness of their complicity in it, and they privileged the applicants of others whose qualifications were no better. Similarly, then, those who would be hired in such a situation have no idea of their privilege alongside an equally qualified applicant denied simply on the unacknowledged basis of race.

Many women know this story well as job applicants, but we may not have imagined how the story could be retold as a narrative about racism. We do know that we vie with one another for a limited number of employment positions in many sectors such as the church or academy. Perhaps one of the places where race and gender connect and collide is in the underlying pretense that justice could be rightly defined by a system in which there are only so many positions available for women. Privilege subtly constructs power as a limited resource that only a few can enjoy at the expense of others rather than an integrative and expansive resource. Women of every race can be allies in calling into question the lie of sexism that punishes all of us. We also need to be vigilant in recognizing our vulnerability to other lies that disclose the multiple stratifying variations of the myth of meritocracy that further divide women.

Perhaps for white women who have seen how the lie of meritocracy disguises the privilege of patriarchy, it is a bit easier to begin to imagine how these concepts of meritocracy and privilege implicate us in the sin of racism. *Racism* is an interlocking system of advantage and corresponding disadvantage based on race.[3] It exists at individual, group, institutional, and cultural/symbolic (e.g., media) levels in active and passive or aversive forms. This definition is critical because it foregrounds the context of power and control from which racism arises and endures. Just as patriarchy could never exist through occasional individual acts by a few men, so we also need to acknowledge that the scope and power of racism points to a similarly interlocking accrual of power and influence rather than the occasional act of a lone purveyor of discrimination. We also know that just as accountability for the enduring power of the sin of sexism is usually obscured by the normative assumptions of privilege, such as the idea that sexism exists because of women's problematic behavior or deficits, so is any true understanding of the origin and continuation of racism. This will require paying attention to those whose interests are served, however unwittingly, by keeping racial privilege in place. White women who wish to be allies in deconstructing racism need to be alert to similar suggestions that racism exists because of the behaviors of those who are disadvantaged by it instead of pursuing those systems and structures served by it. Think, for example, of the energy given to critiquing "welfare mothers" rather than attending to the deep, systemic inequities in housing, education, employment, minimum-wage rather than living-wage policies, child care, and health care that more adequately explain generations of under- or unemployment.

A particularly stunning contradiction of the myth of meritocracy that should claim the attention of every woman is the fact that the best predictor of one's socioeconomic status as an adult is the socioeconomic status of one's father.[4] *Socioeconomic class* describes a relative position in a structurally and historically defined hierarchical network of social relations that predicts levels of access to power and control in multiple contexts of institutional and daily life. Socioeconomic factors also disclose the distortions of privilege that create and sustain inequitable access to goods and services. Clearly, the collisions that women experience across the differences of gender, race, and class expose the dynamic asymmetries of power as privilege variously disguised by the myth of meritocracy to avoid accountability.

Once we recognize how meritocracy functions to maintain privileges for some and to assure the oppressive marginalization of others, then both the priority for confronting privilege and the inadequacy of compassion without justice are clear. Any account of the social construction of race in the American colonies will disclose the European inheritance of an unholy alliance of sexism, racism, and classism from the outset.[5] Power was presumed to be the right of a few rich, white planters. Because the balance of privilege most often lies with us, the implications now for white women, especially those who enjoy economic privilege as well, include a particular accountability for acknowledging whatever privilege is ours and leveraging that privilege to speak truth to power rather than participating in the pretenses of meritocracy. Of course it is also true that accountability for confronting the asymmetries of economic privilege, racism, and heterosexism among women exists within each racial group.

Critical Race Theory

Critical theory is an important resource for surfacing and analyzing the role of power and assessing the asymmetries of power, particularly in relation to the marginalization of various groups of persons. Critical race theory provides valuable resources for European American women in our efforts to deconstruct barriers of racism and develop patterns of accountability that will allow us to work as allies with women of color.

The Cycle of Socialization (fig. 21.1, p. 337) developed by Harro[6] is one of the foundational sources for understanding the process by which persons are socialized into ways of seeing and being that then increasingly shape understanding of self and other as well as related behaviors. Though not developed with theological implications in mind, it is a tool that demonstrates well the formative and interlocking effects of various institutions and central relationships for shaping personal and social identity and agency. For example, it quickly demonstrates that racism is learned behavior that arises and is reproduced through the convergence of multiple relational and institutional sources. It can be similarly useful for imagining how girls are inducted into patriarchal self-understanding. It demonstrates a child's susceptibility to the prevailing norms and practices of her or his culture. This cycle of socialization also demonstrates the increasing and reinforcing power of these interlocking factors that makes transformative change difficult without substantial, intentional support.

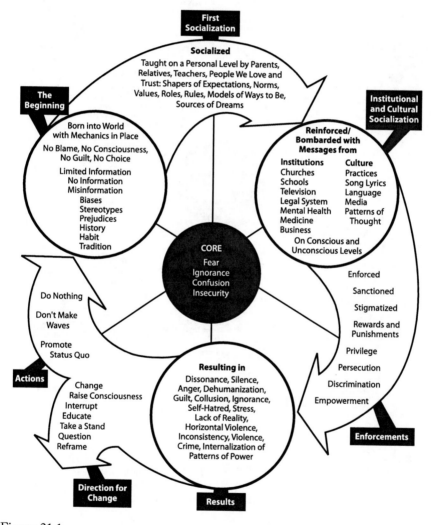

Figure 21.1
"Cycle of Socialization," developed by Bobbie Harro, in Marianne Adams, Lee Anne Bell, and Pat Griffin, eds., *Readings for Diversity and Social Justice: An Anthology on Racism, Antisemitism, Sexism, Heterosexism, Ableism, and Classism*, 2d ed. (New York: Routledge, 2000), 16.

Harro's Cycle of Liberation below (fig. 21.2) suggests a process of reconstructing a more positive and inclusive sense of self (see n. 6).

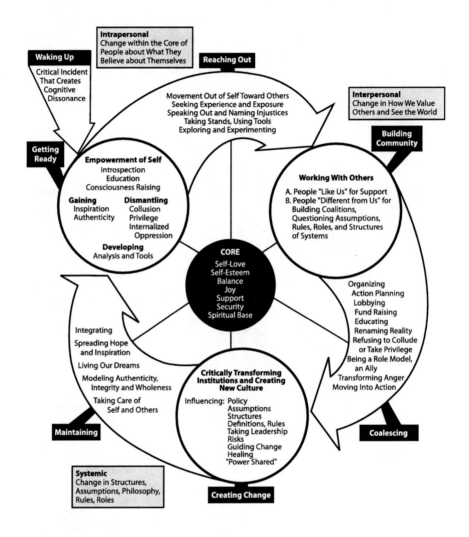

Figure 21.2
"Cycle of Liberation," developed by Bobbie Harro, in Marianne Adams, Lee Anne Bell, and Pat Griffin, eds., *Readings for Diversity and Social Justice: An Anthology on Racism, Antisemitism, Sexism, Heterosexism, Ableism, and Classism,* 2d ed. (New York: Routledge, 2000), 464.

These graphic representations of how children internalize self-understanding shaped by privilege or stigmatizing oppression are useful in underscoring that human beings construct and can reconstruct identities related to oppression and privilege. However, it is also important to stress how formative initial induction into identities such as race and gender is. We need to respect the challenge involved in deconstructing internalized privilege and stigma. In the developmental theory of Robert Kegan, we are reminded of the important role of intentional communities who offer *confirmation* of emerging recognitions around the need to reconstruct our identities and agency in relation to privilege and oppression; *continuity* as we try on new self-understanding and behaviors; and *contradiction* when we misstep in our process of reconstructing our sense of self and related practices.[7]

Critical race theorists have also demonstrated that social identity development theory is helpful for tracking the unsettling experiences related to efforts to deconstruct internalization of privilege or stigma.[8] Importantly, this theory quickly notes that those who recognize dissonance in their experience either related to privilege or oppression may not be able to sustain the hard work of change. Change is not inevitable. Antiracism activist and scholar Beverly Daniel Tatum encourages the use of this theory or related theories of racial identity development as a means of supporting persons who choose to confront either their racial privilege or stigma because it helps to normalize the range of emotions and experiences persons often encounter in processes of such deep change.[9] The chart below (fig. 21.3) illustrates the theory and possible steps that persons may experience in deconstructing the effects of racism and reconstructing a more inclusive identity.

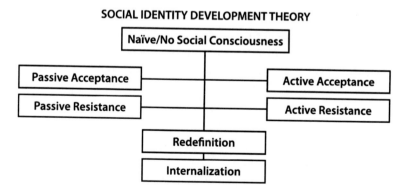

SOCIAL IDENTITY DEVELOPMENT THEORY

Naïve/No Social Consciousness

Passive Acceptance — Active Acceptance

Passive Resistance — Active Resistance

Redefinition

Internalization

Figure 21.3
Rita Hardiman and Bailey W. Jackson, "Racial Identity Development: Understanding Racial Dynamics in College Classrooms and on Campus," *New Directions for Teaching and Learning 52* (Winter 1992): 21–37.

As Harro's Cycle of Socialization also claims, this theory notes that all of us begin at the point of naïveté about our social identity in relation to others. Gradually we actively or passively accept our standing as defined by the dominant culture. For example, children of actively racist parents may learn actively to embrace racial privilege while children of white parents who practice a more passive or aversive racism will probably not recognize how their behaviors reproduce racism. When some precipitating event or events do disclose racial privilege or stigma, white persons may choose actively to resist racist practices but in some contexts we may find active resistance too threatening and choose more passive resistance. If persons stay with this process of change, eventually resistance resolves into a more integrated identity that is redefined by the insights gained through the process of resistance, and persons are free to explore a more positive sense of this newly constructed, more inclusive sense of self. Finally, this theory suggests that the process of redefinition evolves into an internalized, revised sense of self. White women who have embraced feminism will quickly recognize that this theory is readily adaptable to our experiences in externalizing the oppressive power of sexism we received from the dominant culture and embracing a more liberative and positive understanding of our identity as women. Of course, recognizing that we have worked through a process of rejecting one form of oppression will also make apparent that going through this process in relation to one sort of stigma or privilege does not resolve our vulnerability to other such types of internalized privilege or stigma, but it may well help us empathically bridge from our experience of sexism to imagine better the experience of sisters of color. As Young's description of the heterogeneous dimensions of our identity makes clear, even within ourselves we need to resolve colliding sources of privilege and oppression such as race and gender.

Theological Themes

Four intersecting theological themes seem particularly rich for addressing our concern about the asymmetries of privilege and oppression that surround race and gender among European American women and women of color. These theological themes also hold constructive possibilities to explore.

Imago Dei

Our creation in the image of God is foundational for effectively confronting the distortions that asymmetries of power create in relationships and communities. I will focus on several of the ethical assertions that this claim makes for us individually and corporately. Jewish and Christian Scriptures begin in Genesis with the claim that to be is to be in relation. Contemporary relational theory now supports what people of many faiths affirm: that we are inherently relational selves for whom relationships are the primary developmental pathway and that maturity is marked not by autonomy but by interdependence and skills for empathy that reflect an increasingly differentiated self—self-aware and able to recognize and value otherness.[10] We are created as neighbors to live in communities of mutual respect and hospitable care. Two key terms help to capture this ontological and ethical claim: hospitality and neighbor love.

Hospitality. In her book *Making Room,* Christine Pohl[11] reminds us that in the early church hospitality had a deep ethical force, as we overhear in Leviticus 19 where we are told to love our neighbors as ourselves and to treat the stranger/alien who resides among us as a citizen whom we love as ourselves because we too have been aliens. In Christian Scriptures, the primary text for neighbor love, of course, is Luke's story of the good Samaritan. In his sermon on this passage, Martin Luther King Jr. reminds us that neighbor love is our vocation.[12] King notes that the priest and the Levite who pass by the stranger beaten and left to die in the ditch on this dangerous road probably asked themselves, "what might happen to me if I stop?" The Samaritan, he imagines, recognizing the humanity of the man, asked, "What will happen to the man if I do not stop?" We know from the story that the Samaritan, also at risk for his own physical safety in stopping, demonstrated a profound commitment to the well-being of the stranger. Surely he asked himself a second question that reflects the profundity of our relatedness, "What will happen to *me* if I do not stop?" In different ways, the lives of both men were in peril.

The lie that lurks behind the experience of racial privilege for European American women is that we who are privileged can remain unaffected by the oppression of others. As King rightly claimed, nobody can be a somebody if anybody is treated as a nobody.[13] Participating in the oppression of another, even passively, diminishes our own humanity. The Samaritan's action demonstrates this deep recognition that our humanity is intimately related. That is also the profundity of the threefold love command, which insists that love of God binds our well-being and that of our neighbor's together.[14]

Love. We pastoral theologians have much to contribute to any conversation about love—especially when persons make love sound simple. If we keep what we know about love rooted in experience, then we can say that love is about the hardest thing we try to do. In *The Spirit and the Forms of Love,* Daniel Day Williams shared several insights about love that resonate with our work as pastoral theologians, supervisors, and pastors, beginning with the normative claim that the goal of love is "communion in freedom."[15] In their essay "Womanist-Feminist Alliances: Meeting on the Bridge," Marsha Foster Boyd and Carolyn Stahl Bohler[16] well describe the complexity of building authentic trust in the context of their racial difference as these two African American and European American pastoral theologians taught a course together, "Womanist and

Feminist Psychology and Theology." Their experience is instructive especially in their care to hold each other accountable for creating increasing honesty about the reality of racism and the toll it exacted as they pursued a commitment to deepen their trust in each other. Their story reflects the ethical claim of neighbor love and realities of constructing bridges of trust in the context of a racist culture.

Of course, this communion in freedom or mutual regard is immediately complicated because we are asked to love *particular people*, not idealized generalizations that reflect our own projections or the stereotypes by what Young describes as cultural imperialism. As Carroll Watkins Ali[17] rightly reminds us, love occurs in real contexts with persons who are subjects of their own stories. As we seek to build bridges of trust and candor in relationships with women of color, European Americans in particular have to deconstruct the consequences of privilege that protect us from the oppressive realities of racism in order for us to hear the story of a particular sister of color.

Love also presumes our *agency and commitment*. The Samaritan certainly did not simply affirm the general value of humankind. He risked his life and shared his wealth and stayed in connection with the stranger whose need was not short term. When, for example, a Latina colleague shares with us her fear that her ability to use her gifts in ministry is at risk because of institutional racism, it will not do to say simply, "I'm sorry," or even, "You can trust me." Rather, for us whose racial identity is privileged, the challenge is to recognize how the humanity of both our colleague and ourselves is diminished by her fearful need to keep an essential aspect of identity invisible and to use our privilege and our agency in her behalf.

Love is not only particular with implications for our own agency, it is also *causal*. Who we love changes us. Think about supervisory, teaching, and pastoral relationships in which real engagement changes everyone involved and how that experience now shapes the way we practice ministry, understand ourselves, and even our theology. Opening ourselves to colleagues of color means that these relationships make claims on our lives that take us in new directions because, in the reciprocity of relation, we come to see more of ourselves and more of the world we share. We can't love from an uninvolved distance. Love changes us.

This theological imperative to enact love finds support in critical race theory in the concept of "ally."[18] To become allies, we European American women need to take the initiative to deconstruct the way privilege distorts our own identities and practices sufficiently to be comfortable as European Americans even as we also know that unlearning racial privilege will be a lifelong journey of continuing accountability. Allies also acknowledge that we are responsible for knowing our own racial group's story and for learning the history and current experience of oppression of our sisters of color. We also know the importance of listening carefully as they voice their experience of oppression rather than presuming we know it. Of course, as love changes us, we also grow committed to transforming what were unearned privileges into rights that are widely shared. Allies believe we can contribute to positive change and that such change is also in our interest even when we meet resistance from other privileged persons. It is profoundly important to allow the metaphor of neighbor and the particularity, agency, and causality of love to shape the way we practice ministry as allies.

Relational Justice

We cannot speak for long about love without identifying the priority of justice. As the theme of *imago Dei* claims, we are created for life in communities shaped by and toward love. Justice is in the service of love. As Daniel Day Williams put it, "Justice is the order that God's love requires."[19] Justice prizes relationships shaped by mutual respect, advocacy, compassion, and appreciation for the particular gifts of the other. It attends to the way power is exercised not only in relationships but through those structures and systems that amplify the effects of privilege. Justice is served by an integrative power that seeks to enlarge the possibilities of all in contrast to zero-sum notions of power.

As early as 1982, in his book *The Relational Self*, Archie Smith Jr. urged us to move from a focus on individuals that obscures the effects of their context to recognize the web of political, economic, and social dynamics that shapes and often distorts our lives and possibilities.[20] Subsequently Bonnie Miller-McLemore and other feminist and womanist pastoral theologians expanded Smith's ideas. In particular, authors such as Brita Gill-Austern[21] and Jeanne Stevenson-Moessner[22] have noted the way theological norms of mutuality are disrupted by patriarchy and distort women's practices of self-care into patterns of self-sacrifice. Teresa Snorton has helpfully described the way racism and the legacy of patterns that began in slavery further distort African American women's expectations around the balance of self-care and care for others.[23] She also notes how socioeconomic factors arising from racism and images of God shaped by oppression complicate African American women's readiness to practice self-care.

Womanist and feminist practitioners of pastoral care are increasingly aware of the importance of the relation of public policy and care. We are witnesses to what is some of the most painful evidence of a faltering social network that is increasingly unable to provide for the most vulnerable. Womanist pastoral theologians in particular well articulate the importance of listening carefully to the voices of those whose oppression we seek to understand.[24] The shared themes of class, race, and gender prompt an increasingly common recognition of the importance of developing constructive theological skills not only for responding to the particular persons for whom we care, but also for recognizing and addressing the intersecting forces of the larger political and social web that contributes to their oppression.[25] In doing so, we model what Elaine Graham meant by pastoral theology as "saving work."[26] For we hope not only to enlarge understanding and offer compassion, but also to empower those for whom we care to exercise their agency in behalf of love and justice and to challenge the practices of those institutions and structures that contribute to human brokenness. As Carroll Watkins Ali reminds us, survival and liberation are important goals.[27]

Sin

Negation of Relation. While there are many images that have been used to describe sin across the millennia in Christian tradition, two used in recent decades are particularly helpful in addressing the complexity of differences that disclose asymmetries of power and privilege in culture and communities of faith. The two are closely related and each expands the meaning of the other. The first term to which I refer is sin as "the negation of relation," which is proposed in Fumitaka Matsuoka's book *The Color of Faith.*[28]

Matsuoka, a systematic theologian, has given us a powerful phrase that immediately conveys the destructive force of sin. The objectification of another as "other" and the corresponding absolutization of our own identity as normative is exactly what happens when we fail to recognize in another the face of a neighbor whom God also loves and whom God calls us to love as ourselves. We overhear that in the generalizations that use "us and them" language. The passage from Leviticus 19 makes it plain that God's hope is for our enduring memory of our kinship with all people that assures the reciprocity of care and regard. Neighbors are peers. There is no hierarchy of value or privileging of status and rights. Most of the students and colleagues with whom we work that identify with the dominant culture do not set out actively to marginalize or objectify another's identity. Privilege functions to obscure such behavior and meritocracy keeps the reality of privilege out of sight and out of mind. Those who are on the receiving end of being rendered invisible or "less than" know the pain and material costs of negation.

Iris Marion Young's description of the way cultural imperialism occurs when those of us in the dominant culture who are accustomed to defining our reality as if we were its center mistake assimilation of difference on our terms for true dialogue that includes a readiness to be changed by the presence and ideas of another. We are so often unaware of the power of privilege to obscure awareness that we may easily overlook how privilege complicates our capacity truly to perceive and understand the difference our sisters of color represent. The ordinary practices and stereotypes that have arisen as part of the distortions of racism complicate the possibility of real mutuality and accurate empathy.[29]

Sin as Lie. Sin as lie is the second image I find helpful. It is certainly similar to the negation of relation in its insights about how sin obscures the particularity and equal value of the other. Sin as lie refers to the way in which we hide behind certain myths and assumptions that allow us to be comfortable with behavior that, if examined, could not be acceptable. In *The Fall to Violence*, Marjorie Suchocki uses this notion of sin to note how easily we obscure our accountability for abusing our freedom to act in ways that enlarge love of neighbor and how easily we excuse our failures to act.[30] Sin as lie is a powerful way to describe how privilege arises and endures through the powerful national myth of meritocracy. Meritocracy, you remember, is the idea of a level playing field with equal opportunity for all in the United States. It means those who identify with the dominant culture can enjoy its benefits without accepting accountability for those who do not have access to such benefits. You may recall the comment of the late Texas governor, Ann Richards, that George H. W. Bush thought he had hit a home run when he started at third base. That aptly describes how sin as lie functions. The effects of such lies are especially apparent when we overhear norms that function unreflectively in our own or other's generalizations about persons' choices or situation.

Wendy Farley also described sin as lie in her remarkable book *Tragic Vision and Divine Compassion: A Contemporary Theodicy*.[31] Here Farley helps us recognize how this lie arises in human experience and endures in human community. Her typology is an apt description of original sin and our complicity in it because she demonstrates how powerfully we are recruited into lies about ourselves and others long before we have the cognitive ability to reflect critically about our ideas and behavior. Farley describes an unfolding process that will be familiar to us and reminds us of Harro's Cycle of Socialization.

Farley begins with the notion of deception to describe ways that primary relationships shape our capacity to see and understand from the beginning of our childhoods. I'm reminded of the song "You've Got to Be Carefully Taught," from the musical *South Pacific*.[32] You may remember it too. The song describes how by the time they reach six or seven years of age children quickly pick up on the fears and suspicions of difference that they overhear at home and make them their own.

By the time we are moving toward elementary school, deception becomes *callousness*. By this Farley refers to the way calluses protect tender points on our bodies. Lies about inequitable treatment of others require calluses for our consciences so that we have rationales for why some housing is so inferior and some children have noticeably fewer resources at school. Think about the way people took picnic baskets to lynchings in this country or the way persons watched as Jews were forced onto boxcars. Our capacity to eat dinner while the news is on may be another example.

We are taught rationalizations and by the time we realize this, we often opt for the idea of *bondage,* by which Farley means our claim that the problem we now acknowledge is beyond the scope of anything we can do. Our hands are tied; we can't solve something as big as classism or racism or heterosexism in the United States—it just is. Bondage is deepened because racial privilege allows most of us who are white to think of ourselves as individuals rather than a social group so that if we are not actively practicing oppressive behavior, we believe we are not complicit in it.

But Farley rightly insists that sin is an ethical claim, which reminds us that we are accountable for our freedom and our choices. Farley's fourth term in this typology is *guilt*. Privilege did not just happen. Our actions or our failure to act reproduce sin, and our actions can interrupt it. I hope you find as I do that this idea of sin as lie is a tool we can use to explore how oppressive situations arise and endure and what roles we can play in interrupting that oppression.

Embodiment

The dominant culture encourages a disembodied spirituality that does not reflect on the role of affections and physicality in constructing our self-understanding or in imagining who God is and how God is present in our lives and world. But in fact, these complex differences of gender, race, class, and orientation that become oppressive are interwoven in our embodied experience.

I also think about the working-class Latina who has a stroke at age forty-five and can no longer employ the fine motor skills that made her a much-admired seamstress. The realities of social class in this country likely mean that her family has few economic resources to provide a safety net. Her whole self-understanding as a mother and wife is wrapped up in providing for her family. European American, middle-class women who have always had health insurance and whose parents participate in pension plans may well struggle to comprehend this Latina's experience of this health crisis that is also an economic crisis. Compassion that is not informed by attention to the need for structural justice will not be experienced as helpful. The barriers created by racism, the enduring absence of social justice for many persons of color, and the lie of meritocracy that keeps the veil of privilege in place will loom large in efforts to offer effective care in such a situation.

An African American woman CPE supervisor knows painfully well the story of sexual and physical violence that is interwoven in the legacy of slavery. The young European American female she is supervising dares to speak of an acquaintance rape the previous year. How might these converging narratives inform their supervisory relationship? What might these two come to know about God as they explore the tragic sin and suffering that is part of their heritage?

Embodiment functions as a resource for sexism, racism, and heterosexism differently than for classism, because the first three sources of oppression include core aspects of our identity. Classism arises as an arbitrary source of inequality that is part of systemic injustice. Our socioeconomic class status is not about an inescapable aspect of our identity but about inequitable distribution of power, rights, and privileges. Yet classism insinuates itself into embodied experience and the way we come to experience ourselves in this culture by virtue of the class status we inhabit. Embodiment is also a powerful theological and pastoral resource for our work. The complexity of difference significantly affects our experience of the differences we embody. Teresa Snorton[33] offers an excellent illustration of the way racism may distort embodied experience for African American women through racist stereotypes or controlling images such as "mammy," "matriarch," and "welfare mother." Images such as "matriarch" can certainly take on a self-fulfilling power so that, as Snorton notes, African American women may learn to distort notions of strength into efforts to be self-sufficient. Their determination to project a sense of strength may in fact begin to prevent them from receiving the care they need as we all do.

Embodiment may be a subtle category for discerning the effects of racism, but the work of womanist and feminist pastoral theologians suggests that this is a fruitful category for uncovering how race and gender collide. Hopefully it will also be a helpful context for exploring how race and gender can inform more effective instances for mutual care.

Concluding Reflections

European American women who wish to become allies with our sisters of color have helpful theoretical and theological resources for the journey. As this essay has demonstrated, experiences of oppression and privilege often collide within and across social groups that share a common oppression. In pursuing the apparent collision among women across the categories of race and gender, however, we have found a remarkable alignment of theoretical and theological proposals that support efforts of European American women who want to deconstruct racial privilege and share those privileges as rights with sisters of color.

Most encouraging for us European American women is the recognition that in each resource we explored we found a common claim. As relational selves, deconstructing privilege is as critical for the moral and spiritual integrity of the one yielding privilege as it is for well-being of the persons who experience oppression. Theologically, we recognized that our very humanity is interwoven. We are created as neighbors, and our well-being is grounded in our interdependence. The love God intends for us is richest when we are actively engaged in securing justice for one another. Developmentally, we learned that our maturity deepens as we develop the capacity to honor the otherness of our neighbors and this requires acknowledging and appreciating the heterogeneity in our own complex selves. True mutuality, so important for relationships and particularly for relationships across oppressive difference, relies on the critical and deep reflection of those who are privileged and our willingness to externalize privilege in exchange for shared rights. Critical race theorists have developed resources to help us on this journey of deconstructing racial privilege and reconstructing a positive, inclusive racial identity.

Even as we appreciate the value of these resources, we also must acknowledge that theologically and theoretically we are confronted with the perduring character of racial oppression. Deconstructing racial privilege is a crucial step for humankind's wholeness, and it is so difficult that it is a lifelong journey. We can also affirm, as women of faith, that each incremental step toward a more inclusive racial identity amplifies the liberating freedom of God's grace, which in turn strengthens us for the work.

Where Race and Gender Collude

Reconstructing Our History

Jeanne Stevenson-Moessner

The Quest

My quest for common ground among multicultural women began some years ago in California when I heard a story about a spelling bee. The occasion was the meeting of a group called Women in Theological Education sponsored by the Presbyterian Church (U.S.A.). There was a concurrent meeting of African Americans that included Joan Martin and Katie Geneva Cannon. Cannon was telling us part of her life narrative, which included her exclusion from a spelling bee in her hometown in North Carolina. She was not allowed to enter the competition due to her race. She went home and told her mother, "I know I can spell."

Many years and challenges later, the brilliant and accomplished Katie Geneva Cannon was being considered for tenure in her academic institution. While the committee on rank and tenure deliberated, she sat in a waiting room. The chair of the committee appeared and announced that she had achieved tenure. Katie Geneva Cannon told us women that she left the room quietly and chose to absorb the news by herself. The words that came to her that day were these: "I knew I could spell!"

I felt race and gender collide that day. It was a positive limit, not a "negative limit" that feminists mention quite often in their narratives. A negative limit foretells the end of the road; it marks the end of a former direction. In my case, the positive limit marked a fork in the road. Katie Geneva Cannon had walked a part of the road of life that I had never and would never walk; she walked the path of double discrimination. You see, I had been allowed to be in the citywide spelling bee in Memphis, Tennessee, as a white girl.

On the other hand, I have been in southern subcultures of the United States where education for white women was not promoted. For example, I attended a Wednesday night supper at a Protestant church in Tennessee. As I stood in line,

I overheard two parents discussing their daughter's desire to go on for a master's degree. It was decided that an advanced degree would present a "marriage risk." In other words, an educated woman would threaten potential suitors. She was denied the opportunity.

In these same subcultures, I have known situations where sons' graduate education would be paid while daughters within the same white family would be denied family support for advanced degrees. In one instance, when a daughter tried to make it on her own, the family refused to fill out their part of the financial-aid application. In some cases, the young women capitulated to the social system that encapsulated them. In other cases, the young women left town and made their way alone. Although the degree of hardship for the women I have personally known in no way matches the degree of hardship of Katie Geneva Cannon's quest for education, their lives touch hers as women on some parcel of common ground.

My quest for common ground was further activated as I chaired the Racism and Sexism Committee at a denominational seminary in the late 1980s. Issues concerning inclusive language, God images, equal opportunities and equitable salaries in ministry, textbooks and bibliographies representative of diverse constituencies—all were volatile and valuable topics in our theological discourse and in our life together. However, the student members of the committee insisted that we either focus on sexism or racism. In their experience, we as committee members could not focus on both within the academic year. The students called for a vote and won their position. That decision has discomforted me to this day.

Therefore, for my contribution to the discussions winding through this volume, I am going back into history to reconstruct a time when racism and sexism colluded. I could have used the words *copartnered, coincided, collaborated,* or *coalesced.* However, I have chosen the word *collude* because it conveys plotting. Women "out of order" must collude to navigate institutional, familial, societal, class, and even ecclesial structures that prevent them from being all they can be, all that God has created them to be.

The Discovery

One afternoon while taking an American church history course at Princeton Theological Seminary, I discovered a document by a woman named Elizabeth Cady Stanton. This document was located in Speer Library in a box of pamphlets.[1] *The Slave's Appeal,* omitted from the formal bibliography of Stanton's written work, read as if written by a slave woman.[2]

In an attempt to adapt the Decalogue, or Ten Commandments, to the issue of slavery, Stanton spoke in rigorous theological application of nine of the commandments.[3] For example, referring to the Sixth Commandment as found in Exodus 20, she appealed to religious bodies and communities and mission boards that accepted tithes from slaveholders, on behalf of those on southern plantations:

'Thou shalt not kill.' Go to, now, take God's image, put out its eyes, knock out its teeth, burn, and brand, and scarify, and catmaul its flesh! Hang it on trees, or head downwards in deep pits, choke it in stocks, hunt it with pikes and guns, and bows, and hounds! make it a target for your cruel jests, your spite, your spleen! use all your hellish arts to blot out, if you can, the faintest vestige of immortality; then, in white robes, from God's altar, on each returning Sabbath day, with holy unction, read to the kneeling saints!! 'Thou shalt not kill.'

In such graphic language, she spoke as a southern slave. Then I learned she was white like me.

Intrigued by this outspoken woman, I investigated further. Elizabeth Cady Stanton was a product of the Great Revival; at age fifteen, she had been exposed to the teaching and preaching of Charles Finney during the Great Troy Revival of 1831. From an evangelical conversion, she found an environment conducive to reform. Stanton met many abolitionists including Gerrit Smith and Henry Cady Stanton, her future husband. Together with her husband and Lucretia Mott, amid family opposition, she sailed to the London World Anti-Slavery Convention in 1840. When the American women who were delegates and observers were denied seats, the gender issue and the slavery issue both became volatile topics. Many of the early feminists of this period around the Seneca Falls Convention of 1848 were ardent abolitionists first; their commitment to women's rights grew out of both evangelism and abolitionism.[4] The women's rights movement intensified when black males were granted the vote. The Fourteenth Amendment, which was ratified on July 28, 1868, gave African American males citizenship; however, women—all women—were denied citizenship. The Fifteenth Amendment on March 30, 1870, granted the vote to all black males; yet, all women were denied suffrage. The six volumes of History of Women Suffrage document the collective surge of energy as women continued their quest for emancipation.

In this ferment of passionate activity, Stanton wrote about slaves of custom, color, sex, and creed.[5] On May 8, 1860, six months following John Brown's raid on Harper's Ferry, Elizabeth Cady Stanton gave a speech to the American Anti-Slavery Society. She made a significant link between abolition and feminism on the following common ground: "Herein is woman more fully identified with the slave than man can possibly be, for she can take the subjective view. . . . For while the man is born to do whatever he can, for the woman and the negro there is no such privilege. . . . The badge of degradation is the skin and sex. . . ." Stanton continued to address a "proud" minister while using Scripture and a linguistic pivot:

No, proud priest, you may cover your soul in holy robes, and hide your manhood in a pulpit, and, like the Pharisee of old, turn your face away from the sufferings of your race; but I am a Christian—a follower of

Jesus—and 'whatever is done unto one of the *least* of these my sisters is done also unto me.' Though, in the person of the poor trembling slave mother, you have bound me with heavy burdens most grievous to bear, though you have done all you could to quench the spark of immortality, which, from the throne of God, brought me into being . . . yet can I speak to [him] [God]. . . .[6]

By adapting Matthew 25:45 and including "sisters," she made a linguistic pivot in her speech and spoke as the poor, trembling slave mother. Her audience was confused with the ambiguity surrounding the subject of the speech. Did she intend white women or African American women to be the subject? Using a biblical understanding, she merged the two.

The Great Convergence

Where were the slave mothers in this time period? The most prominent slave mother was Sojourner Truth, who was known in circles of abolitionism and women's rights.

Isabella Baumfree (also spelled Bomefree), or Sojourner Truth, was born in 1797 to Elizabeth and James Baumfree, slaves on the Hardenbergh plantation in upstate New York. When Charles Hardenbergh, her second "master," died in 1808, Isabella was sold at age nine to John Neeley. She and a herd of sheep were sold for a total of one hundred dollars. She had five slave masters in all.

After walking off of the estate of "fifth master" John Dumont in 1826 with her daughter, Sophia, and claiming her freedom from slavery, Isabella Baumfree later experienced another form of oppression. Following her transformative religious experience while living in the safety of the Van Wagenen's home, she began to worship in a local Methodist church. In 1829, Isabella left Ulster County with a white evangelical teacher named Miss Gear. Isabella met Elijah Pierson, who gathered a group of followers in his home, the "Kingdom." Isabella was designated the housekeeper. However, after Robert Matthias arrived, he took over the leadership of the group and engaged in bizarre activities, which newspaper accounts described as "cultic." Robert Matthias (dubbed the Imposter) was placed on trial for the murder of one of the cult's followers and was acquitted. However, later, when Elijah Pierson died in strange circumstances, not only was Matthias put on trial but Isabella as well. In the newspaper account of the "Kingdom of Matthias Trial at White Plains, NY," Isabella was portrayed as an accomplice to the questionable death of Pierson.[7] She and Matthias were accused of poisoning Pierson and stealing money from the household. After she and Matthias were acquitted, she later sued for libel.[8] Isabella left a situation of bondage to Robert Matthias and headed east for New York City as the Spirit called. She changed her name to Sojourner Truth after a profound religious awakening and became a traveling preacher.

In her preaching and evangelism, she advocated for the antislavery cause and for women's rights. While she was selling her autobiography, *The Narrative of Sojourner Truth,* in 1850 at the national convention in Worcester, Massachusetts, she first came into formal contact with the women's rights movement. She later attended and spoke at the women's rights meeting in Akron, Ohio, in 1851, and delivered her famous "And a'n't I a woman?" speech. There had been opposition to her speaking, according to Frances Gage.[9] People approached Gage with fear that abolitionism and women's rights as two causes would be all "mixed up."[10] Sojourner later remarked that she was about the only African American [colored] woman who went around speaking about the rights of the African American woman.[11] As a "woman out of order," she claimed common ground.

Where is there evidence of the convergence of Sojourner Truth and Elizabeth Cady Stanton, or any other of the vocal women's rights advocates? In the spring of 1850, Lucy Stone, a graduate of Oberlin College and a hired speaker for the Massachusetts Anti-Slavery Society, attended an antislavery convention in Boston. "At its conclusion an announcement was made, inviting those who were interested in a woman's rights convention to meet in the anteroom. Lucy Stone and Abby Foster were among the nine who appeared. The outcome of this meeting was the first National Woman's Rights Convention, held in Worchester, Massachusetts, in October 1850."[12] At this convention, Lucretia Mott, Lydia Mott, Angelina Grimke, Abby Foster, Ernestine Rose, Lucy Stone, Antoinette Brown, Elizabeth Cady Stanton, and Sojourner Truth all began to work together for equal rights for women. This momentum was criticized by such former colleagues as Wendell Phillips and Gerrit Smith for detracting from the "Negro's Hour."[13] Women were encouraged to put their claims second to men's. However, the women decided to be "out of order" and persist. "The argument that black and white women deserved the vote as much as freedmen had few advocates. The insistence of abolitionists and Republicans that black male suffrage take precedence over female suffrage enraged Stanton."[14] The Eleventh National Women's Rights Convention was set for May 1866. Sojourner stayed with the Stanton family and attended the meeting. Stanton's daughter, Harriet, was ten at the time and remembered reading the morning papers to Sojourner. Sojourner told her: "I can't read little things like letters. I read big things like men."[15]

Once again the disagreement over joining two suffrage causes intensified. Many members of the Anti-Slavery Society wanted to emphasize black male suffrage and postpone momentum for female suffrage. The radical feminists refused to wait. Foremost was Sojourner Truth at the Equal Rights Association meeting in May 1867. Sojourner Truth, "speaking for them [radical feminists] as well as for black women, said they must work for universal suffrage now."[16] She admonished women to step into the water while the water was stirring. Black women would be no better situated than before, she said, if they were denied the vote while black men received it. Then, their men would be masters over them as women.[17] She colluded with other women out of order against the prevailing system of unequal suffrage. However, with support from men like Horace Greeley, the Fourteenth Amendment passed, giving black males the same voting privilege as white males. None of these women mentioned, working so hard for universal suffrage, lived to see women of any color receive the right to vote.

The Intersection

On one occasion, the house of Harriet Beecher Stowe was filled with several eminent clergymen. Harriet was notified that Sojourner Truth had arrived and requested an interview. In an article published in *The Atlantic Monthly* in 1863, Harriet describes this transformative encounter with "Sojourner Truth, the Libyan Sibyl."

> I do not recollect ever to have been conversant with any one who had more of that silent and subtle power which we call personal presence than this woman. In the modern Spiritualistic phraseology, she would be described as having a strong sphere. Her tall form, as she rose up before me, is still vivid to my mind. . . . She seemed perfectly self-possessed and at her ease,—in fact, there was almost an unconscious superiority, not unmixed with a solemn twinkle of humor, in the odd composed manner in which she looked down on me.[18]

Sojourner fell into a state of quiet reflection and eventually broke out with the words, "O Lord! O Lord! Oh, the tears, an' the groans, an' the moans! O Lord!"[19] She related the sufferings she had seen among slaves; the bruising, the tearing, and mangling of the flesh were original observations that were echoed in Elizabeth Cady Stanton's "A Slave's Appeal."

Harriet called Dr. Beecher, Professor Allen, two or three other clergymen, and her family to listen to the sibyl and sage Sojourner. Harriet introduced Sojourner to Dr. Beecher, stating his celebrity as a preacher. "'Is he?' Sojourner said, offering her hand in a condescending manner, and looking down on his white head."[20] She identified herself as a preacher as well. Dr. Beecher proceeded to ask if she preached from the Bible. She stated that she didn't because she could not read a letter. Dr. Beecher then queried as to the source of her homiletics.

> Her answer was given with a solemn power of voice, peculiar to herself, that hushed every one in the room. 'When I preaches, I has jest one text to preach from, an' I always preaches from this one. *My* text is, "WHEN I FOUND JESUS."'

It is another way of saying, "I knew I could spell."

The audience was spellbound as she told of her conversion and gave the narrative of her life with the passion of her personality. Upon dispersing, one clergyman remarked that he had heard more of the gospel in her stories than in most sermons.

Sojourner stayed several days with Harriet Beecher Stowe as a welcome guest. In the published interview, Harriet underscored the strong conversations that occurred in her home, including the topic of women's rights.

Harriet Beecher Stowe has left us with the only published interview with Sojourner Truth. Consider the setting in which it occurred. Into a well-furnished home came a former slave who had not even slept in a bed until she was an adult. On one hand, there is an evening soiree with educated gentry; on the other, there is the mother wit and natural wisdom of a woman with no formal education. As I read the interview, the matters of classism permeated the pages. The disparity between lifestyles is markedly pronounced. Even with the class differences, however, Harriet and Sojourner found a common space, which began with Sojourner's first words to Harriet: "So, this is *you*," she said.[21]

Throughout this volume, contributors have used words to describe a common space: intersection, interweaving, interacting. What I have in mind is like a unique space in Dubuque, Iowa (see fig. 22.1, p. 356). It is not a ring road, that breathtaking circular phenomenon in England, affectionately dubbed a "roundabout" by the British. In other words, the "convergence" or "common ground" I am describing does not require the traveler to go in a circular fashion. The direction is not set. Rather, there are five small arteries as depicted below. One enters the common space beside Finley Hospital, another artery enters beside a bank; yet another street borders an eye clinic, another skirts a church, another hedges a dry cleaners. What is required for a safe and healthy passage across this common terrain is respect for the rights and the timing of the other travelers. In order to make it across this space, the driver of a vehicle must have a careful eye on the other vehicles, approaching from different venues. Turns are taken with respect and vigilance for the presence of others—others who are coming from east, west, north, south, yet now ready to cross a common space, only to venture forth with new possibilities.

I have lived in this city of Dubuque, Iowa, for twelve years; I have never witnessed an accident at this location. I cross this location several times a day; I have never even seen a close call.

Our work on this volume has been like crossing this space of convergence. None of our trajectories have been the same. I do not know the extent of the journey of those who are Native American, Latina, Asian American, Puerto Rican, African American, or Italian. I do know there is a connectedness of concern for some of the world's injustices toward women. A thirteen-year-old rape victim in Mogadishu, Somalia, was stoned to death after being accused of "adultery." Three men had raped her. Dozens of Islamic militants stoned Aisha

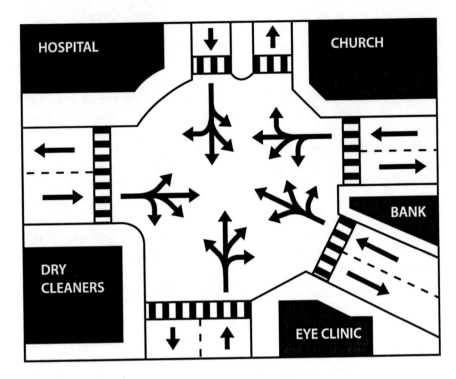

Figure 22.1

Ibrahim Duhulow to death on October 27, 2008, in a packed stadium in Kismayo.[22] Amnesty International cited witnesses of the public stoning. This act of violence occurred as we were writing this volume; although I circulated the information among all contributors, I did not have to ask for responses. I knew how each contributor felt. The continuing violence to women is one reason we write as we do.

In September of 2008, while we were writing this volume, five honor killings occurred in Islamabad, Pakistan.[23] Five women tried to choose their own husbands; three of these women were teenagers. All five were shot, thrown into a ditch, and buried alive by relatives. In conservative parts of Pakistan, the freedom to choose a partner is an insult to the family. Hundreds of women are killed by male relatives every year. Once again, for me, race and gender collide. I cannot identify with the severity of the consequences in this true story. However, race and gender collude as I remember the subtle "arranged marriages" in certain economically privileged subcultures in the southern part of the United

States. Some "society families" expect their children to marry into "society families." There are contemporary dowries involved for the females, dowries that usually consist of their fathers' incomes, their parents' inheritance, or their trust funds. The consequences of marrying outside the subculture are not as severe as for the Pakistani women, obviously, but there is a degree of collusion as women attempt to navigate the "terrain of sexism and classism."

As we find our way in the quest toward freedom, I believe there are at least ten rules for the road. These rules are not written in the language of "Thou shalt not," but, rather, in the affirmation: "I shall." You may ascertain hints of the Decalogue or the Ten Commandments of Exodus 20 in the distance, and you would not be far off course. Here is the way we women journey, we women who come from so many different locations. We take our turn crossing the "common space" and then we go on our way.

Ten Rules for the Road

- I shall behold God.
- I shall bow down to no man, no injustice, no falsehood, no treachery.
- I shall name and honor God.
- I shall respect Sabbath time and rest.
- I shall honor those who have been mother and father to me.
- I shall not be diminished by any method of murder including killing, battery, rape, or incest.
- I shall respect my body.
- I shall not allow my identity, respect, esteem, or self to be stolen.
- I shall speak the truth.
- I shall, in all honesty, claim what is mine.

I know that my journey is not yours; neither is yours mine. We have come from different places, even cultures, and we are headed to various venues of life. But within these pages and within our passions for justice, we have passed for a few moments across common ground. Those moments were shared moments, and I shall not forget them as I wish you Godspeed.

Contributors

Esther E. Acolatse is Assistant Professor of Pastoral Theology at Duke University Divinity School. She holds a BA (Hons) from the University of Ghana, an M.T.S. from Harvard Divinity School, and a Ph.D. in practical theology from Princeton Theological Seminary. She previously taught theology at Loyola College in Baltimore, Maryland.

Adriana P. Cavina lives in Phoenix, Arizona, where she is a certified chaplain and clinical pastoral education supervisor. She has been chair of the International Pastoral Care Network for Social Responsibility, founding member of the Society for Intercultural Pastoral Care and Counseling, and President of the Federation of Evangelical Women in Italy. A native of Italy, Adriana is one of the first Italian women to be ordained as a Baptist pastor, is a published author in Italy, and is an international lecturer on multicultural competencies in spiritual care.

Karla J. Cooper is an African Methodist Episcopal itinerant elder with dual standing in the United Church of Christ. Having traveled extensively throughout Africa and India, she currently serves as pastor of Quinn Chapel AME Church in Lincoln, Nebraska, as well as chaplain and adjunct faculty of Doane College. Cooper has a B.A. from Southeast Missouri State University and a M.Div. from Eden Theological Seminary. She is presently a doctoral student at the University of Nebraska in Lincoln.

Pamela Cooper-White is Ben G. and Nancye Clapp Gautier Professor of Pastoral Theology, Care, and Counseling at Columbia Theological Seminary, Decatur, Georgia. She is the author of *Many Voices: Pastoral Psychotherapy and Theology in Relational Perspective* (2006), *Shared Wisdom: Use of the Self in Pastoral Care and Counseling* (2003), and *The Cry of Tamar: Violence against Women and the Church's Response* (1995) all from Fortress Press. In 2005, she received the American Association of Pastoral Counselors' national award for Distinguished Achievement in Research and Writing. An Episcopal priest and pastoral psychotherapist, she is a clinical fellow in AAPC and serves as publications editor of *The Journal of Pastoral Theology*.

Laura W. Dorsey, board certified in the Association of Professional Chaplains, an ordained Presbyterian minister with twenty years' experience in parish and clinical settings, is chaplain for oncology services at Northside Hospital in Atlanta, Georgia. She is a clinical member of the Association for Clinical Pastoral Education, a member of the ACPE clinical member advisory board, a board-certified member of the Association of Professional Chaplains, and a former student of analytical psychology at the Jungian Institute of Zurich and the Memphis Interregional Seminar. She is the mother of three adult children, grandmother of five, and frequent host to student and church gatherings at Rabbit Hill Farm, where she lives.

Carol Lakota Eastin is an ordained United Methodist elder and fellow in the American Association of Pastoral Counselors. She is the founding pastor of the Native American Fellowship-Dayspring Church. Carol is part of a clergy couple; she and her husband, Bill, have two sons.

Miriam Figueroa was born in Rio Piedras, Puerto Rico, in a Pentecostal pastoral home. She is an ordained minister of the Church of God in Puerto Rico, a member of the executive council of the national Church of God, and an associate pastor in Aguas Buenas. Miriam is the wife of Rev. José Pimentel, mother of three, and a grandmother.

Kathleen J. Greider is Professor of Spiritual Care and Pastoral Counseling at Claremont School of Theology in Claremont, California. Her research and teaching interests include practical and pastoral theology, interculturality, the interplay of social and personal change, and depth psychology. She is the author of *Reckoning with Aggression: Theology, Violence, and Vitality* (1997) and *Much Madness Is Divinest Sense: Wisdom in Memoirs of Soul-Suffering* (2007).

Jacqueline Kelley is Director of Clinical Pastoral Education at Princeton Baptist Medical Center in Birmingham, Alabama. Jacqueline is an ordained United Methodist elder, a board certified member of the Association of Professional Chaplains, a grief counselor at Community Grief Support Services, and an Adjunct Professor at Beeson Divinity School, Samford University.

Yoke-Lye Lim Kwong is an ordained minister, Association for Clinical Pastoral Education supervisor, a board-certified chaplain, and an American Association of Pastoral Counselors pastoral care specialist. She is the director of spiritual care services at Howard Regional Health System, Kokomo, Indiana. She is Malaysian-Chinese-Cantonese, speaks several dialects/languages, and has lived in Southeast Asia, Canada, and the United States. Her journey of immigration energizes her to teach frequently and offer workshops that stimulate awareness in exploring intercultural, interethnic spiritual care and supervision to promote justice, compassion, equality, and inclusion.

Michelle Oberwise Lacock is an ACPE supervisor and ordained United Methodist clergy (Northern Illinois Annual Conference). Michelle currently serves on the board of directors for the Chicago American Indian Center and as chair of the board of directors of the North Central Jurisdiction United Methodist Native American Course of Study. She is published in the *Journal of Supervision and Training in Ministry* and is married with four adult children and one granddaughter.

Insook Lee is Assistant Professor of Pastoral Care and Counseling at Hood Theological Seminary in Salisbury, North Carolina. She is an ordained minister in the Presbyterian Church (USA), a fellow in the American Association of Pastoral Counselors (AAPC), and a mother of two grown children, Ellen and David. She has previous experience in parish ministry for several immigrant churches of Korean-Americans, has served as a pastoral psychotherapist in Atlanta, and is currently conducting research on intercultural approaches to pastoral care and counseling, postcolonial feminist theories, and Asian American concepts of self-identity.

Suk Yeon Lee is an ordained member of the Evangelical Lutheran Church in America. She graduated from Pacific Lutheran Theological Seminary, served as an associate pastor in Concord, California, and earned an M.A. from Graduate Theological Union in Religion and Psychology. She is currently a doctoral student in pastoral counseling at Yonsei University. She is a mother of three children and a licensed pharmacist in Korea.

Barbara J. McClure is Assistant Professor of Pastoral Theology in the Graduate Department of Religion and the Divinity School, Vanderbilt University. Prior to teaching full-time, she worked six years as a pastoral counselor in private practice and seven years as a leader development coach and organizational consultant. Barbara is the author of *Moving Beyond Individualism in Pastoral Care and Counseling: Reflections on Theory, Theology, and Practice*, 2009).

Joretta L. Marshall is Professor of Pastoral Theology, Care, and Counseling at Brite Divinity School in Fort Worth, Texas, and author of several articles and books including *Counseling Lesbian Partners* (2004) and *How Can I Forgive?* (2005). A member of the United Methodist clergy from the Rocky Mountain Conference, Joretta taught previously at Vanderbilt University Divinity School, Iliff School of Theology, and Eden Theological Seminary. An active member in the American Association of Pastoral Counselors, Joretta was President from 2008 to 2010.

Bonnie J. Miller-McLemore is E. Rhodes and Leona B. Carpenter Professor of Pastoral Theology in the Graduate Department of Religion and the Divinity School, Vanderbilt University. Recent publications include *In the Midst of Chaos: Care of Children as Spiritual Practice* (2006), *Faith's Wisdom for Daily Living* (with Herbert Anderson, Augsburg Fortress, 2008), and *Children and Childhood in American Religions* (2008). Ordained in the Christian Church (Disciples of Christ), she has spent recent years actively supporting the development of both practical theology and childhood studies in religion, serving as President of the Association of Practical Theology and cochair of two new units of the American Academy of Religion: the Consultation on Childhood Studies and Religion and the Group on Practical Theology.

Francesca Debora Nuzzolese is Assistant Professor of Pastoral Care and Spiritual Formation at Palmer Theological Seminary, Wynnewood, Pennsylvania, and a pastoral psychotherapist in private practice. She is an ordained European Baptist and is pursuing training in spiritual direction. Her academic interests and pastoral ministry are primarily with women in the subcultures of poverty and neglect; she is interested in the pursuit of their psychospiritual well-being.

Sophia Park grew up in seven countries over four continents. Her research interests include multiculturalism in pastoral care and the dynamics of immigrant families living in multicultural contexts. Sophia works as a counselor at the Care and Counseling Center of Georgia and as a part-time spiritual counselor at Ridgeview Institute in Smyrna, Georgia. As a candidate for ministry in the Presbyterian Church (USA), Sophia is actively engaged in the Korean American community in Atlanta by providing counseling, seminars, and workshops at church retreats. She is raising four children with her husband.

Nancy Ramsay is the Executive Vice President, Dean, and Professor of Pastoral Theology and Pastoral Care at Brite Divinity School, affiliated with Texas Christian University in Fort Worth, Texas, where she has served since 2005. Previously she served as the Harrison Ray Anderson Professor of Pastoral Theology at Louisville Presbyterian Theological Seminary. Her research and writing interests include gender, intimate violence, aging, and addressing forms of oppressive difference such as racism, classism, and heterosexism.

Melinda McGarrah Sharp is completing a doctoral program at Vanderbilt University in religion, psychology, and culture. Her dissertation focuses on caring and violence when intercultural misunderstandings create relational crises. She is interested in postcolonialism and pastoral theology, understanding intercultural relationships, and consultation in clinical ethics as a form of care.

Teresa E. Snorton, the executive director of the Association for Clinical Pastoral Education, Inc., is an ordained minister in the Christian Methodist Episcopal Church. She is a certified supervisor in the ACPE, a board-certified chaplain in the Association for Professional Chaplains, and an active member of the Society for Pastoral Theology. She has degrees from Vanderbilt University, Louisville Presbyterian Theological Seminary, Southern Baptist Theological Seminary, and United Theological Seminary and is a longtime advocate and speaker for multicultural issues in pastoral care and counseling.

Angella M. Pak Son is Associate Professor of Psychology and Religion at Drew Theological School, Madison, New Jersey. She is a clinical member of the American Association of Pastoral Counselors and an ordained minister of the Presbyterian Church (USA). She is in the process of publishing a book on the spirituality of joy.

Jeanne Stevenson-Moessner is Professor of Pastoral Care at Perkins School of Theology, Southern Methodist University, Dallas, Texas. She is a past chair of the Society for Pastoral Theology, a Henry Luce III Fellow, an ordained Presbyterian minister in the Presbyterian Church (USA), a Fellow in the American Association of Pastoral Counselors, and a former missionary. She has published *The Spirit of Adoption: At Home in God's Family* (2003), *A Primer in Pastoral Care* (Fortress Press, 2005), *Prelude to Practical Theology* (2008), edited *Through the Eyes of Women: Insights for Pastoral Care* and *In Her Own Time: Women and Developmental Issues in Pastoral Care* (both Fortress Press, 1996 and 2000), and coedited *Women in Travail and Transition* (Fortress Press, 1990) with Maxine Glaz. Jeanne is married to New Testament scholar David Moessner; they have two children.

Elizabeth Johnson Walker is Associate Professor of Pastoral Care and Counseling at Louisville Presbyterian Seminary in Louisville, Kentucky. She is a licensed Marriage and Family Therapist, Approved Supervisor with the American Association of Marriage and Family Therapy, Member Associate of the American Association of Pastoral Counselors, a former pastor, Corresponding Secretary of the Society for Pastoral Theology, and an ordained elder in the United Methodist Church. She has published articles in *Journal of Pastoral Counseling* and chapers in *Working with Black Youth* (2005) and *Multidimensional Ministry for Today's Black Family* (2007).

Beverly R. Wallace is the assistant to the bishop of the Southeastern Synod and an ordained minister of the Evangelical Lutheran Church in America. With a passion for justice and women's concerns, she most recently coordinated pastoral care and spiritual and emotional health for the Hurricane Katrina recovery effort on the coast of Mississippi. Beverly served as a chaplain at Emory University Hospital, has coauthored several articles, and was coauthor of *African-American Grief* (2005).

Women in this photo are identified on p. ii.

Notes

Preface

1. Esteban R. Montilla and Ferney Medina, *Pastoral Care and Counseling with Latino/as*, Creative Pastoral Care and Counseling (Minneapolis: Fortress Press, 2006), 4.
2. The Associated Press, "Fear of attack keeps students away," Dubuque *Telegraph Herald*, Friday 15, 2009, 7A.
3. Sebnem Arsu, "Turkan Saylan, 73, Turkish Doctor, Educator and Advocate," *The New York Times*, May 23, 2009, A15.

Introduction

1. Jean Baker Miller, *Toward a New Psychology of Women* (Boston: Beacon, 1976), xxii.

Chapter 1: Com|plicated Woman

1. Interview/conversation with Sara Caldéron, Jan. 18. 2008, used by permission. All subsequent quotes from Sara derive from this interview.
2. Gilles Deleuze, *The Fold: Leibniz and the Baroque*, trans. Tom Conley (Minneapolis: University of Minnesota Press, 1993; orig. French pub. 1988), 137.
3. J. K. Rowling, *Harry Potter and the Prisoner of Azkaban* (New York: Scholastic, 1999).
4. Elsewhere, I have made a more extended argument for valuing multiplicity over against the paradigm of "integration" in psychology and psychotherapy: see my original paper, "Interrogating Integration, Dissenting Dis-integration: Multiplicity as a Positive Metaphor in Therapy and Theology," presented to the Person, Culture, and Religion Group, American Academy of Religion, San Diego, November 19, 2007, and forthcoming in the journal *Pastoral Psychology*. For a much more detailed discussion of multiplicity in relation to both constructive theology and pastoral psychotherapy, see also my book *Many Voices: Pastoral Psychotherapy in Relational and Theological Perspective* (Minneapolis: Fortress Press, 2006).
5. Sigmund Freud, "The Ego and the Id" (1923), *Standard Edition of the Complete Psychological Works of Sigmund Freud*, ed. and trans. J. Strachey (New York: Norton, 2000; hereafter cited as *SE*), vol. 19.
6. For a more detailed critique of the heroic paradigm of "depth" in psychoanalysis, see Cooper-White, "Higher Powers and Infernal Regions: Models of Mind in Freud's Interpretation of Dreams and Contemporary Psychoanalysis, and their Implications for Pastoral Care," *Pastoral Psychology* 50, no. 5 (2002): 319–43; see also idem, *Shared Wisdom*, 47–54; and idem, *Many Voices*, 51–62.
7. Sigmund Freud, "The Dynamics of the Transference," (1912), *SE* 12:99–108.
8. This movement identifies as its "originary text" Stephen Mitchell, *Relational Concepts in Psychoanalysis* (Cambridge: Harvard University Press, 1988). Other important examples include Stephen A. Mitchell, *Relationality: From Attachment to Intersubjectivity* (Hillsdale, N.J.: Analytic Press, 2000); Stephen A. Mitchell and Lewis Aron, eds., *Relational Psychoanalysis: The Emergence of a Tradition* (Hillsdale, N.J.: Analytic Press, 1999); Lewis Aron, *A Meeting of Minds: Mutuality in Psychoanalysis* (Hillsdale, N.J.: Analytic Press, 1996); Jessica Benjamin, *The Bonds of Love:*

Psychoanalysis, Feminism, and the Problem of Domination (New York: Pantheon, 1988); and idem, *Like Subjects, Love Objects: Essays on Recognition and Sexual Difference* (New Haven: Yale University Press, 1995); Phillip Bromberg, *Standing in the Spaces: Clinical Process, Trauma, and Dissociation* (Hillsdale, N.J.: Analytic Press, 1998); and the journal *Psychoanalytic Dialogues* (beginning with vol. 1 in 1991).

9. For a more detailed summary in relation to pastoral care and counseling, see Cooper-White, *Shared Wisdom*, especially chap. 3, "The Relational Paradigm: Postmodern Concepts of Countertransference and Intersubjectivity," 35–60; and idem, *Many Voices*, esp. chap. 1, "A Relational Understanding of Persons," 35–66.

10. Philip Bromberg, "'Speak! That I May See You': Some Reflections on Dissociation, Reality, and Psychoanalytic Listening," *Psychoanalytic Dialogues* 4, no. 4 (1994): 517–47.

11. Jody Messler Davies, "Multiple Perspectives on Multiplicity," *Psychoanalytic Dialogues* 8, no. 2 (1998): 195. The relational-psychoanalytic understanding of "dissociation" as potentially nonpathological, and the distancing from the automatic equation of dissocation with trauma, is also discussed in Cooper-White, *Shared Wisdom*, 48–50, in relation to intersubjectivity.

12. Jody Messler Davies, "Dissociation, Repression, and Reality Testing in the Countertransference: False Memory in the Psychoanalytic Treatment of Adult Survivors of Childhood Sexual Abuse," *Psychoanalytic Dialogues* 6, no. 2 (1996): 197.

13. Bromberg, "'Speak! That I May See You'," 517–47, cited in Cooper-White, *Shared Wisdom*, 49 (emphasis added). See also Bromberg, "Standing in the Spaces: The Multiplicity of Self and the Psychoanalytic Relationship," *Contemporary Psychoanalysis* 32 (1996): 509–35; and idem, *Standing in the Spaces: Clinical Process, Trauma, and Dissociation* (Hillsdale, N.J.: Analytic Press, 2001).

14. Clifford Geertz, "'From the Native's Point of View': On the Nature of Anthropological Understanding, in *Local Knowledge: Further Essays in Interpretive Anthropology* (New York: Basic Books, 1983), 59.

15. E.g., Alan Roland, *In Search of Self in India and Japan: Toward a Cross-Cultural Psychology* (Princeton: Princeton University Press, 1988).

16. Daniel Stern, *The Interpersonal World of the Infant* (New York: Basic Books, 1985); Robert Emde, "The Affective Self: Continuities and Transformation from Infancy," in *Frontiers of Infant Psychiatry*, vol. 2, ed. J. D. Call, et al. (New York: Basic Books, 1984), 38–54; "The prerepresentational self and its affective core," *Psychoanalytic Study of the Child* 38 (1983): 165–92; Beatrice Beebe and Frank M. Lachmann, "The Contribution of Mother-Infant Mutual Influence to the Origins of Self- and Object Representations," in *Relational Perspectives in Psychoanalysis*, ed. N. J. Skolnick and S. C. Warshaw (Hillsdale, N.J.: Analytic Press, 1992), 83–117.

17. Stephen A. Mitchell, *Hope and Dread in Psychoanalysis* (New York: Basic Books, 1995), 105.

18. This may be close to what C. G. Jung referred to as the "Self" (capital S), which is greater than the executive "ego" who does the conscious knowing, and incorporates all the disavowed and unknown parts of oneself. But there is a distinction from Jung's concept as well. For Jung, the Self was conceived of as a whole, or potentially whole, and desiring the archetype of Wholeness. There is still one unitive self, or being, implied, and the direction of the unconscious is still imagined largely in terms of downward "depth."

19. Carolyn Saari, "Identity Complexity as an Indicator of Mental Health," *Clinical Social Work Journal* 21, no. 1 (1993): 11–23.

20. For more on the implications of a postmodern subjectivity/intersubjectivity, see also Cooper-White, *Shared Wisdom*, 52–54.

21. Alison Pearson, *I Don't Know How She Does It: The Life of Kate Reddy, Working Mother* (New York: Random House, 2002).

22. Carol Gilligan, *In a Different Voice* (Cambridge: Harvard University Press, 1982).

23. Hillary Clinton, victory speech after winning New Hampshire Democratic Primary, Jan. 8, 2008: "I come tonight with a very, very full heart. And I want especially to thank New Hampshire. Over the last week, I listened to you, and in the process, I found my own voice." In Their Own Words, *New York Times*, Jan. 8, 2008, online at http://www.nytimes.com/2008/01/08/us/politics/08text-clinton.html?fta=y, accessed June 24, 2009.

24. Nelle Morton, *The Journey Is Home* (Boston: Beacon, 1985). Teresa Snorton points out an additional caution that "hearing into speech" can be romanticized when other variables, such as culture, race, and class, are not taken into consideration (personal communication).

25. For a wonderful introduction to the implications of French postmodern feminism for feminist theology, see C. W. Maggie Kim, Susan St. Ville, and Susan Simonaitis, eds., *Transfigurations: Theology and the French Feminists* (Minneapolis: Fortress Press, 1993).

26. Jacques Lacan, "The Mirror Stage as Formative of the Function of the I," *Écrits: The First Complete Edition in English*, trans. Bruce Fink (New York: Norton, 2007; orig. French pub. 1970), 76.

27. Luce Irigaray, "The Power of Discourse and the Subordination of the Feminine," "Così fan Tutte," and "The Mechanics of Fluids," in *This Sex Which Is Not One*, trans. Catherine Porter (Ithaca, N.Y.: Cornell University Press, 1985; orig. French pub. 1977), 83, 89, 111, et passim.

28. Luce Irigaray, "Divine Women," trans. Stephen Muecke, Sydney, Australia: Local Consumption Occasional Paper 8 (1986). See also Grace M. Jantzen, *Becoming Divine: Towards a Feminist Philosophy of Religion* (Bloomington: Indiana University Press, 1999), esp. 1–58.

29. Elizabeth Grosz, "Irigaray and the Divine," in Kim, et al., eds., *Transfigurations*, 210.

30. "Lips" provide a rich metaphor for Irigaray in discussing both touch and reciprocity in her essays "This Sex Which Is Not One" and "When Our Lips Speak Together," in *This Sex Which Is Not One*, 23–33, 205–17; and "The Limits of Transference," in *To Speak Is Never Neutral*, trans. Gail Schwab (London: Routledge, 2002; orig. French pub. 1977), 237–46. See also Diana Tietjens Meyers, *Subjection and Subjectivity: Psychoanalytic Feminism and Moral Philosophy* (New York: Routledge, 1994), 96–91.

31. Irigaray, "The Limits of Transference."

32. Irigaray, "Così fan Tutte," in *This Sex Which Is Not One*, 90.

33. Deleuze, *The Fold*.

34. Cooper-White, *Many Voices*, 56–60, 73–74, 81.

35. Cooper-White, "Higher Powers."

36. Deleuze and Felix Guattari, *A Thousand Plateaus: Capitalism and Schizophrenia*, trans. Brian Massumi (Minneapolis: University of Minnesota Press, 1987/1980), 313. Also discussed in Catherine Keller, *Face of the Deep: A Theology of Becoming* (London: Routledge, 2003), 167–70.

37. Deleuze, *The Fold*, 137; see also 24.

38. Keller, *Face of the Deep*, 232–32 (italics original).

39. Elizabeth Johnson, *She Who Is: The Mystery of God in Feminist Theological Discourse* (New York: Crossroad, 1992), 143, cited in Keller, 232.

40. Gen Doy, *Drapery: Classicism and Barbarism in Visual Culture* (London: I. B. Tauris, 2002), 150.

41. Jane Flax, "Multiples: On the Contemporary Politics of Subjectivity," also quoting Luce Irigaray, in *Disputed Subjects: Essays on Psychoanalysis, Politics and Philosophy* (New York: Routledge, 1993), 93; also cited in Cooper-White, *Shared Wisdom*, 53; see also idem, *Many Voices*, 61–62.

42. Michel Foucault, *The History of Sexuality: An Introduction*, trans. Robert Hurley (London: Penguin, 1978; orig. French pub. 1976), 100; also cited in Jantzen, *Becoming Divine*, 57.

43. Homi Bhabha, *The Location of Culture* (New York: Routledge, 1994), 114. See also Bhabha, "The Third Space" (interview by Jonathan Rutherford), in Rutherford, ed., *Identity: Community, Culture, Difference* (London: Lawrence and Wishart, 1990), 207–21. For a summary of how Bhabha's formulation of hybridity differs from a romanticized ideal of "diversity" free of conflict, see Cooper-White, *Many Voices*, 45.

44. Gayatri Chakravorty Spivak, "Can the Subaltern Speak? Speculations on Widow Sacrifice," *Wedge* 7, no. 8 (1985): 120–30; see also idem, *A Critique of Postcolonial Reason: Toward a History of the Vanishing Present* (Cambridge: Harvard University Press, 1999); and idem, *The Spivak Reader: Selected Works of Gayatri Chakravorty Spivak*, ed. Donna Landry and Gerald MacLean (New York: Routledge, 1996).

45. Luis N. Rivera-Pagán, "Doing Pastoral Theology in a Post-Colonial Context: Some Observations from the Caribbean," *Journal of Pastoral Theology* 17, no. 2 (2007): 1–27; presented to the 2007 Annual Study Conference, Society for Pastoral Theology, San Juan, Puerto Rico, June 2007.

46. E.g., Irigaray, "The Sex Which Is Not One," 28.

47. For further discussion of this theme, see Elaine Graham, *Making the Difference: Towards a Theology of Gender* (New York: Continuum, 1995), 221.

48. Ibid., 223; see also Judith Butler, *Gender Trouble: Feminism and the Subversion of Identity* (London: Routledge, 1990); and idem, *Bodies that Matter: On the Discursive Limits of Sex* (London: Routledge, 1993); Flax, e.g., "The Play of Justice," in *Disputed Subjects*, 111–28; Jantzen, *Becoming Divine*, 57.

49. Irigaray, "Mechanics of Fluids," 99.

50. Butler, *Gender Trouble*, 32; also cited in Keller, 179.

51. Irigaray, *Speculum of the Other Woman*, trans. Gillian Gill (Ithaca, N.Y.: Cornell University Press, 1985; orig. French pub. 1974); see also Julia Kristeva, *Revolution in Poetic Language*, trans. Margaret Waller (New York: Columbia University Press, 1984; orig. French pub. 1974). For further references to the use of this term see http://science.jrank.org/pages/9861/Jouissance-Feminist-Political-Applications-Jouissance.html, accessed March 12, 2009.

52. Term from Jacques Derrida, *Of Grammatology*, trans. Gayatri Chakravorty Spivak (Baltimore: Johns Hopkins University Press, 1976; orig. French pub. 1967).

53. Jacques Derrida, *Writing and Difference*, trans. Alan Bass (Chicago: University of Chicago Press, 1978).

54. Graham, *Making the Difference*, 227; also citing Seyla Benhabib, *Situating the Self* (Cambridge: Polity, 1992); and Don Browning, *A Fundamental Practical Theology: Descriptive and Strategic Proposals* (Minneapolis: Fortress Press, 1991), 2–10. For a further elaboration of Graham's "theology of practice," see Graham, *Transforming Practice: Pastoral Theology in an Age of Uncertainty* (London: Mowbray, 1996; reprinted Eugene, Ore.: Wipf and Stock, 2002).

55. Deleuze, *The Fold*, 3.

56. Bromberg, "'Speak! That I May See You'."

57. Cooper-White, *Many Voices*.

58. In *Many Voices*, I have elaborated a theology of multiplicity, including a new formulation of pastoral trinitarian language: "God as Creative Profusion, God as Incarnational Desire, and God as Living Inspiration," in chap. 3, "A Relational Understanding of God," 67–94. Other constructive theological approaches to multiplicity of the divine include Keller, *Face of the Deep*; Jantzen, *Becoming Divine*; and most recently, Laurel C. Schneider, *Beyond Monotheism: A Theology of Multiplicity* (New York: Routledge, 2008). All of these approaches take seriously the postmodern feminist critique of oneness and propose alternative visions that move beyond Enlightenment categories of universality, truth, and singular rationality.

59. Irigaray, "The Limits of Transference," 238.

Chapter 2: Just Care

1. I am making implicit references to the work of some of the practical theologians who have helped me understand the importance of methodology to authentic pastoral theology and praxis. They are as follows: Don Browning's *A Fundamental Practical Theology: Descriptive and Strategic Proposals* (Minneapolis: Fortress Press, 1991); John Patton's *From Ministry to Theology: Pastoral Action and Reflection* (Nashville: Abingdon, 1990); and the scholarship of feminist and womanist theologians as collected in Bonnie J. Miller-McLemore and Brita L. Gill-Austern, eds., *Feminist and Womanist Pastoral Theology* (Nashville: Abingdon, 1999).

2. Journalist Pat McBroom reports on a research project conducted by six sociologists at the University of California at Berkeley. According to their findings, over the past twenty years the United States has "dismantled" many of its historic structures for spreading wealth out among the people. This explains the growing gap between rich Americans and everyone else in the country. "The current level of inequality is neither inevitable nor tied to talent; it is a matter of choice," the sociologists seem to conclude after a year of combining their expertise to expose the root causes of inequality. Their analysis traces the outlines of far-reaching changes in the balance of power between workers, corporations, and communities that once allowed most Americans to share in expanding affluence. It also provides a new perspective on why working people have lost so much

ground since the 1970s, even while productivity has continued to rise, and it offers some solutions. Two of the structures that have been dismantled, according to these sociologists, are strong unions and the rootedness of corporations in given communities. Neither has been lost because of so-called natural forces in the economy, but because of political decisions, the authors say. They argue that the resulting imbalance has led to an increasing concentration of wealth at the top. "The United States is now more unequal than at any point in the last 75 years," the sociologists write. "We are choosing our level of inequality by the rules we make, including how we regulate corporations and unions, how we distribute the tax burden and how we set wages." News Release, 4/2/96 (Public Information Office: The University of California, 1996).

3.　For a current overview on the relationships between health issues and socioeconomic inequalities, see Vincente Navarro, ed., *The Political Economy of Social Inequalities: Consequences for Health and Quality of Life* (Amityville, N.Y.: Baywood, 2002). The link between mistreatment at work and at home and the development of poor self-esteem, especially for women, is skillfully articulated by Barbara Ehrenreich in *Nickel and Dimed: On (Not) Getting By in America* (New York: Metropolitan Books, 2001), and by Solange De Santis, *Life on the Line: One Woman's Tale of Work, Sweat and Survival* (New York: Doubleday, 1999). For a sociological diagnosis of powerlessness, see Michael Lerner, *Surplus Powerlessness* (Oakland: The Institute for Labor & Mental Health, 1986).

4.　For current attempts at engaging the psychospiritual needs of the poor, see James Newton Poling, *Render unto God: Economic Vulnerability, Family Violence, and Pastoral Theology* (St. Louis: Chalice, 2002); Pamela D. Couture, *Blessed are the Poor? Women's Poverty, Family Policy, and Practical Theology* (Nashville: Abingdon, 1991); idem, *Seeing Children, Seeing God: A Practical Theology of Children and Poverty* (Nashville: Abingdon, 2000); the late Judith Orr's unpublished dissertation, "A dialectical understanding of the psychological and moral development of working-class women with implications for pastoral counseling" (Claremont School of Theology, 1991); and Orr's chapter contribution, "Socioeconomic Class and the Life Span Development of Women," in *In Her Own Time: Women and Developmental Issues in Pastoral Care*, ed. Jeanne Stevenson-Moessner (Minneapolis: Fortress Press, 2000), 45–63. Orr's work has greatly inspired my own research and pastoral work with women of the lower classes.

5.　One of the most popular biographies of Antonio Gramsci in the English language is by Giuseppe Fiori, *Antonio Gramsci: Life of a Revolutionary* (New York: Dutton, 1971). It is constructed with the help of live interviews and personal and formal correspondence with Gramsci's family and friends still living. For his theory of reeducation, see Teodros Kiros, *Toward the Construction of a Theory of Political Action* (Lanham, Md.: University Press of America, 1985).

6.　While it can be argued that men of particular ethnicities and races are just as vulnerable to socioeconomic injustice and disparity, the variable of gender unquestionably intensifies the predicament of women and children, hence the alarming phenomenon called the "feminization of poverty."

7.　On intersubjective theory, see the works of Robert D. Stolorow, Bernard Brandchaft, and George E. Atwood, *Psychoanalytic Treatment: An Intersubjective Approach* (Hillsdale, N.J.: Analytic Press, 1987); idem, *The Intersubjective Perspective* (Northvale, N.J.: Jason Aronson, 1994); and Storolow and Atwood, *Contexts of Being: The Intersubjective Foundations of Psychological Life* (Hillsdale, N.J.: Analytic Press, 1992).

8.　Daniel N. Stern, *The Interpersonal World of the Infant* (New York: Basic Books, 1985); also of practical relevance is his *Diary of a Baby: What Your Child Sees, Feels and Experiences* (New York: Basic Books, 1990).

9.　Mary E. Hunt, *Fierce Tenderness: A Feminist Theology of Friendship* (New York: Crossroad, 1991).

10.　Ibid., 100.

11.　Ibid., 101.

12.　Ibid., 102.

13.　Ibid., 105.

14.　This list is born from observation and reflection on my pastoral practice with women of the lower socioeconomic classes, but it finds ample confirmation in conservative and current statistics and research, which evidence the higher and wider phenomenon of victimization of women due specifically to their gender. For further information, see Jean Baker Miller, *Toward a New Psychology of Women* (Boston: Beacon, 1986).

15. The diagram is adapted from Norma Gluckstern's own diagram—which tries to capture the therapeutic process through the "Personal/Institutional change groups" for oppressed women. Her own work and analysis are presented by Judith Orr as a viable therapeutic option for working-class women. See Orr's dissertation, p. 368f.

Chapter 3: A Womanist Legacy of Trauma, Grief, and Loss

1. Paul C. Rosenblatt and Beverly R. Wallace, "Narratives of Grieving African Americans about Racism in the Lives of Deceased Family Members," *Death Studies* 29, no. 3 (2005): 217–35.

2. Michelle Wallace, *Black Macho and the Myth of the Superwoman* (New York: Dial, 1990).

3. Paul C. Rosenblatt and Beverly R. Wallace, *African American Grief* (New York: Brunner-Routledge, 2005).

4. Sharon H. Smith, "'Fret No More My Child . . . For I'm All Over Heaven All Day:' Religious Beliefs in the Bereavement of African American Middle-Aged Daughters Coping with the Death of an Elderly Mother," *Death Studies* 26 (2002): 309–23; idem, "'Now That Mom Is in the Lord's Arms, I Just Have to Live the Way She Taught Me:' Reflections on an Elderly, African American Mother's Death," *Journal of Gerontological Social Work* 32, no. 2 (1999): 41–51.

5. Margaret S. Stroebe and Henk Schut, "Models of Coping with Bereavement: A Review," in Margaret S. Stroebe, Robert Hanson, Wolfgang Stroebe, and Henk Schut, eds., *Handbook of Bereavement Research* (Washington, D.C.: American Psychological Association, 2001), 375–404.

6. Sidney Z. Moss and Robert Rubinstein, "Middle-Aged Son's Reaction to Father's Death," *Omega* 35 (1997): 43–65.

7. Regina E. Romero, "The Icon of the Strong Black Woman: The Paradox of Strength," in *Psychotherapy with African American Women*, eds. L. Jackson and B. Greene (New York: Guilford, 1996), 225–39.

8. R. Neimeyer, N. Keese, and B. Fortner, "Loss and Meaning Reconstruction: Propositions and Procedures," in *Traumatic and Non-Traumatic Bereavement*, ed. S. Rubin, R. Malkinson, and C. E. Wittum (Madison: International University Press, 1998), 5–40; Paul C. Rosenblatt, "A Social Constructionist Perspective on Cultural Differences in Grief," in Stroebe, et al., eds., *Handbook of Bereavement Research*, 285–300; Smith, "Now That Mom Is in the Lord's Arms," 41–51.

9. Neimeyer, et al., "Loss and Meaning Reconstruction," 5–40.

10. Stroebe and Schut, "Models of Coping with Bereavement," 375–404.

11. Moss and Rubinstein, "Middle-aged Son's Reaction to Father's Death," 43-65.

12. Romero, "The Icon of the Strong Black Woman," 226–27.

13. Interview with Sarah by the author on several different occasions in 2008.

14. Alice Walker, *In Search of Our Mother's Garden: Womanist Prose* (New York: Harcourt Brace Jovanovich, 1983), xi–xii.

15. Ibid.

16. Romero, "The Icon of the Strong Black Woman," 225–39.

17. Delores S. Williams, *Sisters in the Wilderness: The Challenge of Womanist God-Talk* (Maryknoll, N.Y.: Orbis, 1993).

18. Romero, "The Icon of the Strong Black Woman," 226–32.

19. Hamilton I. McCubbin, Marilyn A. McCubbin, Anne I. Thompson, Sae-Young Han, and Chad T. Allen, 1997 Commemorative Lecture, American Association of Family & Consumer Sciences, October 1, 1997, published in *Journal of Family and Consumer Sciences*, Fall 1997.

20. Jessica Henderson Daniel, "The Courage to Hear: African American Women's Memories of Racial Trauma," in *Psychotherapy with African American Women*, eds. L. C. Jackson and B. Greene (New York: Guilford, 1996), 126–44.

21. D. J. Gandy, *Sacred Pampering Principles: An African-American Women's Guide to Self-Care and Inner Renewal* (New York: Quill, 1997).

22. Romero, "The Icon of the Strong Black Woman," 229–32.

23. Ibid, 232.

24. D. C. Dance, *Honey, Hush! An Anthology of African American Women's Humor* (New York: Norton, 1998).

25. Romero, "The Icon of the Strong Black Woman," 227.

26. Ibid, 228.

27. Patricia H. Collins, *Black Feminist Thought: Knowledge, Consciousness, and the Politics of Empowerment* (London: HarperCollins Academic, 1990); bell hooks, *Sisters of the Yam: Black Women and Self-Recovery* (Boston: South End, 1993).

28. Jacqueline Grant, *White Women's Christ and Black Women's Jesus: Feminist Christology and Womanist Response* (Atlanta: Scholars Press, 1989).

29. Collins, *Black Feminist Thought*, 67–90.

30. Ibid, 7.

31. Ibid, 70–75.

32. Teresa E. Snorton, "The Legacy of the African-American Matriarch: New Perspectives for Pastoral Care," in *Through the Eyes of Women: Insights for Pastoral Care*, ed. Jeanne Stevenson-Moessner (Minneapolis: Fortress Press, 1996), 50–65.

33. Ibid., 62.

34. Ibid., 63.

35. E. J. Bell and S. M. Nkomo, "Armoring: Learning to Withstand Racial Oppression," *Journal of Comparative Family Studies*, 29, no. 2 (1998): 285–95.

36. Ibid.

37. Ibid.

38. Leslie C. Jackson, "The New Multiculturalism and Psychodynamic Theory: Psychodynamic Psychotherapy and African American Women," in Jackson and Greene, eds., *Psychotherapy with African American Women*, 1–14.

39. Beverly Greene, "Sturdy Bridges: The Role of African-American Mothers in the Socialization of African-American Children," *Women and Therapy* 10, nos. 1-2 (1994): 205–25; Kumera Shorter-Gooden and Leslie C. Jackson, "The Interweaving of Cultural and Intrapsychic Issues in the Therapeutic Relationship," in Jackson and Greene, eds., *Psychotherapy with African American Women*, 15–32; Romero, "The Icon of the Strong Black Woman," 237.

40. Bell and Nkomo, "Armoring," 285–95.

41. Rosenblatt and Wallace, *African American Grief*.

42. Dena Rosenbloom and Mary Beth Williams, *Life After Trauma: A Workbook for Healing* (New York: Guilford, 1999), 17.

43. Ibid, 21.

44. Paul L. Toth, Rex Stockton, and Fredrick Browne, "College Student Grief and Loss," in *Loss and Trauma: General and Close Relationship Perspectives*, ed. J. H. Harvey and E. D. Miller (Philadelphia: Brunner-Routledge, 2000), 237–48.

45. Rosenblatt and Wallace, *African American Grief*, 1.

46. Rosenblatt and Wallace, "Narratives of Grieving African Americans about Racism in the Lives of Deceased Family Members," in ibid., 217–35.

47. Smith, "Fret No More My Child," 309–23.

48. Martha B. Robbins, "Women and Motherloss," in Stevenson-Moessner, ed., *Through the Eyes of Women*, 167–78.

49. Ibid.

50. Bridgett M. Davis, "Speaking of Grief: Today I Feel Real Low, I Hope You Understand," in *The Black Women's Health Book: Speaking for Ourselves*, ed. E. C. White (Seattle: Seal Press, 1990), 219–25.

51. Smith, "Fret No More My Child," 309–23.

52. Ibid.

53. Rosenblatt and Wallace, "Narratives of Grieving African Americans," 217–35.

54. Stroebe and Schut, "Models of Coping with Bereavement," 375–404.

55. Snorton, "The Legacy of the African-American Matriarch," 50–65.

56. Rosenblatt and Wallace, *African American Grief*.

57. Tanya L. Sharpe, "Sources of Support for African-American Family Members of Homicide," in *The Journal of Ethnic and Cultural Diversity in Social Work* (2008): 1–28.

58. Romero, "The Icon of the Strong Black Woman," 237.

59. Audre Lorde, "Living with Cancer," in White, ed., *The Black Women's Health Book*, 27–37.

60. R. Davis, "Discovering 'Creative Essence' in African American Women: The Construction of Meaning Around Inner Resources," *Women's Studies International Forum* 21, no. 5 (1998): 493–504.

61. Julia A. Boyd, *In the Company of My Sisters: Black Women and Self-Esteem* (Boston: Dutton, 1993).

62. Snorton, "The Legacy of the African-American Matriarch," 50–65.

63. Stroebe and Schut, "Models of Coping with Bereavement," 375–404.

64. C. B. Williams, "African American Women: Afrocentrism and Feminism: Implications for Therapy," *Women & Therapy* 3, no. 4 (1999): 1–16.

65. R. D. Matthew, "Using Power from the Periphery: An Alternative Theological Model for Survival in Systems," in *A Troubling in My Soul: Womanist Perspectives on Evil and Suffering*, ed. Emilie M. Townes (Maryknoll, N.Y.: Orbis, 1993), 92–106.

Chapter 4: Pastoral Care of Korean American Women

1. I would like to express my deepest appreciation to my peer reviewer, Bonnie Miller-McLemore, for her generous, thoughtful, and insightful review of my manuscript and her pioneering work in the issues of mothering.

2. Heinz Kohut, *The Analysis of the Self* (New York: International Universities Press, 1971); *The Restoration of the Self* (New York: International Press, 1977); *The Search for the Self: Selected Writings of Heinz Kohut: 1950–1978*, ed. Paul H. Ornstein (New York: International Universities Press, 1978); *Self Psychology and the Humanities: Reflections on a New Psychoanalytic Approach*, ed. Charles B. Strozier (New York: Norton, 1984); and *How Does Analysis Cure?* ed. Arnold Goldberg (Chicago: University of Chicago Press, 1984).

3. J. Bowlby, *Attachment and Loss*, vol. 1: *Attachment* (New York: Basic Books, 1969); and vol. 2: *Separation: Anxiety and Anger* (New York: Basic Books, 1973).

4. Margaret S. Mahler, *On Human Symbiosis and the Vicissitudes of Individuation* (New York: International Universities Press, 1968).

5. D. W. Winnicott, *Playing and Reality* (London and New York: Routledge, 1971).

6. Erik Erikson, *Childhood and Society*, 2nd ed. (New York: Norton, 1963); *Identity: Youth and Crisis* (New York: Norton, 1968); and *The Life Cycle Completed* (New York: Norton, 1998).

7. Kohut, *The Restoration of the Self*, 171–91.

8. Jean Baker Miller points out three different dynamics that maintain the permanent inequality between the dominant and subordinate groups in the society. They are: (1) the dominant group defines the subordinate group to be innately defective and inferior; (2) the dominant group defines the psychological characteristics of the subordinate group for the benefit of the dominant group; and (3) the dominant group takes all measures to prevent the subordinate group from challenging the permanent inequality (*Toward a New Psychology of Women*, 2nd ed. [Boston: Beacon, 1986], 3–12).

9. John H. Berthrong and Evelyn N. Berthrong, *Confucianism: A Short Introduction* (Oxford: One Word, 2000), 169. For a detailed discussion of the influence of Confucianism on Korean American women, see my article "Confucianism and the Lack of the Development of the Self Among Korean American Women," in *Pastoral Psychology* 54, no. 4 (March 2006): 325–36. See also Li-Hsiang Lisa Rosenlee's *Confucianism and Women: A Philosophical Interpretation* (Albany: State University of New York Press, 2006) for a juxtaposition of Confucianism (Chinese) and feminism in rethinking Confucianism as a feminist ethical theory emphasizing both relational and substantial self, reciprocity and complementarity as the basic form of human relationships, and the virtue of *ren* as the ideal personhood.

10. Ibid., 9.

11. Yung-Chung Kim, ed. and trans., *Women of Korea: A History from Ancient Times to 1945* (Seoul: Ewha Womans University Press, 1982), 53.

12. Ibid., 89.

13. Xinzhong Yao, *An Introduction to Confucianism* (Cambridge, UK: Cambridge University Press, 2000), 183.

14. Charisse Jones and Kumea Shorter-Gooden, *Shifting: The Double Lives of Black Women in America* (New York: HarperCollins, 2003), 7; italics mine.

15. Sa-Soon Yun, "Confucian Thought and Korean Culture," in *Korean Cultural Heritage: Thought and Religion*, vol. 2, ed. Chu-Hwan Son (Seoul: The Korea Foundation, 1996), 113; as cited in Yao, *An Introduction to Confucianism*, 115.

16. A comparative study using samples from both Seoul, South Korea, and Detroit, Michigan, concludes that, in spite of the long length of their stay in the United States (average length of stay was sixteen years), Korean American samples living in Detroit exhibited a similar level of adherence to the traditional Confucian values as those in Seoul (Kyung Ja Hyun, "Sociocultural Change and Traditional Values: Confucian Values Among Koreans and Korean Americans," *International Journal of Intercultural Relations*, 25 [2001]: 203–29).

17. Frank A. John and Colleen L. Johnson, "Role Strain in High Commitment Career Women," *Journal of the American Academy of Psychoanalysis* 4, no. 1 (1976): 16.

18. Mirra Komzrovsky, *Women in College: Shaping New Feminine Identities* (New York: Basic Books, 1986), 253.

19. Ailee Moon, "Attitudes Toward Ethnic Identity, Marriage, and Familial Life among Women of Korean Descent in the United States, Japan, and Korea," in *Korean American Women: From Tradition to Modern Feminism*, ed. Yong I. Song and Ailee Moon (Westport, Conn: Praeger, 1998), 65–72; Pyong Gap Min, "The Korean American Family," in *Ethnic Families in America: Patterns and Variations*, 3rd ed., eds. Charles H. Mindel, Robert W. Habenstein, and Roosevelt Wright Jr. (New York: Elsevier Science, 1988).

A comparative study of mothering between the first and 1.5 generations of Korean Americans confirms this finding by its claim that, with both the first and 1.5 generations, the Korean American's gender-role division took precedence over the economic necessity in attributing mothering to primarily women (Sungsook Moon, "Immigration and Mothering: Case Studies from Two Generations of Korean Immigrant Women," *Gender and Society* 17, no. 6 [December 2003]: 840–60).

20. Moon, "Attitudes Toward Ethnic Identity"; Won Moo Hurh and Kwang Chung Kim, *Korean Immigrants in America* (London and Toronto: Associated University Presses, 1984); Kwang Chung Kim and Won Moo Hurh, "Employment of Korean Immigrant Wives and the Division of Household Tasks," in *Korean Women in Transition: At Home and Abroad*, ed. Eui-Young Yu and Earl H. Phillips (Los Angeles: California State University, 1987), 199–218; idem, "The Burden of Double Roles: Korean Immigrant Wives in the USA," *Ethnic and Racial Studies* 11 (1988): 151–67; Pyong Gap Min, "Korean Immigrant Wives' Overwork," *Korean Journal of Population and Development* 91 (1992): 557–92; idem, "The Burden of Labor on Korean American Wives in and Outside the Family," in *Korean American Women*, 89–101; and Eui-Young Yu, "Korean American Women: Demographic Profiles and Family Roles," in *Korean Women in Transition*, 183–97.

21. Eui-Young Yu, "Koreans in America: Social and Economic Adjustments," in *The Korean Immigrant in America*, eds. Byong-Suh Kim and Sang Hyun Lee (Montclair: The Association of Korean Christian Scholars in North America, 1980), 75–98; Pyong Gap Min and Young I. Song, "Demographic Characteristics and Trends of Post-1965 Korean Immigrant Women and Men," in *Korean American Women*, 45–63.

22. Min and Song, "Demographic Characteristics and Trends of Post-1965 Korean Immigrant Women and Men," 58. See also "Separation and Divorce among Korean Immigrant Families" (*Korean American Women*, 151–59) by Siyon Rhee, whose study concludes that domestic violence is the most prominent reason for divorce of Korean American women.

23. E. Chun, "The Korean Battered Spouse: Where to Go for Help," *Korean Journal* 1, no. 3 (1990): 22–23; as cited in Rhee, "Separation and Divorce," 157. For a more detailed discussion on the topic, see Yong I. Song and Ailee Moon, "The Domestic Violence against Women in Korean Immigrant Families: Cultural, Psychological, and Socioeconomic Perspectives" (*Korean American Women*, 161–73).

24. Andrew Sung Park, "The Formation of Multicultural Religious Identity Within Persons in Korean-American Experience," *Journal of Pastoral Theology* 13, no. 2 (Fall 2003): 36.

25. See Sung Sil Lee Sohng, "A Critical Feminist Inquiry in a Multicultural Context" (*Korean American Women*, 11–21), for a further discussion of how, in addition to sexism caused by traditional Confucian ideology, both societal injustice (racism) and cultural particularity should be a part of the interpretation of Korean American women's experiences.

26. Kelly Oliver, *The Colonization of Psychic Space: A Psychoanalytic Social Theory of Oppression* (Minneapolis: University of Minnesota Press, 2004), 3. A notable work on this topic by Frantz Fanon is *Black Skin, White Masks*, trans. Charles Lam Markmann (New York: Grove, 1967).

27. Oliver discusses Frantz Fanon's writings on the colonization of the psychic space of black men by their white counterparts and its harmful effect on the subjectivity of black men: "If European notions of alienation are inherent in the formation of subjectivity and agency, debilitating alienation undermines subjectivity and agency" (ibid., 26) and "prevents [a black man] from making himself a lack of being" (ibid., 4).

28. Kohut, *The Analysis of the Self*, 66.

29. Ibid., 65–66.

30. For a study on the influence of mother's embracement of the traditional supportive role and father's unfulfilled ambition on Korean American daughters, see Jenny Hyun Chung Pak, *Korean American Women: Stories of Acculturation and Changing Selves* (New York & London: Routledge, 2006).

31. Several studies have noted a higher rate of depressive state found in the Korean American samples as compared to the average rate found in other samples of studies on depression (Joseph D. Hovey, Sheena Kim, and Laura D. Seligman, "The Influences of Cultural Values, Ethnic Identity, and Language Use on the Mental Health of Korean American College Students," *The Journal of Psychology* 140, no. 5 (2006): 499–511; Yunjin Oh, Gary F. Koeske, and Esther Sales, "Acculturation, Stress, and Depressive Symptoms Among Korean Immigrants in the United States," *Journal of Social Psychology* 142 (2002): 511–26; and W. H. Kuo, "Prevalence of Depression Among Asian-Americans," *Journal of Nervous and Mental Disease* 172 (1984): 449–57.). The study by Hovey, Kim, and Seligman shows the highest ratio of two to one between the study of Korean American samples and that of others.

32. Herbert Anderson and Bonnie Miller-McLemore, *Faith's Wisdom for Daily Living*, (Minneapolis: Augsburg Fortress, 2008), 31–69.

33. Sang Hyun Lee, "Called to Be Pilgrims: Toward a Theology within the Korean Immigrant Context," in *The Korean Immigrant in America*, 38.

34. Woon Moo Hurh and Kwang Chung Kim, "Religious Participation of Korean Immigrants in the United States," *Journal for the Scientific Study of Religion* 29, no. 1 (1990): 28.

35. For instance, Brita L. Gill-Austern has noted the following comprehensive list of the negative impact of women's self-sacrifice and self-denial on women: (1) women whose loving has consistent patterns of self-sacrifice commonly lose touch with their own needs and desires; (2) women's self-sacrifice and self-denial leads to a loss of a sense of self and a loss of voice; (3) the fall-out from self-sacrifice is often a reservoir of resentment, bitterness, and anger as women come more and more to feel victimized; (4) love as self-sacrifice frequently leads to overfunctioning on behalf of others, underfunctioning on behalf of self, which contributes to a loss of sense of self-esteem and a sense of one's own direction; (5) self-sacrificing love can undermine the capacity for genuine mutuality and intimacy; (6) love as self-sacrifice and self-denial creates great stress and strain; (7) love understood as self-sacrifice can lead women to abdicate their public responsibility to use their God-given gifts on behalf of the greater community and for the common good; and (8) love understood as self-sacrifice and self-denial can unwittingly contribute to exploitation and domination of relationships by the more powerful party (Brita L. Gill-Austern, "Love Understood as Self-Sacrifice and Self-Denial: What Does It Do to Women?" in *Through the Eyes of Women: Insights for Pastoral Care*, ed. Jeanne Stevenson-Moessner [Minneapolis: Fortress Press, 1996], 310–15).

36. Barbara Hilkert Andolsen, "Agape in Feminist Ethics," *The Journal of Religious Ethics* 9, no. 1 (1981): 69–83. See also *Mutuality Matters: Family, Faith, and Just Love*, eds. Herbert Anderson, Edward Foley, Bonnie Miller-McLemore, and Robert Schreiter (Lanham, Md.: Rowman & Littlefield, 2004), for various discussions on the construction of the notion of mutuality from the perspective from love, marriage, family, and ministry.

37. Gill-Austern, "Love Understood as Self-Sacrifice and Self-Denial," 310–15.

38. Ibid., 90–93.

39. Bonnie J. Miller-McLemore, *Also a Mother: Work and Family as Theological Dilemma* (Nashville: Abingdon, 1994), 166.

40. Bonnie J. Miller-McLemore, *In the Midst of Chaos: Caring for Children as Spiritual Practice,* (San Francisco: John Wiley, 2007), 90.

41. Bonnie J. Miller-McLemore, "Two Views of Mothering: Birthing and Mothering as Powerful Rites of Passage," in *In Her Own Time: Women and Developmental Issues in Pastoral Care,* ed. Jeanne Stevenson-Moessner (Minneapolis: Fortress Press, 1989), 184. See also *In the Midst of Chaos,* 121–25.

42. Michael E. Kerr and Murray Bowen, *Family Evaluation: An Approach Based on Bowen Theory* (New York: Norton, 1988).

43. Jeanne Stevenson-Moessner, "From Samaritan to Samaritan: Journey Mercies," in *Through the Eyes of Women,* 322–33.

44. Jamie Lew, "Korean American High School Dropouts: A Case Study of Their Experiences and Negotiations of Schooling, Family, and Communities," in *Invisible Children in the Society and Its School,* 3rd ed., ed. Sue Books (Mahwah, N.J.: Lawrence Erlbaum Assoc., 2007), 103–16.

45. Miller-McLemore, *In the Midst of Chaos,* 21–37.

46. Cho's family and their church could have played an important role in intervention and healing of Cho's mental ailment and possibly prevented such atrocity if they were open to and informed about mental health issues.

47. Tong-He Koh, "Religion as a Variable in Mental Health: A Case for Korean Americans," in *Korean Americans and Their Religions: Pilgrims and Missionaries from a Different Shore,* ed. Ho-Youn Kwon, Kwang Chung Kim, and R. Stephen Warner (University Park: Pennsylvania State University Press, 2001), 102; *Diagnostic and Statistical Manual of Mental Disorders: DSM-IV-TR,* 4th ed. (Washington, DC: American Psychiatric Association, 2000), 356.

48. Koh, "Religion as a Variable in Mental Health," 102; Stanley Sue and James K. Morishima, *The Mental Health of Asian Americans* (San Francisco: Jossey-Bass, 1982), 55–56. See *Asian Americans and Christian Ministry,* ed. Inn Sook Lee and Timothy D. Son (Seoul, Korea: Voice, 1999), for discussions on theological, identity, pastoral care, and spiritual issues of Korean Americans and churches.

49. Mikyong Kim-Goh, "Korean Women's Hwa-Byung: Clinical Issues and Implications for Treatment," in *Korean American Women: From Tradition to Modern Feminism,* 225–33.

Chapter 5: Gyn|Ecology

1. Alice Lesch Kelly, "The Struggle to Move beyond 'Why Me?'" in *The New York Times,* Health, May 5, 2007, 1.

2. Barbara A Goff, Barbara J. Matthews, Eric H. Larson, C. Holly, A. Andrilla, Michelle Wynn, Denise M. Lishner, Laura-Mae Baldwin, "Predictors of Comprehensive Surgical Treatment in Patients With Ovarian Cancer," in *CANCER, Interdisciplinary International Journal of the American Cancer Society* 109, no. 10 (May 15, 2007): 2031.

3. Kathleen M. O'Connor, "Jeremiah," in *The Women's Bible Commentary,* ed. Carol A. Newsom and Sharon H. Ringe (Louisville: Westminster John Knox, 1992), 169–77.

4. Maxine Glaz, "A New Pastoral Understanding of Women," in *Women in Travail and Transition: A New Pastoral Care,* eds. Maxine Glaz and Jeanne Stevenson-Moessner (Minneapolis: Fortress Press, 1991), 15.

5. Mary James Dean and Mary Louise Cullen, "Woman's Body: Spiritual Needs and Theological Presence," in *Women in Travail and Transition,* eds. Glaz and Jeanne Stevenson-Moessner, 86.

6. Clinical Pastoral Education (CPE) is interfaith professional education for ministry. It brings theological students and ministers of all faiths (pastors, priests, rabbis, imams, and others) into supervised encounter with persons in crisis. Out of an intense involvement with persons in need, and the feedback from peers and teachers, students develop new awareness of themselves as persons and of the needs of those to whom they minister. From theological reflection on specific

human situations, they gain a new understanding of ministry. Within the interdisciplinary team process of helping persons, they develop skills in interpersonal and interprofessional relationships. See http://www.acpe.edu/faq.htm, accessed December 10, 2008.

7. O'Connor, "Jeremiah," 175.

8. Jack Tresidder, *Symbols* (San Francisco: Chronicle, 1998), 59.

9. "Gyn" is an abbreviation for gynecology, a branch of medicine that deals with women, their disease, hygiene, and medical care.

10. Hilda J. Brucker, "Breaking Through the Silence," *Points North* (September 2007): 124.

11. Yomi S. Wronge, "Disparity in Breast Cancer Testing: Blacks Less Likely to Have Mammograms," *The Record* (Bergen County, N.J.), April 22, 2006, A10.

12. Esther M. John, Alexander Miron, Gail Gong, Amanda I. Phipps, Anna Felberg, Frederick P. Li, Dee West, and Alice S. Whittemore, "Prevalence of Pathogenic BRCA1 Mutation Carriers in 5 US Racial/Ethnic Groups," *Journal of the American Medical Association* 298, no. 24 (December 26, 2007): 2869.

13. Jessica Queller, "Pretty Is What Changes: Impossible Choices, the Breast Cancer Gene, and How I Defied My Destiny," *The Turtle Creek News*, April 18, 2008, 17.

14. Frank N. Magill and Dayton Kohler, eds., *Masterpieces of World Literature* (New York: Harper & Brothers, 1949), 314.

15. Pearl S. Buck, *The Good Earth* (New York: Simon & Schuster, 1931), 182.

16. Norma Broude and Mary D. Garrard, eds., *Feminism and Art History: Questioning the Litany* (New York: Harper & Row, 1982), 270–76.

17. Gerda Lerner, *The Creation of Feminist Consciousness: From the Middle Ages to Eighty-seventy* (New York: Oxford University Press, 1993), 117.

18. Alice Walker, introduction to "The Welcome Table," in *Listening for God: Contemporary Literature and the Life of Faith*, ed. Paula J. Carlson and Peter S. Hawkins (Minneapolis: Augsburg Fortress, 1994), 107.

19. Joan Borysenko, *A Woman's Book of Life* (New York: Riverhead, 1996), 214.

20. Brucker, "Breaking Through the Silence," 125.

21. The Center for Social Innovation, Women's Healthy Environment Network (Toronto: WHEN, 2007), 2, http://www.womenshealthenvironments.ca/, accessed June 24, 2009.

22. J. A. Roberts, Douglas Brown, Thomas Elkins, and David Larson, "Factors influencing views of patients with gynecologic cancer about end of life decisions," *American Journal of Obstetrics and Gynecology* (September 9, 1996), 166.

23. Howard Thurman, *Deep Is the Hunger* (New York: Harper & Row, 1951), 24.

24. Michael Lerner, *Choices in Healing* (Cambridge: MIT Press, 1994).

25. John Patton, *From Ministry to Theology: Pastoral Action and Reflection* (Nashville: Abingdon, 1990), 110.

26. Jay M. Milstein, "Introducing Spirituality in Medical Care," *Journal of the American Medical Association* 299, no. 20 (May 28, 2008): 2440.

27. James D. Andrews, *Cultural, Ethnic, and Religious Manual* (Winston-Salem: Jamarda Resources, 1999), 63. Native Americans may avoid direct eye contact with nurses, physicians, and elders as a sign of respect. Direct eye contact and staring is sometimes considered impolite or aggressive. This is true for Southeast Asians, Chinese, and Koreans. Male figures are the spokesmen. For Asians, Indians, and Hindus the husband is the primary decision maker. A mother-in-law is also considered authoritarian.

28. "Full code" takes place when an all-out effort to resuscitate a patient is initiated. This may include a combination of stimulants to the veins, intravenous catheter into the neck, pumping of upper body, breathing mask and /or ventilator, tube into mouth and down windpipe, and electrical paddles placed on the chest.

29. Andrews, *Cultural, Ethnic, and Religious Manual*, 63.

30. Boston Women's Health Book Collective, *Our Bodies, Our Selves* (New York: Simon & Schuster, 1971), 618.

31. Dietrich Bonhoeffer, *Letters and Papers from Prison* (New York: Macmillian, 1971), 174.

32. Dietrich Bonhoeffer, *Spiritual Care* (Minneapolis: Fortress Press, 1985), 58-59.

33. O'Conner, "Jeremiah," 176–77.

34. Maxine Glaz, "A New Pastoral Understanding of Women," in Glaz and Stevenson-Moessner, eds., *Women in Travail and Transition*, 15.

35. Ann Belford Ulanov, *Spiritual Aspects of Clinical Work* (Einsiedeln: Daimon Verlag, 2004), 403.

36. Howard Clinebell, *Ecotherapy: Healing Ourselves, Healing the Earth* (Minneapolis: Fortress Press, 1996), 2-3, quoting Brian Swimme and Thomas Berry, *The Universe Story: From the Primordial Flaring Forth to the Ecozoic Era, a Celebration of the Unfolding Cosmos* (San Francisco: HarperSanFrancisco, 1992), 237.

37. Margaret Kornfeld, *Cultivating Wholeness* (New York: Continuum, 2002), 10.

38. Reuel Howe, *The Miracle of Dialogue* (New York: Seabury, 1963), 76.

Chapter 6: We Hold Our Stories in Blankets

1. Joy Harjo, "The Blanket Around Her" in Rayna Green, ed., *That's What She Said: Contemporary Poetry and Fiction by Native American Women* (Bloomington: Indiana University Press, 1984), p. 127.

2. Pendleton blankets are blankets that are made by Pendleton Woolen Mills in Pendleton, Oregon. The company was founded in 1896 to make trade blankets for the Native Americans. These blankets are used today by the Native American community as honor gifts for important occasions. Located online at http://www.collectorsguide.com/fa/fa026.shtml, accessed March 16, 2009.

3. Rebecca Kugel and Lucy Eldersveld Murphy, "Searching for Cornfields—and Sugar Groves," in *Native Women's History in Eastern North America before 1900: A Guide to Research and Writing*, ed. Rebecca Kugel and Lucy Eldersveld Murphy (Lincoln: University of Nebraska Press, 2007), xv.

4. Amnesty International, *Maze of Injustice: The Failure to Protect Indigenous Women from Sexual Violence in the USA* (New York: Amnesty International USA, 2006).

5. Stella U. Ogunwole, *We the People Report: American Indian and Alaska Natives in the United States Census 2000 Special Report*, Censr-28 (Washington, D.C., 2006), http://www.census.gov/prod/2006pubs/censr-28.pdf, accessed June 24, 2009.

6. Ibid., 1.

7. Michael Krauss, "Status of Native American Language Endangerment," in *Stabilizing Indigenous Languages*, ed. Gina Cantoni (Flagstaff: Northern Arizona University Center for Excellence in Education Monograph Series, Perspectives, 1996), 1, http://www.ncela.gwu.edu/pubs/stabilize/i-needs/status.htm, accessed March 16, 2009.

8. Jason McCarty and Jean Sinzdak, "Report Shows Status of Native Women Below the Economic, Political Average," National Council of American Indians press release, 1, http://www.iwpr.org/States2004/PDFs/Press_Release_12_6_04.pdf, accessed March 16, 2009.

9. Ibid.

10. Karina Walters, "From Dis-Placement to Dis-Ease: Embodiment and Expression of Historical Trauma Among Indigenous Women," unpublished lecture presented at the University of Washington, Seattle, Washington, April 26, 2007.

11. Irene Vernon, *Native Americans and HIV/AIDS*, ed. Dolores Subia BigFoot, under the grant number 97-V1-GX-0002 from the Office for Victims of Crime (OVC), U.S. Department of Justice (Oklahoma: University of Oklahoma Health Sciences Center, 2000), 3.

12. McCarty and Sinzdak, "Report Shows Status of Native Women Below the Economic, Political Average," 2.

13. Vernon, *Native Americans and HIV/AIDS*, 3.

14. Maya Dollarhide, "Fighting Domestic Violence and Restoring a Nation," *Voices Unabridged*, E-Magazine on Women and Human Rights Worldwide, April 18, 2007, 1, http://voices-unabridged.org/article.php?id_article=180&numero=12, accessed March 16, 2009.

15. Bonnie Duran, Margaret Sanders, Betty Skipper, Howard Waitzkin, Lorraine Malcoe, Susan Paine, and Joel Yager, "Prevalence and Correlates of Mental Disorders Among Native American Women in Primary Care," *American Journal of Public Health* 94, no. 1 (2004): 77.

16. Joseph Gone and Carmela Alcantara, "Identifying Effective Mental Health Interventions for American Indians and Alaska Natives: A Review of the Literature," *Cultural Diversity and Ethnic Minority Psychology* 13, no. 4 (2007): 358.

17. "Indian Health Fact Sheet," United States Department of Health & Human Services: Indian Health Service (January 2007), 1.

18. The Western Shoshone are located in Idaho, Nevada, Utah, Death Valley, and Panamint Valley, California. For further information see http://www.temoaktribe.com/history.shtml.

19. Walters, "From Dis-Placement to Dis-Ease," 14.

20. The role of a woman may be defined by her female life-cycle, such as age and motherhood, status in the tribe, or her responsibilities and authority. Kugel and Lucy Murphy, eds., *Native Women's History in Eastern North America before 1900*, xviii.

21. Suanne Ware-Diaz agreed to be interviewed by the authors for this article.

22. Mary's name has been changed to protect her confidentiality and location.

23. Judith Nies, *Native American History* (New York: Ballantine, 1996), 50.

24. Genograms are constructed by mapping the relationships within a person's family system, usually three generations, which helps both the student and the supervisor to understand the "larger picture" of the family system's current and historical problems. Monica McGoldrick, *Genograms: Assessment and Intervention*, 2nd ed. (New York: Norton, 1999), 2.

25. Ibid.

26. James Wilson, *The Earth Shall Weep: A History of Native America* (New York: Grove, 1998), 21.

27. Ibid., 22.

28. Ibid., 23.

29. Jack Weatherford, *Indian Givers: How the Indians of the Americas Transformed the World* (New York: Fawcett Columbine, 1988), 70.

30. Ibid., 115.

31. Vernon, *Native Americans and HIV/AIDS*, 1.

32. The Cherokee were forcibly removed from their land in the Carolinas in 1838 and were made to walk to Oklahoma during the cold winter months. Men, women, and children, old and young, walked many months often without the proper clothing for the winter. Many died on the long walk. John Ehle, *Trail of Tears: The Rise and Fall of the Cherokee Nation* (New York: Anchor, 1988).

33. Ibid.

34. For further reading on the destruction, please read David Stannard, *American Holocaust: The Conquest of the New World* (New York: Oxford University Press, 1992).

35. Lewis Meriam, *The Problem of Indian Administration, or The Meriam Report of 1928* (Baltimore: Johns Hopkins University Press and The Institute for Government Research Studies in Administration, 1928).

36. Ibid.

37. For more information, Stephen L. Pevar, *The Rights of Indians and Tribes: The Authoritative ACLU to Indian and Tribal Rights*, 3rd ed. (New York: New York University Press, 2004).

38. Eleanor Burke Leacock, "Women's Status in Egalitarian Society," in Kugel and Murphy, eds., *Native Women's History in Eastern North America before 1900*, 93.

39. Judith Nies, *Native American History*, 78.

40. Ibid.

41. Ibid, 278.

42. Rebecca Lyons stated, "Nothing is as personal as the clothes we wear. Clothing can be seen as a vessel that holds the human spirit." See Emil Her Many Horses, ed., *Identity by Design: Tradition, Change, and Celebration in Native Women's Dresses*, National Museum of the American Indian, Smithsonian Institution (New York: HarperCollins, 2007), 11.

43. Ibid., 336.

44. Kugel and Murphy, eds., *Native Women's History in Eastern North America before 1900*, xvii.

45. Ibid., xxi.

46. Nies, *Native American History*, 311.

47. Ibid., 380.

48. Ibid., 396.

49. Kugel and Murphy, eds., *Native Women's History in Eastern North America before 1900*, xxi.

50. Tweedy Sombaro, Dine', is an ordained elder in the United Methodist Church and agreed to be interviewed by the authors for this chapter.

51. Name omitted for confidentiality.

52. Ibid.

53. Susan Hazen-Hammond, *Spider Woman's Web: Traditional Native American Tales About Women's Power* (New York: Perigee, 1999).

54. The Chicago American Indian Center is the oldest American Indian Center in the United States; the center provides many opportunities for women to find support services and cultural educational events. Online at http://www.aic-chicago.org, accessed March 16, 2009.

55. Lewis Mehl-Madrona, *Narrative Medicine: The Use of History and Story in the Healing Process* (Rochester, Vt.: Bear, 2007), 123.

56. Bonnie Duran, et al., Prevalence and Correlates of Mental Disorders Among Native American Women in Primary Care," 74.

57. Thomas King, *The Truth about Stories* (Minneapolis: University of Minnesota Press, 2003), 10.

58. "Embedded theologies are often put into words when visitors offer comfort to the bereaved. 'She's in heaven with God's angels,' someone might say, standing before the casket. In contrast deliberative theologies are deliberately thought out; the 'host associated elements' are sorted out—the memories unpacked, the beliefs appraised, the feelings, values, and hopes identified and evaluated." Carol Doehring, *The Practice of Pastoral Care* (Louisville: Westminster John Knox, 2006), 112.

59. Ibid., 97.

60. Christie Cozad Neuger, *Counseling Women: A Narrative, Pastoral Approach* (Minneapolis: Fortress Press, 2001), 86–92.

61. Sally's name changed due to confidentiality.

62. Ben Okri, *A Way of Being Free* (London: Phoenix House), 46.

63. We have found Carrie Doehring's seven moments on how pastoral caregivers can offer care to be beneficial in the care of Native American women. The seven moments are listed on p. 10 in her book *The Practice of Pastoral Care* and then developed in the ensuing chapters.

64. Seven Circles Heritage Center, 8817 W. Southport Rd., Edwards, Ill. 61528, is a multicultural, interfaith center originally formed by Native Americans. Online at http://www.7circlesheritage.org, accessed

65. Huston Smith, *A Seat at the Table*, ed. Phil Cousineau (Berkeley: University of California Press, 2006), xviii.

66. Maria Napoli, *Holistic Health Care for Native Women: An Integrated Model* (Tempe: Arizona State University, School of Social Work, 2002), 4. Online at http://www.pubmedcentral.nih.gov/articlerender.fcgi?artid=1447281, accessed

67. Gina Jones, Maryellen Baker, and Mildred "Tinker" Schuman. *The Healing Blanket: Stories, Values, and Poetry from Ojibwe Elders and Teachers* (Center City, Minn.: Hazelden, 1998), 134.

68. Rose's name has been changed for confidentiality.

69. Christa Wells, "Held," sung by Natalie Grant on the album *Awaken*, Curb Records, 2008, ASIN B0011W24A0.

70. Carol and Bill's son, John, died at the age of seventeen from a rare form of liver cancer in 1998.

71. Seven Circles Heritage Center, Edwards Ill., see n. 66, above.

72. Ragatha Calentine is on the curriculum design team and faculty of Flying with Eagles, a Native American Youth Leadership Training Program of the North East Region Native American International Caucus, United Methodist Church. She is a youth worker and accomplished storyteller.

73. Lakota Project is a grassroots urban outreach program based in Rapid City, South Dakota. Its mission is to teach Lakota language and values and to strengthen the Lakota family. Online at http://www.lakotaproject.org, accessed March 16, 2009, accessed

74. Native American UMC Dayspring Church was chartered in 2005 in the Illinois Great Rivers Conference, United Methodist Church. It is the first church of its kind in Illinois. Online at http://www.nafdayspring.com, accessed

75. From the coming-of-age ceremony held for young girls in the Seven Circles community.

76. For many years Ho Chunk elder Casper Mallory was, before his death, the spiritual elder for the Return to Pimiteoui Pow Wow, Peoria, Ill. He was the uncle of Hayna Sine, the emcee of the powwow, and sister of Ruth Sine, our teacher and beloved elder. Casper's spirit is with us always in the Circle.

77. Gina Jones, "Let the Blanket Remind You," in Jones, et al., *The Healing Blanket*, 138.

Chapter 7: When Race, Gender, and Orientation Meet

1. We will not, in this chapter, argue about whether homosexuality is a sin. The authors agree that it is not. Lesbians, gay men, bisexuals, and transgendered people are God's children who are fully created in the image of God. There is nothing lacking in their personhood nor is there a disease or defect they must overcome in order to be whole. There are many resources that examine the biblical and theological merits of our perspective. See, for example, Karen Oliveto, Kelly Turney, and Traci West, *Talking about Homosexuality: A Congregational Resource* (Cleveland: Pilgrim, 2005); Jack Rogers, *Jesus, the Bible, and Homosexuality: Explode the Myths, Heal the Church* (Louisville: Westminster John Knox, 2006).

2. For insights into the construction of gender, sexual orientation, and race/ethnicity see: Judith Butler, *Gender Trouble: Feminism and the Subversion of Identity* (New York: Routledge, 1999); Lee Butler, *Liberating our Dignity, Saving our Souls* (St. Louis: Chalice, 2006); Horace Griffin, *Their Own Receive Them Not: African American Lesbians and Gays in Black Churches* (Cleveland: Pilgrim, 2006); Riki Wilchins, *Queer Theory, Gender Theory: An Instant Primer* (Los Angeles: Alyson, 2004).

3. Gary David Comstock, *A Whosoever Church: Welcoming Lesbians and Gay Men into African-American Congregations* (Louisville: Westminster John Knox, 2001); Yvette Flunder, *Where the Edge Gathers: Building a Community of Radical Inclusion* (Cleveland: Pilgrim, 2005).

4. Beverly Greene, "Lesbian Women of Color: Triple Jeopardy," in *Women of Color: Integrating Ethnic and Gender Identities in Psychotherapy*, eds. Lillian Comas-Diaz and Beverly Greene (New York: Guilford, 1994), 389–427.

5. For understandings of the importance of agency, see Katie Cannon, *Black Feminist Ethics* (Atlanta: Scholars, 1988); and Christie C. Neuger, *Counseling Women: A Narrative, Pastoral Approach* (Minneapolis: Fortress Press, 2001). In a similar fashion, Griffin addresses the question of natural law and choice in arguments about homosexuality in *Their Own Receive Them Not*, 76–107.

6. Patricia Hill Collins, *Black Feminist Thought: Knowledge, Consciousness, and the Politics of Empowerment* (Boston: Unwin Hyman, 1990).

7. See the work of Gershen Kaufman and Lev Raphael, *Coming Out of Shame: Transforming Gay and Lesbian Lives* (New York: Broadway, 1966).

8. Griffin, *Their Own Receive Them Not*, 212 ff.

9. For a powerful exploration of the dynamics in building collegial relationships, see Marsha Foster Boyd and Carolyn Stahl Bohler, "Womanist-Feminist Alliances: Meeting on the Bridge," in *Feminist and Womanist Pastoral Theology*, eds. Bonnie J. Miller-McLemore and Brita L. Gill-Austern (Nashville: Abingdon, 1999), 189–210.

10. See the work by Connie Roop and Peter Roop, *In Their Own Words: Sojourner Truth* (New York: Scholastic, 2003).

11. See, for example, the early work of Oliver Cox, *Caste, Class and Race: A Study in Social Dynamics* (New York: Doubleday, 1948), and the more recent work of bell hooks, *Where We Stand: Class Matters* (New York: Routledge, 2000), and Michael Omi and Howard Winant, *Racial Formation in the United States: From the 1960s to the 1990s*, 2nd ed. (New York: Routledge, 1994).

12. See Michel Foucault, *The History of Sexuality*, trans. Robert Hurley (New York: Pantheon, 1978).

13. Griffin, *Their Own Receive Them Not*, x.

14. See E. Patrick Johnson and Mae G. Henderson, "Introduction: Queering Black Studies, 'Quaring' Black Studies," in *Black Queer Studies*, eds. E. Patrick Johnson and Mae G. Henderson (Durham: Duke University Press, 2006), 1–20.

15 Boyd and Bohler, "Womanist-Feminist Alliances," 189–210.

16. "The Combahee River Collective Statement," in *Home Girls: A Black Feminist Anthology*, ed. Barbara Smith (New York: Kitchen Table, 1983), 272.

Chapter 8: Womanist Pastoral Care Using Narrative Therapy in Addressing Multicultural Issues

1. Jacques Audinet, "Diversity, Geography, Cultures," in *The Human Face of Globalization: From Multicultural to Mestizaje*, trans. Frances Dal Chele (Lanham, Md.: Rowman & Littlefield, 1999), 7–20.

2. Ibid.,12.

3. Ibid.,13.

4. Monica McGoldrich, Joe Giordano, Nydia Garcia-Preto, eds., *Ethnicity and Family Therapy* (New York: Guilford, 2005), 1.

5. Ibid., 20.

6. Ibid.,13.

7. K. Samuel Lee, "Becoming Multicultural Dancers: The Pastoral Practitioner in a Multicultural Society," *Journal of Pastoral Care* 5, no. 44 (2001): 392–93.

8. Ibid.

9. Derald Wing Sue, Rosie P. Bingham, Lisa Porche-Burke, and Melba Vasquez, "The Diversification of Psychology: A Multicultural Revolution," *American Psychologist* 54, no. 12 (1999): 1061–69.

10. Online at http://www.census.gov, accessed June 24, 2009.

11. Sue, et al., "The Diversification of Psychology," 1063.

12. Online at http://www.census.gov, accessed June 24, 2009.

13. Letty M. Russell, "From Garden to Table," in Letty M. Russell, Kwok Pui-lan, Ada María Isasi-Díaz, and Katie Geneva Cannon, eds., *Inheriting Our Mother's Gardens: Feminist Theology in Third World Perspective* (Louisville: Westminster, 1988), 155.

14. McGoldrich et al., eds., *Ethnicity & Family Therapy*, 2.

15. Ibid.

16. Derald Wing Sue, *Counseling the Culturally Diverse: Theory and Practice* (Hoboken, N.J.: Wiley, 2008), 177.

17. Ibid.

18. Emmanuel Lartey, *In Living Color: An Intercultural Approach to Pastoral Care and Counseling* (London: Jessica Kingsley, 2003), 69.

19. Sue, *Counseling the Culturally Diverse*, 179.

20. Lartey, *In Living Color*, 91.

21. Russell, "From Garden to Table," 143–44.

22. Ada Mari a Isasi-Díaz, "A Hispanic Garden in a Foreign Land," in Russell, et al., eds., *Inheriting Our Mother's Gardens*, 93.

23. Mitsuye Yamada, "Invisibility is an Unnatural Disaster: Reflections of an Asian American Woman," in Cherrie Moraga and Gloria Anzaldua, eds., *The Bridge Called My Back: Writings by Radical Women of Color* (New York: Kitchen Table, Women of Color Press, 1983), 36–40.

24. Judit Moschkovich, "But I Know You American Woman," in Moraga and Anzaldua, eds., *The Bridge Called My Back*, 79, 80.

25. Barbara Cameron, "Gee, You Don't Seem Like An Indian from the Reservation," in Moraga and Anzaldua, eds., *The Bridge Called My Back*, 47–49.

26. Atoosa Nowrouzi, Clinical Pastoral Education first-year resident, Princeton Baptist Health System, Birmingham, Alabama. Unpublished paper, 2008.

27. Williadean Crear, written May 3, 2007, Clinical Pastoral Education first-year resident, Princeton Baptist Health System, Birmingham, Alabama. Original unpublished poem. Part of

my CPE curriculum is the integration of womanist theology, narrative therapy, and family systems theory into a social-concern didactic. As an opportunity to help my students grow, I encouraged them to participate in the development of this paper by submitting their expression of their experience as a woman in a multicultural society. Atoosa and Williadean submitted original works.

28. Lartey, *In Living Color*, 30–31.

29. Linda H. Hollies, ed., *Womanist Care: How to Tend to the Souls of Women*, vol. 1 (Joliet, Ill.: WTWMI Publications, 1991), xiii.

30. Emile M. Townes, *A Troubling in My Soul: A Womanist Perspective on Evil and Suffering* (New York: Orbis, 1993), 130.

31. Jacqueline Grant, *White Women's Christ and Black Women's Jesus* (Atlanta: Scholars Press, 1989), 205.

32. Townes, *A Troubling in My Soul*, 164.

33. Fred L. Hord and Jonathan S. Lee, *I Am Because We Are: Reading in Black Philosophy* (Amherst: University of Massachusetts Press, 1995), 7–8.

34. Ibid., 11.

35 J. Laird, "Theorizing Culture: Narrative Ideas and Practice Principles," in Monica McGoldrick, ed., *Re-visioning Family Therapy: Race, Culture, and Gender* (New York: Guilford, 1998), 33.

36. Ibid., 31.

37. Jill Freedman and Gene Combs, *Narrative Therapy: The Social Construction of Preferred Realities* (New York: Norton, 1996), 47, 1.

38. Russell, "From Garden to Table," 151–52.

39. Don C. Locke, *Increasing Multicultural Understanding* (Thousand Oaks, Calif.: SAGE, 1998), 18.

40. Homer Jernigan, Ph.D., "Clinical Pastoral Education with Students from Other Cultures: The Role of the Supervisor," *Journal of Pastoral Care* 54, no.2 (Summer 2000), 140.

41. Freedman and Combs, *Narrative Therapy*, 136.

42. Walter Brueggemann, *Power, Providence and Personality: Biblical Insights Into Life and Ministry* (Louisville: Westminster John Knox, 1990), 41.

43. Edward P. Wimberly, *African American Pastoral Care* (Nashville: Abingdon, 1991), 12.

Chapter 9: *La Veglia*—Keeping Vigil

1. *La veglia* is an Italian expression meaning "keeping vigil." It denotes an old Italian folk custom to gather outside each house door in the summer evenings. It provided a time and a place to strengthen friendships, build community, and share personal vicissitudes and comment on political events. The custom has now disappeared from the village life. As it was practiced in country villages, mostly men and women would sit in separate circles, chatting along through the evening hours and discussing topics of separate interest.

2. Romance languages, such as French, Spanish, and Italian, have two "grammatical genders," male and female. Since grammar requires the whole sentence to agree with the subject, a male noun will have a sentence agreed in the male gender and a female noun in the female gender. In contrast, Anglo-Saxon languages have three "grammatical genders," male, female, and neuter, such as German with *der, die, das* and English with *he, she, it*. These languages seldom require grammatical gender agreement in the sentence.

3. In Italian a simple sentence such as "I came home tired last night" will sound *sono tornato stanco ieri sera* if the speaker is male, and *sono tornata stanca ieri sera* if the speaker is female.

4. See Luce Irigaray, *An Ethics of Sexual Difference*, trans. Carolyn Burke and Gillian C. Gill (Ithaca, New York: Cornell University Press, 1993); idem, *Key Writings* (New York: Continuum, 2004); Margaret Whitford, ed., *The Irigaray Reader* (Oxford: Blackwell, 1991).

5. Luce Irigaray, *Je, Tu, Nous: Toward a Culture of Difference*, trans. Allison Martin (New York: Routledge, 1993), 32.

6. Luce Irigaray, *Oltre I Propri Confini*, (Milano: Baldini Castoldi, 2007), 29, 32; trans. mine.

7. See Diotima, *Il Pensiero della Differenza Sessuale* (Milano: La Tartaruga, 1987); Luisa Muraro, *L'Ordine Simbolico della Madre* (Milano: Editori Riuniti, 1991); idem, *Lingua Materna, Scienza Divina* (Napoli: D'Auria, 1995); idem, *Il Dio delle Donne* (Milano: Mondadori, 2003).

8. See Elena Gianini Belotti, *Dalla Parte delle Bambine* (Milano: Feltrinelli, 1973); Diotima, *Mettere al Mondo il Mondo* (Milano: La Tartaruga, 1990).

9. Adriana Cavarero, "Per Una Teoria della Differenza Sessuale," in Diotima, *Il Pensiero della Differenza Sessuale*, 45; trans. mine.

10. Ibid., 46.

11. Ibid., 48.

12. Ibid., 52, 53.

13. At the same time, and in the wake of the political actions of the feminist movement in Italy, the Italian government appointed a Commission for Equal Opportunities that had the task, among others, of addressing the problem of the language. So, in due time, new words were coined to describe women in professional roles until then occupied by men and expressed through masculine nouns. Beside *direttore* ("director"), we now have *direttora;* beside *ricercatore* ("researcher"), we now have *ricercatora;* beside *scrittore* ("writer"), we now have *scrittora;* and so on. It is interesting to note that roles traditionally occupied by women already had a feminine noun to describe them, such as *professoressa* ("teacher"), *sarta* ("dressmaker"), *parrucchiera* ("hairdresser"), beside the masculine counterparts *professore, sarto, parrucchiere.*

14. Carol Gilligan, *In a Different Voice: Psychological Theory and Women's Development* (Cambridge: Harvard University Press, 1993).

15. Luce Irigaray, *Essere Due* (Torino: Bollati Boringhieri, 1994), 68; trans. mine.

16. Twenty years after the work of *Diotima* and *Sophia*, some of the linguistic changes brought about by them have become integral part of the Italian language. Nobody ever hesitates to name a woman a *pastora*. The impact of the cultural transformation of the role of women has taken instead a road characterized by many twists and turns. The intellectual spark has been subdued. A new generation of women has taken full advantage of the space offered to them in the workforce by changed gender-role expectations, but full equality is still an ongoing political issue and a debated cultural process.

Chapter 10: Aggression in Korean American Women

1. Philip Rieff, *The Triumph of the Therapeutic: Uses of Faith After Freud* (New York: Harper & Row, 1966), 2.

2. David Switzer describes a crisis theory in his book *The Minister as Crisis Counselor* (Nashville: Abingdon, 1986). According to his theory, in a crisis old and inadequate methods of coping are challenged. Because of the novelty of the situation, there is a lack of success with the usual coping mechanisms. A feeling of helplessness and ineffectiveness results. Then the person goes deep into a reserve of strength and extends the range of behavior in attempting to maintain ego integrity. If successful, the methods of dealing effectively with a new and threatening situation have been learned and have been brought into the repertoire of response. The very nature of crisis is that it forces change and readjustment. A person learns new methods of coping that become part of increased adaptability, resiliency, and strength. This is the positive side of crisis. There is the potential for new insights; not only a solution of the problems but also a reorganization of personality around a new center and on a higher level (38).

3. I am using psychoanalytic theories of aggression because I believe that those psychoanalytic theories well describe human aggression in a form of innate, indestructible "energy" of being human, which any social system and institution cannot annihilate completely.

4. Rieff, *The Triumph of the Therapeutic*, 237.

5. Ibid.

6. Ibid., 46.

7. Ibid., 14.

8. Ibid., 11.

9. Don Browning, *Religious Thought and the Modern Psychologies: A Critical Conversation in the Theology of Culture* (Philadelphia: Fortress Press, 1987), 62.

10. Carl Rogers, *On Becoming a Person: A Therapist's View of Psychotherapy* (Boston: Houghton Mifflin, 1961), 189.

11. Self-actualization "refers to a drive or tendency evident within all organic and human life to grow, develop, mature, and thereby actualize or realize the potentialities of the organism and the self. Carl Rogers and Abraham Maslow developed the notion of self-actualization/self-realization in the 1960s, through their separate but similar growth-oriented personality theories. For Carl Rogers, a human relationship of complete acceptance and understanding—'unconditional positive regard'—is prerequisite to actualizing the self's inherent potentialities. If a person receives conditional regard—socially imposed 'conditions of worth'—then self-actualization is compromised." The quotation is from D. L. Silver, "Self-Actualization/Self-Realization," in Rodney Hunter, ed., *Dictionary of Pastoral Care and Counseling* (Nashville: Abingdon, 1990), 1126.

12. W. Slote and G. Devos, *Confucianism and the Family* (Albany: State University of New York Press, 1998), 75.

13. Ibid., 123.

14. Ibid., 133.

15. Ibid., 123.

16. Henry Parens, *The Development of Aggression in Early Childhood* (New Jersey: Jason Aronson, 1979).

17. Ibid., 25.

18. Ibid.

19. In the following discussion of historical understanding of human aggression, I mostly use Parens's discussion of this topic as written in *The Development of Aggression in Early Childhood*.

20. Ibid., 41.

21. Sigmund Freud, *Civilization and its Discontents*, ed. Ernest Jones, trans. Joan Riviere (London: Hogarth, 1951), 102.

22. Parens, *The Development of Aggression in Early Childhood*, 41.

23. Gertrude Blanck and Rubin Blanck, *Ego Psychology: Theory and Practice* (New York: Columbia University Press, 1994), 14.

24. Parens, *The Development of Aggression in Early Childhood*, 61.

25. Blanck and Blanck, *Ego Psychology*, 28.

26. Parens, *The Development of Aggression in Early Childhood*, 42.

27. Ibid., 83.

28. Ibid.

29. Ibid.

30. Ibid., 58.

31. Ibid., 164 (italics are mine).

32. Ibid., 69.

33. Ibid., 83.

34. Ibid., 17.

35. Ibid., 19.

36. Yeol Kyu Kim, *Anger of Koreans* (Seoul: Humanist, 2004), 187.

37. DSM-IV states that "the term *culture-bound syndrome* denotes recurrent, locality-specific patterns of aberrant behavior and troubling experience that may or may not be linked to a particular DSM-IV diagnostic category. Many of these patterns are indigenously considered to be 'illness,' or at least afflictions, and most have local names. Although presentations conforming to the major DSM-IV categories can be found throughout the world, the particular symptoms, course, and social response are very often limited to specific societies or culture areas and are localized, folk, diagnostic categories that frame coherent meanings for certain repetitive, patterned, and troubling sets of experiences and observations" (*Diagnostic and Statistical Manual of Mental Disorders*, 4th ed. [Washington, D.C.: American Psychiatric Association, 1994], 844).

38. Christopher K. Chung, M.D., an assistant professor and director of psychiatric emergency services at Harbor-UCLA Medical Center in Torrance, California, described the Korean

phenomenon of *hwa-byung* (literally, fire disease) as "more specifically, suppressed anger syndrome." He contended that *hwa-byung* could be universal and that, if a term for such a syndrome as *hwa-byung* exists in a certain culture, the possibility exists that "this syndrome can be better understood from a culture-general perspective." This quotation is from Sandra L. Somers, "Examining Anger in 'Culture-Bound' Syndromes," *Psychiatric Times* 15, no. 1 (January 1, 1998); e-journal: http://psychiatrictimes.com/display/article/10168/55206, accessed March 19, 2009.

39. Somers, "Examining Anger in 'Culture-Bound' Syndromes."

40. Ibid.

41. Ibid.

42. Ibid.

43. Ibid.

44. Yeol Kyu Kim, *Anger of Koreans*, 199.

45. Choong-Koo Park, "Gender Discriminating Culture and Korean Church," *Christian Thoughts* (February 1995): 153.

46. Feminist scholars show that these teachings could easily become subject to enormous abuse and that "this theological paradigm [the relationship between Christ and the church] reinforces the cultural-patriarchal pattern of subordination" in Christian marriage. The quotation is from Elisabeth Schüssler Fiorenza, *In Memory of Her: A Feminist Theological Reconstruction of Christian Origins* (New York: Crossroad, 1994), 269. Fiorenza argues that Christ's self-giving love for the church is to be the model for the love relationship of the husband with his wife. Patriarchal domination is thus radically questioned. . . . Nevertheless, it must be recognized that this christological modification of the husband's patriarchal position and duties does not have the power, theologically, to transform the patriarchal pattern of the household code, even though this might have been the intention of the author. Instead, Ephesians christologically cements the inferior position of the wife in the marriage relationship" (270). See also Elizabeth Johnson, "Ephesians," in *The Women's Bible Commentary*, ed. Carol Newsom and Sharon H. Ringe (Louisville: Westminster John Knox), 338–42.

47. Kathleen Greider, *Reckoning with Aggression: Theology, Violence, and Vitality* (Louisville: Westminster John Knox, 1997), 58.

48. Kathleen Greider, "Too Militant? Aggression, Gender, and the Construction of Justice," in *Through the Eyes of Women: Insights for Pastoral Care*, ed. Jeanne Stevenson-Moessner (Minneapolis: Fortress Press, 1996), 128.

49. Greider bases her biblical analysis on her study of women's experience and seeks how women's experience can illuminate biblical texts and other theological and religious sources.

50. Greider, *Reckoning with Aggression*, 8.

51. Ibid.

52. Ibid., 5.

53. Ibid., 78.

54. Ibid.

55. Jean Miller, "Construction of Anger in Women and Men," in *Women's Growth in Connection: Writings from the Stone Center*, ed. Judith V. Jordan, et al. (New York: Guilford, 1991), 199.

56. In Korean society, the feeling of "shame" is a very strong emotion that threatens the social and self-identity of an individual. Korean women are taught to kill themselves rather than "shame" their family and ancestors. In ancient times, Korean women of prestigious families actually carried a small silver knife (*Eun-Jang-Do*) with them for that purpose, such as if they were raped.

57. Walter Wink, *The Powers That Be: Theology for a New Millennium* (New York: Doubleday, 1998), 37.

58. Ibid., 39.

59. Ibid., 31.

60. Walter Wink thinks of "demons" as the spirituality of systems and structures that have betrayed their divine vocations: "Corporations and governments are creatures whose sole purpose is to serve the general welfare. When they refuse to do so, their spirituality becomes diseased. They become demonic" (ibid., 5). His understanding of "spirituality" does not have a supernatural dimension. Rather, it is similar to an "ethos" or "ideology," which is an invisible entity of a visible, "material" element of an institution.

61. Ibid., 30. From this perspective, I am not arguing in this paper that every patriarchal system is intrinsically demonic, though I believe that a patriarchal system can easily turn into a "demonic" system for women who are excluded from the power structure. In pastoral care of Korean American women, I have worked with many clients who were content with their subservient roles and who did not have any motivation and intention to liberate themselves completely from this patriarchal system, though they complained and suffered its "nonhumanizing" uses of power to oppress them. According to Wink, "demonic" is not a system itself but the abuse of its power. So the question, "Is a patriarchal system intrinsically demonic or is its misuse or abuse of power demonic?" is another topic of research that is beyond the purpose of this paper.

62. In fact, I have seen many cases among my clients where Korean American wives are much more efficient than their husbands in running businesses in an immigrant context. The husbands often used to work in professional jobs or companies in Korea while their wives were homemakers. In an immigrant context, however, both husbands and wives have to work together to secure financial status. Many Korean immigrants are currently working in the nonprofessional areas such as running grocery stores, cleaning shops, or restaurants. In these nonprofessional businesses, husbands are often found ineffective because they are so accustomed to their previous social status as "important" persons. Meanwhile, wives are more flexible and do not care about whether people may think of them as important or not. As a consequence, wives are better in dealing with American customers (who sometimes put down minorities) and in general interpersonal skills with American people. Husbands gradually come to depend upon their wives for practical details that are necessary for successful business.

Chapter 11: Pastoral Care with Korean Goose Moms

1. http://www.geocities.com/roman.jost/Korea_Allgemein/Traditional_Korean_Wedding_English.htm

2. The term *goose family* is not an official term, but it was added in the newly published Korean dictionary *Hunminjungeum* (Golden Star, 2004). Other scholars called it "transnational family" or "multinational household" or "new global long distance family" (Cho, 2004). In this article, I will refer to the husband as goose dad, the wife as goose mom, and the family as goose family.

3. To protect the identities in these case studies, I have changed the names.

4. Bonnie J. Miller-McLemore, *In the Midst of Chaos: Raising Children as Spiritual Practice*, Practices of Faith (San Francisco: Jossey-Bass, 2007), 81–82.

5. Ibid., 83, quoting Horace Bushnell, *Christian Nurture* (New York: Scribner, 1861; reprint, Eugene, Ore.: Wipf & Stock, 2000), 237.

6. *Yealyealmon* were dedicated to women who killed themselves following their deceased husbands or who physically sacrificed themselves to take care of their sick families. A woman who showed a good example as a wise mother and good wife was remembered by the gate.

7. Bonnie J. Miller-McLemore and Herbert Anderson, "Salvaging Sacrifice," in *Faith Wisdom in Daily Living*, Lutheran Voices (Minneapolis: Augsburg Fortress, 2008), 55, quoting Christine E. Gudorf, "Parenting, Mutual Love, and Sacrifice," in *Women's Consciousness and Women's Conscience: A Reader in Feminist Ethics*, ed. Barbara Hilkert Andolsen, Christine E. Gudorf, and Mary D. Pellauer (San Francisco: Harper & Row, 1985), 176, 185–86.

8. Ibid., 57, quoting Beverly Wildung Harrison, "The Power of Anger in the Work of Love: Christian Ethics for Women and Other Strangers," in *Making the Connections: Essays in Feminist Social Ethics*, ed. Carol S. Robb (Boston: Beacon, 1985), 19, emphasis in the text (reprinted from *Union Seminary Quarterly Review* 36 [1981]: 41–57).

9. Miller-McLemore and Anderson, "Salvaging Sacrifice," 57; and Harrison, "The Power of Anger in the Work of Love," 19.

10. Miller-McLemore and Anderson, "Salvaging Sacrifice," 57.

11. Ibid., 59, quoting Rita Nakashima Brock, *Journeys by Heart: A Christology of Erotic Power* (New York: Crossroad, 1988), 50, 53, 56, 69, 70.

12. *Merriam-Webster's Collegiate Dictionary*, 11th ed. (Springfield, Mass: Merriam-Webster, 2003), 1099.

13. Ibid., 60.

14. Ibid., 64, quoting Barbara Hilkert Andolsen, "Agape in Feminist Ethics," *The Journal of Religious Ethics* 9, no. 1 (1981): 69–83, quote on p. 80.

15. Ibid., 64–65.

16. Herbert Anderson, "Between Rhetoric and Reality: Women and Men as Equal Partners," in *Mutuality Matters: Family, Faith, and Just Love*, ed. Herbert Anderson, Edward Foley, Bonnie Miller-McLemore, and Robert Schreiter (New York: Rowman & Littlefield, 2004), 73.

17. Carolyn Osiek, "Who Submits to Whom? Submission and Mutuality in the Family," in *Mutuality Matters*, Anderson, et al., eds., 58.

18. Pauline Kleingeld and Joel Anderson, "Justice as a Family Value," unpublished English version of "Die gerechtigkeitsorientierte Familie: Jenseits der Spannung zwischen Liebe und Gerechtigkeit," in *Person zu Person*, ed. Beate Rössler and Axel Honneth (Frankfurt: Suhrkamp, 2008), 1.

19. Ibid., 3.

20. Ibid.

21. Ibid., 4.

22. Ibid., 6.

23. Ibid., 9.

24. Jeanne Stevenson-Moessner, "A New Pastoral Paradigm and Practice," in *Women in Travail and Transition: A New Pastoral Care*, ed. Maxine Glaz and Jeanne Stevenson-Moessner (Minneapolis: Fortress Press, 1991), 207.

25. Brita L. Gill-Austern, "Love Understood as Self-Denial: What Does It Do to Women?" in *Through the Eyes of Women: Insights for Pastoral Care*, ed. Jeanne Stevenson-Moessner (Minneapolis: Fortress Press, 1996), 313.

26. K. Samuel Lee, "Navigating between two Cultures: the Bicultural Family's Lived Realities," in *Mutuality Matters*, Anderson, et al., eds., 107.

27. Ibid., 108.

28. Ibid., 114; original concept was proposed by Jung Young Lee.

29. Ibid., 115.

30. Ibid., quoting Susan Okin, "Is Multiculturalism Bad?" in *Is Multiculturalism Bad for Women?* ed. Joshua Cohen, Matthew Howard, and Martha Nussbaum (Princeton: Princeton University Press, 1999), 8–24.

31. Ibid., 11.

32. http://www.northernshaolinacademy.com/new/images/FiveElementsDiagram.jpg, accessed June 25, 2009.

33. Augustus Y. Napier and Carl A. Whitaker, *The Family Crucible* (New York: Harper & Row, 1978), 93.

34. Herbert Anderson, *The Family and Pastoral Care*, Theology and Pastoral Care (Philadelphia: Fortress Press, 1984), 60.

Chapter 12: Pentecostal and Female in Puerto Rico

1. E. A. Wilson, "Lugo, Juan L.," in Stanley M. Burgess and Eduard M. Van Der Maas, eds., *The New International Dictionary of Pentecostal and Charismatic Movements* (Grand Rapids: Zondervan, 2003), 845.

2. Ibid.

3. Roberto Domínguez, *Pioneros de Pentecostés Norteamérica y las Antillas, tercera edición* (Barcelona, España: CLIE, 1990), 15–56.

4. Dr. Helen Santiago, *Las Campañas Evangelísticas de T.L. Osborn (1950–1951) y la "pentecostalización" del protestantismo puertorriqueño*, unpublished manuscript (Trujillo Alto, Puerto Rico, 2005), 1–4.

5. Ada María Isasi-Díaz, *En la Lucha: In the Struggle* (Minneapolis: Fortress Press, 2004), 34.

6. The Church of God (Cleveland, Tennessee) is a centralized church. The church in Puerto Rico follows the same administrative structure of the central church in Cleveland. There are three levels of credentials for ministers: exhorters, ordained ministers, and bishops. Women can only be exhorters and ordained ministers but not bishops. At the General Assembly held every two years ministers meet to attend the business meetings. Only bishops comprise the general voting body. Women are excluded from voting and discussion at that meeting. Women can vote to ratify what that body has accepted. If an issue is not accepted in that general voting body, it will not be considered for the ratification process. On the other hand, it is worth saying that only bishops can be elected for the highest positions in the Church of God: General Overseer and its assistants and the Council of Eighteen. Women are excluded from these bodies. No representation of women is to be found at that level. Cf. Kimberly Ervin Alexander and R. Hollis Gause, *Women in Leadership: A Pentecostal Perspective* (Cleveland, Tenn.: Center for Pentecostal Leadership and Care, 2006).

7. Isasi-Díaz, *En la Lucha*, 161.

8. Ibid., 164.

9. Eldin Villafañe. *El Espíritu Liberador: Hacia una Ética Social Pentecostal Hispanoamérica* (Buenos Aires-Grand Rapids: Nueva Creación y Eerdmans, 1996), 188.

10. Delores Williams, *Sisters in the Wilderness: The Challenge of Womanist God-Talk* (New York: Orbis, 2001).

11. Cecil Cone, *The Identity Crisis in Black Theology* (Nashville: The African Methodist Episcopal Church, 1975), 23. In Williams, *Sisters in the Wilderness*, 152.

12. Williams, *Sisters in the Wilderness*, 188.

13. It is meant that African American biblical tradition is created. It is black people taking from the written text what the community considered to be normative for its life and what they took to be the true word of God in the Bible. This is often passed along in fragments. See Williams, *Sisters in the Wilderness*, chap. 7 n.18.

14. Williams, *Sisters in the Wilderness*, 188.

15. Elisabeth Schüssler Fiorenza invites students of the Bible to read it with suspicion. She argues that women are taught to study Scripture with a hermeneutic of respect, acceptance, and obedience. This feminist theologian has defended that a hermeneutic practice of deconstruction that is capable of analyzing cultural and linguistic practices that are in function of dominance need to be acquired by Bible students, especially women. When doing so, the reader will question, critique, and demystify ideas and concepts that hinder the "most profound truth." Elisabeth Schüssler Fiorenza, *Los Caminos de la Sabiduría* (Santander: Sal Terrae, 2004), 231–33.

16. See n. 6 above.

17. Casiano Floristan, *Teología Práctica* (Salamanca: Ediciones Sígueme, 2002), 9–12.

18. I had the opportunity of asking twenty-five of our 253 churches in the island if they have women in their local councils (Church and Pastor's Council). All of them answered in the affirmative. This was noted in a research paper presented in the Interamerican University of Puerto Rico, as a requisite for the course "Pastoral Theology and Ethics" taught by professor Felipe Martinez Arroyo. Miriam E. Figueroa, "Exclusion of Women in Positions of Authority in the Church of God Mission Board in PR," November, 2004.

19. Ada María Isasi, "Justificación," in Virginia Fabella y R.S. Sugirtharajah, *Diccionario de teologías del Tercer Mundo* (Navarra, España: Verbo Divino, 2002), 188.

20. Roberto A. Rivera, *Introducción a las Disciplinas Espirituales* (Nashville: Abingdon, 2008), 104.

21. Justo L. González, *Mañana: Christian Theology from a Hispanic Perspective* (Nashville: Abingdon, 1990), 47–48.

22. Elisabeth Schüssler Fiorenza, "On the Open Road to Galilee," in *Women's Spirituality: Resources for Christian Development*, ed. Joann Wolski Conn (New York: Paulist, 1996), 384.

Chapter 13: What About All Those Angry Black Women?

1. Carl Jung, *The Development of Personality*, Collected Works of C. G. Jung, vol. 17 (London: Routledge, 1967, 1991).

2. Peter S. Jensen, David Mrazek, Penelope K. Knapp, Laurence Steinberg, Cynthia Pfeffer, John Schowalter, and Theodore Shapiro, "Evolution and revolution in child psychiatry: ADHD [attention-deficit hyperactivity syndrome] as a disorder of adaptation," *Journal of the American Academy of Child and Adolescent Psychiatry* 36, no. 12 (December 1997): 1672.

3. Charles Johnson and Patricia Smith, *Africans in America: America's Journey through Slavery* (New York: Harcourt Brace, 1998), 70.

4. Ibid., 41.

5. Ibid., 112.

6. Ibid., 47.

7. Ibid., 199. Pennsylvania banned perpetual slavery in 1780, freeing all slaves born after 1780 when they reached the age of twenty-eight. Rhode Island and Connecticut began gradual emancipation in 1794. New York and New Jersey implemented slavery bans in 1785 and 1786, respectively.

8. Ibid., 323.

9. Ibid., 364.

10. Paula Giddings, *When and Where I Enter: The Impact of Black Women on Race and Sex in America* (New York: Morrow, 1984), 44–45, quoting *Aunt Sally, or the Cross: The Way to Freedom* (Cincinnati: American Reform Tract and Book Society, 1858), 9; Bethany Veney, *The Narrative of Bethany Veney, A Slave Woman* (Worcester, Mass., 1889), 26; and Linda Brent, *Incidents in the Life of a Slave Girl* (New York: Harvest/Harcourt Brace Jovanovich, 1973), 57.

11. Patricia Hill Collins, *Black Feminist Thought: Knowledge, Consciousness and the Politics of Empowerment* (New York: Routledge and Kegan Paul, 1990), 67ff.

12. W. E. B. Du Bois, "Of Our Spiritual Strivings," in *The Souls of Black Folk*, 100th anniversary ed. (New York: Signet Classic reprint, 1995), 45.

13. Joseph L. White and Thomas Parham, *The Psychology of Blacks: An African-American Perspective* (Englewood Cliffs, N.J.: Prentice Hall, 1990), 47.

14. U.S. Census Bureau, U.S. Census Table PINC-03: Educational Attainment—People 25 Years Old and Over, by Total Money Earnings in 2005, Work Experience in 2005, Age, Race, Hispanic Origin and Sex, http://pubdb3.census.gov/macro/032006/perinc/new03_000.htm, accessed on June 25, 2009.

15. Callie Rennison and Sarah Welchans, Bureau of Justice Statistics, Special Report: Intimate Partner Violence, May 2000, NCJ 178247, p. 3, at http://www.ojp.usdoj.gov/bjs/pub/pdf/ipv.pdf, accessed June 25, 2009

16. Bureau of Justice Statistics, Homicide Trends in the US: Trends in Intimate Homicides, FBI Supplementary Homicide Reports, 1976–2005, available at http://www.ojp.usdoj.gov/bjs/homicide/intimates.htm, accessed June 25, 2009.

17. Statistic from womenshealth.gov, Web site of The National Women's Health Information Center, http://www.4woman.gov/minority/africanamerican/, accessed March 20, 2009.

18. Dr. L. H. Welchel, "The Genies of the Black Preacher Before Emancipation," unpublished lecture, Atlanta, Ga., January 14, 2009.

19. Daphne C. Wiggins, *Righteous Content: Black Women's Perspectives of Church and Faith* (New York: New York University Press, 2004).

20. In *Soul Theology: The Heart of American Black Culture* (San Francisco: Harper & Row, 1986), Henry Mitchell and Nicholas Cooper-Lewter identify these core beliefs in African American religion: the Providence of God, the Justice of God, the Omnipotence of God, the Omniscience of God, the Goodness of God and Creation, the Grace of God, the Equality of Persons, and the Perseverance of Persons. God is viewed as all-knowing and all-powerful.

21. Andrew D. Lester, *The Angry Christian: A Theology for Care and Counseling* (Louisville: Westminster John Knox, 2003), 113.

22. Ma'at ("That which is straight") was the systematized sacred-spiritual ideal of ancient Kemet. It was the underlying current that intricately connected all things including human

behavior. It was the universal ethical principle of ancient Egyptian religion, denoting 'justice,' 'order,' and 'truth.' Ma'at was connected to the entire existence of the universe, and was not limited to ethics for human beings alone. Ma'at was the perfect order, toward which man should strive. It was, therefore, considered essential to live according to the principles of Ma'at so as not to disturb the very fabric of creation. Since the ancient Kemetic society believed that the universe was an ordered and rational place, Ma'at became the embodiment of the seven principles: Truth, Justice, Righteousness, Order, Balance, Harmony and Reciprocity." Online at http://cuip.net/schools/woodlawn/2_virtues.html, accessed March 20, 2009.

23. Lester, *The Angry Christian*, 135.

24. bell hooks, *Killing Rage* (New York: Holt, 1996), 16.

25. Evelyn L. Parker, ed., *The Sacred Selves of Adolescent Girls: Hard Stories of Race, Class and Gender* (Cleveland: Pilgrim, 2006), 44.

26. Maya Angelou, *And Still I Rise* (New York: Random House, 1978); bell hooks, *Ain't I A Woman: Black Women and Feminism* (Cambridge: South End Press, 1981); idem, *Feminist Theory: From Margin to Center* (Cambridge: South End Press, 1984); idem, *Talking Back: Thinking Feminist, Thinking Black* (Cambridge: South End Press, 1989); and idem, *Sisters of the Yam: Black Women and Self-Recovery* (Cambridge: South End Press, 1993); Delores S. Williams, *Sisters in the Wilderness: The Challenge of Womanist God-Talk* (Maryknoll, N.Y.: Orbis, 1993).

27. Parker, *The Sacred Selves of Adolescent Girls*, 69.

Chapter 14: Unraveling the Relationship Myth in the Turn Toward Autonomy

1. See David Bakan, *The Duality of Human Existence* (Chicago: Rand McNally, 1966); Sandra Bem, "The Measurement of Psychological Androgyny," *Journal of Personality and Social Psychology* 42 (1974): 155–62.

2. Nancy Chodorow, "Family Structure and Feminine Personality," in *Woman, Culture, and Society*, eds. Michelle Z. Rosaldo and Louise Lamphere (Stanford: Stanford University Press, 1974), 43–66; idem, *The Reproduction of Mothering: Psychoanalysis and the Sociology of Gender* (Berkeley: University of California Press, 1978); Jessica Benjamin, *The Bonds of Love: Psychoanalysis, Feminism, and the Problem of Domination* (New York: Pantheon, 1988).

3. See, for example, Carol Gilligan, *In a Different Voice* (Cambridge: Harvard University Press, 1992); Judith V. Jordan, et al., eds., *Women's Growth in Connection* (New York: Guilford, 1991).

4. Wendi L. Gardner and Shira Gabriel, "Gender Differences in Relational and Collective Interdependence: Implications for Self-Views, Social Behavior, and Subjective Well-Being," in *The Psychology of Gender*, eds. Anne Beal, Alice Eagly, and Robert Sternberg (New York: Guilford, 2004), 171.

5. I note here the need to attend to individual differences and the "between and within" groups variances on self-construals.

6. Erik H. Erikson, *Childhood and Society* (New York: Norton, 1986), 219 (emphasis mine).

7. Martin Buber, *The Knowledge of Man* (Amherst, N.Y.: Humanity Books, 1998).

8. Martin Buber, *I and Thou* (New York: Scribner, 1970), 112.

9. Ibid., 114. It needs to be noted here that in his discourse on "Dialogue" and the dialogic moment, Buber points out that in order for real dialogue ensuing from love to pertain, "you must have been, you must be with yourself." Of course, Buber's reflections on the relational sphere extend beyond "one-on-one" interpersonal relationships (what is often assumed because of his concept of I and Thou) into the social sphere. See his *Between Man and Man* (New York: Macmillan, 1948), especially 21ff.

10. Family-systems theory affirms the effect of lack of differentiation from one's family of origin on later intimate adult relationships. See Murray Bowen, "Toward the Differentiation of Self in One's Family of Origin," in *Family Therapy in Clinical Practice* (Northvale, N.J.: Jason Aronson, 1978); and Edwin H. Friedman, *Generation to Generation: Family Process in the Church and Synagogue* (New York: Guilford, 1985), for further insights.

11. The story of the "Giving Tree," a tree conceptualized as female who dies after meeting all the needs of the boy, and the moral lesson from it is not lost on little boys and girls. The story gives a good example of this kind of teaching.

12. See Christine Neuger, "A Feminist Perspective on Pastoral Counseling with Women," in *Clinical Handbook of Pastoral Counseling*, vol 2, eds. Robert Wicks and Richard Parson (New York: Paulist, 1993), 201; Juliana Adu-Gyamfi, "Sex Status, Cognitive Styles, and Psychiatric Symptoms," unpublished dissertation (Legon: University of Ghana, 1989). The study by Adu-Gyamfi conducted in Ghana over a two-year span on gender, cognitive style, and psychiatric symptoms is of particular interest here because it underscores the pervasiveness of the depressive feelings many women carry with them. Adu-Gyamfi was unsure whether her data and analysis could be accurate because as it stood, it meant that all the women in her sample were depressed at some level (from a private conversation with the researcher in 1986).

13. See Dana Crowley Jack, *Silencing the Self: Women and Depression* (New York: HarperCollins, 1991), 5, 16, 21. The title of the book is aptly named to reflect the reason and source of the depression in women. When the self is silenced and not allowed to struggle intrapsychically and interpersonally into being on its own terms, depression becomes its reactive mode. In this way, that self comes to be known almost by hiding.

14. See Jean Baker Miller, "The Development of Women's Sense of Self," in Jordan, *Women's Growth in Connection*, 11–26.

15. Ibid., 15.

16. I am not disputing the possibility of women's growth toward connectedness. Studies in the biological basis of behavior indicate that the differences between males and females "are driven by the actions of the reproductive hormones in the central nervous system," but while biology is privileged in these findings, "it is not rigidly deterministic," for nurture affects the biological predispositions toward any behavior. In short, what is learned can be unlearned, and perhaps a form of cognitive therapy can be incorporated into counseling with women who need to unlearn the undue emphases on the relational ethos for their own growth and development. See Elizabeth Hampson and Susan Moffat, "The Psychology of Gender: Cognitive Effects of Reproductive Hormones on the Adult Nervous System," in Beal, et al., eds., *The Psychology of Gender*, 38–64.

17. There are more female panhandlers in Accra, for instance, more of whom are porting infants than would be expected in such a collectivistic culture. The traditional *kayayei* (porters in the marketplaces) with infants on their backs and heavy loads atop their heads is a fairly common sight as well. Though one acknowledges the underlying socioeconomic factors, one must also acknowledge the contribution of colonialism in disrupting familial ways of life in Africa, and the fact that the postcolonial effects of gendered living have not been attended to in any appreciable manner. Thus, a precolonial ethos that prevails in a postcolonial milieu shortchanges the less powerful. What it means to be masculine and feminine in postcolonial Africa as a whole is yet to be named, confronted, and renegotiated for the mutual benefit of both genders. The most obvious effect is seen in the socioeconomic sector and is largely due to the disparity in literacy and opportunities for education. Although literacy figures for Ghana indicate that 74.8 percent of the overall population is literate, with 82.7 percent of males literate, and 67.1 percent of females, the 2001 National Population and Housing Census showed that "43.4 per cent of those who are three years old or more have never been to school and 49.9 per cent of the adult population of 15 years or more are totally illiterate"; see "Human Development Indicators," on http://www.ghanaweb.com/GhanaHomePage/general, which quotes *2000 Population and Housing Census, A Special Report on 20 Largest Localities* (Ghana Statistical Services, 2002), http://www.statsghana.gov.gh/KeySocial.html, both accessed June 25, 2009.

18. Mercy Amba Oduyoye, *Daughters of Anowa: African Women and Patriarchy* (Maryknoll, N.Y.: Orbis, 1995).

19. Ibid., 61.

20. This phenomenon has been described in the literature as "fear of success" (see Matina S. Horner, "Toward an Understanding of Achievement-Related Conflicts in Women," *Journal of Social Issues* 28 [1972]: 157–75), but later research indicates that fear of success was due more to the contextual factors that hitherto assumed intrapsychic factors as a result of early childhood learning about succeeding outside gender-proscribed roles. Current "role boundary maintenance theory"

gives a more complete understanding of what pertains here in the African context. See John Condry and Sharon Dyer, "Fear of Success Attribution of Cause to the Victim," *Journal of Social Issues* 32 (1976): 72, citing David Tresmer's research, which later appeared in his *Fear of Success* (New York: Plenum, 1977), 49–82.

21. Many may be familiar with the stories surrounding Kweku Ananse, the spider and the traditional trickster, of many Ghanaian folktales. In this regard, *anansesem* seeks to hoodwink people into believing lies about themselves so the teller can get ahead. Thus, communities completely ignore other proverbs and "folktalk" that calls for some equity among people. So one often hears the proverb, "All are God's children, none is the child of earth," pointing to the equality and worth of all in God's sight. At the same time, disparity exists between people based on their gender, and gender stratification is taken for granted. Meanwhile, women in black Africa continue to perform economic roles as part of or in addition to their mothering roles. At the same time, the myth of their playing secondary and dependent roles still goes on. Women continue to be "culture's bondswoman" and are required to take a subservient place to man in a bid to retain a corporate identity for the benefit of all.

22. Robert Kegan, *The Evolving Self: Problem and Process in Human Development* (Cambridge: Harvard University Press, 1982).

23. See essays by Mary Lynn Dell, Carolyn Wilbur Treadway, and Bonnie Miller-McLemore in *In Her Own Time: Women and Developmental Issues in Pastoral Care*, ed. Jeanne Stevenson-Moessner (Minneapolis: Fortress Press, 2000).

24. Female circumcision in some tribal and religious settings in Africa has gained recognition in the West where most assume it is a ritual that is pervasive in all of Africa; however, it is more germane to particular northern and often Islamized tribes. It is worthy to note that this ritual is performed by these same tribal groups who have settled in Western countries such as the United States.

25. See Teresa Hargrave Bremer and Michele Andrisin Wittig, "Fear of Success: A Personality Trait or a Response to Occupational Deviance and Role Overload?" *Sex Roles* 6, no. 1 (1980): 27–46.

26. The lack of progress in many African settings can be correlated to the inability and lack of opportunity to form autonomous selves without the attending conflicted intrapsychic tensions. In addition, guilt paralyzes the individual and leads to inertia in many cases.

27. Chodorow, *The Reproduction of Mothering*.

28. Virginia Held, *Feminist Morality: Transforming Culture, Society, and Politics* (Chicago: University of Chicago Press, 1993), 60.

29. Oduyoye, *Daughters of Anowa*, 81.

30. Evelyn Fox Keller, *Reflections on Gender and Science* (New Haven: Yale University Press, 1985), 99.

31. The notion of surrender here is borrowed from the psychoanalytic literature, where surrender is contrasted with submission—a volitional state that may oftentimes come under the manipulation of the other. See Emmanuel Ghent, M.D., "Masochism, Submission, Surrender—Masochism as a Perversion of Surrender," *Contemporary Psychoanalysis* 26 (1990): 108–36.

Chapter 15: Pastoral Care for the 1.5 Generation

1. The term *1.5 generation* generally refers to people who immigrate to a new country, usually at a young age, bringing with them characteristics from their home country, but also continuing to assimilate into the new country (see below, p. XX).

2. Space is the invisible area where intersubjective endeavors through relationships occur. For example, new space is created through actual utterance of words as well as through new intellectual, emotional, and spiritual understandings. New insight or understanding creates and enlarges one's space, opening up to more possibilities to think and act.

3. "Dynamic" is in contrast to the dominant cultural spaces where there are fixed rules and static values that determine who is an insider and who is an outsider.

4. Mary Eunjoo Kim, *Preaching the Presence of God: A Homiletic from an Asian American Perspective* (Valley Forge: Judson, 1996), 41.

5. Jennifer Oldstone-Moore, *Confucianism* (New York: Oxford University Press, 2002), 97–98.

6. Ibid.

7. Xinzhong Yao, *An Introduction to Confucianism* (Cambridge: Cambridge University Press, 2000), 181.

8. Ibid., 283.

9. Ibid.

10. Kim, *Preaching the Presence of God*, 41.

11. Many Asian parents do not initiate deep, emotional talk with their children. They see their role not as a counselor but as a guide and a provider.

12. Unlike in the Philipines and India, where English is one of the official state languages, Korea has only one official language spoken in schools—Korean. In fact, many Korean immigrants are educated and have a professional background, but their skills are not transferable without proficient English language skills. Therefore, many are forced into downward mobility by opening their own businesses, which requires longer hour works. For more information see Kyeyoung Park, *The Korean American Dream: Immigrants and Small Business in New York City* (Ithaca: Cornell University Press, 1995).

13. I am aware that many people have implicated mental illness as a cause of his behavior. I am not refuting such a claim but only highlighting his cultural context, of being caught in between, as an important factor that possibly contributed to the outcome.

14. Cho withdrew, "folding inward" into his own space, oppressing himself, without allowing himself to reach out to others.

15. There are many other "successful" Korean American 1.5 generations serving in various sectors of American public and corporate life. However, the regard of being "successful" 1.5 generation should not be limited to one's academic or professional achievement in the public sector. 1.5-generation mothers who are able to mirror several different cultural identities in their children as well as model them in their own lives are very "successful."

16. This is from an observer's perspective based on data that was available to me from the Korean, Korean American, and Western media, such as The Hankyoreh, Hankooki.com, DongA. com, *The Washington Post, The New York Times*, and ABC News.

17. Jung Young Lee, *Marginality: The Key to Multicultural Theology* (Minneapolis: Fortress Press, 1995), 43. Robert E. Park and Everette Stonequist borrowed insights from George Simmel and Werner Sombert to describe the individual who lives in two societies or two cultures and is a member of neither.

18. Heinz Kohut, *The Analysis of the Self* (New York: International Universities Press, 1971), xiv.

19. This has been demonstrated from history through systematically making discriminating laws not only to control the Asian population but to exclude them in the wealth building until 1965. See Meizhu Lui, Barbara Robles, Betsy Leondar-Wright, Rose Brewer, and Rebecca Adamson, *The Color of Wealth: The Story Behind the U.S. Racial Wealth Divide* (New York: New Press, 2006).

20. Kim, *Preaching the Presence of God*, 39.

21. Ibid.

22. Ibid., 45.

23. Jung Young Lee used "in-both" and "in-beyond" in referring to his concept of the "New Marginal" person who lives in both cultures but also has the ability to transform cultures. See Lee, *Marginality*.

24. Ibid., 63.

25. Carol Meyers, "Temple, Jerusalem," in *Anchor Bible Dictionary* (New York: Doubleday, 1992), 6:350–68.

26. E. P. Sanders notes that the majority of Jews in the land of Israel at the time of Jesus observed the rules of purity (i.e., holiness); see Sanders, *Judaism: Practice and Belief, 63 B.C.E.–66 C.E.* (London: SCM, 1992), 214–30.

27. Jesus said, "The Son of Man has come eating and drinking; and you say, 'Behold, a gluttonous man, and a drunkard, a friend of tax-collectors and sinners!'" (Luke 7:34).

28. These can be extended to include women who feel caught in between family and work, gays and lesbians who do not feel accepted in the dominant culture, disabled persons, and many others who feel in between cultures and subcultures.

Chapter 16: Counseling Grace

1. Heinz Kohut, *The Analysis of the Self* (New York: International Universities Press, 1971).

2. Elizabeth J. Walker, "A Model of Counseling With Some African American Women Clients," unpublished Ph.D. dissertation, Interdenominational Theological Center, Atlanta, Georgia, 2000.

3. John Newton, "Amazing Grace," in *The Book of Hymns* (Nashville: The United Methodist Publishing House, 1966), 92.

Chapter 17: Silent Cry

1. A term generally used by the Chinese to name the United States of America. See Ronald Takaki, *A Different Mirror: A History of Multicultural America* (New York: Back Bay, 1993), 415.

2. "Feathers from a Thousand Li Away," see Amy Tan, *The Joy Luck Club* (New York: Ivy, 1989), 3.

3. Asians and Pacific Islanders are people who originated from the Far East, Southeast Asia, the Indian Subcontinent, or the Pacific Islands. Peter C. Phan, a leading Catholic Vietnamese theologian, writes, "By any measure Asian American Christian theology, as distinct from studies in Asian religions, is still in its infancy, compared with Black and Hispanic (Latino/a) theologies, for instance. Currently the number of Asian American theologians and Asian doctoral students in theology, as distinct from seminarians, is minuscule and their scholarly output small" (*Christianity with an Asian Face: Asian American Theology in the Making* [Maryknoll, N.Y.: Orbis, 2003], xi). Christianity practiced in the East is different from the West. For resources on Eastern Christianity, see Scott W. Sunquist, David Wu Chu Sing, and John Chew Hiang Chee, eds., *A Dictionary of Asian Christianity* (Grand Rapids: Eerdmans, 2001); and Phan, *Christianity with an Asian Face*. In Eastern Christianity, there has been some awareness on the part of Asian male theologians and biblical scholars about Asian women's oppression. However, due to the male privilege in the patriarchal family and social system, it places on Asian women the full ownership of their process of liberation. This reality is reflected in the work of Soo-Young Kwon and Anthony Duc Le, "Relationship building in Clinical Pastoral Education: A Confucian Reflection from Asian Chaplains," *Journal of Pastoral Care* 58, no. 3 (Fall 2004): 203–14. "Though the article, written by two Asian men, discusses the Asian (Confucian) perspective in general, it must be noted that there may be differences pertaining to gender within the Asian population. We hope that future articles written by Asian women will explore more thoroughly the role of gender within the same cultural patterns." Here the authors give the readers the impression that they are not responsible to address female issues. The Multicultural Task Force of the Association of Clinical Pastoral Education (ACPE) was appointed in fall 2004 to develop "cultural competencies" for ACPE Supervisors and their programs. Though the task force members represented a community of diversity, unfortunately, no female Asian supervisor was invited to participate in this groundbreaking work. On the contrary, it included an Asian male who was not an ACPE supervisor.

4. *Yin-Yang* is a Taoist concept that unites all opposites. According to *Yin-Yang*, our life and destiny are closely interwoven with the workings of two polarities: positive and negative energy forces, known as *chi* (translated as "human breath or spirit"). Harmony is the state of the balance of these opposites. In human relationships, balancing and harmonizing is what gives essence to a prosperous life.

5. The term is used in the 2005 ACPE (Association for Clinical Pastoral Education) Standards. It is defined as "an attitude of respect when approaching people of different cultures, which entails engagement in a process of self-reflection and self-critique requiring an ability to move beyond one's own biases." *2005 Standards, Association of Clinical Pastoral Education* (Decatur, Ga.: ACPE, 2005), 23.

6. For a collection of this Chinese poetry, see Him Mark Lai, Genny Lim, and Judy Young, *Island: Poetry and History of Chinese Immigrants on Angel Island, 1910–1940* (Seattle: University of Washington Press, 1980).

7. Equal Employment Opportunity Commission Title VII of the Civil Rights Act of 1964 states that it is unlawful to discriminate against any employee or applicant because of the individual's national origin. No one can be denied equal employment opportunity because of birthplace, ancestry, culture, or linguistic characteristics common to a specific ethnic group. In August 2003 the EEOC and Workplace partners launched a new initiative to protect employment rights of Asian Americans, called TIGAAR (The Information Group for Asian American Rights). See Shamita Das Dasgupta, ed., *A Patch Shawl: Chronicles of South Asian Women* (New Brunswick, N.J.: Rutgers University Press, 1998). In her research, she cited the works of Teresa Amott and Julie Matthaei, "In reality uptown Chinese [women] were already educationally and socially advantaged in Taiwan and China, and simply transferred these achievements and status to the United States. Indeed . . . discrimination exists even against such "model" immigrants" (211).

8. Chinese names are usually made of three parts. The first is the family name, the second is a generational name, and the third is the specific name of the child (called the first name in America). The Chinese take great care to give names to their children that maintain the family's pride, luck, and vision for their children. Many Chinese adopt English names to adapt to the dominant culture without their parents' involvement. For the parents, this act is experienced as cultural alienation on two levels: their rights as parents are being undermined, and their children's loyalty to uphold the culture is challenged.

9. Ken Uyeda Fong, *Pursuing the Pearl: A Comprehensive Resource for Multi-Asian Ministry* (Valley Forge: Judson, 1995), 180.

10. All names are fictitious; identifying information has been changed to protect the identities of persons in this story.

11. *Xei xong xon tan* is a Chinese proverb; it means to care for someone sensitively through a contextual understanding.

12. Chung Hyun Kyung, *Struggle to Be the Sun Again: Introducing Asian Women's Theology* (Maryknoll, N.Y.: Orbis, 1990), 35.

13. Ibid., 54.

14. Ibid., 57.

15. Peter C. Phan and Jung Young Lee, eds., *Journeys at the Margin: Toward an Autobiographical Theology in American-Asian Perspective* (Collegeville, Minn.: Liturgical, 1999), 31.

Chapter 18: Women, Professional Work, and Diversity

1. Key elements of this case have been changed to protect the identity of the client, though the issues remain as they were presented to me.

2. Sue Kirchoff and Barbara Hagenbaugh, "Immigration: A fiscal boon or financial strain?" in *USA TODAY,* January 22, 2004.

3. Daniel Goleman, Richard Boyatzis, Annie McKee, *Primal Leadership: Learning to Lead with Emotional Intelligence* (Cambridge: Harvard Business School Press, 2004).

4. Mary C. Waters, "Immigrant Families at Risk: Factors that Undermine Chances for Success," in *Immigration and the Family: Research and Policy on U.S. Immigrants,* ed. Alan Booth, Ann C. Crouter, and Nancy Landale (Mahwah, N.J.: Lawrence Erlbaum Association, 1997), 86–87.

5. Sally C. Selden and A. Frank Selden, "Diversity in Public Organizations: Moving toward a Multicultural Model," in *Modern Organizations: Theory and Practice,* 2nd ed., ed. Ali Farazmand (Westport, Conn.: Praeger, 2002), 183–206.

6. Mary Lou de Leon Siantz, "Factors That Impact Developmental Outcomes of Immigrant Children," in Booth, et al., eds., *Immigration and the Family*, 155.

7. Cynthia Garcia Coll Katherine Magnuson, "Psychological Experience of Immigration: A Developmental Perspective," in Booth, et al., eds., *Immigration and the Family*, 101–02.

8. Siantz, "Factors That Impact Developmental Outcomes of Immigrant Children," 155.

9. Waters, "Immigrant Families at Risk," 86–87.

10. Caroline B. Bretell and Patricia A. DeBergeois, "Anthropology and the Study of Immigrant Women," in *Seeking Common Ground: Multidisciplinary Studies of Immigrant Women in the United States*, ed. Donna Gabaccia (Westport, Conn.: Praeger, 1992), 53.

11. Ibid., 43–49.

12. Ibid., 33.

13. Waters, "Immigrant Families at Risk," 84. For example, many women with college degrees or above who were employed as professors in their home countries take lower-level jobs upon entering the U.S. workforce. Others, though, make lateral moves or take on responsibilities new to them, such as managing others. Rita J. Simon, "Sociology and Immigrant Women," in Gabaccia, ed., *Seeking Common Ground*, 25.

14. Simon, "Sociology and Immigrant Women," 26.

15. Lisa Lowe, "Work, Immigration, Gender: New Subjects of Cultural Politics," *Social Justice*, 25, no. 3 (1998): 5.

16. Siantz, "Factors That Impact Developmental Outcomes of Immigrant Children," 153–56.

17. Lowe, "Work, Immigration, Gender," 3.

18. Selden and Selden, "Diversity in Public Organizations," 195.

19. Ibid., 196.

20. The World Council of Churches has been "chided" for confusing capitalism and free enterprise or economic liberalism. The nuance of this distinction is outside the purview of this essay and will not be undertaken here. Edward Duff, *The Social Thought of the World Council of Churches* (London: Longmans, Green, 1956).

21. "Dis-ease" is a broad term commonly used to indicate the sense that things are "not right" with a person and her world: feelings of alienation, the sense of being exploited, and existential uneasiness are examples of the dis-ease I invoke here. It can indicate depression and other mental illness, though it need not point to a specific, diagnosable condition as might be found in the *Diagnostic and Statistical Manual-IV-TR* (Washington, D.C.: American Psychiatric Association, 2000).

22. H. Richard Niebuhr, *The Responsible Self: An Essay in Christian Moral Philosophy* (New York: Harper & Row, 1963/1978). Niebuhr argues here for the importance of persons to be engaged and responsive to God's work in the social order.

23. Daniel Goleman, "It May Be a Good Job, but Is It 'Good Work'?" in *The New York Times*, November 18, 2008, Business, 2. See also Howard Gardner, Mihaly Csikszentmihalyi, William Damon, *Good Work: When Excellence and Ethics Meet* (New York: Basic, 2002).

24. I am using the word *institution* to mean an organized practice (such as a marriage) or a social body (such as a financial services company) "established to meet a basic human need, social function, or felt desire. . . . [Institutions] have to be constructed and maintained by intentional human actions" (Max Stackhouse, "Institution/Institutionalization," in *The Westminster Dictionary of Christian Ethics*, ed. James F. Childress and John Macquarrie (Philadelphia: Westminster, 1986), 304). Ethicist Susan Moller Okin and pastoral theologian Edward Wimberly suggest that the family is the first institution that holds and forms us. Developmental theorists such as Erik Erikson, Heinz Kohut, Harry Stack Sullivan, and Kenneth Gergen agree that persons always come into being in the context of interpersonal, sociocultural, and political relationships and that the self is inextricable from the institutions that create the living human web (see Bonnie Miller-McLemore, "The Living Human Web: Pastoral Theology at the Turn of the Century," in *Through the Eyes of Women: Insights for Pastoral Care*, ed. Jeanne Stevenson-Moessner [Minneapolis: Fortress Press, 1996]).

25. Howard Clinebell and Larry Graham are among those who would argue that pastoral theologians are not only called to care for persons but for all of God's creation, including the inanimate world as well. See Howard Clinebell, *Ecotherapy: Healing Ourselves, Healing the Earth*

(Minneapolis: Fortress Press, 1996); and Larry K. Graham, *Care of Persons, Care of Worlds: A Psychosystems Approach to Pastoral Care and Counseling* (Nashville: Abingdon, 1992).

26. Graham, *Care of Persons, Care of Worlds*, 11.

27. For a fuller discussion of this, see my book *Beyond Individualism in Pastoral Care and Counseling: Reflections on Theory, Theology and Practice* (Eugene, Ore.: Wipf and Stock, forthcoming, 2009).

28. Freud makes this argument most clearly in Sigmund Freud, *Civilization and Its Discontents,* trans. and ed. James Strachey (New York: Norton, 1961), esp. chap. 4.

29. David H. Jensen, *Responsive Labor: A Theology of Work* (Louisville: Westminster John Knox, 2007), ix.

30. David W. Miller, *God at Work: The History and Promise of the Faith at Work Movement* (New York: Oxford University Press, 2007), 79–80.

31. Stackhouse, "Institution/Institutionalization," 304.

32. While persons who labor unpaid—for example, in the domestic sphere caring for and educating children—certainly are working, my focus here is on contexts of wage-earning work. Pastoral theologian Larry K. Graham argues that the "forces" that impinge on human well-being "are larger than individual persons and have cultural, ideological and systemic dimensions, which powerfully shape concrete persons and their options. . . . To treat the individual in isolation from these forces is often to throw a straw into the wind. These very forces need challenge and modification along with the changes necessary in individual persons" (Graham, *Care of Persons, Care of Worlds,* 11). John Rawls defines basic structures this way: "The basic structure of a society is the way in which the main political and social institutions of a society fit together into one system of social cooperation, and the way they assign basic rights and duties and regulate the division of advantages that arise from social cooperation over time. The political constitution within an independent judiciary, the legally recognized forms of property, and the structure of the economy (for example, as a system of competitive markets with private property in the means of production), as well as the family in some form, all belong to the basic structure. The basic structure is the background social framework within which the activities of associations and individuals take place." John Rawls, *Justice as Fairness: A Restatement,* p. 10, as quoted in Iris Marion Young, "Taking the Basic Structure Seriously," *Symposium: John Rawls and the Study of Politics* 4, no. 1 (March 2006): 91.

33. Young, "Taking the Basic Structure Seriously," 94.

34. Bonnie Miller-McLemore, "The Living Human Web," 9–26. As Ian Burkitt, a social constructivist, asserts, "the idea that there is a basic division between society and the individual is nonsense. All efforts to find the 'relationship' between the 'two' are wasted, for when we look at society and the individual we are viewing exactly the same thing—social being—from two different angles." Burkitt, *Social Selves: Theories of the Social Formation of Personality* (Thousand Oaks, Calif.: Sage, 1991), 1.

35. Archie Smith, *The Relational Self: Ethics and Therapy from a Black Church Perspective* (Nashville: Abingdon, 1982), 59.

36. Smith, *The Relational Self;* Edward Wimberly, *Counseling African American Marriages and Families* (Louisville: Westminster John Knox, 1997); Pamela Couture, *Seeing Children, Seeing God: A Practical Theology of Children and Poverty* (Nashville: Abingdon, 2000); idem, *Blessed are the Poor? Women's Poverty, Family Policy, and Practical Theology* (Nashville: Abingdon, 1991); James Newton Poling, *The Abuse of Power: A Theological Problem* (Nashville: Abingdon, 1991); and idem. *Render Unto God: Economic Vulnerability, Family Violence, and Pastoral Theology* (St. Louis: Chalice, 2002).

37. Ali Farazmand, "Introduction: The Multifaceted Nature of Modern Organizations," in Farazmand, ed., *Modern Organizations*, xv–xxix.

38. Ann Swidler, "Saving the Self: Endowment versus Depletion in American Institutions," in *Meaning and Modernity: Religion, Polity and the Self,* ed. Richard Madsen, et al. (Berkeley: University of California Press, 2002), 54.

39. Bonnie Miller-McLemore coined the term "the living human web" to describe the appropriate focus of pastoral theological attention. In this she expanded Anton Boisen's interest in caring for the "living human document." See Miller-McLemore, "The Living Human Web."

40. This is in line with other pastoral theologians' thinking. See Larry K. Graham, *Care of Persons, Care of Worlds*; Nancy Ramsay, "Contemporary Pastoral Theology: A Wider Vision for the Practice of Love," in *Pastoral Care and Counseling: Redefining the Paradigms*, ed. Nancy J. Ramsay (Nashville: Abingdon, 2004), 155–76; Bonnie Miller-McLemore, "Pastoral Theology as Public Theology: Revolutions in the 'Fourth Area,'" in Ramsay, ed., *Pastoral Care and Counseling*, 45–64.

41. Books and articles on leading healthy congregations abound. For example, see almost any entry in the *Journal of Religious Leadership*, and books such as Ronald W. Richardson's *Creating a Healthier Church: Family Systems Theory, Leadership, ad Congregational Life*, Creative Pastoral Care and Counseling (Minneapolis: Fortress Press, 1996).

42. Nancy Ramsay, "A Time of Ferment and Redefinition," in *Pastoral Care and Counseling*, 1–43.

43. E. Brooks Holifield, *A History of Pastoral Care in America: From Salvation to Self Realization* (Nashville: Abingdon, 1983); and E. Brooks Holifield, "History of Protestant Pastoral Care (United States)," in *Dictionary of Pastoral Care and Counseling*, gen. ed. Rodney J. Hunter (Nashville: Abingdon, 1996), 511–15. Ramsay, "A Time of Ferment and Redefinition," 10.

44. Young, "Taking the Basic Structure Seriously," 96.

45. See, for example, Edward Farley, *Good and Evil: Interpreting a Human Condition* (Minneapolis: Fortress Press, 1990).

46. Walter Wink, *Engaging the Powers: Discernment and Resistance in a World of Domination* (Minneapolis: Fortress Press, 1992), 1.

47. Though this idea is found in the work of theologians such as Edward Farley and Marjorie Suchocki and sociologists such as Peter Berger, Walter Wink popularized the term in his series *Naming the Powers: The Language of Power in the New Testament* (Philadelphia: Fortress Press, 1984); *Unmasking and Powers: The Invisible Powers that Determine Human Existence* (Philadelphia: Fortress Press, 1986); and *Engaging the Powers*. Wink articulates a vision of Powers referred to in the New Testament. He writes, "They are visible *and* invisible, earthly *and* heavenly, spiritual *and* institutional. The Powers possess an outer, physical manifestation (buildings, portfolios, personnel, trucks, fax machines) and an inner spirituality, or corporate culture, or collective personality" (Wink, *Engaging the Powers*, 3 [italics in the original]). When the Powers become integrated and committed to "idolatrous values," they make up the "Domination System," or Evil.

48. This is a paraphrase of Walter Wink. Wink argues the point that the Powers surround us on every side, are necessary and useful (and that we can do nothing without them), but that they support and perpetuate both good and evil simultaneously)Wink, *Engaging the Powers*, 3).

49. Ibid.

50. Organizational theorists posit a continuum of diversity in organizational life from segregated institutions (intentionally racist and exclusionary) to fully inclusive and genuinely multicultural institutions in which all members fully participate; share power with diverse racial, cultural, and economic groups to determine mission, structure, constituency, policies, and practices; and resist social oppression in all forms. Bailey W. Jackson ("The Theory and Practice of Multicultural Organization Development in Education," in M. Ouellet, ed. *Teaching Inclusively: Resources for Course, Departmental and Institutional Change* [Stillwater: New Forums, 2005]), for example, suggests a six-stage continuum of organizational development in which Stage One is exclusionary, e.g., the system is "openly devoted to maintaining the majority group's dominance and privilege, and these values are typically manifested in the system's mission and membership criteria" (10). Stage Four is the Affirming System, which "is committed to eliminating the discriminatory practices and inherent advantage given members of the majority group by actively recruiting and promoting members of those social groups typically denied access to the system" (12); and Stage Six is the Multicultural System, which "acts on a commitment to eradicate social oppression in all forms within the system; includes the members of diverse cultural and social groups as full participants, especially in decisions that shape the system. [It also] follows through on broader external social responsibilities including support of efforts to eliminate all forms of social oppression and to educate others in multicultural perspectives" (13).

51. Ibid., 24.

52. This work is particularly important in order for women to thrive. See *Women's Growth in Connection: Writings from the Stone Center,* Judith V. Jordan, Alexandra G. Kaplan, Jean Baker Miller, Irene P. Stiver, Janet L. Surrey, eds. (New York: Guilford, 1991).

53. It should be remembered that a genuinely multicultural organization is always an ideal and something to aspire to, never fully realized. See Jackson, "The Theory and Practice of Multicultural Organization Development in Education," 17.

54. These are practices I develop more fully in another article ("Pastoral Theology as the Art of Paying Attention: Widening the Horizons," *International Journal of Practical Theology* 12, no. 2 (2008): 189–210. Catholic practical theologian Brian Hall and his associates have spent more than thirty years researching values and their impact on personal and organizational well-being. They have identified and catalogued 125 values they place on a developmental continuum from early stage values such as Safety/Security to more mature values such as Global Sustainability. Brian Hall, *Values Shift: A Guide to Personal and Organizational Transformation* (Rockport, Mass.: Twin Lights, 1995), 21.

55. Teresa Amott, Julie Matthaei, *Race, Gender, and Work: A Multicultural Economic History of Women in the United States* (Boston: South End Press, 1991). This is in line, too, with Nancy Ramsay's view of pastoral theology as compassionate resistance. See Nancy Ramsay, "Compassionate Resistance: An Ethic for Pastoral Care and Counseling." *The Journal of Pastoral Care* 52, no. 3 (Fall 1998): 217–26. Ramsay suggests pastoral theologians think of themselves as those who, besides supporting, also participate in (re)forming and advocating. Formation is defined by Ramsay as acts that expand our imaginations and understanding, thereby assisting the subjects of care to "engage in personal, relational or public challenges" (Ramsay, "A Time of Ferment and Redefinition," 3). She also recommends advocacy, or acts that have "liberative intentions" such as "shaping institutional and governmental policies that may diminish or support the social ecology of human life" (ibid., 4). Developing socially adequate practices of formation and advocacy would appropriately bring pastoral theologians into the very midst of public arenas of human experience—of which the organizations where we work are one significant element. Indeed, Bonnie Miller-McLemore asserts that public policy and structural issues that determine the health of human persons are as important to attend to as dynamics of individual emotional well-being (Miller-McLemore, "Pastoral Theology as Public Theology: Revolutions in the 'Fourth Area,'" in Ramsay, ed., *Pastoral Care and Counseling,* 45–64).

56. David Miller argues in *God at Work* that, in general, religion is gaining acceptance in the U.S. workplace. For religion and the immigrant experience, see Brettell and DeBergeios, *Seeking Common Ground,* 52. Of the millions of immigrants entering the workforce in the future, Steven Warner argues that the great majority of newcomers are Christian; this emboldens my argument that pastoral theologians belong alongside folks—especially, perhaps, those foreign born—to address the injustices in the companies for whom they work. As fellow people of faith we might have a perspective and language that these employees would understand and welcome. See R. Stephen Warner, "Coming to America: Immigrants and the Faith they Bring," *The Christian Century* 212, no. 3 (Feb. 10, 2004): 20–23.

57. Bonnie Miller-McLemore affirms work that confronts evil and contests violent, abusive behaviors "that perpetuate undeserved suffering and false stereotypes that distort the realities of people's lives. . . . [That] involves advocacy and tenderness on behalf of the vulnerable, giving resources and means to those previously stripped of authority, voice, and power . . . [and] fosters solidarity among the vulnerable." Miller-McLemore, "Feminist Theory in Pastoral Theology," in Bonnie J. Miller-McLemore and Brita L. Gill-Austern, eds., *Feminist and Womanist Pastoral Theology* (Nashville: Abingdon, 1999), 80.

58. The two most significant works to come out of the Stone Center at Wellesley College attest to the importance of this work for the well-being of women. See Jordan, et al., eds., *Women's Growth in Connection;* and Judith V. Jordan, ed., *Women's Growth in Diversity: More Writings from the Stone Center* (New York: Guilford, 1997).

Chapter 19: Soul Care Amid Religious Plurality

1.   Diana L. Eck, *A New Religious America: How A "Christian Country" Has Become the World's Most Religiously Diverse Nation* (San Francisco: HarperSanFrancisco, 2001).

2.   The literature in chaplaincy on interreligious encounter has tended to focus on specific situations of supervision or caregiving between persons of different traditions. See, for example, Nina C. Davis, "Zen Buddhist and Christian Co-Supervisors: A Reflection on CPE—Is Multi-faith and Multicultural CPE Possible?" *Journal of Supervision and Training in Ministry* 23 (2003): 60–65; Homer L. Jernigan, "Clinical Pastoral Education with Students from Other Cultures: The Role of the Supervisor," *Journal of Pastoral Care* 54, no. 2 (Summer 2000): 135–45; and Helmut Weiss, ed., *Intercultural and Inter-Faith Communication: Materials from the International Seminar 2005* (Düsseldorf: Society for Intercultural Pastoral Care and Counseling, 2006). Resources that present snapshots of the core beliefs and common practices of a variety of religions are also begin-ning to appear: see, for example, Neville A. Kirkwood, *A Hospital Handbook on Multicultural-ism and Religion*, rev. ed. (Harrisburg, Pa.: Morehouse, 2005); Sue Wintz and Earl P. Cooper, "A Quick Guide for Cultural and Spiritual Traditions" (Schaumburg, Ill.: Association of Pro-fessional Chaplains, 2003), http://www.professionalchaplains.org/uploadedFiles/pdf/learning-cultural-sensitivity.pdf, accessed December 28, 2008.

Literature that seeks to articulate a somewhat more overarching theoretical approach to inter-religious soul care is also beginning to emerge: Robert G. Anderson and Mary A. Fukuyama, eds., *Ministry in the Spiritual and Cultural Diversity of Health Care: Increasing the Competency of Chaplains* (Binghamton, N.Y.: Haworth, 2004); Daniel S. Schipani and Leah Dawn Bueckert, eds., *Spiritual Caregiving in the Hospital: Windows to Chaplaincy Ministry* (Kitchener, Ont., and Elkhart, Ind.: Pandora Press, in association with Institute of Mennonite Studies, 2006); Dagmar Grefe, "Patch Where it Hurts: Towards a 'Global' Didactic of Interreligious Encounters in Spiritual Care and Counseling," Ph.D. dissertation, Claremont School of Theology, 2007; Leah Dawn Bueckert and Daniel S. Schipani, eds., *You Welcomed Me: Interfaith Spiritual Care in the Hospital* (Elkhart, Ind.: Associated Mennonite Biblical Seminary, 2009); Daniel S. Schipani and Leah Dawn Bueckert, eds., *Interfaith Spiritual Care: Understandings and Practices* (Kitchener, Ont.: Pandora, 2009).

3.   An example of the small literature in counseling that attends to the particularity of clients' religious identity (the religious identity of the counselor is not addressed) is P. Scott Richards and Allen E. Bergin, eds., *Handbook of Psychotherapy and Religious Diversity* (Washington, D.C.: American Psychological Association, 2000). There is a growing counseling literature that inten-tionally avoids addressing religion and its distinct expressions, instead trying to identify commonly held values, beliefs, and practices deemed to be "spiritual." It is noteworthy that though pastoral counseling has defined itself as a practice in which religious particularity and diversity is respected and fostered, religious plurality and interreligious encounter are not commonly addressed in the pastoral counseling literature.

4.   The primary example is Dayle A. Friedman, ed., *Jewish Pastoral Care: A Practical Handbook from Traditional and Contemporary Sources*, 2nd ed. (Woodstock, Vt.: Jewish Lights, 2005).

5.   The focus of this essay and my choices of foci for reflection within this large area in need of "excavation" emerge from my personal and professional location as a Christian teaching soul care at a historically Christian theological school on the outskirts of Los Angeles, the most religiously diverse region in this most religiously diverse country. More and more often my students are not Christian, have been shaped by more than one religious tradition, are preparing for chaplaincies and social service in religiously diverse settings, and/or encounter religious diversity within their own religious communities—including within Christian parishes. My students and I study and learn together at Claremont School of Theology, which in 2008 revised its mission statement in light of the religious pluralism in which we are immersed. See "New Statements of Mission, Vision, and Values," http://www.cst.edu/about_claremont/news_new%20mission%20statement.php, accessed December 27, 2008.

6.   Interreligious encounter is a relatively familiar dynamic in chaplaincy, so my focus here is on other settings.

7. Many Jews prefer use of the Hebrew term *Shoah* (השואה) over "Holocaust" to refer to the genocide of Jews in the period before and during World War II.

8. George Kilcourse, "U.S. Interchurch Families: Ecumenism with a Human Face," *One in Christ: A Catholic Ecumenical Review* 24, no. 3 (1988): 249.

9. Ibid.

10. Ibid.

11. This issue is discussed at length in Ernest Falardeau, "Mutual Recognition of Baptism and Pastoral Care of Interchurch Families," *Journal of Ecumenical Studies* 28, no. 1 (Winter 1991): 63–73.

12. Kilcourse, "U.S. Interchurch Families," 245. Given this rate of disaffiliation, Christian pastoral caregivers' neglect of religious plurality within families appears to contribute to the decline of church attendance in the United States. Some families do find ways to benefit from their religious plurality: Brita Gill-Austern evocatively describes how, though it is not her primary religious home because she is Christian, participating in the life of Congregation Beth El with her Jewish husband and children has enriched her faith. Brita L. Gill-Austern, "The Braid of Generations: A Model of Family Ministry," in *Tending the Flock: Congregations and Family Ministry*, eds. K. Brynolf Lyon and Archie Smith Jr. (Louisville: Westminster John Knox, 1998), 55–77.

13. K. Samuel Lee, "The Teacher-Student in Multicultural Theological Education: Pedagogy of Collaborative Inquiry," *Journal of Supervision and Training in Ministry* 22 (2002): 81–99.

14. Of course, some people are not merely bireligious but multireligious, weaving together in their life narrative beliefs and practices from more religious traditions than two.

15. For an exploration of this notion from a pastoral counseling perspective, see Pamela Cooper-White, *Many Voices: Pastoral Psychotherapy in Relational and Theological Perspective* (Minneapolis: Fortress Press, 2007).

16. For an example of research that documents this impetus to religiously plural identity, see Courtney Bender and Wendy Cadge, "Constructing Buddhism(s): Interreligious Dialogue and Religious Hybridity," *Sociology of Religion* 67, no. 3 (2006): 229–47.

17. Siroj Sorajjakool's work is enriched by this form of religious plurality. See especially Siroj Sorajjakool, *Wu Wei, Negativity, and Depression: The Principle of Non-Trying in the Practice of Pastoral Care* (Binghamton, N.Y.: Haworth, 2001), and *Do Nothing: Inner Peace for Everyday Living—Reflections on Chuang Tzu's Philosophy* (West Conshohocken, Pa.: Templeton Foundation Press, 2009).

18. See, for example, KangHack Lee, "Christian Spiritual Direction in the Confucian Culture: A Korean Perspective," *Reflective Practice: Formation and Supervision in Ministry* 28 (2008): 192–208; and Hee Ann Choi, *Korean Women and God: Experiencing God in a Multi-religious Colonial Context* (Maryknoll, N.Y.: Orbis, 2005). As her title indicates, Choi also explores the role of colonialism in the creation of Korean religious plurality.

19. Much of Lee Butler's work emphasizes the interrelatedness of traditional African values and African American Christianity. See Lee H. Butler Jr., *Liberating Our Dignity, Saving our Souls* (St. Louis: Chalice, 2006), and *A Loving Home: Caring for African American Marriage and Families* (Cleveland: Pilgrim, 2000).

20. Howard W. Stone and James O. Duke, *How to Think Theologically*, 2nd ed. (Minneapolis: Fortress Press, 2006), esp. 13–21.

21. Peter Yuichi Clark, "Exploring the Pastoral Dynamics of Mixed-Race Persons," *Pastoral Psychology* 52, no. 4 (March 2004): 315–28. The suggestions for care are discussed on pp. 324–28.

22. Ibid., 325.

23. Duane Bidwell's article on his experiences in ministry as a Buddhist-Christian provides a moving example. Duane R. Bidwell, "Practicing the Religious Self: Buddhist-Christian Identity as Social Artifact," *Buddhist-Christian Studies* 28 (2008): 3–12.

24. Clark, "Exploring the Pastoral Dynamics of Mixed-Race Persons," 327. Clark also suggests that for Christians, a process-oriented theology is beneficial for soul care, because of its affirmation of "God's and our continuous creativity in facing each potential moment of existence" (327).

25. Paul F. Knitter, *Introducing Theologies of Religions* (Maryknoll, N.Y.: Orbis, 2000). Knitter's remarkably lucid discussion deserves to be read carefully and in full by all pastoral caregivers interested in interreligious caregiving. Knitter's work asks us to take more seriously and seek to comprehend in an even-handed way the theological (religious?) diversity within Christianity. It would be helpful to learn from colleagues in traditions other than Christianity how these approaches compare to and/or differ from approaches to religious pluralism in their traditions.

26. It is my custom to use the formulation "G-d" to refer to divinity, rather than spelling the word in its entirety. Following its use in Judaism, this incomplete spelling symbolizes the humility we are advised to practice when speaking of the divine and the incapacity of humans to know the divine completely. (I use the full spelling when quoting others who use it.)

27. Knitter, *Introducing Theologies of Religions*, 19.

28. "Countertransference" refers to the relational dynamic in which caregivers' thoughts and feelings affect their relationships with care seekers, sometimes without the caregivers' awareness.

29. Joseph F. Viti, "A Journey of Soul Companioning: Personal, Vocational, and Ministry Reflections," in Bueckert and Schipani, eds., *You Welcomed Me*, 15.

30. See, for example, a series of essays published in the journal *Christian Bioethics*: Corinna Delkeskamp-Hayes, "Generic Versus Catholic Hospital Chaplaincy: The Diversity of Spirits as a Problem of Inter-Faith Cooperation," *Christian Bioethics* 9, no. 1 (2003): 3–21; Brad F. Mellon, "Faith-to-Faith at the Bedside: Theological and Ethical Issues in Ecumenical Clinical Chaplaincy," *Christian Bioethics* 9, no. 1 (2003): 57–67; Corinna Delkeskamp-Hayes, "The Price of Being Conciliatory: Remarks about Mellon's Model for Hospital Chaplaincy Work in Multi-Faith Settings," *Christian Bioethics* 9, no. 1 (2003): 69–78.

31. These perspectives comprise a slight variation of the action-reflection-action cycle often proposed as a framework for practical theological analysis of and response to human need; I have specified "reflection" as being comprised more precisely of two practices: *evaluation* of action, which informs *preparation* for future action. As in other practical theological methods, these perspectives are not sequential or discrete—the perspectives are closely interrelated, and we can begin with any of the perspectives, as appropriate to the caregiving situation. Schipani and Bueckert also call for and articulate a practical theological approach to interreligious soul care. Daniel S. Schipani and Leah Dawn Bueckert, "Interfaith Spiritual Caregiving: The Case for Language-Care," in their edited volume *Spiritual Caregiving in the Hospital*, 261.

32. Clyde Kluckholn and Henry Murray, *Personality in Nature, Society, and Culture* (New York: Knopf, 1948).

33. Judith A. Berling, *Understanding Other Religious Worlds: A Guide for Interreligious Education* (Maryknoll, N.Y.: Orbis, 2004), 39, citing Clifford Geertz, *Local Knowledge: Further Essays in Interpretive Anthropology*, 2nd ed. (New York: Basic, 2000), 58.

34. Though he does not address religious diversity, it is a factor to be included in the power analysis Eric Law persuasively argues is required for interculturality. Eric H. F. Law, *The Wolf Shall Dwell with the Lamb: A Spirituality for Leadership in a Multicultural Community* (St. Louis: Chalice, 1993), 53–61.

35. Robert G. Anderson, "The Search for Spiritual/Cultural Competency in Chaplaincy: Five Steps that Mark the Path," in *Ministry in the Spiritual and Cultural Diversity of Health Care: Increasing the Competency of Chaplains*, eds. Robert G. Anderson and Mary A. Fukuyama (Binghamton, N.Y.: Haworth, 2004), 14–15.

36. Schipani and Bueckert, "Interfaith Spiritual Caregiving," 246.

37. Ibid., 259–60.

38. Berling, *Understanding Other Religious Worlds*, 39.

39. Schipani and Bueckert, "Interfaith Spiritual Caregiving," 246.

40. Anderson, "The Search for Spiritual/Cultural Competency in Chaplaincy," 15.

41. Ibid., 14.

42. Ibid., 15.

43. Ibid., 12–13; Schipani and Bueckert, "Interfaith Spiritual Caregiving," 257–58.

44. A.J. van den Blink, "Empathy and Diversity: Problems and Possibilities," *Journal of Pastoral Theology* 3 (1993): 5.

45. Seminarians are often left in this condition by the first years of their study (though it can happen to caregivers with many years experience as well)—with former beliefs questioned and reformation of religious identity barely begun, it is difficult, even threatening, to be fully present to care seekers, colleagues, or supervisors who are confident in their beliefs.

46. van den Blink, "Empathy and Diversity," 7.

47. Schipani and Bueckert, "Interfaith Spiritual Caregiving," 257–58.

48. Anderson, "The Search for Spiritual/Cultural Competency in Chaplaincy," 13.

49. The literature in soul care regularly notes that research has shown a close correlation between a lack of self-care and both burnout and ethical misconduct by religious leaders. From that perspective, we can see that self-care is not best understood as remedial but as foundational and preventative. Especially given that resources to prepare us for ethical interreligious practice are just beginning to appear, self-care is especially important to lay the energetic groundwork for mindful, moral practice with persons whose religious traditions we may know only barely.

50. Anderson, "The Search for Spiritual/Cultural Competency in Chaplaincy," 13.

51. David W. Augsburger, *Pastoral Counseling across Cultures* (Philadelphia: Westminster, 1986), 22–24.

52. Beth Porter, a Christian, describes a two-year process of assisting Ellen, a Jewish woman with developmental disabilities living in the mostly Christian community of L'Arche Daybreak, to prepare for her Bat Mitzvah. Porter's essay provides an honest example of the time and effort it takes to learn enough about another religious tradition to be helpful to a care seeker. But the essay is also encouraging, because it shows how working with a care seeker makes the process more fruitful and potentially transformative not just of persons but of their communities. Beth Porter, "L'Arche Daybreak: An Example of Interfaith Ministry among People with Developmental Disabilities," *Journal of Pastoral Care* 52, no. 2 (Summer 1998): 157–65.

Chapter 20: Are There Limits to Multicultural Inclusion?

1. We appreciate feedback received on earlier drafts from Jeanne Stevenson-Moessner, Teresa Snorton, Angella Son, and other women involved in this book project as well as colleagues at Vanderbilt University, Ellen Armour and Brooke Ackerly.

2. See Rita Nakashima Brock, "Introduction," *Setting the Table: Women in Theological Conversation*, ed. Rita Nakashima Brock, Claudia Camp, and Serene Jones (St. Louis: Chalice, 1995), 17–19. Brock adopts this phrase from her reading of Peggy McIntosh, "Interactive Phases of Curricular Re-Vision: A Feminist Perspective," Working Paper No. 124, 1983, Wellesley College Center for Research on Women, Wellesley, MA.

3. As will become evident as the chapter develops, there are many different kinds of feminism and many different definitions of multiculturalism.

4. Jeanne Stevenson-Moessner, Introduction, p. 2, above.

5. This is a slight alternation of Gayatri Chakravorty Spivak's criticism of the colonial pattern of "white men saving brown women from brown men" in "Can the Subaltern Speak?" in *Marxism and the Interpretation of Culture*, eds. Cary Nelson and Lawrence Grossberg (Urbana: University of Illinois Press, 1988), 296–97, cited by Kwok Pui-lan, "Unbinding Our Feet: Saving Brown Women and Feminist Religious Discourse," in *Postcolonialism, Feminism, and Religious Discourse*, eds. Laura E. Donaldson and Kwok Pui-lan (New York: Routledge, 2002), 64.

6. Christopher G. Ellison and Darren E. Sherkat, "Conservative Protestantism and Support for Corporal Punishment," *American Sociological Review* 58 (1993): 131–44; Christopher G. Ellison, John P. Bartkowski, and Michelle L. Segal, "Conservative Protestantism and the Parental Use of Corporal Punishment," *Social Forces* 74 (1996): 1003–28. James Dobson has been a primary player in promoting this position. See his *The New Dare to Discipline* (Wheaton: Tyndale House, 1996); updated from the original *Dare to Discipline* (Wheaton: Tyndale House, 1970). For a recent examination of evangelical fathering see W. Bradford Wilcox, *Soft Patriarchs, New Men: How Christianity Shapes Fathers and Husbands* (Chicago: University of Chicago Press, 2004).

7. The only other nation that has not signed is Somalia, but, unlike the United States, it does not have capacity to ratify treaties; see http://www.unicef.org/crc/, and http://www2.ohchr.org/english/bodies/crc/crcs48.htm, both accessed March 24, 2009. See also Jill Marie Gerschutz and Margaret P. Karns, "Transforming Visions into Reality: The Convention on the Rights of the Child," in *Children's Human Rights: Progress and Challenges for Children Worldwide*, ed. Mark Ensalaco and Linda C. Majka (Lanham, Md.: Rowman & Littlefield, 2005), 31.

8. National Center for Home Education, "Oppose the UN Convention on the Rights of the Child," Issues Alert 1999, updated 2007, http://www.hslda.org/docs/nche/000000/00000021.asp, accessed March 25, 2009.

9. "The Campaign for US Ratification of the Convention on the Rights of the Child," http://childrightscampaign.org/crcindex.php?sNav=index_snav.php&sDat=index_dat.php; see also http://www.amnestyusa.org/children/crn_faq.html, both accessed March 25, 2009.

10. John P. Bartkowski and Christopher G. Ellison, "Conservative Protestants on Children and Parenting," in *Children and Childhood in American Religions*, ed. Don S. Browning and Bonnie J. Miller-McLemore (Camden: Rutgers University Press, forthcoming 2009).

11. Elizabeth Gershoff and Robert Larzelere, "Is Corporal Punishment an Effective Means of Discipline?" American Psychological Association Media Information, http://www.apa.org/releases/spanking.html, accessed March 25, 2009; Murray A. Straus, *Beating the Devil Out of Them: Corporal Punishment in American Families* (San Francisco: Lexington, 1994); idem, "Spanking and the Making of a Violent Society," *Pediatrics* 98 (1996): 837–42; Philip Greven, *Spare the Child: The Religious Roots of Punishment and the Psychological Impact of Physical Abuse* (New York: Vintage, 1990); and Donald Capps, *The Child's Song: The Religious Abuse of Children* (Louisville: Westminster John Knox, 1995). Interestingly, the United Methodist Church claims to be the first and only denomination to make an official statement against corporal punishment of children in 2004, http://www.stophitting.com/index.php?page=unitedmethodist, accessed March 25, 2009.

12. "Convention on the Rights of the Child," http://untreaty.un.org/English/TreatyEvent2001/pdf/03e.pdf, accessed March 25, 2009; Office of the United Nations High Commissioner for Human Rights, *Legislative History of the Convention on the Rights of the Child*, 2 vols. (New York and Geneva: United Nations, 2007).

13. See Brooke A. Ackerly, *Universal Human Rights in a World of Difference* (Cambridge, UK: Cambridge University Press, 2008).

14. Devaki Jain, *Women, Development, and the UN: A Sixty-Year Quest for Equality and Justice* (Bloomington: Indiana University Press, 2005), 29.

15. Editors Uma Narayan and Julia J. Bartkowiak ask this question in the introduction to *Having and Raising Children: Unconventional Families, Hard Choices, and the Social Good* (University Park: Pennsylvania State University Press, 1999), 6.

16. Mark Ensalaco and Linda C. Majka, "Introduction," in Ensalaco and Majka, eds., *Children's Human Rights*, 1–6.

17. *Wisconsin v. Yoder*, 406 U. S. 205 (1972), http://supreme.justia.com/us/406/205/case.html, accessed March 25, 2009; Shawn Francis Peters, *The Yoder Case: Religious Freedom, Education, and Parental Rights* (Lawrence: University Press of Kansas, 2003); Seyla Benhabib, *The Claims of Culture: Equality and Diversity in the Global Era* (Princeton: Princeton University Press, 2002), 124.

18. See "Fact Sheet: The Rights of Girls," from UNICEF, http://www.unicef.org/spanish/crc/images/Rights_of_girls.pdf, accessed March 25, 2009. See also Gayatri Chakravorty Spivak, *Thinking Academic Freedom in Gendered Post-Coloniality* (Capetown: University of Capetown, 1992); and Susan Moller Okin, "Gender Equality and Cultural Differences," *Political Theory*, 22, no. 1 (February 1994): 11–13.

19. For examples of early books on children, see Andrew D. Lester, *Pastoral Care with Children in Crisis* (Philadelphia: Westminster, 1985); and Herbert Anderson and Susan B. W. Johnson, *Regarding Children: A New Respect for Childhood and Families* (Louisville: Westminster John Knox, 1994). For examples of work on abuse of children, see James N. Poling, *The Abuse of Power: A Theological Problem* (Nashville: Abingdon, 1991); Nancy Ramsay, "Sexual Abuse and Shame: The Travail of Recovery," in *Women in Travail and Transition: A New Pastoral Care*, ed. Maxine Glaz and Jeanne Stevenson-Moessner (Minneapolis: Fortress Press, 1991), 109–25; Capps, *The Child's*

Song; and Stephen Pattison, "'Suffer Little Children': The Challenge of Child Abuse and Neglect to Theology," *Theology and Sexuality* 9 (1998): 36–58.

20. Loretta M. Kopelman, "Female Circumcision/Genital Mutilation and Ethical Relativism," *Second Opinion* 20, no. 2 (1994): 56.

21. Elizabeth Heger Boyle, *Female Genital Cutting: Cultural Conflict in the Global Community* (Baltimore: Johns Hopkins University Press, 2002), 73–74.

22. Celia W. Dugger, "A Refugee's Body Is Intact but Her Family Is Torn," *New York Times*, September 11, 1996, A1; Fauziya Kassindja and Layli Miller Bashir, *Do They Hear You When You Cry* (New York: Delacorte, 1998).

23. Corinne A. Kratz, "Seeking Asylum, Debating Values, and Setting Precedents in the 1990s: The Cases of Kassindja and Abankwah in the United States," in *Transcultural Bodies: Female Genital Cutting in Global Context*, eds. Ylva Hernlund and Bettina Shell-Duncan (New Brunswick: Rutgers University Press, 2007), 173.

24. Kratz, "Seeking Asylum," 178.

25. Susan Moller Okin, "Is Multiculturalism Bad for Women?" in *Is Multiculturalism Bad for Women?* eds. Joshua Cohen, Matthew Howard, and Martha Nussbaum (Princeton: Princeton University Press, 1999), 9, 13–14, 24.

26. Ibid., 11–12, 23–24.

27. Saskia Sassen, "Culture beyond Gender," in Cohen, et al., eds., *Is Multiculturalism Bad for Women?* 77–78. For early womanist and feminist theological work on this point, see Delores S. Williams, *Sisters in the Wilderness: The Challenge of Womanist God-Talk* (Maryknoll, N.Y.: Orbis, 1993); Jacquelyn Grant, *White Women's Christ and Black Women's Jesus* (Atlanta: Scholars, 1989); Susan Thistlethwaite, *Sex, Race, and God: Christian Feminism in Black and White* (New York: Crossroad, 1989); and Ellen Armour, *Deconstruction, Feminist Theology, and the Problem of Difference: Subverting the Race/Gender Divide* (Chicago: University of Chicago Press, 1999).

28. Joshua Cohen, Matthew Howard, and Martha Nussbaum, "Introduction" in Cohen, et al., eds., *Is Multiculturalism Bad for Women?* 4–5.

29. Martha C. Nussbaum, "A Plea for Difficulty," in Cohen, et al., eds., *Is Multiculturalism Bad for Women?* 105, 108–09. For Nussbaum's "capabilities" approach to some of these questions, see *Sex and Social Justice* (Oxford: Oxford University Press, 1999), and *Women and Human Development: The Capabilities Approach* (Cambridge: Cambridge University Press, 2000).

30. Benhabib, *The Claims of Culture*, esp. 40–42, and idem, "In Defense of Universalism—Yet Again! A Response to Critics of Situating the Self," *New German Critique* 62 (Spring-Summer 1994): 173–89. On Nussbaum, see Ylva Hernlund and Bettina Shell-Duncan, "Transcultural Positions: Negotiating Rights and Culture," in Ylva Hernlund and Bettina Shell-Duncan, eds., *Transcultural Bodies: Female Genital Cutting in Global Contexts* (New Brunswick, N.J.: Rutgers University Press, 2007), 25.

31. David A. Crocker, "Functioning and Capability: The Foundations of Sen's and Nussbaum's Development Ethic," *Political Theory* 20, no. 4 (November 1992): 592 (emphasis in original).

32. Mary Dietz, "Current Controversies in Feminist Theory," *Annual Review of Political Science* 6 (2003): 417–18.

33. Ibid., 417.

34. Ibid., 419.

35. Ibid., 417, 422.

36. Okin, "Gender Equality and Cultural Differences," 5; Jane Flax, "Race/Gender and the Ethics of Difference: A Reply to Okin's 'Gender Inequality and Cultural Differences,'" *Political Theory* 23, no. 3 (August 1995): 500–10; Susan Moller Okin, "Response to Jane Flax," *Political Theory* 23, no. 3 (August 1995): 514–15.

37. Flax, "Race/Gender and the Ethics of Difference," 500–10.

38. Jeanne Stevenson-Moessner and Maxine Glaz, "Preface," in Glaz and Stevenson-Moessner, eds., *Women in Travail and Transition*, vi.

39. Emmanuel Y. Lartey, *In Living Color: An Intercultural Approach to Pastoral Care and Counselling* (London: Cassell, 1997), vi. He expands on this in the second edition by adding one new chapter that spells out the difference between the four terms (London: Jessica Kingsley, 2003).

40. Emmanuel Y. Lartey, *Pastoral Theology in an Intercultural World* (Cleveland: Pilgrim, 2006), 11.

41. Lartey, *In Living Color*, 128–29.

42. Ibid., 10.

43. Kwok Pui-lan, "Feminist Theology as Intercultural Discourse," in *The Cambridge Companion to Feminist Theology*, ed. Susan Frank Parsons (Cambridge: Cambridge University Press, 2002), 21, emphasis added.

44. Williams, *Sisters in the Wilderness*, 67.

45. Carroll A. Watkins Ali, "A Womanist Search for Sources," in Bonnie J. Miller-McLemore and Brita L. Gill-Austern, eds., *Feminist and Womanist Pastoral Theology* (Nashville: Abingdon, 1999), 52.

46. Patricia Hill Collins, *Black Feminist Thought: Knowledge, Consciousness, and the Politics of Empowerment*, 2nd ed. (New York: Routledge, 2000), vii, 18.

47. Ibid., 1–8.

48. Ibid., 283.

49. Fred C. Gingrich, "Pastoral Counseling in the Philippines: A Perspective from the West," in James Reaves Farris, ed., *International Perspectives on Pastoral Counseling* (Binghamton, N.Y.: Haworth, 2002), 35–37.

50. Ibid., 36.

51. Howard Clinebell, "Preface," in *International Perspectives on Pastoral Counseling*, ed. James Reaves Farris (Binghamton, N.Y.: Haworth, 2002), xv–xix.

52. Pamela Couture, *Child Poverty: Love, Justice, and Social Responsibility* (St. Louis: Chalice, 2007), 92–93.

53. Amartya Sen, *Development as Freedom*, 74, cited in Cynthia Holder-Rich, "Development as Freedom or Freedom as Development? A Christian Dialogue with Amartya Sen's *Development as Freedom*," *Journal for Southern Africa* 110 (July 2001): 89–96; Martha Nussbaum, *Frontiers of Justice*, 290, cited in Alyssa R. Bernstein, "Nussbaum versus Rawls: Should Feminist Human Rights Advocates Reject the Law of Peoples and Endorse the Capabilities Approach?" in *Global Feminist Ethics*, ed. Rebecca Whisnant and Peggy DesAutels (Lanham, Md.: Rowman & Littlefield, 2008), 117–38.

54. Crocker, "Functioning and Capability," 607 (emphasis in original).

55. Bonnie J. Miller-McLemore, *Let the Children Come: Reimagining Childhood from a Christian Perspective* (San Francisco: Jossey-Bass, 2003); and idem, *In the Midst of Chaos: Caring for Children as Spiritual Practice*, Practices of Faith (San Francisco: Jossey-Bass, 2007). In a "transitional hierarchy," children should not be held as morally responsible as adults who have far greater means and opportunity to perfect their abilities to do good or evil. Inversely, parents enter a period of "transitional renunciation" that puts at least an initial check on one's own needs to meet the more acute needs of a vulnerable child. Jean Baker Miller uses a similar phrase, "temporary inequality," in her *Toward a New Psychology of Women* (Boston: Beacon, 1976).

56. See Yael Tamir, "Siding with the Underdogs," in Cohen, et al., eds., *Is Multiculturalism Bad for Women?* 51.

57. Cohen, Howard, and Nussbaum, "Introduction," in Cohen, et al., eds., *Is Multiculturalism Bad for Women?* 4.

58. Katha Pollitt, "Whose Culture?" in Cohen, et al., eds., *Is Multiculturalism Bad for Women?* 27.

59. Laura E. Donaldson and Kwok Pui-lan, "Introduction," in *Postcolonialism, Feminism, and Religious Discourse*, eds. Donaldson and Kwok, 28.

60. Nussbaum, *Sex and Social Justice*, 30.

61. Meyda Yegenoglu, *Colonial Fantasies: Towards a Feminist Reading of Orientalism* (Cambridge: Cambridge University Press, 1998), 105–06, cited by Kwok Pui-lan, "Unbinding Our Feet," 76.

62. Rachel Burr, "Children's Rights: International Policy and Lived Practice," in *An Introduction to Childhood Studies*, ed. Mary Jane Kehily (Berkshire, UK: Open University Press, 2004), 159.

63. Nussbaum, *Sex and Social Justice*, 30.

64. Will Kymlicka, "Liberal Complacencies," in Cohen, et al., eds., *Is Multiculturalism Bad for Women?* 34.

65. Bhikhu Parekh, "A Varied Moral World," in Cohen, et al., eds., *Is Multiculturalism Bad for Women?* 73–74. See also Bhikhu Parekh, *Rethinking Multiculturalism: Cultural Diversity and Political Theory* (Cambridge: Harvard University Press, 2002).

66. Pollitt, "Whose Culture?" 29. For more on internal cultural diversity, see political theorists Seyla Benhabib, *The Claims of Culture*; Uma Narayan, *Dislocating Cultures: Identities, Traditions, and Third-World Feminism* (New York: Routledge, 1997). For a theological perspective, see Kathryn Tanner, *Theories of Culture*, Guides to Theological Inquiry (Minneapolis: Fortress Press, 1997).

67. Bonnie Honig, " 'My Culture Made Me Do It,' " in Cohen, et al., eds., *Is Multiculturalism Bad for Women?* 37.

68. Homi K. Bhabha, "Liberalism's Sacred Cow," in Cohen, et al., eds., *Is Multiculturalism Bad for Women?* 79.

69. Sarah Song, "Majority Norms, Multiculturalism, and Gender Equality," *American Political Science Review* 99, no. 4 (November 2005): 474.

70. For example, see Laura M. Purdy, "Boundaries of Authority: Should Children Be Able to Divorce Their Parents?" in *Having and Raising Children: Unconventional Families, Hard Choices, and the Social Good*, ed. Uma Narayan and Julia J. Bartkowiak (University Park: Pennsylvania State University Press, 1999), 153–62.

71. Nussbaum, *Sex and Social Justice*, 14.

72. See Song, "Majority Norms." Song convincingly demonstrates how gender and culture enter into legal arguments and decisions in the United States context.

73. Honig, " 'My Culture Made Me Do It,' " 39. See also Saba Mahmood, "Agency, Performativity, and the Feminist Subject," in *Bodily Citations: Religion and Judith Butler*, ed. Ellen T. Armour and Susan M. St. Ville (New York: Columbia University Press, 2006), 177–221.

74. See also Meyda Yegenoglu, "Sartorial Fabric-ations: Enlightenment and Western Feminism," in Donaldson and Pui-Lan, eds., *Postcolonialism, Feminism, and Religious Discourse*, 82-99.

75. Azizah Y. al-Hibri, "Is Western Patriarchal Feminism Good for Third World/Minority Women?" in Cohen, et al., eds., *Is Multiculturalism Bad for Women?* 44.

76. Okin, "Reply," 123.

77. Cass R. Sunstein, "Should Sex Equality Law Apply to Religious Institutions?" in Cohen, et al., eds., *Is Multiculturalism Bad for Women?* 87–88.

78. To this point, as we were preparing this article for publication, the *New York Times* featured an article about whether complex issues and emotions surrounding hymen restoration surgery is liberative or oppressive for young adult Muslim women living in Europe; see Elaine Sciolino and Squad Mekhennet, "In Europe, Debate Over Islam and Virginity," June 11, 2008, http://www.nytimes.com/2008/06/11/world/europe/11virgin.html?ex=1213934400&en=a7f7cc9cd5d49de9&ei=5070&emc=eta1, accessed March 25, 2009.

79. Honig, " 'My Culture Made Me Do It,' " 38, 40.

80. Robert Post, "Between Norms and Choices," in Cohen, et al., eds., *Is Multiculturalism Bad for Women?* 68.

81. Kratz, "Seeking Asylum," 196.

82. Brooke Ackerly, *Political Theory and Feminist Social Criticism* (Cambridge: Cambridge University Press, 2000); also personal conversation.

Chapter 21: Where Race and Gender Collide

1. Iris Marion Young, *Justice and the Politics of Difference* (Princeton: Princeton University Press, 1990), 63–65.

2. Marianne Bertrand and Sendhil Mullainathan, *Are Emily and Brendan More Employable than Lakisha and Jamal? A Field Experiment on Labor Market Discrimination*, working paper 9873 (Cambridge, Mass.: National Bureau of Economic Research, 2003).

3. David Wellman, *Portraits of White Racism*, 2nd ed. (Cambridge: Cambridge University Press, 1993).

4. Jodie Kliman and William Madsen, "Social Class and the Family Life Cycle," in *The Expanded Family Life Cycle*, 3rd ed., ed. Betty Carter and Monica McGoldrick (Boston: Allyn and Bacon, 1999).

5. Ronald Takaki, *A Different Mirror: A History of Multicultural America* (Boston: Back Bay, 1993).

6. "Cycle of Socialization," and "Cycle of Liberation" are developed by Bobbie Harro, in Marianne Adams, Lee Anne Bell, and Pat Griffin, eds., *Readings for Diversity and Social Justice: An Anthology on Racism, Antisemitism, Sexism, Heterosexism, Ableism, and Classism*, 2d ed. (New York: Routledge, 2000), 16, 464.

7. Robert Kegan, *The Evolving Self* (Cambridge: Harvard University Press, 1982), 158–59.

8. Rita Hardiman and Bailey Jackson, "Model of Social Identity Development," in *Teaching for Diversity and Social Justice*, ed. Adams, et al., Appendix 2A.

9. Beverly Daniel Tatum, "Talking About Race, Learning About Racism: An Application of Racial Identity Development Theory in the Classroom," in *Harvard Educational Review* 62, no. 1 (1992): 1–24.

10. Judith Jordan, Alexandra Kaplan, Jean Baker Miller, Irene Stiver, and Janet Surrey, *Women's Growth in Connection* (New York: Guilford, 1991).

11. Christine Pohl, *Making Room: Recovering Hospitality as a Christian Tradition* (Grand Rapids: Eerdmans, 1999).

12. Martin Luther King Jr., "On Being a Good Neighbor," in *Strength to Love* (Philadelphia: Fortress Press), 26–35.

13. Martin Luther King Jr., "Letter from Birmingham City Jail," in *A Testament of Hope: The Essential Writings and Speeches of Martin Luther King, Jr.*, ed. James M. Washington (New York: HarperCollins, 1986), 289–302.

14. Jeanne Stevenson-Moessner, "A New Pastoral Paradigm and Practice," in *Women in Travail and Transition: A New Pastoral Care*, ed. Maxine Glaz and Jeanne Stevenson-Moessner (Minneapolis: Fortress Press, 1991), 200–01.

15. Daniel Day Williams, *The Spirit and the Forms of Love* (New York: Harper & Row, 1968), 114–22.

16. Marsha Foster Boyd and Carolyn Stahl Bohler, "Womanist-Feminist Alliances: Meeting on the Bridge," in *Feminist and Womanist Pastoral Theology*, ed. Bonnie J. Miller-McLemore and Brita L. Gill-Austern (Nashville: Abingdon, 1999), 189–210.

17. Carroll Watkins Ali, *Survival and Liberation: Pastoral Theology in African American Context* (St. Louis: Chalice, 1999), 123.

18. "Characteristics of an Ally," in *Teaching for Diversity and Social Justice*, ed., Adams, et al., Appendix 6G.

19. Williams, *The Spirit and the Forms of Love*, 250.

20. Archie Smith Jr., *The Relational Self: Ethics and Therapy from a Black Church Perspective* (Nashville: Abingdon, 1982).

21. Brita Gill-Austern, "Love Understood as Self-Sacrifice and Self-Denial: What Does It Do to Women?" in *Through the Eyes of Women: Insights for Pastoral Care*, ed. Jeanne Stevenson-Moessner (Minneapolis: Fortress Press, 1996), 304–21.

22. Jeanne Stevenson-Moessner, "From Samaritan to Samaritan: Journey Mercies," in *Through the Eyes of Women*, ed. Stevenson-Moessner, 322–32.

23. Teresa Snorton, "Self-Care for the African American Woman," in *In Her Own Time: Women and Developmental Issues in Pastoral Care*, ed. Jeanne Stevenson-Moessner (Minneapolis: Fortress Press, 2000), 285–94.

24. Carolyn McCrary, "The Wholeness of Women," in *The Journal of the Interdenominational Theological Center* 25, no. 3 (Spring 1998): 258–94.

25. Pamela Couture, *Seeing Children, Seeing God: A Practical Theology of Children and Poverty* (Nashville: Abingdon, 2000).

26. Elaine Graham, *Transforming Practice: Pastoral Theology in an Age of Uncertainty* (Mowbray: London, 1996).

27. Ali, *Survival and Liberation*.

28. Fumitaka Matsuoka, *The Color of Faith* (Cleveland: United Church Press, 1998).

29. Beverly Daniel Tatum, "Racial Identity Development and Relational Theory: The Case of Black Women in White Communities," in *Women's Growth in Diversity*, ed. Judith Jordan (New York: Guilford, 1997), 92.

30. Marjorie Suchocki, *The Fall to Violence* (New York: Continuum, 1994).

31. Wendy Farley, *Tragic Vision and Divine Compassion: A Contemporary Theodicy* (Louisville: Westminster John Knox, 1990).

32. Richard Rodgers and Oscar Hammerstein, "You've Got to Be Carefully Taught," in *South Pacific* (New York: BMG Music, 1958).

33. Teresa Snorton, "The Legacy of the African-American Matriarch: New Perspectives for Pastoral Care," in *Through the Eyes of Women*, ed. Stevenson-Moessner, 50–65.

Chapter 22: Where Race and Gender Collude

1. This document is located in the Rev. W. B. Sprague Collection, 194 (3rd Ser.) no. 7. *The Slave's Appeal* is also on microfiche at Firestone Library, Princeton University, Princeton, New Jersey, in the Anti-Slavery Depository holding.

2. *The Slave's Appeal* was omitted from the list of works compiled by Stanton's son and daughter, *Elizabeth Cady Stanton, as revealed in her letters, diary, and reminiscences*, ed. Theodore Stanton and Harriet Blatch, vol. 1, in the Appendix (New York and London: Harper & Bros., 1922), 354–62. Elisabeth Griffith, who wrote a biography of Stanton, *In Her Own Right: The Life of Elizabeth Cady Stanton* (New York: Oxford University Press, 1984), 101, quotes from a document that she erroneously called *A Slave's Appeal*.

3. For a full treatment of all nine of the Commandments, see Jeanne Stevenson-Moessner, "Elizabeth Cady Stanton, Reformer to Revolutionary: A Theological Trajectory," *Journal of the American Academy of Religion* 62, no. 3 (Fall 1994): 673–97.

4. Donald W. Dayton, "The Evangelical Roots of Feminism," in *Discovering an Evangelical Heritage* (New York: Harper & Row, 1976).

5. *Elizabeth Cady Stanton as Revealed in Her Letters, Diary and Reminiscences*, 78.

6. Ibid.

7. "Kingdom of Matthias Trial at White Plains, NY," in *The Farmers' Cabinet*, April 24, 1835, Amherst, New Hampshire.

8. Saunders Redding, "Sojourner Truth," in *Notable American Women, 1607–1950*, vol. 3, ed. Edward T. James (Cambridge: Harvard University Press, 1971), 480.

9. Elizabeth Cady Stanton, Susan B. Anthony, and Matilda Joslyn-Gage, eds., *History of Woman Suffrage: Vol. 1, 1848–1861* (New York: Fowler and Wells, 1881), 115.

10. Ibid.

11. Stanton, et al., eds., *History of Woman Suffrage: Vol. 2, 1861–1876*, 194.

12. Miriam Gurko, *The Ladies of Seneca Falls: The Birth of the Woman's Rights Movement* (New York: MacMillan, 1974), 138.

13. Ibid., 214.

14. Griffith, *In Her Own Right*, 124,

15. Stanton, et al., eds., *History of Woman Suffrage: Vol. 2*, 152.

16. Gurko, *The Ladies of Seneca Falls*, 214–15.

17. Ibid., 215.

18. Harriet Beecher Stowe, "Sojourner Truth, The Libyan Sibyl," *The Atlantic Monthly* 11 (Boston: Ticknor and Fields, 1863): 473.

19. Ibid., 474.

20. Ibid.

21. Ibid., 473.

22. The Associated Press, "Group: Rape victim stoned to death," in Dubuque *Telegraph Herald*, Sunday, November 2, 2008, 10A.

23. The Associated Press, "Pakistan investigates 5 'honor killings'," in Dubuque *Telegraph Herald*, Tuesday, September 2, 2008.

Index

9 780800 664442